TEST ITEM FILE

LINDA FLORA
Montgomery County Community College

THERESA HORNSTEIN
Lake Superior College

KELLI PRIOR
Finger Lakes Community College

ANNE GALBRAITH
University of Wisconsin-LaCrosse

STEPHEN T. KILPATRICK
University of Pittsburgh at Johnstown

GREG PRYOR
Francis Marion University

EIGHTH EDITION

Biology

LIFE ON EARTH

AUDESIRK   AUDESIRK   BYERS

PEARSON
Benjamin Cummings

San Francisco Boston New York
Cape Town Hong Kong London Madrid Mexico City
Montreal Munich Paris Singapore Sydney Tokyo Toronto

Project Manager: Crissy Dudonis
Acquisitions Editor: Jeff Howard
Executive Managing Editor: Kathleen Schiaparelli
Assistant Managing Editor: Gina M. Cheselka
Production Editor: Ashley M. Booth
Supplement Cover Manager: Paul Gourhan
Supplement Cover Designer: Victoria Colotta
Manufacturing Buyer: Ilene Kahn
Associate Director of Operations: Alexis Heydt-Long

ISBN-10: 0-13-195768-6

ISBN-13: 978-0-13-195768-8

1 2 3 4 5 6 7 8 —OPM— 11 10 09 08 07

www.aw-bc.com

Contents

Chapter 1   An Introduction of Life on Earth

1) All of the following are scientific principles that underlie scientific inquiry except

    A) natural causality.

    B) uniformity in space and time.

    C) natural selection.

    D) common perception.

    E) All of these are true.

Answer: C
Diff: 1   Page Ref: 1.1
Skill: Factual

2) Examples of natural causality include

    A) mice arise from sweaty underwear and wheat husks.

    B) maggots grow from rotting meat.

    C) epilepsy is a disease of the brain.

    D) the existence of elves.

    E) All of these are true.

Answer: C
Diff: 1   Page Ref: 1.1
Skill: Application

3) Science cannot answer certain moral questions because

    A) scientists are not smart enough.

    B) scientists have no moral values.

    C) moral values differ among individuals.

    D) morality requires deductive reasoning.

    E) there aren't enough variables.

Answer: C
Diff: 1   Page Ref: 1.1
Skill: Conceptual

4) Which of the following is true about scientific theories?

    A) They have been thoroughly tested.

    B) They are developed by inductive reasoning.

    C) They are used to support observations using deductive reasoning.

    D) They can be either supported or modified by new observations.

    E) All of these are correct.

Answer: E
Diff: 1   Page Ref: 1.1
Skill: Factual

5) Which of these would NOT be scientific?

    A) determine differences in species composition between two parks

    B) immunize people with different vaccines to determine the effectiveness against flu virus

    C) send tadpoles up in the space shuttle to see how gravity affects development

    D) use different tomatoes in spaghetti sauce to determine which produces the best taste

    E) use different advertising methods for a product to determine which produces the best purchasing results

Answer: D
Diff: 3   Page Ref: 1.1
Skill: Application

6) The scientific method includes all of the following EXCEPT

    A) experimentation.

    B) a testable theory.

    C) an observation.

    D) a hypothesis.

    E) conclusions.

Answer: B
Diff: 2   Page Ref: 1.1
Skill: Conceptual

7) We use the scientific method every day. Imagine your car doesn't start one morning before school. Which of these is a reasonable *hypothesis* regarding the problem?

    A) I'm going to be late.

    B) I'm out of gas.

    C) Check if your lights were left on.

    D) Kick the tires.

    E) Add a quart of oil.

Answer: B
Diff: 2   Page Ref: 1.1
Skill: Application

8) A scientific theory

    A) is a general explanation for a natural phenomena.

    B) is an educated guess.

    C) is less reliable than a hypothesis.

    D) will never be changed.

    E) none of the above

Answer: A
Diff: 2   Page Ref: 1.1
Skill: Factual

9) A scientific explanation that is tentative and requires more investigation is termed a/an

    A) theory.

    B) fact.

    C) control.

    D) hypothesis.

    E) observation.

Answer: D
Diff: 2   Page Ref: 1.1
Skill: Factual

10) A carefully formulated scientific explanation that is based on a large accumulation of observations and is in accord with scientific principles is termed a/an

    A) hypothesis.

    B) theory.

    C) fact.

    D) control.

    E) postulate.

Answer: B
Diff: 2   Page Ref: 1.1
Skill: Factual

11) All the following are features of the scientific method EXCEPT

    A) hypothesis formulation.

    B) observation and experimentation.

    C) supernatural causes.

    D) inductive and deductive reasoning.

    E) forming conclusions.

Answer: C
Diff: 2   Page Ref: 1.1
Skill: Conceptual

12) You are testing treatments for AIDS sufferers and find that 75% respond very well and 25% show no improvement or decline in health after your experimental treatment. You should

    A) conclude you have proven the effectiveness of the drug.

    B) conclude that only 75% of AIDS victims should be treated.

    C) review the results, modify the drug or the dosage, and repeat the experiment.

    D) discontinue experimentation because 25% of patients did not improve.

    E) begin work on an entirely new drug.

Answer: C
Diff: 3   Page Ref: 1.1
Skill: Application

13) Alexander Fleming observed a patch of mold that bacteria were not able to grow near. Which of these was his hypothesis?

   A) The mold used all of the nutrients so that the bacteria couldn't grow.

   B) The mold produced a substance that killed nearby bacteria.

   C) The bacteria changed their DNA when growing near the mold.

   D) The mold was dead.

Answer: B
Diff: 2   Page Ref: 1.1
Skill: Conceptual

14) There are very few laws, but many theories in biology. Why?

   A) It is a difference in terminology; they are actually the same thing.

   B) A theory is supported by repeated tests and by extensive evidence, but cannot be proven; laws must be proven to be true.

   C) Laws are true all the time, theories are true only most of the time.

   D) Laws are hypotheses that have been proven; theories are hypotheses that haven't been tested yet.

   E) A theory is a tentative explanation, a law is an explanation that has been shown to be true at least once.

Answer: B
Diff: 3   Page Ref: 1.1
Skill: Conceptual

15) One ml of an experimental drug diluted in a saline solution is injected into 20 pregnant mice to determine possible side effects. Which of the following is a suitable "control" for this experiment?

   A) 20 male mice injected with 1 ml of saline

   B) 20 male mice injected with 1 ml of the drug

   C) 20 pregnant mice injected with 2 ml of the drug

   D) 20 non–pregnant mice injected with 1 ml of the drug

   E) 20 pregnant mice injected with 1 ml of saline

Answer: E
Diff: 2   Page Ref: 1.1
Skill: Application

16) Which of the following is a hypothesis rather than a theory?

    A) Matter is composed of atoms.

    B) Living things are made of cells.

    C) Modern organisms descended from pre-existing life forms.

    D) Male birds with long tails have more mates than male birds with short tails.

    E) All of these are theories.

Answer: D
Diff: 2   Page Ref: 1.1
Skill: Conceptual

17) Faith-based assertions are not considered scientific theories because

    A) faith-based assertions can be proven.

    B) faith-based assertions can be disproven.

    C) scientific theories can be disproven.

    D) scientific theories are not modifiable.

    E) faith-based assertions can become scientific theories.

Answer: C
Diff: 1   Page Ref: 1.1
Skill: Factual

18) Which correctly indicates the sequence of increasing organization?

    A) molecule, cell, organelle, organ

    B) organelle, tissue, cell, organ

    C) atom, molecule, tissue, cell

    D) organ, tissue, cell, molecule

    E) cell, tissue, organ, organ system

Answer: E
Diff: 1   Page Ref: 1.1
Skill: Factual

19) Natural laws are the same regardless of when or wear one is. True or False?

Answer: TRUE
Diff: 1   Page Ref: 1.1
Skill: Factual

20) Experimentation to answer a scientific question leads to more questions. True or False?

Answer: TRUE
Diff: 1   Page Ref: 1.1
Skill: Factual

21) A good experiment should look at as many variables as possible. True or False?

Answer: FALSE
Diff: 2   Page Ref: 1.1
Skill: Conceptual

22) A hypothesis is much more general than a scientific theory. True or False?

Answer: FALSE
Diff: 2   Page Ref: 1.1
Skill: Conceptual

23) Design a simple experiment based on the observation that people taking Drug X for headaches also seem to have lower cholesterol. Include a hypothesis statement and your actual experimental design for the study.

Answer: Students should include a controlled variable, repetition and a hypothesis statement.
Diff: 3   Page Ref: 1.1
Skill: Application

24) All scientific study begins with observations and the formation of testable _____.

Answer: hypotheses
Diff: 2   Page Ref: 1.1
Skill: Conceptual

25) To test the effect of vitamin D on growth, two groups of rats were raised under identical conditions and fed the same diet, but one of the groups also received daily injections of vitamin D. The injections of vitamin D in this experiment are considered the _____.

Answer: variable
Diff: 2   Page Ref: 1.1
Skill: Application

26) A large group of similar, interbreeding organisms is defined as a _____.

Answer: species
Diff: 1   Page Ref: 1.1
Skill: Factual

27) A group of species in a given area belong to the same _____.

Answer: population
Diff: 1   Page Ref: 1.1
Skill: Factual

28) The smallest unit of life is the _____.

Answer: cell
Diff: 1   Page Ref: 1.1
Skill: Factual

29) Evolution is described as change from pre-existing life forms to modern-day organisms. What actually changed?

    A) rate of reproduction

    B) ability of organisms to cope with external stimuli

    C) energy and nutrition demands of the organisms

    D) genetic makeup of the species

    E) the species' physical appearance

Answer: D
Diff: 2   Page Ref: 1.2
Skill: Conceptual

30) Which of the following is/are important to the theory of evolution?

    A) environmental change

    B) variation in traits within a population

    C) mutation

    D) inheritance of traits

    E) all of these

Answer: E
Diff: 2   Page Ref: 1.2
Skill: Conceptual

31) Which is NOT an example of evolution?

    A) development of antibiotic-resistant bacteria

    B) flightless birds on islands without predators

    C) This year's flu is different from last year's flu.

    D) A dog learns how to open the cabinet where its food is kept.

    E) Most commercial pesticides are effective for 2-3 years.

Answer: D
Diff: 3   Page Ref: 1.2
Skill: Application

32) Mutation is essential to

    A) an organism's survival.

    B) evolution.

    C) sexual reproduction.

    D) growth.

    E) gamete formation.

Answer: B
Diff: 2   Page Ref: 1.2
Skill: Conceptual

33) A mutation is

    A) a physical deformity.

    B) a change in DNA sequence.

    C) a dose of radiation.

    D) a defective egg or sperm cell.

    E) the inability to speak.

Answer: B
Diff: 1   Page Ref: 1.2
Skill: Factual

34) In a word, evolution means _____.

    A) selection

    B) improvement

    C) mutation

    D) change

    E) nature

Answer: D
Diff: 1   Page Ref: 1.2
Skill: Conceptual

35) The concept of evolution is based upon

    A) genetic variation within a population.

    B) inheritance of variations by offspring of parents with the variations.

    C) survival and reproductive success of organisms with favorable variations.

    D) all genetic variation in a population is equally successful.

    E) all of the above

Answer: C
Diff: 2   Page Ref: 1.2
Skill: Conceptual

36) All of the following are examples of adaptations, EXCEPT

    A) mice learning a maze to get food.

    B) larger teeth in beavers for gnawing wood.

    C) different beak shape for birds that eat seeds vs. insects.

    D) insects that resemble twigs.

    E) flower coloration that attracts pollinators.

Answer: A
Diff: 2   *Page Ref: 1.2*
Skill: Application

37) Suppose a life form contains an enzyme that repairs DNA errors. The result is a decrease in mutations. This trait would most impact the organism's ability to

    A) obtain energy.   B) evolve.

    C) move.   D) maintain homeostasis.

Answer: B
Diff: 3   *Page Ref: 1.2*
Skill: Application

38) Mutations

    A) can occur during the copying of the DNA.

    B) are a change in the sequence of DNA.

    C) may improve the chances of survival for an organism.

    D) Both A and B are correct.

    E) All of the above are correct.

Answer: E
Diff: 2   *Page Ref: 1.2*
Skill: Factual

39) Variation among organisms is due to adaptations. True or False?

Answer: FALSE
Diff: 2   *Page Ref: 1.2*
Skill: Conceptual

40) Adaptations aid in the survival and reproduction of an organism in a particular environment. True or False?

Answer: TRUE
Diff: 1   *Page Ref: 1.2*
Skill: Factual

41) The _____ molecule stores all the hereditary information of an organism.

Answer: DNA
Diff: 1   Page Ref: 1.2
Skill: Factual

42) Errors or changes in the DNA molecule "blueprint" are called _____.

Answer: mutations
Diff: 2   Page Ref: 1.2
Skill: Factual

43) In terms of natural selection what does the phrase "survival of the fittest" mean?

Answer: Those members of a species better adapted to a particular environment are better able to survive to reproduce and pass their genes on to their offspring. Fitness is related to reproductive fitness.
Diff: 3   Page Ref: 1.2
Skill: Conceptual

44) Evolution is based on adaptations that aid in survival and reproduction of a species. List three different adaptations.

Answer: There are many correct answers. Some acceptable answers are: roots of plants (help land plants gain water); fleshy fish fins that allowed for movement across a surface; wings of eagles (aid in hunting)
Diff: 3   Page Ref: 1.2
Skill: Conceptual

45) The three natural processes that underlie evolution are _____.

Answer: genetic variation, inheritance, natural selection
Diff: 1   Page Ref: 1.2
Skill: Factual

46) Which of the following is/are characteristic of living organisms?

   A) organized structure

   B) responsiveness to stimuli

   C) maintenance of homeostasis

   D) B and C are correct.

   E) A, B, and C are correct.

Answer: E
Diff: 2   Page Ref: 1.3
Skill: Factual

47) All of the following are TRUE of ALL eukaryotic organisms except

    A) They are made of many cells linked together.

    B) They can grow.

    C) They reproduce themselves.

    D) They obtain nutrients and energy from their environment.

    E) All of these are true.

Answer: D
Diff: 2   Page Ref: 1.3
Skill: Factual

48) You drink a glass of lemonade, but your body's pH does not change. This is an example of how organisms

    A) maintain homeostasis.

    B) maintain organization.

    C) adapt to their environment.

    D) are immune to acid.

    E) are what they eat.

Answer: A
Diff: 2   Page Ref: 1.3
Skill: Application

49) Humans born without sweat glands usually do not survive. Why not?

    A) Sweating is an important mechanism for maintaining temperature homeostasis.

    B) Sweat glands create openings in the skin where gas exchange occurs.

    C) Sweating is an important way of ridding the body of excess water.

    D) Sweating is important for purging impurities from the body.

    E) Sweat builds up in the body which causes swelling and tissue damage.

Answer: A
Diff: 2   Page Ref: 1.3
Skill: Application

50) An organism's ability to maintain internal stability when the external environment changes is termed

    A) natural selection.

    B) mutation.

    C) responsiveness.

    D) metabolism.

    E) homeostasis.

Answer: E
Diff: 1   Page Ref: 1.3
Skill: Factual

51) You observe a plant on your windowsill that is growing at an angle toward the outside. This is an example of a living thing

    A) maintaining homeostasis.   B) responding to stimuli.

    C) reproducing.   D) evolving.

Answer: B
Diff: 1   Page Ref: 1.3
Skill: Application

52) Using his antennae, the male moth finds female moths by following a trail of airborne chemicals, called pheromones, upwind to the female producing them. This is an example of how living things

    A) acquire nutrients.

    B) grow.

    C) reproduce.

    D) respond to stimuli.

    E) maintain homeostasis.

Answer: D
Diff: 2   Page Ref: 1.3
Skill: Application

53) A typical animal would be characterized by all of the following EXCEPT

    A) the presence of eukaryotic cells.

    B) the ability to acquire nutrition through ingestion.

    C) the ability to grow and reproduce.

    D) the ability to maintain homeostasis.

    E) All of these are true.

Answer: E
Diff: 2   Page Ref: 1.3
Skill: Conceptual

54) Why do animals require "food" for survival?

    A) Food is a source of energy.

    B) Necessary chemicals are provided by food.

    C) Food is a primary source of water for all animals.

    D) A and B

    E) A, B, and C

Answer: D
Diff: 2   Page Ref: 1.3
Skill: Conceptual

55) The main difference between an autotroph and a heterotroph is

    A) how they reproduce.   B) how they respond to stimuli.

    C) the placement of their organelles.   D) how they obtain energy.

Answer: D
Diff: 1   Page Ref: 1.3
Skill: Factual

56) The energy that sustains nearly all life ultimately comes from sunlight. True or False?

Answer: TRUE
Diff: 1   Page Ref: 1.3
Skill: Factual

57) Photosynthetic bacteria are examples of autotrophs. True or False?

Answer: TRUE
Diff: 2   Page Ref: 1.3
Skill: Conceptual

58) In 2020, you are the top biologist at a research station studying biodiversity in Costa Rica. A young scientist brings you a sample from a new, previously unexplored collection site. She asks you to look at the sample and determine if it is indeed a living organism. As you begin your investigations you must first decide what characteristics define life from non–life. How would you characterize a living organism to be able to differentiate it from something that is non–living? Consider some of the aspects of life that you learned in your biology courses as an undergraduate.

Answer: The student should be able to describe several of the characteristics of a living organism in their answer.
Diff: 2   Page Ref: 1.3
Skill: Factual

59) Organisms respond to both internal and external stimuli. Describe the difference between these two types of stimuli and give an example of each.

Answer: variable
Diff: 1   Page Ref: 1.3
Skill: Factual, Application

Choose the characteristic of a living organism that best corresponds to the numbered statement. Selections may be used once, more than once, or not at all.

A. Growth
B. Reproduction
C. Homeostasis
D. Evolve
E. Response to stimuli

60) A sunflower follows the sun as it move across the sky during the day.

Answer: E
Diff: 2   Page Ref: 1.3
Skill: Conceptual

61) A puppy is born weighing 5 lb and eventually becomes a 75 lb golden retriever.

Answer: A
Diff: 2   Page Ref: 1.3
Skill: Conceptual

62) Humans sweat when the temperature gets hot so that they can cool themselves.

Answer: C
Diff: 2   Page Ref: 1.3
Skill: Conceptual

63) At the beginning of the week a plant is 3 inches tall, and at the end of the week it is 4 inches.

Answer: A
Diff: 2   Page Ref: 1.3
Skill: Conceptual

64) A paramecium will move from direct light.

Answer: E
Diff: 2   Page Ref: 1.3
Skill: Conceptual

65) A bacterium divides into two bacteria which are identical to, but smaller than, the original bacterium.

Answer: B
Diff: 2   Page Ref: 1.3
Skill: Conceptual

66) Over time the neck length of the giraffe has increased as only those giraffes with longer necks survived by eating the leaves high up on the trees and were able to reproduce and pass those long neck genes on to the next generation.

Answer: D
Diff: 2   Page Ref: 1.3
Skill: Conceptual

67) List four characteristics of living things and give an example to illustrate each.

Answer: There are many possible answers for this question. The following includes some acceptable answers: Living things are both complex and organized (Ex. cells have organelles with specific organization); Living things respond to stimuli (plants grow toward light); Living things maintain homeostasis (human body maintains body temperature); Living things acquire and use energy (plants use photosynthesis); Living things grow (animals grow during their lifetime); Living things reproduce (organisms produce offspring); Living things have the capacity to evolve (bacteria have evolved antibiotic resistance)
Diff: 2   Page Ref: 1.3
Skill: Application

68) Of the following levels of organization, Archaea have

A) atoms.

B) molecules.

C) organs.

D) A and B

E) A, B, and C

Answer: D
Diff: 2   Page Ref: 1.1, 1.4
Skill: Application

69) In evolutionary terms, which cell listed is considered to be most primitive?

A) protistan

B) prokaryotic

C) autotrophic

D) heterotrophic

E) eukaryotic

Answer: B
Diff: 2   Page Ref: 1.4
Skill: Factual

70) To which kingdom would a multicellular, eukaryotic, photosynthetic organism belong?

   A) protista

   B) fungi

   C) plantae

   D) animalia

   E) none of the above

Answer: C
Diff: 2   Page Ref: 1.3, 1.4
Skill: Factual

71) The basic difference between a prokaryotic cell and a eukaryotic cell is that the prokaryotic cell

   A) possesses membrane-bound organelles.

   B) lacks DNA.

   C) lacks a nuclear envelope.

   D) is usually considerably larger.

   E) is structurally more complex.

Answer: C
Diff: 2   Page Ref: 1.4
Skill: Factual

72) The Bacteria and Eukarya domains are distinguished by

   A) all members of Bacteria being single-celled and all members of Eukarya being multicellular.

   B) Bacteria getting nutrients via absorption and eukarya by photosynthesis.

   C) the fact that only Eukarya have the ability to grow and reproduce.

   D) the absence or presence of organelles and a nucleus in Bacteria.

   E) none of the above

Answer: D
Diff: 2   Page Ref: 1.4
Skill: Conceptual

73) Which kingdom has eukaryotic members?

    A) Kingdom Protista

    B) Kingdom Fungi

    C) Kingdom Plantae

    D) Kingdom Animalia

    E) All have some eukaryotic members.

Answer: E
Diff: 2   Page Ref: 1.4
Skill: Factual

74) Which kingdom possesses unicellular animal-like members as well as unicellular plant-like members?

    A) Kingdom Fungi

    B) Kingdom Animalia

    C) Kingdom Protista

    D) Kingdom Plantae

    E) all of the above

Answer: C
Diff: 2   Page Ref: 1.4
Skill: Factual

75) A cell that lacks organelles is a(n)

    A) member of the Kingdom Plantae.   B) animal cell.

    C) prokaryotic cell.   D) eukaryotic cell.

Answer: C
Diff: 2   Page Ref: 1.4
Skill: Factual

76) Prokaryotic cells are distinguishable from eukaryotic cells by the presence of a nucleus. True or False?

Answer: FALSE
Diff: 1   Page Ref: 1.4
Skill: Factual

77) Single-celled organisms that lack a nucleus belong to the two domains _____ and _____.

Answer: Archaea; Bacteria
Diff: 2   Page Ref: 1.4
Skill: Factual

78) Cell containing a nucleus are _____ and cells without a nucleus are _____.

Answer: eukaryotes; prokaryotes
Diff: 2   Page Ref: 1.4
Skill: Conceptual

79) The experiments of Francesco Redi

    A) disproved maggots and flies were related.

    B) disproved the idea of spontaneous generation.

    C) disproved the scientific method.

    D) used the scientific method to prove the idea of spontaneous generation.

    E) used his experiments to determine that flies come from maggots.

Answer: B
Diff: 2   Page Ref: Scientific Inquiry
Skill: Factual

80) Francesco Redi designed an experiment to test the notion of spontaneous generation. In his experiment, he left the first jar of meat open to the air and covered the second jar. The first jar would be called the

    A) experimental jar.   B) control jar.

    C) conclusive jar.   D) hypothetical jar.

Answer: B
Diff: 2   Page Ref: Scientific Inquiry
Skill: Conceptual

81) Biodiversity is the total number of organisms in an ecosystem. True or False?

Answer: FALSE
Diff: 1   Page Ref: Earth Watch
Skill: Factual

Chapter 2 Atoms, Molecules, and Life

1) A substance with specific properties that cannot be broken down or converted to another substance is a(n)

   A) element.

   B) molecule.

   C) ion.

   D) compound.

   E) mixture.

   Answer: A
   Diff: 1   Page Ref: 2.1
   Skill: Factual

2) If you examined the universe, the Earth, and the human body, which of the following combinations of elements would you find most common?

   A) C, O, Na, He, P, S

   B) C, Na, O, N, H, Mg

   C) Cl, Ca, C, H, O, P

   D) K, H, C, S, O, P

   E) S, P, O, N, H, C

   Answer: E
   Diff: 2   Page Ref: 2.1
   Skill: Factual

3) What determines the atomic number of an atom?

   A) number of electrons in the outermost energy level

   B) total number of energy shells

   C) arrangement of neutrons in the atomic nucleus

   D) number of protons in the atomic nucleus

   E) the total number of electrons and neutrons

   Answer: D
   Diff: 2   Page Ref: 2.1
   Skill: Factual

4) Which four elements make up approximately 96% of living matter?

    A) carbon, hydrogen, nitrogen, oxygen

    B) carbon, sulfur, phosphorus, hydrogen

    C) carbon, sodium, chlorine, magnesium

    D) carbon, oxygen, sulfur, calcium

    E) oxygen, hydrogen, calcium, sodium

Answer: A
Diff: 2   Page Ref: 2.1
Skill: Factual

5) You have been hired as a chemist. Your first task at your new job is to examine a newly discovered atom. The paperwork you are given states that its atomic number is 110. What does this mean?

    A) The atom contains 110 protons.

    B) The atom contains 55 electrons.

    C) The atom contains 55 protons and 55 neutrons.

    D) The atom is an isotope.

Answer: A
Diff: 2   Page Ref: 2.1
Skill: Application

6) Iron is an important trace element in human body cells. Imagine you are a biochemist trying to characterize what is known about iron atoms, in an effort to learn more about human physiology. You learn that iron has an atomic number of 26. What does this tell you about iron?

    A) An iron atom has 13 electrons and 13 protons.

    B) An iron atom has 13 protons and 13 neutrons.

    C) An iron atom has 26 protons.

    D) An iron atom is unable to become an isotope.

Answer: C
Diff: 2   Page Ref: 2.1
Skill: Application

7) Carbon–14 is often used for carbon dating, where scientists measure the rate of carbon–14 decay to determine the age of items. It contains six protons and eight neutrons. During the process of carbon–14 decay, one of its eight neutrons becomes a proton and an electron is emitted. Which of the following is the BEST explanation of what has occurred?

   A) The resulting atom is still has an unstable nucleus.

   B) The resulting atom is now a different element because the number of protons has changed.

   C) The resulting atom is still carbon–14.

   D) An ionic bond has formed.

   Answer: B
   Diff: 3   Page Ref: 2.1
   Skill: Conceptual

8) Radioactive isotopes are useful biological tools that are often used to

   A) measure the size of fossils.   B) detect brain tumors.

   C) build up a store of calcium in a cell.   D) increase the pH of blood.

   Answer: B
   Diff: 2   Page Ref: 2.1/Scientific Inquiry
   Skill: Application

9) An isotope of the element fluorine is commonly used in positron emission tomography (PET) scans. The non–isotope form of fluorine has 9 electrons, 9 protons and 10 neutrons. Based on your knowledge of isotopes, which of the following could be true about the fluorine isotope used in PET scans?

   A) The isotope form has only 8 electrons.

   B) The isotope form can have 8 or 10 protons.

   C) The isotope form has 9 neutrons.

   D) The isotope form has the same number of protons, neutrons and electrons as the non–isotope form.

   Answer: C
   Diff: 2   Page Ref: 2.1
   Skill: Application

10) An element is the fundamental structural unit of matter. True or False?

   Answer: FALSE
   Diff: 1   Page Ref: 2.1
   Skill: Factual

11) Isotopes are atoms of the same element that vary in the number of protons. True or False?

   Answer: FALSE
   Diff: 1   Page Ref: 2.1
   Skill: Factual

12) Each atom has an equal number of electrons and protons. True or False?

Answer: TRUE
Diff: 1   Page Ref: 2.1
Skill: Factual

13) The chemical properties of an element are determined by the number of _____ its atoms contain.

Answer: electrons
Diff: 2   Page Ref: 2.1
Skill: Factual

14) An isotope is atoms of the same element that have different numbers of _____.

Answer: neutrons
Diff: 1   Page Ref: 2.1
Skill: Factual

15) The second electron shell is considered to be full when it contains _____ electrons.

Answer: eight
Diff: 1   Page Ref: 2.1
Skill: Factual

16) Why is a helium atom (Atomic #2) more stable than a hydrogen atom (Atomic #1)?

A) Two electrons completely fill its outermost electron shell.

B) Eight electrons completely fill its outermost electron shell.

C) The outermost electron shell is half-empty.

D) Helium atoms react readily with oxygen.

E) Hydrogen atoms react to form helium.

Answer: A
Diff: 2   Page Ref: 2.2
Skill: Conceptual

17) Which of the following factors is the most significant when considering the reactivity of an atom?

A) An atom is the smallest particle of an element.

B) A molecule is the smallest unit of a compound.

C) Atoms are held together by interactions between electrons.

D) The number of protons affects the size of the atom.

E) Atoms with many neutrons may be radioactive.

Answer: C
Diff: 2   Page Ref: 2.2
Skill: Conceptual

18) Sodium (Na), atomic number 11, has a tendency to lose an electron in the presence of chlorine. After losing the electron, Na will have _____ protons in its nucleus.

    A) 10   B) 11   C) 12   D) 21   E) 22

Answer: B
Diff: 3   *Page Ref: 2.2*
Skill: Conceptual

19) For an atom to achieve maximum stability and become chemically inert, what must occur?

    A) Its outermost energy shell must be filled with electrons.

    B) The number of electrons must equal the number of protons.

    C) Sharing of electron pairs is necessary.

    D) Ionization is required.

    E) It must be inert.

Answer: A
Diff: 2   *Page Ref: 2.2*
Skill: Conceptual

20) An atom's nucleus is composed of

    A) protons.

    B) neutrons.

    C) protons and electrons.

    D) protons and neutrons.

    E) neutrons and electrons.

Answer: D
Diff: 1   *Page Ref: 2.2*
Skill: Factual

21) How does one explain the formation of ions?

    A) sharing of electrons

    B) gain or loss of electrons

    C) gain or loss of protons

    D) sharing of protons

    E) gain or loss of neutrons

Answer: B
Diff: 2   *Page Ref: 2.2*
Skill: Factual

22) You have been hired as a chemist and are examining the paperwork of a newly discovered atom. You read that this atom has a tendency to lose 2 electrons. Based on what you know, this would result in the formation of

    A) a polar molecule.   B) an ion.

    C) a water molecule.   D) an isotope.

Answer: B
Diff: 2   Page Ref: 2.2
Skill: Application

23) The formation of sodium chloride (NaCl) is the result of

    A) covalent bonding.

    B) chemical unreactivity.

    C) attraction between opposite charges.

    D) the lack of chemical attraction.

    E) both A and C

Answer: C
Diff: 2   Page Ref: 2.2
Skill: Factual

24) Atoms or molecules which have gained or lost electrons are termed

    A) acids.

    B) bases.

    C) polymers.

    D) ions.

    E) buffers.

Answer: D
Diff: 2   Page Ref: 2.2
Skill: Factual

25) Biological molecules primarily are joined by

    A) peptide bonds.

    B) ionic bonds.

    C) hydrogen bonds.

    D) disulfide bonds.

    E) covalent bonds.

Answer: E
Diff: 2   Page Ref: 2.2
Skill: Factual

26) Phosphorus has an atomic number of fifteen, so what will be the distribution of its electrons?

   A) The first energy level will have eight and the second will have seven.

   B) The first energy level will have two, the second will have eight, and the third will have five.

   C) The first energy level will have two and the second will have thirteen.

   D) The first, second, and third energy levels will each have five electrons.

   E) Electron arrangement cannot be determined from the atomic number.

Answer: B
Diff: 2   Page Ref: 2.2
Skill: Conceptual

27) Sulfur is an essential element in the human body and studying its characteristics is important in understanding human physiology. Sulfur atoms have 6 electrons in their outer shell. Based on this information, which of the following may be true?

   A) Sulfur can form important molecules using covalent bonds.

   B) Sulfur is inert.

   C) Sulfur is an important isotope of hydrogen.

   D) Sulfur has 8 electrons in its outer shell and forms ions.

Answer: A
Diff: 2   Page Ref: 2.2
Skill: Conceptual

28) Which of the following could potentially be a free radical?

   A) oxygen (atomic number = 8)   B) helium (atomic number = 2)

   C) argon (atomic number = 9)   D) neon (atomic number = 10)

Answer: A
Diff: 2   Page Ref: 2.2
Skill: Application

29) Free radicals are considered dangerous because

   A) they attack the atomic nucleus.

   B) they emit dangerous radiation.

   C) they steal electrons from other atoms causing them to become free radicals.

   D) they damage oxygen and cause it to become an antioxidant.

Answer: C
Diff: 2   Page Ref: 2.2
Skill: Factual

30) Scientists now recommend a diet rich in antioxidants to stay healthy. What occurs at the atomic level to explain the reasoning behind this recommendation?

A) Antioxidants stop the chain reaction of cellular damage caused by free radicals.

B) Antioxidants cause an increase in pH which is necessary.

C) Antioxidants steal electrons which gives cells extra energy.

D) Antioxidants are inert and do not interact with free radicals.

Answer: A
Diff: 2   Page Ref: 2.2
Skill: Application

31) Which of the following BEST explains why an atom may not form compounds readily?

A) The atom has no electrons.

B) The atom has an uneven number of protons.

C) The atom has seven electrons in its outer shells.

D) The atom's outer energy levels are completely full.

Answer: D
Diff: 2   Page Ref: 2.2
Skill: Application

32) NASA's Deep Space 1 probe used ion propulsion technology to propel it into outer space. Ion propulsion uses an electrical charge to ionize atoms such as xenon. These ions are funneled from the exhaust of the craft at such high speeds that it is pushed in the opposite direction and propelled into space. The electrical charge that is used to ionize xenon atoms most likely

A) cause protons to become neutrons.

B) cause electrons to be released from the atoms.

C) cause neutrons to be released from the atoms.

D) change the atoms into radioactive isotopes.

Answer: B
Diff: 2   Page Ref: 2.2
Skill: Application

33) The element carbon has an atomic number of six. Carbon would most likely

A) form an ionic bond.

B) form four covalent bonds.

C) form two covalent bonds.

D) donate two electrons to another atom.

Answer: B
Diff: 2   Page Ref: 2.2
Skill: Application

34) Calcium has an atomic number of 20. A calcium ion could have

A) 20 electrons.   B) 18 electrons.

C) 10 electrons.   D) cannot be determined

Answer: B
Diff: 1   Page Ref: 2.2
Skill: Application

35) Carbon has an atomic number of six. Carbon would most likely

A) share electrons.

B) gain electrons.

C) lose electrons.

D) share protons.

E) lose protons.

Answer: A
Diff: 1   Page Ref: 2.2
Skill: Application

36) What does H^1O^1H represent?

A) atom of water

B) mixture including water

C) molecule of water

D) planetary model of water

E) ionic bonding of water

Answer: C
Diff: 2   Page Ref: 2.2
Skill: Conceptual

37) All the following are true of hydrogen gas, H_2, EXCEPT (H atomic number = 1)

A) H_2 is stable.

B) H_2 is covalently bonded.

C) H_2 shares one pair of electrons.

D) H_2 is polar.

E) All of the above are true.

Answer: D
Diff: 2   Page Ref: 2.2
Skill: Conceptual

38) Polar covalent bonds form when

   A) electrons are shared unequally between atoms.

   B) more than one pair of electrons is shared.

   C) ions are formed.

   D) an acid and base are combined.

   E) atoms from two molecules are attracted to each other.

Answer: A
Diff: 1   Page Ref: 2.2
Skill: Factual

39) Which of these bonds is characterized by equal sharing of electrons?

   A) C–H   B) O–H   C) H–Cl   D) Ch=O   E) N–H

Answer: A
Diff: 3   Page Ref: 2.2
Skill: Factual

40) Which of the following represents a molecule characterized by polar covalent bonding?

   A) NaCl   B) H_2 C) H_2O D) C–C   E) CH_4

Answer: C
Diff: 3   Page Ref: 2.2
Skill: Factual

41) What bond(s) is(are) easily disrupted in aqueous (water) solutions?

   A) covalent

   B) polar covalent

   C) ionic

   D) A and B are correct.

   E) A, B, and C are correct.

Answer: C
Diff: 2   Page Ref: 2.2
Skill: Conceptual

42) If sulfur has an atomic number of 16, how many covalent bonds does it form?

   A) 0   B) 2   C) 4   D) 6   E) 8

Answer: B
Diff: 2   Page Ref: 2.2
Skill: Conceptual

43) The part of the atom of greatest biological interest is the

   A) proton.

   B) electron.

   C) neutron.

   D) innermost electron shell.

   E) none of the above

Answer: B
Diff: 2   Page Ref: 2.2
Skill: Conceptual

44) Which pair has similar chemical properties?

   A) ^1H and ^{22}Na

   B) ^{12}C and ^{28}Si

   C) ^{16}O and ^{32}S

   D) ^{12}C and ^{14}C

   E) ^1H and ^2He

Answer: D
Diff: 3   Page Ref: 2.2
Skill: Conceptual

45) A single covalent chemical bond represents the sharing of how many electrons?

   A) 1   B) 2   C) 3   D) 4   E) 6

Answer: B
Diff: 2   Page Ref: 2.2
Skill: Factual

46) Polar molecules

   A) have an overall negative electric charge.

   B) have an equal distribution of electric charge.

   C) have an overall positive electric charge.

   D) have an unequal distribution of electric charge.

   E) are ions.

Answer: D
Diff: 1   Page Ref: 2.2
Skill: Factual

47) The hydrogen bond between two water molecules arises because water is

    A) polar.

    B) nonpolar.

    C) a liquid.

    D) a small molecule.

    E) hydrophobic.

Answer: A
Diff: 1   Page Ref: 2.2
Skill: Conceptual

48) _____ often form(s) as a result of polar bonds.

    A) Ionic bonds

    B) Hydrogen bonds

    C) Peptide bonds

    D) Ice

    E) Water

Answer: B
Diff: 1   Page Ref: 2.2
Skill: Factual

49) Which statement is an accurate description of water molecules?

    A) They are charged and polar.

    B) They are charged and nonpolar.

    C) They are uncharged and polar.

    D) They are uncharged and nonpolar.

    E) They are ionically bonded.

Answer: C
Diff: 2   Page Ref: 2.2
Skill: Factual

50) Which of the following is an example of hydrogen bonding?

    A) The bond between O and H in a single molecule of water.

    B) The bond between O of one water molecule and H of a second water molecule.

    C) The bond between O of one water molecule and O of a second water molecule.

    D) The bond between H of one water molecule and H of a second water molecule.

    E) The bond between the H of a water molecule and the H of a hydrogen molecule.

Answer: B
Diff: 2   Page Ref: 2.2
Skill: Factual

51) Which of the following results from a transfer of electron(s) between atoms?

A) nonpolar covalent bond

B) polar covalent bond

C) ionic bond

D) hydrogen bond

E) electron–proton interaction

Answer: C
Diff: 1   Page Ref: 2.2
Skill: Factual

52) Which of the following results from an unequal sharing of electrons between atoms?

A) nonpolar covalent bond

B) polar covalent bond

C) ionic bond

D) hydrogen bond

E) electron–proton interaction

Answer: B
Diff: 1   Page Ref: 2.2
Skill: Factual

53) Which of the following best explains the attraction of water molecules to each other?

A) nonpolar covalent bond

B) polar covalent bond

C) ionic bond

D) hydrogen bond

E) electron–proton interaction

Answer: D
Diff: 1   Page Ref: 2.2
Skill: Conceptual

54) Which of the following would be least affected by the presence of water?

A) nonpolar covalent bond

B) polar covalent bond

C) ionic bond

D) hydrogen bond

E) electron–proton interaction

Answer: A
Diff: 2   Page Ref: 2.2
Skill: Conceptual

55) What is the difference between covalent and ionic bonds?

Answer: Covalent bonds are the sharing of electrons between atoms while ionic bonds are the electric charge attraction between two ions.
Diff: 2   Page Ref: 2.2
Skill: Conceptual

56) Which type of chemical bond is the most important for biological molecules? Why?

Answer: Covalent bonds are most important for biological molecules because they form the strongest types of bonds, especially in aqueous environments.
Diff: 2   Page Ref: 2.2
Skill: Conceptual

57) Draw the following atoms: make sure that you clearly represent all three subatomic particles and show the electron shells for each:
    Nitrogen (atomic number = 7) Hydrogen (atomic number = 1)

Answer: Nitrogen contains seven protons, seven neutrons and seven electrons; Hydrogen contains one proton, one neutron and one electron.
Diff: 2   Page Ref: 2.2
Skill: Conceptual

58) Draw the following atoms: make sure that you clearly represent all three subatomic particles and show the electron shells for each:
    Nitrogen (atomic number = 7) Hydrogen (atomic number = 1)

Using the atoms drawn, draw the covalent bond(s) that would allow for the atoms to be most stable.

Answer: Nitrogen contains seven protons, seven neutrons and seven electrons; Hydrogen contains one proton, one neutron and one electron. Drawing should show hydrogens covalently bonded to nitrogen (NH_3).
Diff: 2   Page Ref: 2.2
Skill: Conceptual

59) The attraction between a slight positive charge on a hydrogen atom and the slight negative charge of a nearby atom is a _____.

Answer: hydrogen bond
Diff: 2   Page Ref: 2.2
Skill: Factual

60) What happens when hydrochloric acid (HCl) is added to pure water?

    A) The HCl molecules separate into H^+ and Cl^- ions.

    B) The water has a decrease of H^+ ions.

    C) The HCl molecules float on top of the water.

    D) The concentration of OH^- ions increases.

    E) The pH of the solution increases.

Answer: A
Diff: 2   Page Ref: 2.3
Skill: Factual

61) An atom of nitrogen attracts electrons more strongly than an atom of hydrogen. Which of the following BEST describes ammonia (NH_3)?

    A) The nitrogen is more slightly positive.

    B) The nitrogen is strongly negative.

    C) The hydrogens are more slightly positive.

    D) The hydrogens are strongly negative.

    E) Charges balance out and none of the atoms has any charge.

Answer: C
Diff: 2   Page Ref: 2.3
Skill: Application

62) If a substance measures 7 on the pH scale, that substance

    A) has equal concentration of H^+ and OH^- ions.

    B) may be lemon juice.

    C) has greater concentration of OH^- than H^+ ions.

    D) probably lacks OH^- ions.

    E) is basic.

Answer: A
Diff: 2   Page Ref: 2.3
Skill: Conceptual

63) A neutral solution

    A) has no H^+.

    B) has no OH^-.

    C) has equal amounts of H^+ and OH^-.

    D) is hydrophobic.

    E) has a pH of 0.

Answer: C
Diff: 2   Page Ref: 2.3
Skill: Factual

64) How do buffers work?

    A) soak up extra acid and base

    B) accept or release H^+

    C) accept or release OH^-

    D) convert H^+ and OH^- to water

    E) monitor the blood pH

Answer: B
Diff: 3   Page Ref: 2.3
Skill: Conceptual

65) The human body must maintain a constant pH. In the blood, bicarbonate serves as a(n) _____ to help maintain the necessary pH.

    A) acid   B) buffer   C) base   D) solvent

Answer: B
Diff: 2   Page Ref: 2.3
Skill: Application

66) Milk of magnesia is often used to treat stomach upset. It has a pH of 10. Based on this information, which of the following is true?

    A) Milk of magnesia is a base.

    B) Milk of magnesia is hydrophobic.

    C) Milk of magnesia is an acid.

    D) Milk of magnesia has the exact same pH as the stomach acid.

Answer: A
Diff: 2   Page Ref: 2.3
Skill: Application

67) What is meant by saying water has a high specific heat?

    A) It can absorb a lot of energy without changing temperature.

    B) It grows hot very quickly.

    C) The boiling point of water is very low.

    D) Water can only heat up to a certain temperature.

    E) Water freezes easily.

Answer: A
Diff: 3   Page Ref: 2.3
Skill: Factual

68) Which property (or properties) of water enables water to function as a moderator of temperature for living organisms?

    A) high specific heat

    B) high heat of vaporization

    C) high heat of fusion

    D) A and B

    E) A, B, and C

Answer: E
Diff: 2   Page Ref: 2.3
Skill: Factual

69) The fact that salt dissolves in water is BEST explained by

    A) the charged nature of water molecules.

    B) the polar nature of water molecules.

    C) the hydrophobic nature of salt.

    D) the ionic nature of water molecules.

    E) the hydrophobic nature of the water.

Answer: B
Diff: 2   Page Ref: 2.3
Skill: Conceptual

70) Hydrophilic molecules

    A) form hydrogen bonds among themselves.

    B) are neutral and nonpolar.

    C) readily dissolve in water.

    D) A and C

    E) A, B, and C

Answer: D
Diff: 2   Page Ref: 2.3
Skill: Factual

71) Water will dissolve all of these EXCEPT

    A) sugar.

    B) salt.

    C) CH_3-CH_2-OH.

    D) CH_3-COOH.

    E) $CH_3-CH_2-CH_2-CH_3$.

Answer: E
Diff: 3   Page Ref: 2.3
Skill: Conceptual

72) Water is considered a good solvent because

    A) it can hydrogen bond with other polar molecules.

    B) it dissolves ionically bonded molecules.

    C) it dissolves all organic molecules.

    D) A and B

    E) all of these

Answer: D
Diff: 2   Page Ref: 2.3
Skill: Conceptual

73) Water moves through a plant because of the property of

    A) high heat of fusion.

    B) high heat of vaporization.

    C) high specific heat.

    D) adhesion.

    E) cohesion.

Answer: E
Diff: 2   Page Ref: 2.3
Skill: Conceptual

74) Why are water molecules cohesive?

    A) because they create surface tension

    B) because they form hydrogen bonds

    C) because they contain hydrogen

    D) because they stick to other polar molecules

    E) because they are repelled by nonpolar molecules

Answer: B
Diff: 2   Page Ref: 2.3
Skill: Conceptual

75) If the acidic level of human blood increases, how is homeostasis maintained?

    A) Bicarbonate (HCO_3^-) releases H^+ ions that combine with excess OH^- ions to form H_2O.

    B) H^+ ion–donor levels increase.

    C) Bicarbonate (HCO_3^-) accepts H^+ and forms carbonic acid.

    D) Answers A, B, and C all are correct.

Answer: C
Diff: 2   Page Ref: 2.3
Skill: Conceptual

76) As ice melts, it

    A) absorbs heat from its surroundings.   B) becomes less dense.

    C) increases its property of cohesion.   D) increases its heat of vaporization.

Answer: A
Diff: 2   Page Ref: 2.3
Skill: Factual

77) What determines the cohesiveness of water molecules?

    A) hydrogen bonds

    B) ionic bonds

    C) covalent bonds

    D) hydrophobic interactions

    E) All of the above are correct.

Answer: A
Diff: 2   Page Ref: 2.3
Skill: Conceptual

78) If you place a paper towel in a dish of water, the water will move up the towel by capillary action. What property of water gives rise to capillary action?

    A) Water molecules separate into H^+ and OH^- ions.

    B) Water is a good solvent.

    C) Water molecules have hydrophobic interactions.

    D) Water can form hydrogen bonds.

    E) Water takes up large amounts of heat when it vaporizes.

Answer: D
Diff: 2   Page Ref: 2.3
Skill: Application

79) Sweating is a useful cooling device for humans because

    A) water takes up a great deal of heat in changing from its liquid state to its gaseous state.

    B) water takes up a great deal of heat in changing from its solid state to its liquid state.

    C) water can exist in three states at temperatures common on Earth.

    D) water is an outstanding solvent.

    E) water ionizes readily.

Answer: A
Diff: 2   Page Ref: 2.3
Skill: Conceptual

80) In general, a substance that carries an electrical charge can dissolve in water. Given this fact, which of the following would most likely NOT dissolve in water?

    A) ionic compounds   B) polar covalent molecules

    C) nonpolar molecules   D) NaCl

Answer: C
Diff: 2   Page Ref: 2.3
Skill: Application

81) You place a paper clip on the surface of a bowl of water. You observe that the paper clip remains suspended on the surface. This is due to the

    A) surface tension of the water.   B) fact the water is a good solvent.

    C) polarity of the water.   D) density of the water.

Answer: A
Diff: 1   Page Ref: 2.3
Skill: Application

82) The specific heat of water is ten times greater than that of iron. You place a metal pot full of water on the stove to heat it up. You touch the metal handle of the pot of when the water is still only lukewarm. Which of the following BEST describes what will happen?

A) You find that the handle is cooler than the water in the pot.

B) You burn your finger and pull your hand away from the very hot handle.

C) You find that both the water and the handle are the same temperature.

D) You determine that metal pots full of water produce acids and bases.

Answer: B
Diff: 2   Page Ref: 2.3
Skill: Application

83) You place a beaker of turpentine on a hot plate next to a beaker of water. Which of the following pieces of information do you need to know in order to hypothesize which will heat up faster?

A) the specific heat of each liquid

B) the heat of vaporization of each liquid

C) the pH of each liquid

D) the number of hydroxide ions in each liquid

Answer: A
Diff: 2   Page Ref: 2.3
Skill: Conceptual

84) You drop a handful of salt into a glass of water. Which of the following BEST describes what is happening inside the glass at the molecular level?

A) The positively charged hydrogen ends of the water molecules are attracted to sodium ions.

B) The positively charged hydrogen ends of the water molecules are attracted to chloride ions.

C) Sodium and chloride ions form a covalent bond.

D) Water and sodium form a covalent bond.

Answer: B
Diff: 1   Page Ref: 2.3
Skill: Conceptual

85) Your friend does a belly flop into the pool. The stinging pain he feels is most likely due to the

A) surface tension of water.   B) fact that water is a good solvent.

C) pH of the water.   D) hydrophobicity of your friend's skin.

Answer: A
Diff: 1   Page Ref: 2.3
Skill: Factual

86) Which of the following is the most dense?

   A) liquid water

   B) water vapor

   C) ice

   D) All of the above forms of water have the same density.

Answer: A
Diff: 1   Page Ref: 2.3
Skill: Factual

87) A living thing composed mostly of water can withstand sunny, hot weather without their body temperature soaring quickly. Which of the following BEST explains why?

   A) Water has a high specific heat.   B) Water has a low specific heat.

   C) Water is a good solvent.   D) Water is a poor solvent.

Answer: A
Diff: 1   Page Ref: 2.3
Skill: Factual

88) Acids have pH values below 7, while bases have pH values above 7. True or False?

Answer: TRUE
Diff: 2   Page Ref: 2.3
Skill: Conceptual

89) Water molecules are held together by ionic bonds. True or False?

Answer: FALSE
Diff: 2   Page Ref: 2.3
Skill: Conceptual

90) Water surface tension is a result of the adhesive nature of water molecules. True or False?

Answer: FALSE
Diff: 1   Page Ref: 2.3
Skill: Conceptual

91) A buffer is essential in living systems to maintain a constant pH. True or False?

Answer: TRUE
Diff: 1   Page Ref: 2.3
Skill: Factual

92) Most liquids become less dense upon solidification, but water is different in that it becomes more dense when it solidifies. True or False?

Answer: FALSE
Diff: 2   Page Ref: 2.3
Skill: Conceptual

93) The water strider skates along the surface of water due to a property of liquids called
_____.

Answer: surface tension
Diff: 2   Page Ref: 2.3
Skill: Factual

94) Molecules that are electrically attracted to water molecules are _____.

Answer: hydrophilic
Diff: 2   Page Ref: 2.3
Skill: Factual

95) What property of water is responsible for the ability of plants to get water from their roots up
to their leaves?

Answer: Cohesion
Diff: 1   Page Ref: 2.3
Skill: Application

96) How does a base differ from an acid?

Answer: A base is a solution with a concentration of OH– ions greater than H+ (pH greater than
7) and an acid has a H+ concentration that exceeds its OH– ion concentration (pH less
than 7).
Diff: 2   Page Ref: 2.3
Skill: Conceptual

97) Imagine you are trying to make a homemade salad dressing and place several drops of olive
oil into a container of water. You stir the solution but the oil doesn't readily mix. Instead you
continue to observe a glistening clump of oil that floats on the surface. Explain what is
happening at the molecular level. (Your answer should include the term hydrophobic.)

Answer: When oil molecules are in together in water, their nonpolar surfaces are hydrophobic
and nestle together. They are surrounded by water molecules that form hydrogen
bonds with one another but not the oil.
Diff: 3   Page Ref: 2.3
Skill: Conceptual

Chapter 3 Biological Molecules

1) Which of the following is NOT an organic molecule?

   A) protein

   B) nucleic acid

   C) monosaccharide

   D) carbon monoxide

   E) lipids

Answer: D
Diff: 1   Page Ref: 3.1
Skill: Conceptual

2) You are telling your friend about what you've learned about organic molecules. You told her that organic molecules are all made up of carbon backbones with hydrogens. She doesn't understand how there can be so many different organic molecules if they all are made up of the same basic components. What do you tell her to explain?

   A) Different organic molecules vary because they possess different isotopes of carbon.

   B) Different organic molecules vary because they possess different functional groups.

   C) Organic molecules actually all have the same structure, they simply move differently.

   D) Organic molecules are different because of different types of hydrogen bonds that form.

Answer: B
Diff: 2   Page Ref: 3.1
Skill: Conceptual

3) Carbon provides a versatile backbone for macromolecules. With an atomic number of 6, carbon can form up to _____ different _____ bonds.

Answer: 4; covalent
Diff: 2   Page Ref: 3.1
Skill: Factual

4) _____ molecules are synthesized by living organisms.

Answer: Organic
Diff: 2   Page Ref: 3.1
Skill: Factual

5) Many fruits and vegetables are described as organic when they have been grown without the use of pesticides. Your chemistry professor tells you that the term "organic" has a different meaning to her. Describe what organic means to this chemist.

   Answer: To a chemist, organic refers to a molecule that contains a carbon backbone with bonded
           hydrogen atoms.
Diff: 2   Page Ref: 3.1
Skill: Application

6) Which of the following BEST explains the molecular complexity of living organisms?

A) The large number of different monomers allows the construction of many polymers.

B) Each organism has its own unique set of monomers for use in constructing polymers.

C) Condensation reactions can create different polymers because they can use virtually any molecules in the cell.

D) While there are not many macromolecules in cells, each one has many different functions.

E) A small number of monomers can be assembled into large polymers with many different sequences.

Answer: E
Diff: 1   Page Ref: 3.2
Skill: Conceptual

7) Large biological molecules are synthesized by removing

A) carbon.

B) covalent bonds.

C) water.

D) oxygen.

E) peptides.

Answer: C
Diff: 1   Page Ref: 3.2
Skill: Factual

8) What type of chemical reaction results in the breakdown of organic polymers into their respective subunits?

A) condensation

B) oxidation

C) hydrolysis

D) ionization

E) reduction

Answer: C
Diff: 2   Page Ref: 3.2
Skill: Factual

9) Which of the following reactions requires the removal of water to form a covalent bond?

A) glycogen → glucose subunits

B) dipeptide → alanine + glycine

C) cellulose → glucose

D) glucose + galactose → lactose

E) fat → fatty acids + glycerol

Answer: D
Diff: 2   Page Ref: 3.2
Skill: Conceptual

10) What do carbohydrates, lipids, and proteins have in common?

A) Monomers of these organic molecules form polymers by way of condensation reactions.

B) Covalent bonding holds these molecules together.

C) Each of these organic molecules has a carbon backbone with various functional groups attached.

D) All are important components of an animal's diet.

E) all of the above

Answer: E
Diff: 2   Page Ref: 3.2
Skill: Conceptual

11) Which of the following correctly matches an organic polymer with its respective monomers?

A) protein and amino acids

B) carbohydrates and polysaccharides

C) hydrocarbon and monosaccharides

D) lipid and steroids

E) DNA and ATP

Answer: A
Diff: 2   Page Ref: 3.2
Skill: Factual

12) Which of the following BEST summarizes the relationship between dehydration reactions and hydrolysis?

A) Dehydration reactions assemble polymers and hydrolysis breaks them down.

B) Hydrolysis occurs during the day and dehydration happen at night.

C) Dehydration reactions can occur only after hydrolysis.

D) Hydrolysis creates monomers and dehydration reactions destroy them.

E) Dehydration reactions occur only in animals and hydrolysis reactions occur only in plants.

Answer: A
Diff: 2   Page Ref: 3.2
Skill: Conceptual

13) In condensation reactions, the atoms that make up a water molecule are derived from

A) oxygen.

B) only one of the reactants.

C) both of the reactants.

D) carbohydrates.

E) enzymes.

Answer: C
Diff: 2   Page Ref: 3.2
Skill: Conceptual

14) Look at the following chemical reaction. Which arrow represents hydrolysis?
Glucose + fructose -------- 1.-------> sucrose + water
                    <-------- 2. -----

A) 1   B) 2   C) both   D) neither

Answer: B
Diff: 2   Page Ref: 3.2
Skill: Conceptual

15) Look at the following chemical reaction. Which molecule is the disaccharide?
Glucose + fructose -------- 1.-------> sucrose + water
                    <-------- 2. -----

A) glucose   B) water   C) sucrose   D) fructose

Answer: C
Diff: 2   Page Ref: 3.2
Skill: Factual/Conceptual

16) Hydrolysis could be correctly described as the

   A) heating of a compound in order to drive off its excess water and to concentrate its volume.

   B) the breaking of a long–chain compound into its subunits by adding water to its structure between the subunits.

   C) constant removal of hydrogen atoms from the surface of a carbohydrate.

   D) None of the above are true.

Answer: B
Diff: 2   Page Ref: 3.2
Skill: Conceptual

17) Keratin and silk are examples of _____ while glucose and sucrose are examples of _____.

   A) proteins; lipids   B) proteins; carbohydrates

   C) carbohydrates; proteins   D) nucleic acids; lipids

Answer: B
Diff: 1   Page Ref: 3.2
Skill: Factual

18) Your instructor tells you that dehydration synthesis involves the removal of a hydrogen ion and the removal of a hydroxyl (OH-) group. She calls on you and asks you to determine what happens next. What should you say?

   A) A large biological molecule is split apart.

   B) The hydrogen ion and hydroxyl group interact to form water.

   C) A monosaccharide is released.

   D) The hydrogen ion immediately becomes an isotope.

Answer: B
Diff: 2   Page Ref: 3.2
Skill: Conceptual

19) _____ determine the characteristics and chemical reactivity of organic molecules.

Answer: Functional groups
Diff: 1   Page Ref: 3.2
Skill: Conceptual

20) Many macromolecules are formed by the connection of monomer units in a _____ reaction (removal of water); the reverse process occurs via a _____ reaction (addition of water).

Answer: dehydration; hydrolysis
Diff: 2   Page Ref: 3.2
Skill: Factual

21) The fiber in your diet is really

   A) protein.   B) ATP.   C) starch.   D) cartilage.   E) cellulose.

   Answer: E
   Diff: 2   Page Ref: 3.3
   Skill: Factual

22) Chitin is an example of a _____.

   A) polymer

   B) polysaccharide

   C) carbohydrate

   D) A and B

   E) all of these

   Answer: E
   Diff: 1   Page Ref: 3.3
   Skill: Factual

23) Where is glycogen stored in vertebrate animals?

   A) liver and muscles

   B) brain and kidneys

   C) heart and bones

   D) pancreas and blood

   E) liver and heart

   Answer: A
   Diff: 2   Page Ref: 3.3
   Skill: Factual

24) An example of a structural polysaccharide is

   A) table sugar.

   B) chitin.

   C) starch.

   D) glucose.

   E) glycogen.

   Answer: B
   Diff: 2   Page Ref: 3.3
   Skill: Factual

25) Which of the following provides long-term energy storage for plants?

    A) glucose   B) glycogen   C) starch   D) cellulose   E) ATP

Answer: C
Diff: 2   *Page Ref: 3.3*
Skill: Factual

26) Lactose is a disaccharide of glucose and galactose, and its digestion requires the actions of the enzyme lactase If the lactose is taken in as part of the diet, but not digested by lactase, this sugar is then metabolized by bacteria in the intestine, leading to the symptoms of lactose intolerance. Lactose intolerance, therefore, results from

    A) a lack of hydrolysis of lactose.

    B) a lack of dehydration synthesis of lactose.

    C) a low blood glucose level.

    D) an inability of the body to produce glucose.

Answer: A
Diff: 2   *Page Ref: 3.3*
Skill: Application

27) In humans, the first phase of cavity formation involves the *S. mutans* bacteria in the mouth causing the hydrolysis of sucrose (sugar). Which of the following would be the result of this reaction?

    A) glucose and fructose   B) starch and water

    C) lactose   D) nucleic acids

Answer: A
Diff: 2   *Page Ref: 3.3*
Skill: Factual/Application

28) Which of the following can serve as both energy source and as structural support for cells?

    A) proteins   B) carbohydrates   C) lipids   D) nucleic acids

Answer: B
Diff: 2   *Page Ref: 3.3*
Skill: Conceptual

29) Which of the following is composed of monosaccharide monomer units?

    A) proteins   B) carbohydrates   C) lipids   D) nucleic acids

Answer: B
Diff: 1   *Page Ref: 3.3*
Skill: Factual

30) When the level of glucose in your blood is high, your body is able to store excess glucose in the liver by forming glycogen. When blood glucose levels fall, this stored glucose can be released. Based on this information, which of the following is true?

    A) Glucose is a polysaccharide that can join to form the monosaccharide glycogen to store excess.

    B) Glucose is not an organic molecule while glycogen is.

    C) Glycogen is a polysaccharide formed by joining excess monosaccharides of glucose.

    D) Glycogen is a highly branched functional group that forms a larger glucose polymer.

Answer: B
Diff: 3   Page Ref: 3.3
Skill: Conceptual

31) What are the four major types of macromolecules?

Answer: carbohydrates, lipids, proteins, and nucleic acids
Diff: 2   Page Ref: 3.3
Skill: Factual

32) Why do cows have the ability to breakdown cellulose into glucose and humans can not digest cellulose?

Answer: Cows also lack the ability to break down cellulose but they do have special bacteria and fungi in their digestive tract that break down cellulose for them.
Diff: 2   Page Ref: 3.3
Skill: Conceptual

33) What are the two main functions of carbohydrates in a living system? Give an example of each.

Answer: energy storage (ex. glucose, starch, glycogen) and structural support (ex. chitin)
Diff: 2   Page Ref: 3.3
Skill: Factual

34) Starch is to glycogen what _____ is to _____.

    A) oil; fat

    B) glucose; chitin

    C) adenine; DNA

    D) carbon; protein

    E) hydrolysis; condensation

Answer: A
Diff: 3   Page Ref: 3.4
Skill: Conceptual

35) Which type of lipid is most important in biological membranes?

A) fats

B) steroids

C) phospholipids

D) oils

E) triglycerides

Answer: C
Diff: 2   Page Ref: 3.4
Skill: Conceptual

36) Which of the following is insoluble in water?

A) olive oil

B) DNA

C) sucrose

D) salt

E) amino acids

Answer: C
Diff: 2   Page Ref: 3.4
Skill: Factual

37) Cholesterol, testosterone, estrogen and ecdysone are all examples of

A) fatty acids.

B) proteins.

C) steroids.

D) hormones.

E) waxes.

Answer: C
Diff: 2   Page Ref: 3.4
Skill: Factual

38) How does one account for the nonpolar, hydrophobic nature of fats?

A) Fats lack both double and triple bonds.

B) The fatty acids are linked to large long–chained alcohols.

C) Carboxyl groups (–COOH) are not present in fats.

D) Carbon and hydrogen atoms share electrons equally.

E) Glycerol is not water soluble.

Answer: D
Diff: 2   Page Ref: 3.4
Skill: Conceptual

39) When one gram of each of the following is oxidized, which yields the greatest amount of energy?

   A) sucrose

   B) glucose

   C) glycerol

   D) hemoglobin

   E) fat

Answer: E
Diff: 2   Page Ref: 3.4
Skill: Factual

40) Of what are fats composed?

   A) three glycerols and their fatty acids

   B) three fatty acids and one glycerol

   C) one glycogen and two phospholipids

   D) two fatty acids and one carboxyl acid

   E) three oils and one glycerol

Answer: B
Diff: 2   Page Ref: 3.4
Skill: Factual

41) Phospholipids are unusual and important to cell structure because

   A) they are part of DNA.

   B) they contain fatty acids.

   C) they have a polar and a nonpolar end.

   D) they are found only in animals.

   E) they are an important energy carrier molecule.

Answer: C
Diff: 2   Page Ref: 3.4
Skill: Factual

42) You go to the store and buy some lard for cooking. You notice when you get home that the lard is solid at room temperature. What does this tell you about the fats in lard?

   A) The fats in lard are not organic molecules.

   B) The lard is composed of saturated fats.

   C) The fats are mostly phospholipids.

   D) The lard is composed of unsaturated fats.

Answer: B
Diff: 2   Page Ref: 3.4
Skill: Application

43) New government regulations require that foods containing *trans* fats be labeled appropriately. A *trans* fat is formed when food manufacturers turn liquid oils into solid fats by adding hydrogen to vegetable oils. How would this hydrogenation process produce a solid fat?

    A) Adding the hydrogen allows fats to form a tertiary and quatenary structure.

    B) Adding the hydrogen allows the fatty acid chains to pack together to form solid lumps.

    C) Adding the hydrogen causes a phospholipid to form.

    D) The extra hydrogen forms a wax molecule.

    Answer: B
    Diff: 2   Page Ref: 3.4
    Skill: Application

44) The fat substitute Olestra contains a sucrose backbone with six to eight fatty acids attached. How is this different from a naturally occurring fat?

    A) Naturally occurring fats contain a glycerol and three fatty acids.

    B) Naturally occurring fats contain a glycerol, two fatty acids and a phosphate group.

    C) Naturally occurring fats contain a sucrose backbone and three fatty acid chains.

    D) Olestra and natural fats have the same structure, they just have different tastes.

    Answer: A
    Diff: 2   Page Ref: 3.4 /Healthwatch
    Skill: Conceptual

45) Two classes of organic compounds typically provide energy for living systems. Representatives of these two classes are

    A) fats and amino acids.

    B) amino acids and glycogen.

    C) amino acids and ribose sugars.

    D) fats and polysaccharides.

    E) nucleic acids and phospholipids.

    Answer: D
    Diff: 2   Page Ref: 3.4
    Skill: Conceptual

46) You have isolated a liquid from a sample of beans. You add the liquid to a beaker of water and shake vigorously. After a few minutes, the water and the other liquid separate into two layers. To which class of biological macromolecules does the unknown liquid most likely belong?

A) carbohydrates

B) lipids

C) proteins

D) enzymes

E) nucleic acids

Answer: B
Diff: 2   Page Ref: 3.4
Skill: Application

47) In a biological membrane, the phospholipids are arranged with the fatty acid chains facing the interior of the membrane. As a result, the interior of the membrane is

A) hydrophobic.

B) hydrophilic.

C) charged.

D) polar.

E) filled with water.

Answer: A
Diff: 2   Page Ref: 3.4
Skill: Conceptual

48) Which of the following macromolecules possess large nonpolar regions making them insoluble in water?

A) proteins   B) carbohydrates   C) lipids   D) nucleic acids

Answer: C
Diff: 2   Page Ref: 3.4
Skill: Conceptual

49) A member of which of the following macromolecule groups is crucial to the structure and function of the cell membrane?

A) proteins   B) carbohydrates   C) lipids   D) nucleic acids

Answer: C
Diff: 2   Page Ref: 3.4
Skill: Conceptual

50) Which of the following is true about waxes?

   A) They are a type of carbohydrate.

   B) They are a food source and most animals have enzymes for breaking them down.

   C) They are saturated and solid at room temperature.

   D) They are unsaturated and most similar to proteins.

Answer: C
Diff: 2   Page Ref: 3.4
Skill: Conceptual

51) Fatty acids with more than one carbon–carbon double bond are called _____.

Answer: polyunsaturated
Diff: 1   Page Ref: 3.4
Skill: Factual

52) Phospholipids have hydrophilic _____ regions and hydrophobic _____ regions.

Answer: head; tail
Diff: 2   Page Ref: 3.4
Skill: Conceptual

53) Why is it an advantage for animals that migrate long distances to store energy as lipids rather than carbohydrates?

Answer: Lipids (fats) weigh less and store three times as much energy as carbohydrates.
Diff: 2   Page Ref: 3.4
Skill: Conceptual

54) Describe the differences between saturated and unsaturated fatty acids. Which is most likely to be solid at room temperature? Why?

Answer: Saturated fats have only single C–C bonds whereas unsaturated have at least one double C–C bond. Therefore, the saturated fatty acids are most likely to be solid at room temperature since the fatty acid chains can be more tightly packed together.
Diff: 2   Page Ref: 3.4
Skill: Conceptual

55) Imagine you were able to hold a handful of phospholipids and you drop those phospholipids into a beaker of water. Based on their chemical properties, how would these phospholipids arrange themselves in the beaker. Explain why.

Answer: The heads of the phospholipids are hydrophilic while the tails are hydrophobic. Therefore, the tails would try to get away from the water by forming a bilayer with other phospholipids tails, forming an interior space closed off from the water. The heads would face outward toward the water. This would look similar to a cell membrane.
Diff: 2   Page Ref: 3.4
Skill: Conceptual

56) Explain how a saturated fat looks different from an unsaturated fat.

Answer: A saturated fat has 3 fatty acids that are saturated with hydrogens and the tails are able to be straight and packed together closely. Unsaturated fats are not fully saturated with hydrogens and contains bonds that cause bends or kinks in the 3 fatty acid chains, so that they cannot pack tightly together.
Diff: 2   Page Ref: 3.4
Skill: Factual

57) The group of biological molecules most diverse in function is

A) carbohydrates.

B) lipids.

C) proteins.

D) nucleic acids.

E) organelles.

Answer: C
Diff: 1   Page Ref: 3.5
Skill: Factual

58) Organisms contain thousands of different proteins composed of _____ different amino acids.

A) 4

B) 20

C) 100

D) 1000

E) approx. 5000

Answer: B
Diff: 2   Page Ref: 3.5
Skill: Factual

59) What determines the specific function of a protein?

A) exact sequence of amino acids

B) number of disulfide bonds

C) a hydrophilic "head" attached to a hydrophobic "tail"

D) fatty acids as monomers

E) the number of peptide bonds it contains

Answer: A
Diff: 2   Page Ref: 3.5
Skill: Factual

60) Specifically, a peptide bond forms between which groups?

    A) amino and aldehyde groups

    B) carboxyl and amino groups

    C) hydroxyl and carboxyl groups

    D) phosphate and hydroxyl groups

    E) carboxyl and aldehyde groups

Answer: B
Diff: 2   Page Ref: 3.5
Skill: Factual

61) What maintains the secondary structure of a protein?

    A) peptide bonds

    B) disulfide bonds

    C) hydrogen bonds

    D) ionic bonds

    E) all of these

Answer: C
Diff: 2   Page Ref: 3.5
Skill: Factual

62) Complex three–dimensional tertiary structures of globular proteins are characterized by

    A) an absence of hydrophilic amino acids.

    B) a helical shape.

    C) a lack of cysteines in amino acid sequence.

    D) disulfide bridges.

    E) interactions among peptide chains.

Answer: D
Diff: 2   Page Ref: 3.5
Skill: Factual

63) Hemoglobin represents which level of protein organization?

    A) primary structure

    B) secondary structure

    C) tertiary structure

    D) quaternary structure

    E) None of these; hemoglobin is a polysaccharide.

Answer: D
Diff: 2   Page Ref: 3.5
Skill: Factual

64) Which of these is an example of a protein?

    A) hemoglobin

    B) cellulose

    C) estrogen

    D) ATP

    E) all of these

Answer: A
Diff: 1   Page Ref: 3.5
Skill: Factual

65) Which type of molecule would be most abundant in a typical cell?

    A) hydrocarbon

    B) protein

    C) water

    D) lipid

    E) carbohydrate

Answer: C
Diff: 2   Page Ref: 3.5
Skill: Conceptual

66) Sequence information in DNA determines which of the following conformational components of proteins?

    A) primary

    B) secondary

    C) tertiary

    D) A, B, and C

    E) none of the above

Answer: D
Diff: 2   Page Ref: 3.5
Skill: Conceptual

67) What type of amino acid side chain would you expect to find on the surface of a protein embedded in a cell membrane?

A) cysteine

B) hydrophobic

C) hydrophilic

D) charged

E) polar, but not charged

Answer: B
Diff: 2   Page Ref: 3.5
Skill: Conceptual

68) How is a denatured protein different from a normal protein?

A) A denatured protein does contain amino acids.

B) A denatured protein has no secondary or tertiary structure.

C) A denatured protein is composed of nucleotides.

D) A denatured protein contains many disulfide bridges.

Answer: B
Diff: 1   Page Ref: 3.5
Skill: Factual

69) Which of the following macromolecules is composed of amino acid subunits?

A) proteins   B) carbohydrates   C) lipids   D) nucleic acids

Answer: A
Diff: 1   Page Ref: 3.5
Skill: Factual

70) Which of the following may possess primary, secondary, tertiary and quaternary structure?

A) proteins   B) carbohydrates   C) lipids   D) nucleic acids

Answer: A
Diff: 2   Page Ref: 3.5
Skill: Conceptual

71) Your classmate is trying to keep all the facts about biological molecules straight. She is confused about proteins and asks you to explain how the terms amino acid and protein are related. What do you tell her?

    A) Proteins are made up of a chain of amino acids.

    B) Amino acids are formed by joining together many proteins.

    C) Proteins are a portion of an amino acid.

    D) Proteins are chains of carbohydrates and amino acids are a type of carbohydrate.

Answer: A
Diff: 2   Page Ref: 3.5
Skill: Conceptual

72) Your friend is trying to learn about how to kill bacteria. She reads that preservatives such as citric acid are added to foods because the acidic environment kills bacteria by denaturing their proteins. She thinks this sounds like a lot of scientific jargon and asks if you know what this means. How can you explain?

    A) Denaturing their proteins means that bacteria explode.

    B) The acid causes the cells to shrivel, also known as denature.

    C) Denaturing means that the proteins of the bacteria lose their structure and can't function, so the bacteria die.

    D) Denaturing refers to the fact that the bacterial cells will divide too quickly and die.

Answer: C
Diff: 3   Page Ref: 3.5
Skill: Conceptual

73) The linear arrangement of amino acids in the polypeptide chain is referred to as the _____ structure of the protein.

Answer: primary
Diff: 1   Page Ref: 3.5
Skill: Factual

74) In the final three-dimensional structure of a protein, _____ amino acids are more likely to be found in the interior of the molecule.

Answer: hydrophobic
Diff: 2   Page Ref: 3.5
Skill: Conceptual

75) Explain why a protein that functions fine in the cytosol of a cell may not function if placed in the cell membrane.

Answer: Proteins must have a particular three-dimensional shape in order to function properly. This shape would change when the protein was placed in the cell membrane.
Diff: 3   Page Ref: 3.5
Skill: Conceptual

76) How do amino acids differ from each other?

    Answer: Amino acids have different functional groups.
    Diff: 2   *Page Ref: 3.5*
    Skill: Factual

77) You have curly hair and your brother has straight hair. Describe how the proteins of your curly hair are different than the proteins of his straight hair.

    Answer: The keratin proteins in your curly hair have disulfide bridges in certain locations that cause the keratin to have bends or curls. The disulfide bonds in your brother's straight here occur in locations that don't cause bends in the keratin so there are no curls.
    Diff: 3   *Page Ref: 3.5*
    Skill: Application

78) The "backbone" of a nucleic acid molecule is made of

    A) nitrogenous bases.

    B) alternating sugar and phosphate groups.

    C) purines.

    D) pyrimidines.

    E) nucleosides.

    Answer: B
    Diff: 1   *Page Ref: 3.6*
    Skill: Factual

79) DNA carries genetic information in its

    A) helical form.

    B) sequence of bases.

    C) tertiary structure.

    D) phosphate groups.

    E) sugar groups.

    Answer: B
    Diff: 1   *Page Ref: 3.6*
    Skill: Factual

80) Where do covalent bonds form between two deoxyribose nucleotides?

    A) between a phosphate group and adenine

    B) between deoxyribose and a phosphate group

    C) between adenine and thymine

    D) between the phosphate groups of both

    E) between deoxyribose and a base

Answer: B
Diff: 2   Page Ref: 3.6
Skill: Factual

81) Adenosine triphosphate is an example of a(n)

    A) carbohydrate.

    B) protein.

    C) lipid.

    D) nucleic acid.

    E) inorganic molecule.

Answer: D
Diff: 2   Page Ref: 3.6
Skill: Factual

82) A nucleotide is

    A) phospholipid, sugar, base.

    B) phosphate, protein, base.

    C) phosphate, sugar, base.

    D) phospholipid, sugar, protein.

    E) none of these

Answer: C
Diff: 1   Page Ref: 3.6
Skill: Factual

83) Which of these is NOT a nucleic acid?

    A) RNA   B) DNA

    C) ATP   D) All of these ARE nucleic acids.

Answer: D
Diff: 1   Page Ref: 3.6
Skill: Factual

84) You have discovered a new virus and have isolated its nucleic acids. What feature could you look for to determine if the nucleic acids of this virus are RNA or DNA?

   A) If it is RNA, it will contain uracil.

   B) If is RNA, it will contain thymine.

   C) If it is DNA, the virus will not contain proteins.

   D) If it is RNA, there will be no adenine.

Answer: A
Diff: 2   Page Ref: 3.6
Skill: Application

85) Which of the following macromolecules is composed of monomer units containing a sugar, a phosphate group, and a nitrogen–containing base?

   A) proteins   B) carbohydrates   C) lipids   D) nucleic acids

Answer: D
Diff: 1   Page Ref: 3.6
Skill: Factual

86) Which of these macromolecule contains coded genetic information?

   A) proteins   B) carbohydrates   C) lipids   D) nucleic acids

Answer: D
Diff: 2   Page Ref: 3.6
Skill: Conceptual

87) Which nucleic acid functions as an energy carrier in the cell?

Answer: ATP
Diff: 2   Page Ref: 3.6
Skill: Factual

88) RNA differs from DNA in that it contains the sugar ribose and uses the nitrogen containing base _____.

Answer: uracil
Diff: 2   Page Ref: 3.6
Skill: Factual

89) Think about a Big Mac or a Whopper. What biological molecules are you eating? What if you got fries with that?

Answer: Burger contains proteins and fats; Bun contains carbohydrates; Lettuce contains carbohydrates and nucleic acids of plant; mayonnaise contains fats; Fries contain lipids, carbohydrates.
Diff: 3   Page Ref: 3.6
Skill: Application

90) Scientists consider prions to be "puzzling" proteins. Which of the following helps to explain why?

    A) Prions are the same as normal proteins but are denatured more easily than typical proteins.

    B) Infectious prions can have the same amino acid sequence but a different structure than non-infectious proteins.

    C) Infectious prions are not denatured by heat.

    D) A,B and C are all explanations.

    E) B and C are explanations.

Answer: E
Diff: 2   Page Ref: Case Study Revisited
Skill: Conceptual

91) Prions are known to cause

    A) mad cow disease.　　　　　　　　　B) colds.

    C) herpes.　　　　　　　　　　　　　　D) sickle cell anemia.

Answer: A
Diff: 2   Page Ref: Case Study Revisited
Skill: Factual

Chapter 4 Cell Structure and Function

1) Which does NOT agree with part of the cell theory?

    A) Insects are composed of cells.

    B) Paramecia come from Paramecia.

    C) Bacteria are the smallest possible organisms.

    D) Minerals are important for good health.

    E) Spontaneous generation cannot occur.

Answer: D
Diff: 2   Page Ref: 4.1
Skill: Conceptual

2) All of the following are components of the modern cell theory except

    A) All living organisms are made up of one or more cells.

    B) The smallest living organisms are single cells, and cells are the functional units of
       multicellular organisms.

    C) All cells arise from pre-existing cells.

    D) Bacterial cells are eukaryotic.

    E) All of these are true.

Answer: D
Diff: 2   Page Ref: 4.1
Skill: Factual

3) What is not characteristic of a prokaryotic cell?

    A) a plasma membrane

    B) a nuclear membrane

    C) ribosomes

    D) enzymes

    E) DNA

Answer: B
Diff: 2   Page Ref: 4.1
Skill: Conceptual

4) Discuss the three main components of modern cell theory that evolved from Rudolf Virchow's
   ideas from the 1850s.

    Answer: All living organisms are composed of one or more cells, the cell is the smallest
             functional unit of life and all cells come from preexisting cells.
    Diff: 2   Page Ref: 4.1
    Skill: Conceptual

5) Of the objects listed, which is the smallest that you can see with the unaided eye?

   A) DNA molecule

   B) frog embryo

   C) virus

   D) ribosomes

   E) human skin cell

Answer: B
Diff: 2   Page Ref: 4.2
Skill: Conceptual

6) Phospholipids

   A) are found in cell membranes.

   B) are completely hydrophilic.

   C) are completely hydrophobic.

   D) are made on the ribosomes.

   E) All of these are true.

Answer: A
Diff: 2   Page Ref: 4.2
Skill: Factual

7) The cells that line the intestine have highly folded plasma membranes on the absorptive surface of the intestine because

   A) this will increase volume, making the cells more efficient.

   B) this will increase surface area to volume ratio.

   C) these cells are most likely active in secretion.

   D) large amounts of plasma membrane will be needed for endocytosis.

Answer: B
Diff: 3   Page Ref: 4.2
Skill: Application

8) All cells possess all the following components EXCEPT

   A) cytoplasm.

   B) genetic material.

   C) nuclear membrane.

   D) plasma cell membrane.

   E) ribosomes.

Answer: C
Diff: 2   Page Ref: 4.2
Skill: Factual

9) Regarding cell type, which one of the following is unlike the others?

    A) the freshwater protist, *Paramecium*

    B) cell of the green plant, Elodea

    C) *Streptococcus* bacterial cell

    D) a cell from a mushroom (a type of fungus)

    E) a human heart muscle cell

Answer: C
Diff: 2   Page Ref: 4.2
Skill: Conceptual

10) What is the meaning of the term "prokaryotic"?

    A) "false nucleus"

    B) "before the nucleus"

    C) "true nucleus"

    D) "small nucleus"

    E) "before the cell"

Answer: B
Diff: 2   Page Ref: 4.2
Skill: Factual

11) The cytoplasm of eukaryotic cells contains

    A) water.

    B) dissolved nutrients.

    C) organelles.

    D) enzymes.

    E) all of these

Answer: E
Diff: 1   Page Ref: 4.2
Skill: Factual

12) Only eukaryotic cells obtain energy and nutrients from the environment. True or False?

Answer: FALSE
Diff: 1   Page Ref: 4.2
Skill: Factual

13) What components do all cells possess?

Answer: DNA (at some point in their life cycle), a cell membrane, and cytoplasm
Diff: 2   Page Ref: 4.2
Skill: Conceptual

14) Describe the main functions of the plasma membrane.

Answer: The main functions of the plasma membrane are to isolate cell internal environment from external environment; regulate the flow of materials into and out of the cell; and, allow interaction with other cells.
Diff: 2   Page Ref: 4.2
Skill: Conceptual

15) Why are cells generally small in size?

Answer: To maintain sufficient surface area for the exchange of nutrients and wastes with the external environment.
Diff: 2   Page Ref: 4.2
Skill: Conceptual

16) Most of the cell's metabolic activities occur in the cell _____.

Answer: cytoplasm
Diff: 1   Page Ref: 4.2
Skill: Factual

17) Cells having a nucleus are referred to as _____ cells and those lacking a true nucleus are called _____ cells.

Answer: eukaryotic; prokaryotic
Diff: 1   Page Ref: 4.2
Skill: Factual

18) A cell that contains large numbers of ribosomes, would produce a large number of _____ molecules.

Answer: protein
Diff: 2   Page Ref: 4.2
Skill: Conceptual

19) Flagellated bacteria

A) can move internal organelles more efficiently than non-flagellated types.

B) can attach to host cells more effectively because of the flagella.

C) can move toward a favorable environment.

D) divide more quickly non-flagellated types.

E) All of the above are correct.

Answer: C
Diff: 2   Page Ref: 4.3
Skill: Conceptual

20) Membrane receptors are proteins that would be synthesized on ribosomes

  A) on the rough endoplasmic reticulum.

  B) on the smooth endoplasmic reticulum.

  C) on the Golgi complexes.

  D) found in the cytoplasm.

  E) found in the nucleus.

Answer: A
Diff: 2   Page Ref: 4.3
Skill: Conceptual

21) Secreted proteins would be synthesized on ribosomes

  A) on the rough endoplasmic reticulum.

  B) on the smooth endoplasmic reticulum.

  C) on the Golgi complexes.

  D) found in the cytoplasm.

  E) found in the nucleus.

Answer: A
Diff: 2   Page Ref: 4.3
Skill: Conceptual

22) A mutant plant cell with no chloroplasts

  A) would not be green.

  B) would still be able to convert carbohydrate to energy.

  C) would still be able to capture energy as sunlight.

  D) would synthesize new chloroplasts in the ER.

  E) Both A and B are correct.

Answer: E
Diff: 2   Page Ref: 4.3
Skill: Conceptual

23) Plastids are found in

  A) bacterial cells.

  B) plant cells.

  C) animal cells.

  D) fungi.

  E) A and B are both correct.

Answer: B
Diff: 2   Page Ref: 4.3
Skill: Factual

24) Which of the following is NOT a function of plastids?

   A) store photosynthetic products

   B) store pigments

   C) carry out photosynthesis

   D) extract energy from food and convert it to ATP

   E) All of the above are functions of plastids.

Answer: D
Diff: 2   Page Ref: 4.3
Skill: Conceptual

25) Of the following cell components which is composed primarily of protein?

   A) cytoskeleton

   B) DNA

   C) cytosol

   D) mitochondria

   E) Golgi complex

Answer: A
Diff: 2   Page Ref: 4.3
Skill: Factual

26) The cytoskeleton is to the cell what

   A) bones are to humans.

   B) a frame is to a house.

   C) a desk is to an office.

   D) A and B

   E) all of these

Answer: D
Diff: 3   Page Ref: 4.3
Skill: Conceptual

27) What primarily determines the shape of cells that lack cell walls?

   A) nucleus

   B) cytosol

   C) endoplasmic reticulum

   D) cytoskeleton

   E) ribosomes

Answer: D
Diff: 2   Page Ref: 4.3
Skill: Factual

28) All the following are important functions of the cytoskeleton EXCEPT

A) storage of food molecules.

B) support of organelles.

C) movement of organelles.

D) maintenance of shape.

E) maintenance of organization in the cell.

Answer: A
Diff: 2   Page Ref: 4.3
Skill: Factual

29) Fibers of the cytoskeleton are composed primarily of

A) nucleic acids.

B) polysaccharides.

C) lipids.

D) ER.

E) proteins.

Answer: E
Diff: 2   Page Ref: 4.3
Skill: Factual

30) Which of the following is NOT a known function of the cytoskeleton?

A) to maintain a critical limit on cell size

B) to provide mechanical support to the cell

C) to maintain a characteristic shape of the cell

D) to hold mitochondria and other organelles in place

E) to assist in cell motility

Answer: A
Diff: 2   Page Ref: 4.3
Skill: Conceptual

31) Drugs that inhibit microtubules will

A) stop organelle movement.

B) inhibit cell division.

C) prevent the formation of new cilia and flagella.

D) kill the cell.

E) all of the above

Answer: E
Diff: 2   Page Ref: 4.3
Skill: Conceptual

32) Which of the following does NOT possess a double membrane?

   A) mitochondrion

   B) nuclear envelope

   C) ribosome

   D) plastid

   E) chloroplast

Answer: C
Diff: 2   Page Ref: 4.3
Skill: Conceptual

33) Which organelle does one expect to be most abundant in cardiac muscle cells?

   A) mitochondria

   B) lysosomes

   C) Golgi complexes

   D) smooth ER

   E) plastids

Answer: A
Diff: 2   Page Ref: 4.3
Skill: Conceptual

34) A nucleolus is

   A) an extra nucleus in the cell.

   B) a darkly staining area in the nucleus where ribosomes are made.

   C) an area where the nucleus is synthesized.

   D) a membrane-bound organelle.

   E) the area in a prokaryote where DNA is concentrated.

Answer: B
Diff: 1   Page Ref: 4.3
Skill: Factual

35) The nuclei of eukaryotic cells are characterized by

   A) a single-layered membrane.

   B) one or more nucleoids.

   C) a double membrane.

   D) a non-porous membrane.

   E) all of these

Answer: C
Diff: 2   Page Ref: 4.3
Skill: Factual

36) Choose the correct pathway of information flow in the cell.

    A) RNA → DNA → protein   B) DNA → RNA → protein

    C) ER → DNA → RNA → protein   D) ER → DNA → Golgi → protein

Answer: B
Diff: 2   Page Ref: 4.3
Skill: Conceptual

37) What is the difference between "free" and "attached" ribosomes?

    A) Free ribosomes are in the cytoplasm while attached ribosomes are anchored to the endoplasmic reticulum.

    B) Free ribosomes produce proteins that remain in the cytosol while attached ribosomes produce proteins that may be exported from the cell.

    C) Free ribosomes produce proteins that are exported from the cell while attached ribosomes make proteins for mitochondria and chloroplasts.

    D) A and C

    E) A and B

Answer: E
Diff: 2   Page Ref: 4.3
Skill: Conceptual

38) If all the lysosomes within a cell suddenly ruptured, what could occur?

    A) The macromolecules in the cell cytosol would begin to degrade.

    B) The number of proteins in the cytosol would begin to increase.

    C) The DNA within the mitochondria would begin to degrade.

    D) The mitochondria and chloroplasts would begin to divide.

    E) There would be no change in the normal function of the cell.

Answer: A
Diff: 2   Page Ref: 4.3
Skill: Conceptual

39) If you identified a cell with large amounts of rough ER, which would NOT be a logical conclusion about that cell?

    A) Large quantities of enzymes for biochemical processes are manufactured by that cell.

    B) Membrane proteins and phospholipids are made to replace other membranous components in the cell.

    C) Digestive enzymes for export are manufactured by that cell.

    D) Membrane lipids are produced by that cell.

    E) Large amounts of protein hormone are exported by the cell.

Answer: D
Diff: 2   Page Ref: 4.3
Skill: Conceptual

40) Cells that primarily produce steroid hormones, such as testosterone and estrogen, for export have large quantities of

    A) cytoplasmic ribosomes.

    B) smooth endoplasmic reticulum.

    C) plasma membranes.

    D) hydrolytic enzymes.

    E) DNA.

Answer: B
Diff: 2   Page Ref: 4.3
Skill: Conceptual

41) Ribosomes are the site of synthesis of

    A) DNA.   B) RNA.   C) proteins.   D) nucleoli.   E) glucose.

Answer: C
Diff: 1   Page Ref: 4.3
Skill: Factual

42) An organelle capable of synthesis of nuclear membrane is the

    A) endoplasmic reticulum (ER).

    B) nucleus itself.

    C) Golgi complex.

    D) mitochondrion.

    E) chloroplast.

Answer: A
Diff: 2   Page Ref: 4.3
Skill: Factual

43) Which of the following is associated with rough ER?

    A) chlorophyll

    B) ribosomes

    C) lipid synthesis

    D) plasma membrane

    E) DNA

Answer: B
Diff: 2   Page Ref: 4.3
Skill: Factual

44) Endoplasmic reticulum is the site of synthesis of

    A) lipids.

    B) testosterone.

    C) more ER.

    D) Choices A and B are correct.

    E) Choices A, B, and C are correct.

Answer: E
Diff: 2   Page Ref: 4.3
Skill: Factual

45) The Golgi packages materials into _____ for transport or export.

    A) organelles

    B) plastids

    C) vesicles

    D) microns

    E) nucleoli

Answer: C
Diff: 2   Page Ref: 4.3
Skill: Factual

46) Which cellular component packages hydrolytic enzymes and forms lysosomes?

    A) Golgi complex

    B) smooth ER

    C) mitochondrion

    D) cytoskeleton

    E) rough ER

Answer: A
Diff: 2   Page Ref: 4.3
Skill: Factual

47) How does a cell rid itself of defective or malfunctioning organelles?

    A) They are engulfed by plastids and stored until export from cell is possible.

    B) Defective parts accumulate until the cell itself dies.

    C) Lysosomes assist in the removal of defective organelles by digesting them.

    D) Ribosomes play a significant role in the removal of malfunctioning parts by absorbing the parts.

    E) They are exported by exocytosis.

Answer: C
Diff: 2   Page Ref: 4.3
Skill: Conceptual

48) Which statement most accurately describes the interaction between ER, ribosomes and Golgi bodies in the export of protein from the cell?

    A) Golgi bodies manufacture proteins which travel through the ER to be packaged by the ribosomes for export.

    B) ER manufactures proteins which are carried by ribosomes to the Golgi bodies for export.

    C) ER manufactures proteins which are carried by Golgi bodies to the ribosomes for export.

    D) Ribosomes manufacture proteins which travel through the ER to be packaged by the Golgi bodies for export.

    E) Ribosomes make proteins that travel through the Golgi bodies to the ER which exports them.

Answer: D
Diff: 2   Page Ref: 4.3
Skill: Conceptual

49) What "buds off" of the Golgi complex?

    A) nuclei

    B) cytoskeleton

    C) ribosomes

    D) new cells

    E) vesicles

Answer: E
Diff: 2   Page Ref: 4.3
Skill: Factual

50) An organelle associated with carbohydrate synthesis is the

    A) Golgi complex.

    B) ribosome.

    C) centriole.

    D) nucleolus.

    E) nucleus.

Answer: A
Diff: 2   Page Ref: 4.3
Skill: Factual

51) A cell with a large number of lysosomes would most likely be active in

    A) synthesis and secretion of secretory proteins.

    B) cell division.

    C) movement.

    D) phagocytosis.

    E) active transport.

Answer: D
Diff: 2   Page Ref: 4.3
Skill: Conceptual

52) Researchers have been able to study the pathway of a secreted protein by "tagging" it with a fluorescent marker. Using this method, you would observe fluorescence moving from the ER to which organelle?

    A) nuclear membrane

    B) lysosome

    C) plasma membrane

    D) mitochondria

    E) Golgi complex

Answer: E
Diff: 2   Page Ref: 4.3
Skill: Conceptual

53) What is the function of a plant cell vacuole?

    A) storage of wastes

    B) support of the cell

    C) excretion of wastes

    D) A and B

    E) B and C

Answer: D
Diff: 2   *Page Ref: 4.3*
Skill: Factual

54) A cell adapted for waste storage and disposal would probably contain a large number of

    A) mitochondria.

    B) vacuoles.

    C) ER.

    D) nuclei.

    E) ribosomes.

Answer: B
Diff: 2   *Page Ref: 4.3*
Skill: Conceptual

55) The utilization of "food" in the mitochondria, with the associated formation of ATP, is termed

    A) aerobic metabolism.

    B) metabolic rate.

    C) diffusion.

    D) metabolic processing of fuels.

    E) catabolism.

Answer: A
Diff: 2   *Page Ref: 4.3*
Skill: Factual

56) Which of the following is/are evidence that mitochondria and chloroplasts were once free-living organisms?

   A) They produce ATP.

   B) They contain their own DNA.

   C) Both capture the energy of sunlight to make ATP.

   D) A and B

   E) A, B, and C

Answer: D
Diff: 3   Page Ref: 4.3
Skill: Conceptual

57) Which of the following is NOT TRUE about both mitochondria and chloroplasts?

   A) Both are capable of ATP synthesis.

   B) Both capture the energy of sunlight to meet metabolic demands.

   C) Both possess their own DNA.

   D) Both are surrounded by a double membrane.

   E) Both may have originally been independent organisms.

Answer: B
Diff: 2   Page Ref: 4.3
Skill: Conceptual

58) Which pair of organelles is responsible for energy supply to eukaryotic cells?

   A) ribosomes and mitochondria

   B) chloroplasts and ribosomes

   C) Golgi bodies and ribosomes

   D) mitochondria and lysosomes

   E) chloroplasts and mitochondria

Answer: E
Diff: 2   Page Ref: 4.3
Skill: Factual

59) Aerobic metabolism occurs in the

    A) ribosome.

    B) chloroplast.

    C) mitochondrion.

    D) cytosol.

    E) nucleus.

Answer: C
Diff: 2   Page Ref: 4.3
Skill: Factual

60) In metabolically active cells, you would expect to find a large number of

    A) Golgi bodies.

    B) chloroplasts.

    C) vesicles.

    D) microtubules.

    E) mitochondria.

Answer: E
Diff: 2   Page Ref: 4.3
Skill: Conceptual

61) Which organelle extracts energy from food molecules and stores it in the high-energy bonds of ATP?

    A) mitochondrion

    B) chloroplast

    C) ribosome

    D) centriole

    E) ER

Answer: A
Diff: 2   Page Ref: 4.3
Skill: Factual

62) Where in the unicellular organism *Euglena* would you expect to find the greatest concentration of mitochondria?

    A) site of lysosome production

    B) near the nuclear membrane

    C) area surrounding basal bodies

    D) within the chloroplasts

    E) near the ribosomes

Answer: C
Diff: 2   Page Ref: 4.3
Skill: Conceptual

63) Which of the following is capable of converting light energy to chemical energy?

    A) chloroplasts

    B) mitochondria

    C) amyloplasts

    D) vacuoles

    E) Golgi bodies

Answer: A
Diff: 1   Page Ref: 4.3
Skill: Factual

64) A biologist ground up some plant cells and then centrifuged the mixture. She obtained some organelles from the pellet in the test tube that took up CO_2 and gave off O_2. The organelles are most likely

    A) nuclei.

    B) ribosomes.

    C) chloroplasts.

    D) mitochondria.

    E) Golgi bodies.

Answer: C
Diff: 3   Page Ref: 4.3
Skill: Application

65) Which of the following relationships between cell structures and their respective functions is NOT correct?

   A) cell wall – support and protection

   B) chloroplasts – chief site of cellular respiration

   C) nucleus – site of genetic control of information

   D) ribosomes – site of protein synthesis

   E) mitochondria – formation of ATP for the cell

Answer: B
Diff: 2   Page Ref: 4.3
Skill: Conceptual

66) A cell has the following molecules and structures: enzymes, DNA, ribosomes, plasma membrane, and mitochondria. It could be a cell from

   A) a bacterium.

   B) an animal, but not a plant.

   C) a plant, but not a animal.

   D) a plant or animal.

   E) any kind of organism.

Answer: D
Diff: 3   Page Ref: 4.3
Skill: Conceptual

67) Sphingomyelin is a common phospholipid found in the brain, liver, and spleen. Sphingomyelin is probably produced in which organelle?

   A) rough endoplasmic reticulum

   B) smooth endoplasmic reticulum

   C) ribosomes

   D) Golgi complexes

   E) lysosomes

Answer: B
Diff: 2   Page Ref: 4.3
Skill: Conceptual

68) A cell from a wheat plant would contain which of the following?

    A) cell wall

    B) chloroplast

    C) mitochondria

    D) A and B

    E) A, B and C

    Answer: E
    Diff: 2   Page Ref: 4.3
    Skill: Conceptual

69) RNA carries information for protein synthesis from the DNA in the nucleus to the ribosomes in the cytoplasm. To get from the nucleus to the cytoplasm, RNA must pass through _____.

    Answer: nuclear pores
    Diff: 2   Page Ref: 4.3
    Skill: Factual

70) The _____ extracts energy from food molecules, while the _____ captures solar energy.

    Answer: mitochondria; chloroplast
    Diff: 2   Page Ref: 4.3
    Skill: Factual

71) The _____ has the ability to digest organelles once they become defective or malfunctioning.

    Answer: lysosome
    Diff: 2   Page Ref: 4.3
    Skill: Conceptual

72) The _____ is an organelle, which serves as a sort of "postal depot" where some of the proteins synthesized on ribosomes and rough ER are processed.

    Answer: Golgi apparatus
    Diff: 2   Page Ref: 4.3
    Skill: Conceptual

73) Briefly describe the interrelationship of structure and function among the rough ER, smooth ER, and Golgi complex.

    Answer: SER is the site of synthesis of phospholipids and cholesterol used in making membranes; RER makes proteins and phospholipids to use as membrane components. Pieces of ER bud off and travel to the Golgi apparatus and finally, to export.
    Diff: 3   Page Ref: 4.3
    Skill: Application

74) A protein molecule is to be exported from the cell. Describe the pathway that the protein takes from the point of synthesis to export.

Answer: A protein to be exported will be synthesized on the rough endoplasmic reticulum. From there it will travel via transport vesicle to the Golgi apparatus for processing. From the Golgi it will travel, again via vesicle, to the plasma membrane for release outside the cell.

Diff: 2   Page Ref: 4.3
Skill: Conceptual

75) When a cell grows in size it must produce more plasma membrane material. How does the cell do this?

Answer: ER vesicle to the Golgi apparatus vesicle to fuse with the plasma membrane.

Diff: 3   Page Ref: 4.3
Skill: Conceptual

76) How is the vacuole involved in support of non–woody parts of the plant?

Answer: The vacuole allows for the build up of turgor pressure in the plant cells that prevents wilting.

Diff: 3   Page Ref: 4.3
Skill: Factual

77) In plant cells, glucose is produced by photosynthesis in the _____ (organelle) and converted to usable energy in the form of ATP in the _____ (organelle).

Answer: chloroplast; mitochondria

Diff: 2   Page Ref: 4.3
Skill: Conceptual

78) Why is the cytoskeleton such an important structural component of cells?

Answer: The cytoskeleton maintains cell shape, facilitates cell and organelle movement and is involved in cell division.

Diff: 2   Page Ref: 4.3
Skill: Conceptual

79) Although both extensions from the cytoplasm serve to move the cell or move fluid past the cell, the _____ are often short and numerous, while the _____ are longer and few in number.

Answer: cilia; flagella

Diff: 2   Page Ref: 4.3
Skill: Conceptual

80) Briefly describe the similarities and differences between cilia and flagella. Give an example of an organism that is ciliated and one that is flagellated. Where do you find ciliated and flagellated cells in humans?

Answer: Both are slender extensions of the cell membrane. Flagella are longer than cilia and usually fewer in number. Both are made from a "9 + 2" array of microtubules, and both arise from centrioles that move to the plasma membrane to form basal bodies. Cilia provide a force that is parallel to the plasma membrane, and function in moving substances across the surface of the cell, and sometimes in movement of the entire cell. Flagella exert a force perpendicular to the plasma membrane and are involved in movement of the entire cell. The respiratory tract contains ciliated cells and human sperm are flagellated.

Diff: 3   Page Ref: 4.3
Skill: Application

81) Compare/contrast plant and animal cell structure. Include at least two similarities and two differences.

Answer: See Table 4.1 for a listing of the differences. The student should mention some of the following characteristics: plant cells have chloroplasts, cell wall, central vacuole; animal cells have lysosomes; both types of cell have rough and smooth ER, nucleus, ribosomes, mitochondria, etc.

Diff: 2   Page Ref: 4.3
Skill: Conceptual

Select the organelle that is the most appropriate match for the numbered statement. Letters may be used once, more than once or not at all.

A. Mitochondria
B. Golgi bodies
C. Rough endoplasmic reticulum
D. Lysosomes
E. Smooth endoplasmic reticulum

82) Digests damaged organelles.

Answer: D
Diff: 2   Page Ref: 4.3
Skill: Factual

83) Sorts our mixtures of protein and sends them to their proper destination.

Answer: B
Diff: 2   Page Ref: 4.3
Skill: Factual

84) Site of protein synthesis.

Answer: C
Diff: 2   Page Ref: 4.3
Skill: Factual

85) Site of cellular respiration.

Answer: A
Diff: 2   Page Ref: 4.3
Skill: Factual

86) Makes steroid hormones.

Answer: E
Diff: 2   Page Ref: 4.3
Skill: Factual

87) Responsible for most of a muscle cell's ATP generation.

Answer: A
Diff: 2   Page Ref: 4.3
Skill: Factual

88) DNA is located in which of the following?

A) prokaryotic cells

B) plant cells

C) animal cells

D) chloroplasts

E) all of the above

Answer: E
Diff: 2   Page Ref: 4.3, 4.4
Skill: Conceptual

89) Prokaryotic as well as eukaryotic cells possess

A) mitochondria.

B) chloroplasts.

C) a cytoskeleton.

D) ribosomes.

E) a nucleus.

Answer: D
Diff: 2   Page Ref: 4.3, 4.4
Skill: Factual

90) Which is a difference between prokaryotes and eukaryotes?

   A) Prokaryotes have RNA, eukaryotes have DNA.

   B) Prokaryotes have DNA, eukaryotes have RNA.

   C) Prokaryotes have a nucleus, eukaryotes have a nucleoid.

   D) Prokaryotes have a nucleoid, eukaryotes have a nucleus.

   E) Prokaryotes have a cell wall, eukaryotes do not.

Answer: D
Diff: 2   Page Ref: 4.3, 4.4
Skill: Conceptual

91) Which of the following correctly identify components that are the same in both plant cells and bacterial cells?

   A) nucleus, DNA, plasma membrane, ribosomes

   B) cytoplasm, endoplasmic reticulum, DNA, plasma membrane, ribosomes

   C) cytoplasm, DNA, plasma membrane, ribosomes

   D) cytoplasm, nucleolus, DNA, plasma membrane

   E) cytoplasm, nucleoid, DNA, plasma membrane, ribosomes

Answer: C
Diff: 2   Page Ref: 4.3, 4.4
Skill: Conceptual

92) Which of the following cell structures would be found in an animal cell, but not in a bacterial cell?

   A) DNA

   B) cell wall

   C) plasma membrane

   D) ribosomes

   E) endoplasmic reticulum

Answer: E
Diff: 2   Page Ref: 4.3, 4.4
Skill: Conceptual

93) If you removed the pili from a bacterial cell, which of the following would you expect to happen?

    A) The bacterium could no longer swim.

    B) The bacterium could no longer adhere to other cells.

    C) The bacterium could no longer regulate the movement of molecules into and out of the cell.

    D) The bacterium would dry out.

    E) The shape of the bacterium would change.

Answer: B
Diff: 2   *Page Ref: 4.4*
Skill: Conceptual

94) Penicillin destroys bacteria by interfering with cell wall synthesis. What will occur as a result?

    A) The underlying cell membrane will become exposed.

    B) The cell will be more sensitive to osmotic changes in the environment.

    C) Mitochondria within the cell will be damaged.

    D) A new cell wall will be synthesized by ribosomes.

    E) Both A and B are correct.

Answer: E
Diff: 2   *Page Ref: 4.4*
Skill: Conceptual

95) Describe the difference between the nucleolus, nucleus and nucleoid regions in cells.

    Answer: Nucleus contains the DNA in eukaryotes and the nucleolus region in the nucleus is the site of ribosome synthesis while the nucleoid region is the site in prokaryotic cells where the DNA is contained in the cytoplasm.
Diff: 2   *Page Ref: 4.3, 4.4*
Skill: Conceptual

96) The _____ may help some pathogenic bacteria evade their host's immune system and attach to host cells.

    Answer: capsule or slime layers
Diff: 2   *Page Ref: 4.4*
Skill: Conceptual

97) The DNA in a prokaryotic cell is contained in the _____ region of the cytoplasm.

    Answer: nucleoid
Diff: 1   *Page Ref: 4.4*
Skill: Factual

98) Prokaryotic cells do not have mitochondria so they cannot make ATP energy. True or False?

Answer: False
Diff: 1   Page Ref: 4.4
Skill: Factual

99) Differences between light and electron microscopes include

A) light microscopes using lenses.

B) electron microscopes using beams of electrons.

C) light microscopes being more powerful than electron microscopes.

D) A and B

E) A, B, and C

Answer: D
Diff: 1   Page Ref: Scientific Inquiry
Skill: Factual

100) Cells are called "cells" because Robert Hooke first thought they looked tiny rooms or cells occupied by monks. True or False?

Answer: True
Diff: 1   Page Ref: Scientific Inquiry
Skill: Factual

Chapter 5 Cell Membrane Structure and Function

1) The compounds in biological membranes that form a barrier to the movement of materials across the membrane are

    A) internal proteins.

    B) carbohydrates.

    C) lipids.

    D) nucleic acids.

    E) external proteins.

Answer: C
Diff: 2   Page Ref: 5.1
Skill: Conceptual

2) The _____ portion of the cell membrane is responsible for the isolating functions of the membrane, while the _____ portion regulates exchange and communication with the environment.

    A) lipid; protein

    B) cholesterol; lipid

    C) protein; cholesterol

    D) carbohydrate; lipid

    E) nucleic acid; lipid

Answer: A
Diff: 2   Page Ref: 5.1
Skill: Conceptual

3) When a mouse cell and a human cell are fused, the membrane proteins of the two cells become uniformly distributed over the surface of the hybrid cell. This occurs because

    A) many proteins can move around within the bilayer.

    B) all proteins are anchored within the membrane.

    C) proteins are asymmetrically distributed within the membrane.

    D) all proteins in the plasma membrane are extrinsic.

    E) different membranes contain different proteins.

Answer: A
Diff: 3   Page Ref: 5.1
Skill: Application

4) Phospholipids spontaneously form a bilayer in an aqueous solution. Why do the heads of the phospholipids point out and the tails point to each other?

    A) The tails are nonpolar and form hydrogen bonds with each other.

    B) The tails are repelled by the aqueous environment.

    C) The heads are attracted to the water inside and outside.

    D) A and C

    E) B and C

Answer: E
Diff: 2   Page Ref: 5.1
Skill: Conceptual

5) How are plasma membranes BEST described?

    A) a double layer of phospholipid molecules with hydrophobic tails directed toward cytoplasm of the cell

    B) a single layer of phospholipid molecules with water molecules attached along one side

    C) a double layer of phospholipid molecules with hydrophilic heads directed toward each other

    D) a double layer of phospholipid molecules with hydrophobic tails oriented toward each other

    E) a single layer of phospholipids with tails pointed to the inside of the cell

Answer: D
Diff: 2   Page Ref: 5.1
Skill: Factual

6) The hydrophobic tails of a phospholipid bilayer are oriented toward the

    A) interior of the plasma membrane (i.e. each other).

    B) extracellular fluid surrounding the cell.

    C) cytoplasm of the cell.

    D) nucleus of the cell.

    E) both B and C

Answer: A
Diff: 2   Page Ref: 5.1
Skill: Factual

7) Which of the following accounts for the fluid aspect of the fluid mosaic model of plasma membranes?

   A) The individual phospholipid molecules are not bonded to each other so movement of certain proteins and lipids is possible within the bilayer.

   B) The plasma membrane is "fluid" because of movement of substances across the membrane.

   C) The bilayer permits diffusion of certain lipid-soluble substances.

   D) The membrane is water soluble.

   E) One of the components of the membrane is water.

   Answer: A
   Diff: 2   *Page Ref: 5.1*
   Skill: Conceptual

8) According to the fluid mosaic model of cell membranes, which of the following is a TRUE statement about membrane phospholipids?

   A) They move laterally along the plane of the membrane.

   B) They frequently flip-flop from one side of the membrane to the other.

   C) They occur in an uninterrupted bilayer, with membrane proteins restricted to the surface of the membrane.

   D) They are free to depart from the membrane and are dissolved in the surrounding solution.

   E) They have hydrophilic tails in the interior of the membrane.

   Answer: A
   Diff: 2   *Page Ref: 5.1*
   Skill: Conceptual

9) In biological membranes, the phospholipids are arranged in

   A) a bilayer with the fatty acids pointing toward each other.

   B) a bilayer with the fatty acids facing outward.

   C) a single layer with the fatty acids facing the interior of the cell.

   D) a single layer with the phosphorus-containing region facing the interior of the cell.

   E) a bilayer with the phosphorus groups in the interior of the membrane.

   Answer: A
   Diff: 2   *Page Ref: 5.1*
   Skill: Factual

10) The hydrophilic regions of a membrane protein are most likely to be found

    A) only in muscle cell membranes.

    B) associated with the fatty acid region of the lipids.

    C) in the interior of the membrane.

    D) exposed on the surface of the membrane.

    E) attached to carbohydrates and facing the interior of a cell.

Answer: D
Diff: 2   *Page Ref: 5.1*
Skill: Conceptual

11) Suppose that plasma membranes were single layers of phospholipids with heads facing the external environment. The interior of this hypothetical cell would have to be

    A) hydrophilic.

    B) hydrophobic.

    C) polar.

    D) nonpolar.

    E) B and D

Answer: E
Diff: 2   *Page Ref: 5.1*
Skill: Conceptual

12) What would happen if the plasma membrane were composed solely of phospholipids and no proteins?

    A) All movement of molecules across the membrane would cease.

    B) Diffusion and osmosis would continue to occur.

    C) Facilitated diffusion, active transport, and osmosis would not occur.

    D) Movement of molecules across the membrane would not be affected.

    E) Immune reactions would not be affected.

Answer: B
Diff: 3   *Page Ref: 5.1*
Skill: Application

13) ISO membranes are inside-out membrane vesicles used by researchers for membrane studies. As a molecule diffuses into the vesicle, it will encounter the layers of the membrane in the following order

A) head–tail–head–tail

B) tail–head–head–tail

C) head–tail–tail–head

D) tail–head–tail–head

E) head–head–tail–tail

Answer: C
Diff: 3   Page Ref: 5.1
Skill: Conceptual

14) What structure in the membrane causes plasma membranes to resist freezing?

A) polar heads of the phospholipids

B) channel proteins

C) cholesterol

D) saturated fatty acid tails

E) unsaturated fatty acid tails

Answer: E
Diff: 2   Page Ref: 5.1
Skill: Factual

15) Within the fluid mosaic of a plasma membrane, what is the role of transport and channel proteins?

A) They prevent passage of amino acids.

B) They allow movement of salts and sugars through the plasma membrane.

C) They may set off cellular changes such as cell division or hormone secretion.

D) They are cell–surface attachment sites.

E) They identify the cell.

Answer: B
Diff: 2   Page Ref: 5.1
Skill: Factual

16) Recognition proteins are most important for

    A) facilitated diffusion of molecules.

    B) active transport of molecules.

    C) maintaining membrane integrity.

    D) maintaining membrane fluidity.

    E) distinguishing foreign cells from "self" cells.

Answer: E
Diff: 2   Page Ref: 5.1
Skill: Factual

17) In general, which of the following is largely responsible for moving substances across the plasma membrane, communicating with other cells and identifying the cell?

    A) phospholipids

    B) carbohydrates

    C) proteins

    D) nucleic acids

    E) cytoskeleton

Answer: C
Diff: 2   Page Ref: 5.1
Skill: Factual

18) What prevents your immune system from attacking your own cells?

    A) inadequate enzymes

    B) fever

    C) cholesterol

    D) recognition proteins

    E) receptor proteins

Answer: D
Diff: 2   Page Ref: 5.1
Skill: Factual

19) Cystic fibrosis is a genetic disease that leads to the production of excessive thick mucous in the respiratory tract, leading to frequent and serious respiratory infections. The defect is due to the production of a faulty membrane protein for the transport of the chloride ion. The protein is still in the membrane; it just doesn't function normally. What type of membrane protein is being affected in this case?

    A) recognition protein

    B) carrier protein

    C) receptor protein

    D) channel protein

    E) protein filaments in the cytoplasm

Answer: D
Diff: 3   *Page Ref: 5.1*
Skill: Conceptual

20) The dominant type of lipid found in cell membranes is

    A) steroids.

    B) triglycerides.

    C) phospholipids.

    D) glycerol.

    E) waxes.

Answer: C
Diff: 1   *Page Ref: 5.1*
Skill: Factual

21) Membranes form because

    A) hydrophilic groups on phospholipids form H-bonds with water.

    B) hydrophobic groups on phospholipids form H-bonds with water.

    C) hydrophobic groups on phospholipids cannot form H-bonds with water.

    D) A and B

    E) A and C

Answer: E
Diff: 2   *Page Ref: 5.1*
Skill: Conceptual

22) Sodium ions are positively charged and therefore are

   A) hydrophilic.

   B) hydrophobic.

   C) hydropathic.

   D) amphipathic.

   E) A and D

Answer: A
Diff: 1   Page Ref: 5.1
Skill: Conceptual

23) Which of the following would not be found in a membrane?

   A) cellulose

   B) cholesterol

   C) phospholipid

   D) channel protein

   E) receptor protein

Answer: A
Diff: 1   Page Ref: 5.1
Skill: Factual

24) Cell membranes do all of the following except

   A) isolate the cell's contents from the external environment.

   B) communicate with other cells.

   C) regulate movement of substances between the cell and the extracellular fluid.

   D) provide attachments between cells.

   E) provide the shape and structure to a cell.

Answer: E
Diff: 2   Page Ref: 5.1
Skill: Factual

25) Which of the following types of membrane proteins are responsible for facilitated diffusion?

   A) transport proteins

   B) recognition proteins

   C) enzymes

   D) receptor proteins

   E) attachment proteins

Answer: A
Diff: 1   Page Ref: 5.1, 5.2
Skill: Factual

26) Which of the following types of membrane proteins are responsible for connecting cells to each other?

    A) transport proteins

    B) recognition proteins

    C) enzymes

    D) receptor proteins

    E) attachment proteins

Answer: E
Diff: 1   Page Ref: 5.1
Skill: Factual

27) Which of the following types of membrane proteins are responsible for conveying external messages such as those sent by a hormone signal?

    A) transport proteins

    B) recognition proteins

    C) enzymes

    D) receptor proteins

    E) attachment proteins

Answer: D
Diff: 1   Page Ref: 5.1
Skill: Factual

28) The antibiotic, polymyxin B, attaches itself to the phospholipids in the phospholipid bilayer and increases the permeability of the membrane. Describe what will occur as a result.

Answer: The plasma membrane will lose its ability to be a selectively permeable barrier. Substances will leak out of the cell, and some previous excluded substances may enter. Eventually, the cell will die.
Diff: 3   Page Ref: .5.1
Skill: Application

29) How does the plasma membrane act as gatekeeper for the cell?

Answer: Separate internal and external cell environments; regulate the exchange of substances between external environment and the cytoplasm; communicate with other cells
Diff: 3   Page Ref: 5.1
Skill: Factual

30) The major lipids in biological membranes are called _____.

Answer: phospholipids
Diff: 1   Page Ref: 5.1
Skill: Factual

31) The phospholipid contains two different parts, a _____ head and a pair of _____ tails.

Answer: polar and/or hydrophilic; nonpolar and/or hydrophobic
Diff: 2   Page Ref: 5.1
Skill: Factual

32) The net movement of molecules from a high concentration to a low concentration is BEST described by which of the following?

A) diffusion

B) active transport

C) osmosis

D) facilitated diffusion

E) exocytosis

Answer: A
Diff: 1   Page Ref: 5.2
Skill: Factual

33) For diffusion to occur, there must be

A) a membrane.

B) a gradient.

C) water.

D) ATP.

E) all of these

Answer: B
Diff: 1   Page Ref: 5.2
Skill: Factual

34) *Vibrio cholerae* releases a toxin (cholera toxin) that blocks a channel protein in the membranes of cells that line the intestine. This toxin prevents the movement of positively charged sodium ions out of the intestine and into these cells. If the sodium ions cannot move into the cells, how would this affect the movement of water?

A) Water would leave the intestines and enter the cells by diffusion.

B) Water would leave the intestines and enter the cells by osmosis.

C) Water would leave the cells and enter the intestines by diffusion.

D) Water would leave the cells and enter the intestines by osmosis.

E) The movement of water would not be affected.

Answer: D
Diff: 3   Page Ref: 5.2
Skill: Application

35) Transport processes (for example, diffusion and active transport) occur across which of the following membranes?

    A) plasma membranes

    B) chloroplast membranes

    C) mitochondrial membranes

    D) ER membranes

    E) all of these

Answer: E
Diff: 2   Page Ref: 5.2
Skill: Conceptual

36) In reference to diffusion, "passive" really means

    A) without a membrane.

    B) in the air.

    C) no gradient.

    D) very slowly.

    E) no energy required.

Answer: E
Diff: 1   Page Ref: 5.2
Skill: Factual

37) You fill a shallow tray with water and place a drop of red ink in one end of the tray and a drop of green ink in the other end. Which of the following is TRUE at equilibrium?

    A) The red ink is uniformly distributed in one half of the tray and the green ink is uniformly distributed in the other half of the tray.

    B) The red and green inks are both uniformly distributed throughout the tray.

    C) Each ink is moving down its concentration gradient.

    D) The concentration of each ink is higher at one end of the tray than at the other end.

    E) No predictions can be made without knowing the size of the ink molecules.

Answer: B
Diff: 3   Page Ref: 5.2
Skill: Application

38) Carbon dioxide crosses the plasma membrane by simple diffusion. What determines the rate at which carbon dioxide enters the cell?

    A) the concentration of carbon dioxide on each side of the membrane

    B) the amount of energy being produced by the cell

    C) the amount of transport protein in the membrane

    D) the amount of carbon dioxide outside of the cell

    E) the amount of oxygen being exported from the cell

Answer: A
Diff: 2   Page Ref: 5.2
Skill: Conceptual

39) What is active transport?

    A) diffusion of molecules within a cell

    B) movement of molecules into or out of a cell against a concentration gradient

    C) movement of molecules into or out of a cell down a concentration gradient

    D) the movement of molecules into or out of a cell using special proteins and not requiring an expenditure of energy

    E) rapid movement of molecules in a solution

Answer: B
Diff: 2   Page Ref: 5.2
Skill: Factual

40) When substances move through a plasma membrane and down gradients of concentration this is called

    A) active transport.

    B) passive transport.

    C) pinocytosis.

    D) exocytosis.

    E) entropy.

Answer: B
Diff: 2   Page Ref: 5.2
Skill: Factual

41) To say a cell is *selectively permeable* means

    A) it has different sized perforations in the membrane.

    B) it is permeable to different substances than other cells.

    C) only certain molecules can pass through.

    D) sometimes water passes through, and sometimes it can't.

    E) permeability depends on gradient differences.

Answer: C
Diff: 2   Page Ref: 5.2
Skill: Factual

42) What happens when diffusion moves molecules across the plasma membrane?

    A) The cell gains needed materials and gets rid of excess materials very quickly.

    B) Most molecules are capable of crossing the phospholipid bilayer at any location and at basically the same rate.

    C) Energy input is required to transport molecules.

    D) The rate of diffusion cannot be influenced by the cell.

    E) The process is very slow and is driven by concentration gradients.

Answer: E
Diff: 2   Page Ref: 5.2
Skill: Conceptual

43) Which of the following may influence the rate of simple diffusion across a differentially permeable membrane?

    A) size of molecule

    B) lipid solubility of the molecule

    C) concentration gradient

    D) A and C are correct.

    E) All are correct.

Answer: E
Diff: 2   Page Ref: 5.2
Skill: Factual

44) Molecules which permeate a plasma membrane by facilitated diffusion

   A) require an expenditure of energy.

   B) require the aid of transport proteins.

   C) move from an area of low concentration to an area of high concentration.

   D) do so much more quickly than those crossing by simple diffusion.

   E) all of these

Answer: B
Diff: 2   Page Ref: 5.2
Skill: Factual

45) A molecule that can diffuse freely through a phospholipid bilayer is probably

   A) hydrophilic.

   B) positively charged.

   C) hydrophobic.

   D) negatively charged.

   E) a sugar.

Answer: C
Diff: 2   Page Ref: 5.2
Skill: Conceptual

46) Molecules assisted by carrier proteins may cross a differentially permeable membrane by

   A) facilitated diffusion.

   B) active transport.

   C) osmosis.

   D) endocytosis.

   E) simple diffusion.

Answer: A
Diff: 1   Page Ref: 5.2
Skill: Factual

47) The diffusion of water molecules across a differentially permeable membrane is termed

   A) facilitated diffusion.

   B) hydrolysis.

   C) active transport.

   D) exocytosis.

   E) osmosis.

Answer: E
Diff: 1   Page Ref: 5.2
Skill: Factual

48) If red blood cells are taken from the body and placed in a hypertonic solution, what happens to the cells?

    A) The cells swell and burst because water moves into the cells.

    B) The cells shrivel up because water leaves the cells.

    C) The cells remain unchanged due to equal solute concentration inside and outside the cells.

    D) The cells remain unchanged due to equal water concentrations inside and outside the cells.

    E) They become white blood cells.

Answer: B
Diff: 2   Page Ref: 5.2
Skill: Conceptual

49) Inside a "cell" you construct, you place a 1 M sugar solution. You place the cell in a 2 M sugar solution. What happens?

    A) Water enters the cell because there is more water outside than inside.

    B) Water leaves the cell because there is more water inside than outside the cell.

    C) Water leaves and enters at the same rate.

    D) Sugar diffuses in and water diffuses out until equilibrium is reached.

    E) None of the above are correct.

Answer: C
Diff: 2   Page Ref: 5.2
Skill: Application

50) A freshwater protozoan, such as *Paramecium*, tends to _____ because it lives in a _____ environment.

    A) gain water; hypotonic

    B) lose water; hypertonic

    C) gain water; hypertonic

    D) lose water; hypotonic

    E) gain water; isotonic

Answer: A
Diff: 2   Page Ref: 5.2
Skill: Conceptual

51) Solutions that cause water to enter cells by osmosis are termed

    A) hypertonic.

    B) isotonic.

    C) hypotonic.

    D) permeable.

    E) hydrophilic.

Answer: C
Diff: 2   Page Ref: 5.2
Skill: Factual

52) The blood plasma of a man who drinks saltwater will become _____ to his red blood cells, whereas the red blood cells will be _____ to the blood plasma.

    A) isotonic; isotonic

    B) hypertonic; isotonic

    C) hypotonic; hypertonic

    D) hypertonic; hypotonic

    E) isotonic; hypertonic

Answer: D
Diff: 2   Page Ref: 5.2
Skill: Application

53) The slowest rate of diffusion of dye particles in water will occur in which situation?

    A) dye particles in water at 10°C

    B) dye particles in water at 20°C

    C) dye particles in water at 30°C

    D) dye particles in water at 40°C

    E) dye particles in water at 80°C

Answer: A
Diff: 2   Page Ref: 5.2
Skill: Conceptual

54) Suppose you have two glucose solutions separated by a differentially permeable membrane. A concentration gradient of glucose across a membrane means (assuming there are no other solutes in the solution)

   A) there are more glucose molecules per unit volume on one side of the membrane than the other.

   B) the solutions are isotonic.

   C) one solution is hypertonic.

   D) one solution has a lower concentration of water molecules.

   E) A, C, and D are correct.

Answer: E
Diff: 2   Page Ref: 5.2
Skill: Conceptual

55) Beaker A has a 10% sucrose solution, and beaker B has an 8% sucrose solution. Choose the correct statement.

   A) Beaker A is isotonic to Beaker B.

   B) Beaker B is hypertonic to Beaker B.

   C) Beaker B is hypotonic the Beaker A.

   D) Beaker A is hypertonic to Beaker B.

   E) Both C and D are correct.

Answer: E
Diff: 2   Page Ref: 5.2
Skill: Conceptual

56) In 1966, two researchers published work that describes an experiment carried out with isolated membrane vesicles from chloroplasts. These membrane vesicles were soaked in an acidic solution (pH 4) until the inside of the vesicle also became pH 4. By what mechanism does the hydrogen ion cross the vesicle membrane?

   A) facilitated diffusion

   B) osmosis

   C) simple diffusion

   D) active transport

   E) endocytosis

Answer: A
Diff: 3   Page Ref: 5.2
Skill: Conceptual

57) In 1966, two researchers published work that describes an experiment carried out with isolated membrane vesicles from chloroplasts, in order to study the reactions of photosynthesis. These membrane vesicles were soaked in an acidic solution (pH 4) until the inside of the vesicle also became pH 4. The researchers then transferred the vesicles to pH 10 solution. What do you think happened?

A) Water moved from inside the vesicle to outside by osmosis.

B) Hydrogen ions moved out of the vesicle by simple diffusion.

C) Hydrogen ions moved into the vesicle through a channel.

D) Hydrogen ions moved out of the vesicle through a channel.

E) No movement of hydrogen ions or water occurred.

Answer: D
Diff: 3   Page Ref: 5.2
Skill: Application

58) Two aqueous solutions are separated by a semipermeable membrane. Solution A is 10% starch and solution B is 5% starch. What will occur?

A) Water will diffuse from solution A to solution B.

B) Water will diffuse from solution B to solution A.

C) Starch will diffuse from solution A to solution B.

D) Starch will diffuse from solution B to solution A.

E) Both B and D will occur.

Answer: B
Diff: 2   Page Ref: 5.2
Skill: Application

59) The rate of facilitated diffusion of a molecule across a membrane will increase as the concentration difference of the molecule across the membrane increases to a certain point. Eventually, an increase in concentration of molecule will not cause any further increase in facilitated diffusion. This is because

A) facilitated diffusion requires ATP energy.

B) as the concentration difference increases, molecules interfere with one another.

C) there are a limited number of carrier proteins in the membrane.

D) increased concentration difference causes a situation far from equilibrium.

E) the diffusion constant depends on the concentration difference.

Answer: C
Diff: 2   Page Ref: 5.2
Skill: Conceptual

60) Osmosis moves water from a region of

    A) high concentration of dissolved material to a region of low concentration.

    B) low concentration of dissolved material to a region of high concentration.

    C) hypertonic solution to a region of hypotonic solution.

    D) negative osmotic potential to a region of positive osmotic potential.

    E) low concentration of water to a region of high concentration of water.

Answer: B
Diff: 2   *Page Ref: 5.2*
Skill: Factual

61) Glucose is a six-carbon sugar that diffuses slowly through artificial phospholipid bilayers. The cells lining the small intestine, however, rapidly move large quantities of glucose from the glucose-rich food into their glucose-poor cytoplasm. Using this information, which transport mechanism is most probably functioning in the intestinal cells?

    A) simple diffusion

    B) exocytosis

    C) active transport

    D) facilitated diffusion

    E) osmosis

Answer: D
Diff: 2   *Page Ref: 5.2*
Skill: Conceptual

62) Two similar-sized animal cells are placed in a 0.5% sucrose solution. Cell A enlarges in size for a while, then stops; cell B continues to enlarge and finally ruptures. Which of the following was TRUE at the beginning of the experiment?

    A) Cell A was hypotonic to the solution and cell B was hypertonic.

    B) Cell A was hypertonic to the solution and cell B was hypotonic.

    C) Cell A was hypertonic to cell B.

    D) Cell B was hypertonic to cell A.

    E) Cells A and B were isotonic to each other.

Answer: D
Diff: 3   *Page Ref: 5.2*
Skill: Application

63) The cytoplasm of a certain cell, such as a neuron, already has a high concentration of K$^+$ ions. How can K$^+$ ions continue to enter the cell?

    A) active transport

    B) facilitated diffusion

    C) osmosis

    D) endocytosis

    E) infusion

Answer: A
Diff: 2   *Page Ref: 5.2*
Skill: Conceptual

64) O$_2$ and CO$_2$ enter or leave a plant cell by

    A) osmosis.

    B) diffusion.

    C) facilitated diffusion.

    D) active transport.

    E) facilitated transport.

Answer: B
Diff: 1   *Page Ref: 5.2*
Skill: Factual

65) Active transport requires

    A) transport proteins.

    B) ATP.

    C) a membrane.

    D) a gradient.

    E) all of these

Answer: E
Diff: 1   *Page Ref: 5.2*
Skill: Factual

66) The process whereby white blood cells engulf bacteria is termed

   A) adhesion.

   B) exocytosis.

   C) pinocytosis.

   D) phagocytosis.

   E) ingestion.

Answer: D
Diff: 1   Page Ref: 5.2
Skill: Factual

67) Which process accounts for the movement of solids into some animal cells?

   A) active transport

   B) facilitated diffusion

   C) diffusion

   D) osmosis

   E) phagocytosis

Answer: E
Diff: 2   Page Ref: 5.2
Skill: Factual

68) What does a cell use exocytosis for?

   A) to move away from danger

   B) to release substances from the cell

   C) to incorporate nutrients

   D) to pump hydrogen molecules across the membrane

   E) to create new cells

Answer: B
Diff: 2   Page Ref: 5.2
Skill: Factual

69) If you forget to water your favorite plant, all of the following will occur at a cellular level except

    A) water moves out of the cytosol by osmosis.

    B) water moves out of the vacuole by osmosis.

    C) turgor pressure builds up in the cells.

    D) the plasma membrane shrinks away from the cell walls.

    E) plasmolysis occurs.

Answer: C
Diff: 2   *Page Ref: 5.2*
Skill: Factual

70) Gases cross membranes by

    A) diffusion.

    B) facilitated diffusion.

    C) active transport.

    D) B and C

    E) A, B, and C

Answer: A
Diff: 1   *Page Ref: 5.2*
Skill: Factual

71) If a frog egg cell is placed into a hypotonic solution it will

    A) shrivel by osmosis.

    B) swell by osmosis.

    C) shrivel by facilitated diffusion.

    D) swell by facilitated diffusion.

    E) shrivel by active transport.

Answer: B
Diff: 2   *Page Ref: 5.2*
Skill: Conceptual

72) Which of the following requires ATP?

    A) diffusion

    B) facilitated diffusion

    C) active transport

    D) A and B

    E) B and C

Answer: C
Diff: 1   *Page Ref: 5.2*
Skill: Factual

73) Carrier molecules in the plasma membrane are only required for active transport. True or False?

Answer: FALSE
Diff: 2   *Page Ref: 5.2*
Skill: Conceptual

74) Osmosis is the diffusion of water molecules across differentially permeable membranes. True or False?

Answer: TRUE
Diff: 1   *Page Ref: 5.2*
Skill: Factual

75) After a dye diffuses equally throughout a glass of water, the dye molecules are no longer moving. True or False?

Answer: FALSE
Diff: 2   *Page Ref: 5.2*
Skill: Conceptual

76) The movement of molecules across a cell membrane in which no energy is required (i.e. diffusion) is called _____ transport and the movement of molecules across the membrane in which energy (i.e. ATP) is required is called _____ transport.

Answer: passive; active
Diff: 2   *Page Ref: 5.2*
Skill: Factual

77) Compare and contrast:
   a. Facilitated diffusion/active transport
   b. Osmosis/simple diffusion

   Answer: Facilitated diffusion and active transport both require membrane transport proteins. However, facilitated diffusion does not require energy and moves substances down a concentration gradient. Active transport requires energy and moves substances against a concentration gradient. Osmosis and simple diffusion are both passive processes. However, osmosis refers to the movement of water down its concentration gradient across a semipermeable membrane. No membrane is required for simple diffusion.
   Diff: 2   Page Ref: 5.2
   Skill: Conceptual

78) Design an experiment to show the effect of hypertonic, hypotonic and isotonic solutions on cells. Hint: Use differentially permeable membranes and remember to include a hypothesis, experimental design and how the results would be recorded and also state what the expected results would be for your experiment.

   Answer: Students should design an experiment in which a solution is placed in a differentially permeable membrane and then placed in a hypertonic, hypotonic and isotonic solution. An appropriate hypothesis and experimental design should be included with appropriate results for the experiment proposed.
   Diff: 3   Page Ref: 5.2
   Skill: Application

79) Why is the biological membrane referred to as being selectively permeable?

   Answer: only allow some molecules to pass through while barring others
   Diff: 2   Page Ref: 5.2
   Skill: Factual

80) Compare and contrast the terms diffusion and osmosis.

   Answer: Osmosis is the diffusion of water (diffusion is a more general term for the movement of molecules along a concentration gradient from high to low concentration).
   Diff: 2   Page Ref: 5.2
   Skill: Conceptual

81) Facilitated diffusion and active transport both require _____ for the movement of molecules across the membrane.

   Answer: transport proteins
   Diff: 2   Page Ref: 5.2
   Skill: Factual

82) Suppose a bag made of a differentially permeable membrane was filled with a 5% solution of glucose and sealed. What would happen if the bag was placed in 1) pure water or 2) 10% glucose solution?

Answer: In condition 1 the bag would swell (water in) and in condition 2 the bag would shrink (water out).
Diff: 3   Page Ref: 5.2
Skill: Application

83) Why does the cell perform endocytosis in addition to active and passive transport mechanisms?

Answer: Endocytosis is required for the transport of large proteins, microbes, or extracellular fluid and specific molecules all larger than the molecule size transported by active and passive transport.
Diff: 2   Page Ref: 5.2
Skill: Conceptual

84) Distinguish between the three types of endocytosis.

Answer: Pinocytosis is for fluid intake, receptor–mediated endocytosis is for the uptake of specific molecules, and phagocytosis is used to uptake large particles into the cell.
Diff: 2   Page Ref: 5.2
Skill: Factual

85) _____ is used by cells to pick up large particles like bacteria.

Answer: Phagocytosis
Diff: 2   Page Ref: 5.2
Skill: Factual

86) Both plant cells and animal cells will swell if placed in a hypotonic solution. However, only the animal cell will burst. Explain.

Answer: Water will enter both cells due to osmosis. In the animal cell, water will continue to enter as long as the extracellular solution is hypotonic, causing the animal cell to eventually burst. The stiff cell wall, found in plant cells but not animal cells, will not expand indefinitely. At some point, as the cytoplasm of the plant cell expands, the cell wall will exert a back pressure on the cell. Further water uptake will be prevented and therefore, the plant cell will not burst.
Diff: 2   Page Ref: 5.2
Skill: Conceptual

87) Specialized cell junctions include

   A) gap junctions.

   B) tight junctions.

   C) desmosomes.

   D) A, B, and C

   E) A and B

Answer: D
Diff: 2   Page Ref: 5.3
Skill: Factual

88) The electric signal for a muscle to contract passes rapidly from one muscle cell to the next by way of

   A) tight junctions.

   B) desmosomes.

   C) gap junctions.

   D) internal proteins.

   E) external proteins.

Answer: C
Diff: 2   Page Ref: 5.3
Skill: Conceptual

89) Adhesion of animal tissues is accomplished by cell-to-cell junctions called

   A) desmosomes.

   B) tight junctions.

   C) gap junctions.

   D) plasmodesmata.

   E) cell plates.

Answer: A
Diff: 2   Page Ref: 5.3
Skill: Factual

90) The urinary bladder is protected from leaking due to cell-to-cell junctions called

   A) desmosomes.

   B) tight junctions.

   C) gap junctions.

   D) plasmodesmata.

   E) stretch receptors.

Answer: B
Diff: 2   Page Ref: 5.3
Skill: Factual

91) Protein channels that provide passage for hormones and nutrients between animal cells are termed

   A) desmosomes.

   B) tight junctions.

   C) gap junctions.

   D) plasmodesmata.

   E) capillaries.

Answer: C
Diff: 2   Page Ref: 5.3
Skill: Factual

92) You observe a cell under a microscope and you can clearly see a cell wall, a vacuole, and cytoplasmic connections. These cytoplasmic connections are

   A) gap junctions.

   B) desmosomes.

   C) plasmodesmata.

   D) tight junctions.

   E) osmotic channels.

Answer: C
Diff: 2   Page Ref: 5.3
Skill: Factual

93) When very small viruses infect a plant cell by crossing its membrane, the viruses often spread rapidly throughout the entire plant without crossing additional membranes. Explain how this occurs.

   Answer: The virus spreads throughout the plant traveling cell to cell via the plasmodesmata junctions.
Diff: 2   Page Ref: 5.3
Skill: Conceptual

94) Compare and contrast the intercellular junctions that allow communication between plant and animal cells.

Answer: Gap junctions in animal cells and plasmodesmata in plant cells—both are involved to coordinate the actions of adjacent cells.
Diff: 2   Page Ref: 5.3
Skill: Conceptual

95) In plant cells, _____ allow for communication between cells and in animal cells the _____ serve the same purpose.

Answer: plasmodesmata; gap junctions
Diff: 2   Page Ref: 5.3
Skill: Conceptual

96) The cells of the intestinal epithelium (lining) are joined to one another by _____ that prevent substances from passing between the cells of this tissue.

Answer: tight junctions
Diff: 2   Page Ref: 5.3
Skill: Factual

97) In _____, membranes of adjacent cells are held together by proteins and carbohydrates, much like glue.

Answer: desmosomes
Diff: 2   Page Ref: 5.3
Skill: Factual

Chapter 6 Energy Flow in the Life of a Cell

1) Which of the following has the greatest amount of kinetic energy?

   A) tank of gasoline

   B) moving car

   C) hot car engine

   D) cool air surrounding the engine

   E) an unlit firecracker

   Answer: B
   Diff: 2   Page Ref: 6.1
   Skill: Factual

2) Which of the following has potential energy?

   A) water droplet on top of a waterfall

   B) glucose molecule

   C) diver on a springboard

   D) 9V battery

   E) all of the above

   Answer: E
   Diff: 2   Page Ref: 6.1
   Skill: Conceptual

3) All the following statements are true of the FIRST law of thermodynamics EXCEPT

   A) the amount of useful energy decreases.

   B) the first law of thermodynamics is often called the law of the conservation of energy.

   C) the total amount of energy within an isolated system remains the same.

   D) one form of energy may be converted to a different form of energy.

   E) All are true of the first law.

   Answer: A
   Diff: 2   Page Ref: 6.1
   Skill: Factual

4) In an isolated system, all the following are true of the SECOND law of thermodynamics EXCEPT

    A) useful energy decreases.

    B) spontaneous changes result in a more uniform distribution of energy.

    C) all chemical reactions are exergonic.

    D) there is a natural tendency toward greater disorder of the organization of matter.

    E) All are true of the second law.

Answer: C
Diff: 2   Page Ref: 6.1
Skill: Factual

5) Entropy is a measure of

    A) increase in orderliness.

    B) gain of high-level energy.

    C) increase in potential energy.

    D) increase in randomness.

    E) increase in kinetic energy.

Answer: D
Diff: 2   Page Ref: 6.1
Skill: Factual

6) How is your body able to counteract the effects of entropy?

    A) regular exercise

    B) sunbathing

    C) eating a balanced diet

    D) bathing regularly

    E) buffers

Answer: C
Diff: 2   Page Ref: 6.1
Skill: Factual

7) Each of the following requires twelve carbon atoms. Which of the arrangements demonstrates carbon atoms with the greatest entropy?

   A) twelve molecules of carbon dioxide, CO_2

   B) one molecule of the disaccharide, maltose, $C_{12}H_{22}O_{11}$

   C) two molecules of the monosaccharide glucose, $C_6H_{12}O_6$

   D) four molecules of the monosaccharide, pyruvate $C_3H_4O_3$

   E) It is impossible to determine.

Answer: A
Diff: 3   Page Ref: 6.1
Skill: Conceptual

8) Energy that is not converted to useful energy is usually given off as

   A) radioactivity.

   B) electricity.

   C) light.

   D) heat.

   E) entropy.

Answer: D
Diff: 2   Page Ref: 6.1
Skill: Factual

9) During photosynthesis, plants convert light energy to chemical energy. This is an illustration of

   A) increasing entropy.

   B) chemical equilibrium.

   C) the first law of thermodynamics.

   D) the second law of thermodynamics.

   E) a spontaneous reaction.

Answer: C
Diff: 2   Page Ref: 6.1
Skill: Conceptual

10) Which of the following BEST illustrates the first law of thermodynamics?

A) the process of photosynthesis where solar energy is converted to chemical energy

B) the burning of fossil fuels to heat a home

C) the use of gasoline to allow your car to run

D) a marathoner eating a high carbohydrate meal and then running a race the next day

E) all of the above

Answer: E
Diff: 2   Page Ref: 6.1
Skill: Conceptual

11) Which of the following is part of the first law of thermodynamics?

A) Energy cannot be created or destroyed.

B) Kinetic energy is stored energy.

C) Energy cannot be transferred or transformed.

D) Exergonic reactions are coupled with endergonic reactions.

E) Potential energy equals kinetic energy in a reaction.

Answer: A
Diff: 2   Page Ref: 6.1
Skill: Conceptual

12) Why is it possible for living organisms to comply with the second law of thermodynamics?

A) Chemical reactions inside cells mostly cause an increase of high-level energy.

B) Living organisms are totally isolated systems which are not subjected to the laws of physics.

C) Sunlight functions as an ultimate source of energy for most forms of life on Earth.

D) Living organisms are unique in that they do not require energy for survival.

E) Organisms are able to function efficiently on heat energy alone.

Answer: C
Diff: 2   Page Ref: 6.1
Skill: Conceptual

13) What is the *ultimate* source of energy for most forms of life on Earth?

    A) heat energy

    B) solar energy

    C) thermal energy

    D) chemical energy

    E) nuclear energy

Answer: B
Diff: 1   Page Ref: 6.1
Skill: Factual

14) Law of Conservation of Energy states that although the form of energy used remains the same the total amount of energy changes. True or False?

Answer: FALSE
Diff: 2   Page Ref: 6.1
Skill: Factual

15) Energy is defined as the capacity to do work. True or False?

Answer: TRUE
Diff: 1   Page Ref: 6.1
Skill: Factual

16) Kinetic energy is like sitting at the top of a hill and potential energy is coasting down that hill on your bike. True or False?

Answer: FALSE
Diff: 2   Page Ref: 6.1
Skill: Conceptual

17) Briefly describe the difference between kinetic energy and potential energy and give an example of each.

Answer: Students should mention that kinetic energy is the energy of motion (examples include heat, light, electricity, a car moving) whereas potential energy is stored (examples include energy in chemical bonds, batteries, child sitting at the top of a slide).
Diff: 2   Page Ref: 6.1
Skill: Conceptual

18) Briefly describe the two laws of thermodynamics.

Answer: The Law of the Conservation of energy states that although the form of energy changes the total amount remains the same and the second law states that as energy changes from one form to another, the same amount of useful energy decreases.
Diff: 2   Page Ref: 6.1
Skill: Conceptual

19) What is a simple definition of energy from the biological perspective? Give some examples of where energy is used in a cell.

Answer: Energy is the ability to do work and the cell uses energy to synthesize molecules, move objects and generate heat—several other examples could be used.

Diff: 2   Page Ref: 6.1
Skill: Factual

20) The second law of thermodynamics states that the _____, or disorder, of the universe is constantly increasing.

Answer: entropy
Diff: 2   Page Ref: 6.1
Skill: Factual

21) Energy transformations are not 100% efficient; often energy in the form of _____ is released, which fulfills the second law of thermodynamics.

Answer: heat
Diff: 2   Page Ref: 6.1
Skill: Factual

22) The energy of movement is _____ energy and stored energy is referred to as _____ energy.

Answer: kinetic; potential
Diff: 2   Page Ref: 6.1
Skill: Factual

23) Sitting at the top of a slide a child has _____ energy and when sliding down she is using _____ energy.

Answer: potential; kinetic
Diff: 2   Page Ref: 6.1
Skill: Conceptual

24) In exergonic chemical reactions

A) reactants have more energy than products.

B) energy is stored by the reactions.

C) reactants have less energy then products.

D) reactants and products possess equal amounts of energy.

E) Both A and B are correct.

Answer: A
Diff: 3   Page Ref: 6.2
Skill: Conceptual

25) When solid sodium hydroxide is added to water, the solution gets hot. This is an example of

   A) an endergonic process.

   B) an exergonic process.

   C) an enzyme–catalyzed process.

   D) a release of activation energy.

   E) a conversion of kinetic energy to potential energy.

   Answer: B
   Diff: 2   Page Ref: 6.2
   Skill: Conceptual

26) Why is photosynthesis considered an endergonic reaction in an isolated plant?

   A) Activation energy is not required.

   B) Photosynthesis does not comply with the physical laws of the universe.

   C) because sugar has less energy than the sun

   D) Protein catalysts are not needed.

   E) Low–energy reactants are converted into high–energy products.

   Answer: E
   Diff: 3   Page Ref: 6.2
   Skill: Conceptual

27) The BEST description of a coupled reaction is

   A) two reactions that occur simultaneously.

   B) a reaction that occurs right after another reaction.

   C) two reactions that occur in the same organelle.

   D) reactions that occur during sexual reproduction.

   E) two reactions that involve one providing energy for the other.

   Answer: E
   Diff: 2   Page Ref: 6.2
   Skill: Conceptual

28) Why is photosynthesis a coupled reaction?

   A) The exergonic reaction occurs in the plant, and the endergonic reaction occurs in the soil.

   B) The exergonic reaction occurs in the plant, and the endergonic reaction occurs in the sun.

   C) Photosynthesis requires a couple of reactants: carbon dioxide and water.

   D) An exergonic reaction occurs in the sun, and an endergonic reaction occurs in the plant.

   E) Sunlight energy is lost as heat.

   Answer: D
   Diff: 2   Page Ref: 6.2
   Skill: Conceptual

29) An _____ chemical reaction releases energy while an _____ reactions requires an input of energy.

    A) exergonic; endergonic

    B) endergonic; exergonic

    C) enzymatic; endergonic

    D) endergonic; enzymatic

    E) equilibrium; exergonic

Answer: A
Diff: 1   *Page Ref: 6.2*
Skill: Factual

30) In the liver, the polysaccharide glycogen is broken down into glucose monomers. The glucose molecules are then released into the blood when blood sugar levels need to be raised. This process is an example of a(n)

    A) endergonic reaction.   B) exergonic reaction.

    C) thermokinetic reaction.   D) potential reaction.

Answer: B
Diff: 2   *Page Ref: 6.2*
Skill: Application

31) Imagine you are conducting an experiment on a yeast enzyme known as sucrase. This enzyme is used by yeast cells to break sucrose into glucose and fructose. What type of reaction is this?

    A) metergonic reaction   B) exergonic reaction

    C) endergonic reaction   D) spontaneous reaction

Answer: B
Diff: 2   *Page Ref: 6.2*
Skill: Application

32) The photosynthetic reaction is considered to be an endergonic reaction. True or False?

Answer: TRUE
Diff: 2   *Page Ref: 6.2*
Skill: Factual

33) The burning of sugar is an example of an endergonic reaction and photosynthesis is an example of an exergonic reaction. True or False?

Answer: FALSE
Diff: 2   *Page Ref: 6.2*
Skill: Factual

34) In cells, endergonic reactions are often coupled with enzymatic reactions that store energy. True or False?

   Answer: FALSE
   Diff: 2   Page Ref: 6.2
   Skill: Conceptual

35) In chemical reactions, the _____ are converted into products.

   Answer: reactants
   Diff: 1   Page Ref: 6.2
   Skill: Factual

36) In chemical reactions _____ reactions release energy and _____ reactions require an input of energy.

   Answer: exergonic; endergonic
   Diff: 3   Page Ref: 6.2
   Skill: Conceptual

37) The burning of sugars as fuels for runners is an example of an _____ chemical reaction whereas the production of sugars during photosynthesis is an example of an _____ chemical reaction.

   Answer: exergonic; endergonic
   Diff: 2   Page Ref: 6.2
   Skill: Conceptual

38) Describe an analogy to distinguish between endergonic and exergonic chemical reactions.

   Answer: There are many possible examples, for example, rolling a boulder up a hill requires
          input of energy (an endergonic process), while the same boulder, once given a push,
          rolls down the hill spontaneously (exergonic process).
   Diff: 2   Page Ref: 6.2
   Skill: Conceptual

39) Coupled reactions are important components of human physiology. Give an example of a coupled reaction in the human body and describe.

   Answer: A coupled reaction is when an exergonic reaction provides the energy needed to drive
          an endergonic reaction. Examples will vary. One example is the chemical breakdown of
          sugars in the human body (exergonic reactions) are used to fuel essential endergonic
          reactions such as muscle contractions.
   Diff: 3   Page Ref: 6.2
   Skill: Conceptual

40) The most common energy carrier molecule of living organisms is

    A) ATP.

    B) inorganic phosphate.

    C) DNA.

    D) glucose.

    E) NADPH.

Answer: A
Diff: 1   Page Ref: 6.3
Skill: Conceptual

41) A "high-energy" bond in an ATP molecule is located between

    A) adenine and ribose.

    B) two phosphate groups.

    C) ribose and first phosphate group.

    D) adenine and first phosphate group.

    E) both B and C

Answer: B
Diff: 2   Page Ref: 6.3
Skill: Factual

42) When a muscle cell demands energy to perform its work of contraction, what happens to ATP?

    A) ATP manufactures more ATP.

    B) ATP enters a metabolic pathway.

    C) ATP is broken down.

    D) ATP is phosphorylated.

    E) ATP catalyzes the reaction.

Answer: C
Diff: 2   Page Ref: 6.3
Skill: Conceptual

43) Which of the following is not a common energy carrier in the cell?

    A) ADP   B) phosphate

    C) electron carriers   D) ATP

Answer: A
Diff: 2   Page Ref: 6.3
Skill: Conceptual

44) When a high-energy bond of ATP is broken, primarily what happens to the released energy?

    A) It is lost as light energy.

    B) It functions as a second messenger.

    C) It polarizes the cell.

    D) It converts inorganic phosphates into energy carrier molecules.

    E) It drives endergonic reactions in the cell.

Answer: E
Diff: 2   Page Ref: 6.3
Skill: Conceptual

45) Which molecule results in short-term storage of energy?

    A) glycogen

    B) fat

    C) sucrose

    D) adenosine triphosphate

    E) protein

Answer: D
Diff: 2   Page Ref: 6.3
Skill: Factual

46) ATP is an energy carrier. Where is the energy actually located?

    A) attached to the phosphate group

    B) in the bonds between phosphate groups

    C) attached to the nucleotide

    D) inside the phosphate

    E) between the sugar and the phosphate

Answer: B
Diff: 2   Page Ref: 6.3
Skill: Factual

47) Energy is transferred from one location to another in the cell

    A) in the form of ATP.

    B) in electrons in an electron carrying molecule.

    C) as ADP.

    D) by high energy wires.

    E) Both A and B are correct.

Answer: E
Diff: 2   Page Ref: 6.3
Skill: Conceptual

48) ADP stores energy in its chemical bonds and is able to use that energy for work in the cell. True or False?

Answer: FALSE
Diff: 2   Page Ref: 6.3
Skill: Factual

49) Briefly describe how ATP acts as an energy carrier in cells.

Answer: ATP stores energy in its chemical bonds and releases the energy when needed with the breaking of the third phosphate bond (forming ADP and phosphate).
Diff: 2   Page Ref: 6.3
Skill: Conceptual

50) The molecule _____ is the major energy carrier in cells.

Answer: ATP
Diff: 1   Page Ref: 6.3
Skill: Factual

51) ATP is considered a short–term form of energy for the cell, while _____ represents more stable, long term energy stores.

Answer: carbohydrates (sucrose, glycogen) or fats
Diff: 2   Page Ref: 6.3
Skill: Factual

52) Special molecules like NAD^+ and FAD transport _____ in cells, which can then be used as energy in the cell.

Answer: electrons
Diff: 2   Page Ref: 6.3
Skill: Factual

53) How would you describe the structural difference between ATP and ADP?

Answer: Both ATP and ADP contain an adenosine and a sugar. In ATP, 3 phosphate groups are attached while in ADP only 2 phosphate groups are attached.
Diff: 2   Page Ref: 6.3
Skill: Conceptual

54) Most reactions in the body occur too slowly to sustain life. This is because

    A) all reactions in the body are endergonic.

    B) many reactions require large inputs of activation energy.

    C) no catalysts are present in body cells.

    D) most biological catalysts are not active at body temperatures (37°C).

    E) there is not enough ATP in body cells.

Answer: B
Diff: 2   Page Ref: 6.4
Skill: Conceptual

55) Which of the following lowers the activation energy of a biochemical reaction?

    A) presence of catalysts

    B) high temperature

    C) low concentration of reactants

    D) altering pH to 7

    E) high concentration of products

Answer: B
Diff: 2   Page Ref: 6.4
Skill: Factual

56) All the following statements pertaining to catalysts are true EXCEPT

    A) biological catalysts are specific enzymes.

    B) catalysts increase activation energy requirements.

    C) catalysts increase reaction rate.

    D) catalysts are not permanently altered during reaction.

    E) catalysts can be used over and over again.

Answer: B
Diff: 2   Page Ref: 6.4
Skill: Factual

57) The reactant is an enzyme catalyzed reaction is the

    A) substrate.

    B) active site.

    C) product.

    D) inhibitor.

    E) activation energy.

Answer: A
Diff: 2   Page Ref: 6.4
Skill: Factual

58) Why are enzymes important?

A) because they are proteins

B) because they can evade the laws of thermodynamics

C) because they bind to substrates

D) because they allow reactions to occur at body temperature

E) because they increase body temperature

Answer: D
Diff: 2   Page Ref: 6.4
Skill: Conceptual

59) Place the steps of enzyme catalysis in the correct order.
1. Substrate and enzyme change shape
2. Substrate enters the active site
3. Enzyme reverts to original configuration
4. Product is expelled

A) 1, 2, 3, 4   B) 1, 3, 4, 2   C) 2, 1, 4, 3   D) 2, 1, 3, 4   E) 2, 3, 1, 4

Answer: C
Diff: 2   Page Ref: 6.4
Skill: Conceptual

60) Which of these statements regarding enzymes is FALSE?

A) Enzymes are proteins that function as biological catalysts.

B) Enzymes display specificity for certain molecules to which they attach.

C) Enzymes provide energy for the reactions they catalyze.

D) The activity of enzymes can be regulated by factors in their environment.

E) An enzyme may be used many times over for a specific reaction.

Answer: C
Diff: 2   Page Ref: 6.4
Skill: Conceptual

61) Which of the following functions as a biological catalyst?

A) energy carrier molecule

B) amino acid

C) enzyme

D) substrate

E) steroids

Answer: C
Diff: 2   Page Ref: 6.4
Skill: Factual

62) Which statement BEST describes the relationship between an enzyme and a reactant molecule?

A) The relationship is temporary.

B) Covalent chemical bonds stabilize the relationship.

C) The enzyme and reactant molecule are both permanently changed.

D) The resultant product and the enzyme are permanently bonded together.

E) The reactant cannot function without the enzyme.

Answer: A
Diff: 2   Page Ref: 6.4
Skill: Conceptual

63) Which enzyme characteristic BEST explains the fact that animals have enzymes that break apart starch molecules but not cellulose despite the fact that both basically are made up of glucose subunits?

A) Enzyme activity is regulated.

B) Enzymes usually speed up chemical reactions.

C) Enzymes are not permanently changed by the reactions they promote.

D) Enzymes are highly specific.

E) All enzymes are proteins.

Answer: D
Diff: 2   Page Ref: 6.4
Skill: Conceptual

64) End products of biosynthetic pathways often act to block the initial step in that pathway. This phenomenon is called

A) allosteric activation.

B) denaturation.

C) irreversible inhibition.

D) feedback inhibition.

E) substrate activation.

Answer: D
Diff: 2   Page Ref: 6.4
Skill: Conceptual

65) Competitive and noncompetitive enzyme inhibitors differ with respect to

A) the precise location on the enzyme to which they bind.

B) their pH.

C) their binding affinities.

D) their energies of activation.

E) none of the above

Answer: A
Diff: 2   Page Ref: 6.4
Skill: Conceptual

66) Which of the following will bind to the active site of an enzyme?

A) substrate

B) competitive inhibitor

C) allosteric inhibitor

D) non competitive inhibitor

E) Both A and B are correct.

Answer: E
Diff: 2   Page Ref: 6.4
Skill: Conceptual

67) The optimum reaction rate of a particular enzyme occurs at pH 7.3 at 37°C. This reaction would probably occur faster by

A) decreasing the pH and increasing the temperature.

B) increasing the temperature to 39° and keeping the pH at 7.3.

C) increasing the pH and maintaining the temperature at 37°.

D) increasing both temperature and pH.

Answer: B
Diff: 2   Page Ref: 6.4
Skill: Conceptual

68) Certain vitamins, such as niacin, act as _____ in enzyme catalyzed reactions.

A) substrates

B) allosteric activators

C) coenzymes

D) inhibitors

E) catalysts

Answer: C
Diff: 2   Page Ref: 6.4
Skill: Conceptual

69) Coenzymes function by

A) bonding to the enzyme and weakening the bonds of the substrate.

B) binding to the substrate and weakening the bonds of the enzyme.

C) binding two or more substrates and joining them.

D) helping substrates find enzymes.

E) joining together to form an enzyme.

Answer: A
Diff: 2   Page Ref: 6.4
Skill: Conceptual

70) Which is the organic molecule that is sometimes required for certain enzyme activity?

A) an accessory enzyme

B) an allosteric enzyme

C) a coenzyme

D) a functional group

E) an activator

Answer: C
Diff: 2   Page Ref: 6.4
Skill: Conceptual

71) The hydrolysis of sucrose to glucose and fructose is a spontaneous reaction. However, if you dissolve sucrose in water and keep the solution overnight at room temperature, there is no detectable conversion to glucose and fructose. Why?

A) The reaction is at equilibrium.

B) The energy of the products is higher than the energy of the reactants.

C) The activation energy of the reaction decreases.

D) The reaction is endergonic.

E) The reaction requires a catalyst.

Answer: E
Diff: 2   Page Ref: 6.4
Skill: Conceptual

72) For many enzymes the rate of product formation increases as the concentration of substrate increases. Eventually the rate of the reaction reaches a maximum, where further increases in the concentration of substrate have no effect. Why?

A) At high concentrations of substrate, all of the enzyme molecules are bound to substrate molecules.

B) At high concentrations of substrate, the activation energy of the reaction increases.

C) At high concentrations of substrate, the activation energy of the reaction decreases.

D) The enzyme is no longer specific for substrate.

E) At high concentrations of substrate, the reaction is endergonic.

Answer: A
Diff: 3   Page Ref: 6.4
Skill: Conceptual

73) FAD is an example of

A) a protein.

B) an electron carrier.

C) an enzyme.

D) an enzyme–substrate complex.

E) an active site.

Answer: B
Diff: 2   Page Ref: 6.4
Skill: Conceptual

74) The addition of the competitive inhibitor slows down a particular reaction. How could you overcome the effects of the inhibitor and increase the rate of the reaction?

A) add more inhibitor

B) add more substrate

C) lower the temperature of the reaction

D) add a coenzyme

E) allow the reaction to reach equilibrium

Answer: B
Diff: 3   Page Ref: 6.4
Skill: Conceptual

75) Imagine you are conducting an experiment on a yeast enzyme known as sucrase. This enzyme is used by yeast cells to break the disaccharide sucrose into glucose and fructose. You decide to conduct an experiment to test whether the sucrase enzyme can break down the artificial sweetener sucralose. Sucralose has some similarity to sucrose structure but is different in that three of its hydroxyl groups are missing and replaced with chlorine atoms instead. Will the sucrase enzyme be able to interact with sucralose as a substrate?

    A) Yes, enzymes such as sucrase are not specific for their substrate.

    B) No, an enzyme must have its specific substrate in order to interact with it.

    C) No because sucralose is found in diet foods.

    D) Yes, all enzymes in human cells can interact with artificial sweeteners.

Answer: B
Diff: 3   Page Ref: 6.4
Skill: Application

76) Sulfa antibiotics damage bacteria by affecting a certain bacterial enzyme. The sulfa antibiotic looks similar to a substrate normally required by the bacterial cells to live. The sulfa antibiotic occupies the active site of the required enzyme and blocks entry of its normal substrate. This prevents the bacteria from making nucleotides that are required for their reproduction and survival. Based on this information, the action of sulfa antibiotics is an example of

    A) electron carriers.   B) competitive inhibition.

    C) denaturing of proteins.   D) activation energy.

Answer: B
Diff: 3   Page Ref: 6.4
Skill: Application

77) Preservatives such as citric acid are added to foods to interfere with bacterial growth. This creates an acidic pH in the food. Why does this affect the bacteria that are present?

    A) An acidic environment encourages endergonic reactions in the bacterial cells.

    B) An acidic environment increases activation energy more quickly in bacteria.

    C) An acidic environment causes bacterial enzymes to denature.

    D) An acidic environment causes the bacteria to grow more rapidly.

Answer: C
Diff: 3   Page Ref: 6.4
Skill: Application

78) The metabolism of a cell is the sum of all its chemical reactions. True or False?

Answer: TRUE
Diff: 1   Page Ref: 6.4
Skill: Factual

79) The usual source of activation energy for a reaction is potential energy stored by the cell. True or False?

Answer: FALSE
Diff: 2   Page Ref: 6.4
Skill: Factual

80) Why does increasing the temperature of a chemical reaction generally increase the rate of the reaction?

Answer: Increasing temperature increases kinetic energy of the reactants causing the molecules to interact more frequently and with sufficient speed to overcome the activation energy of the reaction.
Diff: 2   Page Ref: 6.4
Skill: Conceptual

81) Explain how enzymes decrease the activation energy required for biological processes in our bodies.

Answer: Enzymes decrease activation energy by a combination of factors including substrate orientation, formation of temporary chemical bonds, electrostatic interactions, and bond distortion.
Diff: 2   Page Ref: 6.4
Skill: Conceptual

82) Describe the properties of a biological catalyst.

Answer: Catalysts (enzymes) serve to speed up only those reactions that would occur spontaneously anyway and are not consumed in the reaction, nor are they permanently changed after the reaction is completed.
Diff: 2   Page Ref: 6.4
Skill: Conceptual

83) _____ are biological catalysts.

Answer: Enzymes
Diff: 2   Page Ref: 6.4
Skill: Factual

84) The enzyme phosphoglucoisomerase catalyses the conversion of glucose-6-phosphate to fructose-6-phosphate. The region on phosphoglucoisomerase where glucose-6-phosphate binds is called the _____.

Answer: active site
Diff: 2   Page Ref: 6.4
Skill: Conceptual

85) Normally an enzyme has maximal enzyme activity at 37°C, but once it has been heated to 100°C and then cooled back down to 37°C the enzyme is no longer active. Why?

Answer: The enzyme's three–dimensional shape would have been distorted and the active site was no longer able to bind the appropriate substrates in the reaction.

Diff: 3   *Page Ref: 6.4*
Skill: Conceptual

Chapter 7 Capturing Solar Energy: Photosynthesis

1) Before photosynthesis evolved, _____ was rare in Earth's atmosphere.

   A) N_2 B) CO_2 C) O_2 D) H_2O E) air

Answer: C
Diff: 2   Page Ref: 7.1
Skill: Factual

2) The products of photosynthesis are

   A) glucose and water.

   B) carbon dioxide, water, and energy.

   C) glucose and carbon dioxide.

   D) carbon dioxide, chlorophyll, and oxygen.

   E) glucose and oxygen.

Answer: E
Diff: 2   Page Ref: 7.1
Skill: Factual

3) What structural feature of a leaf allows a leaf to obtain CO_2 from the air?

   A) stomata

   B) epidermis

   C) cuticle

   D) mesophyll

   E) chloroplast

Answer: A
Diff: 2   Page Ref: 7.1
Skill: Factual

4) The vast majority of chloroplasts found in a leaf are located where?

   A) vascular bundles

   B) cuticle

   C) epidermis

   D) stroma

   E) mesophyll

Answer: E
Diff: 2   Page Ref: 7.1
Skill: Factual

5) Specifically, molecules of chlorophyll are located in membranes of sacs called

A) cristae.

B) thylakoids.

C) stroma.

D) grana.

E) vesicles.

Answer: B
Diff: 1   Page Ref: 7.1
Skill: Factual

6) What factors influence the rate of photosynthesis?

A) light intensity

B) temperature

C) CO_2

D) water availability

E) all of these

Answer: E
Diff: 2   Page Ref: 7.1
Skill: Conceptual

7) All of the following compounds are required (i.e., are necessary constituents for chemical reactions) at some state of green plant photosynthesis, EXCEPT

A) ATP.

B) NADP.

C) water.

D) oxygen.

E) carbon dioxide.

Answer: D
Diff: 2   Page Ref: 7.1
Skill: Conceptual

8) The cellular organelle of eukaryotic organisms which is responsible for photosynthetic activity is the

   A) nucleus.

   B) mitochondrion.

   C) chloroplast.

   D) endoplasmic reticulum.

   E) ribosome.

Answer: C
Diff: 1   Page Ref: 7.1
Skill: Factual

9) Imagine a scientist discovers a mutant plant seedling that appears to lack stomata. What would be the effect of this?

   A) CO_2 would not be able to enter as a reactant for photosynthesis.

   B) Water would not be able to enter the plant cells.

   C) Visible wavelengths of light would be unable to reach the chloroplasts.

   D) Additional ATP would be produced by the cells of the plant seedling and the plant would grow taller.

Answer: A
Diff: 2   Page Ref: 7.1
Skill: Conceptual

10) Imagine a plant in your garden doesn't receive an adequate amount of water. Which of the following would be most affected by this?

   A) the light dependent reactions of photosynthesis

   B) the light independent reactions of photosynthesis

   C) both the light dependent and light independent reactions of photosynthesis

   D) Photosynthesis would not be affected by this.

Answer: C
Diff: 2   Page Ref: 7.1
Skill: Conceptual

11) The grana are disk-shaped, interconnected membranous sacs embedded in the stroma that form thylakoids when stacked on one another. True or False?

Answer: FALSE
Diff: 2   Page Ref: 7.1
Skill: Factual

12) The majority of the leaf's chloroplasts are found in the mesophyll cells. True or False?

Answer: TRUE
Diff: 1   Page Ref: 7.1
Skill: Factual

13) Give the chemical equation for photosynthesis. For each reactant, indicate where the plant acquires it. For each product, note during what part of photosynthesis it is produced.

Answer: The chemical equation for photosynthesis is:
$$6CO_2 + 6H_2O + light\ energy \rightarrow C_6H_{12}O_6 + 6O_2$$
CO_2 comes through the stomata, water comes from the vascular bundles (or veins) to the mesophyll cells, and chlorophyll molecules embedded in the thylakoid membrane of the chloroplast absorb sunlight. The glucose is produced during the light–independent reactions and the oxygen is produced during the light–dependent reactions.
Diff: 2   Page Ref: 7.1
Skill: Conceptual

14) Explain how the leaf is adapted for capturing energy from the sun and acquiring carbon dioxide and water.

Answer: CO_2 comes through adjustable pores, or stomata, and water comes from the vascular bundles (or veins) to the mesophyll cells. Leaves are broad and flat, and provide a large surface area to the sun. Chlorophyll molecules embedded in the thylakoid membrane of the chloroplast absorb sunlight.
Diff: 2   Page Ref: 7.1
Skill: Conceptual

15) Light dependent reactions occur in the _____ and light independent reactions occur in the _____ of the chloroplast of a typical mesophyll leaf cell.

Answer: thylakoids; stroma
Diff: 2   Page Ref: 7.1
Skill: Conceptual

16) The cells in the _____ layer of the leaf contain the majority of a leaf's chloroplasts.

Answer: mesophyll
Diff: 2   Page Ref: 7.1
Skill: Factual

17) The process of photosynthesis converts solar energy into _____ energy stored in the bonds of glucose.

Answer: chemical
Diff: 1   Page Ref: 7.1
Skill: Factual

18) Albino corn has no chlorophyll. You would expect these seedlings to

   A) capture light energy in the white end of the spectrum.

   B) fail to thrive.

   C) synthesize glucose indefinitely, using stored ATP and NADPH.

   D) undergo the C$_4$ pathway.

   E) use accessory pigments such as carotenoids to capture light.

   Answer: B
   Diff: 3   Page Ref: 7.2
   Skill: Conceptual

19) The energy source in photosynthesis is

   A) glucose.

   B) ultraviolet light.

   C) visible light.

   D) air.

   E) oxygen.

   Answer: C
   Diff: 2   Page Ref: 7.2
   Skill: Conceptual

20) Energy is passed around different chlorophyll molecules until it reaches a specific chlorophyll molecule called the

   A) reaction center.

   B) photoelectric point.

   C) electron carrier molecule.

   D) accessory pigment.

   E) nucleus.

   Answer: A
   Diff: 2   Page Ref: 7.2
   Skill: Factual

21) Where are carotenoid pigments found?

   A) in the mitochondria

   B) in the stroma of the chloroplasts

   C) in the thylakoid membranes of the chloroplasts

   D) in the nucleus

   Answer: C
   Diff: 2   Page Ref: 7.2
   Skill: Factual

22) The pigment(s) that absorb light energy to drive photosynthesis is/are

    A) chlorophyll.

    B) carotenoids.

    C) anthocyanins.

    D) A and B

    E) all of these

Answer: D
Diff: 2   Page Ref: 7.2
Skill: Factual

23) A pigment that absorbs red and blue light and reflects green light is

    A) phycocyanin.

    B) carotenoid.

    C) xanthophyll.

    D) melanin.

    E) chlorophyll.

Answer: E
Diff: 1   Page Ref: 7.2
Skill: Factual

24) Which of the following is NOT true of chlorophyll?

    A) It is green in color.

    B) It absorbs light at the red and blue ends of the spectrum.

    C) It is the main photosynthetic pigment in plants.

    D) It is found in mitochondria.

    E) It does not absorb green wavelengths of light.

Answer: D
Diff: 2   Page Ref: 7.2
Skill: Factual

25) You are experimenting with different types of lighting for your indoor green plants. Which of the following colors of light will be most effective?

   A) green

   B) orange–yellow

   C) blue

   D) red–green

   E) red–blue

Answer: E
Diff: 2   Page Ref: 7.2
Skill: Conceptual

26) Which statement is TRUE regarding the light–dependent reactions?

   A) They rely on energy provided by glucose synthesis.

   B) Oxygen is required.

   C) Without water, the system would shut down.

   D) ATP and NADPH are needed.

   E) Without photosystem I, photosystem II could not occur.

Answer: C
Diff: 2   Page Ref: 7.2
Skill: Conceptual

27) The replacement electrons for the reaction center of photosystem II come from

   A) photosystem I.

   B) H_2O.

   C) glucose.

   D) O_2.

   E) NADPH.

Answer: B
Diff: 2   Page Ref: 7.2
Skill: Factual

28) Which sequence accurately reflects the flow of electrons in photosynthesis?

   A) Photosystem I → Photosystem II → H_2O → NADP

   B) Photosystem II → Photosystem I → NADP → H_2O

   C) H_2O → Photosystem II → Photosystem I → NADP

   D) Photosystem I → Photosystem II → NADP → H_2O

   E) H_2O → Photosystem I → Photosystem II → NADP

Answer: C
Diff: 2   Page Ref: 7.2
Skill: Conceptual

29) The ATP and the NADPH synthesized during the light dependent reactions are

   A) dissolved in the cytoplasm.

   B) transported to the mitochondria.

   C) pumped into a compartment within the thylakoid membrane.

   D) transported into the nucleus.

   E) dissolved in the stroma.

Answer: E
Diff: 3   Page Ref: 7.2
Skill: Conceptual

30) What is produced in the electron transport system associated with photosystem II?

   A) NADPH   B) ATP   C) glucose   D) O_2 E) CO_2

Answer: B
Diff: 2   Page Ref: 7.2
Skill: Factual

31) Light–dependent photosynthetic reactions produce

   A) ATP, NADPH, O_2.

   B) ATP, NADPH, CO_2.

   C) Glucose, ATP, O_2.

   D) Glucose, ATP, CO_2.

   E) ATP, NADPH, H_2O.

Answer: A
Diff: 2   Page Ref: 7.2
Skill: Factual

32) Where does the O_2 released during photosynthesis come from?

    A) CO_2

    B) H_2O

    C) ATP

    D) $C_6H_{12}O_6$

    E) RuBP

Answer: B
Diff: 2   Page Ref: 7.2
Skill: Factual

33) During the process of photosynthesis, solar energy is converted into

    A) chemical energy.

    B) heat energy.

    C) thermal energy.

    D) mechanical energy.

    E) nuclear energy.

Answer: A
Diff: 2   Page Ref: 7.2
Skill: Conceptual

34) The light–dependent reactions of photosynthesis result in which of the following?

    A) oxidation of CO_2

    B) reduction of H_2O

    C) phosphorylation of ADP

    D) oxidation of chlorophyll

    E) oxidation of glucose

Answer: C
Diff: 2   Page Ref: 7.2
Skill: Conceptual

35) What is the role of water in photosynthesis?

   A) to maintain turgor pressure

   B) to provide electrons

   C) to provide oxygen

   D) to provide H_2

   E) all of these

Answer: B
Diff: 2   Page Ref: 7.2
Skill: Conceptual

36) Which of the following is a source of electrons used for reduction reactions by green plants?

   A) glucose   B) CO_2 C) RuBP   D) O_2 E) H_2O

Answer: E
Diff: 2   Page Ref: 7.2
Skill: Conceptual

37) According to the chemiosmotic theory, hydrogen ions cross the thylakoid membranes from the stroma by

   A) osmosis.

   B) facilitated diffusion.

   C) active transport.

   D) simple diffusion.

   E) phosphorylation.

Answer: C
Diff: 3   Page Ref: 7.2
Skill: Conceptual

38) The energy of the movement of electrons down their concentration gradient via electron transport within chloroplasts and mitochondria is used to generate molecules of

   A) H_2O.   B) CO_2.   C) glucose.   D) ATP.   E) O_2.

Answer: D
Diff: 2   Page Ref: 7.2
Skill: Conceptual

39) The energy of the movement of electrons down a concentration gradient via electron transport within the thylakoid membrane generates

   A) H_2O.   B) CO_2.   C) glucose.   D) O_2.   E) ATP.

Answer: E
Diff: 2   Page Ref: 7.2
Skill: Conceptual

40) Which process of photosynthesis is linked to the production of ATP?

    A) photosystem II

    B) generation of NADPH

    C) splitting of a water molecule

    D) fixing of carbon

    E) synthesis of O_2

Answer: A
Diff: 2   Page Ref: 7.2
Skill: Conceptual

41) Suppose you are studying photosynthesis in a research lab. You grow your plants in a chamber with a source of water that has a radioactively labeled oxygen atom. What photosynthetic product will be radioactive?

    A) ATP   B) glucose   C) oxygen   D) NADPH   E) RuBP

Answer: C
Diff: 2   Page Ref: 7.2
Skill: Conceptual

42) Glucose synthesis requires which of the following?

    A) Sunlight must be present.

    B) Products of energy–capturing reactions must be available.

    C) The concentration of O_2 must be significantly higher than that of CO_2.

    D) Mitochondria must provide energy as ATP.

    E) all of the above

Answer: B
Diff: 2   Page Ref: 7.2
Skill: Conceptual

43) Which of the following is TRUE about the light–dependent reactions?

    A) NADPH and ATP are both synthesized on an electron transport chain that connects photosystem I and photosystem II.

    B) Photosystem I generates ATP, while photosystem II generates NADPH.

    C) Photosystem II generates ATP, while photosystem I generates NADPH.

    D) ATP is the final electron acceptor.

Answer: C
Diff: 2   Page Ref: 7.2
Skill: Factual

44) Which of the following statements about the light reactions of photosynthesis is FALSE?

    A) The splitting of water molecules provides a source of electrons.

    B) Chlorophyll (and other pigments) absorb light energy which excites electrons.

    C) An electron transport chain is used to create a proton gradient.

    D) The proton gradient is used to reduce NADP.

    E) ATP is synthesized.

Answer: D
Diff: 2   *Page Ref: 7.2*
Skill: Conceptual

45) The NADPH required for carbon dioxide fixation is formed

    A) by the reduction of oxygen.

    B) by the hydrolysis of ATP.

    C) during the light reactions.

    D) only in C_4 plants.

    E) in the mitochondria.

Answer: C
Diff: 2   *Page Ref: 7.2*
Skill: Conceptual

46) The primary function of the light reactions of photosynthesis is

    A) to produce energy-rich glucose from carbon dioxide and water.

    B) to produce energy-rich ATP and NADPH.

    C) to produce NADPH used in respiration.

    D) to convert light energy to the chemical energy of lipids.

    E) to use the ATP to make glucose.

Answer: B
Diff: 2   *Page Ref: 7.2*
Skill: Conceptual

47) You are carrying out an experiment on an aquatic plant in your fish tank. You decide to expose the plant to varying wavelengths of light to determine which wavelength is best for the light dependent reactions. Which of the following products could you measure to determine what wavelength of light is optimum for the light dependent reactions?

    A) oxygen bubbles   B) water molecules

    C) carbon dioxide   D) sucrose

Answer: A
Diff: 2   *Page Ref: 7.2*
Skill: Application

48) You are carrying out an experiment on several aquatic plants in your fish tank. You decide to expose 2 of the plants to green light and 2 of the plants to blue light. You want to determine which type of light is best for the light dependent reactions so you decide to measure the amount of oxygen bubbles produced to reach your conclusions. Which of the following results would be expected?

   A) There would be more bubbles from the plants in green light compared to blue light.

   B) There would be more bubbles from the plants in blue light compared to green light.

   C) There would be the same number of bubbles from plants in either blue or green light.

   D) There would be no bubbles produced in either situation.

Answer: B
Diff: 3   Page Ref: 7.2
Skill: Application

49) The photosystems are involved in the light–dependent reactions of photosynthesis. True or False?

Answer: TRUE
Diff: 2   Page Ref: 7.2
Skill: Factual

50) Carbon dioxide is required in the light–dependent reaction. True or False?

Answer: FALSE
Diff: 2   Page Ref: 7.2
Skill: Factual

51) The carotenoids and other accessory pigments in the chloroplast help harvest light energy toward the reaction center chlorophyll molecules. True or False?

Answer: TRUE
Diff: 2   Page Ref: 7.2
Skill: Conceptual

52) _____ is the main light–capturing molecule in chloroplasts and is responsible for giving most leaves their characteristic green color.

Answer: Chlorophyll
Diff: 1   Page Ref: 7.2
Skill: Factual

53) What is the role of the green pigment chlorophyll in photosynthesis?

Answer: Critical in light–dependent reactions to harness light energy and begin the flow of electrons which in turn creates the proton gradient allowing for chemiosmosis[1]ATP formation which is required for the light–independent reactions.
Diff: 2   Page Ref: 7.2
Skill: Conceptual

54) In the process of photosynthesis, _____ and _____ are required from the light dependent reactions to completely reduce carbon dioxide to glucose in the Calvin cycle.

Answer: ATP; NADPH
Diff: 2   Page Ref: 7.2
Skill: Factual

55) During the light–dependent reactions of photosynthesis, the synthesis of _____ is coupled to the diffusion of protons.

Answer: ATP
Diff: 2   Page Ref: 7.2
Skill: Factual

56) Describe the two major component of a photosystem. What is the function of each?

Answer: The *light-harvesting complex* absorbs light and passes the energy to a specific chlorophyll molecule called the reaction center. The *electron transport system* is a series of electron carrier molecules that are responsible for directly donating electrons to the electron carrier molecule $NADP^+$ and indirectly driving the synthesis of ATP.
Diff: 2   Page Ref: 7.2
Skill: Conceptual

57) Light harvesting pigments in the chloroplast include chlorophyll and the accessory pigments, _____.

Answer: carotenoids
Diff: 1   Page Ref: 7.2
Skill: Factual

58) The _____ is composed of a light–harvesting complex and an electron transport system.

Answer: photosystem
Diff: 1   Page Ref: 7.2
Skill: Factual

59) Imagine you are conducting a photosynthesis experiment on a plant in the lab. You block any sunlight (or artificial light) from reaching the plant. Explain the specific effect this will have on the light dependent reactions.

Answer: Light will not be present to hit the chlorophyll and electrons will not be excited. Therefore the light reactions will not occur and no energy will be produced to be used in the dark reactions.
Diff: 1   Page Ref: 7.2
Skill: Conceptual

60) In C$_3$ photosynthesis, what fixes the carbon?

   A) RuBP   B) PEP   C) PGA   D) PGAL   E) ATP

Answer: A
Diff: 2   Page Ref: 7.3
Skill: Conceptual

61) How many molecules of CO$_2$ are fixed to form one molecule of glucose?

   A) 2   B) 3   C) 6   D) 9   E) 12

Answer: C
Diff: 2   Page Ref: 7.3
Skill: Conceptual

62) The term "cycle" is used to describe the light-independent reactions (Calvin–Benson cycle) because

   A) the same reactions occur every time.

   B) CO$_2$ is fixed.

   C) the process begins and ends with RuBP.

   D) glucose is synthesized during the process.

   E) the process depends on products from the light–dependent reactions.

Answer: C
Diff: 2   Page Ref: 7.3
Skill: Conceptual

63) Where is glucose synthesized?

   A) thylakoids

   B) cytoplasm

   C) matrix

   D) stroma

   E) intermembrane compartment

Answer: B
Diff: 2   Page Ref: 7.3
Skill: Factual

64) What is the correct order for the reactions of the Calvin–Benson cycle?

    A) carbon fixation, regeneration of RuBP, synthesis of G3P

    B) synthesis of G3P, regeneration of RuBP, carbon fixation

    C) carbon fixation, synthesis of G3P, regeneration of RuBP

    D) regeneration of RuBP, carbon fixation, synthesis of G3P

    E) synthesis of G3P, carbon fixation, regeneration of RuBP

Answer: C
Diff: 2   Page Ref: 7.3
Skill: Factual

65) Which of the following occurs during the light–independent reactions of photosynthesis?

    A) Water is converted into hydrogen and water.

    B) Carbon dioxide is converted into sugars.

    C) Chlorophyll acts as an enzyme only in the dark.

    D) Nothing occurs, the plant rests in the dark.

    E) none of the above

Answer: B
Diff: 2   Page Ref: 7.3
Skill: Conceptual

66) All of the following are part of the Calvin–Benson cycle EXCEPT

    A) carbon fixation.

    B) synthesis of G3P.

    C) generation of ATP.

    D) regeneration of RuBP.

    E) All of the above are part of the cycle.

Answer: C
Diff: 2   Page Ref: 7.3
Skill: Conceptual

67) Suppose the stomata of a typical C3 plant close in the middle of the day. What will occur?

    A) The rate of photosynthesis will decrease.

    B) There will be no effect on photosynthesis.

    C) The rate of photosynthesis will increase because water is being conserved.

    D) Oxygen will be rapidly consumed.

    E) Carbon dioxide release will increase.

Answer: A
Diff: 2   Page Ref: 7.3
Skill: Conceptual

68) Which of the following are required for the C_3 cycle?

 A) CO_2

 B) RuBP enzyme

 C) ATP

 D) NADPH

 E) all of the above

Answer: E
Diff: 2   Page Ref: 7.3
Skill: Conceptual

69) Which of the following provides O_2 as an end product?

 A) light–dependent reaction

 B) light–independent reaction

 C) cellular respiration

 D) glycolysis

 E) phosphorylation

Answer: A
Diff: 2   Page Ref: 7.3
Skill: Factual

70) In the C_3 cycle, where does the carbon come from to form glucose?

 A) from ATP and NADPH

 B) from chlorophyll

 C) from atmospheric CO_2

 D) from enzymes

 E) from water

Answer: C
Diff: 2   Page Ref: 7.3
Skill: Factual

71) What happens to CO_2 when it moves into the stroma?

    A) The CO_2 gives up its O_2.

    B) It immediately passes on to the thylakoids.

    C) It becomes a carbohydrate.

    D) The CO_2 becomes a by-product of cellular respiration.

    E) It is converted to water.

Answer: C
Diff: 2   Page Ref: 7.3
Skill: Factual

72) In green plants, the primary function of the Calvin cycle is to

    A) use ATP to release carbon dioxide.

    B) use NADPH to release carbon dioxide.

    C) split water and release oxygen.

    D) transport glucose out of the chloroplast.

    E) construct simple sugars from carbon dioxide.

Answer: E
Diff: 2   Page Ref: 7.3
Skill: Factual

73) Glucose is made during which of the following reactions?

    A) light-dependent reactions only

    B) light-independent reactions only

    C) both light dependent and independent reactions

    D) neither the light or dark reactions

Answer: B
Diff: 2   Page Ref: 7.3
Skill: Factual

74) During photosynthesis when is CO_2 is utilized?

    A) during the light-dependent reactions only

    B) during the light-independent reactions only

    C) during both light dependent and independent reactions

    D) CO_2 is not utilized during either the light dependent or independent reactions.

Answer: B
Diff: 2   Page Ref: 7.3
Skill: Factual

75) ATP is required during which of the following reactions?

    A) during the light–dependent reactions only

    B) during the light–independent reactions only

    C) during both light dependent and independent reactions

    D) ATP is not required during either the light dependent or independent reactions.

Answer: B
Diff: 2   Page Ref: 7.3
Skill: Factual

76) Enzymes are required during which of the following reactions?

    A) during the light–dependent reactions only

    B) during the light–independent reactions only

    C) during both light dependent and independent reactions

    D) Enzymes are not required during either the light dependent or independent reactions.

Answer: C
Diff: 2   Page Ref: 7.3
Skill: Factual

77) Water is required during which of the following reactions?

    A) during the light–dependent reactions only

    B) during the light–independent reactions only

    C) during both light dependent and independent reactions

    D) Water is not required during either the light dependent or independent reactions.

Answer: A
Diff: 2   Page Ref: 7.3
Skill: Factual

78) NADPH is synthesized during which of the following reactions?

    A) during the light–dependent reactions only

    B) during the light–independent reactions only

    C) during both light dependent and independent reactions

    D) NADPH is not utilized during either the light dependent or independent reactions.

Answer: A
Diff: 2   Page Ref: 7.3
Skill: Conceptual

79) You are conducting an experiment to track what happens to the carbons from CO_2 molecules used in the light independent reactions of photosynthesis. You add a radioactive tag to the carbons of the CO_2 reactants and then collect the products following the reactions. Which products would then be radioactive?

    A) ATP

    B) water

    C) glucose

    D) both B and C

    E) both A and B

Answer: C
Diff: 3   Page Ref: 7.3
Skill: Application

80) Why is no glucose produced if a plant is kept for long periods in the dark, even though the sugar producing reactions are called light–independent?

Answer: The light–independent reactions require ATP and NADPH produced from the light–dependent reactions to drive the synthesis of glucose in the Calvin cycle reactions.
Diff: 2   Page Ref: 7.3
Skill: Conceptual

81) Is glucose a direct product of the Calvin–Benson cycle reactions?

Answer: No, G3P is the carbohydrate produced and two of these molecules must combine to form one molecule of glucose.
Diff: 2   Page Ref: 7.3
Skill: Conceptual

82) Which component of the Calvin–Benson cycle is recycled and why is this important for the light–independent reactions?

Answer: The RuBP molecule is recycled and this is essential for the cycle nature of the process to be maintained.
Diff: 2   Page Ref: 7.3
Skill: Conceptual

83) Imagine you are conducting a photosynthesis experiment on a plant in the lab. You block any sunlight (or artificial light) from reaching the plant. Your teacher tells you that this will affect even the light independent reactions. Your classmate leans over to you and asks "If those reactions are not light dependent, how will they be affected?" What answer should you give him?

    A) The light independent reactions won't be affected at all. The teacher must be confused.

    B) The light independent reactions will be affected because light must hit the stroma as a reactant in generating glucose.

    C) The light dependent reactions are needed to generate the energy required to make glucose.

    D) The light independent reactions require light so that water can be made. Without that water production, the plant dies.

Answer: C
Diff: 3   *Page Ref: 7.4*
Skill: Application

84) Differentiate the light–dependent reactions of photosynthesis from the light–independent reactions.

Answer: The student should discuss how the light–dependent reactions capture solar energy and convert it to energy carrier molecules, ATP and NADPH, while in the light–independent reactions the ATP and NADPH is used to drive the chemical reactions required for the synthesis of glucose.
Diff: 2   *Page Ref: 7.4*
Skill: Conceptual

85) Photosystem II generates _____ and Photosystem I generates _____, both of which are required by the light–dependent reactions.

Answer: ATP; NADPH
Diff: 2   *Page Ref: 7.4*
Skill: Conceptual

86) How are the light–dependent and light–independent reactions related to one another?

Answer: The light–dependent reactions produce the ATP and NADPH required to drive the light–dependent reactions which results in the synthesis of sugar (glucose).
Diff: 2   *Page Ref: 7.4*
Skill: Conceptual

87) What happens to the photosynthetic reactions when there is no sunlight present?

Answer: ATP and NADPH levels from the light dependent reactions become limiting and that in turn can lead to the decrease in sugar production from the light independent reactions.
Diff: 2   *Page Ref: 7.4*
Skill: Conceptual

88) In the reduction of CO_2 during C_4 photosynthesis, which of the following initially combined with CO_2?

A) PGA   B) RuBP   C) PGAL   D) NADH   E) PEP

Answer: E
Diff: 2   Page Ref: 7.5
Skill: Factual

89) Where does one expect to find the reactions of a C_4 pathway occurring in a plant such as corn?

A) mesophyll cells

B) bundle–sheath cells

C) epidermal cells

D) A and B

E) B and C

Answer: D
Diff: 2   Page Ref: 7.5
Skill: Factual

90) In the C_4 cycle, what is the source of carbon?

A) NADPH

B) glucose

C) water

D) carbon dioxide

E) ATP

Answer: D
Diff: 2   Page Ref: 7.5
Skill: Conceptual

91) What kind of habitat does a C_4 pathway plant favor?

A) hot and dry

B) cool and moist

C) totally aquatic

D) wet and cloudy

E) cool and dry

Answer: A
Diff: 2   Page Ref: 7.5
Skill: Factual

92) Photorespiration is bad for a plant because

    A) O_2 is required.

    B) CO_2 is synthesized.

    C) RuBP is degraded.

    D) glucose is synthesized.

    E) no ATP is produced.

Answer: E
Diff: 2   *Page Ref: 7.5*
Skill: Factual

93) Where does the C_4 cycle get its name?

    A) Only four carbons are used in the cycle.

    B) It is a four-step process.

    C) Four CO_2 molecules are released.

    D) The first product in the cycle has four carbons.

    E) PEP is a four-carbon molecule.

Answer: D
Diff: 2   *Page Ref: 7.5*
Skill: Factual

94) If C_4 photosynthesis prevents photorespiration, why haven't all plants evolved to use the C_4 pathway?

    A) All plants *will* evolve to be C_4 in time.

    B) C_4 produces some toxic byproducts.

    C) C_4 is not advantageous in all climates.

    D) Only some plants use C_4 photosynthesis.

    E) C_4 is only advantageous in high oxygen habitats.

Answer: C
Diff: 2   *Page Ref: 7.5*
Skill: Conceptual

95) When water supplies are plentiful for the plant

   A) the stomata remain open.

   B) CO_2 uptake will increase.

   C) the stomata will close.

   D) O_2 uptake will increase.

   E) Both A and B are correct.

Answer: E
Diff: 2   Page Ref: 7.5
Skill: Conceptual

96) C_3 plants are adapted to _____ conditions, while C_4 plants are adapted to _____ environmental conditions.

   A) dry; wet

   B) wet; dry

   C) temperate; cool and rainy

   D) high light; low light

   E) drought; rainy

Answer: B
Diff: 2   Page Ref: 7.5
Skill: Factual

97) In C_4 photosynthesis, where does the carbon come from to synthesize glucose?

   A) from ATP and NADPH

   B) from chlorophyll

   C) from enzymes

   D) from water

   E) from atmospheric CO_2

Answer: E
Diff: 2   Page Ref: 7.5
Skill: Factual

98) Under dry conditions, a C_4 plant is more photosynthetically efficient than a C_3 plant. True or False?

Answer: TRUE
Diff: 2   Page Ref: 7.5
Skill: Factual

99) The combination of oxygen with RuBP during the light-independent reactions, rather than carbon dioxide, is called _____.

Answer: photorespiration
Diff: 2   *Page Ref: 7.5*
Skill: Factual

100) Some plants, called the _____ plants, have evolved a way to reduce photorespiration.

Answer: C_4
Diff: 1   *Page Ref: 7.5*
Skill: Factual

101) During the process of _____, RuBP combines with oxygen instead of carbon dioxide.

Answer: photorespiration
Diff: 2   *Page Ref: 7.5*
Skill: Factual

102) In C_3 plants, the Calvin cycle occurs in the chloroplasts of _____ cells, but in C_4 plants the cycle occurs in the _____ cells.

Answer: mesophyll; bundle sheath
Diff: 2   *Page Ref: 7.5*
Skill: Factual

103) Many plants have evolved leaves that have adjustable pores, called _____, which allow for gas exchange and water loss.

Answer: stomata
Diff: 2   *Page Ref: 7.5*
Skill: Factual

104) Why does photorespiration reduce photosynthesis efficiency?

Answer: Photorespiration does not produce any useful cellular energy and it prevents the synthesis of glucose in C_3 plants.
Diff: 2   *Page Ref: 7.5*
Skill: Conceptual

105) What is photorespiration? Describe how C_4 plants have evolved the ability to reduce photorespiration.

Answer: Photorespiration occurs when RuBP combines with O_2 rather than CO_2 not allowing the plant to fix carbon and produce glucose. C_4 plants use a two stage carbon-fixation pathway where PEP is used instead of RuBP which specifically reacts with CO_2 and not O_2; the CO_2 is then shuttled to the bundle-sheath cells and creates a high CO_2 concentration that favors the regular C_3 cycle reactions without competition from O_2.
Diff: 3   *Page Ref: 7.5*
Skill: Conceptual

106) The dinosaurs died off from a lack of sunlight. What does this statement imply about the extinction of the dinosaurs?

Answer: Two hypotheses about the extinction of dinosaurs (meteor hit or massive volcano eruptions) both would have led to reduced sunlight which would have had an immediate impact on photosynthesis (limiting the light–dependent reactions and thereby limiting photosynthesis) and reducing the food source for herbivores which then limited the food source for the carnivores (chain reaction type event).

Diff: 2   Page Ref: 7.5
Skill: Conceptual

Chapter 8   Harvesting Energy: Glycolysis and Cell Respiration

1) At the end of glycolysis, the original carbons of the glucose molecule form

A) six molecules of carbon dioxide.

B) two molecules of NADH.

C) two molecules of pyruvic acid.

D) two molecules of citric acid.

E) two molecules of fructose.

Answer: C
Diff: 2   Page Ref: 8.1
Skill: Conceptual

2) The anaerobic breakdown of glucose is called

A) fermentation.

B) respiration.

C) phosphorylation.

D) chemiosmosis.

E) Krebs cycle.

Answer: A
Diff: 2   Page Ref: 8.1
Skill: Factual

3) What results if glucose is metabolized under completely anaerobic conditions?

A) Pyruvic acid immediately enters the Krebs cycle.

B) Pyruvic acid is converted by fermentation into CO_2 and ethanol or lactic acid.

C) Pyruvic acid is converted back to fructose until the concentration of oxygen increases.

D) Pyruvic acid leaves the fluid portion of the cytoplasm and enters the mitochondrial matrix.

E) Pyruvic acid is converted to NADH.

Answer: B
Diff: 2   Page Ref: 8.1
Skill: Factual

4) ATP is

    A) a short–term, energy-storage compound.

    B) the cell's principle compound for energy transfers.

    C) synthesized within mitochondria.

    D) the molecule all living cells rely on to do work.

    E) all of the above

Answer: E
Diff: 2   Page Ref: 8.1
Skill: Conceptual

5) The main function of cell respiration is to produce

    A) CO_2.

    B) glucose.

    C) ATP.

    D) NADH and $FADH_2$.

    E) all of the above

Answer: C
Diff: 2   Page Ref: 8.1
Skill: Conceptual

6) Briefly compare and contrast the processes of cellular respiration and photosynthesis.

    Answer: Student should include the fact that carbon dioxide and water are used with light energy to produce glucose during photosynthesis and then in cellular respiration the glucose is broken down into carbon dioxide and water and energy in the form of ATP. Both processes use chemiosmosis to produce ATP.
Diff: 3   Page Ref: 8.1
Skill: Conceptual

7) How does the lack of oxygen influence energy availability in animals?

    Answer: Low oxygen results in little ATP production via chemiosmosis.
Diff: 2   Page Ref: 8.1
Skill: Factual

8) Over half of the energy produced by the breakdown of glucose is released as _____ and the remaining energy is converted to _____.

    Answer: heat; ATP
Diff: 2   Page Ref: 8.1
Skill: Factual

9) The organelles responsible for the bulk of ATP production in cellular respiration are the
_____.

Answer: mitochondria
Diff: 2   Page Ref: 8.1
Skill: Factual

10) During glycolysis, what is the net gain of ATP molecules produced?

A) 2   B) 4   C) 34   D) 36   E) 38

Answer: A
Diff: 2   Page Ref: 8.2
Skill: Factual

11) Which event occurs in the fluid portion of the cytoplasm of a cell undergoing glucose metabolism?

A) Krebs (citric acid) cycle

B) electron transport

C) chemiosmosis

D) Acetyl CoA formation

E) glycolysis

Answer: E
Diff: 2   Page Ref: 8.2
Skill: Factual

12) What molecule is common to both C_3 photosynthesis and the process of glycolysis?

A) pyruvate

B) G3P

C) Acetyl CoA

D) fructose

E) NADPH

Answer: B
Diff: 3   Page Ref: 8.2
Skill: Factual

13) Where does fermentation occur within a cell undergoing anaerobic metabolism of glucose?

    A) surface of cell membrane

    B) stroma of chloroplast

    C) mitochondrial matrix

    D) fluid portion of the cytoplasm

    E) nucleus

Answer: D
Diff: 2   Page Ref: 8.2
Skill: Factual

14) You are playing a long tennis match and your muscles begin to switch to anaerobic respiration. Which of the following is NOT a bad consequence?

    A) Your cells convert NADH to NAD^+.

    B) Lactic acid is produced.

    C) ATP production declines.

    D) Oxygen debt increases.

    E) All of these ARE problems.

Answer: A
Diff: 2   Page Ref: 8.2
Skill: Conceptual

15) After fermentation, lactic acid is converted to pyruvic acid in the

    A) blood stream.

    B) liver.

    C) muscles.

    D) heart.

    E) lungs.

Answer: B
Diff: 2   Page Ref: 8.2
Skill: Factual

16) What is the significance of the conversion of pyruvic acid to lactic acid during fermentation?

A) Pyruvic acid becomes available to enter matrix reactions.

B) The citric acid cycle is initiated.

C) NAD^+ is regenerated for use in glycolysis.

D) The oxidation of pyruvic acid becomes possible.

E) ATP is produced.

Answer: C
Diff: 2   Page Ref: 8.2
Skill: Conceptual

17) In vertebrate animal cells, where does the synthesis of lactic acid occur?

A) fluid portion of the cytoplasm

B) surface of ribosomes

C) mitochondrial matrix

D) mitochondrial inner membranes

E) nucleus

Answer: A
Diff: 2   Page Ref: 8.2
Skill: Factual

18) How does one account for the bubbles that "tickle your nose" when one drinks a glass of champagne?

A) Bubbles of CO_2 are trapped due to the chemistry of aerobic respiration by yeast cells.

B) Lactic acid fermentation accounts for the bubbles in a bottle of sparkling wine such as champagne.

C) The champagne was bottled while the yeast were still alive and fermenting, so bubbles of CO_2 were trapped.

D) The bubbles are simply air bubbles which resulted from the wine-making process.

E) The bubbles were formed by the yeast cells during glycolysis.

Answer: C
Diff: 2   Page Ref: 8.2
Skill: Conceptual

19) How do fatigued human muscle cells repay an "oxygen debt"?

   A) Cells produce more oxygen.

   B) The cells convert glucose into pyruvic acid.

   C) The tired cells increase production of ATP.

   D) The cells decrease CO_2 production.

   E) Lactic acid is converted back into pyruvic acid by the cells.

Answer: E
Diff: 2   Page Ref: 8.2
Skill: Conceptual

20) Which of the following statements is TRUE of glycolysis followed by fermentation?

   A) It produces a net gain of ATP.

   B) It produces a net gain of NADH.

   C) It is an aerobic process.

   D) It can be performed only by bacteria.

   E) It produces more ATP than aerobic respiration.

Answer: A
Diff: 2   Page Ref: 8.2
Skill: Conceptual

21) Which kind of metabolic poison would interfere with glycolysis?

   A) An agent that reacts with oxygen and depletes its concentration in the cell.

   B) An agent that binds to pyruvate and inactivates it.

   C) An agent that closely mimics the structure of glucose, but is not capable of being metabolized.

   D) An agent that reacts with NADH and oxidizes it to NAD^+.

   E) An agent that inhibits the formation of acetyl coenzyme A.

Answer: C
Diff: 2   Page Ref: 8.2
Skill: Conceptual

22) Which of the following is common to both fermentation and cellular respiration?

A) Krebs cycle

B) reduction of pyruvate into lactate

C) conversion of pyruvate to Acetyl CoA

D) glycolysis

E) electron transport

Answer: D
Diff: 2   Page Ref: 8.2
Skill: Conceptual

23) The end product of glycolysis is

A) pyruvate.

B) the starting point for the citric acid cycle.

C) the starting point for the fermentation pathway.

D) A and B

E) A, B and C

Answer: E
Diff: 2   Page Ref: 8.2
Skill: Conceptual

24) During cell respiration, the pyruvate produced in glycolysis is

A) transported to the mitochondria.

B) broken down to CO_2 and water.

C) the source of electrons for NADH and $FADH_2$.

D) converted to Acetyl CoA.

E) all of the above

Answer: E
Diff: 2   Page Ref: 8.2
Skill: Conceptual

25) Where does the synthesis of pyruvic acid occur during glycolysis?

A) cristae

B) ribosomes

C) matrix

D) intermembrane compartment

E) fluid portion of the cytoplasm

Answer: E
Diff: 2   Page Ref: 8.2
Skill: Factual

26) In the first reaction of glycolysis, glucose receives a phosphate group from ATP. This reaction is

    A) respiration.

    B) fermentation.

    C) exergonic.

    D) endergonic.

    E) none of the above

Answer: D
Diff: 2   Page Ref: 8.2
Skill: Conceptual

27) For bacteria to continue growing rapidly when they are shifted from an environment containing oxygen to an anaerobic environment, they must

    A) increase the rate of the citric acid cycle.

    B) produce more ATP per molecule of glucose during glycolysis.

    C) produce ATP using NADH.

    D) increase the rate of transport of electrons down the respiratory chain.

    E) increase the rate of glycolytic reactions.

Answer: E
Diff: 2   Page Ref: 8.2
Skill: Conceptual

28) In the absence of oxygen, a yeast cell undergoes fermentation and uses 100 molecules of glucose. How much net ATP will be generated?

    A) 36   B) 100   C) 200   D) 300   E) 400

Answer: C
Diff: 3   Page Ref: 8.2
Skill: Application

29) During the fermentation of one molecule of glucose, the net production of ATP is

    A) one molecule.

    B) two molecules.

    C) three molecules.

    D) six molecules.

    E) eight molecules.

Answer: B
Diff: 2   Page Ref: 8.2
Skill: Factual

30) Both plants and animals perform

    A) glycolysis.

    B) fermentation.

    C) Krebs cycle.

    D) photosynthesis.

    E) A, B and C are correct.

Answer: E
Diff: 2   Page Ref: 8.2
Skill: Conceptual

31) In human cells (muscle cells) the fermentation process produces

    A) lactic acid.

    B) 12 molecules of ATP.

    C) pyruvic acid.

    D) an excessive amount of energy.

    E) none of the above

Answer: A
Diff: 2   Page Ref: 8.2
Skill: Factual

32) Products of the fermentation process can include

    A) carbon dioxide.

    B) ethanol.

    C) lactic acid.

    D) all of the above

    E) none of the above

Answer: D
Diff: 2   Page Ref: 8.2
Skill: Factual

33) The products of glycolysis are

    A) ATP, NADH, pyruvate.

    B) ATP, NADH, pyruvate, $FADH_2$.

    C) ATP, NADH, Acetyl CoA.

    D) ATP, NADH, $FADH_2$, CO_2.

    E) ATP and pyruvate.

Answer: A
Diff: 3   Page Ref: 8.2
Skill: Factual

34) How does baker's yeast in bread dough make the bread rise?

Answer: Bread rises due to the production of carbon dioxide during alcohol fermentation.
Diff: 2   Page Ref: 8.2
Skill: Application

35) Why is it important to regenerate NAD^+ molecules during fermentation?

Answer: Glycolysis would stop when all the NAD^+ molecules were used up resulting in no energy production for that cell.
Diff: 2   Page Ref: 8.2
Skill: Conceptual

36) _____ is the only stage in glucose metabolism that does not require oxygen to proceed.

Answer: Glycolysis
Diff: 2   Page Ref: 8.2
Skill: Conceptual

37) Two possible end products of fermentation are _____ as is produced by our muscle cell under anaerobic conditions and _____ by yeast under anaerobic conditions.

Answer: lactic acid; carbon dioxide and alcohol
Diff: 2   Page Ref: 8.2
Skill: Conceptual

38) The conversion of glucose to lactic acid is a form of _____.

Answer: fermentation
Diff: 2   Page Ref: 8.2
Skill: Factual

39) Yeast in a bottle of champagne produce _____ and _____.

Answer: alcohol; carbon dioxide
Diff: 2   Page Ref: 8.2
Skill: Factual

40) During which part of aerobic respiration is the oxygen actually used?

   A) glycolysis

   B) fermentation

   C) Krebs cycle

   D) conversion of pyruvic acid to Acetyl CoA

   E) electron transport system

Answer: E
Diff: 2   Page Ref: 8.3
Skill: Factual

41) Why do you breathe more heavily during exercise?

   A) because your cells need more O_2

   B) because your cells are producing more CO_2

   C) because your cells need more glucose

   D) A and B

   E) all of the above

Answer: D
Diff: 2   Page Ref: 8.3
Skill: Conceptual

42) *Specifically*, what process yields the CO_2 that is exhaled during breathing?

   A) glycolysis

   B) C_3 cycle

   C) conversion of pyruvate to Acetyl CoA and the Krebs cycle

   D) chemiosmosis

   E) fermentation

Answer: C
Diff: 2   Page Ref: 8.3
Skill: Conceptual

43) The metabolic breakdown of one molecule of glucose harvests the greatest amount of energy during

   A) glycolysis.

   B) Krebs cycle.

   C) matrix reactions.

   D) fermentation.

   E) electron transport.

Answer: E
Diff: 2   Page Ref: 8.3
Skill: Factual

44) How many CO_2 molecules are generated from each pyruvate that enters the mitochondria?

   A) 1   B) 2   C) 3   D) 4   E) 5

Answer: C
Diff: 2   Page Ref: 8.3
Skill: Conceptual

45) In order to be able to continue, each turn of the Krebs cycle must regenerate

    A) Acetyl CoA.

    B) NADH and $FADH_2$.

    C) citrate.

    D) pyruvate.

    E) ATP.

Answer: C
Diff: 2   Page Ref: 8.3
Skill: Conceptual

46) In individuals on high protein, low carbohydrate diets, amino acids such as alanine, glycine, and serine, can be converted to pyruvate by deanimation (removal of the amino group). How many ATP, NADH, and $FADH_2$ will be generated from one molecule of alanine?

    A) 1 $FADH_2$, 3 NADH, and 1 ATP

    B) 2 $FADH_2$, 6 NADH, and 2 ATP

    C) 2 ATP and 1 NADH

    D) 2 $FADH_2$, 3 NADH, and 2 ATP

    E) 1 $FADH_2$, 1 NADH, and 1 ATP

Answer: A
Diff: 2   Page Ref: 8.3
Skill: Application

47) Which of the following is an example of an electron carrier molecule?

    A) citric acid

    B) CO_2

    C) Acetyl CoA

    D) NADH

    E) ATP

Answer: D
Diff: 2   Page Ref: 8.3
Skill: Factual

Biology: Life on Earth, 8e

48) The electron transport chain receives electrons directly from

    A) NADH.

    B) $FADH_2$.

    C) ATP.

    D) A and B

    E) all of these

Answer: D
Diff: 2   Page Ref: 8.3
Skill: Factual

49) In the matrix reactions, what happens to the original carbons in pyruvic acid?

    A) They form the backbone chain of citric acid.

    B) They form the ring structure of oxaloacetic acid.

    C) They are incorporated into molecules of NADH and $FADH_2$.

    D) They end up in molecules of CO_2.

    E) They form glucose.

Answer: D
Diff: 2   Page Ref: 8.3
Skill: Factual

50) Chemiosmosis in mitochondria directly results in the synthesis of

    A) NADH.   B) $FADH_2$.   C) H_2O.   D) CoA.   E) ATP.

Answer: E
Diff: 2   Page Ref: 8.3
Skill: Factual

51) What is the final electron acceptor in cellular respiration?

    A) ATP

    B) NADH

    C) carbon dioxide

    D) oxygen

    E) $FADH_2$

Answer: D
Diff: 2   Page Ref: 8.3
Skill: Factual

52) The insecticide rotenone inhibits one of the steps of the electron transport system in mitochondria. What is the immediate result?

    A) Transport of pyruvate into the mitochondria will increase.

    B) The cells will utilize oxygen more rapidly.

    C) The rate of the Krebs cycle reactions will increase.

    D) Electron transport will increase.

    E) The rate of fermentation will increase.

Answer: E
Diff: 2   Page Ref: 8.3
Skill: Conceptual

53) In the matrix, oxygen combines with _____ to form _____.

    A) electrons; water

    B) hydrogen ions; water

    C) electrons and hydrogen ions; water

    D) carbon; CO_2

    E) electrons and carbon; CO_2

Answer: C
Diff: 2   Page Ref: 8.3
Skill: Factual

54) From the beginning of glycolysis to the end of the Krebs cycle, what has the cell gained from the breakdown of each molecule of glucose?

    A) two molecules of pyruvate

    B) 4 ATP, 10 NADH, and 2 $FADH_2$

    C) 2 ATP and 6 NADH

    D) 2 ATP, 4 NADH and 2 $FADH_2$

    E) 2 ATP, lactate, and NAD^+

Answer: B
Diff: 2   Page Ref: 8.3
Skill: Conceptual

55) The cells of which of these organs undergo aerobic respiration?

    A) heart

    B) lungs

    C) skin

    D) kidneys

    E) all of these

Answer: E
Diff: 2   Page Ref: 8.3
Skill: Conceptual

56) Oxygen is necessary for cellular respiration because oxygen

    A) combines with electrons and hydrogen ions to form water.

    B) combines with carbon to form carbon dioxide.

    C) combines with carbon dioxide and water to form glucose.

    D) reduces glucose to form carbon dioxide and water.

    E) combines with electrons to form CO_2.

Answer: A
Diff: 2   Page Ref: 8.3
Skill: Factual

57) When oxygen is present

    A) most cells utilize aerobic cellular respiration.

    B) most animal cells will carry on fermentation and produce lactic acid.

    C) most bacteria and yeasts carry on fermentation.

    D) two ATP molecules are produced for each glucose molecule.

    E) most animals will convert CO_2 to glucose.

Answer: A
Diff: 2   Page Ref: 8.3
Skill: Conceptual

58) ATP can be used to drive nonspontaneous reactions because

    A) nonspontaneous reactions are exergonic.

    B) the breakdown of ATP to ADP is exergonic.

    C) the breakdown of ATP to ADP is endergonic.

    D) when ATP is broken down to ADP, phosphate is released.

    E) ADP possesses more free energy than ATP.

Answer: B
Diff: 2   Page Ref: 8.3
Skill: Conceptual

59) The portion of aerobic respiration that produces the most ATP per molecule of glucose is

    A) chemiosmosis.

    B) the citric acid cycle.

    C) glycolysis.

    D) lactic acid fermentation.

    E) alcohol fermentation.

Answer: A
Diff: 2   Page Ref: 8.3
Skill: Factual

60) In yeast, if the electron transport system is shut down because of a lack of oxygen, glycolysis will probably

    A) shut down.

    B) increase.

    C) produce more ATP per molecule of glucose.

    D) produce more NADH per molecule of glucose.

    E) produce more acetyl coenzyme A.

Answer: B
Diff: 2   Page Ref: 8.3
Skill: Conceptual

61) As a biker pumps up a hill to the finish line of a race, his leg muscles are most likely

    A) using cellular respiration to produce maximal ATP levels.

    B) using more oxygen for maximal ATP production.

    C) using lactic acid fermentation for ATP production.

    D) both A and B

    E) all of the above

Answer: C
Diff: 2   Page Ref: 8.3
Skill: Application

62) Which parts of the mitochondria are directly involved in the synthesis of ATP during chemiosmosis?

    A) matrix

    B) inner mitochondrial membrane

    C) outer mitochondrial membrane

    D) A and B

    E) A, B and C

Answer: D
Diff: 2   Page Ref: 8.3
Skill: Conceptual

63) If ATP is made in the mitochondria, how does it provide energy for reactions in the cytoplasm of the cell?

    A) ATP is pumped out from the intermembrane space of the mitochondria to the cytoplasm.

    B) ATP diffuses out of the mitochondria into the cytoplasm.

    C) ATP is used to make glucose, which is transported to the cytoplasm.

    D) The energy in ATP is converted to NADH, which travels to the cytoplasm.

    E) ATP is converted to ADP, which can be transported to the cytoplasm and converted back into ATP.

Answer: B
Diff: 3   Page Ref: 8.3
Skill: Factual

64) Which of the following most closely matches the correct order of main events of cellular respiration?

    A) glycolysis, pyruvate enters mitochondrion, Krebs cycle, major ATP production, electron transport

    B) glycolysis, major ATP production, pyruvate enters mitochondrion, electron transport, Krebs cycle

    C) glycolysis, Krebs cycle, electrons transport system, major ATP production

    D) Krebs cycle, electron transport, major ATP production, glycolysis

    E) major ATP production, pyruvate enters mitochondrion, Krebs cycle, electron transport

Answer: C
Diff: 2   Page Ref: 8.3
Skill: Conceptual

65) The products of the Krebs cycle include

    A) ATP.

    B) carbon dioxide.

    C) energy carriers.

    D) B and C only

    E) all of the above

Answer: E
Diff: 2   Page Ref: 8.3
Skill: Conceptual

66) The part of a mitochondrion that structurally compares to the stroma of a chloroplast is the

    A) grana.

    B) matrix.

    C) thylakoids.

    D) cristae.

    E) outer membrane.

Answer: B
Diff: 2   Page Ref: 8.3
Skill: Factual

67) The cristae of the mitochondria can be compared functionally to the thylakoid membranes of the chloroplast because both contain a system for

    A) enzyme synthesis.

    B) pyruvate production.

    C) glucose synthesis.

    D) anaerobic respiration.

    E) electron transport.

Answer: E
Diff: 2   Page Ref: 8.3
Skill: Factual

68) During which of the following processes is <u>NO</u> ATP produced?

A) glycolysis

B) Krebs cycle

C) ETS

D) ATP is made during each of the processes above.

E) ATP is not made during any of the processes above.

Answer: D
Diff: 2   Page Ref: 8.3
Skill: Factual

69) The most ATP is produced during which of the following processes?

A) glycolysis

B) Krebs cycle

C) ETS

D) An equal amount of ATP is produced during each of the processes above.

Answer: C
Diff: 2   Page Ref: 8.3
Skill: Factual

70) Which of the following processes occur(s) in the cytoplasm?

A) glycolysis

B) Krebs cycle

C) ETS

D) Both A and B occur in the cytoplasm.

E) All of the above occur in the cytoplasm.

Answer: A
Diff: 2   Page Ref: 8.3
Skill: Factual

71) Which of the following processes occur(s) in a membrane?

A) glycolysis

B) Krebs cycle

C) ETS

D) None of the above occur in a membrane.

Answer: C
Diff: 2   Page Ref: 8.3
Skill: Factual

72) Which of the following processes require(s) oxygen directly?

A) glycolysis   B) Krebs cycle   C) ETS   D) fermentation

Answer: C
Diff: 2   Page Ref: 8.3
Skill: Factual

73) Which of the following processes require(s) enzymes?

A) glycolysis

B) Krebs cycle

C) ETS

D) all of these

E) none of these

Answer: D
Diff: 2   Page Ref: 8.3
Skill: Factual

74) Which of the following processes involves ATP synthesizing enzymes associated with hydrogen ion channels?

A) glycolysis

B) Krebs cycle

C) ETS

D) all of these

E) none of these

Answer: C
Diff: 2   Page Ref: 8.3
Skill: Factual

75) The term chemiosmosis is associated with which process?

A) glycolysis

B) Krebs cycle

C) ETS

D) all of these

E) none of these

Answer: C
Diff: 2   Page Ref: 8.3
Skill: Factual

76) During which of the following processes is CO_2 produced?

A) glycolysis

B) Krebs cycle

C) ETS

D) all of these

E) none of these

Answer: B
Diff: 2   Page Ref: 8.3
Skill: Factual

77) During which of the following processes is glucose synthesized?

A) glycolysis

B) Krebs cycle

C) ETS

D) all of these

E) none of these

Answer: E
Diff: 2   Page Ref: 8.3
Skill: Factual

78) Which of the following processes involve(s) citric acid?

A) glycolysis

B) Krebs cycle

C) ETS

D) all of these

E) none of these

Answer: B
Diff: 2   Page Ref: 8.3
Skill: Factual

79) Which of the following processes occur(s) in plants?

A) glycolysis

B) Krebs cycle

C) ETS

D) all of these

E) none of these

Answer: D
Diff: 2   Page Ref: 8.3
Skill: Conceptual

80) Chemiosmosis links a hydrogen gradient to the production of ATP. True or False?

Answer: TRUE
Diff: 2   *Page Ref: 8.3*
Skill: Factual

81) Glycolysis and the Krebs cycle reactions occur in the mitochondria. True or False?

Answer: FALSE
Diff: 2   *Page Ref: 8.3*
Skill: Factual

82) Carbon dioxide is considered a waste product of cellular respiration. True or False?

Answer: TRUE
Diff: 2   *Page Ref: 8.3*
Skill: Factual

83) The process of fermentation is energetically more efficient than cellular respiration. True or False?

Answer: FALSE
Diff: 2   *Page Ref: 8.3*
Skill: Factual

84) Explain the relationship among the respiratory system, the circulatory system, and cellular respiration. How are they tied together?

Answer: Oxygen is inhaled and travels to the tissues in the body via the circulatory system. The oxygen is used in cell respiration to provide ATP. CO_2 is produced during cellular respiration and is transported back to the lungs via the circulatory system, and is exhaled during breathing.
Diff: 3   *Page Ref: 8.3*
Skill: Conceptual

85) _____ is a series of reactions, occurring under aerobic conditions, in which large amounts of ATP are produced.

Answer: Cellular respiration
Diff: 2   *Page Ref: 8.3*
Skill: Factual

86) Most of the ATP produced during cellular respiration is generated in the _____ after the movement of hydrogen ions through ATP-synthesizing proteins in the inner membrane of the mitochondrion.

Answer: mitochondrial matrix
Diff: 2   *Page Ref: 8.3*
Skill: Factual

87) _____ is the process by which hydrogen ions move via a concentration gradient through ATP–synthesizing enzymes resulting in the production of ATP.

Answer: Chemiosmosis
Diff: 2   Page Ref: 8.3
Skill: Factual

88) In the process of cellular respiration, a molecule of _____ is completely broken down to form _____, _____, and _____.

Answer: glucose; H_2O; ATP; carbon dioxide
Diff: 2   Page Ref: 8.3
Skill: Factual

89) Louis Pasteur (a French biochemist) investigated the metabolism of yeast which can survive under aerobic or anaerobic conditions. He observed that the yeast consumed sugar at a much faster rate under anaerobic conditions than it did under aerobic conditions. Explain this Pasteur effect.

Answer: Under anaerobic conditions fermentation is being used producing only 2 ATP/glucose, whereas under aerobic conditions cellular respiration is used producing 34–36 ATP/glucose so more glucose is required under anaerobic conditions to yield the same amount of ATP for the yeast.
Diff: 2   Page Ref: 8.3
Skill: Application

90) You are running five miles to get some exercise. Describe how your muscle cells are getting energy. Discuss the processes involved and detail the differences that will occur at the start of your run and toward the end of your run.

Answer: Student should address the shift from aerobic cellular respiration to anaerobic lactic acid fermentation as oxygen becomes scarce for the muscle cells.
Diff: 2   Page Ref: 8.3
Skill: Application

91) Briefly describe the three main steps of aerobic glucose metabolism.

Answer: glycolysis (glucose to pyruvate), Krebs cycle (pyruvate to CO_2), electron transport chain (electrons from Krebs cycle through the electron transport chain to the terminal electron acceptor of O_2 – ATP production via chemiosmosis)
Diff: 2   Page Ref: 8.3
Skill: Factual

92) Respiration rates are measured by the amount of oxygen per gram of tissue and it was determined that a warm blooded mouse has 2.5 ml O_2/gram tissue/hour whereas a cold blooded crayfish has a 0.047 ml O_2/gram tissue/hour. Why is there such a dramatic difference?

Answer: Warm blooded animals require more energy to maintain a higher body temperature and greater metabolic rate.
Diff: 3   Page Ref: 8.3
Skill: Application

93) In the 1940s, some physicians prescribed low doses of a drug called dinitrophenol to help patients lose weight. This unsafe method was abandoned after a few patients died. DNP uncouples the chemiosomotic machinery by making the lipid bilayer of the inner mitochondrial membrane leaky to hydrogen ions. Explain how this causes weight loss.

Answer: No proton gradient is established so little ATP is produced even through the process of cellular respiration. So the patient must burn more stored (fat) energy to try to give the body enough energy.

Diff: 3   Page Ref: 8.3
Skill: Application

Chapter 9 DNA: The Molecule of Heredity

1) The hereditary material that is present in all cells is

    A) protein.   B) RNA.   C) DNA.   D) R-strain.   E) S-strain.

Answer: C
Diff: 1   *Page Ref: 9.1*
Skill: Factual

2) What was the main point of Griffith's experiments with pneumonia in mice?

    A) Mice exposed to the S-strain bacterium became resistant to the R-strain bacterium.

    B) There is a substance present in dead bacteria that can cause a heritable change in living bacteria.

    C) The genetic material was definitively proven in these experiments to be DNA.

    D) S-strain bacteria can cause pneumonia.

    E) Heat destroys the hereditary material.

Answer: B
Diff: 2   *Page Ref: 9.1*
Skill: Conceptual

3) What is the relationship among DNA, a gene, and a chromosome?

    A) A chromosome contains hundreds of genes which are composed of protein.

    B) A chromosome contains hundreds of genes which are composed of DNA.

    C) A gene contains hundreds of chromosomes which are composed of protein.

    D) A gene is composed of DNA, but there is no relationship to a chromosome.

    E) A gene contains hundreds of chromosomes which are composed of DNA.

Answer: B
Diff: 2   *Page Ref: 9.1*
Skill: Conceptual

4) In Griffith's experiments, what happened when heat–killed S–strain *pneumococcus* were injected into a mouse along with live R–strain *pneumococcus*?

   A) DNA from the live R–strain was taken up by the heat–killed S–strain, converting them to R–strain and killing the mouse.

   B) DNA from the heat-killed S–strain was taken up by the live R–strain, converting them to S–strain and killing the mouse.

   C) Proteins released from the heat–killed S–strain killed the mouse.

   D) RNA from the heat–killed S–strain was translated into proteins that killed the mouse.

   E) nothing

Answer: B
Diff: 2   Page Ref: 9.1
Skill: Conceptual

5) When Griffiths experimented with two types of S. pneumoniae, he found that

   A) the virulent strain killed the mice but the avirulent strain did not.

   B) if the virulent strain was heat–killed before injection, the mice would live.

   C) if the avirulent strain was mixed with the heat–killed virulent strain before injection, the mice would die.

   D) A and B

   E) A, B and C

Answer: E
Diff: 2   Page Ref: 9.1
Skill: Factual

6) Avery, MacLeod, and McCarty continued Griffith's work with S. pneumoniae and concluded from their experiments that DNA was the hereditary material. What would happen to mice after injection of heat–killed virulent bacteria mixed with live avirulent bacteria after treatment with DNase if protein was the hereditary material instead of DNA?

   A) The mice would die.

   B) The mice would live.

   C) Not enough information provided to answer the question.

Answer: A
Diff: 3   Page Ref: 9.1
Skill: Conceptual

7) Eukaryotic chromosomes are composed mostly of DNA. True or False?

Answer: FALSE
Diff: 1   Page Ref: 9.1
Skill: Factual

8) In eukaryotic cells, chromosomes are composed of both DNA and proteins. True or False?

Answer: TRUE
Diff: 2   Page Ref: 9.1
Skill: Factual

9) _____ carries the blueprints for all forms of life on Earth.

Answer: DNA
Diff: 2   Page Ref: 9.1
Skill: Factual

10) By the late 1800s scientists had determined that heritable information existed as discrete units called genes, which were located on _____.

Answer: chromosomes
Diff: 2   Page Ref: 9.1
Skill: Factual

11) Chromosomes contain both _____ and _____ and in the early 20th century scientists were unsure which of these carried the heritable units called genes.

Answer: DNA; protein
Diff: 2   Page Ref: 9.1
Skill: Factual

12) Briefly describe the experiments done by Griffith and by Avery, McCarty and MacLeod. What was the relevance of these studies?

Answer: Students should describe the transforming agent Griffith found that converted R–strain bacteria to S–strain bacteria and that the AMM experiments were then able to determine that the transforming agent was DNA. Both series of experiments led to the connection between genes and DNA.
Diff: 2   Page Ref: 9.1
Skill: Conceptual

13) DNA has

A) A, U, G, and C bases.

B) only C and T bases.

C) only A and G bases.

D) C, T, A, and G bases.

E) both U and T bases.

Answer: D
Diff: 2   Page Ref: 9.2
Skill: Factual

14) If amounts of bases in a DNA molecule are measured, we find

    A) A = C and G = T.

    B) A = G and C = T.

    C) T = A and C = G.

    D) no two bases would be equal in amount.

    E) that all bases are equal in amount.

Answer: C
Diff: 2   Page Ref: 9.2
Skill: Factual

15) The DNA of a certain organism has guanine as 30% of its bases. What percentage of its bases would be adenine?

    A) 0%   B) 10%   C) 20%   D) 30%   E) 40%

Answer: C
Diff: 2   Page Ref: 9.2
Skill: Application

16) Which is NOT found in DNA?

    A) deoxyribose sugar

    B) adenine

    C) phosphate group

    D) phospholipid group

    E) thymine

Answer: D
Diff: 2   Page Ref: 9.2
Skill: Factual

17) The correct structure of a nucleotide is

    A) phosphate–5 carbon sugar–nitrogen base.

    B) phospholipid–sugar–base.

    C) phosphate–sugar–phosphate–sugar.

    D) adenine–thymine and guanine–cytosine.

    E) base–phosphate–glucose.

Answer: A
Diff: 2   Page Ref: 9.2
Skill: Factual

18) The rules formulated by Chargaff state that

   A) A = T and G = C in any molecule of DNA.

   B) A = C and G = T in any molecule of DNA.

   C) A = G and C = T in any molecule of DNA.

   D) A = U and G = C in any molecule of RNA.

   E) DNA and RNA are made up of the same four nitrogenous bases.

Answer: A
Diff: 1   Page Ref: 9.2
Skill: Factual

19) If cytosine makes up 22% of the nucleotides in a sample of DNA from an organism, then adenine would make up what percent of the bases?

   A) 22

   B) 44

   C) 28

   D) 56

   E) It cannot be determined with the information given.

Answer: C
Diff: 2   Page Ref: 9.2
Skill: Application

20) In an analysis of the nucleotide composition of DNA to see which bases are equivalent in concentration, which of the following would be TRUE?

   A) A = C

   B) A = G and C = T

   C) A + C = G + T

   D) A + T = C + G

   E) Both B and C are correct.

Answer: C
Diff: 2   Page Ref: 9.2
Skill: Application

21) By the early 1950s, many biologists realized that the key to understanding inheritance lay in the structure of

    A) DNA.

    B) protein.

    C) enzymes.

    D) chromosomes.

    E) ribosomes.

Answer: A
Diff: 2   Page Ref: 9.2
Skill: Factual

22) The X-ray diffraction pattern for DNA suggested to Wilkins and Franklin all of the following features about DNA EXCEPT

    A) a DNA molecule is helical.

    B) a DNA molecule has a diameter of 2 nanometers.

    C) one full turn of the DNA helix occurs every 3.4 nanometers.

    D) the phosphate-sugar "backbone" of the molecule is on the outside of the DNA helix.

    E) A pairs with T and G pairs with C in a DNA molecule.

Answer: E
Diff: 2   Page Ref: 9.2
Skill: Factual

23) In DNA, phosphate groups bond to

    A) adenine.

    B) ribose.

    C) pyrimidine bases.

    D) other phosphate groups.

    E) deoxyribose.

Answer: E
Diff: 2   Page Ref: 9.2
Skill: Factual

24) The sequence of subunits in the DNA "backbone" is

      A) --base--phosphate--base--phosphate--base--phosphate-.

      B) --phosphate--sugar--phosphate--sugar--phosphate--sugar.

      C) --sugar--base--sugar--base--sugar--base--sugar--base-.

      D) --base--sugar--phosphate--base--sugar--phosphate-.

      E) --base--phosphate--sugar--base--phosphate--sugar-.

Answer: B
Diff: 2   Page Ref: 9.2
Skill: Factual

25) The rules for base pairing in DNA are

      A) A = C and G = T in amount.

      B) A with C, and G with T.

      C) A with G, and C with T.

      D) A with T, and G with C.

      E) A = G and C = T in amount.

Answer: D
Diff: 2   Page Ref: 9.2
Skill: Factual

26) Complementary base pairs are held together by

      A) peptide bonds.

      B) hydrogen bonds.

      C) disulfide bonds.

      D) covalent bonds.

      E) ionic bonds.

Answer: B
Diff: 2   Page Ref: 9.2
Skill: Factual

27) The two polynucleotide chains in a DNA molecule are attracted to each other by

      A) covalent bonds between carbon atoms.

      B) hydrogen bonds between bases.

      C) peptide bonds between amino acids.

      D) ionic bonds between "R" groups in amino acids.

      E) covalent bonds between phosphates and sugars.

Answer: B
Diff: 2   Page Ref: 9.2
Skill: Factual

28) In a DNA molecule, base pairing occurs between

    A) adenine and thymine.

    B) adenine and guanine.

    C) guanine and uracil.

    D) thymine and cytosine.

    E) adenine and uracil.

Answer: A
Diff: 2   Page Ref: 9.2
Skill: Factual

29) For the DNA sequence GCCTAT in one polynucleotide chain, the sequence found in the other polynucleotide chain is

    A) CGGATA.

    B) GCCATA.

    C) CGGAUA.

    D) ATTCGC.

    E) GCCTAT.

Answer: A
Diff: 2   Page Ref: 9.2
Skill: Application

30) How does the Watson and Crick model of DNA structure help explain DNA replication?

    A) Deoxyribose sugar always bonds to a nitrogenous base.

    B) Precise base pairing allows the base sequence to be copied.

    C) Phosphate groups always bond to deoxyribose sugar.

    D) The number of purines equals the number of pyrimidines.

    E) Four types of bases are found in DNA.

Answer: B
Diff: 2   Page Ref: 9.2
Skill: Conceptual

31) In the comparison of a DNA molecule to a twisted ladder, the uprights of the ladder represent

A) nitrogenous bases linked together.

B) deoxyribose linked to phosphates.

C) deoxyribose linked to sulfates.

D) nitrogenous bases linked to phosphates.

E) hydrogen bonds between bases.

Answer: B
Diff: 2   Page Ref: 9.2
Skill: Conceptual

32) In the comparison of a DNA molecule to a twisted ladder, the rungs of the ladder represent

A) nitrogenous bases linked together.

B) deoxyribose linked to phosphates.

C) deoxyribose linked to sulfates.

D) nitrogenous bases linked to phosphates.

E) the backbones of the molecule.

Answer: A
Diff: 2   Page Ref: 9.2
Skill: Conceptual

33) Which of the following does NOT follow from the Watson and Crick base pairing rules?

A) A = T in amount.

B) G = C in amount.

C) A + G = T + C in amount.

D) A + T = G + C in amount.

E) All the above choices are correct answers.

Answer: D
Diff: 2   Page Ref: 9.2
Skill: Conceptual

34) Which component of a nucleotide present within a DNA molecule could be removed without breaking the polynucleotide chain?

    A) ribose

    B) deoxyribose

    C) phosphate

    D) uracil

    E) thymine

Answer: E
Diff: 2   Page Ref: 9.2
Skill: Conceptual

35) It became apparent to Watson and Crick after completion of their model that a DNA molecule could carry a vast amount of hereditary information in its

    A) sequence of bases.

    B) phosphate–sugar backbone.

    C) complementary base pairing.

    D) side groups of nitrogenous bases.

    E) different five–carbon sugars.

Answer: A
Diff: 2   Page Ref: 9.2
Skill: Conceptual

36) Why did scientists at first think that DNA would be a poor candidate for the hereditary material?

    A) Griffith's experiments suggested protein was the hereditary material.

    B) Studies showed that viruses lacking DNA passed genetic traits to the next generation.

    C) DNA was made of only four kinds of subunits.

    D) The work of Franklin and Wilkins showed that DNA could not be the hereditary material.

    E) None of the above is correct.

Answer: C
Diff: 2   Page Ref: 9.2
Skill: Conceptual

37) Pick the best choice for the following statement about DNA:
Like a spiral staircase.

    A) deoxyribose

    B) phosphate

    C) double helix

    D) hydrogen bonds

    E) covalent bonds

Answer: C
Diff: 2   Page Ref: 9.2
Skill: Conceptual

38) Pick the best choice for the following statement about DNA:
Joins sugar to phosphate.

    A) deoxyribose

    B) phosphate

    C) double helix

    D) hydrogen bonds

    E) covalent bonds

Answer: E
Diff: 2   Page Ref: 9.2
Skill: Conceptual

39) Pick the best choice for the following statement about DNA:
Joins adenine and thymine, and also guanine and cytosine.

    A) deoxyribose

    B) phosphate

    C) double helix

    D) hydrogen bonds

    E) covalent bonds

Answer: D
Diff: 2   Page Ref: 9.2
Skill: Conceptual

40) Pick the best choice for the following statement about DNA:
Watson and Crick are credited with its discovery.

   A) deoxyribose

   B) phosphate

   C) double helix

   D) hydrogen bonds

   E) covalent bonds

Answer: C
Diff: 2   Page Ref: 9.2
Skill: Conceptual

41) Pick the best choice for the following statement about DNA:
Covalently bonded to nitrogen–containing base.

   A) deoxyribose

   B) phosphate

   C) double helix

   D) hydrogen bonds

   E) covalent bonds

Answer: A
Diff: 2   Page Ref: 9.2
Skill: Conceptual

42) Pick the best choice for the following statement about DNA:
Units of the "uprights" of the DNA ladder that do NOT attach to the nitrogen bases.

   A) deoxyribose

   B) phosphate

   C) Double helix

   D) hydrogen bonds

   E) covalent bonds

Answer: B
Diff: 2   Page Ref: 9.2
Skill: Conceptual

43) How many base pairs are in a gene?

A) 2

B) 4

C) thousands

D) billions

E) 100

Answer: C
Diff: 2   Page Ref: 9.2
Skill: Factual

44) How many possible sequences of bases are in a DNA molecule?

A) 2

B) 4

C) thousands

D) billions

E) 100

Answer: D
Diff: 2   Page Ref: 9.2
Skill: Factual

45) How many different kinds of base pairs are in DNA?

A) 2

B) 4

C) thousands

D) billions

E) 100

Answer: A
Diff: 2   Page Ref: 9.2
Skill: Factual

46) How many different kinds of nucleotides are in DNA?

A) 2

B) 4

C) thousands

D) billions

E) 100

Answer: B
Diff: 2   Page Ref: 9.2
Skill: Factual

47) Chargaff found that the amounts of the four bases vary from species to species, but the amount of adenine always equals the amount of guanine and the amount of thymine always equals the amount of cytosine. True or False?

Answer: FALSE
Diff: 2   Page Ref: 9.2
Skill: Conceptual

48) A strand of DNA is a polymer of nucleotides held together by hydrogen bonds. True or False?

Answer: FALSE
Diff: 2   Page Ref: 9.2
Skill: Conceptual

49) The basic subunits of DNA are the _____.

Answer: nucleotides
Diff: 2   Page Ref: 9.2
Skill: Factual

50) What are the three main components of a DNA nucleotide?

Answer: A DNA nucleotide contains a sugar (deoxyribose), a phosphate group and a nitrogen-containing base.
Diff: 2   Page Ref: 9.2
Skill: Application

51) The DNA of chromosomes is composed of two strands, wound about each other in a _____.

Answer: double helix
Diff: 2   Page Ref: 9.2
Skill: Factual

52) The X-ray crystallographs of the British scientists _____ were essential for the discovery of the structure of the DNA molecule.

Answer: Wilkins and Franklin
Diff: 2   Page Ref: 9.2
Skill: Factual

53) Name the four types of nitrogen-containing bases found in DNA. Discuss which bases are complementary to one another and describe how the bases are held together in the double helix of DNA.

Answer: Adenine is complementary to Thymine and Guanine is complementary to Cytosine. The bases are held together via hydrogen bonds.
Diff: 2   Page Ref: 9.2
Skill: Conceptual

54) A stretch of DNA 10 nucleotides long can have how many possible sequences of the four bases?

A) one

B) four

C) ten

D) hundreds

E) more than a million

Answer: E
Diff: 2   Page Ref: 9.3
Skill: Conceptual

55) The number of subunits in a DNA molecule is more important to its function than the sequence. True or False?

Answer: FALSE
Diff: 1   Page Ref: 9.3
Skill: Factual

56) Which of the following is TRUE of the genetic information in the cells of your body?

A) Different kinds of cells contain different genetic information.

B) Each type of cell contains only the genetic information it needs to be that type of cell.

C) The genetic information in almost all of your cells is identical.

D) The genetic information changes in a predictable manner as you grow and develop.

E) None of the above are true.

Answer: C
Diff: 2   Page Ref: 9.4
Skill: Conceptual

57) When a cell divides

A) each daughter cell receives a nearly perfect copy of the parent cell's genetic information.

B) each daughter cell receives exactly half the genetic information in the parent cell.

C) each daughter cell receives the same amount of genetic information that was in the parent cell, but it has been altered.

D) genetic information is randomly parceled out to the daughter cells.

E) None of the above are true.

Answer: A
Diff: 1   Page Ref: 9.4
Skill: Conceptual

58) If a cell has replicated its DNA, which of the following is usually TRUE?

    A) The cell is irreversibly committed to divide.

    B) The cell will never divide.

    C) The cell has recently divided.

    D) The DNA has become fragmented.

    E) It is a daughter cell.

Answer: A
Diff: 1   Page Ref: 9.4
Skill: Conceptual

59) The timing of DNA replication and cell division is regulated carefully for which of the following reasons?

    A) so that the DNA is replicated only one time prior to each cell division

    B) so that cells that will never divide do not replicate their DNA

    C) so that the cell does not try to replicate its DNA if it lacks enough energy and raw materials to complete the process

    D) All of the above are reasons for the regulation of DNA replication.

    E) None of the above are true.

Answer: D
Diff: 2   Page Ref: 9.4
Skill: Conceptual

60) When DNA polymerase is in contact with thymine in the parental strand, what does it add to the growing daughter strand?

    A) deoxyribose

    B) phosphate group

    C) adenine

    D) single–ring pyrimidine

    E) uracil

Answer: C
Diff: 2   Page Ref: 9.4
Skill: Conceptual

61) Semiconservative DNA replication means

    A) the old DNA is completely broken down.

    B) the old DNA remains completely intact.

    C) A pairs with T and G pairs with C.

    D) only half of the DNA is replicated.

    E) each new DNA molecule has half of the old one.

Answer: E
Diff: 2   Page Ref: 9.4
Skill: Factual

62) All of the following occur during DNA replication EXCEPT

    A) separation of parental DNA strands.

    B) use of parental DNA as a template.

    C) formation of chromatids.

    D) synthesis of totally new double-stranded DNA molecules.

    E) use of DNA polymerase enzymes.

Answer: D
Diff: 2   Page Ref: 9.4
Skill: Conceptual

63) If a cell has one DNA molecule containing only radioactive nitrogen, and the cell is placed in culture medium containing only regular nitrogen, how many cells will contain some DNA with radioactive nitrogen after four rounds of cell replication?

    A) one   B) two   C) four   D) eight   E) sixteen

Answer: B
Diff: 2   Page Ref: 9.4
Skill: Application

64) The feature of the Watson-Crick model of DNA structure that explains its ability to function in replication is

    A) that each strand contains all the information present in the double helix.

    B) the structural and functional similarities of DNA and RNA.

    C) that the double helix is right-handed and not left-handed.

    D) that DNA replication does not require enzymes.

    E) the fact that the nitrogen bases are exposed on the outside of the molecule.

Answer: A
Diff: 2   Page Ref: 9.4
Skill: Conceptual

65) When chromosomes replicate

    A) the two DNA strands separate and each is used as a template for synthesis of a new strand.

    B) new synthesis occurs in only one direction from where it begins.

    C) one strand of the DNA is completely replicated first, and then the second strand is replicated.

    D) there is not enough DNA to distribute to the two daughter cells.

    E) All of these are correct.

Answer: A
Diff: 2   Page Ref: 9.4
Skill: Factual

66) In semiconservative replication a DNA molecule serves as a template for a new DNA molecule which either consists of both parental strands of DNA or both newly synthesized strands of DNA. True or False?

Answer: FALSE
Diff: 2   Page Ref: 9.4
Skill: Conceptual

67) DNA helicase is involved in rewinding the strands of DNA into a helix after replication. True or False?

Answer: FALSE
Diff: 2   Page Ref: 9.4
Skill: Factual

68) DNA polymerase has the ability to match the nucleotide base in the parental strand with a free nucleotide that is complementary to that base and then forms the covalent bonds between the nucleotides in the growing daughter strand of DNA. True or False?

Answer: TRUE
Diff: 2   Page Ref: 9.4
Skill: Factual

69) _____ is the process whereby a molecule of DNA copies itself.

Answer: DNA replication
Diff: 2   Page Ref: 9.4
Skill: Factual

70) DNA is copied within eukaryotic cells in the process of _____ to produce two identical DNA molecules.

Answer: replication
Diff: 2   Page Ref: 9.4
Skill: Factual

71) DNA replication uses _____ base pairing to ensure genetic constancy.

Answer: complementary
Diff: 2   *Page Ref: 9.4*
Skill: Conceptual

72) Briefly describe the basic process of DNA replication.

Answer: DNA helicase unwinds the double helix of the parental DNA molecule and DNA polymerase pairs free nucleotides to be complementary to the parental DNA strand. The new nucleotides are then joined together to form two new strands of DNA paired with each of the original parental strands.
Diff: 2   *Page Ref: 9.4*
Skill: Conceptual

73) Which of the following is TRUE about the accuracy of DNA replication?

A) Many errors are made during DNA replication, but this does not matter because of the immense size of the DNA molecule.

B) Many errors are made during DNA replication, but this does not matter because repair enzymes will mend the errors.

C) The few errors made by DNA polymerase are usually corrected by repair enzymes.

D) DNA polymerase makes very few errors, so no repair enzymes are needed.

E) DNA polymerase always makes a perfect copy of the original DNA.

Answer: C
Diff: 2   *Page Ref: 9.5*
Skill: Conceptual

74) A cell that lacks the ability to make DNA repair enzymes

A) will be able to correctly replicate its DNA, but it will need more time to do so.

B) will be completely unable to replicate its DNA.

C) will replicate its DNA as well as a cell with intact repair enzymes.

D) will replicate its DNA as rapidly as a normal cell, but the resulting DNA will have more errors in it.

E) None of the above are true.

Answer: D
Diff: 3   *Page Ref: 9.5*
Skill: Conceptual

75) DNA polymerase, before any proofreading by repair enzymes, makes on average one mistake for every

    A) 100 base pairs.

    B) 1000 base pairs.

    C) 10,000 base pairs.

    D) million base pairs.

    E) billion base pairs.

Answer: C
Diff: 2   Page Ref: 9.5
Skill: Factual

76) Newly replicated DNA strands contain on average one mistake for every

    A) 100 base pairs.

    B) 1000 base pairs.

    C) 10,000 base pairs.

    D) million base pairs.

    E) billion base pairs.

Answer: E
Diff: 2   Page Ref: 9.5
Skill: Factual

77) The DNA in your body's cells can accumulate errors for which of the following reasons?

    A) Mistakes are made during DNA replication.

    B) Some DNA spontaneously breaks down at normal body temperature.

    C) Ultraviolet light in sunlight damages DNA.

    D) All of the above are reasons DNA can accumulate errors.

    E) None of the above are true.

Answer: D
Diff: 2   Page Ref: 9.5
Skill: Factual

78) The sequence 5'-ACGTACGT-3' altered to 5'-ACGCACGT-3' could have arisen as a result of

    A) a point mutation.

    B) a deletion mutation.

    C) an insertion mutation.

    D) A or B

    E) A, B or C

Answer: A
Diff: 3   *Page Ref: 9.5*
Skill: Application

79) The sequence 5'-ACGTACGT-3' altered to 5'-ACGACGT-3' could have arisen as a result of

    A) a point mutation.

    B) a deletion mutation.

    C) an insertion mutation.

    D) A or B

    E) A, B or C

Answer: B
Diff: 3   *Page Ref: 9.5*
Skill: Application

80) DNA replication occurs without errors due to the complementary base pairing used in the copying process. True or False?

Answer: FALSE
Diff: 2   *Page Ref: 9.5*
Skill: Conceptual

81) Most mutations are harmful, although some can be beneficial. True or False?

Answer: TRUE
Diff: 1   *Page Ref: 9.5*
Skill: Factual

82) Inversions are movements of DNA from one chromosome to another. True or False?

Answer: FALSE
Diff: 1   *Page Ref: 9.5*
Skill: Factual

83) DNA polymerase and other repair enzymes _____ the newly synthesized DNA strand during and after the replication process.

Answer: proofread
Diff: 2   *Page Ref: 9.5*
Skill: Conceptual

84) How do scientists know that "proofreading" occurs during and after the DNA replication process?

Answer: DNA polymerase mismatches bases about every 10,000 base pairs but the actual mutation rate is one in every billion base pairs.
Diff: 3   Page Ref: 9.5
Skill: Conceptual

85) When Hershey and Chase labeled phage T2 with radioactive phosphorus (P –32), they concluded that the phage injects DNA and not protein into its host because the

A) radioactive DNA ended up inside the bacterium.

B) radioactive protein ended up inside the bacterium.

C) both of these

D) none of these

Answer: A
Diff: 2   Page Ref: Scientific Inquiry
Skill: Conceptual

86) If we radioactively label the DNA of bacteriophage and then allow them to infect bacteria, where should the radioactivity end up?

A) outside the bacterial cells   B) inside the bacterial cells

C) inside the nuclei of the bacterial cells   D) inside the nuclei of the bacteriophage

Answer: B
Diff: 2   Page Ref: Scientific Inquiry
Skill: Conceptual

87) Watson and Crick did no actual experiments to determine the structure of DNA. True or False?

Answer: TRUE
Diff: 1   Page Ref: Scientific Inquiry
Skill: Factual

88) In one strand of DNA the nucleotide sequence is 5'–ATGC–3'. The complementary sequence in the other strand must be

A) 5'–CGTA–3'.   B) 5'–ATGC–3'.   C) 5'–GCAT–3'.   D) one of these

Answer: C
Diff: 2   Page Ref: A Closer Look
Skill: Application

89) Which of the following are NOT involved in the DNA replication process?

A) DNA helicase

B) DNA ligase

C) DNA replicase

D) DNA polymerase

E) All of the above are involved.

Answer: C
Diff: 2   Page Ref: A Closer Look
Skill: Factual

90) DNA ligase is important in the replication process as it can bind together small segments of DNA. True or False?

Answer: TRUE
Diff: 2   Page Ref: A Closer Look
Skill: Factual

91) During DNA replication, the continuous daughter strand is the leading strand. True or False?

Answer: TRUE
Diff: 2   Page Ref: A Closer Look
Skill: Factual

92) At one end of a double helix, one strand has a free sugar (3') group and the other has a free phosphate (5') group. This means that the strands are _____.

Answer: antiparallel
Diff: 1   Page Ref: A Closer Look
Skill: Factual

93) _____ breaks the hydrogen bonds between complementary base pairs during DNA replication.

Answer: DNA helicase
Diff: 1   Page Ref: A Closer Look
Skill: Factual

94) Segments of DNA that are made during replication are joined together by _____.

Answer: DNA ligase
Diff: 1   Page Ref: A Closer Look
Skill: Factual

Chapter 10 Gene Expression and Regulation

1) The sequence of nitrogen-containing bases on one strand of DNA most directly determines the sequence of

    A) fatty acids in a fat molecule.

    B) amino acids in a protein molecule.

    C) sugars in a polysaccharide molecule.

    D) All of the above choices are correct.

    E) bases in a protein molecule.

Answer: B
Diff: 2   Page Ref: 10.1
Skill: Factual

2) The sequence of nitrogen-containing bases on one strand of DNA could determine the

    A) sequence of nitrogen-containing bases in mRNA.

    B) sequence of amino acids in protein.

    C) sequence of nitrogen-containing bases in the other DNA strand.

    D) All of the above choices are correct.

    E) sequence of amino acids in the mRNA.

Answer: D
Diff: 2   Page Ref: 10.1
Skill: Factual

3) The "one-gene one-enzyme" hypothesis concluded that

    A) each type of gene codes for a single type of protein.

    B) specific enzymes give rise to specific genes.

    C) only certain genes function in cells.

    D) enzymes regulate gene activity.

    E) DNA → RNA → protein.

Answer: A
Diff: 2   Page Ref: 10.1
Skill: Factual

4) When comparing DNA and RNA, we find

A) no sugar is present in either molecule.

B) hydrogen bonding is important only in DNA.

C) only DNA has a backbone of sugars and phosphates.

D) adenine pairs with different bases in DNA and RNA.

E) thymine pairs with different bases in DNA and RNA.

Answer: D
Diff: 2   Page Ref: 10.1
Skill: Factual

5) Which of these is found in RNA but NOT in DNA?

A) adenine

B) uracil

C) thymine

D) phosphate groups

E) deoxyribose sugar

Answer: B
Diff: 2   Page Ref: 10.1
Skill: Factual

6) Both DNA and RNA

A) are single-stranded molecules.

B) contain the same four types of nitrogen-containing bases.

C) have the same five-carbon sugars.

D) contain phosphate groups.

E) cannot both be present in a cell simultaneously.

Answer: D
Diff: 2   Page Ref: 10.1
Skill: Factual

7) The number of consecutive mRNA bases needed to specify an amino acid is

A) 3.

B) 4.

C) 20.

D) 64.

E) a variable number.

Answer: A
Diff: 2   Page Ref: 10.1
Skill: Factual

8) The number of different possible codons is

   A) 3.

   B) 4.

   C) 20.

   D) 64.

   E) unknown.

Answer: D
Diff: 2   Page Ref: 10.1
Skill: Factual

9) If a bacterial protein has 30 amino acids, how many nucleotides are needed to code for it?

   A) 30   B) 60   C) 90   D) 120   E) 600

Answer: C
Diff: 2   Page Ref: 10.1
Skill: Application

10) Which of the following molecules functions to transfer information from one generation to the next?

   A) DNA   B) mRNA   C) tRNA   D) proteins   E) lipids

Answer: A
Diff: 2   Page Ref: 10.1
Skill: Factual

11) If the sequence of bases in a section of DNA is TAGGCTAA, what is the corresponding sequence of bases in mRNA?

   A) ATCCGATT

   B) TAGGCTAA

   C) CGAAUCGG

   D) AATCGGAT

   E) AUCCGAUU

Answer: E
Diff: 2   Page Ref: 10.1
Skill: Factual

12) The number of nucleotides in a codon is

   A) 3.

   B) 4.

   C) 20.

   D) 64.

   E) a variable number.

Answer: A
Diff: 2   Page Ref: 10.1
Skill: Factual

13) Which of the choices is coded for by the shortest piece of DNA?

   A) a tRNA having 75 nucleotides

   B) a mRNA having 50 codons

   C) a protein having 40 amino acids

   D) a protein with 2 polypeptides, each having 35 amino acids

   E) a mRNA having 100 bases

Answer: A
Diff: 2   Page Ref: 10.1
Skill: Factual

14) In *Neurospora*, a fungus, a pathway synthesizes the amino acid Z from W with E1, E2, and E3 serving as enzymes that catalyze the three reactions as shown:

   E1 E2 E3
   W → X → Y → Z

Mutants that have a defective gene for E2 will grow on media that contains

   A) W or X.

   B) Y or Z.

   C) W, X, Y, or Z.

   D) X.

   E) none of these

Answer: B
Diff: 3   Page Ref: 10.1
Skill: Application

15) The genetic code

    A) is different in different organisms.

    B) is read in sets of three bases called codons.

    C) is used during transcription of RNA.

    D) A and C

    E) B and C

Answer: B
Diff: 2   Page Ref: 10.1
Skill: Factual

16) How does an RNA molecule differ from a DNA molecule?

Answer: RNA is normally single-stranded whereas DNA is double-stranded. RNA has the sugar ribose whereas DNA has the sugar deoxyribose. RNA uses the base uracil whereas DNA uses thymine.
Diff: 2   Page Ref: 10.1
Skill: Factual

17) The process of copying genetic information from DNA to RNA is called

    A) translation.

    B) transformation.

    C) replication.

    D) transcription.

    E) polymerization.

Answer: D
Diff: 2   Page Ref: 10.2
Skill: Factual

18) The function of the promoter is

    A) to signal the RNA polymerase where to start transcribing the DNA.

    B) to signal the RNA polymerase which strand of the DNA to read.

    C) to signal the RNA polymerase where to stop transcribing the DNA.

    D) A and B

    E) A, B and C

Answer: D
Diff: 2   Page Ref: 10.2
Skill: Factual

19) Which of the following molecules functions to transfer information from the nucleus to the cytoplasm?

    A) DNA   B) mRNA   C) tRNA   D) proteins   E) lipids

Answer: B
Diff: 2   Page Ref: 10.2
Skill: Factual

20) Transcription is the process of

    A) synthesizing a DNA molecule from an RNA template.

    B) assembling an RNA molecule without a template.

    C) synthesizing an RNA molecule using a DNA template.

    D) synthesizing a protein using information from a mRNA.

    E) replicating a single-stranded DNA molecule.

Answer: C
Diff: 2   Page Ref: 10.2
Skill: Factual

21) A transcription start signal is called

    A) an initiation codon.

    B) a promoter.

    C) an origin.

    D) a start site.

    E) a nonsense codon.

Answer: B
Diff: 1   Page Ref: 10.2
Skill: Factual

22) Uracil pairs with

    A) thymine.   B) adenine.   C) guanine.   D) cytosine.   E) uracil.

Answer: B
Diff: 2   Page Ref: 10.2
Skill: Factual

23) What mRNA carries from the nucleus is

    A) enzymes.

    B) ribosomes.

    C) information.

    D) amino acids.

    E) tRNA.

Answer: C
Diff: 2   Page Ref: 10.2
Skill: Factual

24) RNA can be distinguished from DNA because RNA

    A) has one polynucleotide chain per molecule.

    B) has the base uracil.

    C) has the sugar ribose.

    D) All of the above choices are correct.

    E) is never found in the nucleus.

Answer: D
Diff: 2   Page Ref: 10.2
Skill: Conceptual

25) If a tRNA molecule specialized for transfer of the amino acid valine has the anticodon CAG, with what codon will it couple?

    A) GAC   B) GTC   C) TUG   D) GUC   E) CAG

Answer: D
Diff: 2   Page Ref: 10.2
Skill: Conceptual

26) Suppose one strand of a "mini-gene" has the following base sequence:
TACCCGGATTCA
The polypeptide encoded by this gene has how many amino acids?

    A) 2   B) 4   C) 6   D) 12

Answer: B
Diff: 2   Page Ref: 10.2
Skill: Application

27) Suppose one strand of a "mini-gene" has the following base sequence:
TACCCGGATTCA
The *last codon* in the mRNA will be

A) UGA.   B) AGT.   C) AGU.   D) TCA.

Answer: C
Diff: 2   *Page Ref: 10.2*
Skill: Application

28) In a wild-type strain of fruit flies, the size of a gene from the start to the stop codon is 2000 DNA bases. An experiment indicates that the mRNA molecule transcribed from this gene is much smaller than that, only 1200 bases. The most likely explanation is

A) a mutation has caused the formation of a stop codon in the gene.

B) the mRNA has been degraded.

C) there are introns in the DNA that have been spliced out of the mRNA.

D) a long tail has been added to the mRNA.

E) Any of these could explain the size difference.

Answer: C
Diff: 3   *Page Ref: 10.2*
Skill: Conceptual

29) For a eukaryotic chromosome, which of the following is true?

A) RNAs of different genes can be transcribed off either DNA strand, but are always made 5'→3'.

B) RNAs of different genes can be transcribed off either DNA strand, but are always made 3'→5'.

C) RNAs of all genes are synthesized 5'→3' off the same DNA strand.

D) RNAs of all genes are synthesized 3'→5' off the same DNA strand.

E) Different genes can be transcribed off either strand, some in the 5'→3' direction and some in the 3'→5' direction.

Answer: A
Diff: 3   *Page Ref: 10.2*
Skill: Conceptual

30) Messenger RNA is single stranded. True or False?

Answer: TRUE
Diff: 2   *Page Ref: 10.2*
Skill: Factual

31) Each gene is specific for a particular type of protein. True or False?

Answer: TRUE
Diff: 2   *Page Ref: 10.2*
Skill: Factual

32) A codon of mRNA consists of three bases which will code for an amino acid. True or False?

Answer: TRUE
Diff: 2   Page Ref: 10.2
Skill: Factual

33) Give the sequence of bases in mRNA for the DNA sequence of TAGGCTAA.

Answer: AUCCGAUU
Diff: 2   Page Ref: 10.2
Skill: Application

34) Describe the three basic processes involved in transcription.

Answer: Initiation involves RNA polymerase binding to a specific promoter region on the template strand of the DNA molecule. Elongation involves RNA polymerase moving along the DNA template strand and adding the appropriate complementary RNA nucleotides. Termination of the process occurs when the RNA polymerase reaches a termination signal on the DNA template strand, and the new mRNA is released to move onto the cytoplasm.
Diff: 2   Page Ref: 10.2
Skill: Factual

35) The strand of the DNA molecule from which RNA is transcribed is called the _____ strand.

Answer: template
Diff: 2   Page Ref: 10.2
Skill: Factual

36) A part of an mRNA molecule with the following sequence (5'-CCGACG-3') is being translated by a ribosome. The following activated tRNA molecules are available. Two of them can correctly match the mRNA so that a dipeptide can form

tRNA anticodon	Amino acid
GGC	proline
CGU	alanine
UGC	threonine
CCG	glycine
ACG	cysteine
CGG	alanine

The dipeptide that will form will be

A) cysteine–alanine.

B) proline–threonine.

C) glycine–cysteine.

D) alanine–alanine.

E) threonine–glycine.

Answer: B
Diff: 2   Page Ref: 10.3
Skill: Application

37) Which occurs in the nucleus?

A) transcription only

B) assembly of amino acids into protein

C) replication of genetic material

D) transcription and replication of genetic material

E) translation only

Answer: D
Diff: 2   Page Ref: 10.3
Skill: Factual

38) The anticodon for AUC is

A) TAG.   B) AUC.   C) GAU.   D) CUA.   E) UAG.

Answer: E
Diff: 2   Page Ref: 10.3
Skill: Application

39) An anticodon is

    A) 4 consecutive nucleotides in tRNA.

    B) 3 consecutive nucleotides in tRNA.

    C) the beginning of a DNA molecule.

    D) 3 consecutive nucleotides in mRNA.

    E) 3 consecutive amino acids in a protein.

Answer: B
Diff: 2   Page Ref: 10.3
Skill: Factual

40) Transfer RNA

    A) is a nucleic acid that alone codes for the primary structure of a protein.

    B) is made directly from DNA during transcription.

    C) is incorporated into the structure of ribosomes.

    D) is larger in size if the protein to be made is longer in amino acid sequence.

    E) transfers amino acids from proteins to mRNA.

Answer: B
Diff: 2   Page Ref: 10.3
Skill: Factual

41) A type of RNA that binds to a specific amino acid is

    A) messenger RNA.

    B) ribosomal RNA.

    C) transfer RNA.

    D) nuclear RNA.

    E) cytoplasmic RNA.

Answer: C
Diff: 2   Page Ref: 10.3
Skill: Factual

42) The process of converting the "message" of mRNA into a sequence of amino acids is called

    A) translation.

    B) transcription.

    C) activation.

    D) replication.

    E) repression.

Answer: A
Diff: 2   Page Ref: 10.3
Skill: Factual

43) The site of protein synthesis is the

   A) smooth endoplasmic reticulum.

   B) nucleus.

   C) nucleolus.

   D) ribosome.

   E) eukaryotic chromosome.

   Answer: D
   Diff: 2   Page Ref: 10.3
   Skill: Factual

44) Each new amino acid is attached to the growing chain by

   A) an ionic bond.

   B) a physical bond.

   C) hydrogen bonds.

   D) an RNA bond.

   E) a peptide bond.

   Answer: E
   Diff: 2   Page Ref: 10.3
   Skill: Factual

45) All of the following are directly involved in translation EXCEPT

   A) ribosomes.

   B) tRNA.

   C) amino acids.

   D) DNA.

   E) mRNA.

   Answer: D
   Diff: 2   Page Ref: 10.3
   Skill: Factual

46) The manufacture of proteins from RNA and amino acids is

   A) activation.

   B) transformation.

   C) replication.

   D) transcription.

   E) translation.

   Answer: E
   Diff: 2   Page Ref: 10.3
   Skill: Factual

47) Suppose one strand of a "mini-gene" has the following base sequence:
TACCCGGATTCA
The *anticodon* of the tRNA that carries the first amino acid will be

    A) AUG.   B) UAC.   C) UCA.   D) AGU.

Answer: B
Diff: 2   Page Ref: 10.3
Skill: Application

48) A sequence of three RNA bases can function as a(n)

    A) codon.

    B) anticodon.

    C) gene.

    D) A and B

    E) A and C

Answer: D
Diff: 2   Page Ref: 10.3
Skill: Factual

49) Ribosomes are a collection of

    A) small proteins that function in translation.

    B) proteins and small RNAs that function in translation.

    C) proteins and tRNAs that function in transcription.

    D) proteins and mRNAs that function in translation.

    E) mRNAs and tRNAs that function in translation.

Answer: B
Diff: 2   Page Ref: 10.3
Skill: Factual

50) The adapters that allow translation of the four-letter nucleic acid language into the 20-letter protein language are called

    A) transfer RNAs.

    B) ribosomal RNAs.

    C) messenger RNAs.

    D) ribosomes.

    E) all of the above

Answer: A
Diff: 2   Page Ref: 10.3
Skill: Factual

51) A charged tRNA enters the protein–synthesizing machinery at the ribosomes by recognition of its

    A) codon.

    B) anticodon.

    C) charge.

    D) amino acid.

    E) none of the above

Answer: B
Diff: 2   Page Ref: 10.3
Skill: Factual

52) What is the minimum number of tRNA molecules required to produce a 60–amino acid polypeptide made up of only ten different kinds of amino acids?

    A) 15   B) 10   C) 30   D) 60   E) 120

Answer: B
Diff: 2   Page Ref: 10.3
Skill: Conceptual

53) A gene may encode information needed by a cell to produce

    A) enzymes.

    B) structural proteins.

    C) hormones.

    D) RNA.

    E) All the above choices are correct.

Answer: E
Diff: 2   Page Ref: 10.3
Skill: Factual

54) Which of the following attaches to specific amino acids?

    A) ribosomal RNA

    B) DNA

    C) messenger RNA

    D) transfer RNA

    E) RNA polymerase

Answer: D
Diff: 2   Page Ref: 10.3
Skill: Factual

55) Which of the following contains nucleotides but no uracil?

    A) ribosomal RNA

    B) DNA

    C) messenger RNA

    D) transfer RNA

    E) RNA polymerase

Answer: B
Diff: 2   Page Ref: 10.3
Skill: Factual

56) Which of the following has anticodons?

    A) ribosomal RNA

    B) DNA

    C) messenger RNA

    D) transfer RNA

    E) RNA polymerase

Answer: D
Diff: 2   Page Ref: 10.3
Skill: Factual

57) Which of the following is made up of amino acids?

    A) ribosomal RNA

    B) DNA

    C) messenger RNA

    D) transfer RNA

    E) RNA polymerase

Answer: E
Diff: 2   Page Ref: 10.3
Skill: Factual

58) Which of the following reads the codons?

    A) ribosomal RNA

    B) DNA

    C) messenger RNA

    D) transfer RNA

    E) RNA polymerase

Answer: D
Diff: 2   Page Ref: 10.3
Skill: Factual

59) Which of the following contains codons?

A) ribosomal RNA

B) DNA

C) messenger RNA

D) transfer RNA

E) RNA polymerase

Answer: C
Diff: 2   Page Ref: 10.3
Skill: Factual

60) Which of the following has two polynucleotide chains?

A) ribosomal RNA

B) DNA

C) messenger RNA

D) transfer RNA

E) RNA polymerase

Answer: B
Diff: 2   Page Ref: 10.3
Skill: Factual

61) Which of the following has deoxyribose sugar?

A) ribosomal RNA

B) DNA

C) messenger RNA

D) transfer RNA

E) RNA polymerase

Answer: B
Diff: 2   Page Ref: 10.3
Skill: Factual

62) Which of the following makes RNA molecules in the nucleus?

A) ribosomal RNA

B) DNA

C) messenger RNA

D) transfer RNA

E) RNA polymerase

Answer: E
Diff: 2   Page Ref: 10.3
Skill: Factual

63) The site of protein synthesis in the cytoplasm is the ribosome. True or False?

Answer: TRUE
Diff: 1   *Page Ref: 10.3*
Skill: Factual

64) Each ribosome is specific for a particular type of protein. True or False?

Answer: FALSE
Diff: 2   *Page Ref: 10.3*
Skill: Factual

65) tRNA consists of a single strand of RNA. True or False?

Answer: TRUE
Diff: 2   *Page Ref: 10.3*
Skill: Factual

66) Each tRNA molecule is only used once. True or False?

Answer: FALSE
Diff: 2   *Page Ref: 10.3*
Skill: Factual

67) tRNA is necessary for transcription to occur. True or False?

Answer: FALSE
Diff: 2   *Page Ref: 10.3*
Skill: Factual

68) In eukaryotic cells, _____ occurs in the nucleus resulting in the production of mRNA which then travels to the cytoplasm for protein synthesis via _____.

Answer: transcription; translation
Diff: 2   *Page Ref: 10.3*
Skill: Factual

69) The anticodon for AUC is _____.

Answer: UAG
Diff: 2   *Page Ref: 10.3*
Skill: Factual

70) Compare and contrast the three major RNA molecules involved in translation.

> Answer: mRNA, tRNA, and rRNA are all single–stranded RNA molecules transcribed from DNA that serve very distinct roles in the translation process. mRNA carries information from the DNA molecule for the sequence of amino acids for the polypeptide. tRNA carries the amino acids that correspond to specific codon units (on the mRNA)[1]through the use of its anticodon. rRNA molecules are important parts of the subunits of the ribosome, which is the site of translation.
> *Diff: 2   Page Ref: 10.3*
> *Skill: Factual*

71) Briefly describe the three stages of translation.

> Answer: Initiation involves the formation of the ribosome; the small ribosomal subunit, the mRNA, and first tRNA (with the anticodon for AUG[1]carrying the amino acid methionine) join together, and then the large ribosomal subunit joins to complete the initiation process. Elongation occurs as the ribosome moves down the mRNA. Then tRNA molecules with the appropriate anticodons bind the appropriate codons, after which the amino acids carried by the tRNA molecules are linked together into a polypeptide chain. Termination occurs when the ribosome reaches a stop codon; the polypeptide chain is released and the ribosome disassembles.
> *Diff: 2   Page Ref: 10.3*
> *Skill: Factual*

72) A random change in a DNA nucleotide base sequence

>   A) has no influence on genetic variation.
>
>   B) is never expressed phenotypically.
>
>   C) constitutes a mutation.
>
>   D) is never beneficial to the organism.
>
>   E) will kill the cell when it occurs.

> Answer: C
> *Diff: 2   Page Ref: 10.4*
> *Skill: Factual*

73) A gene mutation is defined as change in the

>   A) nucleotide sequence of RNA.
>
>   B) nucleotide sequence of DNA.
>
>   C) amino acid sequence in protein.
>
>   D) activation of a gene.
>
>   E) structure of ribosomes.

> Answer: B
> *Diff: 2   Page Ref: 10.4*
> *Skill: Factual*

74) For a mutation to affect evolution, it must occur in

A) somatic cells.

B) prokaryotic cells.

C) diploid cells.

D) gametes.

E) eukaryotic cells.

Answer: D
Diff: 2   Page Ref: 10.4
Skill: Factual

75) Of the following types of mutations, which is considered the LEAST drastic?

A) insertion of one base

B) deletion of two bases

C) a neutral base substitution

D) a stop codon

E) a substitution of a hydrophilic amino acid for a hydrophobic one

Answer: C
Diff: 2   Page Ref: 10.4
Skill: Conceptual

76) A mutation that results in a change in the codon reading pattern could result from

A) a base insertion only.

B) a base deletion only.

C) a base substitution only.

D) deletion of three consecutive bases.

E) either an insertion or a deletion of a base.

Answer: E
Diff: 2   Page Ref: 10.4
Skill: Conceptual

77) Which point mutation would be most likely to have a catastrophic effect on the functioning of a protein?

   A) a base substitution

   B) a base deletion near the start of the coding sequence

   C) a base deletion near the end of the coding sequence

   D) deletion of three bases near the start of the coding sequence

   E) a base insertion near the end of the coding sequence

Answer: B
Diff: 2   Page Ref: 10.4
Skill: Conceptual

78) What kind of mutation occurs when one base is changed to another at a single location in the DNA?

   A) insertion

   B) deletion

   C) substitution

   D) nonsense

   E) neutral

Answer: C
Diff: 1   Page Ref: 10.4
Skill: Factual

79) How can a gene be mutated with no resulting change in the protein that is produced from that gene?

   A) The mutation is at the active site of the protein.

   B) A codon has changed, but it codes for he same amino acid as the original codon.

   C) An entire codon has been removed.

   D) RNA polymerase can edit the mutation from the mRNA produced during translation.

   E) This is impossible. All mutations, by definition, result in altered proteins.

Answer: B
Diff: 2   Page Ref: 10.4
Skill: Conceptual

80) A "mini-gene" has the following sequence: TACCCGTGCACG
If the T at the beginning of the sequence is deleted, what will be the consequence?

A) All of the codons after that point will be changed.

B) Only the amino acid coded for in that codon will be changed.

C) RNA polymerase will skip that codon, but all the others will be read normally.

D) RNA polymerase will correct the deletion and a normal protein will be produced.

E) The first nucleotide is not important, so there will be no change.

Answer: A
Diff: 2   Page Ref: 10.4
Skill: Application

81) A "mini-gene" has the following sequence: TACCCGTGCACG
Which of the following sequences represents a single base substitution?

A) TACCCGTGCACG

B) TACCCGAGCACG

C) TACCCGGCACG

D) TACCCGTGTCACG

E) TACCGTGCTACG

Answer: B
Diff: 1   Page Ref: 10.4
Skill: Application

82) The normal protein for a gene has exactly 100 amino acids. A mutated version of this gene produces a protein only 20 amino acids long. Furthermore, the sequence of amino acids is the same for the first 6 amino acids, but completely different after that point. What kind(s) of mutation could cause this?

A) The start codon is missing.

B) A neutral mutation in the seventh codon.

C) A base substitution in the twenty first codon changes it to a stop codon.

D) An insertion in the seventh codon.

E) This type of mutation is impossible.

Answer: D
Diff: 3   Page Ref: 10.4
Skill: Application

83) Describe the different types of effects that may result from point mutations in the DNA sequence.

Answer: The protein can be unchanged, equivalent, have altered function, or be destroyed by a stop codon (premature). The student's answer should include all these possibilities, and explain why they have their respective effects.
Diff: 2   Page Ref: 10.4
Skill: Factual

84) A random change in DNA nucleotide base sequence is called a _____.

Answer: mutation
Diff: 2   Page Ref: 10.4
Skill: Factual

85) A mutation in which only one nucleotide in the DNA sequence is changed is referred to as a _____ mutation.

Answer: point
Diff: 2   Page Ref: 10.4
Skill: Factual

86) How does a cell use its DNA to create the cell itself?

A) by controlling the environment outside the cell

B) by controlling the production of more DNA

C) by controlling the replication of mitochondria and chloroplasts

D) by controlling the production of cellular proteins

E) Both choices B and D are correct.

Answer: D
Diff: 2   Page Ref: 10.5
Skill: Factual

87) Gene expression is

A) how genes are passed from parent to offspring.

B) the unique set of genes in an individual.

C) the banding pattern seen on a chromosome.

D) the flow of genetic information from genes to proteins.

E) the same as replication.

Answer: D
Diff: 1   Page Ref: 10.5
Skill: Factual

88) Which of the following is TRUE about gene expression?

A) Gene expression remains constant throughout an organism's life span.

B) Different individuals of the same species express all the same genes.

C) Gene expression is not influenced by the environment.

D) Different tissues within an organism express different genes.

E) All of the above statements are false.

Answer: D
Diff: 2   Page Ref: 10.5
Skill: Factual

89) Which of the following is NOT a means of regulating gene expression?

A) regulating the life span of a protein

B) modifying proteins after they are synthesized

C) varying the rate at which messenger RNAs are translated

D) varying the rate at which messenger RNAs are transcribed

E) deleting genes from cells in which they are not needed

Answer: E
Diff: 2   Page Ref: 10.5
Skill: Factual

90) At what level(s) can transcription be regulated in eukaryotic cells?

A) individual genes

B) regions of chromosomes

C) entire chromosomes

D) All of the above are correct.

E) None of the above are correct.

Answer: D
Diff: 2   Page Ref: 10.5
Skill: Factual

91) Calico cats are almost always female. This is because of

A) X–chromosome inactivation.

B) the lack of a Y chromosome in females.

C) activation of the calico gene by the female sex hormone estrogen.

D) the calico gene in males is inactivated by the sex hormone testosterone.

E) a mutation found on the X chromosome.

Answer: A
Diff: 3   Page Ref: 10.5
Skill: Conceptual

92) What is a likely function of condensed regions of chromosomes?

    A) to enhance transcription of the genes in the condensed region

    B) to render the genes in the condensed region inaccessible to RNA polymerase

    C) These regions can be structural and contain no genes.

    D) Both B and C are correct.

    E) None of the above are correct.

Answer: D
Diff: 2   Page Ref: 10.5
Skill: Conceptual

93) How can a single gene code for more than one protein?

    A) Different RNA polymerases transcribe it and produce different proteins.

    B) Different types of ribosomes translate the resulting mRNA, producing different proteins.

    C) Different introns can be removed to produce different proteins.

    D) The exons within a mRNA can be spliced together in different ways.

    E) None of the above are correct.

Answer: D
Diff: 2   Page Ref: 10.5
Skill: Conceptual

94) Your tongue does not grow hair because

    A) different genes are expressed in different tissues.

    B) skin cells have extra DNA that codes for hair proteins.

    C) the genes for hair proteins have been deleted from the cells of your tongue.

    D) saliva prevents hair from growing.

    E) None of the above are correct.

Answer: A
Diff: 2   Page Ref: 10.5
Skill: Conceptual

95) Steroid hormones have the ability to regulate transcription. True or False?

Answer: TRUE
Diff: 1   Page Ref: 10.5
Skill: Factual

96) Highly condensed and compact regions of DNA are more easily transcribed than the decondensed regions. True or False?

Answer: FALSE
Diff: 2   Page Ref: 10.5
Skill: Factual

97) The Barr body is the X chromosome in the cell chosen to be expressed while the other X chromosome is inactivated. True or False?

Answer: FALSE
Diff: 2   Page Ref: 10.5
Skill: Factual

98) In females an entire X chromosome is inactivated in each cell. The inactivated X chromosome is called the _____.

Answer: Barr body
Diff: 2   Page Ref: 10.5
Skill: Factual

99) Discuss five main strategies a typical eukaryotic cell might use to regulate gene expression.

Answer: Student should mention transcription rate regulation, alternative splicing, mRNA stability, protein modification after translation, and protein stability.
Diff: 2   Page Ref: 10.5
Skill: Factual

100) The production of proteins by a cell surprisingly requires very little energy. True or False?

Answer: FALSE
Diff: 2   Page Ref: A Closer Look
Skill: Factual

Chapter 11 The Continuity of Life: Cellular Reproduction

1) The genetic material in bacteria consists of

    A) several circular DNA molecules.

    B) one circular RNA molecule.

    C) many rod–like DNA molecules with protein.

    D) one circular DNA molecule.

    E) DNA in mitochondria.

Answer: D
Diff: 2   Page Ref: 11.1
Skill: Factual

2) A bacterial cell splits into two new cells by

    A) duplication.

    B) forming a cell plate.

    C) forming a cell furrow.

    D) mitosis.

    E) fission.

Answer: E
Diff: 2   Page Ref: 11.1
Skill: Factual

3) The daughter cells of binary fission are

    A) structurally identical.

    B) chromosomally different.

    C) genetically identical.

    D) structurally identical and genetically identical.

    E) not genetically the same as the parent cell.

Answer: C
Diff: 2   Page Ref: 11.1
Skill: Factual

4) Which of the following organisms does NOT reproduce cells by mitosis and cytokinesis?

    A) cow

    B) bacterium

    C) mushroom

    D) cockroach

    E) banana tree

Answer: B
Diff: 2   Page Ref: 11.1
Skill: Conceptual

5) During the "S" portion of interphase, what is the cell doing?

    A) resting

    B) general cell metabolism

    C) synthesizing DNA

    D) making a spindle

    E) undergoing differentiation

Answer: C
Diff: 2   Page Ref: 11.1
Skill: Factual

6) When does chromosome replication occur in a eukaryotic cell?

    A) prophase

    B) metaphase

    C) anaphase

    D) interphase

    E) telophase

Answer: D
Diff: 2   Page Ref: 11.1
Skill: Factual

7) The longest period of a cell's life cycle is

    A) prophase.

    B) telophase.

    C) interphase.

    D) anaphase.

    E) metaphase.

Answer: C
Diff: 2   Page Ref: 11.1
Skill: Factual

8) Which of the following does NOT take place during the G_1 or G_2 phases of the cell cycle?

    A) synthesis of ATP

    B) growth of the cell

    C) cellular respiration

    D) enzyme activity

    E) replication of DNA

Answer: E
Diff: 2   Page Ref: 11.1
Skill: Conceptual

9) When are spindle proteins made?

    A) G1

    B) S

    C) G2

    D) cytokinesis

    E) all of the above

Answer: C
Diff: 2   Page Ref: 11.1
Skill: Factual

10) When does DNA synthesis occur?

    A) G1

    B) S

    C) G2

    D) cytokinesis

    E) all of the above

Answer: A
Diff: 2   Page Ref: 11.1
Skill: Factual

11) When does general cell metabolism occur?

    A) G1

    B) S

    C) G2

    D) cytokinesis

    E) all of the above

Answer: E
Diff: 2   Page Ref: 11.1
Skill: Factual

12) How are binary fission and mitosis both examples of asexual reproduction?

Answer: Offspring cells are formed from a single parent with the uniting of male and female gametes.
Diff: 2   Page Ref: 11.1
Skill: Conceptual

13) The production of cells that are genetically similar to the parents occurs through the process of _____.

Answer: asexual reproduction
Diff: 2   Page Ref: 11.1
Skill: Conceptual

14) Eggs and sperms cells are examples of _____ produced via the process of meiotic cell division.

Answer: gametes
Diff: 2   Page Ref: 11.1
Skill: Factual

15) Describe the main stages of the eukaryotic cell cycle.

Answer: G_1—growth, decision to divide; S—DNA replication; G_2—growth; mitosis—nuclear division; and cytokinesis—division of the cell
Diff: 2   Page Ref: 11.1
Skill: Factual

16) During which stages of the cell cycle will chromosomes be composed of two attached chromatids?

Answer: From the G_2 of interphase through metaphase[1]separation occurs at the start of anaphase.
Diff: 2   Page Ref: 11.1
Skill: Conceptual

17) Diploid cells of the fruit fly *Drosophila* have 8 chromosomes. How many chromosomes does a *Drosophila* gamete have?

   A) one   B) two   C) four   D) eight   E) sixteen

Answer: C
Diff: 2   Page Ref: 11.2
Skill: Conceptual

18) Human body cell nuclei contain

   A) 46 pairs of chromosomes.

   B) 44 pairs of chromosomes.

   C) 23 unpaired chromosomes.

   D) 22 pairs of chromosomes.

   E) 23 pairs of chromosomes.

   Answer: E
   Diff: 2   Page Ref: 11.2
   Skill: Factual

19) A eukaryotic chromosome is made up of

   A) DNA only.

   B) protein and nucleic acid.

   C) ventromeres and centrioles.

   D) loops of naked DNA.

   E) DNA and RNA only.

   Answer: B
   Diff: 2   Page Ref: 11.2
   Skill: Factual

20) The cells of the intestinal epithelium are continually dividing, replacing dead cells lost from the surface of the intestinal lining. If you examined a population of intestinal epithelial cells under the microscope, most of the cells would

   A) be in meiosis.

   B) be in mitosis.

   C) be in interphase.

   D) have condensed chromosomes.

   E) B and D

   Answer: C
   Diff: 2   Page Ref: 11.2
   Skill: Conceptual

21) Cell reproduction in prokaryotic cells differs from eukaryotic cells in that

    A) prokaryotic cells reproduce asexually but eukaryotic cells do not.

    B) each prokaryotic cell has a circular chromosome but the chromosomes of eukaryotic cells are linear.

    C) prokaryotic cells lack nuclei and do not replicate their DNA before dividing but eukaryotic cells have nuclei and replicate their DNA before dividing.

    D) prokaryotic chromosomes have DNA and protein but eukaryotic chromosomes are made of only DNA.

    E) They do not differ significantly in any way.

Answer: B
Diff: 2   Page Ref: 11.2
Skill: Conceptual

22) If there are 12 chromosomes in an animal cell in the G_1 stage of the cell cycle, what is the diploid number of chromosomes for this organism?

    A) 6   B) 12   C) 24   D) 36   E) 48

Answer: B
Diff: 2   Page Ref: 11.2
Skill: Application

23) If a normal diploid cell has eight chromosomes, then

    A) there are eight homologous pairs of chromosomes per diploid cell.

    B) there are eight chromatids per diploid cell between S phase and mitosis of the cell cycle.

    C) there are four chromosomes per cell after meiosis.

    D) sperm cells made from this cell would have eight chromosomes.

    E) None of these are correct.

Answer: C
Diff: 3   Page Ref: 11.2
Skill: Application

24) Homologous pairs of chromosomes

    A) consist of two chromosomes the same size and with the same genes.

    B) consist of two chromosomes having identical alleles.

    C) consist of two chromosomes that came from one parent.

    D) are found in sperm and eggs.

    E) are found in haploid cells.

Answer: A
Diff: 2   Page Ref: 11.2
Skill: Conceptual

25) The pea has a haploid number of seven chromosomes; the diploid number would be _____.

Answer: 14
Diff: 2   Page Ref: 11.2
Skill: Conceptual

26) What does the term diploid mean?

Answer: Cells contain two types of each chromosome (homologues) one from each gamete —the exception being the sex chromosomes.
Diff: 2   Page Ref: 11.2
Skill: Conceptual

27) When a DNA molecule doubles during the S phase of the cell cycle, a chromosome is then comprised of two joined _____.

Answer: sister chromatids
Diff: 2   Page Ref: 11.2
Skill: Factual

28) Which of these sequences correctly describes the cell cycle?

A) $G_1 \rightarrow G_2 \rightarrow S \rightarrow$ prophase $\rightarrow$ metaphase $\rightarrow$ anaphase $\rightarrow$ telophase

B) $S \rightarrow G_2 \rightarrow$ prophase $\rightarrow$ metaphase $\rightarrow$ anaphase $\rightarrow$ telophase $\rightarrow G_1$

C) $G_1 \rightarrow S \rightarrow G_2 \rightarrow$ prophase $\rightarrow$ anaphase $\rightarrow$ metaphase $\rightarrow$ telophase

D) prophase $\rightarrow$ metaphase $\rightarrow$ telophase $\rightarrow$ anaphase $\rightarrow G_1 \rightarrow S \rightarrow G_2$

E) $G_1 \rightarrow S \rightarrow G_2 \rightarrow$ metaphase $\rightarrow$ prophase $\rightarrow$ anaphase $\rightarrow$ telophase

Answer: B
Diff: 2   Page Ref: 11.3
Skill: Conceptual

29) A cell is cleaved into two approximately equal halves, each with about the same amount of cytoplasm, during

A) G_2 phase.

B) cytophase.

C) cytokinesis.

D) spindle apparatus formation.

E) interphase.

Answer: C
Diff: 2   Page Ref: 11.3
Skill: Factual

30) During mitotic anaphase, chromatids migrate

A) from the poles of the cell toward the metaphase plate.

B) from the metaphase plate toward the poles.

C) toward the nuclear envelope.

D) along with their sister chromatids toward one pole.

E) along with the other member of the homologous pair toward the metaphase plate.

Answer: B
Diff: 2   Page Ref: 11.3
Skill: Factual

31) The microtubules of the mitotic spindle attach to a specialized structure in the centromere region of each chromosome, called the

A) kinetochore.

B) nucleosomes.

C) equatorial plate.

D) nucleotide.

E) centrosome.

Answer: A
Diff: 2   Page Ref: 11.3
Skill: Factual

32) How do daughter cells at the end of mitosis and cytokinesis compare with their parent cell when it was in G_1 of the cell cycle?

A) The daughter cells have half the amount of cytoplasm and half the amount of DNA.

B) The daughter cells have half the number of chromosomes and half the amount of DNA.

C) The daughter cells have the same number of chromosomes and half the amount of DNA.

D) The daughter cells have the same number of chromosomes and the same amount of DNA.

E) The daughter cells may have new combinations of genes due to crossing over.

Answer: D
Diff: 2   Page Ref: 11.3
Skill: Conceptual

33) The formation of a cell plate is beginning across the middle of a cell and nuclei are reforming at opposite ends of a cell. What kind of a cell is this?

A) an animal cell in metaphase

B) an animal cell in telophase

C) an animal cell undergoing cytokinesis

D) a plant cell in metaphase

E) a plant cell undergoing cytokinesis

Answer: E
Diff: 2   Page Ref: 11.3
Skill: Conceptual

34) Cell division usually occurs as two events, namely

A) interphase and mitosis.

B) mitosis and cytokinesis.

C) nuclear division and chromosomal division.

D) interphase and cytoplasmic division.

E) interphase and cytokinesis.

Answer: B
Diff: 2   Page Ref: 11.3
Skill: Factual

35) Cells that result from mitosis have identical

A) kinds of proteins.

B) numbers of proteins.

C) genetic information.

D) kinds and numbers of proteins.

E) numbers of mitochondria.

Answer: C
Diff: 2   Page Ref: 11.3
Skill: Factual

36) Sister chromatids are

    A) duplicate chromosomes held together by a common centromere.

    B) specialized gamete-forming cells.

    C) non-functional chromosomes.

    D) homologous pairs of chromosomes.

    E) different in their genetic content.

Answer: A
Diff: 2   *Page Ref: 11.3*
Skill: Factual

37) Mitosis in humans usually results in the formation of

    A) 2 diploid cells.

    B) 4 diploid cells.

    C) 2 haploid cells.

    D) 4 haploid cells.

    E) sperm or egg cells.

Answer: A
Diff: 2   *Page Ref: 11.3*
Skill: Factual

38) During which stage of mitosis do chromosomes line up at the equator of the spindle apparatus?

    A) prophase

    B) metaphase

    C) anaphase

    D) telophase

    E) The chromosomes do not line up at all.

Answer: B
Diff: 2   *Page Ref: 11.3*
Skill: Factual

39) Which of the following does NOT occur during prophase?

   A) The nuclear membrane disintegrates.

   B) Nucleoli break up.

   C) The spindle apparatus forms.

   D) The chromosomes condense.

   E) DNA replicates.

   Answer: E
   Diff: 2   Page Ref: 11.3
   Skill: Conceptual

40) During which stage of mitosis do sister chromatids move away from each other?

   A) prophase

   B) metaphase

   C) anaphase

   D) telophase

   E) They do not move away from each other at all.

   Answer: C
   Diff: 2   Page Ref: 11.3
   Skill: Factual

41) Cytokinesis is evident in animal cells when

   A) constriction occurs around the equator.

   B) chromosomes are observable.

   C) cell plate formation occurs.

   D) a spindle apparatus forms.

   E) prophase begins.

   Answer: A
   Diff: 2   Page Ref: 11.3
   Skill: Factual

42) Cell plate formation is accomplished by

   A) endoplasmic reticulum.

   B) spindle fibers.

   C) cytoskeleton.

   D) Golgi complex.

   E) mitochondria.

   Answer: D
   Diff: 2   Page Ref: 11.3
   Skill: Conceptual

43) Suppose a slide containing 100 cells is made from a random sample of cells growing in a petri plate. The average time for a complete cell cycle to occur in the petri plate is 24 hours. Ten cells on the slide are in prophase, three are in metaphase, six in anaphase, eight in telophase, and 73 are in interphase. How many hours, on average, does a cell in the petri plate spend in interphase?

  A) 73 hours

  B) 24 hours

  C) 17.5 hours

  D) 6.5 hours

  E) One cannot tell from the information given.

Answer: C
Diff: 3   Page Ref: 11.3
Skill: Application

44) All of the following are characteristics of telophase of mitosis, EXCEPT

  A) cytokinesis begins.

  B) each chromosome is made of two chromatids.

  C) the nuclear membrane reappears.

  D) chromosomes begin to uncoil.

  E) microtubules disappear.

Answer: B
Diff: 2   Page Ref: 11.3
Skill: Conceptual

45) If there are 20 centromeres in a cell, how many chromosomes are there?

  A) 10   B) 20   C) 30   D) 40   E) 50

Answer: B
Diff: 2   Page Ref: 11.3
Skill: Application

46) In general, the division of the cell, called _____, follows immediately upon mitosis.

Answer: cytokinesis
Diff: 2   Page Ref: 11.3
Skill: Factual

47) If cells in the process of dividing are subjected to colchicine, a drug that interferes with the functioning of the spindle apparatus (such that the spindle is unable to attach to the sister chromatids), at which stage will mitosis be arrested?

Answer: The cells will be arrested in prophase.
Diff: 2   Page Ref: 11.3
Skill: Application

48) A cell containing 92 chromatids at the start of mitosis would, at its completion, produce cells with _____ chromosomes.

Answer: 46
Diff: 2   *Page Ref: 11.3*
Skill: Conceptual

49) Vinblastine is a drug that interferes with the assembly of microtubules. It is widely used for chemotherapy in treating cancer patients whose cancer cells are actively dividing to form tumors. Suggest a hypothesis to explain how vinblastine slows tumor growth.

Answer: Blocks mitosis and the cells cannot divide slowing the growth of the tumor.
Diff: 2   *Page Ref: 11.3*
Skill: Application

50) Checkpoint proteins

A) normally cause cells to grow.

B) normally stop cells from growing.

C) normally prevent cells from repairing DNA damage.

D) normally cause mutations in DNA.

Answer: B
Diff: 2   *Page Ref: 11.4*
Skill: Conceptual

51) Cyclin proteins

A) can bind to CDK proteins.

B) can activate CDK proteins.

C) are made at constant levels throughout the cell cycle.

D) A and B

E) A, B and C

Answer: D
Diff: 2   *Page Ref: 11.4*
Skill: Factual

52) Sexual reproduction by necessity involves which two processes?

A) meiosis and fertilization

B) mutation and translocation

C) nondisjunction and pleiotropy

D) mitosis and fertilization

E) differentiation and specialization

Answer: A
Diff: 2   *Page Ref: 11.5*
Skill: Conceptual

53) During asexual reproduction, the genetic material of the parent is passed on to the offspring by

    A) homologous pairing.

    B) meiosis and fertilization.

    C) mitosis and cytokinesis.

    D) meiosis and cytokinesis.

    E) going to G_0 in the cell cycle.

Answer: C
Diff: 2   *Page Ref: 11.1, 11.5*
Skill: Conceptual

54) Asexual reproduction produces genetically identical individuals because

    A) chromosomes do not have to replicate.

    B) it involves chromosome replication without cytokinesis.

    C) no meiosis or fertilization takes place.

    D) the only cell division that occurs is meiosis.

    E) cytokinesis occurs prior to mitosis.

Answer: C
Diff: 2   *Page Ref: 11.1, 11.5*
Skill: Conceptual

55) Meiosis can occur

    A) in all organisms.

    B) only in diploid organisms.

    C) only in multicellular organisms.

    D) only in haploid organisms.

    E) only in unicellular organisms.

Answer: B
Diff: 2   *Page Ref: 11.5*
Skill: Conceptual

56) Suppose you have two kinds of koi fish in your koi pond: solid gold fish with normal short tails, and calico-colored fish with long, droopy tails. How would you proceed if you wanted to produce solid gold koi with long, droopy tails?

A) Interbreed the gold koi fish among themselves, hoping that a mutation for droopy tails would arise.

B) Breed gold koi fish with calico ones until some gold-colored offspring with droopy tails appear.

C) Breed the calico, droopy-tailed koi among themselves, hoping that a mutation for gold koi with droopy tails would appear.

D) Breed both types of koi with white, normal-tailed koi until the desired traits appear in the offspring.

E) It would be impossible to have a koi with gold color and a droopy tail.

Answer: B
Diff: 3   Page Ref: 11.5
Skill: Conceptual

57) Which of the following is a consequence of sexual reproduction, as compared to asexual reproduction?

A) The offspring will be very similar to each other.

B) There will be few offspring with undesirable traits.

C) There will be more genetic diversity among the offspring.

D) The offspring will have a diploid chromosome number twice that of their parents.

E) There will be fewer mutations.

Answer: C
Diff: 2   Page Ref: 11.1, 11.5
Skill: Conceptual

58) Which of the following is an advantage of sexual reproduction?

A) increased number of beneficial mutations

B) rapid production of genetically identical offspring

C) elimination of most harmful genes

D) decreased genetic variability

E) reshuffling of genes combines different alleles in beneficial ways

Answer: E
Diff: 2   Page Ref: 11.5
Skill: Factual

59) Which of the following is probably TRUE of the first eukaryotic cells to evolve?

   A) They were diploid, but soon lost half their chromosomes to become haploid.

   B) They were diploid and unable to divide by normal mitosis.

   C) They were haploid and able to undergo meiosis.

   D) They were haploid, but soon two of these haploid cells fused to form a diploid cell.

   E) They were neither haploid nor diploid, since these terms have no meaning for such primitive eukaryotic cells.

Answer: D
Diff: 2   Page Ref: 11.5
Skill: Factual

60) Which of the following is a haploid?

   A) zygote

   B) gamete (sex cell)

   C) muscle cell

   D) embryo

   E) brain cell

Answer: B
Diff: 2   Page Ref: 11.5
Skill: Conceptual

61) In sexually reproducing organisms, the source of chromosomes in the offspring is

   A) almost all from one parent, usually the father.

   B) almost all from one parent, usually the mother.

   C) half from the father and half from the mother.

   D) the X comes from the mother and the autosomes come from the father.

   E) a random mixing of chromosomes from both parents.

Answer: C
Diff: 2   Page Ref: 11.5
Skill: Factual

62) Genetically diverse offspring result from

   A) mitosis.

   B) cloning.

   C) sexual reproduction.

   D) cytokinesis.

   E) anaphase.

Answer: C
Diff: 2   Page Ref: 11.5
Skill: Conceptual

63) If a liver cell of an animal has 24 chromosomes, then the sperm cells of this animal would also have 24 chromosomes. True or False?

Answer: FALSE
Diff: 2   Page Ref: 11.5
Skill: Conceptual

64) Which does NOT happen during meiosis?

   A) independent assortment

   B) production of diploid cells

   C) synapsis

   D) crossing-over

   E) segregation

Answer: B
Diff: 2   Page Ref: 11.6
Skill: Conceptual

65) Gametes differ from body cells in

   A) having only one member of each pair of homologous chromosomes.

   B) being haploid.

   C) functioning in sexual reproduction.

   D) having half the amount of genetic material.

   E) All the above choices are correct.

Answer: E
Diff: 2   Page Ref: 11.6
Skill: Conceptual

66) All of the following take place during meiosis EXCEPT

    A) two S phases of interphase.

    B) crossing over.

    C) reduction of chromosome number from 2n to 1n.

    D) segregation of homologous chromosomes.

    E) pairing of similar chromosomes during Prophase I.

Answer: A
Diff: 2   *Page Ref: 11.6*
Skill: Factual

67) Meiosis

    A) occurs in most somatic cells of animals.

    B) produces spores or gametes, depending on the organism.

    C) produces diploid cells.

    D) occurs during the S phase of the cell cycle.

    E) occurs in animals but not in plants.

Answer: B
Diff: 2   *Page Ref: 11.6*
Skill: Conceptual

68) Meiosis

    A) is a purely random division of chromosomes.

    B) doubles the number of chromosomes.

    C) reduces the number of chromosomes by half.

    D) does not change the number of chromosomes.

    E) allows chromosomes to split in half.

Answer: C
Diff: 2   *Page Ref: 11.6*
Skill: Conceptual

69) Meiosis results in the production of

    A) diploid cells with unpaired chromosomes.

    B) diploid cells with paired chromosomes.

    C) haploid cells with unpaired chromosomes.

    D) haploid cells with paired chromosomes.

    E) None of the above choices is correct.

Answer: C
Diff: 2   *Page Ref: 11.6*
Skill: Factual

70) During anaphase of meiosis I, what segregates?

    A) sister chromatids

    B) the spindle

    C) homologous chromosomes

    D) non-allelic genes

    E) the nucleolus

Answer: C
Diff: 2   *Page Ref: 11.6*
Skill: Factual

71) Reciprocal exchange of genetic material between similar chromosomes is called

    A) synapsis.

    B) segregation.

    C) tetrad formation.

    D) meiosis.

    E) crossing-over.

Answer: E
Diff: 2   *Page Ref: 11.6*
Skill: Factual

72) The earliest event of meiosis among those listed is

    A) chromosomes move to the equator of the spindle.

    B) chromatids separate and migrate to opposite poles.

    C) crossing over occurs.

    D) homologous chromosomes pair up along their lengths.

    E) segregation occurs.

Answer: D
Diff: 2   *Page Ref: 11.6*
Skill: Conceptual

73) Chromosomes exchange genetic material by

    A) segregation.

    B) mitosis.

    C) synapsis.

    D) fertilization.

    E) crossing over.

Answer: E
Diff: 2   *Page Ref: 11.6*
Skill: Factual

74) Between the two divisions of meiosis there is

   A) crossing–over.

   B) a pairing of homologous chromosomes.

   C) replication of selected genes.

   D) segregation and independent assortment of chromosomes.

   E) no chromosome replication.

Answer: E
Diff: 2   Page Ref: 11.6
Skill: Factual

75) The products of meiosis are

   A) one nucleus containing twice as much DNA as the parent nucleus.

   B) two genetically identical cells.

   C) four nuclei containing half as much DNA as the parent nucleus.

   D) four genetically identical nuclei.

   E) two genetically identical nuclei.

Answer: C
Diff: 2   Page Ref: 11.6
Skill: Conceptual

76) The four haploid nuclei found at the end of meiosis differ from one another in their exact genetic composition. Some of this difference is the result of

   A) cytokinesis.

   B) DNA replication.

   C) sister chromatid separation.

   D) spindle formation.

   E) crossing over.

Answer: E
Diff: 2   Page Ref: 11.6
Skill: Conceptual

77) Chromosome number is reduced during meiosis because the process consists of

    A) two cell divisions without any chromosome replication.

    B) a single cell division without any chromosome replication.

    C) two cell divisions in which half of the chromosomes are destroyed.

    D) two cell divisions and only a single round of chromosome replication.

    E) four cell divisions with no chromosome replication.

Answer: D
Diff: 2   Page Ref: 11.6
Skill: Factual

78) Just after telophase I, each cell contains

    A) one full set of chromosomes, each with two chromatids.

    B) two full sets of chromosomes, each with two chromatids.

    C) one full set of chromosomes, each with a single chromatid.

    D) two full sets of chromosomes, each with a single chromatid.

    E) None of the above choices is correct.

Answer: A
Diff: 2   Page Ref: 11.6
Skill: Factual

79) A diploid cell contains 6 chromosomes. After meiosis I, each of the cells contains

    A) 3 maternal and 3 paternal chromosomes each time.

    B) a mixture of maternal and paternal chromosomes totaling 3.

    C) 6 maternal and 6 paternal chromosomes each time.

    D) a mixture of maternal and paternal chromosomes totaling 6.

    E) 3 pairs of chromosomes.

Answer: B
Diff: 2   Page Ref: 11.6
Skill: Application

80) An organism has a diploid chromosome number of 10. A cell, from this organism, in metaphase I of meiosis has

   A) 10 pairs of chromosomes.

   B) 20 chromosomes.

   C) 10 chromatids.

   D) 5 chromosomes.

   E) 10 chromosomes.

Answer: E
Diff: 2   Page Ref: 11.6
Skill: Application

81) Homologous chromosomes pair up (synapsis) during

   A) mitosis.

   B) meiosis I.

   C) meiosis II.

   D) mitosis and meiosis II.

   E) protein synthesis.

Answer: B
Diff: 2   Page Ref: 11.6
Skill: Factual

82) The chromosome number is reduced from diploid to haploid during

   A) mitosis.

   B) meiosis I.

   C) meiosis II.

   D) interphase.

   E) S phase of mitosis.

Answer: B
Diff: 3   Page Ref: 11.6
Skill: Factual

83) Which occurs in meiosis I but NOT in meiosis II?

    A) Diploid daughter cells are produced.

    B) Chromosomes without chromatids line up at the equator.

    C) Centromeres divide.

    D) Synapsis of homologous chromosomes occurs.

    E) The spindle apparatus forms.

Answer: D
Diff: 2   Page Ref: 11.6
Skill: Conceptual

84) An exchange of corresponding DNA segments occurs during

    A) prophase.

    B) anaphase II.

    C) prophase II.

    D) anaphase I.

    E) prophase I.

Answer: E
Diff: 2   Page Ref: 11.6
Skill: Factual

85) Chromosomes of a homologous pair separate from each other during

    A) anaphase I.

    B) anaphase II.

    C) metaphase I.

    D) prophase II.

    E) metaphase II.

Answer: A
Diff: 2   Page Ref: 11.6
Skill: Factual

86) The two cells at the end of meiosis I

    A) rarely continue into meiosis II.

    B) function as gametes.

    C) are diploid.

    D) are haploid.

    E) can continue as body cells.

Answer: D
Diff: 2   Page Ref: 11.6
Skill: Factual

87) At the end of telophase II, each of the four resulting cells has

    A) one full set of chromosomes, each with two chromatids.

    B) two full sets of chromosomes, each with two chromatids.

    C) one full set of chromosomes, each with a single chromatid.

    D) two full sets of chromosomes, each with a single chromatid.

    E) the same genetic constitution as the body cells that produced it.

Answer: C
Diff: 2   Page Ref: 11.6
Skill: Conceptual

88) The second meiotic division causes which of the following?

    A) $2n \rightarrow 1n$

    B) $1n \rightarrow 1n$

    C) $2n \rightarrow 2n$

    D) $1n \rightarrow 2n$

    E) None of the above choices is correct.

Answer: B
Diff: 2   Page Ref: 11.6
Skill: Conceptual

89) Centromeres split during

    A) anaphase I and anaphase II of meiosis.

    B) anaphase of mitosis and anaphase I of meiosis.

    C) anaphase of mitosis and anaphase II of meiosis.

    D) the S portion of interphase.

    E) cytokinesis of mitosis and meiosis II.

Answer: C
Diff: 2   Page Ref: 11.6
Skill: Factual

90) Which occurs during meiosis II but NOT meiosis I?

    A) independent assortment of chromosomes

    B) centromeres divide

    C) diploid number reduced to haploid number

    D) crossing–over

    E) All of the above choices are correct.

Answer: B
Diff: 2   Page Ref: 11.6
Skill: Factual

91) The main function of meiosis II is

 A) separate sister chromatids during anaphase.

 B) reduce the number of gametes by half.

 C) reduce the number of chromosomes by half.

 D) increase genetic variability by crossing over.

 E) to allow homologous chromosomes to pair up.

Answer: A
Diff: 2   *Page Ref: 11.6*
Skill: Factual

92) Sister chromatids move away from each other during

 A) anaphase I.

 B) cytokinesis.

 C) metaphase II.

 D) telophase II.

 E) anaphase II.

Answer: E
Diff: 2   *Page Ref: 11.6*
Skill: Factual

93) Each sperm cell of a horse contains 32 chromosomes. How many chromosomes are there in each of the horse's body cells?

 A) 16

 B) 32

 C) 16 pairs

 D) 64

 E) either 16 or 64, depending on the cell type

Answer: D
Diff: 2   *Page Ref: 11.6*
Skill: Conceptual

94) If there are 12 chromosomes in a cell that has just completed meiosis II, what is the diploid number of chromosomes for that organism?

A) 6

B) 12

C) 24

D) 24 pairs

E) either 6 or 24, depending on the cell type

Answer: C
Diff: 2   Page Ref: 11.6
Skill: Conceptual

95) Haploid cells

A) can result from meiosis.

B) have one member of each pair of homologous chromosomes.

C) function as gametes or spores in sexually reproducing organisms.

D) cannot be produced by mitosis.

E) Both choices A and C are correct.

Answer: E
Diff: 2   Page Ref: 11.6
Skill: Conceptual

96) Which of the following statements is FALSE?

A) Meiosis separates homologous chromosomes in a diploid cell to produce haploid daughter cells containing one copy of each type of chromosome.

B) During prophase I, homologous chromosomes pair up and exchange DNA.

C) During meiosis II, paired homologous chromosomes move up to the equator of the cell.

D) During anaphase I, homologous chromosomes separate.

E) In meiosis II, the sister chromatids of each chromosome separate.

Answer: C
Diff: 2   Page Ref: 11.6
Skill: Conceptual

97) Which of the following occurs in mitosis but NOT in meiosis?

A) Cells genetically identical to parents are made.

B) centrioles divide

C) crossing over

D) independent assortment of chromosomes

E) pairing up of similar chromosomes during prophase

Answer: A
Diff: 2   Page Ref: 11.3, 11.6
Skill: Conceptual

98) Meiosis reduces the chromosome number by

A) discarding some of the chromosomes.

B) reducing the length of each chromosome by half.

C) duplicating DNA once, followed by two cell divisions.

D) independent assortment of chromosomes during meiosis I.

E) the formation of polar bodies.

Answer: C
Diff: 2   Page Ref: 11.6
Skill: Factual

99) Organisms with haploid life cycles do not normally undergo meiosis. True or False?

Answer: TRUE
Diff: 2   Page Ref: 11.7
Skill: Factual

100) Plants usually have life cycles that include both multicellular diploid and haploid stages. True or False?

Answer: TRUE
Diff: 2   Page Ref: 11.7
Skill: Factual

101) Which is NOT a source of variety in sexually reproducing species?

A) crossing over

B) DNA replication

C) distribution of chromosomes in gametes

D) fertilization

E) independent assortment of chromosomes during meiosis I

Answer: B
Diff: 2   Page Ref: 11.8
Skill: Conceptual

102) Which of the following contributes to genetic diversity?

   A) mitosis

   B) random fertilization

   C) independent alignment of chromosomes during metaphase I of meiosis

   D) B and C above both contribute to genetic diversity.

   E) A, B, and C above all contribute to genetic diversity.

Answer: D
Diff: 2   Page Ref: 11.8
Skill: Factual

103) The independent alignment of chromosomes during metaphase I of meiosis results in an increased number of

   A) combinations of genetic traits.

   B) chromosomes.

   C) gametes.

   D) successful fertilizations.

   E) synapses.

Answer: A
Diff: 2   Page Ref: 11.8
Skill: Conceptual

104) The haploid chromosome number (n) of *Drosophila* is 4. How many possible arrangements of chromosomes are possible in the gametes owing only to independent assortment?

   A) 2   B) 4   C) 8   D) 16   E) 32

Answer: D
Diff: 2   Page Ref: 11.8
Skill: Application

105) What are the major sources of genetic variation in sexual reproduction?

   A) shuffling of homologues during meiosis I

   B) crossing over

   C) random fusion of gametes

   D) A and B both contribute genetic variation.

   E) A, B, and C all contribute genetic variation.

Answer: E
Diff: 2   Page Ref: 11.8
Skill: Factual

106) Pea plants have 7 pairs of chromosomes. Considering the effects of both random shuffling of homologues during meiosis I and random fertilization, how many different combinations of chromosomes are possible among the offspring from a random cross between two pea plants?

A) 64

B) 128

C) 256

D) over 10,000

E) over 100,000

Answer: D
Diff: 3   Page Ref: 11.8
Skill: Application

107) If an organism carries a mutation that prevents crossing over, which of the following would you predict is likely to happen?

A) The gametes produced would accumulate lethal mutations, so the organism would be sterile.

B) The gametes would have fewer chromosomes than usual.

C) The gametes would have lower genetic variability than usual.

D) No gametes would be produced.

E) There would be no effect; the gametes would be the same as in a normal organism.

Answer: C
Diff: 2   Page Ref: 11.8
Skill: Conceptual

108) Unlike mitosis, sexual reproduction increases variation in a population by recombining chromosomes and the genes they contain. True or False?

Answer: TRUE
Diff: 2   Page Ref: 11.8
Skill: Conceptual

109) Briefly describe where genetic variability arises in sexually reproducing organisms.

Answer: Students should discuss independent assortment of chromosomes, crossing over during meiosis, and random gamete fertilization. Mutations during replication may also be discussed.
Diff: 2   Page Ref: 11.8
Skill: Conceptual

110) How do meiosis and sexual reproduction produce genetic variability?

Answer: Students should include shuffling of homologues during meiosis, crossing over during prophase I and random gamete fusion in their answer.
Diff: 2   Page Ref: 11.8
Skill: Conceptual

111) Offspring that are genetically identical to their parents are referred to as _____.

Answer: clones
Diff: 2   Page Ref: Scientific Inquiry
Skill: Factual

Chapter 12 Patterns of Inheritance

1) Gregor Mendel concluded that each pea has two units for each trait, and each gamete contains one unit. Mendel's "units" are now referred to as _____.

A) genes

B) characters

C) alleles

D) transcription factors

E) none of the above

Answer: A
Diff: 1   Page Ref: 12.1
Skill: Factual

2) A _____ is a portion of DNA that resides at a particular locus or site on a chromosome and encodes a particular function.

Answer: gene
Diff: 1   Page Ref: 12.1
Skill: Factual

3) Peas were a good organism of choice for Mendel because

A) they cannot self-fertilize.

B) they cannot cross-fertilize.

C) he could study one trait at a time.

D) the traits were difficult to visualize.

E) All of these are correct.

Answer: C
Diff: 1   Page Ref: 12.2
Skill: Factual

4) The region of the chromosome occupied by a gene is called a _____.

Answer: locus
Diff: 1   Page Ref: 12.3
Skill: Factual

5) What is the ratio of phenotypes in the offspring produced by the cross *Aa* x *Aa*? Assume complete dominance for the trait.

  A) 100% dominance

  B) 100% recessive

  C) 75% dominant: 25% recessive

  D) 50% dominant: 50% recessive

  E) 25% dominant: 75% recessive

Answer: C
Diff: 1   Page Ref: 12.3
Skill: Application

6) If the allele for inflated pea pods (*I*) is dominant to the allele for constricted (*i*), the cross *Ii* x *ii* is expected to produce

  A) all with inflated pods.

  B) all with constricted pods.

  C) half with inflated and half with constricted pods.

  D) 3/4 with inflated and 1/4 with constricted pods.

  E) 3/4 with constricted and 1/4 with inflated pods.

Answer: C
Diff: 1   Page Ref: 12.3
Skill: Application

7) According to the Law of Segregation

  A) each individual carries a single copy of each "factor."

  B) pairs of factors fuse during the formation of gametes.

  C) pairs of factors separate during the formation of gametes.

  D) the sex chromosomes of males and females differ.

  E) there is an independent assortment of non–homologous chromosomes during meiosis.

Answer: C
Diff: 2   Page Ref: 12.3
Skill: Factual

8) According to the Law of Segregation, in an organism with the genotype *Aa*

    A) all the gametes will have gene *A*.

    B) all the gametes will have gene *a*.

    C) half the gametes will have *A* and half will have *a*.

    D) 3/4 of the gametes will have *A* and 1/4 will have *a*.

    E) 1/4 of the gametes will have *A* and 3/4 will have *a*.

Answer: C
Diff: 1   Page Ref: 12.3
Skill: Conceptual

9) A recessive gene is one

    A) that is not expressed as strongly as a dominant allele.

    B) whose effect is masked by a dominant allele.

    C) that appears only in a heterozygote.

    D) that produces no effect when present in the homozygous condition.

    E) that must be lethal in the homozygous condition.

Answer: B
Diff: 1   Page Ref: 12.3
Skill: Factual

10) Which of the following statements is FALSE?

    A) Individuals with the same phenotype might have different genotypes.

    B) Matings between individuals with dominant phenotypes cannot produce offspring with recessive phenotypes.

    C) Matings between individuals with recessive phenotypes usually do not produce offspring with dominant phenotypes.

    D) Individuals with the same genotype might have different phenotypes.

    E) All of the above choices are correct.

Answer: B
Diff: 2   Page Ref: 12.3
Skill: Conceptual

11) If, in a heterozygous individual, only one allele is expressed in the phenotype, that allele is

    A) normal.

    B) haploid.

    C) potent.

    D) recessive.

    E) dominant.

Answer: E
Diff: 1   Page Ref: 12.3
Skill: Factual

12) The physical manifestation of an organism's genes is its

    A) environment.

    B) genotype.

    C) phenotype.

    D) genetic code

    E) number of chromosomes.

Answer: C
Diff: 1   Page Ref: 12.3
Skill: Factual

13) A cross produced 915 offspring with normal pigment and 310 with albinism. Conclusion?

    A) One of the parents was homozygous for albinism.

    B) Both parents were heterozygous.

    C) One parent was homozygous for normal pigmentation.

    D) Both parents were albinos.

    E) 605 albino zygotes must have failed to develop.

Answer: B
Diff: 2   Page Ref: 12.3
Skill: Application

14) When the two gametes that fuse to form a zygote contain different alleles of a given gene, the offspring is

    A) haploid.

    B) heterozygous.

    C) abnormal.

    D) homozygous.

    E) a new species.

Answer: B
Diff: 1   Page Ref: 12.3
Skill: Factual

15) If we cross two pea plants each heterozygous for yellow seed color genes, the expected ratio of yellow : green among the offspring will be

    A) 25% yellow : 75% green.

    B) 50% yellow : 50% green.

    C) 75% yellow : 25% green.

    D) 100% yellow.

    E) 100% green.

Answer: C
Diff: 1   Page Ref: 12.3
Skill: Application

16) What type of allele produces its effects only in homozygous individuals?

    A) recessive

    B) dominant

    C) incompletely dominant

    D) diploid

    E) haploid

Answer: A
Diff: 1   Page Ref: 12.3
Skill: Factual

17) When alleles move into different gametes, this demonstrates

   A) dominance.

   B) independent assortment.

   C) fertilization.

   D) crossing-over.

   E) segregation.

Answer: E
Diff: 2   Page Ref: 12.3
Skill: Factual

18) If a round pea has a wrinkled parent, the round pea is

   A) *RR.*   B) *Rr.*   C) *rr.*   D) haploid.   E) recessive.

Answer: B
Diff: 2   Page Ref: 12.3
Skill: Conceptual

19) Mendel's Law of Segregation states that

   A) members of a pair of alleles move away from each other during gamete formation.

   B) each gamete receives a full complement of chromosomes.

   C) there may be alternative forms of the same gene.

   D) genes end up in respective gametes by chance.

   E) genes in the same chromosome must stay together.

Answer: A
Diff: 2   Page Ref: 12.3
Skill: Factual

20) When Mendel used true-breeding white flowers and true-breeding purple flowers as the parental generation, he obtained which of the following results?

   A) All the offspring had white flowers.

   B) All the offspring had purple flowers.

   C) 3/4 of the flowers produced were purple and 1/4 were white.

   D) 3/4 of the flowers produced were white and 1/4 were purple.

   E) 1/2 of the flowers produced were white and 1/2 were purple.

Answer: B
Diff: 1   Page Ref: 12.3
Skill: Factual

21) The genetic makeup of an individual is its

   A) phenotype.

   B) sex cells.

   C) mutation.

   D) gene pool.

   E) genotype.

Answer: E
Diff: 1   Page Ref: 12.3
Skill: Factual

22) The results of a test cross reveal that all the offspring resemble the parent being tested. This parent must be

   A) heterozygous.

   B) recessive.

   C) self-pollinated.

   D) homozygous.

   E) haploid.

Answer: D
Diff: 1   Page Ref: 12.3
Skill: Application

23) A Mendelian test cross is used to determine whether

   A) an allele is dominant or recessive.

   B) flowers are purple or white.

   C) the genotype or phenotype is more important.

   D) an individual is homozygous or heterozygous.

   E) segregation or independent assortment is occurring.

Answer: D
Diff: 1   Page Ref: 12.3
Skill: Conceptual

24) Yellow-seeded pea plants may be homozygous or heterozygous. To find out which, we can cross the plants with

    A) true-breeding yellow-seeded plants.

    B) true-breeding green-seeded plants.

    C) heterozygous green-seeded plants.

    D) heterozygous yellow-seeded plants.

    E) the same genotype.

Answer: B
Diff: 2   Page Ref: 12.3
Skill: Conceptual

25) In a test cross, what percentage of the offspring will have the same genotype as the tested parent if the parent is homozygous?

    A) 25%   B) 50%   C) 75%   D) 100%   E) 0%

Answer: D
Diff: 1   Page Ref: 12.3
Skill: Conceptual

26) What is the genotype of a dominant individual if some of its offspring show the recessive phenotype?

    A) *DD*

    B) *Dd*

    C) *dd*

    D) cannot tell without more information

    E) either *DD* or *Dd*

Answer: B
Diff: 1   Page Ref: 12.3
Skill: Conceptual

27) Crossing spherical-seeded pea plants with dented-seeded pea plants resulted in progeny that all had spherical seeds. This indicates that the dented seed trait is

    A) codominant.

    B) dominant.

    C) recessive.

    D) A and B

    E) A and C

Answer: C
Diff: 2   Page Ref: 12.3
Skill: Conceptual

28) Cleft chin is an autosomal dominant trait. A man homozygous for the cleft chin marries a woman with a round chin. What proportion of their female progeny will show the trait?

A) 0%   B) 25%   C) 50%   D) 75%   E) 100%

Answer: E
Diff: 2   Page Ref: 12.3
Skill: Application

29) A pea plant with red flowers is test crossed and one half of the resulting progeny have red flowers, while the other half have white flowers. You know that the genotype of the test crossed parent was

A) *RR*.

B) *Rr*.

C) *rr*.

D) either *RR* or *Rr*.

E) cannot tell unless the genotypes of both parents are known.

Answer: B
Diff: 1   Page Ref: 12.3
Skill: Application

30) Classical albinism results from a recessive allele. Which of the following is the expected offspring from a normally pigmented male with an albino father and an albino wife?

A) 75% normal; 25% albino

B) 75% albino; 25% normal

C) 50% normal; 50% albino

D) all normal

E) all albino

Answer: C
Diff: 2   Page Ref: 12.3
Skill: Conceptual

31) In garden peas, the allele for tall plants is dominant over the allele for short plants. A true–breeding tall plant is crossed with a short plant and one of their offspring is test crossed. Out of 20 offspring resulting from the test cross, about _____ should be tall.

A) 0   B) 5   C) 10   D) 15   E) 20

Answer: C
Diff: 2   Page Ref: 12.3
Skill: Application

32) In crossing a homozygous recessive with a heterozygote, what is the chance of getting a homozygous recessive phenotype in the F1 generation?

A) 0%   B) 25%   C) 50%   D) 75%   E) 100%

Answer: C
Diff: 1   Page Ref: 12.3
Skill: Factual

33) If two parents are carriers of albinism (an autosomal recessive trait), what is the chance that their fourth child will have a homozygous genotype?

A) 0%   B) 25%   C) 50%   D) 75%   E) 100%

Answer: C
Diff: 2   Page Ref: 12.3
Skill: Application

34) All of the following combinations are possible in the gametes of an organism that is *AaBb* EXCEPT

A) *AB*.   B) *aB*.   C) *aa*.   D) *ab*.   E) *Ab*.

Answer: C
Diff: 2   Page Ref: 12.4
Skill: Conceptual

35) Martians normally have three eyes (*E*), but the rare "humanoid" mutation (*e*) causes monsters with two eyes to be born. Eye color in Martians is inherited similarly to humans, with brown eyes (*B*) being dominant to blue (*b*). Assuming these two genes are carried on separate chromosomes, what must the genotypes of two normal, brown–eyed parents be if they have a blue-eyed, humanoid son?

A) *EEBB* and *eebb*

B) both *EeBb*

C) *eeBB* and *EEbb*

D) both *eebb*

E) You cannot tell from the information provided.

Answer: B
Diff: 2   Page Ref: 12.4
Skill: Application

36) You cross a pea plant with yellow, smooth seeds with one having wrinkled, green seeds. You examine the seeds of 967 offspring, and find some have yellow, smooth seeds and some have yellow, wrinkled seeds, but no green seeds of either type show up. What is the genotype of the yellow-seeded parent? (*Y* = yellow, *y* = green; *S* = smooth, *s* = wrinkled)

A) *YYSs*   B) *YYss*   C) *YYSS*   D) *YySs*   E) *YySS*

Answer: A
Diff: 2   Page Ref: 12.4
Skill: Application

37) In pea plants, tall plants are dominant over short, and green pods are dominant over yellow. If you were to cross true-breeding tall, green-podded plants with true-breeding short, yellow-podded plants, and then were to cross the F1 individuals among themselves, what proportion of the F2 offspring would you expect to be tall and yellow-podded?

    A) 1/16   B) 1/4   C) 3/16   D) 3/4   E) 9/16

Answer: C
Diff: 2   Page Ref: 12.4
Skill: Conceptual

38) If you cross pea plants that are heterozygous for purple flowers and yellow seeds (*PpYy*), and you examine 800 offspring for flower and seed color, about how many do you expect to have white flowers and green seeds?

    A) all of them (800)

    B) 450

    C) 400

    D) 50

    E) none

Answer: D
Diff: 2   Page Ref: 12.4
Skill: Application

39) In Labrador retrievers, black coat color is dominant to chocolate coat color. Labradors also are prone to a serious eye ailment, called progressive retinal atrophy (PRA), which is recessive to normal vision. If two black Labradors with normal vision are mated, and one puppy in a litter of seven entirely black puppies has PRA, what are the likely genotypes of the parents?

    A) Both parents are homozygous for both traits.

    B) One parent is heterozygous for PRA, whereas the other does not carry the trait.

    C) Both parents are heterozygous for both traits.

    D) Both parents are heterozygous carriers of PRA, but we can't determine what their coat-color genotype is.

    E) We can't say anything about the parental genotypes. The PRA in the puppy arose through spontaneous mutation.

Answer: D
Diff: 3   Page Ref: 12.4
Skill: Application

40) The independent inheritance of two or more distinct traits is called the _____.

Answer: law of independent assortment
Diff: 1   Page Ref: 12.4
Skill: Factual

41) What is a physical requirement in order for independent assortment of alleles for two different genes to occur?

Answer: The genes must be on different chromosomes.
Diff: 3   Page Ref: 12.4
Skill: Conceptual

42) Describe where in the process of meiosis independent assortment of genes occur.

Answer: Homologous pairs of chromosomes align randomly along the metaphase plate during metaphase I, and separate during anaphase I.
Diff: 2   Page Ref: 12.4
Skill: Conceptual

43) What are the possible genotypes in a gamete of an organism that is *HhTt* if the two genes are located on separate chromosomes?

Answer: *HT, Ht, hT,* and *ht*
Diff: 1   Page Ref: 12.4
Skill: Conceptual

44) Although the law of independent assortment is generally applicable, when two loci are on the same chromosome the phenotypes of the progeny sometimes do not fit the phenotypes predicted. This is due to

A) translation.

B) inversions.

C) chromatid abnormalities.

D) linkage.

E) reciprocal chromosome exchange.

Answer: D
Diff: 2   Page Ref: 12.5
Skill: Conceptual

45) You self–pollinate heterozygous purple–flowered, long–pollened pea plants, and get mostly purple–flowered short–pollened plants and white–flowered long–pollened plants, with a very few purple–flowered, long–pollened or white–flowered, short–pollened plants. What is the most likely explanation?

A) One of the genes in question resides on a sex chromosome.

B) The genes are linked.

C) Long pollen is often lethal, so few plants with long pollen survive to adulthood.

D) This is a normal random variation from the expected ratio for independent assortment.

E) The purple allele influences pollen to become shorter.

Answer: B
Diff: 3   Page Ref: 12.5
Skill: Application

46) Which of the following is TRUE of genes that are found near each other on the same chromosome?

   A) They tend to be inherited together.

   B) They are linked.

   C) They will be expressed differently in males than in females.

   D) None of the above are true.

   E) Both A and B above are true.

Answer: E
Diff: 2   Page Ref: 12.5
Skill: Conceptual

47) When genes are linked, the reason a few of the recombinant genotypes still occur in the offspring is because of

   A) mutation.

   B) linkage.

   C) crossing over.

   D) natural selection.

   E) independent assortment.

Answer: C
Diff: 2   Page Ref: 12.5
Skill: Conceptual

48) Imagine you do a test cross between a purple-flowered pea plant having serrated leaves (a dominant trait) and a white-flowered pea plant having smooth edges. If the purple-flowered plant is heterozygous for both traits, the expected ratio in the offspring is 1 purple-serrated:1 purple-smooth:1 white serrated:1 white smooth. Instead, you see is 4 purple-serrated:1 purple-smooth:1 white serrated:4 white smooth. What is the explanation of this ratio?

   A) There is incomplete dominance.

   B) The genes are linked.

   C) The genes are linked and there is incomplete dominance.

   D) There has been a mutation during the cross.

   E) None of the above explain these results.

Answer: B
Diff: 3   Page Ref: 12.5
Skill: Application

49) What would be true if linkage of two genes were complete?

    A) Crossing over between the two genes would never occur.

    B) The genes would assort independently.

    C) All possible combinations of alleles in the gametes would be produced.

    D) All possible combinations of alleles in the offspring would be produced.

    E) None of the above would be true.

Answer: A
Diff: 2   Page Ref: 12.5
Skill: Conceptual

50) Describe a reason for when the pattern of inheritance breaks the law of independent assortment.

Answer: Alleles that are found close together on the same chromosome tend to be inherited together. This is called gene linkage.
Diff: 2   Page Ref: 12.5
Skill: Conceptual

51) What occurs to result in linked genes not being inherited together?

Answer: Recombination of chromosomes during crossover during Prophase I.
Diff: 2   Page Ref: 12.5
Skill: Conceptual

52) Humans possess

    A) 2 pairs of sex chromosomes and 46 pairs of autosomes.

    B) 2 pairs of sex chromosomes and 23 pairs of autosomes.

    C) 1 pair of sex chromosomes and 46 pairs of autosomes.

    D) 1 pair of sex chromosomes and 23 pairs of autosomes.

    E) 1 pair of sex chromosomes and 22 pairs of autosomes.

Answer: E
Diff: 1   Page Ref: 12.6
Skill: Factual

53) A human sperm cell receives autosomes and

    A) exactly the same genetic information as a body cell.

    B) an X chromosome always.

    C) either an X or a Y chromosome.

    D) a Y chromosome always.

    E) both an X and a Y chromosome.

Answer: C
Diff: 1   *Page Ref: 12.6*
Skill: Factual

54) In humans, the sex of the offspring is determined by the

    A) autosomes carried by the egg cell.

    B) autosomes carried by the sperm cell.

    C) sex chromosome carried by the egg cell.

    D) sex chromosome carried by the sperm cell.

    E) cytoplasm carried by the egg cell.

Answer: D
Diff: 2   *Page Ref: 12.6*
Skill: Conceptual

55) White eyes in male fruit flies is determined by a

    A) dominant gene on the Y.

    B) recessive gene on the Y.

    C) dominant gene on the X.

    D) recessive gene on the X.

    E) a gene in the autosomes.

Answer: D
Diff: 1   *Page Ref: 12.6*
Skill: Factual

56) A female fruit fly whose male parent has white eyes

    A) must have red eyes.

    B) must have white eyes.

    C) must have a gene for white eyes.

    D) can have only white-eyed offspring.

    E) must be heterozygous for eye-color genes.

Answer: C
Diff: 2   *Page Ref: 12.6*
Skill: Application

57) Traits controlled by sex-linked recessive genes are expressed more often in males because

A) males inherit these genes from their fathers.

B) males always carry two copies of these genes.

C) all male offspring of a female carrier get the gene.

D) the male has only one gene for the trait.

E) males get more doses of the recessive gene than do females.

Answer: D
Diff: 2   Page Ref: 12.6
Skill: Conceptual

58) A recessive allele on the X chromosome causes colorblindness. A non-colorblind woman (whose father is colorblind) marries a colorblind man. What is the chance their son will be colorblind?

A) 0%   B) 25%   C) 50%   D) 75%   E) 100%

Answer: C
Diff: 3   Page Ref: 12.6
Skill: Application

59) Hemophilia is a sex-linked recessive gene causing a blood disorder. What are the chances that the daughter of a normal man and a heterozygous woman will have hemophilia?

A) 0%   B) 25%   C) 50%   D) 75%   E) 100%

Answer: A
Diff: 3   Page Ref: 12.6
Skill: Application

60) A colorblind boy has a normal mother and a colorblind father. From which parent did he get the colorblind gene?

A) father

B) mother

C) Either parent could have given him the gene.

Answer: B
Diff: 3   Page Ref: 12.6
Skill: Application

61) A man who carries a harmful sex-linked (on the X chromosome) gene will pass the gene on to

    A) all of his daughters.

    B) half of his daughters.

    C) half of his sons.

    D) all of his sons.

    E) all of his children.

Answer: A
Diff: 2   Page Ref: 12.6
Skill: Application

62) Colorblindness is more common in men than in women because

    A) men have only one X chromosome.

    B) the gene is located on the Y chromosome.

    C) women cannot inherit the gene from their fathers.

    D) crossing-over occurs only in women.

    E) men get more copies of the gene than do women.

Answer: A
Diff: 2   Page Ref: 12.6
Skill: Conceptual

63) Why would you predict that half of the human babies born will be males and half will be females?

    A) because of the segregation of the X and Y chromosomes during male meiosis

    B) because of the segregation of the X chromosomes during female meiosis

    C) because all eggs contain an X chromosome

    D) A and B

    E) A and C

Answer: A
Diff: 2   Page Ref: 12.6
Skill: Conceptual

64) An individual who is a "carrier" for a sex-linked trait like hemophilia

    A) is always female.

    B) is heterozygous for recessive condition.

    C) shows the dominant phenotype.

    D) can pass the gene on to his/her daughters.

    E) All the above choices are correct.

Answer: E
Diff: 2   Page Ref: 12.6
Skill: Conceptual

65) Hemophilia is a genetic disease that has plagued the royal houses of Europe since the time of Queen Victoria, who was a carrier. Her granddaughter Alexandria married Nicholas II, the last czar of imperial Russia. Alexandria was a carrier for hemophilia; Nicholas was normal. Their son, Alexis, was afflicted with the disease. Alexis and his four sisters were all killed in 1917. It is most likely that

    A) none of the four sisters carried the hemophilia gene.

    B) at least one of the sisters was a carrier of the gene.

    C) all four sisters were carriers of the hemophilia gene.

    D) at least one of the sisters had hemophilia like Alexis.

    E) Alexis inherited the hemophilia gene from Nicholas II.

Answer: B
Diff: 3   Page Ref: 12.6
Skill: Conceptual

66) A type of muscular dystrophy shows sex-linked recessive inheritance. Affected persons usually die by the age of 15-20. Suppose that a boy with the disease lives long enough to marry a woman heterozygous for the trait. If they have a son, what is the probability that he will have the disease?

    A) 25%   B) 50%   C) 75%   D) 100%   E) 0%

Answer: B
Diff: 2   Page Ref: 12.6
Skill: Application

67) Two people with normal vision have two sons, one colorblind and one normal. If this couple then has six daughters, what percentage of the daughters should have normal color vision?

    A) 25%   B) 50%   C) 75%   D) 100%   E) 0%

Answer: D
Diff: 3   Page Ref: 12.6
Skill: Application

68) Hemophiliacs have blood that does not coagulate well and often die at a young age. The gene for the disease is recessive and sex-linked. Which of the following is the BEST prediction about the offspring of a hemophiliac male and a nonhemophiliac female who is a carrier for the disease?

    A) All children would be hemophiliac.

    B) All females would be hemophiliac.

    C) All males would be hemophiliac.

    D) Hemophiliac children would occur in a 3:1 ratio, normal to hemophiliac.

    E) Some males and females could be hemophiliac.

Answer: E
Diff: 3   Page Ref: 12.6
Skill: Application

69) Only males can express sex-linked traits. True or False?

Answer: FALSE
Diff: 2   Page Ref: 12.6
Skill: Conceptual

70) Males always inherit sex-linked traits from their fathers. True or False?

Answer: FALSE
Diff: 2   Page Ref: 12.6
Skill: Conceptual

71) Sex-linked traits affect only sexual characteristics. True or False?

Answer: FALSE
Diff: 2   Page Ref: 12.6
Skill: Conceptual

72) In humans there are 22 pairs of _____ and one pair of _____.

Answer: autosomes; sex chromosomes
Diff: 2   Page Ref: 12.6
Skill: Factual

73) Blood typing is often used as evidence in paternity cases in court. In one case, the mother had blood type B and the child had blood type O. Which of the following blood types could the father NOT have?

A) A

B) B

C) AB

D) O

E) Both choices C and D are correct.

Answer: C
Diff: 2   Page Ref: 12.7
Skill: Application

74) In snapdragons, red x white → pink. What is expected for the cross pink x red?

A) 1/2 red and 1/2 pink

B) all pink

C) 1/2 red and 1/2 white

D) all red

E) 3/4 red and 1/4 pink

Answer: A
Diff: 2   Page Ref: 12.7
Skill: Application

75) In snapdragons, red x white → pink. What proportion of pink flowers are expected from the cross pink x pink?

A) no pink   B) 1/4 pink   C) 1/2 pink   D) 3/4 pink   E) all pink

Answer: C
Diff: 2   Page Ref: 12.7
Skill: Application

76) In snapdragons, red x white → pink. This pattern of inheritance is explained by

A) complete dominance.

B) incomplete dominance.

C) hybridization.

D) multiple alleles.

E) genetic interaction.

Answer: B
Diff: 1   Page Ref: 12.7
Skill: Factual

77) Codominance occurs when

   A) both of the alleles in a heterozygote are expressed phenotypically in an individual.

   B) expression of 2 different alleles alternates from one generation to the next.

   C) a heterozygote expresses an intermediate phenotype.

   D) offspring exhibit several different phenotypic expressions of a single trait.

   E) None of the above choices is correct.

Answer: A
Diff: 1   Page Ref: 12.7
Skill: Factual

78) When the expression of a trait is influenced by the action of many genes, the pattern of inheritance is called

   A) complete dominance.

   B) incomplete dominance.

   C) multiple alleles.

   D) discontinuous variation.

   E) polygenic inheritance.

Answer: E
Diff: 2   Page Ref: 12.7
Skill: Factual

79) Human eye color is the result of

   A) polygenic inheritance.

   B) codominance.

   C) simple dominance.

   D) sex-linked recessive inheritance.

   E) genes and environmental effects.

Answer: A
Diff: 1   Page Ref: 12.7
Skill: Factual

80) Smurfs live in widely separated groups and rarely interbreed, so geneticists know very little about them. On one occasion, two smurfs from different groups did mate. A big-footed, white smurf mated with a small-footed, blue smurf. Three offspring resulted: one big-footed and blue and two small-footed and blue. Which statement about the inheritance of color in smurfs is most likely to be correct?

    A) Blue is dominant to white.

    B) White is dominant to blue.

    C) White and blue are codominant.

    D) A and C

    E) You cannot reach any conclusions.

Answer: A
Diff: 2   Page Ref: 12.7
Skill: Application

81) Smurfs live in widely separated groups and rarely interbreed, so geneticists know very little about them. On one occasion, two smurfs from different groups did mate. A big-footed, white smurf mated with a small-footed, blue smurf. Three offspring resulted: one big-footed and blue and two small-footed and blue. Which statement about the inheritance of footedness in smurfs is most likely to be correct?

    A) Big is dominant to small.

    B) Small is dominant to big.

    C) Big and small are codominant.

    D) A and C

    E) You cannot reach any conclusions.

Answer: E
Diff: 3   Page Ref: 12.7
Skill: Application

82) In Mendel's experiments, if the gene for tall (T) plants was incompletely dominant over the gene for short (t) plants, what would be the result of crossing two Tt plants?

    A) 25% tall; 50% intermediate; 25% short

    B) 50% tall; 25% intermediate; 25% short

    C) 25% tall; 25% intermediate; 50% short

    D) All the offspring would be tall.

    E) All the offspring would be intermediate.

Answer: A
Diff: 2   Page Ref: 12.7
Skill: Application

83) Human skin color is the result of

    A) one pair of genes showing incomplete dominance.

    B) codominance.

    C) simple dominance.

    D) sex-linked recessive inheritance.

    E) polygenic inheritance.

Answer: E
Diff: 2   Page Ref: 12.7
Skill: Factual

84) If an individual who is homozygous for type B blood marries a heterozygous type A individual, what is the chance that their first child will have type AB blood?

    A) 0%   B) 25%   C) 50%   D) 75%   E) 100%

Answer: C
Diff: 2   Page Ref: 12.7
Skill: Application

85) Studies show the greatest similarity on IQ test scores is between

    A) parents and children.

    B) brothers and sisters.

    C) identical twins raised in the same environment.

    D) fraternal twins raised in different environments.

    E) all children attending the same school.

Answer: C
Diff: 2   Page Ref: 12.7
Skill: Factual

86) In snapdragons, heterozygotes have pink flowers, and the two homozygous individuals are red or white. When a red flowered plant is crossed with a white flowered plant, what proportion of the offspring will have pink flowers?

Answer: 100%
Diff: 1   Page Ref: 12.7
Skill: Application

87) In human blood types the alleles for A and B are said to be _____ because they are both expressed.

Answer: codominant
Diff: 1   Page Ref: 12.7
Skill: Factual

88) The blood types of humans are an example of _____.

Answer: multiple alleles
Diff: 1   Page Ref: 12.7
Skill: Factual

89) The resulting pink flowers which occur after crossing red and white snapdragons is most likely a result of _____.

Answer: incomplete dominance
Diff: 1   Page Ref: 12.7
Skill: Factual

90) Pedigree analysis

   A) documents transmission of a genetic characteristic over two or more generations.

   B) reveals whether a trait is dominant or recessive.

   C) involves procedures of molecular biology.

   D) A and B

   E) A, B and C

Answer: E
Diff: 2   Page Ref: 12.8
Skill: Factual

91) Sickle-cell anemia is caused by a

   A) recessive sex-linked gene.

   B) dominant autosomal gene.

   C) simple dominant gene.

   D) combined interaction of several genes.

   E) recessive autosomal gene.

Answer: E
Diff: 1   Page Ref: 12.9
Skill: Factual

92) Human females who receive sex-linked genes always express them. True or False?

Answer: FALSE
Diff: 1   Page Ref: 12.9
Skill: Factual

93) A female who is heterozygous for a recessive, sex linked character is a _____ for that character.

Answer: carrier
Diff: 1   Page Ref: 12.9
Skill: Factual

94) Which of the following causes sterility in a human?

A) XXX   B) XYY   C) XXY   D) XY   E) XX

Answer: C
Diff: 2   Page Ref: 12.10
Skill: Factual

95) Of the following, which is the LEAST common chromosome disorder among live born infants?

A) Turner's syndrome

B) Klinefelter's syndrome

C) Down syndrome

D) Trisomy X

E) They all are equally common.

Answer: A
Diff: 2   Page Ref: 12.10
Skill: Factual

96) Autosomal nondisjunction can result in

A) XYY males.

B) Turner syndrome.

C) Klinefelter syndrome.

D) Trisomy X.

E) Down syndrome.

Answer: E
Diff: 2   Page Ref: 12.10
Skill: Factual

97) The failure of chromosomes to segregate properly during meiosis is called

A) nondisjunction.

B) translocation.

C) replication.

D) inversion.

E) independent assortment.

Answer: A
Diff: 2   Page Ref: 12.10
Skill: Factual

98) Which disorder is characterized by an abnormal number of autosomes?

    A) Turner syndrome

    B) Klinefelter syndrome

    C) Trisomy X syndrome

    D) XYY syndrome

    E) Down syndrome

Answer: E
Diff: 2   Page Ref: 12.10
Skill: Factual

99) Which disorder is characterized by sterile males with some breast development?

    A) Turner syndrome

    B) Klinefelter syndrome

    C) Trisomy X syndrome

    D) XYY syndrome

    E) Down syndrome

Answer: B
Diff: 2   Page Ref: 12.10
Skill: Factual

100) For which disorder can those affected be male or female?

    A) Turner syndrome

    B) Klinefelter syndrome

    C) Trisomy X syndrome

    D) XYY syndrome

    E) Down syndrome

Answer: E
Diff: 2   Page Ref: 12.10
Skill: Factual

101) Which disorder is characterized by short females with webbed necks?

    A) Turner syndrome

    B) Klinefelter syndrome

    C) Trisomy X syndrome

    D) XYY syndrome

    E) Down syndrome

Answer: A
Diff: 2   Page Ref: 12.10
Skill: Factual

102) Which disorder is characterized by the individual having a normal number of sex chromosomes?

    A) Turner syndrome

    B) Klinefelter syndrome

    C) Trisomy X syndrome

    D) XYY syndrome

    E) Down syndrome

Answer: E
Diff: 2   Page Ref: 12.10
Skill: Factual

103) Which disorder is more common among the babies of older mothers?

    A) Turner syndrome

    B) Klinefelter syndrome

    C) Trisomy X syndrome

    D) XYY syndrome

    E) Down syndrome

Answer: E
Diff: 2   Page Ref: 12.10
Skill: Factual

104) Which disorder is the most common chromosome anomaly among newborns?

    A) Turner syndrome

    B) Klinefelter syndrome

    C) Trisomy X syndrome

    D) XYY syndrome

    E) Down syndrome

Answer: E
Diff: 2   Page Ref: 12.10
Skill: Factual

105) Hemophilia is

    A) sex-linked recessive.

    B) simple dominant.

    C) autosomal nondisjunction.

    D) sex chromosomal nondisjunction.

    E) recessive autosomal.

Answer: A
Diff: 1   Page Ref: 12.10
Skill: Factual

106) Red-green colorblindness is

    A) sex-linked recessive.

    B) simple dominant.

    C) autosomal nondisjunction.

    D) sex chromosomal nondisjunction.

    E) recessive autosomal.

Answer: A
Diff: 1   Page Ref: 12.10
Skill: Factual

107) Sickle-cell anemia is

    A) sex-linked recessive.

    B) simple dominant.

    C) autosomal nondisjunction.

    D) sex chromosomal nondisjunction.

    E) recessive autosomal.

Answer: E
Diff: 1   Page Ref: 12.10
Skill: Factual

108) Turner syndrome is

    A) sex-linked recessive.

    B) simple dominant.

    C) autosomal nondisjunction.

    D) sex chromosomal nondisjunction.

    E) recessive autosomal.

Answer: D
Diff: 1   Page Ref: 12.10
Skill: Factual

109) Klinefelter syndrome is

    A) sex-linked recessive.

    B) simple dominant.

    C) autosomal nondisjunction.

    D) sex chromosomal nondisjunction.

    E) recessive autosomal.

Answer: D
Diff: 1   Page Ref: 12.10
Skill: Factual

110) A sex-linked recessive condition resulting in abnormally excessive bleeding is

    A) cystic fibrosis.   B) Down syndrome.

    C) hemophilia.   D) colorblindness.

Answer: C
Diff: 1   Page Ref: 12.10
Skill: Factual

111) A disorder caused by non-disjunction of chromosome 21 resulting in a trisomy 21 child is

    A) cystic fibrosis.   B) Down syndrome.

    C) hemophilia.   D) colorblindness.

Answer: B
Diff: 2   Page Ref: 12.10
Skill: Factual

112) A recessive genetic disorder with salty sweat as one symptom is

    A) cystic fibrosis.   B) Down syndrome.

    C) hemophilia.   D) colorblindness.

Answer: A
Diff: 2   Page Ref: 12.10
Skill: Factual

113) A sex-linked recessive condition causing abnormal color vision is called

    A) cystic fibrosis.   B) Down syndrome.

    C) hemophilia.   D) colorblindness.

Answer: D
Diff: 1   Page Ref: 12.10
Skill: Factual

114) A genetic disease due to the lack of clotting factor(s) is

A) cystic fibrosis.

B) Down syndrome.

C) hemophilia.

D) colorblindness.

Answer: C
Diff: 1   *Page Ref: 12.10*
Skill: Factual

Chapter 13 Biotechnology

1) Which of the following is NOT a goal of biotechnology?

   A) generating economic benefits

   B) efficiently producing biologically important molecules

   C) improving agriculturally important food plants

   D) more effectively treating disease

   E) creating humans with higher intelligence levels

   Answer: E
   Diff: 1   Page Ref: 13.1
   Skill: Conceptual

2) Manipulating the molecular basis of inheritance by recombinant DNA technology is called

   A) Mendelian genetics.

   B) biotechnology.

   C) DNA fingerprinting.

   D) restriction fragment length polymorphism (RFLP).

   E) the polymerase chain reaction (PCR).

   Answer: B
   Diff: 1   Page Ref: 13.1
   Skill: Factual

3) Biotechnology CANNOT be used to

   A) produce large quantities of particular human proteins.

   B) produce effective and safe vaccines.

   C) identify human fetuses with particular genetic diseases.

   D) alter food plants to increase yield.

   E) alter the intelligence levels of newborn infants.

   Answer: E
   Diff: 1   Page Ref: 13.1
   Skill: Conceptual

4) Which of the following results from inserting foreign DNA into an organism to produce a new gene combination?

   A) recombinant DNA

   B) regulatory genes

   C) mutations

   D) translation

   E) gene cloning

Answer: A
Diff: 1   Page Ref: 13.1
Skill: Factual

5) A cell or organism that contains foreign DNA inserted into its own genetic material is termed

   A) transgenic.

   B) polygenic.

   C) engineered.

   D) foreign.

   E) xenophobic.

Answer: A
Diff: 1   Page Ref: 13.1
Skill: Factual

6) Goals of genetic engineering include all of the following EXCEPT

   A) to learn more about genetic inheritance.

   B) to learn more about genetic diseases.

   C) to learn more about bacterial inheritance.

   D) to provide economic and social benefits.

   E) All of the above are goals of genetic engineering.

Answer: E
Diff: 2   Page Ref: 13.1
Skill: Conceptual

7) Define the term biotechnology.

   Answer: Any use or alteration of organisms, cells or biological molecules to achieve specific practical goals.
   Diff: 1   Page Ref: 13.1
   Skill: Conceptual

8) How would it have been possible for ancient Egyptians to be involved in biotechnology?

Answer: Biotechnology includes selective breeding of plants and animals; by definition
biotechnology is any alteration of organisms to achieve specific practical goals.
Diff: 1   *Page Ref: 13.1*
Skill: Conceptual

9) A _____ animal has recombinant DNA integrated into its own genetic material.

Answer: transgenic
Diff: 2   *Page Ref: 13.1*
Skill: Factual

10) Small accessory chromosomes found in bacteria and useful in recombinant DNA procedures
are called

A) plasmids.

B) palindromes.

C) centrioles.

D) bacteriophage.

E) viruses.

Answer: A
Diff: 1   *Page Ref: 13.2*
Skill: Factual

11) Plasmids are

A) non-circular DNA segments in bacteria.

B) small self-replicating DNA molecules in bacteria.

C) made of RNA.

D) found only in single copies within bacteria.

E) necessary in order for bacteria to reproduce.

Answer: B
Diff: 1   *Page Ref: 13.2*
Skill: Factual

12) DNA recombination does NOT occur between different species in nature by

    A) bacterial transformation.

    B) bacteria acquiring plasmids.

    C) viruses transferring DNA between host organisms.

    D) sexual reproduction in animals.

    E) None of the above is a correct choice.

Answer: D
Diff: 1   Page Ref: 13.2
Skill: Conceptual

13) Recombinant DNA technology

    A) will never be of economic importance.

    B) only concerns changing genes in large animals.

    C) is concerned with randomly creating new genes from nucleotides.

    D) is dangerous and will lead to monstrosities.

    E) involves combining existing genes from different organisms in new ways.

Answer: E
Diff: 1   Page Ref: 13.2
Skill: Factual

14) Which of these is NOT a natural method of DNA recombination?

    A) sexual reproduction

    B) genetic transformation in bacteria

    C) viral infection

    D) gene amplification in bacteria

    E) All the above are correct choices.

Answer: D
Diff: 2   Page Ref: 13.2
Skill: Conceptual

15) DNA from different bacteria may be combined using all of the following EXCEPT

    A) transformation.

    B) plasmids.

    C) viruses.

    D) crossing over.

    E) all of the above

Answer: D
Diff: 2   Page Ref: 13.2
Skill: Factual

16) Natural DNA recombination is random and undirected. True or False?

Answer: TRUE
Diff: 1   Page Ref: 13.2
Skill: Conceptual

17) Most natural DNA recombination is beneficial to the organisms in which they occur. True or False?

Answer: FALSE
Diff: 1   Page Ref: 13.2
Skill: Conceptual

18) DNA recombination changes the genetic makeup of organisms. True or False?

Answer: TRUE
Diff: 1   Page Ref: 13.2
Skill: Conceptual

19) Sexual reproduction in humans is a natural method of DNA recombination. True or False?

Answer: TRUE
Diff: 1   Page Ref: 13.2
Skill: Conceptual

20) A recombinant plasmid may contain only human DNA. True or False?

Answer: FALSE
Diff: 1   Page Ref: 13.2
Skill: Conceptual

21) How is it possible for a dead bacterium to influence the DNA in a living bacterium?

Answer: Dead bacteria release plasmids, which can be taken up by other bacteria through the process of transformation passing along any genetic information that was on the plasmid to the live organism.
Diff: 3   Page Ref: 13.2
Skill: Conceptual

22) _____ are small circular pieces of DNA molecules that are often used in the process of transformation.

Answer: Plasmids
Diff: 1   Page Ref: 13.2
Skill: Conceptual

23) In biotechnology research, DNA fragments created by restriction enzyme action are separated from one another by

    A) crossing over.

    B) gel electrophoresis.

    C) centrifugation.

    D) filtering.

    E) the polymerase chain reaction.

Answer: B
Diff: 1   Page Ref: 13.3
Skill: Factual

24) The polymerase chain reaction (PCR) is useful in

    A) analyzing a person's fingerprints.

    B) cutting DNA into many small pieces.

    C) allowing restriction enzymes to cut DNA at palindromes.

    D) creating recombinant plasmids.

    E) making many copies of a small amount of DNA.

Answer: E
Diff: 1   Page Ref: 13.3
Skill: Factual

25) DNA migrates in an electric field because

    A) it is positively charged.

    B) it is negatively charged.

    C) organisms only have a few chromosomes.

    D) different chromosomes carry different charges.

    E) none of the above

Answer: B
Diff: 2   Page Ref: 13.3
Skill: Conceptual

26) The polymerase chain reaction (PCR) allows scientists to do all of the following EXCEPT

    A) make millions of copies of a particular gene.

    B) make gene copies quite rapidly.

    C) make gene copies quite cheaply.

    D) use a very small amount of DNA as starting material.

    E) sequence the bases within a gene as it is being copied.

Answer: E
Diff: 2   Page Ref: 13.3
Skill: Conceptual

27) What is the goal of forensic biotechnology?

    A) to identify specific genes and insert them into organisms such as cattle, crop plants, or bacteria

    B) to identify victims and criminals

    C) to identify carriers of genetic disorders

    D) to correct genetic disorders

    E) to improve crop yields in agriculture

Answer: B
Diff: 2   Page Ref: 13.3
Skill: Conceptual

28) Which of the following is currently used to produce genetic "fingerprints" of people?

    A) the number of introns in a chromosome

    B) the genes responsible for producing the unique fingerprints on a person's fingers

    C) restriction fragment length polymorphisms (RFLPs)

    D) single tandem repeats (STRs)

    E) plasmids

Answer: D
Diff: 2   Page Ref: 13.3
Skill: Factual

29) Specific fragments of DNA on a gel can be visualized using

    A) DNA probes.

    B) restriction enzymes.

    C) electrophoresis.

    D) single tandem repeats (STRs).

    E) PCR.

Answer: A
Diff: 2   Page Ref: 13.3
Skill: Conceptual

30) If the DNA fingerprint of a suspect does not match a blood sample from a crime scene, what can you conclude?

    A) The suspect was never at the crime scene.

    B) The suspect may have been at the crime scene, because DNA fingerprinting has a large error rate.

    C) The blood sample had to come from another person, but the suspect may still have been there.

    D) The blood sample was probably degraded over time.

    E) You cannot get a DNA fingerprint from a blood sample.

Answer: C
Diff: 2   Page Ref: 13.3
Skill: Application

31) DNA is negatively charged because of its

    A) bases.

    B) ribose.

    C) deoxyribose.

    D) phosphates.

    E) large size.

Answer: D
Diff: 2   Page Ref: 13.3
Skill: Factual

32) In the gel below, a plasmid DNA was digested with the restriction enzyme *Pst*I and then loaded into lane 2. Lane 1 contains lambda DNA cut with *Hind*III into the fragment sizes indicated on the left. Lane 3 contains uncut plasmid DNA. Lane 4 is empty.

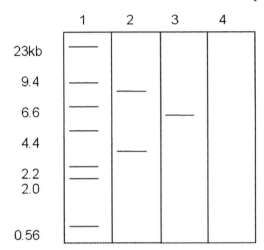

Which of the following statements best describes the results of this gel?

A) *Pst*I cuts the plasmid once to produce a 5kb fragment.

B) *Pst*I cuts the plasmid twice to produce a 5kb fragment.

C) *Pst*I cuts the plasmid once to produce 8 and 3kb fragments.

D) *Pst*I cuts the plasmid twice to produce 8 and 3kb fragments.

Answer: D
Diff: 3   Page Ref: 13.3
Skill: Application

33) Which of the following techniques amplifies a specific region of DNA?

A) PCR

B) gel electrophoresis

C) use of DNA probes

D) DNA profiles

E) none of these

Answer: A
Diff: 2   Page Ref: 13.3
Skill: Conceptual

34) During gel electrophoresis

    A) DNA moves toward the positive electrode.

    B) small DNA fragments move farther into the gel than large ones.

    C) DNA moves through holes in the agarose gel.

    D) A and C

    E) all of these

Answer: E
Diff: 2   Page Ref: 13.3
Skill: Conceptual

35) Which of the following molecular techniques involves "DNA replication in a tube"?

    A) transformation

    B) gel electrophoresis

    C) PCR

    D) A and B

    E) all of these

Answer: C
Diff: 2   Page Ref: 13.3
Skill: Conceptual

36) The following are the results of a PCR–based DNA fingerprinting analysis done at two different loci on blood found at a grisly crime scene. Lane V shows the victim's blood, lane S shows the blood sample from the crime scene, and lanes A through D show blood from four suspects. Which suspect is <u>undoubtedly</u> the killer?

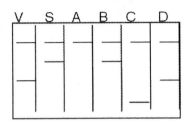

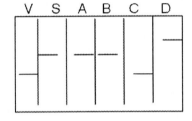

   A) A

   B) B

   C) C

   D) D

   E) none of these

Answer: E
Diff: 3   Page Ref: 13.3
Skill: Application

37) The polymerase chain reaction joins many small DNA molecules into a long chain. True or False?

Answer: FALSE
Diff: 1   Page Ref: 13.3
Skill: Conceptual

38) The "DNA fingerprints" of fraternal twins will be the same. True or False?

Answer: FALSE
Diff: 2   Page Ref: 13.3
Skill: Conceptual

39) Organisms within the same species will possess the same DNA fingerprint, but organisms from different species will have different DNA fingerprints. True or False?

Answer: FALSE
Diff: 1   Page Ref: 13.3
Skill: Conceptual

40) To amplify a specific gene one can use the DNA fingerprinting technique to identify a specific gene and make multiple copies of that gene. True or False?

Answer: FALSE
Diff: 1   Page Ref: 13.3
Skill: Conceptual

41) Describe strategies that can be used to generate multiple copies of a gene that is of interest to a researcher.

Answer: Amplify copies within a bacterium or via PCR amplification.
Diff: 2   Page Ref: 13.3
Skill: Application

42) In gel electrophoresis DNA is separated based upon charge and _____.

Answer: size
Diff: 2   Page Ref: 13.3
Skill: Factual

43) A radioactively labeled DNA _____ can be used to identify a specific piece of DNA in an electrophoresis gel.

Answer: probe
Diff: 2   Page Ref: 13.3
Skill: Factual

44) What is the advantage of using PCR over bacterial cloning to generate large quantities of a specific piece of DNA?

Answer: PCR is faster and cheaper than traditional bacterial cloning.
Diff: 2   Page Ref: 13.3
Skill: Application

45) Compare and contrast DNA fingerprinting with regular ink fingerprinting.

Answer: Both have the ability to distinguish individuals; however, DNA fingerprinting techniques can also be used for expanded applications (e.g. determining endangered species law violations, human evolution and migration patterns).
Diff: 3   Page Ref: 13.3
Skill: Conceptual

46) The enzymes used to cut genes in recombinant DNA research are called

A) DNA polymerases.

B) RNA polymerases.

C) spliceosomes.

D) replicases.

E) restriction enzymes.

Answer: E
Diff: 1   Page Ref: 13.4
Skill: Factual

47) In recombinant DNA technology, plasmids

A) are used to insert foreign DNA into bacteria.

B) show restriction enzymes where to cut bacterial DNA.

C) are necessary for cellular respiration in bacteria.

D) are where protein synthesis occurs in bacteria.

E) are found in the blood of bacteria.

Answer: A
Diff: 1   Page Ref: 13.4
Skill: Conceptual

48) Which pair of enzymes is necessary to make recombinant DNA?

A) DNA polymerase and ligase

B) ligase and restriction enzyme

C) restriction enzyme and DNA polymerase

D) DNA polymerase and RNA polymerase

E) those that cause dehydration synthesis and hydrolysis

Answer: B
Diff: 2   Page Ref: 13.4
Skill: Factual

49) In order to join a fragment of human DNA to bacterial or yeast DNA, both the human DNA and the bacterial (or yeast) DNA must be first treated with the same

A) DNA ligase.

B) DNA polymerase.

C) restriction enzyme.

D) DNA gyrase.

E) none of the above

Answer: C
Diff: 2   Page Ref: 13.4
Skill: Application

50) Restriction enzymes are useful in recombinant DNA studies because they

A) cut DNA at specific locations.

B) join the cut ends of small DNA molecules.

C) can reproduce in bacteria.

D) give plasmids antibiotic properties.

E) can separate pieces of DNA and RNA from each other.

Answer: A
Diff: 2   Page Ref: 13.4
Skill: Conceptual

51) Restriction enzymes

A) randomly sever DNA into small pieces.

B) defend bacteria against viral infections.

C) normally cut bacterial DNA as well as viral DNA.

D) will only cut DNA containing methyl groups.

E) will only work on viruses that attack bacteria.

Answer: B
Diff: 3   Page Ref: 13.4
Skill: Factual

52) Suppose ENZ–1 and ENZ–2 are two different restriction enzymes. If various pieces of DNA are cut with either of these enzymes, which of the following cut DNAs would join together most easily to form recombinant molecules?

    A) human DNA cut with ENZ–1 and gorilla DNA cut with ENZ–2

    B) human DNA cut with ENZ–1 and human DNA cut with ENZ–2

    C) human DNA cut with ENZ–2 and bacterial DNA cut with ENZ–2

    D) bacterial DNA cut with ENZ–1 and gorilla DNA cut with ENZ–2

    E) all of the above choices

Answer: C
Diff: 2   Page Ref: 13.4
Skill: Application

53) If you cut out your gene using *Eco*RI and *Bam*HI, what enzymes will you need to cut this vector in order to clone the gene into the vector?

    A) *Eco*RI only

    B) *Bam*HI only

    C) both *Eco*RI and *Bam*HI

    D) Neither of these enzymes will work to clone the gene into this vector.

Answer: C
Diff: 2   Page Ref: 13.4
Skill: Application

54) A restriction enzyme cut site map of a linear piece of DNA containing a gene that you are trying to clone is shown below. *Eco*RI (E), *Bam*HI (B), and *Pst*I (P). The numbers below the map indicate the fragment sizes that are obtained when cutting with the restriction enzymes shown.

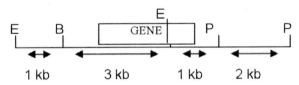

If you cut the DNA that contains the gene with *Pst*I and *Bam*HI, what fragments are obtained?

    A) 1, 2, and 3 kb fragments

    B) 1 and 2 kb fragments

    C) 1 and 3 kb fragments

    D) 1, 2 and 4 kb fragments

    E) 1 and 4 kb fragments

Answer: D
Diff: 3   Page Ref: 13.4
Skill: Application

55) A restriction enzyme cut site map of a linear piece of DNA containing a gene that you are trying to clone is shown below. *Eco*RI (E), *Bam*HI (B), and *Pst*I (P).

*Eco*RI would be a good enzyme to use to clone this gene into the plasmid available. True or False?

Answer: FALSE
Diff: 2   *Page Ref: 13.4*
Skill: Application

56) Restriction enzymes are restricted in that they normally work only on bacterial DNA. True or False?

Answer: FALSE
Diff: 1   *Page Ref: 13.4*
Skill: Conceptual

57) Ligase enzymes are used to covalently bind together pieces of DNA. True or False?

Answer: TRUE
Diff: 1   *Page Ref: 13.4*
Skill: Factual

58) Restriction enzymes cut open DNA at random sites. True or False?

Answer: FALSE
Diff: 1   *Page Ref: 13.4*
Skill: Conceptual

59) Restriction enzymes have the ability to cut DNA at specific sequences. True or False?

Answer: TRUE
Diff: 1   *Page Ref: 13.4*
Skill: Conceptual

60) Enzymes that cleave double-stranded DNA at specific sites are _____.

Answer: restriction enzymes
Diff: 1   *Page Ref: 13.4*
Skill: Factual

61) An important tool of genetic engineering is the use of _____, which is DNA altered by the incorporation of genes from a different organism.

Answer: recombinant DNA
Diff: 1   *Page Ref: 13.4*
Skill: Conceptual

62) _____ animals and plants are those which express DNA derived from another species.

Answer: Transgenic
Diff: 2   Page Ref: 13.4
Skill: Conceptual

63) Which of the following are agricultural application(s) of biotechnology: Herbicide resistant corn, Bt-toxin producing soybean, Banana vaccine against pathogenic *E. coli*, Growth hormone treated cows, Human insulin produced by bacteria?

Answer: Herbicide resistant corn, Bt-toxin producing soybean, Banana vaccine against pathogenic *E. coli*, Growth hormone treated cows
Diff: 2   Page Ref: 13.4
Skill: Conceptual

64) All of the following are benefits of sequencing the human genome EXCEPT

A) Genes were discovered whose functions were completely unknown.

B) More genes that cause disease have been discovered.

C) The number of genetic disorders that can be diagnosed molecularly has increased.

D) Comparisons of the human genome to genomes of other organisms helps determine what makes us human.

E) All of these are benefits of the human genome project.

Answer: E
Diff: 2   Page Ref: 13.5
Skill: Factual

65) The DNA sequence of humans and chimps differs by just over 1%. True or False?

Answer: TRUE
Diff: 2   Page Ref: 13.5
Skill: Factual

66) About 90% of the human genome contains the genes, whereas the remainder contains the promoters and other regions. True or False?

Answer: FALSE
Diff: 2   Page Ref: 13.5
Skill: Factual

67) Differences in RFLP banding patterns indicate that

    A) the two different DNAs being tested possess different base pairs.

    B) mRNA is not transcribed.

    C) the genes map to different chromosomes.

    D) A and C

    E) none of the above

Answer: A
Diff: 1   Page Ref: 13.6
Skill: Conceptual

68) Which of the following has NOT yet been done by using the technique of inserting human genes into bacteria?

    A) making growth hormone to help children grow normally

    B) making insulin to treat diabetics

    C) making blood clotting enzymes to treat hemophiliacs

    D) making cancer cell–killing hormones to treat those with malignancies

    E) making clot–dissolving enzymes to treat those with heart attacks

Answer: D
Diff: 1   Page Ref: 13.6
Skill: Application

69) Which of the following can be used to detect genetic disorders?

    A) restriction fragment length polymorphisms (RFLPs)

    B) arrays of DNA probes on filter paper

    C) single tandem repeats (STRs)

    D) A and B above can both be used.

    E) A, B, and C above can be used.

Answer: D
Diff: 2   Page Ref: 13.6
Skill: Application

70) If you wish to develop a procedure for identifying a genetic disorder caused by 20 different alleles, what method would be most likely to be useful?

   A) restriction fragment length polymorphisms (RFLPs)

   B) arrays of DNA probes on filter paper

   C) single tandem repeats (STRs)

   D) polymerase chain reaction (PCR)

   E) gene therapy

Answer: B
Diff: 2   Page Ref: 13.6
Skill: Application

71) What is a problem that has been encountered when using a virus to insert a functional version of a gene into a person's DNA?

   A) The patient's immune system kills the virus.

   B) The virus can cause another disease.

   C) The person contracts the viral disease, which is lethal.

   D) Cell division no longer works, because the altered chromosome is no longer identical to its homologue.

   E) Both A and B above are correct answers.

Answer: E
Diff: 2   Page Ref: 13.6
Skill: Conceptual

72) Discuss one agricultural and one medical application of biotechnology.

   Answer: Agriculture¹biodiversity, breeding, pest resistance, increase marketability of crops (tomatoes). Medical¹genetic screening, animal models of human diseases, therapeutic proteins (insulin, vaccines), gene therapy.
   Diff: 2   Page Ref: 13.5, 13.6
   Skill: Conceptual

73) Describe how the technique of gene therapy might help someone with an inherited genetic disease.

   Answer: Replace defective genes in somatic cells of the individual with the disease and alter the gametes so that the disease is not passed on to offspring.
   Diff: 2   Page Ref: 13.6
   Skill: Conceptual

74) Which of the following is an example of recombinant DNA technology (more than one answer may be correct)?
A) Herbicide resistant corn
B) Bt-toxin producing soybean
C) Banana vaccine against pathogenic *E. coli*
D) Growth hormone treated cows
E) Human insulin produced by bacteria
F) Human gene therapy

Answer: A, B, C, D, E, F
Diff: 2   Page Ref: 13.5, 13.6
Skill: Conceptual

75) Which of the following Involves cloning of human genes (more than one answer may be correct)?
A) Herbicide resistant corn
B) Bt-toxin producing soybean
C) Banana vaccine against pathogenic *E. coli*
D) Growth hormone treated cows
E) Human insulin produced by bacteria
F) Human gene therapy

Answer: E, F
Diff: 2   Page Ref: 13.5, 13.6
Skill: Conceptual

76) Which of the following is a medical application of biotechnology (more than one answer may be correct)?
A) Herbicide resistant corn
B) Bt-toxin producing soybean
C) Banana vaccine against pathogenic *E. coli*
D) Growth hormone treated cows
E) Human insulin produced by bacteria
F) Human gene therapy

Answer: C, E, F
Diff: 2   Page Ref: 13.5, 13.6
Skill: Conceptual

77) Which of the following was successfully used to treat Ashanti DeSilva who suffered from SCID (severe combined immunodeficiency)?
A) Herbicide resistant corn
B) Bt-toxin producing soybean
C) Banana vaccine against pathogenic *E. coli*
D) Growth hormone treated cows
E) Human insulin produced by bacteria
F) Human gene therapy

Answer: F
Diff: 2   Page Ref: 13.5, 13.6
Skill: Conceptual

78) Controversy has arisen about using genetically engineered bovine growth hormone to increase milk yield in cattle. This points out that

    A) recombinant DNA technology is inherently a bad idea and should be abandoned.

    B) humans are not wise enough to use this technique properly.

    C) society should let scientists decide the proper uses of recombinant DNA technology.

    D) society as a whole should decide the proper uses of recombinant DNA technology.

    E) citizens should not be allowed to decide such issues since they tend to make decisions based on emotion.

Answer: D
Diff: 3   Page Ref: 13.7
Skill: Conceptual

79) Which of the following is NOT a goal of biotechnology?

    A) to understand more about the process of inheritance and gene expression

    B) to provide better understanding and treatment of various human diseases

    C) to generate improved agricultural plants and domestic animals

    D) to prevent the inheritance of human genes judged to be undesirable

    E) All the above choices are valid goals of biotechnology.

Answer: D
Diff: 2   Page Ref: 13.7
Skill: Conceptual

80) Which of the following are differences between traditional (selective breeding) and modern (genetic engineering) biotechnology?

    A) Genetic engineering can be done much more quickly than selective breeding.

    B) Genetic engineering can use genes from unrelated species whereas selective breeding must use genes from the same or very closely related individuals.

    C) Genetic engineering can alter the DNA sequence of existing genes, whereas selective breeding cannot.

    D) All three of the above are differences.

    E) None of the above are differences.

Answer: D
Diff: 2   Page Ref: 13.7
Skill: Conceptual

81) Researchers attempted to improve the balance of amino acids in soybeans by inserting a gene from Brazil nuts. Why have these transgenic soybeans never been grown commercially?

A) The public was misinformed by food–safety advocates, and refused to buy products made from the modified soybeans.

B) The modified soybeans could not grow with the foreign gene present.

C) Some people were allergic to the protein product of the Brazil nut gene.

D) Regulatory hurdles made the modified soybeans too expensive to market profitably.

E) The protein product of the soybean was indigestible to most people.

Answer: C
Diff: 2   Page Ref: 13.7
Skill: Conceptual

82) What is a threat to the environment of transgenic crops?

A) Pollen from transgenic crops could carry the recombinant genes to wild relatives, with unpredictable consequences.

B) Wild animals might eat the transgenic crop and become genetically mutated "monsters."

C) Transgenic crops could escape cultivation and become "superweeds."

D) The products of the modified genes these crops carry are usually toxic and would be released to the environment if the plants die.

E) None of the above are threats.

Answer: A
Diff: 2   Page Ref: 13.7
Skill: Conceptual

83) There are potential risks in performing recombinant DNA research on humans. True or False?

Answer: TRUE
Diff: 1   Page Ref: 13.7
Skill: Conceptual

84) There are potential risks in performing recombinant DNA research on plants. True or False?

Answer: TRUE
Diff: 1   Page Ref: 13.7
Skill: Conceptual

85) Stringent safety rules are unnecessary for recombinant DNA research. True or False?

Answer: FALSE
Diff: 1   Page Ref: 13.7
Skill: Conceptual

86) Discuss some of the bioethical concerns related to screening for genetic diseases.

Answer: Let the student express their opinions concerning this highly controversial topic as long as they support their statements logically.
Diff: 2   Page Ref: 13.7
Skill: Conceptual

87) Without the discovery of the organism *Thermus aquaticus*, the technique of PCR may never have been developed. True or False?

Answer: TRUE
Diff: 1   Page Ref: Scientific Inquiry
Skill: Conceptual

88) Golden Rice was originally developed to provide a source of iron to people for whom rice is their principal food. True or False?

Answer: FALSE
Diff: 1   Page Ref: Biotechnology Watch
Skill: Factual

89) Prenatal diagnosis is available for which of the following disorders?

A) cystic fibrosis

B) Down Syndrome

C) sickle cell anemia

D) all of these

E) none of these

Answer: D
Diff: 2   Page Ref: Health Watch
Skill: Factual

90) Which of the following techniques is most commonly used to prenatally diagnose a genetic disorder such as cystic fibrosis in a fetus?

A) amniocentesis

B) chorionic villus sampling

C) isolation of fetal cells from maternal blood

D) ultrasound

E) All of these are equally commonly used.

Answer: A
Diff: 2   Page Ref: Health Watch
Skill: Factual

Chapter 14 Evolution

1) Plato's view of species

    A) was consistent with the modern concept of evolution.

    B) did not allow for evolutionary change.

    C) included species that do not actually exist.

    D) recognized that each individual in a species is unique.

    E) allowed for limited evolution within species.

Answer: B
Diff: 2   Page Ref: 14.1
Skill: Conceptual

2) Which of these statements is inconsistent with the theory of catastrophism?

    A) Species can go extinct due to natural disasters, such as floods.

    B) Many species have become extinct.

    C) There are millions of undescribed species in the world.

    D) There are no humans in early fossil records.

Answer: D
Diff: 1   Page Ref: 14.1
Skill: Conceptual

3) Which geologist described the age of the Earth as "eternal"?

    A) Lyell   B) Lamarck   C) Buffon   D) Malthus   E) Aristotle

Answer: A
Diff: 1   Page Ref: 14.1
Skill: Factual

4) Lamarck would agree with all of these statements EXCEPT

    A) boa constrictors should have vestigial hind limbs and a pelvic girdle.

    B) daily stretching will make you and your offspring more flexible.

    C) bob-tailed cats evolved after several generations of cats had their tails bitten off.

    D) a man who routinely shaves the hair off his head will have sons who become bald.

    E) giraffes evolved their long necks by stretching.

Answer: A
Diff: 1   Page Ref: 14.1
Skill: Conceptual

5) The incorrect theory that "organisms can modify their bodies through use or disuse of parts, and that these modifications can be passed on to their offspring" was formulated by

A) Hutton.   B) Darwin.   C) Aristotle.   D) Lamarck.   E) Lyell.

Answer: D
Diff: 1   Page Ref: 14.1
Skill: Factual

6) Which scientist devised the theory of uniformitarianism to account for the old age of the Earth?

A) Plato   B) Darwin   C) Cuvier   D) Lamarck   E) Lyell

Answer: E
Diff: 1   Page Ref: 14.1
Skill: Factual

7) The publication date of Darwin's book, *On the Origin of Species by Means of Natural Selection,* was

A) 1809.   B) 1830.   C) 1859.   D) 1869.   E) 1900.

Answer: C
Diff: 1   Page Ref: 14.1
Skill: Factual

8) The author of *On the Origin of Species by Means of Natural Selection* was

A) Mendel.   B) Malthus.   C) Smith.   D) Darwin.   E) Lamarck.

Answer: D
Diff: 1   Page Ref: 14.1
Skill: Factual

9) Darwin and _____ both developed and proposed the theory of evolution by natural selection.

A) Buffon   B) Malthus   C) Wallace   D) Lamarck   E) Hutton

Answer: C
Diff: 1   Page Ref: 14.1
Skill: Factual

10) Who published *On the Origin of Species* in 1859?

    A) Darwin

    B) Lamarck

    C) Darwin and Wallace

    D) Cuvier

    E) Plato

Answer: A
Diff: 1   Page Ref: 14.1
Skill: Factual

11) Who presented the idea of natural selection to the Linnaean Society in 1858?

    A) Darwin

    B) Lamarck

    C) Darwin and Wallace

    D) Cuvier

    E) Plato

Answer: C
Diff: 1   Page Ref: 14.1
Skill: Factual

12) Whose philosophy was based on the "ideal form?"

    A) Darwin

    B) Lamarck

    C) Darwin and Wallace

    D) Cuvier

    E) Plato

Answer: E
Diff: 1   Page Ref: 14.1
Skill: Factual

13) Who proposed the geological theory of catastrophism?

    A) Darwin

    B) Lamarck

    C) Darwin and Wallace

    D) Cuvier

    E) Plato

Answer: D
Diff: 1   Page Ref: 14.1
Skill: Factual

14) Who suggested that giraffes developed their long necks over time by stretching?

     A) Darwin   B) Lamarck   C) Wallace   D) Cuvier   E) Plato

Answer: B
Diff: 1   Page Ref: 14.1
Skill: Factual

15) Fossils are rocks or sediments that

    A) have been shaped by wind or water to resemble lifelike forms.

    B) have been shaped by people to resemble plants or animals.

    C) bear the impressions or shapes of preserved organisms.

    D) all of the above

Answer: C
Diff: 1   Page Ref: 14.1
Skill: Factual

16) Modern geologists estimate that the age of the Earth is about _____ years old.

    A) 4,500

    B) 450,000

    C) 4,500,000

    D) 4,500,000,000

    E) 4,500,000,000,000

Answer: D
Diff: 2   Page Ref: 14.1
Skill: Factual

17) There were biologists before Darwin who proposed mechanisms for evolution. True or False?

Answer: TRUE
Diff: 1   Page Ref: 14.1
Skill: Factual

18) Sea squirts and lampreys, which are both aquatic animals, have a perforated pharynx, a ventral heart, and a notochord at some stage of development. These similarities are BEST explained by

  A) artificial selection.

  B) inheritance of acquired characteristics.

  C) a common ancestry.

  D) uniformitarianism.

  E) the "ladder of Nature."

Answer: C
Diff: 2   Page Ref: 14.2
Skill: Application

19) When unrelated organisms living under similar environmental demands evolve superficially similar structures, it is called

  A) superficial selection.   B) comparative anatomy.

  C) convergent evolution.   D) coevolution.

Answer: C
Diff: 1   Page Ref: 14.2
Skill: Factual

20) Structures that serve little or no purpose in the organism being considered, but are homologous to important structures in other organisms, are referred to as

  A) analogous.   B) mutations.   C) vestigial.   D) convergent.

Answer: C
Diff: 2   Page Ref: 14.2
Skill: Factual

21) The fat–insulated, streamlined bodies of seals and penguins are similar, although these organisms are not closely related. Such superficially similar structures are

  A) vestigial structures.

  B) homologous structures.

  C) genetically similar.

  D) evidence of convergent evolution.

  E) coevolved structures.

Answer: D
Diff: 1   Page Ref: 14.2
Skill: Conceptual

22) Which of the following structures is NOT homologous to the others?

   A) alligator forelimb

   B) bird wing

   C) human arm

   D) insect wing

   E) bat wing

Answer: D
Diff: 2   Page Ref: 14.2
Skill: Conceptual

23) Boa constrictors have tiny pelvic girdles and leg bones within their bodies. Because these structures are nonfunctional "evolutionary baggage," they are called

   A) convergent.

   B) analogous.

   C) maladaptive.

   D) homologous.

   E) vestigial.

Answer: E
Diff: 1   Page Ref: 14.2
Skill: Factual

24) Convergent evolution occurs when

   A) unrelated organisms develop analogous structures.

   B) two or more different species evolve to become one species.

   C) two or more populations merge into one.

   D) analogous structures evolve to be homologous.

   E) none of the above

Answer: A
Diff: 2   Page Ref: 14.2
Skill: Conceptual

25) The fact that whales have pelvic and leg bones indicates

    A) they probably evolved from fish.

    B) ancestral whales had legs.

    C) whales should have functional legs.

    D) having a pelvis is advantageous.

    E) whales did not evolve by natural selection.

Answer: B
Diff: 2   *Page Ref: 14.2*
Skill: Application

26) The human appendix is an example of a(n)

    A) analogous structure.

    B) homologous structure.

    C) vestigial structure.

    D) adaptation.

    E) mutation.

Answer: C
Diff: 1   *Page Ref: 14.2*
Skill: Factual

27) Which of the following are vestigial structures?

    A) fish fins

    B) vertebral columns in snakes

    C) pelvic bones of whales

    D) wings of bats

    E) Only choices A, B, and D are correct.

Answer: C
Diff: 1   *Page Ref: 14.2*
Skill: Conceptual

28) Mammalian appendages with similar bone structures can be used for flying, swimming, running, or grasping. These are examples of _____ structures.

    A) vestigial

    B) embryonic

    C) convergent

    D) artificially selected

    E) homologous

Answer: E
Diff: 2   Page Ref: 14.2
Skill: Conceptual

29) Dolphins (which are mammals) and sharks (which are fish) have stiff dorsal fins projecting from their backs that help them maneuver through water. These structures are BEST described as

    A) analogous structures.   B) homologous structures.

    C) vestigial structures.   D) mutations.

Answer: A
Diff: 1   Page Ref: 14.2
Skill: Application

30) Some animal species found in caves have tiny, nonfunctional eyes. These are BEST described as

    A) analogous structures.   B) homologous structures.

    C) vestigial structures.   D) mutations.

Answer: C
Diff: 1   Page Ref: 14.2
Skill: Application

31) Strong evidence for the common ancestry of all vertebrates is

    A) they all have legs.

    B) their means of reproduction.

    C) the similarity of their embryological stages.

    D) they all evolved from fish.

    E) they all possess DNA.

Answer: C
Diff: 2   Page Ref: 14.2
Skill: Conceptual

32) Karl von Baer's observations of vertebrate embryos suggest that

    A) fish are unrelated to other vertebrates because they are the only vertebrates that develop gills.

    B) fish, turtles, and mice are more closely related to each other than they are to either chickens or humans because they have substantial tails.

    C) chickens and humans are closely related because they lack substantial tails.

    D) all vertebrate species have similar genes for development, with some being active in some species and inactive in others.

Answer: D
Diff: 2   *Page Ref: 14.2*
Skill: Conceptual

33) Which of the following is NOT necessarily strong evidence supporting a common ancestry and close relatedness between two species?

    A) presence of wings and the ability to fly

    B) embryonic development of gill slits

    C) similar nucleotide sequence in the gene that codes for cytochrome c

    D) homologous structures that are used in similar ways

Answer: A
Diff: 2   *Page Ref: 14.2*
Skill: Application

34) Which of the following cellular–level processes does NOT support the claim that all organisms share a common ancestry?

    A) Among all living species, DNA carries genetic information.

    B) Among all living species, RNA translates genes into proteins.

    C) Among all living species, Cytochrome c genes are identical.

    D) Among all living species, ATP is used as a source of energy.

    E) Among all living species, the same 20 amino acids are used to build proteins.

Answer: E
Diff: 2   *Page Ref: 14.2*
Skill: Factual

35) The amino acid sequence of human and chimpanzee hemoglobin is almost identical, yet differs considerably from the hemoglobin of dogs. This statement

    A) supports the theory of evolution.

    B) opposes the theory of evolution.

    C) neither supports nor opposes biological evolution.

Answer: A
Diff: 1   *Page Ref: 14.2*
Skill: Application

36) Assume that it is possible to remove continuous cores of rock from the Earth that are 3000 feet long and contain fossils. The theory of evolution by natural selection would predict what about the fossils found in such cores, as they are examined from top to bottom?

A) Lower fossils are more similar to living species than higher fossils.

B) The number of fossils decreases from top to bottom but the number of species increases.

C) Fossil species remain constant from top to bottom.

D) Higher fossils are more similar to living species than lower fossils.

E) Fossils forms are arranged in random patterns.

Answer: D
Diff: 2   Page Ref: 14.2
Skill: Application

37) The large, productive udders of domesticated milk goats and cows are _____ structures.

A) useless   B) analogous

C) vestigial   D) artificially selected

Answer: D
Diff: 2   Page Ref: 14.2
Skill: Conceptual

38) The wings of insects and bats are _____ structures.

A) homologous   B) analogous

C) vestigial   D) artificially selected

Answer: B
Diff: 2   Page Ref: 14.2
Skill: Conceptual

39) A bat's wing and a sheep's front leg are _____ structures.

A) homologous   B) analogous

C) vestigial   D) artificially selected

Answer: A
Diff: 2   Page Ref: 14.2
Skill: Conceptual

40) Pelvic bones in snakes and whales are _____ structures.

A) homologous   B) analogous

C) vestigial   D) artificially selected

Answer: C
Diff: 2   Page Ref: 14.2
Skill: Conceptual

41) Provide three different types of evidence (from different sub–disciplines in biology) that scientists commonly use to provide support for the theory of evolution.

Answer: Fossils; comparative anatomy; embryological similarity; and modern biochemical and genetic analyses are four possible answers.
Diff: 3   Page Ref: 14.2
Skill: Factual

42) Darwin and Wallace both realized that most species produce many more offspring than is necessary to maintain a constant population. The 'excess' individuals in a population

A) migrate to another location.

B) die before they can reproduce.

C) evolve to become new species.

D) mutate and are able to adapt to new environments.

Answer: B
Diff: 2   Page Ref: 14.3
Skill: Factual

43) Which of the four postulates of Darwin's theory of evolution was not well established when *On the Origin of Species* was first published, but is overwhelmingly supported today?

A) Some differences among individuals in a population are due to genetics, and are heritable.

B) Individuals in a population differ physically from one another, in many ways.

C) Some individuals in a population survive and reproduce better than other individuals.

D) Individuals with advantageous traits survive longest and leave the most offspring.

Answer: A
Diff: 2   Page Ref: 14.3
Skill: Factual

44) Imagine that a population of deer living on an island without any predators was threatened with overpopulation, until wolves were imported. After a couple of years there were fewer deer, but their average running speed and length of their legs had increased. This is an example of

A) inheritance of acquired characteristics.

B) changes due to chance alone.

C) genetic impossibility.

D) unfavorable mutations.

E) natural selection.

Answer: E
Diff: 2   Page Ref: 14.3
Skill: Conceptual

45) Which of the following statements about the genetic basis of evolution is TRUE?

   A) All marathon runners necessarily possess good genes for running because their bodies are in such good physical condition.

   B) Exercise can have a beneficial effect on an individual's genes.

   C) Any physical alterations made to a person's body during their lifetime will not affect their genetic makeup.

   D) Cutting the tails off mice for 100 generations and allowing them to interbreed will result in a population of mice with genes for short tails.

Answer: C
Diff: 3   Page Ref: 14.3
Skill: Application

46) The theory of natural selection states that

   A) all individuals live to reproduce in each generation.

   B) only the largest and strongest individuals survive.

   C) random assortment of genes results in better physical characteristics in the following generations.

   D) the most well-adapted individuals in their environments survive and reproduce, contributing the most genes to the next generation.

   E) individuals that mutate in response to changes in their environment will contribute the most genes to the next generation.

Answer: D
Diff: 2   Page Ref: 14.3
Skill: Factual

47) Natural selection can only act upon a certain trait if the trait is

   A) heritable.

   B) behavioral.

   C) favorable.

   D) morphological.

   E) new.

Answer: A
Diff: 1   Page Ref: 14.3
Skill: Conceptual

48) Which of these conditions was NOT included in Darwin's or Wallace's theory of natural selection?

   A) Physical appearances of individuals vary in a population.

   B) Reproductive rates of individuals vary in a population.

   C) An individual's chance of survival and reproduction depends on its characteristics.

   D) Some physical traits are passed from parents to offspring.

   E) Genetic mutations spontaneously arise in the DNA of individuals.

   Answer: E
   Diff: 1   Page Ref: 14.3
   Skill: Factual

49) If the weather in Virginia changed so dramatically that there is snow on the ground most of the year, what would occur in the local squirrel population?

   A) The weather change would cause a mutation that causes their fur to be white, resulting in white squirrels that survive and reproduce better than gray squirrels.

   B) If a mutation occurred that caused white fur to develop, such white squirrels would likely survive and reproduce better than gray squirrels.

   C) Evolution would produce white squirrels, because white squirrels would survive and reproduce better than squirrels of any other color.

   D) Natural selection would cause a new gene to appear in the population, resulting in squirrels growing white fur when there is snow on the ground and growing gray fur at other times.

   E) Natural selection could not change the population of squirrels in response to such climatic changes.

   Answer: B
   Diff: 3   Page Ref: 14.3
   Skill: Application

50) Natural selection is BEST described as

   A) the ability to generate new traits that better suit the species.

   B) increasing the perfection of a species.

   C) working on existing variation of traits to favor those better suited to the organism's environment.

   D) causing the death of a significant proportion of the population.

   E) driving the species toward an eventual endpoint in which the species possesses the best possible adaptations for that particular environment.

   Answer: C
   Diff: 3   Page Ref: 14.3
   Skill: Conceptual

51) Which of the following is NOT in accord with the process of natural selection?

    A) In an insect that is the favorite prey of bats, a new mutation arises that gives it longer wings, allowing it to fly faster.

    B) The leaves of plants exposed to full sunlight are smaller than the leaves of plants growing in the shade, due to genetic differences between the plants.

    C) A mammal is born with the ability to produce a chemical that attracts members of the opposite sex, and subsequently has greater reproductive success than its siblings.

    D) In an island population, brown–colored individuals of a certain lizard species become more common than green individuals because a hurricane kills off all green individuals.

Answer: D
Diff: 3   Page Ref: 14.3
Skill: Application

52) Which of the following is NOT an example of natural selection?

    A) Plants with thorns are less likely to be eaten by herbivores than other members of the same species that lack thorns.

    B) Bacteria in hospital patients develop resistance to the drugs used to combat them.

    C) Scientists breed cows that give greater amounts of milk than their ancestors.

    D) Fruit fly larvae with an enzyme to break down alcohol are better able to feed on fermenting fruit than those that lack the enzyme.

    E) Female fish that produce more eggs leave more offspring than those that produce fewer eggs.

Answer: C
Diff: 3   Page Ref: 14.3
Skill: Conceptual

53) Inheritable mutations in the genes of an individual arise due to

    A) random chance.

    B) environmental change.

    C) vigorous exercise or effort.

    D) other species in the environment.

    E) artificial selection.

Answer: A
Diff: 1   Page Ref: 14.3
Skill: Factual

54) Which of the following statements about mutations is TRUE?

    A) Mutations have no effect on the survival and reproduction of an organism.

    B) Mutations are almost always better for the organism.

    C) Mutations almost always leave the organism worse off than before.

    D) Mutations are caused by natural selection.

    E) Mutations occur at random and may be good, bad, or have no effect on the organism.

Answer: E
Diff: 1   Page Ref: 14.3
Skill: Conceptual

55) A change in the genetic makeup of a population is called

    A) natural selection.   B) uniformitarianism.

    C) artificial selection.   D) evolution.

Answer: D
Diff: 1   Page Ref: 14.3
Skill: Factual

56) Which of the following statements was NOT one of Darwin's assumptions in his theory of natural selection?

    A) There are more offspring produced in each generation than can possibly survive to adulthood.

    B) Individuals in populations tend to vary in specific traits.

    C) Certain traits of parents are usually passed along to their offspring.

    D) Organisms usually have two copies of each gene for each trait.

    E) Some versions of traits allow the individuals who have them to better survive and reproduce.

Answer: D
Diff: 2   Page Ref: 14.3
Skill: Factual

57) A population of grasshoppers in the Kansas prairie has two color types, green and brown. Typically, the prairie receives adequate water to maintain healthy, green grass. Assume a bird species that eats grasshoppers moves into the prairie. How will this affect natural selection of the grasshoppers? How might this change in a drought year, when the grass turns brown?

Answer: The brown phenotype may be more easily detected by the bird predator and decrease in frequency when the prairie is green. The opposite may be true in drought years when the green phenotype is more visible.
Diff: 3   Page Ref: 14.3
Skill: Application

58) The controlled breeding of domestic plants and animals by humans in order to produce certain physical traits in those organisms is called

  A) natural selection.

  B) agricultural selection.

  C) physical selection.

  D) artificial selection.

  E) all of the above

Answer: D
Diff: 1   Page Ref: 14.4
Skill: Factual

59) Which of the following is an excellent example of artificial selection?

  A) the many different breeds of domestic cats

  B) cheetahs that can outrun their prey

  C) the ability to gain muscle mass by using steroids

  D) green treefrogs that blend perfectly into their leafy surroundings

  E) all of the above

Answer: A
Diff: 2   Page Ref: 14.4
Skill: Application

60) Which of the following would you expect to occur in a captive population of guppies collected from Trinidad, if you allowed them to breed for many generations in an aquarium without any predators?

  A) Female guppies would become more brightly colored.

  B) Female guppies would prefer to mate with the dull-colored males.

  C) The number of dull-colored male guppies would eventually equal the number of bright-colored males.

  D) Male guppies that are bright-colored would have better reproductive success than dull males.

Answer: D
Diff: 3   Page Ref: 14.4
Skill: Application

61) Which of the following is NOT a true scenario that has occurred in insect pests in Florida, due to natural selection?

A) Cockroaches now avoid a poison bait that used to be very effective at killing them.

B) The amount of pesticide applied by farmers has increased in response to resistant pests.

C) The additional amount of pesticides farmers must apply to kill resistant pests costs billions of dollars a year.

D) Roaches that ate a common poison bait became immune to the poison and tripled in size.

Answer: D
Diff: 1   Page Ref: 14.4
Skill: Factual

62) Charles Darwin believed that artificial selection was

A) impossible.

B) unimportant.

C) a process completely identical to natural selection.

D) a common phenomenon in nature.

E) similar in many ways to natural selection.

Answer: E
Diff: 1   Page Ref: 14.4
Skill: Factual

63) The many different breeds of domestic dog were produced by

A) natural selection.   B) artificial selection.

C) physical selection.   D) artificial mutation.

Answer: B
Diff: 1   Page Ref: 14.4
Skill: Factual

64) Imagine that a biologist develops a strain of corn with lower fat content by choosing low fat variants and cross-breeding them over a period of several generations. This is an example of

A) convergent evolution.

B) natural selection.

C) artificial mutation.

D) artificial selection.

E) inheritance of acquired characteristics.

Answer: D
Diff: 2   Page Ref: 14.4
Skill: Conceptual

65) Most commercial pesticides are effective for only 2 to 3 years. This is because

   A) new pests invade the area.

   B) the chemicals induce mutations that provide immunity.

   C) the chemicals mutate and become ineffective.

   D) the pests learn to hide when the chemicals are being applied.

   E) those pests born with mutations that provide immunity will survive and reproduce.

Answer: E
Diff: 3   Page Ref: 14.4
Skill: Application

66) Which of the following would you predict would evolve in guppies taken from streams in Trinidad with predators, and put into streams lacking predators?

   A) Male guppies would become more colorful.

   B) Male guppies would become less colorful.

   C) Male guppies would not change in coloration.

   D) Guppies would evolve to have females prefer even more colorful males.

   E) Guppies would evolve to have females prefer less colorful males.

Answer: A
Diff: 2   Page Ref: 14.4
Skill: Application

67) *Anolis* lizards have been transplanted from an area with many large trees to islands with many small plants. These lizards have

   A) undergone no evolutionary change.

   B) evolved shorter legs.

   C) evolved longer legs.

   D) evolved to be able to run away from predators more quickly.

   E) evolved to be able to maneuver less efficiently.

Answer: B
Diff: 2   Page Ref: 14.4
Skill: Factual

68) Based on the way that natural selection works, what is the BEST way to make use of antibacterial soap?

   A) Always use it because most bacteria will cause illness.

   B) Always use it because it is unlikely that bacteria will evolve to become resistant to it.

   C) Never use it because bacteria will evolve to become resistant to it.

   D) Use it only when you need to be free of bacterial contamination, so bacteria will be less likely to evolve resistance to it.

   E) Never use it because all bacteria are harmless.

Answer: D
Diff: 3   Page Ref: 14.4
Skill: Application

69) Evidence that supports the theory of evolution is found in the studies of

   A) embryos.

   B) biochemistry.

   C) fossils.

   D) artificial selection.

   E) all of these

Answer: E
Diff: 1   Page Ref: 14.2, 14.3, 14.4
Skill: Factual

70) The English economist who wrote that human population "increases in a geometrical ratio" and would soon exceed the Earth's capacity to support it was

   A) Wallace.   B) Mendel.   C) Hutton.   D) Lyell.   E) Malthus.

Answer: E
Diff: 1   Page Ref: Scientific Inquiry
Skill: Factual

71) Both Darwin and Wallace were influenced by Thomas Malthus' writings on

   A) population growth.

   B) uniformitarianism.

   C) genetics.

   D) evolution.

   E) natural selection.

Answer: A
Diff: 1   Page Ref: Scientific Inquiry
Skill: Factual

72) Some of Darwin's most important discoveries were based on studies of birds and tortoises he observed in

    A) Tahiti.

    B) Jamaica.

    C) Ecuador.

    D) the Bahamas.

    E) the Galapagos Islands.

Answer: E
Diff: 1   Page Ref: Scientific Inquiry
Skill: Factual

73) The Galapagos Islands, visited by Darwin, are located where?

    A) off the west coast of Australia

    B) off the west coast of North America

    C) off the west coast of South America

    D) near Southeast Asia

    E) near the center of the south Atlantic Ocean

Answer: C
Diff: 1   Page Ref: Scientific Inquiry
Skill: Factual

74) The existence of species of flightless birds with wings suggests that

    A) they are ancestral to flying birds.   B) they are not related to flying birds.

    C) they descended from flying birds.   D) birds did not evolve from dinosaurs.

Answer: C
Diff: 2   Page Ref: Case Study
Skill: Conceptual

75) Wisdom teeth are not needed in modern humans, but we still possess them because our ancestors relied on them for chewing their food. True or False?

Answer: TRUE
Diff: 1   Page Ref: Case Study
Skill: Factual

Chapter 15   How Organisms Evolve

1) Which of the following can evolve?

   A) individuals   B) populations   C) genes   D) communities

Answer: B
Diff: 1   Page Ref: 15.1
Skill: Conceptual

2) Which of the following categories is the SMALLEST unit capable of evolution?

   A) individual

   B) population

   C) species

   D) community

   E) family

Answer: B
Diff: 1   Page Ref: 15.1
Skill: Conceptual

3) A population is BEST defined as

   A) all individuals of the same species, located throughout the world.

   B) all individuals of the same species, located in a given region of the world.

   C) all individuals of all species, located throughout the world.

   D) all individuals of all species, located in a given region of the world.

   E) those individuals of the same species that have an identical genetic makeup.

Answer: B
Diff: 1   Page Ref: 15.1
Skill: Factual

4) An allele frequency is

   A) the number of all alleles in a population.

   B) the relative proportion of a given allele in a population.

   C) the sum of all genes in a population.

   D) the number of different types of alleles in a population.

Answer: B
Diff: 2   Page Ref: 15.1
Skill: Conceptual

5) The gene pool *for a particular gene* is made up of

    A) all the alleles that occur in the population.

    B) all the alleles for a certain trait that occur in the population.

    C) the sum of all the heterozygous individuals in the population.

    D) the sum of all the homozygous individuals in the population.

    E) all the alleles for a certain trait in a given individual.

Answer: B
Diff: 1   Page Ref: 15.1
Skill: Factual

6) In a very small population of birds, assume 5 out of 20 alleles are the type that code for blue feathers. What is the allele frequency of the "blue feather allele" in this population?

    A) 0.20   B) 0.25   C) 0.40   D) 0.50   E) 5

Answer: B
Diff: 2   Page Ref: 15.1
Skill: Application

7) Which of the following is NOT capable of evolving?

    A) a population of fruit flies

    B) a strain of bacteria

    C) a biology professor

    D) a population of cats in a city

    E) a group of plants of the same species that reproduces asexually

Answer: C
Diff: 2   Page Ref: 15.1
Skill: Application

8) Which of the following statements about evolution is FALSE?

    A) Individuals evolve.

    B) Populations evolve.

    C) An entire species can evolve.

    D) Evolution involves a change of frequency of alleles.

Answer: A
Diff: 2   Page Ref: 15.1
Skill: Conceptual

9) Evolution can be defined as

    A) a change in the genetic makeup of a population over time.

    B) a change in phenotype of an individual over his or her lifetime.

    C) a change in the genetic makeup of an organism over time.

    D) an individual changing into another species.

    E) one species diverging into two species.

Answer: A
Diff: 1   Page Ref: 15.1
Skill: Factual

10) Populations of organisms are constantly evolving, which means they are always

    A) improving.

    B) at equilibrium.

    C) becoming more like humans.

    D) getting bigger.

    E) changing.

Answer: E
Diff: 2   Page Ref: 15.1
Skill: Conceptual

11) Within a large population, if no mutations occur, no migration occurs, all matings are random, and each individual has an equal chance of reproducing, which of the following will probably happen?

    A) Extinction will occur.

    B) A bottleneck will occur.

    C) Natural selection will occur at the normal rate for that species.

    D) A change in allele frequency will lead to rapid evolution.

    E) No evolution will occur.

Answer: E
Diff: 2   Page Ref: 15.1
Skill: Conceptual

12) In the context of evolution, equilibrium means

A) no change in allele frequency.

B) no change in population size.

C) equal numbers of all alleles.

D) equal numbers of males and females.

E) no individuals move into or out of the population.

Answer: A
Diff: 2   Page Ref: 15.1
Skill: Factual

13) Which of the following is NOT a condition of the Hardy–Weinberg Principle?

A) No mutations occur.

B) Natural selection will occur.

C) No gene flow will occur.

D) All mating is random.

E) Individuals will not move into or out of the population.

Answer: B
Diff: 2   Page Ref: 15.1
Skill: Factual

14) In an equilibrium population

A) mutation rates do not change.

B) natural selection occurs.

C) allele frequencies do not change.

D) population size cannot change.

E) rates of gene flow are constant.

Answer: C
Diff: 2   Page Ref: 15.1
Skill: Factual

15) Suppose that the only population of a certain reptile species lives on an African mountain. If you could prevent all movement of individuals out of this large but isolated population, which of the following describes the most likely future of this reptile population?

    A) Evolution will promptly cease.

    B) The population will go extinct after a few generations because of inbreeding.

    C) Evolution will continue because of mutations, assortative mating, and genetic drift.

    D) The bottleneck effect will cause major evolutionary changes in the isolated population.

    E) The population will survive only as long as the environment remains constant.

Answer: C
Diff: 2   Page Ref: 15.2
Skill: Application

16) Imagine that two men and two women settle on an uninhabited island, no new settlers arrive, and nobody leaves the island for many generations. All four of the settlers have brown eyes, but one of the men carries a recessive gene for blue eyes. Eye color has no effect on fitness. If the percentage of blue–eyed individuals on the island increases from zero to 25%, this is probably due to which factor?

    A) artificial selection   B) natural selection

    C) random mutation   D) genetic drift

Answer: D
Diff: 2   Page Ref: 15.2
Skill: Conceptual

17) Imagine that 1 of the original 4 mice that escape from a research lab is blind due to a genetic defect. If the mice breed, and most of the mice born in subsequent generations are blind from birth, this is most likely a case of

    A) artificial selection.

    B) the founder effect.

    C) selective mutation.

    D) an equilibrium population.

    E) natural selection.

Answer: B
Diff: 2   Page Ref: 15.2
Skill: Application

18) Which of the following can cause evolutionary change in a small population?

    A) genetic drift

    B) random mutation

    C) natural selection

    D) all of the above

    E) none of the above

Answer: D
Diff: 1   Page Ref: 15.2
Skill: Factual

19) Which of the following is MOST likely to experience genetic drift?

    A) a population of endangered birds that includes only 5 individuals

    B) a population of common rodents that includes millions of individuals

    C) a species of insect that occurs all across North America

    D) a population of bears that is growing by thousands of individuals each year

    E) a plant species that has spread to many different habitats all around the world

Answer: A
Diff: 1   Page Ref: 15.2
Skill: Conceptual

20) Inbreeding is defined as

    A) reproduction among unrelated individuals.

    B) reproduction within a geographically-isolated population.

    C) sexual reproduction in a large population.

    D) sexual reproduction among closely related individuals.

Answer: D
Diff: 1   Page Ref: 15.2
Skill: Factual

21) Antibiotic resistance is an example of _____ in bacteria.

    A) genetic drift   B) assortative mating

    C) natural selection   D) an equilibrium population

Answer: C
Diff: 1   Page Ref: 15.2
Skill: Factual

22) From an evolutionary point of view, what important process occurs when a young male baboon leaves the troop that he was born in to join another troop?

    A) non-random mating

    B) gene flow

    C) bottleneck effect

    D) natural selection

    E) genetic drift

Answer: B
Diff: 2   Page Ref: 15.2
Skill: Conceptual

23) The 30,000 elephant seals alive today are genetically very similar, due to

    A) natural selection.

    B) artificial selection.

    C) the bottleneck effect.

    D) the founder effect.

    E) random mutation.

Answer: C
Diff: 1   Page Ref: 15.2
Skill: Factual

24) Habitat loss, natural catastrophes, and/or excessive harvesting of a species often results in

    A) increased mutation rates.

    B) population bottlenecks.

    C) increased fitness of individuals.

    D) artificial selection.

    E) increased gene flow.

Answer: B
Diff: 2   Page Ref: 15.2
Skill: Conceptual

25) A small population is likely to evolve because of _____, but this is not likely to be true for large populations.

A) artificial selection

B) genetic drift

C) mutations

D) assortative mating

E) natural selection

Answer: B
Diff: 2   Page Ref: 15.2
Skill: Conceptual

26) A population with _____ is at risk for extinction.

A) many individuals

B) low genetic variation

C) gene flow

D) low levels of genetic drift

E) random mating

Answer: B
Diff: 1   Page Ref: 15.2
Skill: Factual

27) The process by which allele frequencies are altered in a population due to chance is called

A) random evolution.

B) assortative evolution.

C) genetic drift.

D) random mutation.

E) fitness.

Answer: C
Diff: 1   Page Ref: 15.2
Skill: Factual

28) Mutations

    A) can be helpful, neutral, or harmful to individuals.

    B) do not arise due to environmental pressures.

    C) are acted upon by natural selection and genetic drift.

    D) provide the potential for evolution.

    E) all of these

Answer: E
Diff: 1   *Page Ref: 15.2*
Skill: Conceptual

29) Mutations are important because they

    A) provide variation that can result in evolutionary change.

    B) occur in response to environmental demands.

    C) are always beneficial in the individuals affected by them.

    D) usually provide an individual with increased reproductive rates.

Answer: A
Diff: 2   *Page Ref: 15.2*
Skill: Conceptual

30) Gene flow

    A) can involve migration of individuals into other populations.

    B) can spread certain alleles throughout a species.

    C) makes separated populations more alike, genetically speaking.

    D) can influence the evolution of a population.

    E) all of the above

Answer: E
Diff: 1   *Page Ref: 15.2*
Skill: Factual

31) In general, each species of fruit fly found in the Hawaiian archipelago is restricted to a single island. One hypothesis to explain this pattern is that new species formed after a small number of flies colonized each new island. This mechanism is called

    A) sexual selection.

    B) genetic equilibrium.

    C) artificial selection.

    D) the founder effect.

    E) assortative mating.

Answer: D
Diff: 2   *Page Ref: 15.2*
Skill: Conceptual

32) Imagine a population of monkeys in South America whose habitat has been reduced to the point where only 20 individuals survive. This is an example of

   A) genetic drift.

   B) the founder effect.

   C) natural selection.

   D) a population bottleneck.

   E) all of the above

Answer: D
Diff: 1   Page Ref: 15.2
Skill: Factual

33) Genetic drift results in a change in gene frequencies because

   A) gene flow within the population is less than gene flow between populations.

   B) the population is so large that natural selection has little noticeable effect.

   C) the population size is so small that chance occurrences can alter gene frequencies.

   D) the population has not yet stabilized.

Answer: C
Diff: 1   Page Ref: 15.2
Skill: Conceptual

34) Evolution by genetic drift is most obvious in

   A) large populations.

   B) aquatic organisms.

   C) small populations.

   D) invertebrate species.

   E) migratory species.

Answer: C
Diff: 1   Page Ref: 15.2
Skill: Factual

35) Shrews have been documented to travel across frozen lakes and establish populations on previously uninhabited islands. This is an example of

   A) genetic drift.

   B) the founder effect.

   C) a population bottleneck.

   D) coevolution.

   E) assortative mating.

Answer: B
Diff: 1   Page Ref: 15.2
Skill: Factual

36) The Pennsylvania Amish have a very high frequency of an unusual allele that results in short arms and legs, and extra fingers. This high frequency is thought to be the result of

   A) the founder effect.

   B) non-random mutations.

   C) a population bottleneck.

   D) coevolution.

   E) all of the above

Answer: A
Diff: 1   Page Ref: 15.2
Skill: Factual

37) The extreme loss of genetic diversity that has occurred in cheetah populations due to overhunting is the result of

   A) the founder effect.

   B) a population bottleneck.

   C) coevolution.

   D) genetic drift.

   E) natural selection.

Answer: B
Diff: 1   Page Ref: 15.2
Skill: Conceptual

38) Which of the following is an example of assortative mating?

   A) A dominant male elephant mates with most females in a group, excluding other males from mating with the females.

   B) A female mouse chooses a mate because he is the same color that she is.

   C) A female sparrow chooses a mate because he attracts her by singing the correct song.

   D) A female sheep chooses a mate because he has previously mated with many females.

   E) A female lizard chooses to mate with the first male she encounters.

Answer: B
Diff: 3   Page Ref: 15.2
Skill: Application

39) Which of the following can be measured to estimate an organism's evolutionary fitness?

A) the number of offspring it produces over its lifetime that survive to breed

B) the number of offspring it produces over its lifetime

C) the number of eggs it produces over its lifetime

D) the size of its offspring

E) the number of gametes it produces over its lifetime

Answer: A
Diff: 1   Page Ref: 15.2
Skill: Factual

40) A bacterial allele that provides resistance to the antibiotic streptomycin

A) is always beneficial to the bacterial cell.

B) is beneficial to the cell in the presence of streptomycin.

C) is neither beneficial nor detrimental to the cell.

D) is beneficial to the cell in the presence of any antibiotic.

E) is always detrimental to the cell.

Answer: B
Diff: 2   Page Ref: 15.2
Skill: Conceptual

41) Having greater evolutionary fitness means

A) having more offspring.

B) having greater strength.

C) being able to produce more sperm or eggs.

D) being able to survive better.

E) being larger or faster than others.

Answer: A
Diff: 1   Page Ref: 15.2
Skill: Factual

42) The fish in a certain population average 10 mm in length. Imagine a population of predatory birds arrives in the area, but they cannot eat fish longer than 15 mm. After a decade, if the fish average 14 mm in length, what likely happened?

    A) The presence of the predator caused mutations for larger fish to occur.

    B) There was stabilizing selection for fish length.

    C) The longer fish survived and produced more offspring than shorter fish.

    D) There was disruptive selection for fish length.

    E) The fish and the predator coevolved.

Answer: C
Diff: 2   Page Ref: 15.2
Skill: Conceptual

43) Evolutionary adaptations are not always the "best" solution to a problem. Explain how the long necks of giraffes can be both advantageous and disadvantageous.

    Answer: The long neck provides an advantage to males when battling for dominance and feeding on the leaves of tall trees. However, when drinking water from a pool, the giraffe is in a very awkward position and at a disadvantage because it is vulnerable to attack by predators.
Diff: 2   Page Ref: 15.2
Skill: Application

44) A city was intensively sprayed with the chemical DDT to control houseflies. The number of houseflies was immediately greatly reduced. Each year thereafter the city was sprayed again, but the flies gradually increased in numbers until ten years later they were as abundant as they were before the control program began. Provide an evolutionary explanation of what has happened.

    Answer: The few flies that happened to be born with a genetic resistance to DDT survived and then passed this resistance on to their offspring. Subsequent generations of flies were less and less affected by DDT, and natural selection resulted in a population resistant to the chemical that could proliferate even when DDT was applied.
Diff: 3   Page Ref: 15.2
Skill: Application

45) Suppose a small population of deer is introduced to an island. All the original males have 6–10 points on their antlers, and the average male has 8 points. After several generations, if most males have antlers with 10 points and no males have 6 points, this illustrates _____ selection.

    A) directional   B) disruptive   C) stabilizing   D) artificial

Answer: A
Diff: 2   Page Ref: 15.3
Skill: Conceptual

46) If the tallest and shortest individuals of a population of humans do not survive and reproduce as well as the individuals of 'average' height, which type of selection would most likely result?

A) directional selection

B) disruptive selection

C) stabilizing selection

D) artificial selection

Answer: C
Diff: 1   Page Ref: 15.3
Skill: Conceptual

47) In a certain species of salmon, some adult males are extremely large whereas other adult males are very small, compared to the females. There are no intermediate–sized adult males in the population. This is probably due to

A) directional selection.

B) disruptive selection.

C) stabilizing selection.

D) artificial selection.

Answer: B
Diff: 2   Page Ref: 15.3
Skill: Conceptual

48) In one butterfly species, the colors of individuals can range from white to black, with many shades of gray in between. If the butterflies in a mountain population become more and more similar in color over several generations (for example, if most butterflies are the same shade of gray), what kind of evolutionary force is likely acting on the population?

A) directional selection

B) disruptive selection

C) stabilizing selection

D) artificial selection

Answer: C
Diff: 1   Page Ref: 15.3
Skill: Factual

49) Imagine you are studying leaf size in a large population of plants, over several years. In one year of your study, there is a below–average amount of rainfall, and the following year the average leaf size in the population is smaller than before. However, the amount of variation in leaf size is the same and the population size doesn't change. Other scientists have done experiments that show small leaves are better adapted to dry conditions than large leaves. What has most likely occurred?

A) genetic drift

B) directional selection

C) stabilizing selection

D) the founder effect

E) disruptive selection

Answer: B
Diff: 3   Page Ref: 15.3
Skill: Application

50) Evolution by natural selection is

    A) a rare event that has never been observed by scientists.

    B) currently occurring, but only in scientific laboratories.

    C) constantly occurring at the same rate in all organisms.

    D) a process that occurs as a result of differences in fitness.

    E) a process that has occurred only in the past.

Answer: D
Diff: 2   Page Ref: 15.3
Skill: Conceptual

51) The elaborate courtship displays common in the Animal Kingdom are the result of

    A) random mating.

    B) sexual selection.

    C) spontaneous mutations.

    D) stabilizing selection.

    E) disruptive selection.

Answer: B
Diff: 1   Page Ref: 15.3
Skill: Conceptual

52) Which of these is a TRUE statement about natural selection?

    A) Natural selection causes genetic changes in an individual.

    B) Natural selection causes genetic changes in populations.

    C) Evolution causes natural selection.

    D) Environmental change causes the heritable variations in individuals that natural selection acts upon.

    E) Natural selection is the only mechanism of evolution.

Answer: B
Diff: 2   Page Ref: 15.3
Skill: Factual

53) The male peacock's beautiful tail is really a trade-off between

    A) artificial selection and natural selection.

    B) natural selection and genetic drift.

    C) sexual selection and natural selection.

    D) disruptive selection and natural selection.

Answer: C
Diff: 2   Page Ref: 15.3
Skill: Conceptual

54) Which of these interactions can result in natural selection?

    A) competition

    B) predation

    C) assortative mating

    D) all of the above

    E) none of the above

Answer: D
Diff: 1   Page Ref: 15.3
Skill: Conceptual

55) In terms of natural selection, a woman who lives _____ is favored.

    A) 105 years and has 2 children

    B) 50 years and has 5 children

    C) 70 years and has 5 children

    D) 35 years and has 4 children

    E) 25 years and has 6 children

Answer: E
Diff: 2   Page Ref: 15.3
Skill: Application

56) Natural selection selects for, or against, certain

    A) genotypes.

    B) phenotypes.

    C) gene pools.

    D) populations.

    E) all of these

Answer: B
Diff: 1   Page Ref: 15.3
Skill: Factual

57) Natural selection acts on _____ to affect the evolution of _____.

    A) genotypes; mutations

    B) genotypes; populations

    C) genotypes; individuals

    D) phenotypes; populations

    E) phenotypes; individuals

Answer: D
Diff: 2   Page Ref: 15.3
Skill: Factual

58) As predator and prey species acquire new adaptations to help them survive the constant "arms race" that occurs between them, what evolutionary phenomenon is occurring?

A) sexual selection

B) artificial selection

C) coevolution

D) competition

E) genetic drift

Answer: C
Diff: 1   Page Ref: 15.3
Skill: Factual

59) Female finches, which do not sing, tend to choose to mate with males who sing a specific, elaborate song. This is an example of

A) coevolution.

B) fitness.

C) inbreeding.

D) assortative mating.

E) sexual selection.

Answer: E
Diff: 1   Page Ref: 15.3
Skill: Factual

60) Which trait is the BEST example of an adaptation?

A) a new mutation that confers Tay–Sachs disease in humans

B) a mutation resulting in weak branches in a species of tree that lives in windy regions

C) a longer tongue in an insect–eating mammal that feeds on insects that live in shallow burrows

D) a mutation resulting in a heat–resistant enzyme in a bacterium living in a hot spring

E) a shorter neck in a giraffe that lives in an area with many rival males and tall trees

Answer: D
Diff: 1   Page Ref: 15.3
Skill: Conceptual

61) An insect population may evolve adaptations to

   A) tolerate an increased concentration of pesticide in its environment.

   B) avoid being seen by bird predators.

   C) better chew the tough leaves of the plants it eats.

   D) attract members of the opposite sex.

   E) all of the above

Answer: E
Diff: 1   Page Ref: 15.3
Skill: Conceptual

62) The type of selection most likely to act on a well-adapted population in a relatively constant environment is

   A) artificial.

   B) directional.

   C) stabilizing.

   D) disruptive.

   E) none of the above

Answer: C
Diff: 1   Page Ref: 15.3
Skill: Conceptual

63) Which of these is NOT one of the major categories of natural selection?

   A) directional

   B) stabilizing

   C) disruptive

   D) polymorphic

   E) All are categories of natural selection.

Answer: D
Diff: 1   Page Ref: 15.3
Skill: Factual

64) When a species lives within a constant environment for a long time, the "average type" of individual may have the best chance of survival and produce the most offspring. What type of selection is occurring?

    A) sexual

    B) disruptive

    C) stabilizing

    D) directional

    E) artificial

Answer: C
Diff: 1   Page Ref: 15.3
Skill: Factual

65) Giraffe leg and neck length increased under _____ selection, but currently is probably maintained by _____ selection.

    A) directional; disruptive

    B) directional; stabilizing

    C) disruptive; stabilizing

    D) stabilizing; disruptive

    E) disruptive; directional

Answer: B
Diff: 2   Page Ref: 15.3
Skill: Conceptual

66) If two or more phenotypes in a population are both favored by selection, what happens?

    A) balanced polymorphism

    B) directional selection

    C) sexual selection

    D) gene flow

    E) stabilizing selection

Answer: A
Diff: 1   Page Ref: 15.3
Skill: Factual

67) In some butterfly populations, there are equal frequencies of alleles that code for black or yellow coloration. This is an example of

    A) sexual selection.

    B) directional selection.

    C) stabilizing selection.

    D) non-random mutations.

    E) balanced polymorphism.

Answer: E
Diff: 1   Page Ref: 15.3
Skill: Conceptual

68) A new predator is introduced to an area that can feed on any millipedes less than 200mm long. No millipedes that live in that area exceed 15mm in length. What will happen?

    A) All millipedes will be potential prey.

    B) The millipedes will necessarily mutate to be longer.

    C) Millipedes will necessarily evolve to avoid the predator.

    D) Disruptive selection will favor 15mm-long millipedes.

    E) Directional selection will favor predators who consume the smallest millipedes.

Answer: A
Diff: 2   Page Ref: 15.3
Skill: Application

69) Despite causing a life-threatening disease, the sickle-cell allele in some areas of Africa has remained in high frequency in those populations because the sickle-cell allele protects against malaria. In the United States, malaria was eradicated shortly before WWII by eliminating the mosquito that spreads the disease. What is likely to happen to the frequency of the sickle-cell allele in African-Americans living in the United States?

    A) The frequency of the sickle-cell allele will increase.

    B) The frequency of the sickle-cell allele will decrease.

    C) The frequency of the sickle-cell allele will not change.

    D) The sickle-cell allele will disappear from the African-American population.

    E) The normal allele will disappear from the African-American population.

Answer: B
Diff: 3   Page Ref: 15.3
Skill: Application

70) In Central Africa the frequency of the sickle-cell allele has remained stable over the years because the allele protects against malaria. In the United States, malaria was eradicated by eliminating the mosquito that spreads the disease. The decreasing frequency of the sickle-cell allele in African–Americans since malaria was eliminated in the United States is an example of

   A) directional selection.

   B) stabilizing selection.

   C) disruptive selection.

   D) genetic drift.

   E) the founder effect.

   Answer: A
   Diff: 2   Page Ref: 15.3
   Skill: Conceptual

71) Imagine that a species of bird with an intermediate beak size becomes two separate species with large and small beaks, respectively. This is an example of

   A) directional selection.

   B) stabilizing selection.

   C) disruptive selection.

   D) sexual selection.

   E) genetic drift.

   Answer: C
   Diff: 1   Page Ref: 15.3
   Skill: Application

72) Imagine a population of hummingbirds with an intermediate beak size develops longer beaks over time. This is an example of

   A) directional selection.

   B) stabilizing selection.

   C) disruptive selection.

   D) sexual selection.

   E) genetic drift.

   Answer: A
   Diff: 1   Page Ref: 15.3
   Skill: Application

73) Suppose a new mutation that improves metabolic efficiency is lost from a small population of mammals living in a region of seasonal food scarcity, after a hurricane eliminates half the mammal population. This is an example of

    A) directional selection.

    B) stabilizing selection.

    C) disruptive selection.

    D) sexual selection.

    E) genetic drift.

Answer: E
Diff: 3   Page Ref: 15.3
Skill: Application

74) Suppose a population of mostly sand–colored crabs migrates from a sand beach to a pebble beach and evolves a darker, speckled coloration that closely resembles the pebble beach. This is an example of

    A) directional selection.

    B) stabilizing selection.

    C) disruptive selection.

    D) sexual selection.

    E) genetic drift.

Answer: A
Diff: 2   Page Ref: 15.3
Skill: Application

75) Imagine that a mutation for red eye color becomes very common in a population of flies, because female flies in this population prefer to mate with red–eyed males. This is an example of

    A) directional selection.

    B) stabilizing selection.

    C) disruptive selection.

    D) sexual selection.

    E) genetic drift.

Answer: D
Diff: 1   Page Ref: 15.3
Skill: Application

76) When different species closely interact for an extended period of time and develop new adaptations in response to each other, it is called

   A) gene flow.

   B) genetic drift.

   C) sexual selection.

   D) stabilizing selection.

   E) coevolution.

Answer: E
Diff: 1   Page Ref: 15.3
Skill: Factual

77) Which of the following phenomena favors individuals with average phenotypes over those with extreme phenotypes?

   A) gene flow

   B) genetic drift

   C) sexual selection

   D) stabilizing selection

   E) coevolution

Answer: D
Diff: 1   Page Ref: 15.3
Skill: Factual

78) The bright coloration of male birds is often the result of

   A) gene flow.

   B) genetic drift.

   C) sexual selection.

   D) stabilizing selection.

   E) coevolution.

Answer: C
Diff: 1   Page Ref: 15.3
Skill: Factual

79) The net migration of alleles into or out of a population from neighboring populations is called

   A) gene flow.

   B) genetic drift.

   C) sexual selection.

   D) stabilizing selection.

   E) coevolution.

Answer: A
Diff: 1   Page Ref: 15.1, 15.3
Skill: Factual

80) What is due to chance events that change the allele frequencies in small populations?

   A) gene flow

   B) genetic drift

   C) sexual selection

   D) stabilizing selection

   E) coevolution

Answer: B
Diff: 1   Page Ref: 15.2, 15.3
Skill: Factual

81) When one species evolves a new phenotypic feature and another species evolves new adaptations in response, it is called

   A) gene flow.

   B) genetic drift.

   C) sexual selection.

   D) stabilizing selection.

   E) coevolution.

Answer: E
Diff: 1   Page Ref: 15.3
Skill: Factual

82) Natural selection that tends to split a population into two phenotypic groups is referred to as

    A) gene flow.

    B) genetic drift.

    C) balanced polymorphism.

    D) stabilizing selection.

    E) coevolution.

Answer: C
Diff: 1   Page Ref: 15.3
Skill: Factual

83) The nonliving components of an environment, such as weather and water availability, are

    A) biotic components.

    B) abiotic components.

    C) genotypes.

    D) phenotypes.

    E) none of the above

Answer: B
Diff: 1   Page Ref: 15.3
Skill: Factual

84) Multidrug-resistant bacteria

    A) have been eradicated worldwide.

    B) are becoming less widespread.

    C) have always been common in the natural environment.

    D) are not serious threats to human health.

    E) are becoming more widespread.

Answer: E
Diff: 1   Page Ref: Case Study
Skill: Factual

85) According to the Hardy–Weinberg Principle, if 75% of the alleles in the gene pool are A_1 and 25% are A_2, what is the proportion of individuals with genotype A_1A_2 in this population?

A) 0.1875

B) 0.5625

C) 0.375

D) 0.0625

E) none of the above

Answer: C
Diff: 3   *Page Ref: A Closer Look*
Skill: Application

86) According to the mathematical equation used to demonstrate the Hardy–Weinberg Principle, if the alleles for a certain trait in a population are A_1 and A_2, the proportion of individuals with the genotype _____ is represented by $2pq$.

A) A_1A_1 B) A_1A_2 C) A_2A_2 D) A_1 E) A_2

Answer: B
Diff: 3   *Page Ref: A Closer Look*
Skill: Conceptual

87) Which of the following can affect a small, endangered population so severely that it goes extinct?

A) inbreeding

B) limited mating opportunities

C) lost alleles and/or low genetic diversity

D) all of the above

E) none of the above

Answer: D
Diff: 2   *Page Ref: Earth Watch*
Skill: Conceptual

Chapter 16 The Origin of Species

1) Which statement BEST describes why Darwin's proposed evolutionary mechanism of natural selection is not entirely adequate in explaining the diversity of life?

   A) Natural selection cannot cause enough change to result in new species.

   B) Natural selection alone cannot account for how new species form.

   C) Natural selection does not cause the types of changes needed for species formation.

   D) Natural selection is only involved when one species evolves into a new species, not when one species splits into two.

   E) Natural selection is not involved in speciation at all.

Answer: B
Diff: 3   *Page Ref: 16.1*
Skill: Conceptual

2) Before the modern era of science, organisms were assigned to species categories on the basis of

   A) behavioral similarities.

   B) existence of fossils of previous forms.

   C) capability of interbreeding.

   D) similarities in appearance.

   E) geographic location.

Answer: D
Diff: 1   *Page Ref: 16.1*
Skill: Factual

3) What is being described by the phrase: "all the populations of organisms that can potentially interbreed with one another under natural circumstances and are reproductively isolated from other populations"?

   A) genus

   B) species

   C) genotype

   D) community

   E) tribe

Answer: B
Diff: 1   *Page Ref: 16.1*
Skill: Factual

4) Fruit fly species all look similar to each other. If you have a male and female fruit fly how can you prove that they are the same species, according to the biological species concept?

    A) Determine the base sequence of the DNA of their chromosomes.

    B) Examine them closely with a low power microscope comparing their physical characteristics to published species key lists of characteristics.

    C) If they mate when they are put together then they are the same species.

    D) If they mate successfully and their offspring can also mate successfully, they are the same species.

    E) If they can both asexually reproduce and their offspring can also successfully asexually reproduce then they are all the same species.

Answer: D
Diff: 2   Page Ref: 16.1
Skill: Application

5) Which of the following cannot be tested via the biological species concept to see whether all the individual organisms are a single species?

    A) birds that occur in different parts of the United States

    B) a population of dinosaurs preserved in a fossil bed in Montana

    C) different populations of lions in Africa

    D) the so called "races" of humans from all around the world

    E) several different-sized fish in Lake Ontario

Answer: B
Diff: 1   Page Ref: 16.1
Skill: Application

6) Which of these definitions of species most closely matches the biological species concept?

    A) Members of the same species are all morphologically similar.

    B) Members of the same species are all genetically identical.

    C) Members of the same species look almost exactly alike.

    D) Members of the same species are whatever an expert says they are.

    E) Members of the same species can mate and produce fertile offspring.

Answer: E
Diff: 2   Page Ref: 16.1
Skill: Conceptual

7) The biological species concept cannot be applied to

   A) extinct organisms.

   B) sympatric populations.

   C) allopatric populations.

   D) polyploid populations.

   E) species resulting from adaptive radiation.

Answer: A
Diff: 2   Page Ref: 16.1
Skill: Conceptual

8) Populations that were once considered to be separate species are sometimes reassigned to the same species because

   A) it was discovered that they can produce viable and fertile offspring.

   B) they have evolved to look different from each other.

   C) they are no longer capable of interbreeding.

   D) they have evolved to look the same.

   E) they have been found to be genetically identical.

Answer: A
Diff: 1   Page Ref: 16.1
Skill: Conceptual

9) Two fossils may be assigned to different species if

   A) they are anatomically different.

   B) they come from different places.

   C) they come from different time periods.

   D) they show no evidence of being capable of interbreeding.

   E) one appears to be ancestral to the other.

Answer: A
Diff: 2   Page Ref: 16.1
Skill: Conceptual

10) Speciation can occur without dramatic anatomical change. True or False?

Answer: TRUE
Diff: 1   Page Ref: 16.1
Skill: Conceptual

11) Anatomical changes can occur without speciation. True or False?

Answer: TRUE
Diff: 1   Page Ref: 16.1
Skill: Conceptual

12) The biological species concept is based on the tendency of individuals in one group to avoid breeding with individuals outside their group. This phenomenon is referred to as _____.

Answer: reproductive isolation
Diff: 1   Page Ref: 16.1
Skill: Factual

13) Explain why naming and describing species based only on their appearance can be problematic.

Answer: In some cases, individuals that look the same are actually different species. For example, the cordilleran flycatcher and the Pacific slope flycatcher look so similar that birdwatchers have difficulty telling them apart, but they are two different species of birds. In other cases, individuals that look very different are the same species. For example, the myrtle warbler and Audubon's warbler were once classified as separate species because they have different colored throat feathers, but they are the same species.
Diff: 3   Page Ref: 16.1
Skill: Application

14) Two species of squirrels live on either side of the Grand Canyon. It is believed that a long time ago, before being separated by the canyon, they were the same species. This is an example of

A) temporal isolation.

B) behavioral isolation.

C) mechanical isolation.

D) hybrid inviability.

E) allopatric speciation.

Answer: E
Diff: 1   Page Ref: 16.2
Skill: Conceptual

15) Two different species of pine release their pollen at different times. This is an example of

A) geographical isolation.

B) ecological isolation.

C) behavioral incompatibility.

D) temporal isolation.

E) mechanical isolation.

Answer: D
Diff: 1   Page Ref: 16.2
Skill: Conceptual

16) Two species of garter snakes live in the same geographic area. One mainly lives in water and the other mainly on land, so that they rarely encounter each other and do not interbreed. This is an example of what type of genetic isolation?

   A) ecological

   B) temporal

   C) mechanical

   D) behavioral

   E) directional

Answer: A
Diff: 2   Page Ref: 16.2
Skill: Conceptual

17) Female blue-footed boobies of the Galapagos will only mate after a very specific courtship display on the part of the male. He high-steps to advertise his bright blue feet. What isolating mechanism discourages female blue-footed boobies from mating with other species of boobies?

   A) ecological isolation

   B) temporal isolation

   C) behavioral isolation

   D) mechanical isolation

   E) gametic incompatibility

Answer: C
Diff: 1   Page Ref: 16.2
Skill: Conceptual

18) Two species of pines, *Pinus radiata* and *Pinus muricota*, live in the same regions of California and are capable of forming hybrids under laboratory conditions. However, they do not interbreed because one releases pollen in February and the other in April. What is the genetic isolating mechanism involved?

   A) ecological

   B) temporal

   C) gametic

   D) geographic

   E) hybrid inviability

Answer: B
Diff: 1   Page Ref: 16.2
Skill: Conceptual

19) In many species of fireflies, males flash light from their abdomens to attract females. Each species has a different flashing pattern. This is an example of

    A) allopatric speciation.

    B) geographical isolation.

    C) temporal isolation.

    D) natural selection.

    E) behavioral isolation.

Answer: E
Diff: 2   Page Ref: 16.2
Skill: Conceptual

20) Eastern and Western meadowlarks look almost identical and sometimes inhabit the same areas of prairies. These birds recognize members of their own species by distinctive songs and thus do not breed with each other. This is an example of

    A) ecological isolation.

    B) behavioral isolation.

    C) mechanical isolation.

    D) geographic isolation.

    E) temporal isolation.

Answer: B
Diff: 2   Page Ref: 16.2
Skill: Conceptual

21) The many different species of treefrogs that inhabit forests in the eastern U.S. maintain their genetic isolation from other species by breeding at slightly different times, in different places in the forest, and by singing different songs. How are these populations isolated?

    A) behavioral isolation

    B) temporal isolation

    C) ecological isolation

    D) Only A and B are correct.

    E) A, B, and C are correct.

Answer: E
Diff: 2   Page Ref: 16.2
Skill: Conceptual

22) One species of moss in upstate New York produces gametes in May, and another species of moss in the same region produces gametes in June. This is an example of a _____ isolating mechanism.

    A) geographic

    B) temporal

    C) mechanical

    D) behavioral

    E) post-mating

Answer: B
Diff: 2   Page Ref: 16.2
Skill: Conceptual

23) The elaborate courtship rituals of many bird species help to preserve genetic isolation due to

    A) behavioral isolation.

    B) temporal isolation.

    C) mechanical incompatibility.

    D) hybrid inviability.

    E) allopatric separation.

Answer: A
Diff: 2   Page Ref: 16.2
Skill: Conceptual

24) One method of protecting the genetic isolation of a population is the inability of sperm to fertilize eggs of a different species. This is called

    A) ecological isolation.

    B) temporal isolation.

    C) behavioral isolation.

    D) hybrid inviability.

    E) gametic incompatibility.

Answer: E
Diff: 2   Page Ref: 16.2
Skill: Factual

25) The great dane and the chihuahua are both domestic dogs (the same species), but mating between them is limited by

    A) hybrid infertility.

    B) hybrid inviability.

    C) mechanical incompatibility.

    D) behavioral isolation.

    E) heterozygote disadvantage.

Answer: C
Diff: 2   Page Ref: 16.2
Skill: Conceptual

26) Interbreeding two different species of lovebirds produces offspring that are unable to build a nest after they mature, because they lack the appropriate, innate knowledge needed to carry the nesting materials and build a nest. This limits genetic mixing between the species due to

    A) hybrid inviability.

    B) behavioral isolation.

    C) ecological isolation.

    D) mechanical incompatibility.

    E) geographical isolation.

Answer: B
Diff: 2   Page Ref: 16.2
Skill: Conceptual

27) Horses and donkeys can mate successfully to produce mules, which are always sterile. Which genetic isolating mechanism is involved here to prevent horses and donkeys from becoming a single species?

    A) hybrid inviability

    B) hybrid infertility

    C) mechanical isolation

    D) behavioral isolation

    E) temporal isolation

Answer: B
Diff: 2   Page Ref: 16.2
Skill: Conceptual

28) Which of these is NOT an example of gametic incompatibility?

   A) Male and female sex organs do not fit together.

   B) A pollen grain does not germinate on a stigma (female structure).

   C) Lily sperm cannot fertilize tulip eggs.

   D) Trout sperm does not penetrate perch eggs.

   E) A stigma destroys a germinating pollen grain.

Answer: A
Diff: 3   Page Ref: 16.2
Skill: Application

29) If a hybrid is unable to produce sperm because meiosis does not proceed correctly, gene flow between the populations is restricted by

   A) hybrid viability.

   B) hybrid infertility.

   C) gametic isolation.

   D) ecological isolation.

   E) temporal isolation.

Answer: B
Diff: 2   Page Ref: 16.2
Skill: Conceptual

30) When offspring are infertile after breeding occurs between individuals of different species, the genetic identities of the two populations are protected by

   A) mechanical incompatibility.

   B) temporal isolation.

   C) behavioral isolation.

   D) hybrid infertility.

   E) genetic isolation.

Answer: D
Diff: 2   Page Ref: 16.2
Skill: Conceptual

31) Lions and tigers can interbreed and produce offspring called tiglons or ligers that live normal life spans but are sterile. Lions and tigers remain isolated genetically because of

    A) hybrid infertility.

    B) hybrid inviability.

    C) mechanical incompatibility.

    D) behavioral isolation.

    E) heterozygote disadvantage.

Answer: A
Diff: 2   Page Ref: 16.2
Skill: Conceptual

32) Temporal isolation is an example of

    A) a premating isolating mechanism.   B) a postmating isolating mechanism.

    C) both A and B   D) neither A nor B

Answer: A
Diff: 1   Page Ref: 16.2
Skill: Conceptual

33) Gametic incompatibility is an example of

    A) a premating isolating mechanism.   B) a postmating isolating mechanism.

    C) both A and B   D) neither A nor B

Answer: B
Diff: 1   Page Ref: 16.2
Skill: Conceptual

34) When some hybrid organisms do not live long, it is an example of

    A) temporal isolation.

    B) hybrid inviability.

    C) hybrid infertility.

    D) hybrid vigor.

    E) gametic incompatibility.

Answer: B
Diff: 1   Page Ref: 16.2
Skill: Conceptual

35) When hybrid organisms survive but do not produce fertile offspring, it is an example of

A) temporal isolation.

B) hybrid inviability.

C) hybrid infertility.

D) hybrid vigor.

E) gametic incompatibility.

Answer: C
Diff: 1   Page Ref: 16.2
Skill: Conceptual

36) When the pollen of one plant species will not germinate on the flower of another species, it is an example of

A) temporal isolation.

B) hybrid inviability.

C) hybrid infertility.

D) hybrid vigor.

E) gametic incompatibility.

Answer: E
Diff: 1   Page Ref: 16.2
Skill: Conceptual

37) When two organisms come into sexual maturity at different times, it is an example of

A) temporal isolation.

B) hybrid inviability.

C) hybrid infertility.

D) hybrid vigor.

E) gametic incompatibility.

Answer: A
Diff: 1   Page Ref: 16.2
Skill: Conceptual

38) When hybrid offspring are created between species, but are unable to breed successfully, it is referred to as _____.

Answer: hybrid sterility
Diff: 1   Page Ref: 16.2
Skill: Factual

39) Store-bought hybrid tomatoes are very popular with consumers. Suppose you buy a tomato from the grocery store, collect seeds from it, and plant the seeds. If the seeds do not germinate, the seedlings fail to thrive, or the plants die quickly after sprouting, what reproductive isolating mechanism might be responsible?

Answer: hybrid inviability
Diff: 1   Page Ref: 16.2
Skill: Application

40) What are the five premating isolating mechanisms that keep different species from successfully mating?

Answer: geographical isolation, ecological isolation, temporal isolation, behavioral isolation, and mechanical incompatibilities
Diff: 1   Page Ref: 16.2
Skill: Factual

41) If there is no gene flow into a population, it is said to be

A) allopatric.

B) sympatric.

C) a founder population.

D) isolated.

E) the bottleneck effect.

Answer: D
Diff: 1   Page Ref: 16.3
Skill: Factual

42) Since the Pleistocene ice age, deserts have been gradually forming in the southwestern United States. As the original lakes and rivers of this area shrank into isolated streams, ponds, and springs the fishes living in them developed a strong potential for

A) speciation.

B) hybridization.

C) polyploidy.

D) temporal isolation.

E) hybrid inviability.

Answer: A
Diff: 2   Page Ref: 16.3
Skill: Application

43) There are currently many similar–looking but different species on either side of the isthmus of Panama. They probably resulted from

A) sympatric speciation.

B) allopatric speciation.

C) temporal isolation.

D) random mutations.

E) hybridization.

Answer: B
Diff: 1   Page Ref: 16.3
Skill: Conceptual

44) Where would a researcher most likely find examples of allopatric speciation?

A) at the bottom of a river

B) in a forest on the east side of a river

C) in a forest on the west side of a river

D) comparing forests on the east and west sides of a river

E) in the surface waters of a river

Answer: D
Diff: 2   Page Ref: 16.3
Skill: Conceptual

45) When the London underground (subway) system was built in the 19th century, mosquitoes moved into the tunnels and fed upon the blood of the people and small animals that inhabit the subway system. Mosquitoes can freely enter and leave through the tunnel entrances, yet new evidence indicates that the underground mosquitoes are different species than local above–ground mosquitoes. What has most likely happened?

A) temporal isolation

B) population bottleneck

C) allopatric speciation

D) behavioral incompatibility

E) adaptive radiation

Answer: C
Diff: 2   Page Ref: 16.3
Skill: Application

46) Two populations of mountain–dwelling salamanders that are separated by an impassable valley are considered _____.

    A) allopatric

    B) sympatric

    C) divergent

    D) founders

    E) subspecies

Answer: A
Diff: 1   *Page Ref: 16.3*
Skill: Factual

47) What happens when two populations become geographically separated from one another and then genetic divergence occurs?

    A) allopatric speciation

    B) sympatric speciation

    C) temporal isolation

    D) continental drift

    E) founder effect

Answer: A
Diff: 1   *Page Ref: 16.3*
Skill: Conceptual

48) The Kaibab squirrel lives on the north side of the Grand Canyon and the Abert squirrel lives on the south side. Even though these two populations are only miles apart, their gene pools are kept isolated by

    A) mechanical incompatibility.

    B) hybrid infertility.

    C) geographic isolation.

    D) ecological isolation.

    E) temporal isolation.

Answer: C
Diff: 2   *Page Ref: 16.3*
Skill: Application

49) The parasitic *Rhagoletis* flies that show a preference for either hawthorn or apple trees, and are no longer interbreeding populations, illustrate what type of speciation?

   A) allopatric

   B) specialization

   C) polyploidy

   D) founder effect

   E) sympatric

Answer: E
Diff: 1   Page Ref: 16.3
Skill: Factual

50) Which statement BEST describes the reproductive isolation between populations of *Rhagoletis* flies found on apple and hawthorn trees?

   A) Hawthorn trees and apple trees grow in different areas, so the two populations do not encounter each other.

   B) Male flies of one population cannot physically mate with females from the other population.

   C) Hybrid offspring of the two populations are sterile.

   D) Eggs laid by female flies mated with a male from the "wrong" population do not develop.

   E) Apple–liking males are more likely to encounter apple–liking females than hawthorn–liking females.

Answer: E
Diff: 2   Page Ref: 16.3
Skill: Factual

51) When a species invades a new habitat and evolves rapidly into several new species to better exploit new resources, what has occurred?

   A) phyletic speciation

   B) divergent speciation

   C) stabilizing selection

   D) polyploidy

   E) adaptive radiation

Answer: E
Diff: 1   Page Ref: 16.3
Skill: Conceptual

52) A single species of finch from South America was displaced to a new habitat in the Galapagos Islands, and evolved rapidly into several new species as it exploited the new resources. What has occurred in these "Darwin's Finches"?

    A) phyletic speciation

    B) divergent speciation

    C) stabilizing selection

    D) polyploidy

    E) adaptive radiation

Answer: E
Diff: 2   Page Ref: 16.3
Skill: Conceptual

53) Which of the following is an example of adaptive radiation?

    A) bat wings

    B) industrial melanism

    C) Darwin's finches

    D) long giraffe necks

    E) starfish arms

Answer: C
Diff: 2   Page Ref: 16.3
Skill: Factual

54) The origins of 300 or more species of cichlid fish in Lake Malawi can BEST be explained by

    A) polyploidy.

    B) adaptive radiation.

    C) premating isolating mechanisms.

    D) random events.

    E) the fossil record.

Answer: B
Diff: 2   Page Ref: 16.3
Skill: Factual

55) What are the two main factors that affect speciation, according to Ernst Mayr?

Answer: isolation and genetic divergence
Diff: 1   Page Ref: 16.3
Skill: Factual

56) Oceanic islands are not the only geographic habitats that can harbor isolated populations of individuals. What are some other examples of isolated "island" populations?

Answer: Any habitat that is characterized by a boundary that the organism cannot cross is considered an "island." For example, a mountaintop, a small pond in the middle of an arid region, or even a living host (for a parasite) can serve as such islands.

Diff: 2   Page Ref: 16.3
Skill: Application

57) From an evolutionary perspective, explain how 3 species of large, flightless birds (ostriches, rheas, and emus) came to occupy the widely-separated land masses of Africa, South America, and Australia.

Answer: All of these birds evolved from a common 'ratite' ancestor that lived on the supercontinent called Gondwana. In response to the extreme geographical isolation resulting from continental drift, allopatric speciation then occurred, resulting in the 3 unique ratite species that are now found on the 3 different continents.

Diff: 2   Page Ref: 16.3
Skill: Factual

58) In what type of habitat, or under what types of environmental conditions, would you expect adaptive radiation to occur?

Answer: Any habitat in which many different types of unexploited food resources and few or no competitors exist would be ideal for adaptive radiation. This seems to be the case in Darwin's finches of the Galapagos Islands, the cichlids of Lake Malawi, and other classic examples of adaptive radiation.

Diff: 2   Page Ref: 16.3
Skill: Application

59) Researchers believe that at least _____ of the species that have lived on Earth have become extinct.

A) 29.9%   B) 59.0%   C) 75.3%   D) 90.0%   E) 99.9%

Answer: E
Diff: 1   Page Ref: 16.4
Skill: Factual

60) Which of these is NOT considered a cause of extinction?

A) environmental change

B) competition

C) overspecialization

D) All of these may result in extinction.

E) None of these may result in extinction.

Answer: D
Diff: 1   Page Ref: 16.4
Skill: Factual

61) Which statement BEST describes how overspecialization can affect a species?

    A) Highly specialized adaptations allow a species to live anywhere on Earth.

    B) New adaptations will never occur in a highly specialized species.

    C) If the habitat around a specialized species changes, it always evolves new specialized adaptations.

    D) Highly specialized adaptations in a species increase the likelihood of extinction if the environment changes.

    E) Highly specialized adaptations are rare in species that occupy a very limited geographic range.

Answer: D
Diff: 3   Page Ref: 16.4
Skill: Conceptual

62) Which of these is the most important cause of extinction?

    A) specialization

    B) environmental change

    C) disease

    D) predation

    E) competition

Answer: B
Diff: 2   Page Ref: 16.4
Skill: Factual

63) Which species is MOST likely to become extinct?

    A) the white tiger beetle, found throughout several mid-Atlantic United States

    B) Kirtland's warbler, which breeds only in a small area of Michigan

    C) the jack-in-the-pulpit, found throughout the eastern United States and Canada

    D) the northeastern pygmy shrew, found throughout New Jersey and Pennsylvania

    E) carp, found throughout Europe, the United States, and Canada

Answer: B
Diff: 2   Page Ref: 16.4
Skill: Conceptual

64) Overspecialized adaptations

A) promote survival in a wide range of habitats.

B) are the result of natural selection.

C) allow a species to be more adaptable to environmental changes.

D) allow a species to be more independent of other species.

E) are found only in species with very wide geographic ranges.

Answer: B
Diff: 2   Page Ref: 16.4
Skill: Conceptual

65) Which of the following may result in extinction of a species?

A) loss of a prey species

B) increase in population size of a predator species

C) introduction of a competitor species

D) evolutionary change in a predator species

E) All of these may result in extinction.

Answer: E
Diff: 2   Page Ref: 16.4
Skill: Conceptual

66) The most common cause of extinction is

A) asteroid impacts.

B) interactions with other species.

C) overspecialization.

D) habitat change.

E) limited species range.

Answer: D
Diff: 1   Page Ref: 16.4
Skill: Factual

67) What is the BEST explanation for the origin of the unique species recently found in the Annamite Mountains of Vietnam?

   A) adaptive radiation

   B) sympatric speciation

   C) allopatric speciation

   D) temporal isolation

   E) behavioral isolation

Answer: C
Diff: 2   Page Ref: Case Study
Skill: Conceptual

68) The unique species of Vietnam's Annamite Mountains probably evolved by _____ speciation due to _____.

   A) allopatric; diversion of a river

   B) allopatric; formation of mountains

   C) allopatric; glacial activity

   D) sympatric; adaptation to high altitudes

   E) sympatric; adaptation to different food sources

Answer: C
Diff: 2   Page Ref: Case Study
Skill: Factual

69) Evolutionary biologists disagree with each other mostly about

   A) whether natural selection can cause evolution.

   B) whether evolution occurs.

   C) whether speciation happens.

   D) whether habitat change really influences extinction.

   E) the importance of different mechanisms causing evolutionary change.

Answer: E
Diff: 2   Page Ref: Evolutionary Connections
Skill: Conceptual

70) Which statement about hybridization is MOST valid?

A) Different species cannot interbreed at all.

B) Hybrids between two species will often survive and may become a new species themselves.

C) Hybrids between two species are often fertile but inviable.

D) Species hybridization is common in some groups of organisms but not in others.

E) Closely related species can always produce healthy hybrids.

Answer: D
Diff: 2   Page Ref: Earth Watch
Skill: Conceptual

71) Hybridization may promote the extinction of a species because

A) an endangered species may further decline by producing less fit hybrid offspring.

B) it may introduce deleterious genes from one species to another.

C) the two species increase their population sizes, increasing the effects of genetic drift.

D) hybridization increases inbreeding, which decreases the average fitness of the species.

E) the hybrid offspring may outcompete the parental species.

Answer: A
Diff: 3   Page Ref: Earth Watch
Skill: Conceptual

72) All members of the golden hamster species known today are descendants of a single litter collected in Syria in 1939. Its diploid chromosome number is 44. Two other species of hamster, each with a diploid number of 22, overlap in Syria. The golden hamster is thought to be a new species following the mating of a male and female of the two other hamster species. What mechanism might explain this recent event of speciation?

A) adaptive radiation

B) formation of fertile hybrid and halving of the chromosome number of this hybrid

C) polyploidy

D) temporal isolation

E) disruptive selection

Answer: C
Diff: 2   Page Ref: A Closer Look
Skill: Conceptual

73) The organisms most likely to undergo sympatric speciation by polyploidy are

A) mammals.

B) insects.

C) plants.

D) protists.

E) birds.

Answer: C
Diff: 1   Page Ref: A Closer Look
Skill: Factual

74) A European species of marsh grass called *Spartina maritima* has a diploid number ("2N") of 60. A similar species native to North America, *S. alterniflora* has 2N=62. In 1835 the North American species was found growing near the European species near Southampton England, after being accidentally imported. Occasional sterile hybrids were noted. In 1895 a new species, *S. anglica*, was first identified at Southampton and subsequently became very common. The new species has been identified as a fertile hybrid of the original two species. What is the 2N chromosome number of the hybrids that form between the original two species *S. maritima* and *S. alterniflora*?

A) 31   B) 60   C) 61   D) 122   E) 153

Answer: C
Diff: 3   Page Ref: A Closer Look
Skill: Application

75) A horse has a diploid number ("2N") of 64 and a donkey has 2N=62. The hybrid of these two species, mules have 2N=63 and are sterile. Why are mules sterile?

A) Mules cannot physically mate with each other.

B) Mules cannot physically mate with horses and donkeys.

C) Some chromosomes in mules cannot undergo meiosis.

D) Mules are not true hybrids.

E) because horses are not able to form new species

Answer: C
Diff: 2   Page Ref: A Closer Look
Skill: Conceptual

76) Polyploidy is an important mechanism of speciation in plants. True or False?

Answer: TRUE
Diff: 1   Page Ref: A Closer Look
Skill: Conceptual

77) Polyploidy is an important mechanism of speciation in animals. True or False?

Answer: FALSE
Diff: 1   Page Ref: A Closer Look
Skill: Conceptual

Chapter 17 The History of Life

1) Louis Pasteur's experiment illustrated that

   A) microbes will grow spontaneously in a nutrient broth that has been sterilized and sealed.

   B) only some organisms can form spontaneously in nutrient broth.

   C) life began by chemical evolution.

   D) some complex molecules associated with living organisms can be synthesized by heating and cooling a solution of simple molecules and providing an electric spark.

   E) microbes will not grow in a nutrient broth that has been sterilized unless they are allowed to enter by opening the vessel to the air.

   Answer: E
   Diff: 2   *Page Ref: 17.1*
   Skill: Factual

2) The scientist usually given credit for disproving the theory of spontaneous generation of bacteria was

   A) Redi.   B) Oparin.   C) Miller.   D) Pasteur.   E) Urey.

   Answer: D
   Diff: 2   *Page Ref: 17.1*
   Skill: Factual

3) If you open a can of chicken noodle soup and immediately examine it microscopically you will find no microorganisms. If you let the open can sit on the shelf for a few weeks and then examine it you will find lots of microorganisms. The origin of these microorganisms is most likely

   A) spontaneous generation.

   B) improper sterilization of the soup prior to canning.

   C) prebiotic evolution.

   D) endosymbiotic evolution.

   E) airborne microorganisms.

   Answer: E
   Diff: 2   *Page Ref: 17.1*
   Skill: Application

4) The theory that life began in the distant past from non–living molecules that became able to reproduce themselves is called

    A) prebiotic evolution.

    B) prehistoric evolution.

    C) natural selection.

    D) spontaneous evolution.

    E) A and D

Answer: A
Diff: 2   *Page Ref: 17.1*
Skill: Factual

5) It has been proposed that the first atmosphere of Earth had all the following gases EXCEPT

    A) H_2.   B) H_2O.   C) O_2.   D) CH_4.

Answer: C
Diff: 2   *Page Ref: 17.1*
Skill: Factual

6) Oxygen has a _____ influence on the formation of complex organic molecules because it _____.

    A) positive; acts as a coenzyme

    B) positive; causes formation of hydrogen bonds

    C) positive; increases metabolism

    D) negative; prevents photosynthesis

    E) negative; reacts with them and destroys them

Answer: E
Diff: 2   *Page Ref: 17.1*
Skill: Factual

7) What compounds were used in the experiment by Stanley Miller to simulate the early atmosphere of Earth?

    A) oxygen, ammonia, hydrogen, and methane

    B) ammonia, hydrogen, and carbon dioxide

    C) water, oxygen, hydrogen, and methane

    D) water, ammonia, hydrogen, and methane

    E) water, oxygen, ammonia, and methane

Answer: D
Diff: 2   *Page Ref: 17.1*
Skill: Factual

8) What chemicals were produced by Stanley Miller and other researchers in their experiments investigating the origin of life?

   A) amino acids and ATP

   B) short proteins and nucleotides

   C) cells similar to bacteria

   D) Only choices A and B are correct.

   E) Choices A, B, and C are correct.

Answer: D
Diff: 2   Page Ref: 17.1
Skill: Factual

9) All experiments that simulate conditions in the early Earth's atmosphere assume that the early atmosphere did **NOT** contain which gas?

   A) water vapor

   B) methane

   C) oxygen

   D) hydrogen

   E) carbon dioxide

Answer: C
Diff: 1   Page Ref: 17.1
Skill: Factual

10) Some RNA molecules have been discovered that can

   A) degrade proteins.

   B) duplicate lipid molecules.

   C) act as enzymes.

   D) form primitive cells.

   E) convert organic molecules into protocells.

Answer: C
Diff: 1   Page Ref: 17.1
Skill: Factual

11) The first self–replicating molecules were probably _____.

    A) DNA

    B) RNA

    C) ribozymes

    D) enzymes

    E) cells

Answer: B
Diff: 2   *Page Ref: 17.1*
Skill: Factual

12) Laboratory research has shown that if a solution containing lipids and proteins is agitated for a long time, then hollow, membrane-bound structures called _____ are produced.

    A) amino acids

    B) adenosine triphosphates

    C) vesicles

    D) mitochondria

    E) primordial cells

Answer: C
Diff: 1   *Page Ref: 17.1*
Skill: Factual

13) The outer boundary of laboratory–created vesicles are most similar to

    A) complete cells.

    B) RNA.

    C) bacteria.

    D) amino acids.

    E) cell membranes.

Answer: E
Diff: 1   *Page Ref: 17.1*
Skill: Factual

14) The scenario of prebiotic evolution leading to the origin of life on Earth is plausible because

    A) experiments suggest that all of the chemical components of living cells could be formed quickly from inorganic precursors.

    B) there was a vast period of time for simple chemicals to evolve into complex cells.

    C) it has been observed to occur near thermal vents located at the bottom of the ocean.

    D) it has been observed under laboratory conditions.

    E) it has been observed to occur on other planets.

Answer: B
Diff: 2   Page Ref: 17.1
Skill: Conceptual

15) Who first demonstrated prebiotic evolution in the laboratory?

    A) Stanley Miller

    B) Francisco Redi

    C) Louis Pasteur

    D) John B. S. Haldane

    E) Sidney Altman

Answer: A
Diff: 1   Page Ref: 17.1
Skill: Factual

16) Who first disproved the "maggots–from–meat" hypothesis?

    A) Harold Urey

    B) Francisco Redi

    C) Louis Pasteur

    D) Alexander Oparin

    E) Sidney Altman

Answer: B
Diff: 1   Page Ref: 17.1
Skill: Factual

17) Who disproved the "broth-to-microorganisms" hypothesis?

   A) Stanley Miller

   B) Francisco Redi

   C) Louis Pasteur

   D) Alexander Oparin

   E) Sidney Altman

Answer: C
Diff: 1   Page Ref: 17.1
Skill: Factual

18) Who first discovered that cellular reactions can be catalyzed by a ribozyme?

   A) Stanley Miller

   B) Francisco Redi

   C) John Tyndall

   D) Alexander Oparin

   E) Sidney Altman

Answer: E
Diff: 1   Page Ref: 17.1
Skill: Factual

19) Who proposed that prebiotic chemical conditions could lead to the evolution of complex molecules and, eventually, to living organisms?

   A) Stanley Miller

   B) Francisco Redi

   C) Louis Pasteur

   D) Alexander Oparin

   E) Sidney Altman

Answer: D
Diff: 1   Page Ref: 17.1
Skill: Factual

20) Discuss why RNA is considered by many scientists to have been the basis for early forms of life.

   Answer: RNA is capable of both information storage (like DNA) and catalytic activity (like enzymes). RNA can also make exact copies of itself. The ability to reproduce and to enzymatically catalyze reactions are important characteristics of cells. A primitive RNA-based biochemistry might have functioned much as the present "DNA → RNA → protein" system does today.
Diff: 3   Page Ref: 17.1
Skill: Conceptual

21) The oldest fossil organisms presently known have been dated at approximately how many years old?

    A) 4.5 billion

    B) 3.5 billion

    C) 1.7 billion

    D) less than 1.7 billion

    E) greater than 4.5 billion

Answer: B
Diff: 1   Page Ref: 17.2
Skill: Factual

22) The fossil record indicates that the earliest cells lived about

    A) 1.5 million years ago.

    B) 2.5 billion years ago.

    C) 3.5 million years ago.

    D) 3.5 billion years ago.

    E) 6 billion years ago.

Answer: D
Diff: 1   Page Ref: 17.2
Skill: Factual

23) Which is the correct series of events in the evolution of life on Earth?

    A) $O_2 \rightarrow$ photosynthesis $\rightarrow$ aerobic metabolism

    B) aerobic metabolism $\rightarrow$ photosynthesis $\rightarrow O_2$

    C) $O_2 \rightarrow$ aerobic metabolism $\rightarrow$ photosynthesis

    D) photosynthesis $\rightarrow O_2 \rightarrow$ aerobic metabolism

Answer: D
Diff: 2   Page Ref: 17.2
Skill: Conceptual

24) The oxygen that arose in early Earth's atmosphere was likely produced by organisms that were very similar to modern

    A) algae.

    B) protists.

    C) plants.

    D) fungi.

    E) cyanobacteria.

Answer: E
Diff: 1   Page Ref: 17.2
Skill: Factual

25) The earliest fossils resemble modern

    A) protists.

    B) green algae.

    C) eukaryotes.

    D) prokaryotes.

    E) protocells.

Answer: D
Diff: 2   Page Ref: 17.2
Skill: Factual

26) The organisms originally responsible for putting oxygen in Earth's atmosphere lived around

    A) 1.5 million years ago.

    B) 2.2 billion years ago.

    C) 3.5 million years ago.

    D) 3.5 billion years ago.

    E) 6 billion years ago.

Answer: B
Diff: 2   Page Ref: 17.2
Skill: Factual

27) The earliest photosynthetic organisms

    A) probably did not produce oxygen.

    B) probably used water as a source of hydrogen.

    C) probably used hydrogen sulfide as a source of hydrogen.

    D) date back to the time when life first emerged on Earth.

    E) possessed chloroplasts.

Answer: C
Diff: 2   *Page Ref: 17.2*
Skill: Factual

28) If the early Earth's atmosphere contained little or no O_2 then where did most of the O_2 in our modern atmosphere come from?

    A) the oxidation of metals

    B) photosynthesis

    C) respiration

    D) the breakdown of carbon dioxide

    E) the splitting of water vapor by sunlight

Answer: B
Diff: 2   *Page Ref: 17.2*
Skill: Factual

29) Aerobic metabolism is an advantage over anaerobic metabolism because

    A) the destructive chemical action of oxygen is utilized to generate energy.

    B) aerobic respiration can be performed whether oxygen is present or not.

    C) aerobic respiration produces more energy than anaerobic respiration.

    D) both A and C

    E) A, B, and C

Answer: D
Diff: 2   *Page Ref: 17.2*
Skill: Conceptual

30) The accumulation of oxygen gas in the atmosphere after the evolution of photosynthesis caused various species of existing anaerobic microbes to

    A) retreat to habitats that are low in oxygen.

    B) become extinct.

    C) evolve a metabolism that uses oxygen.

    D) both A and C

    E) A, B, and C

Answer: E
Diff: 3   Page Ref: 17.2
Skill: Conceptual

31) Eukaryotic cells evolved about _____ years ago.

    A) 4.5 billion

    B) 3.5 billion

    C) 1.7 billion

    D) 600 thousand

    E) 10 thousand

Answer: C
Diff: 1   Page Ref: 17.2
Skill: Factual

32) _____ may have evolved from aerobic bacteria and _____ may have evolved from photosynthetic cyanobacteria that were engulfed by predatory prokaryotic cells.

    A) Chloroplasts; mitochondria   B) Mitochondria; nuclei

    C) Mitochondria; chloroplasts   D) Cell membranes; chloroplasts

Answer: C
Diff: 1   Page Ref: 17.2
Skill: Factual

33) Many structures in eukaryotic cells, such as mitochondria, chloroplasts, microtubules, flagella, and cilia, are believed to have evolved from

    A) invaginations in the plasma membrane.   B) products of the cell's DNA.

    C) endosymbiotic prokaryotes.   D) protocells.

Answer: C
Diff: 2   Page Ref: 17.2
Skill: Factual

34) The endosymbiotic hypothesis accounts for the origin of which cell structure?

    A) chloroplast

    B) cell wall

    C) chromosome

    D) plasma membrane

    E) ribosome

Answer: A
Diff: 1   Page Ref: 17.2
Skill: Factual

35) The proposal that certain eukaryotic cell structures may have evolved from a prokaryotic symbiosis is called

    A) the protocell hypothesis.   B) the living intermediate hypothesis.

    C) the endosymbiont hypothesis.   D) spontaneous generation.

Answer: C
Diff: 1   Page Ref: 17.2
Skill: Factual

36) Describe how the mitochondrion evolved as an organelle, according to the endosymbiont hypothesis.

    Answer: The mitochondrion probably began as an aerobic bacterium that was engulfed, but not
            digested, by another prokaryotic cell. The two cells began a symbiotic relationship that
            persisted, with the host cell providing protection and nutrients to the aerobic bacterium,
            which in turn provided ATP or similar molecules to its host.
Diff: 2   Page Ref: 17.2
Skill: Conceptual

37) Multicellularity allows organisms to

    A) be photosynthetic.

    B) undergo aerobic respiration.

    C) be big.

    D) be fast.

    E) reproduce more efficiently.

Answer: C
Diff: 2   Page Ref: 17.3
Skill: Factual

38) Probably the greatest advantage to the original, multicellular organisms was

A) increased use of oxygen.

B) increased metabolism.

C) increased food intake.

D) predator avoidance.

E) the ability to photosynthesize.

Answer: D
Diff: 2   Page Ref: 17.3
Skill: Factual

39) The first multicellular eukaryotic fossils were

A) algae.

B) fungi.

C) cyanobacteria.

D) reptiles.

E) amphibians.

Answer: A
Diff: 1   Page Ref: 17.3
Skill: Factual

40) The fossil record indicates that about 600 million years ago, a wide variety of _____ animals had evolved in the oceans.

A) unicellular

B) vertebrate

C) fish-like

D) whale-like

E) invertebrate

Answer: E
Diff: 2   Page Ref: 17.3
Skill: Factual

41) About 530 million years ago, what adaptation evolved to make fish the dominant predators of the sea?

   A) jaws

   B) scales

   C) fins

   D) internal skeleton

   E) eyes

Answer: D
Diff: 2   Page Ref: 17.3
Skill: Factual

42) The first multicellular terrestrial organisms were

   A) plants.

   B) insects.

   C) fungi.

   D) amphibians.

   E) reptiles.

Answer: A
Diff: 2   Page Ref: 17.4
Skill: Factual

43) All of the following are potential problems for organisms that dwell on land rather than water EXCEPT

   A) desiccation.

   B) light availability.

   C) union of sex cells.

   D) body support.

   E) movement.

Answer: B
Diff: 2   Page Ref: 17.4
Skill: Factual

44) Which of the following was NOT an advantage to life on land for the earliest terrestrial species?

   A) More light was available for photosynthesis on land.

   B) Reproduction on land was easier than in water.

   C) Terrestrial soil contained more concentrated nutrients than seawater.

   D) There were few or no predators on land.

   E) There were many available ecological niches.

Answer: B
Diff: 2   Page Ref: 17.4
Skill: Conceptual

45) One advantage that allowed the seed plants to greatly surpass the ferns in colonizing the land was the evolution of

   A) a fibrous root system.   B) a woody stem.

   C) sex without swimming sperm.   D) spores.

Answer: C
Diff: 2   Page Ref: 17.4
Skill: Factual

46) Flowering plants first rose to great prominence in the

   A) Cambrian period.

   B) Precambrian period.

   C) Cretaceous period.

   D) Eocene period.

   E) Paleozoic period.

Answer: C
Diff: 2   Page Ref: 17.4
Skill: Factual

47) Early land plants required adaptations that

   A) aided reproduction.

   B) helped support the plant.

   C) decreased water loss.

   D) none of the above

   E) A, B, and C are true.

Answer: E
Diff: 1   Page Ref: 17.4
Skill: Factual

48) The first land plants were restricted to moist, marshy environments because of

A) the need for stem support.

B) the lack of a cuticle.

C) reproductive cell requirements.

D) the need for nutrients.

E) sensitivity to sunlight.

Answer: C
Diff: 2   *Page Ref: 17.4*
Skill: Factual

49) _____ eliminated the need for water for plant reproduction.

A) Pollen

B) Vascular tissues

C) Flowers

D) Sperm

E) Cones

Answer: A
Diff: 2   *Page Ref: 17.4*
Skill: Factual

50) Which of the following was an advantage for the earliest terrestrial plants?

A) More water was available.

B) More light was available.

C) Less complex reproductive structures were necessary.

D) A and B

E) A, B, and C

Answer: B
Diff: 2   *Page Ref: 17.4*
Skill: Factual

51) The earliest group of land plants whose reproduction did not require water for swimming sperm were the

    A) conifers.

    B) ferns.

    C) club mosses.

    D) algae.

    E) lobefins.

Answer: A
Diff: 2   Page Ref: 17.4
Skill: Factual

52) Which of the following is assumed to be more primitive than a dinosaur and more complex than a shark?

    A) starfish

    B) segmented worm

    C) crayfish

    D) chicken

    E) frog

Answer: E
Diff: 2   Page Ref: 17.4
Skill: Conceptual

53) By examination of fossil evidence, paleontologists believe that mammals evolved from ancestors of modern

    A) sharks.

    B) arthropods.

    C) amphibians.

    D) reptiles.

    E) lobefins.

Answer: D
Diff: 2   Page Ref: 17.4
Skill: Factual

54) The fossil evidence indicates that amphibians evolved from _____.

   A) fish

   B) frogs

   C) reptiles

   D) dinosaurs

   E) mammals

Answer: A
Diff: 2   Page Ref: 17.4
Skill: Factual

55) The exoskeleton of early marine arthropods can be considered a "pre-adaptation" for life on land because that shell

   A) protected against predators.   B) resisted water loss.

   C) absorbed light.   D) reflected ultraviolet radiation.

Answer: B
Diff: 2   Page Ref: 17.4
Skill: Factual

56) Which group of vertebrates was the first to evolve a waterproof egg, allowing the group to move away from water, deeper onto dry land?

   A) lobefins

   B) mammals

   C) birds

   D) primates

   E) reptiles

Answer: E
Diff: 2   Page Ref: 17.4
Skill: Factual

57) Reptiles can inhabit much drier environments than amphibians because of

   A) internal fertilization.

   B) waterproof eggs.

   C) improved lungs.

   D) Only choices A and B are correct.

   E) Choices A, B, and C are correct.

Answer: E
Diff: 2   Page Ref: 17.4
Skill: Factual

58) Birds and mammals have a more active lifestyle than reptiles, due to

    A) internal fertilization.

    B) a high, constant body temperature.

    C) insulation over body surface.

    D) internal fertilization and a high, constant body temperature.

    E) a high, constant body temperature and insulation over body surface.

Answer: E
Diff: 2   Page Ref: 17.4
Skill: Factual

59) The first terrestrial animals probably were

    A) arthropods.

    B) amphibians.

    C) reptiles.

    D) dinosaurs.

    E) mammals.

Answer: A
Diff: 2   Page Ref: 17.4
Skill: Factual

60) Primitive fish called _____ were probably the ancestors of both modern bony fish and _____.

    A) lobefins; reptiles

    B) lobefins; amphibians

    C) sharks; amphibians

    D) arthropods; amphibians

    E) arthropods; reptiles

Answer: B
Diff: 2   Page Ref: 17.4
Skill: Factual

61) The "pre-adaptations" of early arthropods that allowed them to evolve into terrestrial forms were

   A) lungs.

   B) vertebral columns.

   C) kidneys.

   D) exoskeletons.

   E) eggs.

Answer: D
Diff: 1   Page Ref: 17.4
Skill: Factual

62) Which arthropod characteristic "pre-adapted" them to life on land?

   A) multiple legs

   B) compound eyes

   C) exoskeleton

   D) open circulatory system

   E) antennae

Answer: C
Diff: 1   Page Ref: 17.4
Skill: Factual

63) The modern-day group of vertebrates that bridges the evolutionary gap between land-dwelling and water-dwelling organisms is

   A) fish.

   B) amphibians.

   C) reptiles.

   D) whales and dolphins.

   E) aquatic birds.

Answer: B
Diff: 2   Page Ref: 17.4
Skill: Factual

64) Which is **NOT** an adaptation of reptiles to life on land?

    A) scaly skin

    B) internal fertilization

    C) leathery egg shells

    D) efficient lungs

    E) aerobic respiration

Answer: E
Diff: 2   *Page Ref: 17.4*
Skill: Factual

65) The reptiles evolved scaly body coverings as a means for

    A) insulation.

    B) courtship rituals.

    C) heat production.

    D) flight.

    E) protection from drying out.

Answer: E
Diff: 2   *Page Ref: 17.4*
Skill: Factual

66) What allowed mammals to diversify?

    A) global warming

    B) dinosaur extinction

    C) increase in size

    D) glaciation

    E) mammary glands

Answer: B
Diff: 2   *Page Ref: 17.4*
Skill: Factual

67) The earliest group of land animals were the

    A) protists.

    B) amphibians.

    C) lobefins.

    D) arthropods.

    E) lungfish.

Answer: D
Diff: 2   *Page Ref: 17.4*
Skill: Factual

68) The direct descendants of early reptiles are probably

A) birds.

B) amphibians.

C) mammals.

D) both A and C

E) A, B, and C

Answer: D
Diff: 2   Page Ref: 17.4
Skill: Factual

69) What adaptations did ancient algae have to make as they washed ashore and evolved into land plants?

Answer: Waterproof coatings to prevent drying out; vascular tissue to move water from roots to leaves; thick cell walls to stand erect; gametes produced within structures to prevent drying out; development of pollen to eliminate the need for water–based sperm transport.
Diff: 3   Page Ref: 17.4
Skill: Conceptual

70) The generally slow and steady succession of species on Earth has been interrupted by

A) unusually high rates of plate tectonics.

B) genetic equilibrium.

C) balanced polymorphism.

D) extreme specialization of a few species.

E) episodes of mass extinction.

Answer: E
Diff: 2   Page Ref: 17.5
Skill: Factual

71) The worst mass extinction event of all time occurred at the end of the

A) Cretaceous period.

B) Cambrian period.

C) Pleistocene period.

D) Mesozoic period.

E) Permian period.

Answer: E
Diff: 1   Page Ref: 17.5
Skill: Factual

72) Which of the following might occur and cause species to become extinct?

    A) plate tectonics

    B) meteorite impact

    C) climate change

    D) global warming

    E) all of these

Answer: E
Diff: 2   Page Ref: 17.5
Skill: Factual

73) The "Southern Beech" tree is found in such diverse places as Australia, South Africa, and South America. It was not transplanted by people. How did it probably get to these widely-separated localities?

    A) Seeds were carried by birds.

    B) Seeds were blown by the prevailing winds.

    C) These land masses were once connected and later drifted apart.

    D) Simultaneous creation of the same species occurred at different geographical locations.

    E) Glaciers split what was once a continuous huge population of beeches.

Answer: C
Diff: 2   Page Ref: 17.5
Skill: Conceptual

74) Most scientists attribute the mass extinction of the dinosaurs to

    A) sunspots.

    B) gradual climate change.

    C) meteor impact.

    D) predation by mammals.

    E) sea level change.

Answer: C
Diff: 1   Page Ref: 17.5
Skill: Factual

75) If the Cretaceous mass extinction had not occurred, which group of animals would today probably include the largest land animals?

A) amphibians

B) reptiles

C) birds

D) insects

E) bony fish

Answer: B
Diff: 1   Page Ref: 17.5
Skill: Conceptual

76) Which represents the correct time sequence (if not evolutionary sequence) of the evolution of modern humans?

A) *Homo heidelbergensis, H. habilis*, Cro-Magnons, Neanderthals

B) *H. habilis, H. heidelbergensis*, Cro-Magnons, Neanderthals

C) *H. habilis, H. heidelbergensis*, Neanderthals, Cro-Magnons

D) Cro-Magnons, Neanderthals, *H. habilis, H. heidelbergensis*

E) *H. heidelbergensis*, Neanderthals, Cro-Magnons, *H. habilis*

Answer: C
Diff: 2   Page Ref: 17.6
Skill: Factual

77) The human species first appeared in the

A) Quaternary period.

B) Cretaceous period.

C) Jurassic period.

D) Tertiary period.

E) Permian period.

Answer: A
Diff: 2   Page Ref: 17.6
Skill: Factual

78) In addition to *Homo*, another genus within the hominids is

    A) Tarsius.

    B) Lemur.

    C) Cro-Magnon.

    D) Habilis.

    E) *Australopithecus.*

Answer: E
Diff: 1   Page Ref: 17.6
Skill: Factual

79) Which of these characteristics separates primates from other mammals?

    A) placental young

    B) mammary glands

    C) precision grip

    D) parental care of young

    E) tree-dwelling

Answer: C
Diff: 1   Page Ref: 17.6
Skill: Factual

80) Which of the following adaptations has been extremely important in primate evolution?

    A) upright posture

    B) hand structure

    C) binocular vision

    D) A and B

    E) A, B, and C

Answer: E
Diff: 2   Page Ref: 17.6
Skill: Factual

81) An adaptation that is closely associated with hominid evolution is

    A) a backbone.

    B) lungs.

    C) omnivory.

    D) grasping hands.

    E) hair.

Answer: D
Diff: 1   Page Ref: 17.6
Skill: Factual

82) The earliest hominids were in a group called _____.

    A) Australopithecines   B) Cro-Magnons

    C) Neanderthals   D) primates

Answer: A
Diff: 1   Page Ref: 17.6
Skill: Factual

83) The hominids originally evolved in

    A) Africa.

    B) Asia.

    C) Europe.

    D) North America.

    E) Australia.

Answer: A
Diff: 1   Page Ref: 17.6
Skill: Factual

84) What is the significance of upright walking?

    A) It provides better posture.

    B) It improves circulation.

    C) It frees the hands for gathering and carrying food.

    D) It improves social interactions.

    E) It improves digestion.

Answer: C
Diff: 2   Page Ref: 17.6
Skill: Factual

85) What characterizes hominids, but not the other groups of primates?

    A) bipedal locomotion

    B) binocular vision

    C) four chambered heart

    D) grasping hands

    E) facial hair

Answer: A
Diff: 2   Page Ref: 17.6
Skill: Factual

86) The genus *Australopithecus*

   A) gave rise to species of the genus *Homo*.

   B) coexisted with species of *Homo* during their early history.

   C) originated in Africa.

   D) none of the above

   E) A, B, and C are true.

Answer: E
Diff: 2   Page Ref: 17.6
Skill: Factual

87) The species that paleoanthropologists believe may be the most direct ancestor to *Homo sapiens* is

   A) *Homo habilis.*

   B) *Homo ergaster.*

   C) *Homo erectus.*

   D) *Homo neanderthalensis.*

   E) *Homo heidelbergensis.*

Answer: E
Diff: 2   Page Ref: 17.6
Skill: Factual

88) *Homo heidelbergensis* is believed to be the ancestor species of

   A) *Homo ergaster.*

   B) *Homo neanderthalensis.*

   C) *Homo sapiens.*

   D) both A and C

   E) both B and C

Answer: E
Diff: 1   Page Ref: 17.6
Skill: Factual

89) The first hominid species to use stone and bone tools was

    A) *Australopithecus afarensis.*

    B) *Australopithecus robustus.*

    C) *Homo habilis.*

    D) *Homo erectus.*

    E) *Homo sapiens.*

Answer: C
Diff: 1   Page Ref: 17.6
Skill: Factual

90) The scientific name for Neanderthals is

    A) *Homo sapiens.*

    B) *Homo erectus.*

    C) *Homo habilis.*

    D) *Australopithecus robustus.*

    E) *Homo neanderthalensis.*

Answer: E
Diff: 1   Page Ref: 17.6
Skill: Factual

91) Which of the following is the BEST description of the "Neanderthals"?

    A) no tool production, stooped posture, heavily muscled

    B) brains about the same as modern humans (or larger), fully upright posture, heavily muscled

    C) brains about the size of apes, fully upright posture

    D) produced simple tools, stooped posture, small brain

    E) no tools, stooped posture, small brain, heavily muscled

Answer: B
Diff: 2   Page Ref: 17.6
Skill: Factual

92) All surviving humans belong to the species

    A) *Homo erectus.*

    B) *Homo habilis.*

    C) *Homo sapiens.*

    D) *Homo robustus.*

    E) *Australopithecus robustus.*

Answer: C
Diff: 1   Page Ref: 17.6
Skill: Factual

93) The oldest fossils of anatomically modern *Homo sapiens* are _____ years old.

    A) 10,000   B) 50,000   C) 160,000   D) 250,000   E) 2 million

Answer: C
Diff: 1   Page Ref: 17.6
Skill: Factual

94) Cave paintings at Lascaux, France were done by which species of hominid?

    A) *Homo erectus*

    B) *Homo habilis*

    C) *Homo sapiens*

    D) *Australopithecus robustus*

    E) *Australopithecus afarensis*

Answer: C
Diff: 1   Page Ref: 17.6
Skill: Factual

95) Hominid species migrated out of Africa

    A) 10 million years ago.

    B) nearly 2 million years ago.

    C) nearly 800,000 years ago.

    D) about 3000 years ago.

    E) both B and C

Answer: E
Diff: 1   Page Ref: 17.6
Skill: Factual

96) It has been proposed that large brains evolved in *Homo species* because

    A) large-brained individuals were favored by natural selection because they were better in social interactions.

    B) large brain evolution was a consequence of evolution for overall larger body size.

    C) large brains allowed better visual acuity, which was favored by natural selection.

    D) genetic drift increased the frequency of large-brained alleles.

    E) large-brained individuals were better able to outwit and escape predators.

Answer: A
Diff: 2   *Page Ref: 17.6*
Skill: Factual

97) This process involves behaviors that are acquired by learning and can be modified and passed from one generation to the next:

    A) prebiotic evolution.

    B) environmental selection.

    C) pre-adaptation.

    D) natural selection.

    E) cultural evolution.

Answer: E
Diff: 1   *Page Ref: 17.6*
Skill: Conceptual

98) A major human cultural innovation that happened about 10,000 years ago was the

    A) development of domesticated crops and livestock.

    B) development of language.

    C) development of self expression in the form of art.

    D) use of tools.

    E) ability to think in abstract terms.

Answer: A
Diff: 1   *Page Ref: 17.6*
Skill: Factual

99) Geologists can determine the age of a rock by measuring _____ in the rock.

A) the amount of carbon–14

B) the proportion of carbon–14 to nitrogen–14

C) the amount of potassium–40

D) the proportion of potassium–40 to argon–40

E) the amount of argon–40

Answer: D
Diff: 1   Page Ref: Scientific Inquiry
Skill: Factual

100) The hobbit-sized hominid whose fossilized remains were recently discovered on a remote oceanic island belonged to the species

A) *Homo erectus.*

B) *Homo habilis.*

C) *Homo sapiens.*

D) *Homo neanderthalensis.*

E) *Homo floresiensis.*

Answer: E
Diff: 1   Page Ref: Case Study
Skill: Factual

Chapter 18 Systematics: Seeking Order Amidst Diversity

1) In the correct spelling of a scientific name, the first of the two names has its first letter in
_____ case and the entire name is _____.

   A) lower; in italic or underlined

   B) lower; not in italic nor underlined

   C) upper; in italic or underlined

   D) upper; not in italic nor underlined

   E) None of these is correct.

   Answer: C
   Diff: 1   Page Ref: 18.1
   Skill: Factual

2) The second of the two names in an organism's scientific name is the _____.

   A) species   B) genus   C) kingdom   D) order   E) family

   Answer: A
   Diff: 1   Page Ref: 18.1
   Skill: Factual

3) The main reason scientists use Latinized scientific names is

   A) tradition; it has always been done that way.

   B) Linnaeus was a Latin American.

   C) scientific publications are usually in Latin.

   D) worldwide recognition across language barriers.

   E) to make life difficult for students in freshman biology classes.

   Answer: D
   Diff: 2   Page Ref: 18.1
   Skill: Factual

4) The science of reconstructing evolutionary history is called

   A) taxidermy.

   B) gradualism.

   C) pre–adaptation.

   D) systematics.

   E) biology.

   Answer: D
   Diff: 1   Page Ref: 18.1
   Skill: Factual

5) The largest or most inclusive group listed below is

    A) class.   B) order.   C) phylum.   D) genus.   E) family.

Answer: C
Diff: 1   Page Ref: 18.1
Skill: Factual

6) The smallest or least inclusive group of the following is

    A) kingdom.   B) class.   C) genus.   D) order.   E) species.

Answer: E
Diff: 1   Page Ref: 18.1
Skill: Factual

7) Which of the following is the correct way to write the scientific name of the wolf?

    A) *Canis Lupus*

    B) canis lupus

    C) *canis Lupus*

    D) *Canis lupus*

    E) Canis lupus

Answer: D
Diff: 2   Page Ref: 18.1
Skill: Factual

8) *Canis latrans, Canis lupus, Canis familiaris* are all in the same

    A) species.

    B) genus.

    C) family.

    D) B and C

    E) A, B, and C

Answer: D
Diff: 2   Page Ref: 18.1
Skill: Factual

9) If two organisms are members of the same kingdom they MUST also be members of the same

A) phylum.

B) class.

C) genus.

D) all of the above

E) none of the above

Answer: E
Diff: 2   Page Ref: 18.1
Skill: Conceptual

10) In the scientific name of humans, *Homo sapiens*, the name "*Homo*" is the

A) class.   B) species.   C) genus.   D) order.   E) family.

Answer: C
Diff: 1   Page Ref: 18.1
Skill: Factual

11) Which of these groups contains the fewest species?

A) kingdom   B) class   C) phylum   D) order   E) domain

Answer: D
Diff: 2   Page Ref: 18.1
Skill: Factual

12) Historically, most classification has been based on _____ similarity.

A) DNA

B) cytochrome c

C) enzyme

D) behavioral

E) morphological

Answer: E
Diff: 2   Page Ref: 18.1
Skill: Factual

13) How did Darwin's evolutionary theory change the significance of the taxonomic categories of organisms?

   A) Darwin's theory of natural selection has had no effect on taxonomy.

   B) Taxonomic categories are now considered to reflect the evolutionary relationships of organisms.

   C) Darwin described the Kingdoms that we use today which include all organisms.

   D) The relationships between organisms became completely known and many species were renamed.

   E) Taxonomists no longer consider anatomical similarity in classifying organisms.

Answer: B
Diff: 3   Page Ref: 18.1
Skill: Conceptual

14) A major difficulty facing systematists is

   A) the ability to sequence DNA.

   B) placing specimens into the predefined taxonomic categories of species and genus.

   C) understanding the sequence of cell divisions in early embryology of plants and animals.

   D) distinguishing anatomy from physiology in plant evolution.

   E) distinguishing similar features due to common ancestry from those due to convergent evolution.

Answer: E
Diff: 3   Page Ref: 18.1
Skill: Conceptual

15) _____ results in similar anatomical features between organisms that may be misleading when trying to determine species relationships.

   A) Descent from a common ancestor

   B) Convergent evolution

   C) DNA sequence evolution

   D) Chromosomal evolution

   E) Adaptation to different environments

Answer: B
Diff: 2   Page Ref: 18.1
Skill: Conceptual

16) Throughout the history of systematics, what characteristic was most commonly used for determining species relationships?

    A) DNA sequence similarity

    B) capability of interbreeding

    C) geographic proximity

    D) anatomical similarity

    E) chromosomal similarity

Answer: D
Diff: 2   Page Ref: 18.1
Skill: Factual

17) Comparing the chromosomes of chimpanzees and humans has revealed that the two species

    A) are closely related.

    B) should be classified in the same genus.

    C) should be classified as the same species.

    D) should not be classified in the same family.

    E) are only distantly related.

Answer: A
Diff: 2   Page Ref: 18.1
Skill: Conceptual

18) The group "Chordata," to which humans belong, is a _____ name.

    A) species   B) family   C) genus   D) kingdom   E) phylum

Answer: E
Diff: 1   Page Ref: 18.1
Skill: Factual

19) _____ is a term that refers to the "evolutionary history" of an organism.

    A) Phylogeny

    B) Systematics

    C) Biological classification

    D) All of the above

    E) None of the above

Answer: A
Diff: 1   Page Ref: 18.1
Skill: Factual

20) The science of reconstructing evolutionary history is called

   A) phylogeny.

   B) systematics.

   C) biological classification.

   D) all of the above

   E) none of the above

Answer: B
Diff: 1   Page Ref: 18.1
Skill: Factual

21) The Swedish naturalist who established the modern system for classifying organisms was

   A) Aristotle.

   B) Linnaeus.

   C) Whittaker.

   D) Woese.

   E) Darwin.

Answer: B
Diff: 1   Page Ref: 18.1
Skill: Factual

22) The biologist who first proposed that all organisms share a common ancestry was

   A) Aristotle.

   B) Linnaeus.

   C) Whittaker.

   D) Woese.

   E) Darwin.

Answer: E
Diff: 1   Page Ref: 18.1
Skill: Factual

23) Who introduced the "two-part" system (genus and species) that is used when biologists name organisms?

   A) Aristotle

   B) Linnaeus

   C) Whittaker

   D) Woese

   E) Darwin

Answer: B
Diff: 1   Page Ref: 18.1
Skill: Factual

24) Briefly explain why the adoption of a standard, two-part scientific naming system is helpful to biologists.

   Answer: "Common names" can create confusion because 1) the same common name may used for different species, and 2) different common names may be used for the same species. In contrast, standard scientific names can be recognized by biologists worldwide, and help them avoid confusion when discussing organisms. In addition, the two-part name allows biologists to quickly discern whether two species are closely related (that is, whether they are in the same genus).

Diff: 2   Page Ref: 18.1
Skill: Application

25) List the following taxonomic categories from the most specific to the most general:

   genus   domain   family   phylum   order

   Answer: genus → family → order → phylum → domain
Diff: 1   Page Ref: 18.1
Skill: Factual

26) Before 1970, the biological classification system was based on

   A) two kingdoms: Bacteria and Eukarya.

   B) two kingdoms: Monera and Animalia.

   C) two kingdoms: Animalia and Plantae.

   D) three kingdoms: Bacteria, Animalia, and Plantae.

   E) five kingdoms: Monera, Protista, Fungi, Animalia, and Plantae.

Answer: C
Diff: 2   Page Ref: 18.2
Skill: Factual

27) Which Kingdom contains mostly unicellular, eukaryotic organisms?

A) Monera   B) Protista   C) Animalia   D) Fungi   E) Plantae

Answer: B
Diff: 1   Page Ref: 18.2
Skill: Factual

28) What is the primary difference between kingdoms Monera and Protista?

A) Monera are unicellular, whereas protists are multicellular.

B) Monera photosynthesize, but protists do not.

C) Monera are prokaryotes, whereas protists are eukaryotes.

D) Monera are plant-like, whereas protists are animal-like.

E) Monera are more recently evolved than protists.

Answer: C
Diff: 2   Page Ref: 18.2
Skill: Conceptual

29) According to chemical and molecular evidence, members of the Kingdom Fungi are most closely related to which of these groups in the "tree of life"?

A) animals   B) plants   C) Archaea   D) Protista   E) Bacteria

Answer: A
Diff: 3   Page Ref: 18.2
Skill: Conceptual

30) A modern system of classification gives the category name "Domain" to which of these?

A) Prokaryota

B) Eukarya

C) Insects

D) Hominidae

E) Fungi

Answer: B
Diff: 1   Page Ref: 18.2
Skill: Factual

31) The three-domain system of classification replaced the five-kingdom system because

    A) the four eukaryotic kingdoms were found to be much more closely related to each other than was previously thought.

    B) bacteria were found to be completely unrelated to eukaryotes.

    C) the four kingdoms of eukaryotes are more closely related than biologists previously realized.

    D) some bacterial species have recently evolved enough to be considered members of a new domain.

    E) new evidence showed that the "tree of life" split into three groups of organisms early on.

Answer: E
Diff: 2   Page Ref: 18.2
Skill: Conceptual

32) The Kingdom Protista

    A) was once classified in the kingdom Plantae.

    B) consists of prokaryotic organisms.

    C) may soon be divided into several kingdoms, based on new information.

    D) both A and C

    E) A, B, and C

Answer: D
Diff: 2   Page Ref: 18.2
Skill: Factual

33) The scientist who proposed the five-kingdom system of classification to replace the two-kingdom system was

    A) Aristotle.

    B) Linnaeus.

    C) Whittaker.

    D) Woese.

    E) Darwin.

Answer: C
Diff: 1   Page Ref: 18.2
Skill: Factual

34) This scientist who proposed the five-kingdom system of classification was

A) Aristotle.

B) Linnaeus.

C) Whittaker.

D) Woese.

E) Darwin.

Answer: C
Diff: 1   Page Ref: 18.2
Skill: Factual

35) Which of the following is prokaryotic?

A) Archaea

B) Fungi

C) Animalia

D) Plantae

E) None of the above are prokaryotic.

Answer: A
Diff: 1   Page Ref: 18.2
Skill: Factual

36) Which of the following is eukaryotic?

A) Archaea

B) Fungi

C) Bacteria

D) Monera

E) None of the above are eukaryotic.

Answer: B
Diff: 1   Page Ref: 18.2
Skill: Factual

37) Which of the following produces cell walls made of chitin?

A) Archaea

B) Fungi

C) Animalia

D) Plantae

E) none of the above

Answer: B
Diff: 2   Page Ref: 18.2
Skill: Factual

38) Which of the following produces cell walls made of cellulose?

    A) Archaea

    B) Fungi

    C) Animalia

    D) Plantae

    E) none of the above

    Answer: D
    Diff: 2   Page Ref: 18.2
    Skill: Factual

39) Changes to domain or kingdom classifications are _____, while changes to species classifications are _____.

    A) rare; also rare

    B) common; also common

    C) common; rare

    D) rare; common

    E) never made; sometimes made

    Answer: D
    Diff: 1   Page Ref: 18.3
    Skill: Factual

40) What should biologists do when two similar organisms that were originally thought to be separate species are found to interbreed freely and produce normal offspring whenever they occur in the same habitat?

    A) retain the two species' names if the organisms have very different appearances

    B) consider both types to be a single species

    C) develop a new name for the hybrids

    D) separate the two groups until they become dissimilar enough to prevent interbreeding

    Answer: B
    Diff: 3   Page Ref: 18.3
    Skill: Conceptual

41) If genetic studies reveal that a population has genetic sequences in common with two closely related species, but has no unique sequences of its own, then

    A) it should be considered a hybrid of the two species.

    B) it should be assigned separate species status.

    C) it should be assigned to the species with which it shares more sequences.

    D) all three should be assigned to the same species.

    E) all three should be considered subspecies within the same species.

Answer: A
Diff: 2   Page Ref: 18.3
Skill: Application

42) The "phylogenetic species concept" is valid for

    A) sexual reproducing species.

    B) asexual reproducing species.

    C) species that do not reproduce.

    D) Both A and B are correct.

    E) A, B, and C are correct.

Answer: D
Diff: 3   Page Ref: 18.3
Skill: Conceptual

43) The "biological species concept" is problematic because

    A) it cannot be applied to asexual organisms.

    B) it cannot be used for extinct species.

    C) it is difficult to apply to two geographically isolated populations.

    D) All of the above are true.

    E) None of the above are true.

Answer: D
Diff: 2   Page Ref: 18.3
Skill: Conceptual

44) Biodiversity is the greatest among

   A) eukaryotic organisms that live in oceans.

   B) freshwater organisms.

   C) organisms that live in temperate deciduous forests.

   D) organisms that live in temperate rain forests.

   E) organisms that live in tropical rain forests.

Answer: E
Diff: 1   Page Ref: 18.4
Skill: Factual

45) How many species are believed to exist on Earth at the present time?

   A) 7,000 to 10,000

   B) approximately 100,000

   C) approximately 500,000

   D) between 7 million and 100 million

   E) approximately 1.5 million

Answer: D
Diff: 2   Page Ref: 18.4
Skill: Factual

46) DNA analysis of bacterial species suggests that

   A) nearly all bacterial species have already been described by biologists.

   B) most bacterial species have yet to be described by biologists.

   C) there is very little diversity among bacterial species.

   D) there is a great deal of diversity among bacterial species.

   E) Both B and D are true.

Answer: E
Diff: 2   Page Ref: 18.4
Skill: Conceptual

47) Most species that have been described by biologists are animals from temperate regions, because

     A) there are more species of animals than there are species from other kingdoms.

     B) there are more animals in temperate regions than in the tropics.

     C) more biologists have studied these organisms than any other organisms, anywhere else.

     D) animals are more abundant than are any other organisms in temperate regions.

     E) Both C and D are true.

Answer: C
Diff: 2   Page Ref: 18.4
Skill: Conceptual

48) The evidence that the HIV virus originated from non–human primates comes from

     A) historical studies of primitive African societies.

     B) comparisons of DNA base sequences among different viruses.

     C) medical histories of humans.

     D) medical histories of primates in captivity.

     E) comparative morphology of primate and human viruses.

Answer: B
Diff: 2   Page Ref: Case Study
Skill: Factual

49) Some biologists do not consider reptiles to be a monophyletic group because

     A) they evolved independently at several different times in the past and from several different ancestral species.

     B) birds are the direct descendants of some reptiles.

     C) all reptiles do not reproduce sexually.

     D) the ancestors of reptiles are the class Amphibia.

     E) reptiles, birds, amphibians, and fish appeared in the fossil record at approximately the same time.

Answer: B
Diff: 2   Page Ref: Evolutionary Connections
Skill: Conceptual

50) Which of the following is **NOT** a monophyletic group?

A) the Class Mammalia, which includes all mammals

B) the Kingdom Animalia, which includes all animals

C) the Family Semionotidae, which includes fish that may not share a common ancestor

D) you, your parents, and your siblings

E) All of the above are monophyletic groups.

Answer: C
Diff: 2   Page Ref: Evolutionary Connections
Skill: Application

51) Genetics studies of human populations have revealed that

A) *Homo sapiens* probably did not evolve from primates.

B) it is nearly impossible to determine the relatedness of human populations.

C) human populations vary tremendously at the level of DNA sequences.

D) humans have very little genetic variation compared to other mammals.

E) all humans are virtually identical.

Answer: D
Diff: 2   Page Ref: Links to Life
Skill: Factual

52) The greatest genetic diversity among humans is found between some _____ populations.

A) African

B) Asian

C) Australian

D) European

E) North American

Answer: A
Diff: 1   Page Ref: Links to Life
Skill: Factual

53) The most powerful way to infer evolutionary relationships relies on which type of evidence?

A) comparative morphology

B) behavioral similarities

C) measurements of the ability to mate and produce fertile offspring

D) comparative anatomy

E) comparison of DNA base sequences

Answer: E
Diff: 2   Page Ref: Scientific Inquiry
Skill: Factual

54) To study the phylogeny of various populations of the same species, it is best to use data on

    A) anatomical characteristics.

    B) geographic distribution.

    C) slowly evolving DNA segments.

    D) rapidly evolving DNA segments.

    E) DNA segments that do not evolve.

Answer: D
Diff: 2   *Page Ref: Scientific Inquiry*
Skill: Conceptual

Chapter 19 The Diversity of Prokaryotes and Viruses

1) The bacterial cell wall contains

    A) cellulose.

    B) chitin.

    C) peptidoglycan.

    D) pectin.

    E) starch.

Answer: C
Diff: 1   *Page Ref: 19.1*
Skill: Factual

2) How do members of the Archaea differ from the Bacteria?

    A) plasma membrane lipids

    B) cell wall composition

    C) ribosomes

    D) RNA polymerases

    E) all of the above

Answer: E
Diff: 2   *Page Ref: 19.1*
Skill: Factual

3) Peptidoglycan is found in the cell walls of

    A) Bacteria.   B) plants.   C) fungi.   D) viruses.   E) Archaea.

Answer: A
Diff: 1   *Page Ref: 19.1*
Skill: Factual

4) Which of the following statements about the Domain Bacteria is TRUE?

    A) Bacteria lack membrane–bound organelles.

    B) Chloroplasts are found in photosynthetic bacteria.

    C) Bacteria are multicellular microbes.

    D) Bacterial endospores are fragile structures that are easily destroyed.

    E) Bacteria are able to increase their genetic variability by reproducing sexually.

Answer: A
Diff: 2   *Page Ref: 19.1*
Skill: Conceptual

5) The classification of bacteria can be based on

      A) nutrient requirements.

      B) appearance of colonies.

      C) means of locomotion.

      D) pigments.

      E) all of the above

Answer: E
Diff: 2   Page Ref: 19.1
Skill: Factual

6) How do gram–positive bacteria necessarily differ from gram–negative bacteria?

      A) nutrient requirements

      B) appearance of colonies

      C) means of locomotion

      D) staining properties

      E) all of the above

Answer: D
Diff: 2   Page Ref: 19.1
Skill: Factual

7) In which of these environments would you normally find prokaryotes?

      A) an animal's intestinal tract

      B) a single drop of seawater

      C) human skin

      D) a spoonful of soil

      E) all of the above

Answer: E
Diff: 2   Page Ref: 19.1
Skill: Factual

8) Which of the following cells is within the size range of a typical prokaryote?

      A) a cell 2 micrometers in diameter

      B) a cell 25 micrometers in diameter

      C) a cell 100 micrometers in diameter

      D) a cell 700 micrometers long

      E) a cell the size of the period at the end of this sentence

Answer: A
Diff: 2   Page Ref: 19.1
Skill: Conceptual

9) The largest prokaryote, *Thiomargarita*, is _____ micrometers in diameter.

    A) 50

    B) 250

    C) 700

    D) 1000

    E) none of the above

Answer: C
Diff: 1   Page Ref: 19.1
Skill: Factual

10) Briefly explain how the classification of prokaryotes has changed in recent years, due to new technological advances.

    Answer: Until recently, prokaryotes were classified based on their appearance, staining properties, nutrient requirements, and means of locomotion. With new genetic techniques, however, modern microbiologists rely heavily upon comparisons of DNA and RNA sequences when classifying prokaryotic species.
Diff: 2   Page Ref: 19.1
Skill: Application

11) Mobile prokaryotes can move around with the help of

    A) peptidoglycan.

    B) sex pili.

    C) flagella.

    D) plasmids.

    E) endospores.

Answer: C
Diff: 1   Page Ref: 19.2
Skill: Factual

12) Prokaryotic flagella may occur

    A) singly, at one end of the cell.   B) scattered over the cell surface.

    C) as a tuft.   D) all of the above

Answer: D
Diff: 1   Page Ref: 19.2
Skill: Factual

13) How do the flagella of Bacteria differ from the flagella of Archaea?

    A) Bacterial flagella only occur at one end of the cell.

    B) The flagella of Archaea are scattered over the cell surface.

    C) Archaeal flagella are thinner than Bacterial flagella.

    D) Bacterial flagella cannot rotate.

    E) all of the above

Answer: C
Diff: 3   Page Ref: 19.2
Skill: Factual

14) What do the sticky layers of protective slime produced by some bacteria enable them to do?

    A) sexually reproduce

    B) stick together and form biofilms

    C) acquire resistance to antibiotics

    D) move from one location to another

    E) survive extreme conditions for long periods of time

Answer: B
Diff: 1   Page Ref: 19.2
Skill: Factual

15) Which structure allows a bacterium to survive and infect a host even after a long period of desiccation?

    A) protein coat

    B) pili

    C) capsule

    D) slime layer

    E) endospore

Answer: E
Diff: 2   Page Ref: 19.2
Skill: Conceptual

16) Endospores as old as _____ years old have been revived into living bacteria.

    A) 250

    B) 2,500

    C) 25,000

    D) 250,000

    E) 250,000,000

Answer: E
Diff: 2   Page Ref: 19.2
Skill: Factual

17) Some prokaryotes can live in harsh environments such as

    A) boiling water.

    B) a mile below Earth's surface.

    C) Antarctic sea ice.

    D) extremely acidic or alkaline conditions.

    E) all of the above

Answer: E
Diff: 2   Page Ref: 19.2
Skill: Factual

18) Many prokaryotes thrive in _____ environments, which lack oxygen.

    A) aerobic

    B) anaerobic

    C) biofilm

    D) pathogenic

    E) none of the above

Answer: B
Diff: 1   Page Ref: 19.2
Skill: Factual

19) Sex pili are prokaryotic structures that are used

    A) during binary fission.

    B) for movement.

    C) for adhering to surfaces.

    D) during conjugation.

    E) all of these

Answer: D
Diff: 1   Page Ref: 19.2
Skill: Factual

20) Binary fission is the method by which bacteria

 A) survive extreme conditions for long periods of time.

 B) reproduce.

 C) acquire genetic variation.

 D) move to new locations.

 E) metabolize without oxygen.

Answer: B
Diff: 1 Page Ref: 19.2
Skill: Factual

21) Through which process are bacteria able to exchange genetic material?

 A) endospore formation

 B) photosynthesis

 C) conjugation

 D) sexual reproduction

 E) anaerobic respiration

Answer: C
Diff: 2 Page Ref: 19.2
Skill: Conceptual

22) Unlike aerobic prokaryotes, anaerobic prokaryotes can obtain energy when _____ is not available.

 A) nitrogen

 B) oxygen

 C) light

 D) glucose

 E) carbon dioxide

Answer: B
Diff: 2 Page Ref: 19.2
Skill: Conceptual

23) Some bacteria use H_2S instead of H_2O in photosynthesis, and they release

   A) sulfur.

   B) ethanol.

   C) acetic acid.

   D) carbon monoxide.

   E) oxygen.

Answer: A
Diff: 2   Page Ref: 19.2
Skill: Factual

24) A single prokaryotic cell could produce as many as _____ of offspring in a single day.

   A) hundreds

   B) thousands

   C) millions

   D) billions

   E) sextillions (more than any of the above)

Answer: E
Diff: 1   Page Ref: 19.2
Skill: Factual

25) Cyanobacteria are _____ prokaryotes.

   A) chemosynthetic

   B) photosynthetic

   C) heterotrophic

   D) eukaryotic

   E) unpigmented

Answer: B
Diff: 1   Page Ref: 19.2
Skill: Factual

26) In bacteria, the small, circular pieces of DNA that are located outside the chromosome are called

    A) plasmids.

    B) sex pili.

    C) flagella.

    D) endospores.

    E) bacteriophages.

Answer: A
Diff: 1   Page Ref: 19.2
Skill: Factual

27) The mutations that improve the survival and reproduction of organisms, and thus contribute to the evolution of species, arise rapidly in prokaryotes due to their

    A) sexual reproduction.

    B) absence of a nucleus.

    C) cell wall composition.

    D) rapid rates of cell division.

    E) anaerobic metabolism.

Answer: D
Diff: 3   Page Ref: 19.2
Skill: Conceptual

28) When someone develops botulism, the disease–causing organisms responsible are

    A) prokaryotic.

    B) unicellular.

    C) anaerobes.

    D) heterotrophs.

    E) all of the above

Answer: E
Diff: 2   Page Ref: 19.3
Skill: Conceptual

29) Legumes obtain a useful form of _____ from bacteria that live in root nodules.

    A) carbon   B) oxygen   C) nitrogen   D) sulfur   E) hydrogen

Answer: C
Diff: 2   Page Ref: 19.3
Skill: Factual

30) Which of the following plants contains nitrogen–fixing bacteria in their root nodules?

   A) corn   B) soybeans   C) tomatoes   D) potatoes   E) oranges

Answer: B
Diff: 1   Page Ref: 19.3
Skill: Factual

31) Through which process do bacteria recycle nutrients in the environment?

   A) photosynthesis

   B) binary fission

   C) endospore formation

   D) conjugation

   E) decomposition

Answer: E
Diff: 2   Page Ref: 19.3
Skill: Conceptual

32) Oil spills are sprayed with bacterial cultures in order to

   A) kill the bacteria.

   B) make the oil easier to wash away.

   C) degrade the oil.

   D) prevent the oil from sticking to wildlife.

   E) detoxify the oil.

Answer: C
Diff: 2   Page Ref: 19.3
Skill: Conceptual

33) The use of bacteria to break down pollutants is referred to as

   A) biosynthesis.

   B) bioremediation.

   C) nitrogen–fixation.

   D) binary fission.

   E) biofixation.

Answer: B
Diff: 1   Page Ref: 19.3
Skill: Factual

34) Bacteria cause which of these diseases?

    A) pneumonia

    B) syphilis

    C) gonorrhea

    D) strep throat

    E) all of these

Answer: E
Diff: 2   *Page Ref: 19.3*
Skill: Factual

35) Diseases that are caused by bacteria include

    A) botulism.

    B) bubonic plague.

    C) Lyme disease.

    D) tuberculosis.

    E) all of the above

Answer: E
Diff: 2   *Page Ref: 19.3*
Skill: Factual

36) The causative agents of plague, which killed 100 million people during the 14th century, were

    A) rats.   B) fleas.   C) bacteria.   D) viruses.   E) fish.

Answer: C
Diff: 1   *Page Ref: 19.3*
Skill: Factual

37) Disease–causing bacteria are called

    A) Archaea.

    B) protozoa.

    C) viroids.

    D) pathogens.

    E) cyanobacteria.

Answer: D
Diff: 1   *Page Ref: 19.3*
Skill: Factual

38) Lyme disease is caused by _____ that are transmitted to humans by ticks.

    A) prions

    B) viruses

    C) Bacteria

    D) Archaea

    E) cyanobacteria

Answer: C
Diff: 1   Page Ref: 19.3
Skill: Factual

39) Which of these is **NOT** caused by bacteria?

    A) strep throat

    B) tetanus

    C) botulism

    D) Lyme disease

    E) smallpox

Answer: E
Diff: 1   Page Ref: 19.3
Skill: Factual

40) Tetanus is caused by _____ bacteria that grow in deep puncture wounds.

    A) aerobic

    B) anaerobic

    C) photosynthetic

    D) nitrogen–fixing

    E) harmless

Answer: B
Diff: 1   Page Ref: 19.3
Skill: Factual

41) Strep throat is caused by *Streptococcus,* a type of

    A) virus.   B) Bacteria.   C) prion.   D) viroid.   E) Archaea.

Answer: B
Diff: 1   Page Ref: 19.3
Skill: Factual

42) Which of the following is the dreaded "flesh-eating" bacterium?

   A) *Clostridium tetani*

   B) *Streptococcus pneumoniae*

   C) *Borrelia burgdorferi*

   D) *Yersinia pestis*

   E) *Escherichia coli*

Answer: B
Diff: 1   *Page Ref: 19.3*
Skill: Factual

43) Which of the following causes bubonic plague, or "Black Death"?

   A) *Clostridium tetani*

   B) *Streptococcus pneumoniae*

   C) *Borrelia burgdorferi*

   D) *Yersinia pestis*

   E) *Escherichia coli*

Answer: D
Diff: 1   *Page Ref: 19.3*
Skill: Factual

44) Which of the following is a normal inhabitant of a cow's digestive tract that can cause harm to people when it contaminates ground beef?

   A) *Clostridium tetani*

   B) *Streptococcus pneumoniae*

   C) *Borrelia burgdorferi*

   D) *Yersinia pestis*

   E) *Escherichia coli*

Answer: E
Diff: 1   *Page Ref: 19.3*
Skill: Factual

45) Which of the following is TRUE?

  A) Viruses are a kingdom of the Bacteria domain.

  B) Prokaryotes include multicellular heterotrophs.

  C) All members of the Archaea are autotrophic and move by means of flagella.

  D) All bacteria are pathogens (disease causing).

  E) Prokaryotic organisms are classified as Bacteria or Archaea.

Answer: E
Diff: 2   Page Ref: 19.3
Skill: Conceptual

46) Prokaryotes are helpful to humans because they

  A) are used to make various foods.

  B) synthesize essential vitamins within our intestinal tracts.

  C) help plants utilize atmospheric nitrogen.

  D) can clean up toxic waste.

  E) all of the above

Answer: E
Diff: 2   Page Ref: 19.3
Skill: Factual

47) In regards to their relationships with humans, are most species of bacteria beneficial, harmful, or serve no noticeable purpose whatsoever?

Answer: The vast majority of prokaryotic species are beneficial to humans. Only a tiny minority
    are pathogenic, but those species tend to get a lot of our attention!
Diff: 2   Page Ref: 19.1
Skill: Application

48) Which of the following causes acquired immune deficiency syndrome?

  A) viruses   B) Bacteria   C) prions   D) viroids   E) Archaea

Answer: A
Diff: 1   Page Ref: 19.4
Skill: Factual

49) The genetic material of a virus may be

A) DNA.

B) RNA.

C) circular.

D) double–stranded.

E) any of the above

Answer: E
Diff: 1   *Page Ref: 19.4*
Skill: Factual

50) Viruses that attack prokaryotes are called

A) viroids.

B) prions.

C) bacteriophages.

D) host cells.

E) all of the above

Answer: C
Diff: 1   *Page Ref: 19.4*
Skill: Factual

51) Which of the following may be contained in a virus?

A) RNA

B) mitochondria

C) cytoplasm

D) ribosomes

E) all of the above

Answer: A
Diff: 1   *Page Ref: 19.4*
Skill: Factual

52) Short strands of RNA that can cause plant diseases are called

A) viruses.   B) Bacteria.   C) prions.   D) viroids.   E) Archaea.

Answer: D
Diff: 1   *Page Ref: 19.4*
Skill: Factual

53) Which of the following is FALSE?

    A) Viruses are classified in the domain Archaea.

    B) Viruses are smaller than bacteria.

    C) Viruses are not living organisms.

    D) Antibiotics cannot prevent or treat viral diseases.

    E) The genetic material of viruses is not contained in a nucleus.

Answer: A
Diff: 2   *Page Ref: 19.4*
Skill: Conceptual

54) Which of the following has no organelles, ribosomes, or cytoplasm?

    A) a virus

    B) a bacterium

    C) a cyanobacterium

    D) an alga

    E) a plant

Answer: A
Diff: 1   *Page Ref: 19.4*
Skill: Factual

55) A virus basically consists of

    A) RNA or DNA and a membrane.

    B) RNA or DNA and a protein coat.

    C) proteins and a cell membrane.

    D) RNA or DNA and enzymes.

    E) enzymes and a protein coat.

Answer: B
Diff: 1   *Page Ref: 19.4*
Skill: Factual

56) Which of the following consist of a protein coat surrounding a molecule of genetic material?

    A) bacteria   B) prions   C) viruses   D) protists   E) Archaea

Answer: C
Diff: 1   *Page Ref: 19.4*
Skill: Factual

57) Which of these is NOT alive?

    A) a bacterium

    B) a virus

    C) a cyanobacterium

    D) a protist

    E) a plant

Answer: B
Diff: 2   Page Ref: 19.4
Skill: Conceptual

58) Which virus attacks white blood cells?

    A) rabies   B) influenza   C) herpes   D) HIV   E) smallpox

Answer: D
Diff: 1   Page Ref: 19.4
Skill: Factual

59) Antibiotics can only be effective against a

    A) virus.   B) prion.   C) viroid.   D) bacterium.

Answer: D
Diff: 2   Page Ref: 19.4
Skill: Conceptual

60) An organism that lacks all organelles and must always reproduce as an intracellular parasite is
a _____.

    A) prokaryote   B) bacterium   C) virus   D) prion

Answer: C
Diff: 2   Page Ref: 19.4
Skill: Conceptual

61) For which of the following diseases or conditions should antibiotics be used?

    A) smallpox

    B) Lyme disease

    C) AIDS (to combat HIV)

    D) mad cow disease

    E) a common cold

Answer: B
Diff: 2   Page Ref: 19.4
Skill: Application

62) Which of the following is characteristic of HIV?

    A) a plasma membrane

    B) DNA surrounded by a nuclear envelope

    C) peptidoglycan

    D) genetic material enclosed in a protein coat

    E) chloroplasts

Answer: D
Diff: 2   Page Ref: 19.4
Skill: Application

63) Short strands of "naked" RNA that invade the nuclei of plant cells and direct the synthesis of new copies of themselves are

    A) bacteria.   B) prions.   C) viruses.   D) viroids.   E) fungi.

Answer: D
Diff: 1   Page Ref: 19.4
Skill: Factual

64) Viroids

    A) are infectious pieces of RNA.

    B) are infectious pieces of DNA enclosed in a protein coat.

    C) have a plasma membrane.

    D) are infectious chains of amino acids.

    E) attack bacteria.

Answer: A
Diff: 1   Page Ref: 19.4
Skill: Factual

65) Prions are

    A) improperly folded proteins.

    B) viral protein coats.

    C) bacterial proteins.

    D) also known as viroids.

    E) sexually-transmitted bacteria.

Answer: A
Diff: 1   Page Ref: 19.4
Skill: Factual

66) Measles is caused by

    A) bacteria.   B) prions.   C) viruses.   D) viroids.   E) fungi.

Answer: C
Diff: 1   Page Ref: 19.4
Skill: Factual

67) Mad cow disease is caused by

    A) bacteria.   B) prions.   C) viruses.   D) viroids.   E) fungi.

Answer: B
Diff: 1   Page Ref: 19.4
Skill: Factual

68) Creutzfeldt–Jacob disease is caused by

    A) bacteria.   B) prions.   C) viruses.   D) viroids.   E) fungi.

Answer: B
Diff: 1   Page Ref: 19.4
Skill: Factual

69) AIDS is caused by

    A) bacteria.   B) prions.   C) viruses.   D) viroids.   E) fungi.

Answer: C
Diff: 1   Page Ref: 19.4
Skill: Factual

70) Avocado sunblotch is caused by

    A) bacteria.   B) prions.   C) viruses.   D) viroids.   E) fungi.

Answer: D
Diff: 1   Page Ref: 19.4
Skill: Factual

71) Herpes is caused by

    A) bacteria.   B) prions.   C) viruses.   D) viroids.   E) fungi.

Answer: C
Diff: 1   Page Ref: 19.4
Skill: Factual

72) Rabies is caused by

    A) bacteria.   B) prions.   C) viruses.   D) viroids.   E) fungi.

Answer: C
Diff: 1   Page Ref: 19.4
Skill: Factual

73) Assume that a genetic analysis of a sick animal's DNA indicates that part of one chromosome does not belong to the animal. It is foreign DNA, and is not similar to any of the animal's normal genes. Where did it most likely come from?

    A) a prion infection

    B) a bacterial infection

    C) an Archaea infection

    D) a viral infection

    E) a fungal infection

Answer: D
Diff: 3   *Page Ref: 19.4*
Skill: Conceptual

74) Are viruses alive or are they just biologically active chemicals? Explain your reasoning.

    Answer: Viruses simply exist as genetic material (DNA or RNA) surrounded by a protein coat. They are only able to make copies of themselves with the help of a host cell. Viruses are not organized on a cellular level, have no metabolism, no cytoplasm, and no self-made membranes. They cannot synthesize organic molecules. Because they lack these and other characteristics of living organisms, they should not be considered alive.
Diff: 3   *Page Ref: 19.4*
Skill: Conceptual

75) Which of the following is NOT a food-borne bacterium that typically causes food poisoning?

    A) *Bacillus anthracis*

    B) *Escherichia*

    C) *Salmonella*

    D) *Listeria*

    E) *Campylobacter*

Answer: A
Diff: 2   *Page Ref: Links to Life*
Skill: Factual

76) Which is the correct sequence of viral replication?

A) genetic material replication → penetration → transcription → assembly → protein synthesis

B) penetration → transcription → assembly → genetic material replication → protein synthesis

C) penetration → genetic material replication → transcription → assembly → protein synthesis

D) penetration → genetic material replication → transcription → protein synthesis → assembly

E) transcription → penetration → genetic material replication → assembly → protein synthesis

Answer: D
Diff: 3   *Page Ref: A Closer Look*
Skill: Conceptual

Chapter 20   The Diversity of Protists

1) Which of the following groups is eukaryotic?

   A) viruses

   B) bacteria

   C) prions

   D) cyanobacteria

   E) protists

Answer: E
Diff: 1   Page Ref: 20.1
Skill: Factual

2) Which of the following best describes the protists, as a group?

   A) plants

   B) animals

   C) fungi

   D) prokaryotes

   E) any eukaryote that is not a plant, animal, or fungus

Answer: E
Diff: 1   Page Ref: 20.1
Skill: Factual

3) The finger–like projections that some prosists use for capturing prey are called

   A) food vacuoles.

   B) pseudopods.

   C) protozoa.

   D) cysts.

   E) pseudoplasmodia.

Answer: B
Diff: 1   Page Ref: 20.1
Skill: Factual

4) Protists may be

   A) photosynthetic.

   B) parasitic.

   C) predatory.

   D) symbiotic.

   E) any of the above

Answer: E
Diff: 1   Page Ref: 20.1
Skill: Factual

5) Protist photosynthesis relies upon

   A) pseudopods.

   B) chloroplasts.

   C) pseudoplasmodia.

   D) eyespots.

   E) silica.

Answer: B
Diff: 1   Page Ref: 20.1
Skill: Factual

6) Protist reproduction

   A) may be sexual.

   B) cannot be asexual.

   C) may include the development of an embryo.

   D) is never influenced by environmental factors.

   E) All of the above are true statements.

Answer: A
Diff: 2   Page Ref: 20.1
Skill: Conceptual

7) The first protist chloroplast was likely

   A) a virus.

   B) a chemosynthetic bacterium.

   C) a photosynthetic bacterium.

   D) an example of secondary endosymbiosis.

   E) a symbiotic green alga.

Answer: C
Diff: 1   Page Ref: 20.1
Skill: Factual

8) Secondary endosymbiosis can occur when

    A) a virus infects a photosynthetic prokaryote.

    B) a non-photosynthetic protist engulfs a photosynthetic bacterium.

    C) a non-photosynthetic protist engulfs a photosynthetic protist.

    D) a protist evolves to become a prokaryote.

    E) a green alga engulfs a photosynthetic bacterium.

Answer: C
Diff: 2   Page Ref: 20.1
Skill: Conceptual

9) Imagine that you discover a photosynthetic eukaryotic cell containing chloroplasts surrounded by four distinct plasma membranes. The most likely explanation for this observation is

    A) endosymbiosis.

    B) secondary endosymbiosis.

    C) parasitism by chloroplasts.

    D) a protist evolving to become a prokaryote.

    E) None of the above could explain this observation.

Answer: B
Diff: 3   Page Ref: 20.1
Skill: Application

10) The Kingdom Protista is a group that can best be defined as "any eukaryote that is not a plant, animal, or fungus." True or False?

Answer: TRUE
Diff: 1   Page Ref: 20.1
Skill: Conceptual

11) The Kingdom Protista is an inadequately-defined and poorly-organized group that will likely be reorganized by biologists in the near future. True or False?

Answer: TRUE
Diff: 2   Page Ref: 20.1
Skill: Conceptual

12) Some protists, such as amoebas, rely upon finger-like projections called _____ for capturing prey.

Answer: pseudopods
Diff: 1   Page Ref: 20.1
Skill: factual

13) A symbiotic protist lives within the guts of termites and allows the host to digest cellulose. This organism belongs to which group?

    A) apicomplexans

    B) amoebas

    C) archaea

    D) parabasalids

    E) ciliates

Answer: D
Diff: 2   Page Ref: 20.2
Skill: Factual

14) Which protist causes a sexually transmitted disease?

    A) *Trichomonas*

    B) *Trypanosoma*

    C) *Giardia*

    D) *Plasmodium*

    E) *Pfiesteria*

Answer: A
Diff: 1   Page Ref: 20.2
Skill: Factual

15) Both *Trichomonas* and *Giardia* are parasitic protists in the group called

    A) slime molds.

    B) alveolates.

    C) excavates.

    D) diatoms.

    E) euglenids.

Answer: C
Diff: 2   Page Ref: 20.2
Skill: Factual

16) Beavers are major carriers of *Giardia*, a _____ that can cause severe diarrhea to people who drink water that contains the organism's cysts.

    A) foraminiferan

    B) euglenid

    C) dinoflagellate

    D) sporozoan

    E) diplomonad

Answer: E
Diff: 1   Page Ref: 20.2
Skill: Factual

17) A parasitic protist that presents a major health problem to backpackers and hikers if they drink unfiltered stream or lake water is

    A) *Didinium.*

    B) *Trypanosoma.*

    C) *Giardia.*

    D) *Plasmodium.*

    E) *Pfiesteria.*

Answer: C
Diff: 1   Page Ref: 20.2
Skill: Factual

18) Which group of protists includes photosynthetic, unicellular, freshwater organisms that possess eyespots?

    A) apicomplexans

    B) euglenids

    C) brown algae

    D) amoebas

    E) alveolates

Answer: B
Diff: 1   Page Ref: 20.2
Skill: Factual

19) Which group of protists includes photosynthetic, individual cells that lack a rigid cell wall and move via a flagellum?

     A) euglenids

     B) slime molds

     C) amoebas

     D) diatoms

     E) water molds

Answer: A
Diff: 1   Page Ref: 20.2
Skill: Factual

20) The eyespot of a *Euglena* cell allows it to

     A) spot potential predators.

     B) see images in black and white only.

     C) photosynthesize.

     D) orient toward light.

     E) None of these (the eyespots are not functional).

Answer: D
Diff: 1   Page Ref: 20.2
Skill: Factual

21) When you eat sushi rolls wrapped in *nori* (a type of seaweed), you are eating a

     A) photosynthetic protist.

     B) chemosynthetic protist.

     C) harmless protozoan.

     D) predatory protozoan.

     E) none of the above

Answer: A
Diff: 2   Page Ref: 20.2
Skill: Application

22) Which of the following is NOT a characteristic of the organism that causes malaria?

    A) prokaryotic

    B) unicellular

    C) non-photosynthetic

    D) parasitic

    E) protist

Answer: A
Diff: 2   Page Ref: 20.2
Skill: Application

23) Which protist causes African sleeping sickness?

    A) *Didinium*

    B) *Trypanosoma*

    C) *Giardia*

    D) *Plasmodium*

    E) *Pfiesteria*

Answer: B
Diff: 1   Page Ref: 20.2
Skill: Factual

24) Which protist group includes the water molds, diatoms, and brown algae?

    A) euglenids

    B) stramenopiles

    C) diatoms

    D) protozoa

    E) slime molds

Answer: B
Diff: 2   Page Ref: 20.2
Skill: Factual

25) Which group has caused such agricultural problems as downy mildew, potato blight, and an avocado disease?

    A) oomycetes

    B) cyanobacteria

    C) diatoms

    D) protozoa

    E) slime molds

Answer: A
Diff: 1   Page Ref: 20.2
Skill: Factual

26) The oomycte that nearly destroyed the French wine industry in the late 1800s was

    A) a slime mold.

    B) a protozoan.

    C) downy mildew.

    D) a cercozoan.

    E) red tide.

Answer: C
Diff: 1   Page Ref: 20.2
Skill: Factual

27) Which group is the critical foundation of marine food webs?

    A) euglenids

    B) cyanobacteria

    C) diatoms

    D) protozoa

    E) slime molds

Answer: C
Diff: 1   Page Ref: 20.2
Skill: Factual

28) Which group is characterized by gritty, glassy, protective shells?

    A) dinoflagellates

    B) diatoms

    C) slime molds

    D) water molds

    E) brown algae

Answer: B
Diff: 1   Page Ref: 20.2
Skill: Factual

29) Which unicellular protists have silica shells consisting of top and bottom halves that fit together like pill boxes?

    A) euglenids

    B) amoebas

    C) apicomplexans

    D) slime molds

    E) diatoms

Answer: E
Diff: 1   Page Ref: 20.2
Skill: Factual

30) Cellular examination of a cyanobacterium and a diatom reveals than the diatom has _____, which is/are absent in the cyanobacterium.

    A) DNA

    B) silica shells

    C) a plasma membrane

    D) a cell wall with peptidoglycan

    E) cilia

Answer: B
Diff: 2   Page Ref: 20.2
Skill: Conceptual

31) Free-floating, photosynthetic, unicellular members of Protista include

    A) phytoplankton.

    B) cyanobacteria.

    C) ciliates.

    D) brown algae.

    E) amoebas.

Answer: A
Diff: 2   Page Ref: 20.2
Skill: Conceptual

32) Phytoplankton are very important to the aquatic ecosystems because they

    A) produce oxygen.

    B) absorb carbon dioxide.

    C) produce glucose.

    D) All of the above are true.

    E) None of the above are true.

Answer: D
Diff: 1   Page Ref: 20.2
Skill: Conceptual

33) Cyanobacteria and phytoplankton are both

    A) heterotrophic.

    B) multicellular.

    C) eukaryotic.

    D) photosynthetic.

    E) parasitic.

Answer: D
Diff: 2   Page Ref: 20.2
Skill: Application

34) Phytoplankton are

    A) multicellular.

    B) heterotrophic.

    C) prokaryotic.

    D) photosynthetic.

    E) all of these

Answer: D
Diff: 1   Page Ref: 20.2
Skill: Conceptual

35) Which group is responsible for 70% of the photosynthesis on Earth?

    A) cyanobacteria

    B) phytoplankton

    C) ferns

    D) conifers

    E) flowering plants

Answer: B
Diff: 1   Page Ref: 20.2
Skill: Factual

36) Which group is commonly referred to as the "seaweeds"?

    A) cyanobacteria

    B) phytoplankton

    C) brown algae

    D) ciliates

    E) water molds

Answer: C
Diff: 1   Page Ref: 20.2
Skill: Conceptual

37) Individuals of which protist group can grow hundreds of feet long, and almost half a foot per day?

    A) cyanobacteria

    B) phytoplankton

    C) water molds

    D) slime molds

    E) brown algae

Answer: E
Diff: 1   Page Ref: 20.2
Skill: Factual

38) The giant kelp found along the Pacific coast is an example of

    A) cyanobacteria.

    B) phytoplankton.

    C) water molds.

    D) slime molds.

    E) brown algae.

Answer: E
Diff: 1   Page Ref: 20.2
Skill: Factual

39) Which protist group includes the dinoflagellates, apicomplexans, and ciliates?

    A) euglenids

    B) stramenopiles

    C) diatoms

    D) alveolates

    E) protozoa

Answer: D
Diff: 2   Page Ref: 20.2
Skill: Factual

40) Which group of photosynthetic, mostly marine protists were named for the presence of two flagella that create a "whirlpool–like" motion?

    A) dinoflagellates

    B) euglenids

    C) apicomplexans

    D) amoebas

    E) cercozoans

Answer: A
Diff: 2   Page Ref: 20.2
Skill: Application

41) The coral that make up a tropical coral reef can only survive in clear, well-lit waters because of the symbiotic, photosynthetic _____ that live within the tissues of the coral.

    A) dinoflagellates

    B) euglenophyta

    C) amoebas

    D) diatoms

    E) prokaryotes

Answer: A
Diff: 2   Page Ref: 20.2
Skill: Factual

42) When a red tide occurs, huge numbers of these microscopic organisms are filtered out of coastal waters by oysters and clams. This sometimes causes the shellfish to become toxic to people that eat them. The organisms that create the red tide are classified as

    A) slime molds.

    B) diatoms.

    C) dinoflagellates.

    D) red algae.

    E) euglenids.

Answer: C
Diff: 1   Page Ref: 20.2
Skill: Factual

43) Which of the following is eukaryotic, usually acts as a producer in its ecosystem, and spins with its flagella?

    A) a sporozoan

    B) an apicomplexan

    C) a cyanobacterium

    D) a dinoflagellate

    E) a slime mold

Answer: D
Diff: 2   Page Ref: 20.2
Skill: Application

44) Which of the following is the parasite sporozoan that causes malaria if it infects a human host?

    A) *Pfisteria*

    B) *Trichomonas*

    C) *Plasmodium*

    D) *Giardia*

    E) *Paramecium*

Answer: C
Diff: 1   *Page Ref: 20.2*
Skill: Factual

45) Which protozoan group consists of entirely parasitic forms?

    A) apicomplexans

    B) amoebas

    C) ciliates

    D) slime molds

    E) radiolarians

Answer: A
Diff: 1   *Page Ref: 20.2*
Skill: Conceptual

46) Which of the following is a parasitic protist that is spread by *Anopheles* mosquitoes?

    A) *Pfisteria*

    B) *Plasmodium*

    C) *Trichomonas*

    D) *Giardia*

    E) *Paramecium*

Answer: B
Diff: 1   *Page Ref: 20.2*
Skill: Factual

47) The most complex group of unicellular protists is the _____.

    A) ciliates

    B) amoebas

    C) dinoflagellates

    D) apicomplexans

    E) cercozoans

Answer: A
Diff: 1   *Page Ref: 20.2*
Skill: Factual

48) The short, hairlike structures that propel *Paramecium* through the water are called

   A) cilia.

   B) pseudopods.

   C) pseudoplasmodia.

   D) flagella.

   E) vacuoles.

Answer: A
Diff: 1   Page Ref: 20.2
Skill: Factual

49) Plasmodial slime molds are described as acellular because they

   A) have no membranes surrounding their nuclei.

   B) have no nuclei.

   C) lack DNA.

   D) reproduce asexually.

   E) are heterotrophic.

Answer: A
Diff: 1   Page Ref: 20.2
Skill: Factual

50) A pseudoplasmodium is

   A) an acellular slime mold.

   B) an aggregation of mycelia.

   C) a group of cellular slime mold cells.

   D) an extension of the slime mold that engulfs prey.

   E) a disease–causing protist.

Answer: C
Diff: 1   Page Ref: 20.2
Skill: Factual

51) The active, feeding form of a/an _____ is a thin, multinucleate plasmodium.

   A) acellular slime mold

   B) green alga

   C) cyanobacterium

   D) apicomplexan

   E) amoeba

Answer: A
Diff: 1   Page Ref: 20.2
Skill: Factual

52) When dry conditions or starvation stimulate an acellular slime mold to change form, it becomes

    A) a plasmodium.   B) a cellular slime mold.

    C) a water mold.   D) a fruiting body.

Answer: D
Diff: 1   Page Ref: 20.2
Skill: Conceptual

53) The _____ algae represent an important source of carrageenan, which is used to thicken paints, cosmetics and ice cream.

    A) red   B) brown

    C) unicellular green   D) multicellular green

Answer: A
Diff: 1   Page Ref: 20.2
Skill: Factual

54) Which of the following characteristics distinguishes red algae from diatoms and dinoflagellates?

    A) aquatic

    B) multicellular

    C) eukaryotic

    D) protist

    E) photosynthetic

Answer: B
Diff: 1   Page Ref: 20.2
Skill: Conceptual

55) Dysentery can be caused by parasitic, lobose _____ that occur in freshwater in warm climates.

    A) diatoms

    B) ciliates

    C) dinoflagellates

    D) slime molds

    E) amoebas

Answer: E
Diff: 2   Page Ref: 20.2
Skill: Factual

56) The white cliffs of Dover, England were formed over millions of years by the accumulation of calcium carbonate shells from _____.

    A) apicomplexans

    B) euglenids

    C) foraminiferans

    D) cyanobacteria

    E) ciliates

Answer: C
Diff: 1   Page Ref: 20.2
Skill: Factual

57) Which group has silica shells similar to those of diatoms?

    A) apicomplexans

    B) dinoflagellates

    C) ciliates

    D) euglenids

    E) radiolarians

Answer: E
Diff: 1   Page Ref: 20.2
Skill: Factual

58) Which of the following is considered to be most closely related to the plants?

    A) brown algae

    B) slime molds

    C) euglenids

    D) green algae

    E) diatoms

Answer: D
Diff: 1   Page Ref: 20.2
Skill: Factual

59) Which of the following can be photosynthetic?

    A) a diatom

    B) a slime mold

    C) an amoeba

    D) an apicomplexan

    E) a ciliate

Answer: A
Diff: 1   Page Ref: 20.2
Skill: Factual

60) Which of the following may be parasitic in humans?

    A) a diatom

    B) a slime mold

    C) an amoeba

    D) an apicomplexan

    E) an amoeba or an apicomplexan

Answer: E
Diff: 1   Page Ref: 20.2
Skill: Factual

61) Which of the following makes pseudopods?

    A) a diatom

    B) a slime mold

    C) an amoeba

    D) an apicomplexan

    E) a ciliate

Answer: C
Diff: 1   Page Ref: 20.2
Skill: Factual

62) Which of the following evolved from protists?

    A) fungi

    B) plants

    C) animals

    D) all of the above

    E) none of the above

Answer: D
Diff: 1   Page Ref: Evolutionary Connections
Skill: Factual

63) Which protist is an invasive seaweed that has severely impacted the Mediterranean Sea, and threatens many other marine environments?

    A) *Pfisteria*

    B) *Spirogyra*

    C) *Trichomonas*

    D) *Volvox*

    E) *Caulerpa*

Answer: E
Diff: 1   Page Ref: Case Study
Skill: Factual

64) The protists include photosynthetic, parasitic, and pathogenic species. True or False?

Answer: TRUE
Diff: 1   Page Ref: 20.2
Skill: Conceptual

65) Some protists can cause sexually transmitted diseases in humans. True or False?

Answer: TRUE
Diff: 1   Page Ref: 20.2
Skill: Factual

66) Euglenids have functional eyespots that can discern all colors of visible light and the movement of predators. True or False?

Answer: FALSE
Diff: 1   Page Ref: 20.2
Skill: Conceptual

67) Some protists can grow more than 6 inches per day. True or False?

Answer: TRUE
Diff: 1   Page Ref: 20.2
Skill: Factual

68) *Trypanosoma* is a protistan parasite that causes _____ in humans.

Answer: African sleeping sickness
Diff: 1   Page Ref: 20.2
Skill: Factual

69) _____ is a protistan parasite that causes malaria in humans.

Answer: *Plasmodium*
Diff: 1   Page Ref: 20.2
Skill: Factual

70) Malaria is caused by a protist that is transmitted by the bite of _____.

Answer: mosquitoes
Diff: 1   Page Ref: 20.2
Skill: Factual

71) Two groups of protists that have silica shells are the _____ and the _____.

Answer: diatoms; radiolarians
Diff: 1   Page Ref: 20.2
Skill: Factual

72) The group of protistan aquatic organisms known generally as _____ produce most of the world's oxygen.

Answer: phytoplankton
Diff: 2   Page Ref: 20.2
Skill: Conceptual

73) Paralytic shellfish poisoning, or PSP, is caused by the group of protists known as _____.

Answer: dinoflagellates
Diff: 1   Page Ref: 20.2
Skill: Factual

74) Explain the difference between a plasmodium and *Plasmodium*.

Answer: A plasmodium is an acellular slime mold structure made up of thousands of nuclei that are not confined in separate cells. In contrast, *Plasmodium* is the genus of apicomplexan protists that causes malaria.
Diff: 3   Page Ref: 20.2
Skill: Application

75) What would life on Earth be like today, had eukaryotic protists not evolved?

Answer: Without the evolution of protists, life on Earth today would most likely be represented by a diversity of prokaryotes, but no eukaryotes. This is because plants, animals, and fungi evolved from protists that subsequently underwent radical changes in their cellular structure and eukaryotic design.
Diff: 3   Page Ref: Evolutionary Connections
Skill: Conceptual

Chapter 21 The Diversity of Plants

1) Plants are

    A) photosynthetic.

    B) eukaryotic

    C) multicellular.

    D) A and C

    E) all of these

Answer: E
Diff: 1   Page Ref: 21.1
Skill: Factual

2) You find a multicellular, eukaryotic organism which carries on photosynthesis. It would be classified as a(n) _____.

    A) fungus   B) plant   C) animal   D) bacteria   E) protists

Answer: B
Diff: 1   Page Ref: 21.1
Skill: Factual

3) Which of the following are characteristic of plants?

    A) They alternate between sporophyte and gametophyte generations.

    B) They have dependent embryos.

    C) They carry on photosynthesis.

    D) They are eukaryotic and multicellular.

    E) all of the above

Answer: E
Diff: 1   Page Ref: 21.1
Skill: Factual

4) A diploid plant is a(n) _____.

    A) egg

    B) sperm

    C) spore

    D) gametophyte

    E) sporophyte

Answer: E
Diff: 1   Page Ref: 21.1
Skill: Factual

5) The haploid generation of a plant is a(n) _____.

    A) angiosperm

    B) seed

    C) rhizoid

    D) gametophyte

    E) sporophyte

Answer: E
Diff: 1   Page Ref: 21.1
Skill: Factual

6) A plant cell undergoing **meiosis** produces a _____.

    A) gametophyte   B) sporophyte   C) cone   D) sporangium

Answer: A
Diff: 2   Page Ref: 21.1
Skill: Conceptual

7) A fertilized egg is a

    A) sporophyte.

    B) gametophyte.

    C) zygote.

    D) spore.

    E) gamete.

Answer: C
Diff: 1   Page Ref: 21.1
Skill: Factual

8) In plants, the diploid, multicellular organisms is the

    A) sporophyte.

    B) gametophyte.

    C) zygote.

    D) spore.

    E) gamete.

Answer: A
Diff: 1   Page Ref: 21.1
Skill: Factual

9) In plants, the haploid, multicellular organism is the

   A) sporophyte.

   B) gametophyte.

   C) zygote.

   D) spore.

   E) gamete.

Answer: B
Diff: 1   Page Ref: 21.1
Skill: Factual

10) The haploid, single-celled product of mitosis is a

   A) sporophyte.

   B) gametophyte.

   C) zygote.

   D) spore.

   E) gamete.

Answer: E
Diff: 1   Page Ref: 21.1
Skill: Factual

11) A gametophyte is

   A) diploid.

   B) haploid.

   C) triploid.

   D) tetraploid.

   E) unable to survive.

Answer: B
Diff: 2   Page Ref: 21.1
Skill: Application

12) The gametophyte produces _____ by _____.

   A) spores; mitosis

   B) gametes; mitosis

   C) spores; meiosis

   D) gametophytes; mitosis

   E) sporophytes; meiosis

Answer: B
Diff: 1   Page Ref: 21.1
Skill: Factual

13) The first cell after fertilization is the

    A) spore.

    B) sporophyte.

    C) embryo.

    D) seed.

    E) zygote.

Answer: E
Diff: 1   Page Ref: 21.1
Skill: Factual

14) Spores develop into _____.

    A) haploid gametophytes

    B) diploid gametophytes

    C) haploid sporophytes

    D) haploid gametes

    E) diploid sporophytes

Answer: A
Diff: 1   Page Ref: 21.1
Skill: Factual

15) Spores are produced by _____.

    A) gametes

    B) gametophytes

    C) sporophytes

    D) zygotes

    E) other spores

Answer: C
Diff: 1   Page Ref: 21.1
Skill: Factual

16) The products of photosynthesis are

   A) sugars and O_2.

   B) lipids and H_2O.

   C) CO_2 and sugars.

   D) minerals and nitrogen.

   E) CO_2 and phosphorus.

Answer: A
Diff: 1   Page Ref: 21.1
Skill: Factual

17) If all plants were wiped out,

   A) Earth's oxygen levels would decline.

   B) animals and fungi would run out of food.

   C) a primary source of drugs would be lost.

   D) all of the above

Answer: D
Diff: 1   Page Ref: 21.1
Skill: Factual

18) Farmers add organic matter in the form of dead plants to their soils. Why?

   A) Organic matter improves soil's ability to hold water and nutrients.

   B) Organic matter adds oxygen to the soil.

   C) Farm wastes need to be gotten rid of somewhere.

   D) Soils need to have addition minerals added yearly.

   E) all of the above

Answer: A
Diff: 1   Page Ref: 21.1
Skill: Factual

19) During the Dust Bowl years, thousands of acres lost all vegetation due to drought, and the soil just blew away. Why?

   A) Plants draw all the water out of soil and increase erosion.

   B) The plants put too much of a nutrient demand on the soils, weakening its structure.

   C) The roots of living plants help hold soil in place and prevent erosion.

   D) Photosynthesis is detrimental to soil microbes.

Answer: C
Diff: 1   Page Ref: 21.1
Skill: Factual

20) Gametophytes produce haploid gametes via _____.

A) meiosis   B) fertilization   C) mitosis   D) pollination

Answer: C
Diff: 2   Page Ref: 21.1
Skill: Conceptual

21) Potatoes as a species have 48 chromosomes. Which of the following has 48 chromosomes?

A) the potato pollen   B) the potato spores

C) the potato plant   D) the potato eggs

Answer: C
Diff: 3   Page Ref: 21.1
Skill: Application

22) How does photosynthesis benefit non photosynthetic organisms like humans?

Answer: Plants convert solar energy to chemical energy in the form of sugars and starches which provide food for humans. During photosynthesis, oxygen is given off as a waste product. This provides the oxygen we breathe.
Diff: 2   Page Ref: 21.1
Skill: Application

23) Which of the following discoveries support the idea that members of the plant kingdom evolved from an ancestral green algae?

A) The types of chlorophyll found in plants are the same as those in green algae and different from that of other photosynthetic organisms.

B) The cell wall composition of plants and green algae are nearly identical and different from the cell walls of other organisms.

C) DNA studies show plants and green algae share a number of unique gene sequences.

D) Both plants and green algae store food reserves in similar types of molecules.

E) All of these are correct.

Answer: E
Diff: 1   Page Ref: 21.2
Skill: Factual

24) Green algae are assumed to be ancestors of plants because

    A) the fossil ancestors have been discovered.

    B) green algae make chitin and laminarin.

    C) green algae make cellulose and starch.

    D) green algae are almost exclusively marine.

    E) lignin is known to occur in some green algae.

Answer: C
Diff: 1   Page Ref: 21.2
Skill: Factual

25) Land plants are believed to have evolved from _____.

    A) green algae   B) fungi   C) lichens   D) bacteria

Answer: A
Diff: 1   Page Ref: 21.2
Skill: Factual

26) Liverworts and mosses are thought to be some of the earliest land plants because

    A) they have well developed root systems.

    B) they lack vascular elements.

    C) they do not require liquid water for reproduction.

    D) the gametophyte generation is dominant.

    E) all of the above

Answer: B
Diff: 2   Page Ref: 21.2
Skill: Application

27) Both plants and green algae store food as

    A) lignan.

    B) chlorophyll.

    C) starch.

    D) cellulose.

    E) lipids.

Answer: C
Diff: 1   Page Ref: 21.2
Skill: Factual

28) Which of the following is characteristic of plants but NOT algae?

      A) photosynthesis

      B) starch

      C) cellulose

      D) chloroplasts

      E) multicellular, dependent embryos

Answer: E
Diff: 2   Page Ref: 21.2
Skill: Conceptual

29) Which of the following descriptions does NOT apply to ANY plant?

      A) autotrophic

      B) multicellular

      C) parasitic

      D) decomposer

      E) symbiont

Answer: D
Diff: 2   Page Ref: 21.2
Skill: Conceptual

30) Which of the supports the idea that land plants arose from green algae?

      A) Both photosynthesize.

      B) Both use the same kind of chlorophyll.

      C) Green algae live in fresh water environments; plants require fresh water.

      D) Both contain similar accessory pigments.

Answer: A
Diff: 2   Page Ref: 21.2
Skill: Conceptual

31) What is the benefit of having a tall stem?

      A) ease of water movement

      B) more nutrients available

      C) greater support

      D) easier reproduction

      E) less competition for light

Answer: E
Diff: 1   Page Ref: 21.2
Skill: Conceptual

32) Why are the Chlorophyta (green algae) considered to be closer to the true plants than any other group of algae?

Answer: Green algae and plants show similar DNA sequences, have similar cell wall composition, store food reserves in similar forms.
Diff: 2   Page Ref: 21.2
Skill: Conceptual

33) Pollen and seeds evolved in response to

A) an increase in pollinators.

B) flower evolution.

C) moist environments.

D) seed predators.

E) dry land environments.

Answer: E
Diff: 1   Page Ref: 21.3
Skill: Conceptual

34) Which of these is an advantage to a plant that moved onto land?

A) increased CO_2 availability

B) dry environment

C) less support

D) increased heat

E) decreased water availability

Answer: A
Diff: 2   Page Ref: 21.3
Skill: Conceptual

35) To reduce water loss, the outside of leaves is covered with a/an _____.

A) cuticle

B) stomata

C) lignan

D) antheridia

E) rhizoids

Answer: A
Diff: 1   Page Ref: 21.3
Skill: Factual

36) Vessel tubes are rigid because they include _____ in their cell walls.

A) DNA   B) lignin   C) ribose   D) nitrogen   E) starch

Answer: B
Diff: 1   Page Ref: 21.3
Skill: Factual

37) What advantage do seed plants have over spore–forming plants?

Answer: Seeds tolerate drying better and are longer lived than spores. Seeds can take advantage
         of animals for dispersal of the seed whereas spores are too small and non nutritive to
         interest animal carriers.
Diff: 3   Page Ref: 21.3
Skill: Application

38) To control the movement of gases, land plants developed

A) roots.   B) stomata.

C) flowers.   D) vascular tissue.

Answer: B
Diff: 2   Page Ref: 21.4
Skill: Application

39) With respect to plant reproduction, there has been an evolutionary trend toward

A) increased pollen production.

B) smaller flowers.

C) larger fruits.

D) sporophyte dominance.

E) greater seed production.

Answer: D
Diff: 1   Page Ref: 21.4
Skill: Factual

40) You examine a one-inch tall plant you collect in the woods. This plant was part of a several square feet mass of similar small plants. It is very flexible and does not easily stand upright by itself. Upon examining the tiny flat leaf–like structures of this plant you see no veins. There is no evidence of seeds, but at the end of a little stalk on the end of the plant there is some sort of spore bearing structure. To which of these groups does this plant likely belong?

   A) angiosperm

   B) gymnosperm

   C) fern

   D) algae

   E) bryophyte

Answer: E
Diff: 2   Page Ref: 21.4
Skill: Application

41) When walking in a forest you find a plant with what appear to be unfertilized seeds on little scales exposed to the air. Yellow dust–like particles are on the surface of the unfertilized seeds. To what group does this plant belong?

   A) angiosperms

   B) gymnosperms

   C) bryophytes

   D) seedless vascular plants

   E) algae

Answer: B
Diff: 3   Page Ref: 21.4
Skill: Application

42) When walking in a tropical forest you come upon a 6 meter tall plant that shows no evidence of seed production. In which of these groups does the plant most likely belong?

   A) gymnosperms

   B) angiosperms

   C) bryophytes

   D) ferns

   E) algae

Answer: D
Diff: 2   Page Ref: 21.4
Skill: Application

43) A fossil plant is found that appears to have several seeds all completely enclosed in a single outer covering. This plant probably belongs to what group?

    A) gymnosperms

    B) angiosperms

    C) bryophytes

    D) ferns

    E) algae

Answer: B
Diff: 2   Page Ref: 21.4
Skill: Application

44) What is/are advantages to producing broad leaves compared to narrow needle–like leaves?

    A) increased water loss

    B) increases gas exchange

    C) increases surface area for light capture

    D) both A and B

    E) A, B, and C

Answer: C
Diff: 1   Page Ref: 21.4
Skill: Factual

45) Which of the following weather conditions would you expect to have the greatest *negative impact* on sexual reproduction of ferns and mosses?

    A) excessively wet and raining conditions

    B) above average temperatures for several days

    C) excessively dry period for several days

    D) moderate temperatures and rainfall

    E) the shade of a forest

Answer: C
Diff: 2   Page Ref: 21.4
Skill: Conceptual

46) Which of the following weather conditions would you expect to have the greatest *positive impact* on sexual reproduction of ferns and mosses?

    A) excessively wet and raining conditions

    B) above average temperature for several days

    C) excessively dry period for several days

    D) below average temperatures for a few days

    E) the shade of a forest

Answer: A
Diff: 2   Page Ref: 21.4
Skill: Conceptual

47) Which evolutionary plant innovation eliminated the need for sperm to swim through water in order to fertilize an egg, resulting in plants being truly adapted for reproduction on land?

    A) rhizoids

    B) fruit

    C) roots

    D) independent gametophyte

    E) pollen

Answer: E
Diff: 1   Page Ref: 21.4
Skill: Factual

48) If you were hiking and wanted to show off your understanding of the differences between gymnosperms and angiosperms, what characteristics could you see with your naked eye that would help you impress your friends?

    A) flowers or cones

    B) presence or lack of vascular tissues

    C) presence or lack of seeds

    D) presence or lack of tree sized stems

    E) size of the male gametophyte

Answer: A
Diff: 1   Page Ref: 21.4
Skill: Factual

49) Gymnosperms

    A) lack flowers.

    B) lack seeds.

    C) lack eggs and sperm.

    D) lack leaves.

    E) All of these are true.

Answer: A
Diff: 1   *Page Ref: 21.4*
Skill: Factual

50) In flowering plants, what is the relationship of the sporophyte generation to the gametophyte generation?

    A) Sporophyte is dominant, but begins development attached to gametophyte.

    B) Gametophyte is dominant, and sporophyte is retained on gametophyte.

    C) Sporophyte is dominant, and gametophyte is microscopic.

    D) Members of this division do not produce sporophytes.

    E) Members of this division do not produce gametophytes.

Answer: C
Diff: 1   *Page Ref: 21.4*
Skill: Factual

51) An oak tree is a _____.

    A) gametophyte

    B) zygote

    C) sporophyte

    D) spore

    E) all of these

Answer: C
Diff: 1   *Page Ref: 21.4*
Skill: Application

52) The evolutionary trend from the ancestral algae to the more recently evolved seed plants shows

    A) decreased size of the gametophyte.

    B) increased prominence of the sporophyte generation.

    C) decreased duration of the gametophyte generation.

    D) A and B

    E) all of the above

Answer: D
Diff: 1   Page Ref: 21.4
Skill: Factual

53) Which group of land plants is most restricted to moist environments?

    A) vascular plants

    B) tracheophytes

    C) bryophytes

    D) anthophyta

    E) angiosperms

Answer: C
Diff: 1   Page Ref: 21.4
Skill: Conceptual

54) Bryophytes

    A) are mosses and liverworts.

    B) lack true roots and leaves.

    C) have poorly developed conducting tissues.

    D) A and B

    E) all of the above

Answer: E
Diff: 1   Page Ref: 21.4
Skill: Factual

55) Bryophytes have simple structures, called _____, that anchor the plant and absorb water.

   A) roots

   B) mycorrhizae

   C) rhizomes

   D) tracheophytes

   E) rhizoids

Answer: E
Diff: 1   Page Ref: 21.4
Skill: Factual

56) Archegonia are _____.

   A) floatation bladders

   B) reproductive structures

   C) conducting tissues

   D) flowers

   E) root symbionts

Answer: B
Diff: 1   Page Ref: 21.4
Skill: Factual

57) Which of the following are important reproductive adaptations that allow plants to inhabit terrestrial environments?

   A) leaves and stems

   B) seeds and pollen

   C) roots and leaves

   D) gametophytes and sporophytes

   E) flowers and leaves

Answer: B
Diff: 2   Page Ref: 21.4
Skill: Conceptual

58) How do seeds improve the chances of survival of a young plant?

   A) Seeds transport the sperm to an egg without water.

   B) Seeds increase exposure of the embryo to light.

   C) Seeds contain food reserve for embryo.

   D) Seeds increase the accuracy of sperm delivery.

   E) all of the above

Answer: C
Diff: 1   Page Ref: 21.34
Skill: Factual

59) Which of the following types of plants produce seeds?

   A) horsetails

   B) ferns

   C) ginkgo

   D) hornworts

   E) mosses

Answer: D
Diff: 1   Page Ref: 21.4
Skill: Factual

60) Which of the following groups of plants was the first to produce seeds?

   A) angiosperms

   B) bryophytes

   C) gymnosperms

   D) lycophytes

   E) chlorophytes

Answer: C
Diff: 1   Page Ref: 21.4
Skill: Factual

61) Which of the following are gymnosperms?

   A) cycads, ginkgoes, and ferns

   B) cycads, conifers, and ferns

   C) ginkgoes, conifers, and horsetails

   D) conifers, ginkgoes, and ferns

   E) cycads, ginkgoes, and conifers

Answer: E
Diff: 1   Page Ref: 21.4
Skill: Factual

62) Which division has been reduced to one remaining species?

    A) conifers

    B) cycads

    C) ginkgoes

    D) bryophytes

    E) liverworts

Answer: C
Diff: 1   Page Ref: 21.4
Skill: Factual

63) Which plants have been planted extensively in the US as a street tree due to their resistance to pollution?

    A) conifers

    B) cycads

    C) ginkgoes

    D) bryophytes

    E) liverworts

Answer: C
Diff: 1   Page Ref: 21.4
Skill: Factual

64) What group dominated the Carboniferous period and is now burned as coal?

    A) angiosperms

    B) conifers

    C) cycads

    D) seedless vascular plants

    E) algae

Answer: D
Diff: 1   Page Ref: 21.4
Skill: Factual

65) Conifers are primarily _____ pollinated.

    A) bee   B) wind   C) moth   D) water   E) beetle

Answer: B
Diff: 1   Page Ref: 21.4
Skill: Factual

66) What is one major difference between ferns and the other seedless vascular plants?

A) reproductive cycle

B) dominant stage of life

C) leaf shape

D) flower structure

E) vascular system

Answer: C
Diff: 2   Page Ref: 21.4
Skill: Conceptual

67) Which group does not depend on water for reproduction?

A) ferns

B) bryophytes

C) algae

D) club mosses

E) flowering plants

Answer: E
Diff: 1   Page Ref: 21.4
Skill: Factual

68) What is the main function of flower petals?

A) produce gametes

B) photosynthesize

C) provide support

D) attract pollinators

E) discourage herbivores

Answer: D
Diff: 1   Page Ref: 21.4
Skill: Factual

69) All of the following contributed substantially to the success of angiosperms EXCEPT

A) pollinators.

B) broad leaves.

C) vascular system.

D) flowers.

E) fruits.

Answer: C
Diff: 2   Page Ref: 21.4
Skill: Conceptual

70) In angiosperms, the male gametophyte is _____.

   A) pollen

   B) the anther

   C) a flower

   D) sperm

   E) a seed

Answer: A
Diff: 1   *Page Ref: 21.4*
Skill: Factual

71) A fruit is

   A) a seed.

   B) a mature ovary.

   C) a mature ovule.

   D) the female gametophyte.

   E) a plant embryo.

Answer: B
Diff: 1   *Page Ref: 21.4*
Skill: Factual

72) Fruit production requires precious resources; what important benefit do they confer?

   A) feed the embryo

   B) keep the seed moist

   C) means of dispersal of seeds

   D) attract seed eater

   E) prevent grazing on the fruit

Answer: C
Diff: 2   *Page Ref: 21.4*
Skill: Conceptual

73) What is/are the *dis*advantages to production of broad leaves?

   A) increased water loss

   B) increases gas exchange

   C) increased surface area for light capture

   D) A and B

   E) A and C

Answer: A
Diff: 1   *Page Ref: 21.4*
Skill: Factual

74) Most gymnosperms are pollinated by

A) insects.

B) birds.

C) small mammals.

D) wind.

Answer: D
Diff: 1   Page Ref: 21.4
Skill: Factual

75) You've observed a moss sporophyte attached to a gametophyte. To what structure, is the sporophyte attached?

A) an archegonium

B) a flower

C) a female cone

D) the embryo sac

E) an antheridium

Answer: A
Diff: 3   Page Ref: 21.4
Skill: Conceptual

76) All plants have or produce _____.

A) vascular tissue

B) seeds

C) pollen

D) gametes

E) fruits

Answer: D
Diff: 2   Page Ref: 21.4
Skill: Conceptual

77) Which of the following is most likely to be successful and thrive in a desert ecosystem?

A) angiosperm

B) conifer

C) green algae

D) fern

E) moss

Answer: A
Diff: 2   Page Ref: 21.4
Skill: Application

78) The _____ of a fern gametophyte imply that it can be found living in the soil independent of a fern sporophyte.

   A) roots

   B) pollen

   C) swimming sperm

   D) archegonia

   E) rhizoids

Answer: E
Diff: 2   Page Ref: 21.4
Skill: Conceptual

79) Which of the following must produce copious amounts of pollen to ensure successful pollination?

   A) tulip

   B) stinking corpse lily

   C) magnolia tree

   D) pine tree

   E) gardenia

Answer: D
Diff: 2   Page Ref: 21.4
Skill: Application

80) Your friend has asked you to make a fruit salad with the following: a pumpkin, cucumber, tomato, broccoli, and kiwi. Which of them will you leave out because it's not a fruit?

   A) pumpkin

   B) cucumber

   C) tomato

   D) broccoli

   E) kiwi

Answer: D
Diff: 2   Page Ref: 21.4
Skill: Application

81) Which of the following is technically not a fruit?

    A) pumpkin

    B) cucumber

    C) tomato

    D) lettuce

    E) green pepper

Answer: D
Diff: 2   Page Ref: 21.4
Skill: Application

82) Which of the following depends on a method of seed dispersal other the consumption of its fruits?

    A) apple   B) oak   C) maple   D) pine   E) moss

Answer: C
Diff: 3   Page Ref: 21.4
Skill: Application

83) Ginkgoes are classified as a/an

    A) seedless vascular plant.   B) gymnosperm.

    C) angiosperm.   D) bryophyte.

Answer: B
Diff: 1   Page Ref: 21.4
Skill: Factual

84) Cycads are classified as a/an

    A) seedless vascular plant.   B) gymnosperm.

    C) angiosperm.   D) bryophyte.

Answer: B
Diff: 1   Page Ref: 21.4
Skill: Factual

85) Horse tails (scouring rush) are classified as a/an

    A) seedless vascular plant.   B) gymnosperm.

    C) angiosperm.   D) bryophyte.

Answer: A
Diff: 1   Page Ref: 21.4
Skill: Factual

86) Tulips are classified as a/an

    A) seedless vascular plant.   B) gymnosperm.

    C) angiosperm.   D) bryophyte.

Answer: C
Diff: 1   Page Ref: 21.4
Skill: Factual

87) Moss can be described as a/an

    A) seedless vascular plant.   B) gymnosperm.

    C) angiosperm.   D) bryophyte.

Answer: D
Diff: 1   Page Ref: 21.4
Skill: Factual

88) Non-vascular plants which need free standing water for fertilization to occur would be classified as _____.

    A) angiosperm   B) conifer   C) fern   D) bryophyte

Answer: D
Diff: 1   Page Ref: 21.4
Skill: Factual

89) A complete lack of vascular tissue is characteristic of a/an

    A) angiosperm.   B) conifer.   C) fern.   D) bryophyte.

Answer: D
Diff: 1   Page Ref: 21.4
Skill: Factual

90) Pollen production by the anthers of a flower is characteristic of

    A) angiosperms.   B) conifers.   C) ferns.   D) bryophytes.

Answer: A
Diff: 1   Page Ref: 21.4
Skill: Factual

91) Male and female cones are characteristic of

    A) angiosperms.   B) conifers.   C) ferns.   D) bryophytes.

Answer: B
Diff: 1   Page Ref: 21.4
Skill: Factual

92) Non-flowering seed plants are classified as

A) angiosperms.   B) conifers.   C) ferns.   D) bryophytes.

Answer: B
Diff: 1   Page Ref: 21.4
Skill: Factual

93) An apple tree would be classified as a/an

A) angiosperm.   B) conifer.   C) fern.   D) bryophyte.

Answer: A
Diff: 2   Page Ref: 21.4
Skill: Application

94) Explain the difference between an angiosperm seed and a gymnosperm seed.

Answer: Gymnosperm seeds develop in cones and lack fleshy covering. Angiosperm seeds develop within the ovary to form a fruit.
Diff: 2   Page Ref: 21.4
Skill: Factual

95) In some areas of the world where there are large numbers of pines, in the spring everything is covered with a yellow dust that turns out upon examination to be pine pollen. Why must conifers produce so much pollen and why do we not see as much pollen produced by a field of flowers?

Answer: Pines are wind pollinated and must produce large excesses of pollen. Field flowers are insect pollinated and therefore don't have to produce so much pollen.
Diff: 2   Page Ref: 21.4
Skill: Conceptual

96) Explain how bryophytes are an intermediate between green algae and terrestrial plants.

Answer: Bryophytes are land dwelling plants, but must be close to water because they are non-vascular and lack the ability to transport water over long distances. They also produce swimming sperm like green algae which means water must be available for fertilization to occur.
Diff: 1   Page Ref: 21.4
Skill: Conceptual

97) Explain the evolutionary relevance of the seed.

Answer: Seeds increased the ability of plants to thrive on land because the plant embryos are protected from drying out and survive until good growing conditions on the food stored inside the seed. The seed coat helps regulate the timing of seed germination.
Diff: 2   Page Ref: 21.4
Skill: Conceptual

98) What methods do angiosperms use to disperse seed?

Answer: Angiosperms spread their seeds several ways: wind, water, ingestion of fruits by birds and animals; hitching a ride on fur, feathers, and clothing.
Diff: 2   Page Ref: 21.4
Skill: Application

99) Why are ferns not well adapted to desert areas?

Answer: Ferns have very limited vascular elements and are not very effective at transporting water. Most ferns lack a heavy cuticle to prevent drying under low humidity. Ferns require liquid water to transport the sperm.
Diff: 3   Page Ref: 21.4
Skill: Application

100) How do gymnosperms differ from angiosperms?

Answer: Gymnosperms do not produce flowers; angiosperms do.
Diff: 2   Page Ref: 21.4
Skill: Application

101) What characteristics allow conifers to dominate cold, dry habitats?

Answer: Conifers have the ability to photosynthesize year round. Their leaves form small needles protected with a heavy waxy cuticle; Their resin acts as an antifreeze.
Diff: 2   Page Ref: 21.4
Skill: Application

Chapter 22 The Diversity of Fungi

1) Your text talks about massive fungal organisms. One of the most massive organisms in the world may be a basidiomycete occupying 1500 acres in Washington state. How can scientists attempt to verify that this is one in fact huge organism?

Answer: Analyze DNA from the fungus in various parts of the range. If the DNA is identical then there may be only one organism.
Diff: 2   *Page Ref: Case Study*
Skill: Factual

2) Fungal cell walls are different from plant cell walls because fungal walls contain _____.

   A) cellulose, while plant walls have chitin

   B) glycogen, while plant walls have cellulose

   C) glycoprotein, while plant walls have starch

   D) chitin, while plant walls have cellulose

   E) cellulose, while plant walls have pectin

Answer: D
Diff: 1   *Page Ref: 22.1*
Skill: Factual

3) True fungi are characterized by/as _____.

   A) cell walls, feeding by absorption, and usually have filamentous bodies

   B) cell walls, photosynthesis, and usually have filamentous bodies

   C) no cell walls, feeding by absorption, chemosynthesis

   D) no cell walls, parasitic, heterotrophic

   E) cell walls, chemosynthetic, heterotrophic

Answer: A
Diff: 1   *Page Ref: 22.1*
Skill: Factual

4) The body of a fungus is generally composed of _____.

   A) cellulose

   B) vascular tissue

   C) mycorrhizae

   D) mold

   E) hyphae

Answer: E
Diff: 1   *Page Ref: 22.1*
Skill: Factual

5) The cellular threads which form the body of a fungus are called _____.

A) spores

B) roots

C) mycorrhizae

D) mold

E) hyphae

Answer: E
Diff: 1   Page Ref: 22.1
Skill: Factual

6) Which of the following is a polysaccharide produced by both fungi and arthropods?

A) cellulose   B) glycogen   C) glucose   D) fructose   E) chitin

Answer: E
Diff: 1   Page Ref: 22.1
Skill: Factual

7) The majority of fungal biomass is located

A) in fruiting bodies.

B) in the reproductive spores.

C) above ground.

D) in roots.

E) underground.

Answer: E
Diff: 1   Page Ref: 22.1
Skill: Factual

8) When you eat mushrooms on your pizza, you are technically eating the?

A) seeds

B) chloroplasts

C) fungal leaves

D) the mycelium

E) roots

Answer: D
Diff: 2   Page Ref: 22.1
Skill: Conceptual

9) You must decide how to classify a newly discovered organism, but have only the chemicals below to help you make your decision. After testing it with the available chemicals, you find out it glows, doesn't turn blue, and fizzes. How will you classify this organism?
Glowing = the presence of a nuclear envelope
Blue = the presence of chloroplasts
Fizzing = the presence of chitin

   A) bacterium

   B) slime mold

   C) diatom

   D) fungus

   E) zooflagellate

Answer: D
Diff: 3   Page Ref: 22.1
Skill: Application

10) How do fungi usually obtain nutrients?

   A) by digesting it externally and then absorbing it

   B) by photosynthesis

   C) by absorbing it and then digesting it within fungal cells

   D) by chemosynthesis

   E) by producing antibiotics that internally destroy bacteria

Answer: A
Diff: 1   Page Ref: 22.1
Skill: Factual

11) Both bacteria and fungi digest food by _____.

   A) secreting enzymes and then absorb the smaller molecules

   B) forming food vacuoles

   C) only eating already decomposed made of with very large molecules

   D) only eating small organisms that they can engulf

   E) photosynthesis

Answer: A
Diff: 1   Page Ref: 22.1
Skill: Factual

12) Which of the following is a "job" that is NOT performed by any fungi?

  A) decomposer

  B) parasite

  C) predator

  D) producer

  E) pathogen

Answer: D
Diff: 2   Page Ref: 22.1
Skill: Conceptual

13) Fungi and arthropods are similar because both are _____.

  A) comprised of eukaryotic cells

  B) strengthened by chitin

  C) multicellular

  D) heterotrophic

  E) all of the above

Answer: E
Diff: 2   Page Ref: 22.1
Skill: Conceptual

14) Molds easily contaminate foods because fungi _____.

  A) are unaffected by cooking

  B) reproduce using highly mobile, air–borne spores

  C) cannot survive in a refrigerator

  D) have haploid bodies

  E) produce temporary visible reproductive structures

Answer: B
Diff: 1   Page Ref: 22.1
Skill: Conceptual

15) A common characteristic shared by fungi and animals is _____.

   A) the formation of embryos when they reproduce

   B) the internal digestion their food

   C) cell walls composed of chitin

   D) mobility

   E) being heterotrophic

   F) all of the above

Answer: E
Diff: 2   Page Ref: 22.1
Skill: Conceptual

16) During asexual reproduction, fungus produce haploid spores via

   A) mitosis.   B) meiosis.

Answer: A
Diff: 1   Page Ref: 22.1
Skill: Factual

17) During sexual reproduction, fungus produce haploid spores via

   A) mitosis.   B) meiosis.

Answer: B
Diff: 1   Page Ref: 22.1
Skill: Factual

18) You find a new organism. It gains nutrients by secreting enzymes outside of itself and absorbing the digested product. It is eukaryotic and has a cell wall containing chitin. It reproduced with spores. Your new organism should be classified as a/an

   A) arthropod.   B) plant.   C) fungus.   D) bacteria.

Answer: C
Diff: 2   Page Ref: 22.1
Skill: Application

19) Fungi are similar to plants because both _____.

   A) are important producers in their ecosystems

   B) have cell walls surrounding their plasma membranes

   C) liberate nutrients from dead tissues

   D) produce embryos when they reproduce

   E) have chloroplasts in their cells

Answer: B
Diff: 2   Page Ref: 22.1
Skill: Conceptual

20) The conspicuous structures on the surface of a dead tree that indicate a fungus is growing inside are for

   A) pollination.

   B) reproduction.

   C) feeding.

   D) defense.

   E) show only.

Answer: B
Diff: 1   Page Ref: 22.1
Skill: Factual

21) The dominant generation in the fungal life cycle is usually _____.

   A) diploid

   B) haploid

   C) a sporophyte

   D) polyploid

   E) unicellular

Answer: B
Diff: 1   Page Ref: 22.1
Skill: Factual

22) Fungal hyphae usually are

   A) haploid.   B) diploid.

Answer: A
Diff: 1   Page Ref: 22.1
Skill: Factual

23) Sexual reproduction in the fungal life cycle includes which of the following sequences?

   A) haploid zygote that divides by meiosis to form haploid spores

   B) diploid zygote that divides by meiosis to form haploid spores that produce haploid mycelia through mitosis

   C) Haploid gametes divide by meiosis to produce a diploid zygote that grows by mitosis to produce diploid mycelia.

   D) Free swimming gametes fuse to form a diploid zygote that grows by mitosis.

   E) Diploid spores divide by meiosis to form haploid gametes which join to form mycelia.

Answer: B
Diff: 2   Page Ref: 22.1
Skill: Factual

24) From the standpoint of species survival, which reproductive method is better?

    A) sexual spores which are genetically different from the parent fungi

    B) asexual spores which are clones of the parent fungus

Answer: A
Diff: 3   Page Ref: 22.1
Skill: Application

25) As inclement fall weather settles in, fungus tend to reproduce

    A) sexually.   B) asexually.

Answer: A
Diff: 2   Page Ref: 22.1
Skill: Conceptual

26) The mat–like structure composed of hyphal threads which forms the body of most fungi is called

    A) asci.

    B) toadstools.

    C) mycelia.

    D) zygospores.

    E) basidia.

Answer: C
Diff: 1   Page Ref: 22.1
Skill: Factual

27) Originally, fungi were considered to be a type of plant. Now they are classified in their own kingdom. What characteristics differentiate fungi from plants?

Answer: Plant cell walls are based on cellulose, fungal walls are based on chitin. Plants have chloroplasts and carry on photosynthesis; fungi lack chloroplasts and obtain energy from other organisms.
Diff: 2   Page Ref: 22.1
Skill: Application

28) Which of the following is NOT a phylum within Kingdom Fungi?

    A) zygomycota

    B) basidiomycota

    C) ascomycota

    D) zooflagellate

    E) deuteromycota

Answer: D
Diff: 1   Page Ref: 22.2
Skill: Factual

29) Swimming flagellated spores are found in which fungus groups?

    A) zygomycetes

    B) chrytrids

    C) basidiomycetes

    D) ascomycetes

    E) all of these

Answer: B
Diff: 1   Page Ref: 22.2
Skill: Factual

30) Chytrids are uniques among fungi because

    A) they have internal digestion.   B) they live in aquatic environments.

    C) their walls lack chitin.   D) All of the above are unique to chytrids.

Answer: B
Diff: 1   Page Ref: 22.2
Skill: Factual

31) In which environment would you most likely find chytrids?

    A) a warm swamp   B) the back of the refrigerator

    C) a basket of over-ripe fruit   D) well-used gym bag

Answer: A
Diff: 2   Page Ref: 22.2
Skill: Conceptual

32) As revealed by fossils, the most ancient group of fungi is probably the

    A) ascomycetes.

    B) basidiomycetes.

    C) chytridiomycetes.

    D) zygomycetes.

    E) imperfect fungi.

Answer: C
Diff: 1   Page Ref: 22.2
Skill: Factual

33) The worldwide die-off of frogs has been traced to infection by what type of fungus?

A) basidiomycetes

B) ascomycetes

C) zygomycetes

D) imperfect fungi

E) chytrids

Answer: E
Diff: 1   Page Ref: 22.2
Skill: Factual

34) Which common type of fungus is known for its ability to produce diploid zygospores?

A) deuteromycota

B) ascomycota

C) oomycota

D) zygomycota

E) diplomycota

Answer: D
Diff: 1   Page Ref: 22.2
Skill: Factual

35) How are zygospores produced?

A) meiosis of hyphae

B) mitosis of hyphae

C) union of egg and sperm

D) meiosis of megaspore

E) union of 2 haploid hyphae

Answer: E
Diff: 1   Page Ref: 22.2
Skill: Factual

36) When germinate, they must undergo _____ before forming hyphae.

A) meiosis   B) sporulation   C) mitosis   D) fertilization

Answer: A
Diff: 2   Page Ref: 22.2
Skill: Factual

37) Single celled fungi are

    A) basidiomycota.

    B) prokaryotic.

    C) ascospores.

    D) club fungi.

    E) yeast.

Answer: E
Diff: 1   Page Ref: 22.2
Skill: Factual

38) The name "sac fungi" is appropriate for the Ascomycetes because

    A) they produce seeds in sac-like structures.

    B) they grow well in closed bags.

    C) the body of the fungus is a sac-like shape.

    D) it is best to carry them in a sack.

    E) they produce spores in sac-like structures.

Answer: E
Diff: 1   Page Ref: 22.2
Skill: Factual

39) The ascus functions in _____.

    A) sexual reproduction

    B) digestion

    C) vegetative growth

    D) asexual reproduction

    E) photosynthesis

Answer: A
Diff: 1   Page Ref: 22.2
Skill: Factual

40) Yeasts are _____.

    A) bacteria

    B) protists

    C) unicellular fungi

    D) phytoplankton

    E) algae

Answer: C
Diff: 1   Page Ref: 22.2
Skill: Factual

41) A more or less circular ring of mushrooms simultaneously appear in your yard, apparently overnight. The circle is several yards in diameter. The most likely explanation for this circle of mushrooms is

    A) mushroom spores were dropped by a circling bird, thus explaining the circular shape of the group of mushrooms.

    B) the mushroom plants in the center of the circle have been eaten by herbivores.

    C) the mushrooms are all part of the same plant, with mycelia radiating out from the location of a germinated spore.

    D) one mushroom in the circle reproduced sexually to make all the other mushrooms in the circle.

    E) a circle is nature's most perfect shape for asexual reproduction structures.

Answer: C
Diff: 1   Page Ref: 22.2
Skill: Factual

42) The specialized reproductive structures of the basidiomycetes are called

    A) asci.

    B) toadstools.

    C) mycelia.

    D) zygospores.

    E) basidia.

Answer: E
Diff: 1   Page Ref: 22.2
Skill: Factual

43) The specialized reproductive structures of the acsomycetes are called

    A) asci.

    B) toadstools.

    C) mycelia.

    D) zygospores.

    E) basidia.

Answer: E
Diff: 1   Page Ref: 22.2
Skill: Factual

44) Black bread molds produce diploid reproductive structures called

A) asci.

B) toadstools.

C) mycelia.

D) zygospores.

E) basidia.

Answer: E
Diff: 1   Page Ref: 22.2
Skill: Factual

45) A fairy ring is

A) a ring of mushrooms.

B) a ring of basidiomycota spores.

C) a cluster of basidiomycota mycelia.

D) a circle of basidia.

E) a ring of gills on the underside of a mushroom.

Answer: A
Diff: 1   Page Ref: 22.2
Skill: Factual

46) Which of the following is characteristic of or associated with the fungi classified as deuteromycetes?

A) cell walls with peptidoglycan

B) extracellular digestion

C) visible fruiting bodies during sexual reproduction

D) formation of diploid zygospores

E) all of the above

Answer: B
Diff: 2   Page Ref: 22.2
Skill: Conceptual

47) How do Ascomycetes differ from Zygomycetes?

Answer: Ascomycetes reproduce sexually by producing spores in terminal sacs, whereas Zygomycetes produce tough, spiky zygospores.
Diff: 2   Page Ref: 22.2
Skill: Conceptual

48) How do Ascomycetes differ from Basidiomycetes?

Answer: Ascomycetes reproduce sexually by producing several spores in terminal sacs. Basidiomycetes produce club–like structures.

Diff: 2   Page Ref: 22.2
Skill: Conceptual

49) How do Zygomycetes differ from Basidiomycetes?

Answer: Zygomycetes produce tough, spiky zygospores, whereas Basidiomycetes produce club–like structures.

Diff: 2   Page Ref: 22.2
Skill: Conceptual

50) How are chytrids different from other fungi?

Answer: Chytrids are the only group of fungi with flagellated spores and the only group to requires water for fertilization.

Diff: 2   Page Ref: 22.2
Skill: Conceptual

51) Lichens and mycorrhizae are similar in that

A) both form symbiotic relationships with plants which benefit the plants.

B) both parasitize live plants eventually killing them.

C) both are pioneer species which colonize bare rock.

D) saprophytes which decompose dead materials.

Answer: A
Diff: 2   Page Ref: 22.3
Skill: Factual

52) Lichens are

A) algae.

B) archaea.

C) fungi.

D) symbiotic association of algae and archaea.

E) symbiotic association of algae and fungi.

Answer: E
Diff: 1   Page Ref: 22.3
Skill: Factual

53) Mycorrhizae are symbiotic associations between

   A) animals and fungi.

   B) fungi and plant stems.

   C) algae and fungi.

   D) algae and plant roots.

   E) plant roots and a fungus.

Answer: E
Diff: 1   Page Ref: 22.3
Skill: Factual

54) Mycorrhizae provide plants with

   A) phosphorus.

   B) nitrogen.

   C) carbon.

   D) both A & B

   E) all of the above

Answer: D
Diff: 1   Page Ref: 22.3
Skill: Factual

55) Some of the first organisms to colonize barren habitats are

   A) fungi.

   B) plants.

   C) mushrooms.

   D) lichens.

   E) small mammals.

Answer: D
Diff: 1   Page Ref: 22.3
Skill: Factual

56) A very common mutualistic relationship between a fungus and the roots of a plant is

   A) lichen.

   B) nitrogen-fixing.

   C) ascomycete.

   D) saprophyte.

   E) mycorrhizal.

Answer: E
Diff: 1   Page Ref: 22.3
Skill: Factual

57) Often the first to colonize bare rock or lava flows are

   A) algae.

   B) fungi.

   C) lichens.

   D) ferns.

   E) bryophytes.

Answer: C
Diff: 1   *Page Ref: 22.3*
Skill: Factual

58) Mycorrhizae surround and infiltrate which parts of vascular plants?

   A) roots

   B) stems

   C) leaves

   D) flowers

   E) all of the above

Answer: A
Diff: 1   *Page Ref: 22.3*
Skill: Factual

59) Mycorrhizae are

   A) root parasites.

   B) nitrogen fixers.

   C) root–dwelling mutualists.

   D) photosynthetic nodules.

   E) bread molds.

Answer: C
Diff: 1   *Page Ref: 22.3*
Skill: Factual

60) Mycorrhizae associations are

   A) very unusual.

   B) common; at least 80% of the species of plants form these associations.

   C) common only to species like grasses.

   D) absolutely necessary for survival.

   E) common only in nutrient–rich environments.

Answer: B
Diff: 1   *Page Ref: 22.3*
Skill: Factual

61) The photosynthetic component of a lichen is a/an _____.

    A) arthropod

    B) small plant

    C) fungus

    D) alga

    E) person

Answer: D
Diff: 2   Page Ref: 22.3
Skill: Conceptual

62) Fungi which live inside plant leaves and provide protection from insects are

    A) lichens.   B) mychorrhizae.   C) endophytes.   D) saprophytes.

Answer: C
Diff: 1   Page Ref: 22.3
Skill: Factual

63) Fungi are important in recycling woody plants because

    A) fungi digest chloroplasts.

    B) fungi are the only organisms capable of digesting both cellulose and lignan.

    C) woody plants occupy the same environment as fungi.

    D) fungi have internal digestion necessary to digest wood.

Answer: B
Diff: 1   Page Ref: 22.3
Skill: Factual

64) If there were no fungi,

    A) nutrient recycling would stop.

    B) plants would overrun the Earth.

    C) grazing animals would be unable to digest plants.

    D) all of the above

Answer: A
Diff: 3   Page Ref: 22.3
Skill: Conceptual

65) Ascomycetes can damage cotton garments because they produce _____.

   A) penicillin

   B) smuts

   C) cellulase

   D) asci

   E) fruiting bodies

Answer: C
Diff: 2   Page Ref: 22.3
Skill: Factual

66) Which of these human diseases is NOT caused by a fungus?

   A) typhoid

   B) ringworm

   C) athlete's foot

   D) vaginal yeast infection

   E) histoplasmosis

Answer: A
Diff: 1   Page Ref: 22.3
Skill: Factual

67) An example of a parasitic fungal disease is

   A) herpes.

   B) malaria.

   C) trichinosis.

   D) athlete's foot.

   E) sleeping sickness.

Answer: D
Diff: 1   Page Ref: 22.3
Skill: Factual

68) *Claviceps purpurea* is an organism from phylum _____. It infects rye plants and produces toxins (including LSD) that can produce convulsions, hallucinations, and death if consumed by a person.

   A) Ascomycota

   B) Chytriiomycota

   C) Basidiomycota

   D) Deuteromycota

   E) Zygomycota

Answer: A
Diff: 2   Page Ref: 22.3
Skill: Factual

69) Most antibiotics for human use are obtained from

   A) bacteria.

   B) archaea.

   C) fungi.

   D) plants.

   E) chemical factories.

Answer: C
Diff: 1   Page Ref: 22.3
Skill: Factual

70) In the environment, what role do fungi play?

   Answer: Fungi recycle nutrients by decomposing dead organisms, they form symbiotic relationships which provide nutrients to the plants, they act as pioneer species.
Diff: 1   Page Ref: 22.3
Skill: Factual

71) Why do fungi have the ability to decompose materials other organisms cannot?

   Answer: Fungi contain both protease and cellulase enzymes not found in other organisms.
Diff: 1   Page Ref: 22.3
Skill: Factual

72) We tend to think of fungi as being bad. What are some of the beneficial aspects of fungi to plants?

   Answer: Fungi form mycorrhizial association which feed nutrients to plants. Fungi can produce toxins which protect plants from predators.
Diff: 1   Page Ref: 22.3
Skill: Factual

73) The highly toxic *Aspergillus* infects

    A) wheat.   B) milk.   C) peanuts.   D) bread.

Answer: C
Diff: 1   Page Ref: 22.4
Skill: Factual

74) Penicillin comes from

    A) corn smut.   B) ascomycete mold.

    C) *Aspergillus*.   D) *Claviceps purpurea*.

Answer: B
Diff: 1   Page Ref: 22.4
Skill: Factual

75) The majority of plant diseases are caused by

    A) bacteria.   B) fungi.   C) arthropods.

Answer: A
Diff: 1   Page Ref: 22.4
Skill: Factual

76) Rusts and smuts are examples of

    A) fungal plant diseases.   B) lichens.

    C) mycorrhizae.   D) antibiotic sources.

Answer: A
Diff: 1   Page Ref: 22.4
Skill: Factual

77) Fungi are important to humans as

    A) medicines.

    B) foods.

    C) pathogens.

    D) pesticides.

    E) all of the above

Answer: E
Diff: 1   Page Ref: 22.4
Skill: Factual

78) Blue cheeses like Roquefort and Stilton get their unique flavor from

    A) chytrids.   B) ascomycete mold.

    C) *Aspergillus.*   D) *Claviceps purpurea.*

Answer: B
Diff: 1   Page Ref: 22.4
Skill: Factual

79) An end product of yeast fermentation is

    A) carbon dioxide.

    B) carbon monoxide.

    C) sugar.

    D) oxygen gas.

    E) more than one of these

Answer: A
Diff: 1   Page Ref: 22.4
Skill: Factual

80) The primary substrate for alcoholic fermentation is

    A) carbon dioxide.

    B) carbon monoxide.

    C) sugar.

    D) oxygen gas.

    E) more than one of these

Answer: C
Diff: 1   Page Ref: 22.4
Skill: Factual

81) The holes in bread are created by what?

    A) air

    B) alcohol

    C) yeast

    D) oxygen gas

    E) carbon dioxide

Answer: E
Diff: 1   Page Ref: 22.4
Skill: Factual

82) In bread making, what happens to the alcohol produced as the result of yeast fermentation?

A) It is respired into carbon dioxide and water by the yeast.

B) It evaporates.

C) It is contained in the holes of the bread.

D) It is consumed by the human who eats the bread.

E) It is converted to sugar by the yeast.

Answer: B
Diff: 1   Page Ref: 22.4
Skill: Factual

83) For which of the following should you give thanks to the fungi for their role in the production of it?

A) a beer

B) pizza

C) penicillin

D) Stilton cheese

E) all of the above

Answer: E
Diff: 1   Page Ref: 22.4
Skill: Factual

84) *Rhizoctonia leguminicola* is a fungus that grows on red clover. When horses and cattle eat the clover with the fungus growing on it, they salivate excessively. This is excessive saliva production is associated with _____.

A) CO_2 produced by the fungus

B) a toxin produced by the fungus

C) the production of penicillin by the clover

D) alcohol produced by the clover

E) the type of sugar produced by the fungus

Answer: B
Diff: 3   Page Ref: 22.4
Skill: Application

85) The importance of fungi to ecosystems is mostly as a

    A) parasite.

    B) herbivore.

    C) omnivore.

    D) producer.

    E) decomposer.

Answer: E
Diff: 1   Page Ref: 22.4
Skill: Factual

86) If a strong fungicide is released and eliminates all the fungi in an ecosystem, which of the following is likely to happen?

    A) improved growth of plant species

    B) faster breakdown of leaf litter

    C) an accumulation of dead and discarded plant and animal tissues

    D) improved soil fertility

    E) increased rate of photosynthesis

Answer: C
Diff: 2   Page Ref: 22.4
Skill: Conceptual

87) Some fungi are predators (not parasites) on what kind of organism?

    A) humans

    B) wheat

    C) chestnut and elm trees

    D) nematodes (roundworms)

    E) spiders

Answer: D
Diff: 1   Page Ref: Evol Connections
Skill: Factual

88) We tend to think of fungi as being bad. What are some of the beneficial aspects of fungi to humans?

Answer: Fungi provide us with antibiotics. They flavor our foods—blue cheese, miso, etc. They ferment plant products to produce bread, wine, and beer.
Diff: 1   Page Ref: 22.4
Skill: Factual

89) Beer is sometimes referred to as "liquid bread". Can you explain why?

Answer: Both beer and bread are made from yeast fermented grains.
Diff: 3   *Page Ref: 22.4*
Skill: Analysis

90) Why is it unsafe to collect wild mushrooms without expert training?

Answer: Poisonous mushrooms can closely resemble those that are safe to eat. It often requires an expert to differentiate them.
Diff: 3   *Page Ref: Links to Life*
Skill: Analysis

Chapter 23 Animal Diversity I: Invertebrates

1) Little is known about the behavior of the giant squid because

    A) they have only been discovered in the last twenty years.

    B) a live specimen has never been recovered.

    C) a live specimen has not been extensively observed in its natural habitat.

    D) captive specimens behave differently than wild specimens.

    E) very few scientists choose to study them.

Answer: C
Diff: 2   Page Ref: Case Study
Skill: Factual

2) All of these are characteristic of all animals EXCEPT

    A) individuals are multicellular.

    B) individuals are heterotrophic.

    C) cells have no cell wall.

    D) reproduction is primarily sexual.

    E) All are characteristic of all animals.

Answer: E
Diff: 1   Page Ref: 23.1
Skill: Factual

3) Which of these is NOT a characteristic of most animals?

    A) autotrophic

    B) reproduce sexually

    C) Cells have no cell wall.

    D) swift response to stimuli

    E) motility at some stage of the life cycle

Answer: A
Diff: 1   Page Ref: 23.1
Skill: Factual

4) Which of the following is NOT a characteristic of animals?

    A) utilizing sexual reproduction

    B) Cells are eukaryotic.

    C) multicellular

    D) possessing tissues and organs

    E) cellulose cell wall surrounding each cell

Answer: E
Diff: 1   *Page Ref: 23.1*
Skill: Factual

5) Which of the following is NOT a characteristic of animals?

    A) cells without cell walls

    B) rapid response to external stimuli

    C) Individuals are multicellular.

    D) cells with nuclei, mitochondria and chloroplasts

    E) mobility at some stage of their life

Answer: D
Diff: 2   *Page Ref: 23.1*
Skill: Conceptual

6) If motility is considered a characteristic of animals, why are stationary creatures like sponges and crinoids still considered to be animals?

Answer: They have a larval stage that is motile so they meet the criterion of "animals are mobile" because at some point in their life cycle they are. These animals become sessile as adults.
Diff: 1   *Page Ref: 23.1*
Skill: Factual

7) Which of these trends has occurred in the course of animal evolution?

    A) increasing cellular specialization

    B) cephalization

    C) gradual shift from autotrophism to heterotrophism

    D) A and B

    E) A, B, and C

Answer: D
Diff: 1   *Page Ref: 23.2*
Skill: Factual

8) Cephalization in the animal kingdom is

A) development of a body which has paired structures that form a side-to-side mirror image.

B) concentration of sensory structures in the head.

C) the ability to rapidly respond to external stimuli.

D) evolutionary development of a net-like system of veins.

E) development of eyes at the anterior end of the organism.

Answer: B
Diff: 1   Page Ref: 23.2
Skill: Factual

9) One trend in the evolution of animals is the increase in the number of tissue (germ) layers that can be seen during embryonic development. In flatworms and more complex animals, there are _____ layers.

A) 2   B) 3   C) 4   D) 5   E) 6

Answer: B
Diff: 1   Page Ref: 23.2
Skill: Factual

10) The epithelial and nervous tissues develop from which germ layer?

A) ectoderm

B) endoderm

C) mesoderm

D) mesoglea

E) protoplasm

Answer: A
Diff: 1   Page Ref: 23.2
Skill: Factual

11) Which of the following animal phyla is distinguished by a lack of tissues?

A) echinoderms

B) flatworms

C) annelids

D) roundworms

E) sponges

Answer: E
Diff: 1   Page Ref: 23.2
Skill: Factual

12) Which of the following terms is BEST associated with cephalization?

    A) anterior and posterior

    B) dorsal and ventral

    C) protostome and deuterostome

    D) axial and appendicular

    E) none of the above

Answer: A
Diff: 2   *Page Ref: 23.2*
Skill: Conceptual

13) Between the organs and the body wall, complex animals have a body cavity called a

    A) cnidarian.

    B) mesoderm.

    C) mesoglea.

    D) coelom.

    E) thorax.

Answer: D
Diff: 1   *Page Ref: 23.2*
Skill: Factual

14) Which of the following is the MOST ancestral type of body plan?

    A) acoelomate   B) coelomate   C) pseudocoelomate

Answer: B
Diff: 1   *Page Ref: 23.2*
Skill: Factual

15) Which germ layer gives rise to the myometrium (the muscle layer of the uterus)?

    A) ectoderm   B) mesoderm   C) endoderm

Answer: B
Diff: 2   *Page Ref: 23.2*
Skill: Application

16) An organism with cephalization will most likely have _____.

   A) radial symmetry

   B) hooks and suckers

   C) a brain

   D) a gastrovascular cavity

   E) gills

Answer: C
Diff: 2   Page Ref: 23.2
Skill: Conceptual

17) How many tissue layers are in the embryos of sponges?

   A) 0   B) 1   C) 2   D) 3   E) 4

Answer: A
Diff: 1   Page Ref: 23.2
Skill: Factual

18) How many tissue layers are in echinoderm embryos?

   A) 0   B) 1   C) 2   D) 3   E) 4

Answer: D
Diff: 1   Page Ref: 23.2
Skill: Factual

19) How many tissue layers are in arthropod embryos?

   A) 0   B) 1   C) 2   D) 3   E) 4

Answer: D
Diff: 1   Page Ref: 23.2
Skill: Factual

20) How many tissue layers are in the embryo of a coral (a cnidarian)?

   A) 0   B) 1   C) 2   D) 3   E) 4

Answer: C
Diff: 1   Page Ref: 23.2
Skill: Factual

21) Animal systematists are able to reconstruct the early evolutionary history of animal phyla using

    A) the fossil record.

    B) DNA sequence comparisons.

    C) anatomical comparisons.

    D) A and B

    E) B and C

Answer: E
Diff: 1   *Page Ref: 23.2*
Skill: Conceptual

22) The common ancestor of sponges and other animals was probably

    A) unicellular.

    B) multicellular without tissues.

    C) multicellular with tissues, but without organ systems.

    D) multicellular with tissues, and with a few organ systems.

    E) multicellular with tissues, and with many organ systems.

Answer: B
Diff: 2   *Page Ref: 23.2*
Skill: Conceptual

23) All animals with tissues

    A) have symmetrical bodies.

    B) have bilateral symmetry.

    C) have radial symmetry.

    D) have two germ layers.

    E) have three germ layers.

Answer: A
Diff: 2   *Page Ref: 23.2*
Skill: Conceptual

24) Which of the following characteristics is associated with all animals that are bilaterally symmetrical at some point in the life cycle?

   A) lack of organs

   B) gastrovascular cavity

   C) coelom

   D) mesoderm

   E) cephalization

Answer: D
Diff: 2   Page Ref: 23.2
Skill: Factual

25) Which of the following characteristics is associated with animals that are radially symmetrical as adults?

   A) mobility

   B) gastrovascular cavity

   C) sessile or otherwise nonmobile

   D) mesoderm

   E) cephalization

Answer: C
Diff: 2   Page Ref: 23.2
Skill: Factual

26) The major difference between protostomes and deuterostomes is

   A) the presence or absence of a coelom.

   B) the way in which the body cavity forms.

   C) the presence or absence of cephalization.

   D) the type of body symmetry.

   E) the presence or absence of tissues.

Answer: B
Diff: 2   Page Ref: 23.2
Skill: Conceptual

27) Ecdysozoans

    A) have trochophore larva.

    B) include mollusks, annelids, and flatworms.

    C) have a special feeding structure.

    D) have a body cavity that forms from the digestive system.

    E) periodically shed their outer body covering.

Answer: E
Diff: 1   Page Ref: 23.2
Skill: Factual

28) Chordates and echinoderms are both protostomes. True or False?

Answer: FALSE
Diff: 1   Page Ref: 23.2
Skill: Factual

29) Most animal phyla are radially symmetrical. True or False?

Answer: FALSE
Diff: 1   Page Ref: 23.2
Skill: Factual

30) Which of these groups is characterized by having no body cavity?

    A) roundworms

    B) annelids

    C) arthropods

    D) chordates

    E) cnidarians

Answer: E
Diff: 1   Page Ref: 23.3
Skill: Factual

31) Which of these groups is characterized by having a pseudocoelom?

    A) roundworms

    B) annelids

    C) arthropods

    D) chordates

    E) cnidarians

Answer: A
Diff: 1   Page Ref: 23.3
Skill: Factual

32) Which of these groups is characterized by having a true coelom?

    A) sponges

    B) cnidarians

    C) arthropods

    D) flatworms

    E) roundworms

Answer: C
Diff: 1   Page Ref: 23.3
Skill: Factual

33) Which of these groups is characterized by a lack of symmetry (neither radial nor bilateral symmetry)?

    A) sponges

    B) Cnidarians

    C) arthropods

    D) flatworms

    E) chordates

Answer: A
Diff: 1   Page Ref: 23.3
Skill: Factual

34) The simplest multicellular animals that have only a few different cell types are

    A) anemones.

    B) sponges.

    C) jellyfishes.

    D) flatworms.

    E) sea squirts.

Answer: B
Diff: 1   Page Ref: 23.3
Skill: Factual

35) Giant squid belong to which group?

    A) arthropods

    B) mollusks

    C) echinoderms

    D) chordates

    E) platyhelminthes

Answer: B
Diff: 1   *Page Ref: 23.3*
Skill: Factual

36) Segmentation is important in the evolution of animals because

    A) it allows them to be bigger.

    B) it allows for specialization of function.

    C) it increases the number of tissue layers present.

    D) A and B

    E) B and C

Answer: B
Diff: 2   *Page Ref: 23.3*
Skill: Conceptual

37) Sponge cells may be supported by an internal skeleton of spicules composed of _____.

    A) protein

    B) silica

    C) calcium carbonate

    D) B and C

    E) any of A, B, or C

Answer: E
Diff: 1   *Page Ref: 23.3*
Skill: Factual

38) A natural bath sponge is primarily composed of

    A) cellulose.

    B) silica.

    C) collar cells.

    D) chitin.

    E) proteinaceous sponge spicules.

Answer: E
Diff: 1   *Page Ref: 23.3*
Skill: Factual

39) The currents of water (containing food) that pass through a sponge are maintained by

    A) collar cells.

    B) ganglia.

    C) medusa.

    D) the osculum.

    E) a water–vascular system.

Answer: A
Diff: 1   Page Ref: 23.3
Skill: Factual

40) Cnidarians have all of the following structures EXCEPT

    A) a gastrovascular cavity.

    B) spicules.

    C) a nerve net.

    D) an endoderm.

    E) cnidocytes.

Answer: B
Diff: 1   Page Ref: 23.3
Skill: Factual

41) The mobile stage of cnidarians is the _____.

    A) medusa   B) hemocoel   C) polyp   D) cnidocyte   E) radula

Answer: A
Diff: 1   Page Ref: 23.3
Skill: Factual

42) Which cnidarian is ecologically important to more forms of life in the ocean than any other?

    A) polyp   B) hydra   C) anemone   D) jellyfish   E) coral

Answer: E
Diff: 1   Page Ref: 23.3
Skill: Factual

43) Hydra, anemones, and jellyfish are

A) Porifera.

B) Cnidaria.

C) Platyhelminthes.

D) Protista.

E) Flagellates.

Answer: B
Diff: 1   Page Ref: 23.3
Skill: Factual

44) A cnidarian that produces a calcium carbonate protective "house" is a(n)

A) oyster.   B) clam.   C) snail.   D) coral.   E) crab.

Answer: D
Diff: 2   Page Ref: 23.3
Skill: Factual

45) How can flatworms survive without a respiratory system?

A) They are small, allowing diffusion of gases directly to and from cells.

B) They are flat, allowing diffusion of gases directly to and from cells.

C) They are not very metabolically active, and there is no need for a more efficient means of gas exchange.

D) They have a thin, moist covering that facilitates gas exchange.

E) All of these are true.

Answer: E
Diff: 2   Page Ref: 23.3
Skill: Conceptual

46) The _____ are the simplest animals to have an excretory system. (Hint: this system consists of cilia beating within canals.)

A) nematodes

B) flatworms

C) cnidarians

D) echinoderms

E) vertebrates

Answer: B
Diff: 2   Page Ref: 23.3
Skill: Factual

47) Schistosomiasis, a devastating disease which affects about 200 million people in tropical regions, is caused by

    A) nematodes.

    B) parasitic flatworms called blood flukes.

    C) echinoderms.

    D) *Trichinella.*

    E) amoebas.

Answer: B
Diff: 1   Page Ref: 23.3
Skill: Factual

48) The phylum Nematoda includes these very common organisms, some of which are parasitic and most of which are often found in soil.

    A) segmented worms

    B) roundworms

    C) flatworms

    D) Earthworms

    E) all of the above

Answer: B
Diff: 1   Page Ref: 23.3
Skill: Factual

49) The *Trichinella* worm, which causes trichinosis, is a(n) _____.

    A) annelid

    B) platyhelminth

    C) nematode

    D) tapeworm

    E) leech

Answer: C
Diff: 1   Page Ref: 23.3
Skill: Factual

50) Worms with a well-developed circulatory system (including five pairs of hearts) are

A) platyhelminths.

B) annelids.

C) echinoderms.

D) nematodes.

E) eels.

Answer: B
Diff: 1   Page Ref: 23.3
Skill: Factual

51) Which invertebrate animal group is characterized by having a closed circulatory system?

A) Platyhelminthes

B) Nematoda

C) Annelida

D) Echinodermata

E) Arthropoda

Answer: C
Diff: 1   Page Ref: 23.3
Skill: Factual

52) A jointed exoskeleton is a characteristic of

A) insects.

B) annelids.

C) mammals.

D) A and B

E) all of the above

Answer: A
Diff: 1   Page Ref: 23.3
Skill: Factual

53) The dominant animal phylum in terms of diversity and richness is

A) Annelida.

B) Arthropoda.

C) Nematoda.

D) Echinodermata.

E) Chordata.

Answer: B
Diff: 1   Page Ref: 23.3
Skill: Factual

54) A(n) _____ provides support and protection to arthropods.

    A) cytoskeleton

    B) exoskeleton

    C) hydrostatic skeleton

    D) epidermis

    E) shell

Answer: B
Diff: 1   Page Ref: 23.3
Skill: Factual

55) Insects are

    A) annelids.

    B) arthropods.

    C) mollusks.

    D) beetles.

    E) arachnids.

Answer: B
Diff: 1   Page Ref: 23.3
Skill: Factual

56) An animal like a grasshopper can conserve water because it has an elaborately branching system of tubes within its body used for gas exchange. These tubes are called

    A) tracheae.

    B) gills.

    C) book lungs.

    D) flame cells.

    E) kidneys.

Answer: A
Diff: 1   Page Ref: 23.3
Skill: Factual

57) Which class is not in phylum Arthropoda?

    A) Insecta

    B) Arachnida

    C) Crustacea

    D) Gastropoda

    E) All are arthropods.

Answer: D
Diff: 1   *Page Ref: 23.3*
Skill: Factual

58) Which of the following animals are arachnids?

    A) spiders

    B) scorpions

    C) grasshoppers

    D) A and B

    E) all of the above

Answer: D
Diff: 1   *Page Ref: 23.3*
Skill: Factual

59) Which of the following animals uses a radula to scrape food into its mouth?

    A) octopus   B) starfish   C) scallop   D) rat   E) snail

Answer: E
Diff: 1   *Page Ref: 23.3*
Skill: Factual

60) The taxonomic group containing the largest and most intelligent invertebrates is

    A) Cephalopoda.

    B) Gastropoda.

    C) Chordata.

    D) Aves.

    E) Uniramia.

Answer: A
Diff: 1   *Page Ref: 23.3*
Skill: Factual

61) The water-vascular system of echinoderms is used for

A) locomotion and respiration.

B) food capture.

C) transport of blood.

D) A and B

E) all of the above

Answer: D
Diff: 1   Page Ref: 23.3
Skill: Factual

62) The animals most like the ancestral protozoan colonies that likely gave rise to animals are

A) chordates.

B) arthropods.

C) sponges.

D) echinoderms.

E) nematodes.

Answer: C
Diff: 2   Page Ref: 23.3
Skill: Conceptual

63) A sponge is characterized by having all of the following EXCEPT _____.

A) amoeboid cells

B) collar cells

C) spicules

D) mesoderm

E) oscula

Answer: D
Diff: 2   Page Ref: 23.3
Skill: Conceptual

64) Which of the following animal taxa contains organisms that have many well-protected internal organs?

    A) sponges

    B) nematodes

    C) cnidaria

    D) annelids

    E) platyhelminthes

Answer: D
Diff: 2   Page Ref: 23.3
Skill: Conceptual

65) A free-living flatworm can be identified as such by its _____.

    A) tubular gut

    B) hooks

    C) cuticle

    D) eyespots

    E) coelom

Answer: D
Diff: 3   Page Ref: 23.3
Skill: Conceptual

66) Adult echinoderms that have radial symmetry lack _____.

    A) a coelom

    B) a head

    C) tissues

    D) a tubular gut with separate mouth and anus

    E) all of the above

Answer: B
Diff: 2   Page Ref: 23.3
Skill: Conceptual

67) The low energy demands of nematodes allow them to survive without a _____.

    A) reproductive system

    B) tubular gut

    C) body cavity

    D) skeleton

    E) respiratory system

Answer: E
Diff: 2   Page Ref: 23.3
Skill: Conceptual

68) Animals with a gastrovascular cavity don't have a(n) _____.

    A) anus

    B) circulatory system

    C) coelom

    D) respiratory system

    E) all of the above

Answer: E
Diff: 3   Page Ref: 23.3
Skill: Conceptual

69) Which of the following supports the ability of various arthropods to fly, swim, or run vigorously?

    A) gills

    B) tracheae

    C) book lungs

    D) a complex nervous system

    E) all of the above

Answer: E
Diff: 2   Page Ref: 23.3
Skill: Conceptual

70) The _____, unique to the cephalopod class of mollusks, supports their active lifestyle.

   A) closed circulatory system

   B) tubular gut

   C) coelom

   D) hinged shells

   E) radula

Answer: A
Diff: 2   Page Ref: 23.3
Skill: Conceptual

71) A hemocoel or blood cavity is found in or associated with _____.

   A) all animals

   B) an open circulatory system

   C) sponges

   D) cephalopods

   E) acoelomates

Answer: B
Diff: 2   Page Ref: 23.3
Skill: Conceptual

72) The tube feet of echinoderms that are used for walking, prey capture, and gas exchange are "inflated" by the _____ unique to the echinoderms.

   A) coelom

   B) hydrostatic skeleton

   C) tubular gut

   D) water vascular system

   E) hemocoel

Answer: D
Diff: 2   Page Ref: 23.3
Skill: Conceptual

73) A snail is a(n)

    A) arthropod.

    B) mollusk.

    C) chordate.

    D) echinoderm.

    E) none of these

Answer: B
Diff: 1   Page Ref: 23.3
Skill: Factual

74) A clam is a(n)

    A) arthropod.

    B) mollusk.

    C) chordate.

    D) echinoderm.

    E) none of these

Answer: B
Diff: 1   Page Ref: 23.3
Skill: Factual

75) A sea cucumber is a(n)

    A) arthropod.

    B) mollusk.

    C) chordate.

    D) echinoderm.

    E) none of these

Answer: D
Diff: 1   Page Ref: 23.3
Skill: Factual

76) A spider is a(n)

    A) arthropod.

    B) mollusk.

    C) chordate.

    D) echinoderm.

    E) none of these

Answer: A
Diff: 1   Page Ref: 23.3
Skill: Factual

77) A tapeworm is a member of which phylum?

    A) Echinodermata

    B) Mollusca

    C) Annelida

    D) Platyhelminthes

    E) Arthropoda

Answer: D
Diff: 1   Page Ref: 23.3
Skill: Factual

78) A crayfish is a member of which phylum?

    A) Echinodermata

    B) Mollusca

    C) Annelida

    D) Platyhelminthes

    E) Arthropoda

Answer: E
Diff: 1   Page Ref: 23.3
Skill: Factual

79) An oyster is a member of which phylum?

    A) Echinodermata

    B) Mollusca

    C) Annelida

    D) Platyhelminthes

    E) Arthropoda

Answer: B
Diff: 1   Page Ref: 23.3
Skill: Factual

80) A sea urchin is a member of which phylum?

    A) Echinodermata

    B) Mollusca

    C) Annelida

    D) Platyhelminthes

    E) Arthropoda

Answer: A
Diff: 1   Page Ref: 23.3
Skill: Factual

81) An Earthworm is a member of which phylum?

    A) Echinodermata

    B) Mollusca

    C) Annelida

    D) Platyhelminthes

    E) Arthropoda

Answer: C
Diff: 1   *Page Ref: 23.3*
Skill: Factual

82) Members of which phylum are characterized by having tube feet?

    A) Echinodermata

    B) Mollusca

    C) Annelida

    D) Platyhelminthes

    E) Arthropoda

Answer: A
Diff: 1   *Page Ref: 23.3*
Skill: Factual

83) You are in charge of a team of systematists whose job it is to classify a newly discovered animal species. Your initial studies reveal that your specimen lacks tissues and organs, and has no head, body symmetry, body cavity, or segmentation. To what phylum does this animal belong?

    A) Cnidaria

    B) Mollusca

    C) Annelida

    D) Platyhelminthes

    E) Porifera

Answer: E
Diff: 2   *Page Ref: 23.3*
Skill: Application

84) You are in charge of a team of systematists whose job it is to classify a newly discovered animal species. Your initial studies reveal that your specimen has tissues but lacks organs, has no head, body cavity, or segmentation, and has radial symmetry. To what phylum does this animal belong?

A) Cnidaria

B) Mollusca

C) Annelida

D) Platyhelminthes

E) Porifera

Answer: A
Diff: 2   Page Ref: 23.3
Skill: Application

85) You are in charge of a team of systematists whose job it is to classify a newly discovered animal species. Your initial studies reveal that your specimen has tissues, organs, and a head, has no body cavity or segmentation, and has bilateral symmetry. To what phylum does this animal belong?

A) Cnidaria

B) Mollusca

C) Annelida

D) Platyhelminthes

E) Porifera

Answer: D
Diff: 2   Page Ref: 23.3
Skill: Application

86) You are in charge of a team of systematists whose job it is to classify a newly discovered animal species. Your initial studies reveal that your specimen has tissues, organs, a head, and a coelom, has no segmentation, and has bilateral symmetry. To what phylum does this animal belong?

A) Cnidaria

B) Mollusca

C) Annelida

D) Platyhelminthes

E) Porifera

Answer: B
Diff: 2   Page Ref: 23.3
Skill: Application

87) You are in charge of a team of systematists whose job it is to classify a newly discovered animal species. Your initial studies reveal that your specimen has tissues, organs, a head, and a pseudocoelom, has no segmentation, and has bilateral symmetry. To what phylum does this animal belong?

A) Cnidaria

B) Mollusca

C) Annelida

D) Platyhelminthes

E) Nematoda

Answer: E
Diff: 2   Page Ref: 23.3
Skill: Application

88) You are in charge of a team of systematists whose job it is to classify a newly discovered animal species. Your initial studies reveal that your specimen has tissues, organs, and a coelom, has no head or segmentation, and has radial symmetry. To what phylum does this animal belong?

A) Cnidaria

B) Mollusca

C) Echinodermata

D) Platyhelminthes

E) Nematoda

Answer: C
Diff: 2   Page Ref: 23.3
Skill: Application

89) Which of the following phyla contains animals that reproduce asexually?

A) Cnidaria

B) Mollusca

C) Annelida

D) Platyhelminthes

E) Nematoda

Answer: A
Diff: 2   Page Ref: 23.3
Skill: Factual

90) Of the various cnidarian species,

   A) all live as polyps.

   B) all live as medusae.

   C) all have polyps as the juvenile stage and medusae as the adult stage.

   D) all have medusae as the juvenile stage and polyps as the adult stage.

   E) some live as polyps, some as medusae, and some as both in different stages.

Answer: E
Diff: 1   Page Ref: 23.3
Skill: Factual

91) The venomous sea wasp is classified in the phylum

   A) Cnidaria.

   B) Mollusca.

   C) Annelida.

   D) Arthropoda.

   E) Nematoda.

Answer: A
Diff: 2   Page Ref: 23.3
Skill: Factual

92) Animals with an anterior end

   A) reproduce asexually.

   B) are radially symmetrical.

   C) have a coelom.

   D) are cephalized.

   E) have a closed circulatory system.

Answer: D
Diff: 1   Page Ref: 23.3
Skill: Conceptual

93) Parasitic tapeworms, which may infect humans who eat undercooked meat, are members of the phylum

    A) Cnidaria.

    B) Platyhelminthes.

    C) Annelida.

    D) Arthropoda.

    E) Nematoda.

Answer: B
Diff: 2   Page Ref: 23.3
Skill: Factual

94) Charles Darwin once wrote that members of this phylum are particularly important for agriculture because they mix and aerate soil.

    A) Cnidaria

    B) Platyhelminthes

    C) Annelida

    D) Arthropoda

    E) Nematoda

Answer: C
Diff: 2   Page Ref: 23.3
Skill: Factual

95) The members of which taxonomic group are best described as having a large, well-developed brain, excellent vision, and are marine carnivorous predators?

    A) oligochaetes

    B) bivalves

    C) gastropods

    D) insects

    E) cephalopods

Answer: E
Diff: 2   Page Ref: 23.3
Skill: Conceptual

96) Of all of the invertebrate phyla, only members of this phylum can fly.

   A) Cnidaria

   B) Platyhelminthes

   C) Annelida

   D) Arthropoda

   E) Nematoda

Answer: D
Diff: 1   Page Ref: 23.3
Skill: Factual

97) Sponges are radially symmetrical. True or False?

Answer: FALSE
Diff: 1   Page Ref: 23.3
Skill: Factual

98) Flatworms have a coelom that is only partially surrounded with mesoderm. True or False?

Answer: FALSE
Diff: 1   Page Ref: 23.3
Skill: Factual

99) Sea stars (starfish) are bilaterally symmetrical at one point in their life cycle. True or False?

Answer: TRUE
Diff: 1   Page Ref: 23.3
Skill: Factual

100) Explain why natural selection would have favored a closed circulatory system for cephalopods.

Answer: A closed circulatory system more efficiently distributes blood to all the cells ensuring that all cells get an adequate supply of glucose and oxygen for ATP synthesis. Cephalopods are predatory creatures and rely on speed and stealth to catch their prey.
Diff: 2   Page Ref: 23.3
Skill: Conceptual

101) The leeches used by doctors to prevent blood clotting and stimulate blood vessel growth in patients recovering from reconstructive surgery are members of the phylum

    A) Cnidaria.

    B) Platyhelminthes.

    C) Annelida.

    D) Arthropoda.

    E) Nematoda.

Answer: C
Diff: 1   Page Ref: Links to Life
Skill: Factual

102) The maggots used by doctors to remove dead tissue in healing wounds are members of the phylum

    A) Cnidaria.

    B) Platyhelminthes.

    C) Annelida.

    D) Arthropoda.

    E) Nematoda.

Answer: D
Diff: 1   Page Ref: Links to Life
Skill: Factual

Chapter 24 Animal Diversity II: Vertebrates

1) The discovery of a coelacanth in South Africa in 1938 was surprising to biologists because

   A) it has not evolved for more than 80 million years.

   B) it was thought to be extinct.

   C) it was a newly evolved species.

   D) it represents a transition between two major groups of fishes.

   E) it is the first species to have made the transition to land.

   Answer: B
   Diff: 2   Page Ref: Case Study
   Skill: Conceptual

2) All chordates have (a) _____.

   A) ventral, hollow nerve cord

   B) bony endoskeleton

   C) post–anal tail

   D) backbone

   E) gills

   Answer: C
   Diff: 2   Page Ref: 24.1
   Skill: Conceptual

3) Invertebrate chordates do NOT have (a) _____.

   A) dorsal, hollow nerve cord

   B) coelom

   C) post–anal tail

   D) backbone

   E) pharyngeal gill slits

   Answer: D
   Diff: 2   Page Ref: 24.1
   Skill: Conceptual

4) All chordates have _____.

   A) bilateral symmetry

   B) a fully lined body cavity

   C) a dorsal, hollow nerve cord

   D) pharyngeal gill slits

   E) all of the above

Answer: E
Diff: 2   Page Ref: 24.1
Skill: Conceptual

5) The great size and mobility of the vertebrates is associated with _____.

   A) four-chambered hearts

   B) lungs used for respiration

   C) lightweight endoskeletons

   D) uterine development of offspring

   E) increased brain size and complexity

Answer: C
Diff: 2   Page Ref: 24.1
Skill: Conceptual

6) As a species, we seem to be more interested in studying vertebrates than invertebrates, probably because

   A) vertebrates are more diverse than invertebrates.

   B) most people have an innate fear of invertebrate animals.

   C) vertebrates are more complex than invertebrates.

   D) vertebrates are biologically more similar to our own species.

   E) vertebrates are more numerous than invertebrates.

Answer: D
Diff: 1   Page Ref: 24.1
Skill: Conceptual

7) All chordates have _____.

   A) deuterostome development

   B) a ventral nerve cord

   C) a pre-anal tail

   D) gills

   E) a backbone

Answer: A
Diff: 1   Page Ref: 24.1
Skill: Conceptual

8) In all chordates, the notochord

   A) appears only in adults.

   B) appears, at least, at early stages of development.

   C) may or may not appear at all; it is not found in all chordates.

   D) appears only at early stages of development.

   E) is found throughout the life cycle.

Answer: B
Diff: 2   Page Ref: 24.1
Skill: Factual

9) Which of the following statements is true of the chordate respiratory system?

   A) They all develop gills.

   B) Some species develop lungs only, without any appearance of gill slits.

   C) They all have at least gill slits in early developmental stages.

   D) They all develop lungs after developing gills.

   E) Gill slits are an outgrowth of the digestive system.

Answer: C
Diff: 2   Page Ref: 24.1
Skill: Factual

10) Which of the following features do humans share with other chordates?

   A) Humans develop a notochord in early development.

   B) Humans have a nerve cord.

   C) Humans develop gill slits in early development.

   D) Humans develop a tail in early development.

   E) Humans have all of these features.

Answer: E
Diff: 1   Page Ref: 24.1
Skill: Factual

11) Which of the following features is absent in lancelets?

    A) a nerve cord

    B) a backbone

    C) a notochord

    D) gill slits

    E) a tail

Answer: B
Diff: 1   Page Ref: 24.1
Skill: Factual

12) Adult tunicates resemble invertebrate animals more than they resemble vertebrates. Why are they classified as chordates?

    A) Tunicate larvae have a notochord.

    B) Tunicate larvae have a nerve cord.

    C) Tunicate larvae have gill slits.

    D) Tunicate larvae have a tail.

    E) Tunicate larvae have all of the above characteristics.

Answer: E
Diff: 2   Page Ref: 24.1
Skill: Conceptual

13) What is the major difference between invertebrate chordates and vertebrate chordates?

    A) Invertebrate chordates do not have a backbone.

    B) Invertebrate chordates have a backbone composed of cartilage.

    C) Vertebrate chordates do not have gill slits.

    D) Vertebrate chordates do not have a tail.

    E) Invertebrate chordates do not have a notochord.

Answer: A
Diff: 1   Page Ref: 24.1
Skill: Conceptual

14) Vertebrates have successfully adapted to many habitats, probably because

    A) they have more efficient digestion than invertebrates.

    B) adaptations of paired appendages allowed colonization of a variety of niches.

    C) they have larger and more complex brains than invertebrates.

    D) Choices 'A' and 'C' are both correct.

    E) Choices 'B' and 'C' are both correct.

Answer: E
Diff: 2   Page Ref: 24.1
Skill: Conceptual

15) Phylum Chordata includes all these EXCEPT

    A) fish.

    B) birds.

    C) amphibians.

    D) squids.

    E) mammals.

Answer: D
Diff: 1   Page Ref: 24.2
Skill: Factual

16) Which of the following is NOT a group of vertebrates?

    A) Reptilia

    B) Amphibia

    C) Mammalia

    D) Aves

    E) Echinodermata

Answer: E
Diff: 1   Page Ref: 24.2
Skill: Factual

17) Class Chondrichthyes includes

    A) whales.

    B) lampreys.

    C) all fish.

    D) frogs.

    E) sharks.

Answer: E
Diff: 1   Page Ref: 24.2
Skill: Factual

18) Class Aves includes

    A) kangaroos.

    B) birds.

    C) frogs.

    D) reptiles.

    E) dogs.

Answer: B
Diff: 1   Page Ref: 24.2
Skill: Factual

19) Mammals have all of the following characteristics EXCEPT

    A) mammary glands.

    B) hair.

    C) a four-chambered heart.

    D) lungs.

    E) All of the above are mammalian characteristics.

Answer: E
Diff: 1   Page Ref: 24.2
Skill: Factual

20) Which of the following has a ventral nerve cord?

    A) Earthworm

    B) shark

    C) coelacanth

    D) frog

    E) hummingbird

Answer: A
Diff: 2   Page Ref: 24.2
Skill: Application

21) Cartilaginous fish are characterized by having _____.

    A) cartilage skeletons

    B) four-chambered hearts

    C) lungs supplemented by air sacs

    D) a backbone

    E) suckerlike mouths lined with teeth

Answer: A
Diff: 2   Page Ref: 24.2
Skill: Conceptual

22) An animal's ability to live successfully on land is most increased by _____.

A) external fertilization

B) a two-chambered heart

C) moist skin used for gas exchange

D) gills

E) development in a shelled egg

Answer: E
Diff: 2   Page Ref: 24.2
Skill: Conceptual

23) The vulnerability of these semi-terrestrial chordates to both water and air pollutants may be the cause of their dramatic decline in numbers.

A) amphibians

B) arthropods

C) annelids

D) bony fish

E) reptiles

Answer: A
Diff: 1   Page Ref: 24.2
Skill: Conceptual

24) Which of the following analogies is incorrect?

A) limbs – roots

B) lungs – stomata

C) shelled amniote egg – fruit

D) dry, scaly skin – waxy cuticle

E) pollen – sperm

Answer: A
Diff: 3   Page Ref: 24.2
Skill: Application

25) Amphibians are not especially successful land dwellers due to their _____.

A) production of a shelled amniote egg

B) reliance on a moist skin for gas exchange

C) lungs that are supplemented by air sacs

D) two-chambered hearts

E) all of the above

Answer: B
Diff: 2   Page Ref: 24.2
Skill: Conceptual

26) Reptilian embryos will not dry out in a desert habitat because _____.

A) reptiles produce lots of defensive slime

B) reptiles' eggs are protected by a jellylike coating

C) the placenta facilitates gas exchange between the mother and the embryo

D) reptiles produce shelled amniote eggs

E) reptiles are endothermic

Answer: D
Diff: 2   Page Ref: 24.2
Skill: Conceptual

27) The high body temperature of birds and mammals is due to _____.

A) conversion of energy to heat during metabolism

B) the presence of sweat, scent and sebaceous glands

C) the fur that insulates them

D) behaviors like basking in the sun or seeking shade

E) the exchange of gases and nutrients via the placenta

Answer: A
Diff: 2   Page Ref: 24.2
Skill: Conceptual

28) Which of the following is essential to the maintenance of the high metabolism of birds?

A) skin that is used as a respiratory structure

B) four-chambered heart

C) embryonic development in a shelled amniote egg

D) hollow bones

E) extraordinary coordination by a well developed nervous system

Answer: B
Diff: 2   Page Ref: 24.2
Skill: Conceptual

29) Reptiles are better adapted to land dwelling than amphibians because of their _____.

    A) two-chambered heart

    B) moist skin used as a respiratory structure

    C) lungs with greater surface area for gas exchange

    D) embryo's uterine development

    E) all of the above

Answer: C
Diff: 1   Page Ref: 24.2
Skill: Conceptual

30) A tunicate is a(n) _____.

    A) bony fish

    B) cartilaginous fish

    C) jawless fish

    D) amphibian

    E) invertebrate chordate

Answer: E
Diff: 1   Page Ref: 24.2
Skill: Factual

31) A shark is a(n) _____.

    A) bony fish

    B) cartilaginous fish

    C) jawless fish

    D) amphibian

    E) invertebrate chordate

Answer: B
Diff: 1   Page Ref: 24.2
Skill: Factual

32) A lamprey is a(n) _____.

    A) bony fish

    B) cartilaginous fish

    C) jawless fish

    D) amphibian

    E) invertebrate chordate

Answer: C
Diff: 1   Page Ref: 24.2
Skill: Factual

33) A tadpole is a(n) _____.

    A) bony fish

    B) cartilaginous fish

    C) jawless fish

    D) amphibian

    E) invertebrate chordate

Answer: D
Diff: 2   Page Ref: 24.2
Skill: Factual

34) A tuna is a(n) _____.

    A) bony fish

    B) cartilaginous fish

    C) jawless fish

    D) amphibian

    E) invertebrate chordate

Answer: A
Diff: 1   Page Ref: 24.2
Skill: Factual

35) A turtle is a(n) _____.

    A) amphibian

    B) reptile

    C) bird

    D) mammal

    E) mollusk

Answer: B
Diff: 1   Page Ref: 24.2
Skill: Factual

36) A marsupial is a(n) _____.

    A) amphibian

    B) reptile

    C) bird

    D) mammal

    E) mollusk

Answer: D
Diff: 1   Page Ref: 24.2
Skill: Factual

37) An animal that has a four-chambered heart, is endothermic, and does not give birth to live offspring is a(n) _____.

    A) amphibian

    B) reptile

    C) bird

    D) mammal

    E) mollusk

Answer: C
Diff: 1   Page Ref: 24.2
Skill: Conceptual

38) Which of the following statements about jawless fishes is correct?

    A) Both hagfishes and lampreys are in the same taxonomic class.

    B) They do not have scales.

    C) They have neither jaws nor teeth.

    D) Both hagfishes and lampreys are considered vertebrates.

    E) The lamprey lineage is older than the hagfish lineage.

Answer: B
Diff: 2   Page Ref: 24.2
Skill: Conceptual

39) Lampreys have recently spread into the Great Lakes because

    A) competitive species have driven them from the ocean.

    B) fishermen have intentionally introduced them with the hope of farming them for "eel skin."

    C) a fish species that they naturally prey upon has recently been introduced to the Great Lakes.

    D) they have no natural predators in these waters.

    E) a new underground connection between the sea and the Great Lakes has recently opened.

Answer: D
Diff: 2   Page Ref: 24.2
Skill: Application

40) Lampreys have reduced the sizes of many commercial fish populations in the Great Lakes because

A) they are parasites on those fish species.

B) they are predators to many of the same prey species.

C) they share many of the same predators.

D) they are predators of those fish species.

E) they secrete toxins that injure or kill other fish.

Answer: A
Diff: 2   Page Ref: 24.2
Skill: Application

41) A large predatory marine vertebrate covered in scales with a skeleton that lacks bone would be classified in the class or order

A) Actinopterygii.

B) Actinista.

C) Chondrichthyes.

D) Amphibia.

E) Reptilia.

Answer: C
Diff: 2   Page Ref: 24.2
Skill: Application

42) The vertebrate group with the greatest diversity of vertebrates is the class or order

A) Actinopterygii.

B) Actinista.

C) Chondrichthyes.

D) Mammalia.

E) Reptilia.

Answer: A
Diff: 2   Page Ref: 24.2
Skill: Factual

43) Swim bladders are present in

    A) marine mammals.

    B) lobe-finned fishes.

    C) jawless fishes.

    D) ray-finned fishes.

    E) cartilaginous fishes.

Answer: D
Diff: 2   Page Ref: 24.2
Skill: Factual

44) Populations of many ray-finned fish species have declined in recent years due to

    A) parasitism by lampreys.

    B) bacterial disease.

    C) decline of their environment.

    D) loss of their prey species.

    E) overfishing by humans.

Answer: E
Diff: 2   Page Ref: 24.2
Skill: Conceptual

45) Lungfish are classified as

    A) amphibians.

    B) lobe-finned fishes.

    C) jawless fishes.

    D) ray-finned fishes.

    E) cartilaginous fishes.

Answer: B
Diff: 1   Page Ref: 24.2
Skill: Factual

46) A fish with fins containing rod-shaped bones surrounded by muscle is a(n)

    A) lobe-finned fish.

    B) shark.

    C) lamprey.

    D) ray-finned fish.

    E) hagfish.

Answer: A
Diff: 2   Page Ref: 24.2
Skill: Application

47) Which vertebrate group has a three-chambered heart?

 A) lobe-finned fishes

 B) amphibians

 C) mammals

 D) ray-finned fishes

 E) birds

Answer: B
Diff: 2   Page Ref: 24.2
Skill: Conceptual

48) Amphibians cannot be entirely terrestrial because

 A) their digestion is adapted for consuming aquatic prey.

 B) they do not have lungs, but have gills that require water for gas exchange.

 C) they have a three-chambered heart that is not efficient enough for terrestrial existence.

 D) their reproduction requires water to allow fertilization and keep eggs moist.

 E) their limbs are not adapted to support their bodies on land.

Answer: D
Diff: 2   Page Ref: 24.2
Skill: Conceptual

49) A terrestrial vertebrate with scales and a three-chambered heart is a(n)

 A) mammal.

 B) amphibian.

 C) reptile.

 D) lobe-finned fish.

 E) bird.

Answer: C
Diff: 2   Page Ref: 24.2
Skill: Application

50) All reptiles

 A) are exclusively terrestrial.

 B) have four well-developed limbs.

 C) are predatory carnivores.

 D) have teeth.

 E) have a three-chambered heart.

Answer: E
Diff: 2   Page Ref: 24.2
Skill: Conceptual

51) Birds are part of related group of vertebrates that includes all of the

A) amphibians.

B) lobe-finned fishes.

C) mammals.

D) reptiles.

E) ray-finned fishes.

Answer: D
Diff: 1   *Page Ref: 24.2*
Skill: Factual

52) Which characteristic do birds share with mammals?

A) a single ovary in females

B) mammary glands

C) a four-chambered heart

D) sweat glands

E) hollow bones

Answer: C
Diff: 1   *Page Ref: 24.2*
Skill: Conceptual

53) Though they are mammals, monotremes lack

A) ovaries in females.

B) mammary glands.

C) a four-chambered heart.

D) hair.

E) nipples.

Answer: E
Diff: 2   *Page Ref: 24.2*
Skill: Factual

54) Monotremes differ from other mammals in that they

A) do not produce milk.

B) lay eggs.

C) have a four-chambered heart.

D) have hair.

E) have nipples.

Answer: B
Diff: 1   *Page Ref: 24.2*
Skill: Factual

55) The _____ is NOT a marsupial.

A) opossum

B) kangaroo

C) Tasmanian devil

D) echidna

E) wombat

Answer: D
Diff: 1   *Page Ref: 24.2*
Skill: Factual

56) _____ are the mammals with the most number of species.

A) Rodents

B) Primates

C) Whales

D) Bats

E) Marsupials

Answer: A
Diff: 2   *Page Ref: 24.2*
Skill: Factual

57) The major recent problem faced by amphibians is

A) habitat destruction.

B) fungal infection.

C) exposure to environmental toxins.

D) developmental abnormality from UV light exposure.

E) All of these are current problems for amphibians.

Answer: E
Diff: 2   *Page Ref: Earth Watch*
Skill: Application

Chapter 25   Animal Behavior

1) If you teach your dog to sit by giving him a treat for every correct response, this is an example
of

A) habituation.

B) insight learning.

C) operant conditioning.

D) trial and error learning.

Answer: C
Diff: 1   Page Ref: 25.1
Skill: Conceptual

2) After eating at the new Mexican restaurant in town, you develop a mild case of food
poisoning. Consequently, you never go back there again to eat. This is an example of

A) habituation.

B) insight learning.

C) operant conditioning.

D) trial and error learning.

Answer: D
Diff: 2   Page Ref: 25.1
Skill: Conceptual

3) Nesting geese will roll softballs (placed next to their nests by biologists) into their nests,
perhaps because they resemble eggs that might have rolled out of the nest. This kind of
behavior is most likely

A) insight learning.

B) habituation.

C) innate.

D) conditioned.

Answer: C
Diff: 2   Page Ref: 25.1
Skill: Conceptual

4) A scientist who studies natural behavior of animals is called a/an

A) ethologist.

B) psychologist.

C) naturalist.

D) physiologist.

E) sociologist.

Answer: A
Diff: 1   Page Ref: 25.1
Skill: Factual

5) Innate animal behavior is

    A) learned.

    B) instinctive.

    C) not under genetic control.

    D) nonadaptive.

    E) both learned and instinctive.

Answer: B
Diff: 1   Page Ref: 25.1
Skill: Conceptual

6) An adaptive change in behavior as a result of experience is called

    A) instinctive behavior.   B) learned behavior.

    C) innate behavior.   D) random behavior.

Answer: B
Diff: 2   Page Ref: 25.1
Skill: Factual

7) A strong association learned during a sensitive period of an animal's life is referred to as

    A) classical conditioning.

    B) insight learning.

    C) altruism.

    D) imprinting.

    E) habituation.

Answer: D
Diff: 1   Page Ref: 25.1
Skill: Factual

8) Konrad Lorenz taught ducks to behave towards him as though he were their mother by providing the appropriate stimulus during a sensitive period. The learned behavior that resulted from this is called

    A) classical conditioning.

    B) fixed action behavior.

    C) altruism.

    D) habituation.

    E) imprinting.

Answer: E
Diff: 2   Page Ref: 25.1
Skill: Factual

9) "Getting used to" a repeated stimulus so that it no longer evokes a response is called

    A) insight.

    B) habituation.

    C) instinctive behavior.

    D) trial and error learning.

    E) imprinting.

Answer: B
Diff: 1   Page Ref: 25.1
Skill: Factual

10) A decline in response to a harmless, repeated stimulus is called

    A) habituation.

    B) insight learning.

    C) a sensitive period.

    D) instinctive behavior.

    E) imprinting.

Answer: A
Diff: 1   Page Ref: 25.1
Skill: Factual

11) The protist *Stentor* contracts when touched for the first time, but gradually stops retracting if touching is continued. This behavior is considered

    A) habituation.

    B) insight learning.

    C) a sensitive period.

    D) operant conditioning.

    E) imprinting.

Answer: A
Diff: 2   Page Ref: 25.1
Skill: Conceptual

12) B.F. Skinner is most closely associated with research on

A) operant conditioning.

B) insight learning.

C) breeding experiments with pigeons.

D) imprinting experiments with ducks.

E) causing dogs to salivate at the sound of a bell.

Answer: A
Diff: 1   Page Ref: 25.1
Skill: Factual

13) During operant conditioning, an animal learns

A) to perform a response to a new stimulus.

B) to perform a behavior to receive a reward or avoid punishment.

C) to change an imprinted behavior.

D) to imprint upon an inappropriate object.

E) to behave like a different animal.

Answer: B
Diff: 2   Page Ref: 25.1
Skill: Factual

14) Failure to respond to harmless, repetitive stimulation is an example of

A) operant conditioning.

B) insight learning.

C) habituation.

D) trial and error learning.

E) imprinting.

Answer: C
Diff: 2   Page Ref: 25.1
Skill: Factual

15) A newly hatched duck adopts the first large moving object it sees as its mother. This is an example of

   A) operant conditioning.

   B) insight learning.

   C) habituation.

   D) trial and error learning.

   E) imprinting.

Answer: E
Diff: 2   Page Ref: 25.1
Skill: Conceptual

16) Training an animal to respond in a specific way to a stimulus is called

   A) operant conditioning.

   B) insight learning.

   C) habituation.

   D) trial and error learning.

   E) imprinting.

Answer: A
Diff: 2   Page Ref: 25.1
Skill: Conceptual

17) When city dwellers fail to respond to ordinary traffic sounds, it is called

   A) operant conditioning.

   B) insight learning.

   C) habituation.

   D) trial and error learning.

   E) imprinting.

Answer: C
Diff: 2   Page Ref: 25.1
Skill: Factual

18) A child learns which foods taste good or bad by

    A) operant conditioning.

    B) insight learning.

    C) habituation.

    D) trial and error learning.

    E) imprinting.

Answer: D
Diff: 2   *Page Ref: 25.1*
Skill: Factual

19) A worm learns to associate a flash of light with an electric shock by

    A) operant conditioning.

    B) insight learning.

    C) habituation.

    D) trial and error learning.

    E) imprinting.

Answer: A
Diff: 2   *Page Ref: 25.1*
Skill: Conceptual

20) The most complex form of learning is

    A) operant conditioning.

    B) insight learning.

    C) habituation.

    D) trial and error learning.

    E) imprinting.

Answer: B
Diff: 2   *Page Ref: 25.1*
Skill: Factual

21) When an animal forms an association with another animal or object during a sensitive period, it is called

    A) operant conditioning.

    B) insight learning.

    C) habituation.

    D) trial and error learning.

    E) imprinting.

Answer: E
Diff: 2   Page Ref: 25.1
Skill: Conceptual

22) When a duck imprints on its mother, it is

    A) innate behavior.   B) learned behavior.

    C) both innate and learned behavior.   D) neither innate nor learned behavior.

Answer: B
Diff: 2   Page Ref: 25.1
Skill: Factual

23) When a dog drools at the sound of a can opener, it is

    A) innate behavior.   B) learned behavior.

    C) both innate and learned behavior.   D) neither innate nor learned behavior.

Answer: B
Diff: 2   Page Ref: 25.1
Skill: Conceptual

24) When a sea anemone habituates to touch, it is

    A) innate behavior.   B) learned behavior.

    C) both innate and learned behavior.   D) neither innate nor learned behavior.

Answer: B
Diff: 2   Page Ref: 25.1
Skill: Factual

25) Normal fruit fly larvae move away from their food after eating. However, some larvae that were subjected to X-rays remain near or in their food after eating. There is a consistent difference in the DNA of these two types of larvae. What can be concluded about this behavior?

   A) It appears to be entirely learned.

   B) It appears to have a genetic component but is altered by experience.

   C) It has a clear genetic component.

   D) Nothing can be concluded about this behavior from the information provided.

Answer: C
Diff: 2   Page Ref: 25.1
Skill: Conceptual

26) In a classic experiment from the 1930s, a biologist conducted selective breeding experiments involving maze running behavior in rats. He repeatedly bred together males and females that made the fewest mistakes, and he bred together males and females that made the most mistakes. After eight generations, all mice that descended from "maze-smart" parents were better at running the maze than all mice that descended from the "maze-dumb" parents. This study indicates that

   A) maze running is a purely innate behavior in rats.

   B) trial-and-error learning in rats appears to have a genetic component.

   C) maze running is a purely learned behavior.

   D) rats move through a maze randomly.

   E) Nothing can be concluded about maze running behavior in rats from the information provided.

Answer: B
Diff: 3   Page Ref: 25.1
Skill: Application

27) Some distasteful insects like the monarch butterfly have bright, high-contrast color patterns. Most predators, once they have tasted a monarch, will leave all other monarchs alone in the future. As a result, what type of learning is occurring in their predators?

   A) operant conditioning

   B) habituation

   C) insight learning

   D) imprinting

   E) all of the above

Answer: A
Diff: 2   Page Ref: 25.1
Skill: Conceptual

28) A toad that eats a bee and is stung tends to avoid eating bees thereafter. This is an example of
_____.

Answer: trial and error learning
Diff: 2   Page Ref: 25.1
Skill: Factual

29) According to ethologists, learning is defined as _____.

Answer: the capacity to make changes in behavior, on the basis of experience
Diff: 2   Page Ref: 25.1
Skill: Factual

30) Viceroy butterflies, which are non-toxic, have color patterns that closely mimic those of
monarch butterflies, which are toxic. When monarchs are common and viceroys are scarce in
the same environment, viceroys are protected because birds cannot tell them apart from
monarchs. However, if monarchs become scarce and viceroys much more common, what do
you predict will happen?

Answer: Viceroys may be eaten more frequently because few birds have had recent bad
        experiences with monarchs.
Diff: 3   Page Ref: 25.1
Skill: Application

31) When walking your male dog, you notice that he urinated upon every vertical object in his
path. His urine is used to "mark" his territory, and serves as a chemical signal to other dogs.
His urine contains

A) pheromones.   B) hormones.   C) apomones.   D) releasers.

Answer: A
Diff: 2   Page Ref: 25.2
Skill: Conceptual

32) Animals communicate with other animals by

A) sound.

B) visual signals.

C) chemical signals.

D) touch.

E) All the above choices are correct.

Answer: E
Diff: 1   Page Ref: 25.2
Skill: Factual

33) Whales communicate across hundreds of miles by

    A) sight.

    B) sound.

    C) pheromones.

    D) touch.

    E) none of these

Answer: B
Diff: 2   Page Ref: 25.2
Skill: Factual

34) The different calls of vervet monkeys indicate

    A) the type of predator detected.

    B) the type of food available.

    C) sexual differences.

    D) the availability of water.

    E) the size of a territory.

Answer: A
Diff: 1   Page Ref: 25.2
Skill: Factual

35) The greatest long distance communication occurs between

    A) insects.

    B) birds.

    C) whales.

    D) bats.

    E) elephants.

Answer: C
Diff: 2   Page Ref: 25.2
Skill: Factual

36) The shape, size, or color of an animal

    A) plays a role in active visual communication.

    B) plays a role in passive visual communication.

    C) does not communicate information.

    D) relates to the pheromones the animal produces.

    E) is used to mark the boundaries of territories.

Answer: B
Diff: 2   Page Ref: 25.2
Skill: Conceptual

37) What advantage does sound communication have over visual communication?

    A) It is more quickly perceived.

    B) It can communicate better the degree of an animal's readiness for a particular behavior.

    C) It can be transmitted over distances even when physical barriers exist.

    D) It is not as likely to attract predators.

    E) It uses less energy.

Answer: C
Diff: 2   Page Ref: 25.2
Skill: Conceptual

38) Chemicals produced by an individual that influence the behavior of members of the same species are called

    A) hormones.

    B) enzymes.

    C) stimuli.

    D) pheromones.

    E) steroids.

Answer: D
Diff: 1   Page Ref: 25.2
Skill: Factual

39) Pheromones may include

    A) fat deposits in the bodies of beetles.

    B) sounds emitted to warn insects of impending danger.

    C) a form of chemical communication among insects.

    D) signals involved in learned behavior patterns of insects.

    E) light emitted by fireflies during the mating season.

Answer: C
Diff: 2   Page Ref: 25.2
Skill: Factual

40) An example of a pheromone is

    A) trail substances deposited by ants.

    B) bat echolocation (sonar).

    C) light emitted by fireflies.

    D) bird song.

    E) the moaning sounds of whales.

Answer: A
Diff: 2   Page Ref: 25.2
Skill: Factual

41) All the following are pheromones EXCEPT

    A) queen substance produced by honeybees.

    B) light emitted by fireflies.

    C) trail substances produced by ants.

    D) sex attractants produced by Japanese beetles.

    E) urine used by wolves to mark territories.

Answer: B
Diff: 2   Page Ref: 25.2
Skill: Factual

42) A chemical produced in one animal that alters the physiological state of another of the same species is called a

    A) pheromone.

    B) releaser.

    C) hormone.

    D) neurotransmitter.

    E) subliminal suggestion.

Answer: A
Diff: 2   Page Ref: 25.2
Skill: Factual

43) A dog growling is an example of _____ –based communication.

A) passive visual

B) active visual

C) chemical

D) sound

E) physical contact

Answer: D
Diff: 1   Page Ref: 25.2
Skill: Conceptual

44) A cat licking another cat is an example of _____ –based communication.

A) passive visual

B) active visual

C) chemical

D) sound

E) physical contact

Answer: E
Diff: 1   Page Ref: 25.2
Skill: Conceptual

45) A lion spraying urine on a tree is an example of _____ –based communication.

A) passive visual

B) active visual

C) chemical

D) sound

E) physical contact

Answer: C
Diff: 1   Page Ref: 25.2
Skill: Conceptual

46) A bird flashing white patches underneath its wings is an example of _____ –based communication.

    A) passive visual

    B) active visual

    C) chemical

    D) sound

    E) physical contact

Answer: B
Diff: 2   *Page Ref: 25.2*
Skill: Conceptual

47) Often in a tank of goldfish, each fish chases all of the other fish that are smaller. This illustrates

    A) dominance hierarchy.   B) aggressive behavior.

    C) ritualized combat.   D) all of these

Answer: D
Diff: 2   *Page Ref: 25.3*
Skill: Conceptual

48) The dominance hierarchy within a group of animals functions to

    A) eliminate competition.

    B) limit population numbers.

    C) minimize aggression.

    D) increase competition.

    E) increase fighting among members of a population.

Answer: C
Diff: 2   *Page Ref: 25.3*
Skill: Conceptual

49) Aggressive encounters between individuals of the same species

    A) are always a fight to the death.

    B) usually result in one of the individuals being injured.

    C) usually consists of rituals or displays.

    D) do not occur in nature.

    E) only occur when food supplies are low.

Answer: C
Diff: 2   *Page Ref: 25.3*
Skill: Conceptual

50) A territory is established most frequently by

    A) an adult male.

    B) an adult female.

    C) a mated pair of animals.

    D) a social group.

    E) a pregnant female.

Answer: A
Diff: 2   Page Ref: 25.3
Skill: Factual

51) Which is NOT true of male animals that have established a good territory?

    A) They are more likely to reproduce successfully.

    B) They are more likely to range outside of it to get enough food.

    C) They are more likely to attract females.

    D) They must advertise to keep other males out.

    E) They will mark the territory well.

Answer: B
Diff: 2   Page Ref: 25.3
Skill: Conceptual

52) Territories may be defended by

    A) males.

    B) females.

    C) a mated pair.

    D) an entire social group.

    E) any of the above

Answer: E
Diff: 2   Page Ref: 25.3
Skill: Conceptual

53) Defense of an area where important resources for survival are located is termed

    A) appeasement.

    B) passive behavior.

    C) aggression.

    D) kinesis.

    E) territoriality.

Answer: E
Diff: 1   Page Ref: 25.3
Skill: Factual

54) Territoriality

    A) increases the size of a population.

    B) decreases aggression within a population.

    C) results in every individual in a population successfully breeding.

    D) All are correct.

    E) B and C are correct.

Answer: B
Diff: 2   Page Ref: 25.3
Skill: Conceptual

55) The dominant animal in a social hierarchy, such as a wolf pack, is called the

    A) alpha.   B) general.   C) king.   D) predator.   E) master.

Answer: A
Diff: 2   Page Ref: 25.3
Skill: Factual

56) An animal that effects changes to make himself look larger is exhibiting

    A) dominance in a social group.

    B) an aggressive display.

    C) a desire to fight.

    D) a readiness to mate.

    E) a submissive posture.

Answer: B
Diff: 2   Page Ref: 25.3
Skill: Conceptual

57) When a canary is singing in its cage it is

    A) marking its territory.

    B) trying to find mate.

    C) an aggressive display.

    D) both A and B

    E) All of the above are true.

Answer: E
Diff: 2   Page Ref: 25.3
Skill: Conceptual

58) At the start of the breeding season male stickleback fish undergo a number of significant changes. Their bellies become bright red in color and they become aggressive towards other males of the species, establishing and defending territories in which they build nests. While most male–male encounters consist solely of the resident lunging at an intruder, if this fails to drive off the intruder biting may follow. Females will choose to mate with males with large territories and well-constructed nests. Based on the above, what would you expect to happen to the incidence of biting behavior as nest sites become scarcer?

Answer: The incidence of biting should increase.
Diff: 2   Page Ref: 25.3
Skill: Application

59) Female peafowl (peahens) prefer to breed with males (peacocks) with the longest tails. However, the longer the peacock's tail, the less well he can fly and the more likely he is to be eaten by predators. In this case

   A) both sexual selection and natural selection favor larger tails in peacocks.

   B) both sexual selection and natural selection favor smaller tails in peacocks.

   C) sexual selection favors smaller tails but natural selection favors larger tails.

   D) sexual selection favors larger tails but natural selection favors smaller tails.

Answer: D
Diff: 3   Page Ref: 25.4
Skill: Conceptual

60) Male bullfrogs produce loud calls during the mating season to attract females. Most females prefer males with the loudest calls. What can be reasonably concluded about this situation?

   A) The louder a male's call, the higher his fitness.

   B) The loudness of a male's call is not a good predictor of his fitness.

   C) The louder a male's call, the lower his fitness.

   D) We cannot come to any conclusions based on the information given.

Answer: A
Diff: 2   Page Ref: 25.4
Skill: Conceptual

61) Which of the following is NOT an advantage of being a social animal?

   A) increased ability to detect predators

   B) conservation of energy

   C) increased likelihood of finding mates

   D) increased hunting efficiency

   E) All are advantages of being a social animal.

Answer: E
Diff: 1   Page Ref: 25.5
Skill: Factual

62) Disadvantages for animals living in groups include

    A) lower efficiency in finding food.

    B) reduced chance of finding a mate.

    C) decreased risk of disease.

    D) increased chance of being spotted by predators.

Answer: D
Diff: 2   Page Ref: 25.5
Skill: Factual

63) Complex societies involving a caste system (humans excluded) are found among the

    A) fishes.

    B) insects.

    C) amphibians.

    D) birds.

    E) reptiles.

Answer: B
Diff: 2   Page Ref: 25.5
Skill: Factual

64) Foraging honeybees indicate the source of food by

    A) leading other bees to the site.

    B) releasing pheromones.

    C) doing a specific waggle dance.

    D) creating noises with their wings.

    E) a unique verbal language.

Answer: C
Diff: 2   Page Ref: 25.5
Skill: Factual

65) The waggle dance of honeybees is

    A) used to delimit territory.

    B) an indicator of danger to the hive.

    C) an example of courtship behavior.

    D) used to describe the location of food.

    E) used to signal the beginning of mating season.

Answer: D
Diff: 1   Page Ref: 25.5
Skill: Factual

66) Honeybees will sting a bear robbing their hive even though the bees will die after they sting the bear. This is an example of

   A) habituation.   B) conditioning.   C) altruism.   D) territoriality.

   Answer: C
   Diff: 2   *Page Ref: 25.5*
   Skill: Conceptual

67) Worker honeybees are

   A) fertile females.

   B) sterile females.

   C) fertile males.

   D) sterile males.

   E) immature bees of either sex.

   Answer: B
   Diff: 2   *Page Ref: 25.5*
   Skill: Factual

68) Honeybees are rendered sterile by

   A) working too vigorously.

   B) high heat in the hive.

   C) random mutations.

   D) the queen's sex pheromone.

   E) being fed royal jelly.

   Answer: D
   Diff: 2   *Page Ref: 25.5*
   Skill: Factual

69) Which of the following inhibits female honeybee development into a queen honeybee?

   A) lack of royal jelly in the diet during development

   B) The eggs that produced them are not fertilized.

   C) failure of worker bees to maintain the larvae

   D) the presence of royal jelly in the diet

   Answer: A
   Diff: 2   *Page Ref: 25.5*
   Skill: Factual

70) Which of the following illustrates altruism?

A) Parent birds clean out their nest.

B) Birds of a different species care for a cuckoo egg.

C) A mother bird pretends to be wounded to distract a predator away from her young.

D) Parent birds spend much of their time and energy feeding their young.

E) Males sing to attract females as mating partners.

Answer: C
Diff: 2   Page Ref: 25.5
Skill: Conceptual

71) "Kin selection" refers to

A) the selection of a mate.

B) deciding which of the related animals can share the food.

C) deciding which of the related animals can live in the colony.

D) which related animals must live and which must die.

E) an animal promoting the survival of the genes of its close relatives.

Answer: E
Diff: 2   Page Ref: 25.5
Skill: Conceptual

72) Male honeybees are called

A) drones.   B) workers.   C) slaves.   D) waggles.

Answer: A
Diff: 1   Page Ref: 25.5
Skill: Factual

73) The behavior of animals in a social group enhances

A) survival of the species.

B) reproductive success of individuals.

C) propagation of genes for favorable traits.

D) survival of close relatives.

E) All of the above choices are correct.

Answer: E
Diff: 2   Page Ref: 25.5
Skill: Conceptual

74) Twin studies have demonstrated that there is a significant genetic component for all but

A) activity level.

B) alcoholism.

C) intelligence.

D) political attitudes.

E) All of the above exhibit a genetic component.

Answer: E
Diff: 2   Page Ref: 25.5
Skill: Factual

75) Smiling when happy seems to be an expression common to all human societies. This behavior is probably

A) genetic in origin.   B) learned.

C) altruistic.   D) none of the above

Answer: A
Diff: 1   Page Ref: 25.6
Skill: Conceptual

76) McClintock found that the menstrual cycles of female college dorm roommates became synchronous over a six-month period. She also showed that armpit odors from one group of women affect the menstrual cycles of other women, who sniff the odors. This might indicate that

A) women have conscious control over their menstrual cycles.

B) pheromones are involved in some human behaviors.

C) menstrual cycles cannot be influenced by nerve impulses.

D) something in the water in their dorm influenced their cycles.

E) eating the same foods causes menstrual cycles to become synchronous.

Answer: B
Diff: 2   Page Ref: 25.6
Skill: Factual

77) When a two-month-old baby is exposed to a large white paper with two dark eye-sized spots, the baby will

    A) smile.

    B) exhibit fright.

    C) exhibit avoidance actions.

    D) not respond to a stimulus of this nature.

    E) vomit.

Answer: A
Diff: 2   Page Ref: 25.6
Skill: Factual

78) Human facial expressions in response to various emotions

    A) are remarkably similar among different cultures.

    B) vary tremendously from culture to culture.

    C) vary according to sex.

    D) vary according to race.

    E) vary according to age.

Answer: A
Diff: 2   Page Ref: 25.6
Skill: Factual

79) Studies of identical human twins have shown that

    A) they are no more alike than are fraternal twins.

    B) they exhibit vastly different behavioral traits if raised in different environments.

    C) their genes appear to have a great deal of influence on their behavior.

    D) they do not live as long as fraternal twins live.

    E) behavior does not depend on the types of genes present.

Answer: C
Diff: 2   Page Ref: 25.6
Skill: Factual

80) A hungry newborn human infant, touched on the side of her mouth, will turn her head and attempt to suckle. This example of behavior is

   A) learned.

   B) instinctive.

   C) not under genetic control.

   D) nonadaptive.

   E) a combination of all the above choices.

   Answer: B
   Diff: 2   Page Ref: 25.6
   Skill: Conceptual

81) Behaviors that we call "play"

   A) never occur in adults.   B) can be dangerous.

   C) are only observed in humans.   D) cannot be adaptive.

   Answer: B
   Diff: 2   Page Ref: Evolutionary Connections
   Skill: Factual

82) Briefly explain how play behavior might have survival value and thus be affected by natural selection.

   Answer: The survival value of play might be that playful behaviors allow juvenile animals to practice behaviors that will be very important later in life. For example, the play behaviors of many different species of mammals are very similar to the hunting and escaping behaviors of adults. If play behavior has a genetic (innate) component, then natural selection will be expected to favor individuals that play as juveniles.
   Diff: 3   Page Ref: Evolutionary Connections
   Skill: Application

Chapter 26 Population Growth and Regulation

1) The forests of Easter Island

    A) disappeared after humans brought many herbivores to the island.

    B) never existed; the island has always been barren.

    C) disappeared as a result of clearcutting by humans.

    D) have not existed for several million years.

    E) disappeared when humans brought a tree disease to the island.

Answer: C
Diff: 2   Page Ref: Case Study
Skill: Factual

2) When a biologist studies the way organisms interact with each other and with their nonliving environment, she is studying their

    A) physiology.

    B) anatomy.

    C) morphology.

    D) genetics.

    E) ecology.

Answer: E
Diff: 1   Page Ref: 26.0
Skill: Factual

3) In a deciduous oak forest of the American northeast, one example of an abiotic component of the ecosystem would be

    A) nematodes in the soil that feed on plant roots.

    B) nematodes in the soil that feed on dead organic matter.

    C) sunlight that filters through the canopy.

    D) animals such as deer that migrate through the forest but do not eat in the forest.

    E) the understory plant community.

Answer: C
Diff: 1   Page Ref: 26.0
Skill: Conceptual

4) A complex interrelated network of organisms and the surrounding abiotic environment in a defined area is a(n)

    A) community.

    B) ecosystem.

    C) population.

    D) biosphere.

    E) biome.

Answer: B
Diff: 2   Page Ref: 26.0
Skill: Factual

5) The organisms that represent the different species within an ecosystem that interact in various ways comprise the

    A) population.

    B) community.

    C) trophic level.

    D) aggregation.

    E) ecotone.

Answer: B
Diff: 1   Page Ref: 26.0
Skill: Factual

6) All of the following might be studied by an ecologist EXCEPT

    A) effects of increasing atmospheric carbon dioxide levels on forest growth.

    B) effects of spraying DDT on the size of mosquito populations.

    C) how amino acid sequence influences three dimensional shape of proteins.

    D) how members of the Archaea are adapted to life at high temperatures.

    E) recovery of forests after a volcanic eruption.

Answer: C
Diff: 2   Page Ref: 26.0
Skill: Conceptual

7) An aquatic biologist is studying a lake in western Massachusetts in order to document the nitrogen (N) cycle of the lake, and thus she is measuring inputs, turnover, and outputs of N. A second ecologist is studying a larger region of western Massachusetts that is forested, with several lakes, and is studying N transfers between the forest and the lakes. The first ecologist claims that her lake is an ecosystem; the second ecologist also claims that her forested region, with its many lakes, is an ecosystem. Which ecologist is correct, or are they both correct or incorrect?

Answer: They both are correct. An ecosystem is a network of interrelated living things and their physical environment. The boundaries of an ecosystem may be drawn almost anywhere, depending on the scope of the study.

Diff: 3   Page Ref: 26.0
Skill: Conceptual

8) All organisms that reside within an ecosystem and that can potentially interbreed are members of a(n)

    A) population.

    B) community.

    C) trophic level.

    D) aggregation.

    E) ecotone.

Answer: A
Diff: 1   Page Ref: 26.1
Skill: Factual

9) Environmental resistance may limit the size of populations by

    A) increasing both birth and death rates.

    B) decreasing both birth and death rates.

    C) increasing death rates and/or decreasing birth rates.

    D) decreasing death rates and/or increasing birth rates.

    E) changing the biotic potential.

Answer: C
Diff: 2   Page Ref: 26.1
Skill: Conceptual

10) To determine the number of individuals that will be added to a population in a specified time we multiply the growth rate (r) by the _____.

    A) biotic potential

    B) original population size

    C) environmental resistance

    D) final population size

    E) number of immigrants

Answer: B
Diff: 2   Page Ref: 26.1
Skill: Factual

11) If a population of 100 birds increases to 120 birds the following year, $r =$ _____.

    A) 0.16   B) 0.20   C) 1.2   D) 2   E) 20

Answer: B
Diff: 3   Page Ref: 26.1
Skill: Application

12) Which factor would not influence the size a population reaches over time?

    A) number of individuals migrating

    B) number of deaths

    C) age of females at reproduction

    D) distance traveled by migrants

    E) number of births

Answer: D
Diff: 2   Page Ref: 26.1
Skill: Conceptual

13) Environmental resistance is

    A) a series of limits imposed on population growth by only the biotic environment (such as predators or competitors).

    B) a series of limits imposed on population growth by only the abiotic environment.

    C) a series of limits imposed on population growth by both the biotic and abiotic environments.

    D) a factor that decreases both death rates and birth rates.

    E) a factor that increases both death rates and birth rates.

Answer: C
Diff: 2   Page Ref: 26.1
Skill: Conceptual

14) The biotic potential of a population

    A) directly affects environmental resistance.

    B) causes changes in birth rates without affecting death rates.

    C) causes changes in death rates without affecting birth rates.

    D) is the maximum rate at which a population may increase.

    E) both A and C

Answer: D
Diff: 2   Page Ref: 26.1
Skill: Conceptual

15) At the start of a study there were 200 spotted owls in an old-growth forest patch in western Oregon. Over the next year, a biologist tracking the birds observed that 25 new birds hatched, of which 5 died. Thus r for this year was _____.

    A) 0.1   B) 5   C) 20   D) 25   E) 200

Answer: A
Diff: 3   Page Ref: 26.1
Skill: Application

16) Exponential growth occurs when

    A) there is a constant number of births each year and the birth rate is greater than the death rate.

    B) the population grows by a fixed percentage each year.

    C) the rate of emigration is greater than the rate of immigration.

    D) the biotic potential decreases each year.

    E) environmental resistance declines each year.

Answer: B
Diff: 2   Page Ref: 26.1
Skill: Conceptual

17) An ecologist is studying the painted turtle population in a small pond. At the beginning of the year there are 100 individuals. Over the course of one year, 40 turtles are born and 60 die. There is no migration. The birth rate for this population is _____ per year.

    A) 0.4   B) 0.6   C) 20   D) 40   E) 60

Answer: A
Diff: 2   Page Ref: 26.1
Skill: Application

18) An ecologist is studying the painted turtle population in a small pond. At the beginning of the year there are 100 individuals. Over the course of one year, 40 turtles are born and 60 die. There is no migration. What is the growth rate (*r*) of the painted turtle population?

A) –0.4   B) –0.2   C) 0.2   D) 0.4   E) 0.6

Answer: B
Diff: 3   Page Ref: 26.1
Skill: Application

19) Based on the data in the table below, what type of growth curve did this mayfly population follow from 1991 to 1997?

Year	Density (individuals/square meter)
1985	0
1991	0.7
1993	5
1995	40
1997	300
1999	250
2001	200

A) E-curve   B) J-curve   C) K-curve   D) L-curve   E) S-curve

Answer: B
Diff: 2   Page Ref: 26.1
Skill: Application

20) A population size will remain stable if

A) there is a constant number of births each year and the birth rate is greater than the death rate.

B) the population grows by a fixed percentage each year.

C) the rate of emigration is greater than the rate of immigration.

D) the birth rate and death rate are equal, as are the rate of emigration and the rate of immigration.

E) environmental resistance declines each year.

Answer: D
Diff: 2   Page Ref: 26.1
Skill: Conceptual

21) According to the equation for population growth rate, of two populations with equal death rates the population with *r* = 2 will increase more rapidly than a population with *r* = 4. True or False?

Answer: FALSE
Diff: 2   Page Ref: 26.1
Skill: Conceptual

22) A measure of the ability of a population to grow under ideal circumstances is its _____.

Answer: biotic potential
Diff: 1   Page Ref: 26.1
Skill: Factual

23) The sum of all factors that limit the ability of a population to grow are known as _____.

Answer: environmental resistance
Diff: 1   Page Ref: 26.1
Skill: Factual

24) In the equation "population growth = rN," the letter r stands for _____.

Answer: growth rate
Diff: 2   Page Ref: 26.1
Skill: Factual

25) Many species of field mice are able to reproduce several times a year, and produce litters with multiple offspring. However, an ecologist noted that the population size of mice, as measured in a California grassland, did not change from year to year. The factors that keep natural populations from increasing are collectively called the _____.

Answer: environmental resistance
Diff: 2   Page Ref: 26.1
Skill: Factual

26) How is a population growth rate expressed?

Answer: Changes (increase or decrease) in the number of individuals per individual per unit of time.
Diff: 3   Page Ref: 26.1
Skill: Factual

27) Write an equation that describes a situation in which a population remains stable.

Answer: Birth + immigration = death + emigration ; or, r = (birth rate + immigration rate) — (death rate + emigration rate) = 0
Diff: 3   Page Ref: 26.1
Skill: Conceptual

28) Explain what happens in exponential population growth.

Answer: The population grows by a fixed percentage of its size during each time period so that the actual numbers of individuals being added to the population gets larger at an ever increasing rate.
Diff: 2   Page Ref: 26.1
Skill: Conceptual

29) In the United States today there is a trend toward women having their first child in their late 30s or early 40s. In contrast, a few decades ago most women started having children in their early 20s. What effect would you expect this change to have on population growth in the United States? Would it have any effect if the number of children per woman is the same? Explain.

Answer: Population growth would be expected to slow even if the number of offspring per woman remains the same, because the effective generation time has increased. The growth curve would be extended over a slightly longer time scale.
Diff: 3   Page Ref: 26.1
Skill: Conceptual

30) Why would a bacterial population living in an unrestricted environment grow much faster than an eagle population?

Answer: A bacterial population can increase more rapidly than an eagle population because each bacterial cell can reproduce every 20 minutes, whereas eagles reproduce less often and begin reproducing at an older age.
Diff: 2   Page Ref: 26.1
Skill: Conceptual

31) When a population has inhabited an area for a long time and the population size has stabilized because of resource limitations

A) carrying capacity has been reached.

B) density dependence is clearly not involved.

C) predation decreases.

D) density independence occurs.

E) environmental resistance declines.

Answer: A
Diff: 2   Page Ref: 26.2
Skill: Conceptual

32) An insect population grows exponentially until an early winter freeze kills almost all of the insects. The next spring the population grows exponentially again. This type of population growth is known as

A) boom–and–bust cycling.

B) sigmoidal growth.

C) density–dependent growth.

D) density–independent growth.

E) sustained cycling.

Answer: A
Diff: 2   Page Ref: 26.2
Skill: Factual

33) An important density-independent factor limiting population size is _____.

    A) predation

    B) weather

    C) environmental resistance

    D) competition

    E) food quantity

Answer: B
Diff: 2   Page Ref: 26.2
Skill: Factual

34) Which of these is NOT a density-dependent control of population size?

    A) parasitism

    B) predation

    C) competition

    D) freezing temperatures

    E) shortage of food

Answer: D
Diff: 2   Page Ref: 26.2
Skill: Conceptual

35) If a caterpillar eats all of the seedlings in your garden, the caterpillar is acting as a

    A) predator.

    B) parasite.

    C) competitor.

    D) density-independent factor.

    E) saprophyte.

Answer: A
Diff: 2   Page Ref: 26.2
Skill: Conceptual

36) In a maple forest in the spring the ground will often be covered with young maple seedlings which compete for light and nutrients. By fall, most of these have died, leaving only a few survivors. This is an example of _____ competition.

    A) scramble

    B) contest

    C) dominance hierarchy

    D) interspecific

    E) social stress

Answer: A
Diff: 2   Page Ref: 26.2
Skill: Conceptual

37) Most parasites have evolved to _____ their hosts.

    A) kill

    B) only weaken

    C) have no effect on

    D) strengthen

    E) none of these

Answer: B
Diff: 2   Page Ref: 26.2
Skill: Factual

38) What type of competition has occurred when one organism uses social or chemical interactions to limit the access of other individuals to resources?

    A) contest competition

    B) scramble competition

    C) interspecific competition

    D) intramural competition

    E) social competition

Answer: A
Diff: 2   Page Ref: 26.2
Skill: Factual

39) A caribou dies because it was weakened by parasites (like tapeworms) passed from one individual to the next under crowded conditions during an unusually long, cold winter. What factor contributed to the death of the caribou?

   A) density–independent factors

   B) density–dependent factors

   C) abiotic factors

   D) biotic factors

   E) all of the above

Answer: E
Diff: 3   Page Ref: 26.2
Skill: Application

40) Some predators feed preferentially on the most abundant prey. This type of predation is

   A) density–dependent.

   B) density–independent.

   C) competitive.

   D) exponential.

   E) cyclical.

Answer: A
Diff: 2   Page Ref: 26.2
Skill: Conceptual

41) Why do many non–native species, such as a prickly pear cactus brought to Australia from South America, rapidly become abundant when first introduced?

   A) The climate in the new site is more favorable than in its native site.

   B) Non–native species increase their reproductive rate when introduced.

   C) There are fewer predators and parasites capable of attacking the non–native species in the new site.

   D) The carrying capacity at the new site is higher than at the native site.

   E) Growth changes from an S–curve to a J–curve at the new site.

Answer: C
Diff: 2   Page Ref: 26.2
Skill: Conceptual

42) An ecosystem's carrying capacity for a population is determined by all of the following factors EXCEPT

    A) space available to the population.

    B) energy available to the population.

    C) water available to the population.

    D) food available to the population.

    E) growth rate of the population.

Answer: E
Diff: 2   Page Ref: 26.2
Skill: Conceptual

43) The carrying capacity of an ecosystem for a given species is determined by

    A) the number of ecotones in the ecosystem.

    B) the availability of resources in the environment.

    C) the proximity of a "source" population for immigration.

    D) the proximity of a "sink" population for emigration.

    E) the intersection between environmental resistance and biotic potential.

Answer: B
Diff: 2   Page Ref: 26.2
Skill: Factual

44) Parasites affect population sizes of their hosts

    A) in a density-dependent fashion, and usually directly kill the hosts.

    B) in a density-dependent fashion, and do not usually directly kill the hosts.

    C) in a density-independent fashion, and usually directly kill the hosts.

    D) in a density-independent fashion, and do not usually directly kill the hosts.

    E) in a density-dependent fashion, and do not affect host death rates.

Answer: B
Diff: 2   Page Ref: 26.2
Skill: Conceptual

45) During the winter of 1999, minimum temperatures did not get much below freezing in an Oregon pond, and the following summer large mosquito populations were observed. In the winter of 2000, frost came early, and most ponds froze for 3 months. In the following summer, very low mosquito populations were observed. This is an example of

    A) density–independent regulation.

    B) density–dependent regulation.

    C) ecosystem carrying capacity.

    D) community carrying capacity.

    E) exotic regulation.

Answer: A
Diff: 2   Page Ref: 26.2
Skill: Application

46) When mosquitoes are very abundant, purple martins flock to the area and specialize on them. When mosquito populations are not large, purple martins are similarly scarce and feed on other insects. This is an example of

    A) density–independent regulation.

    B) density–dependent regulation.

    C) ecosystem carrying capacity.

    D) community carrying capacity.

    E) exotic regulation.

Answer: B
Diff: 2   Page Ref: 26.2
Skill: Application

47) *Juglans nigra*, or the black walnut, releases an allelopathic (toxic to other plants) compound when its leaves decompose; the result is that few plants can live under the canopy of the tree. Thus the black walnut can be said to engage in

    A) parasitism.

    B) scramble competition.

    C) sociopathic competition.

    D) allele–dependent competition.

    E) contest competition.

Answer: E
Diff: 2   Page Ref: 26.2
Skill: Application

48) A population of wild horses has a growth rate (*r*) of 0.2 per year. If the population starts out with 50 individuals and there is no migration, how many would you expect after one year; after two years?

A) 10; 2   B) 52; 54   C) 60; 70   D) 60; 72   E) 70; 90

Answer: D
Diff: 3   Page Ref: 26.2
Skill: Application

49) A laboratory experiment followed the growth of a flour beetle (*Tribolium* sp.) population over time. At first the population increased dramatically but later growth slowed and the population size leveled off. While food (the wheat flour in which they live) was still abundant, it was noticed that flour beetles resorted to eating their own eggs when densities got high. What can we conclude about cannibalism in this species?

A) It has no effect on the growth of the population as food scarcity is clearly the limiting factor here.

B) It is clearly maladaptive as populations always do best when their densities rise as high as possible.

C) It serves as a density-dependent means of population control.

D) It serves as a density-independent means of population control.

E) We cannot reach any conclusions based on the information provided.

Answer: C
Diff: 3   Page Ref: 26.2
Skill: Application

50) Zebra mussels were introduced into Lake St. Clair around 1988. The following table shows the densities (in grams dry weight per square meter of lake bottom) of populations of native unionid mussels and exotic zebra mussels in the lake before and after this introduction. Both groups feed by filtering small particles from the water. Based on the information given, which of the following best describes the likely relationship between zebra mussels and unionids?

Year	Unionids	Zebra mussels
1986	4.5	0.0
1990	3.7	4.6
1992	1.3	3.4
1994	0.1	3.2

A) Unionids exert a density–dependent control on zebra mussel populations.

B) Unionids exert a density–independent control on zebra mussel populations.

C) Zebra mussels exert a density–dependent control on unionid populations.

D) Zebra mussels exert a density–independent control on unionid populations.

E) Zebra mussels and unionids have no effect on each other.

Answer: C
Diff: 3   Page Ref: 26.2
Skill: Application

51) Zebra mussels were introduced into Lake St. Clair around 1988. The following table shows the densities (in grams dry weight per square meter of lake bottom) of populations of native unionid mussels and exotic zebra mussels in the lake before and after this introduction. Both groups feed by filtering small particles from the water. If a "magic bullet" chemical is developed and employed to kill zebra mussels while leaving all other species unaffected, what do you predict will happen to the unionid populations?

Year	Unionids	Zebra mussels
1986	4.5	0.0
1990	3.7	4.6
1992	1.3	3.4
1994	0.1	3.2

A) They will be unaffected, staying at very low densities.

B) They will continue to decrease until all unionid species go extinct.

C) They will rebound in numbers due to reduced competition.

D) They will initially increase, then decrease again.

E) No predictions can be made based on the information provided.

Answer: C
Diff: 2   Page Ref: 26.2
Skill: Application

52) Dramatic reductions in phosphates flowing into the western basin of Lake Erie during the late 1980s dramatically increased oxygen concentrations in deeper waters of the lake. In response, mayfly nymphs, which had been rare in the lake since oxygen levels first dropped in the 1960s, rebounded as shown in the following table. Which of the following changes could account for the decline in mayflies from 1997 to 2001?

Year	Density (individuals/square meter)	Oxygen (milligrams/liter)
1985	0	1.5
1991	0.7	6.0
1993	5	6.2
1995	40	5.8
1997	300	6.1
1999	250	5.2
2001	200	4.5

A) Mayfly-eating fish populations increased due to a greater availability of their food, increasing mayfly death rates.

B) The decline in dissolved oxygen levels caused decreased birth rates or increased death rates of mayflies.

C) Mayflies exceeded their carrying capacity in 1997, degrading their environment and causing the population to crash.

D) All of the above are possible.

E) None of the above is possible.

Answer: D
Diff: 3   Page Ref: 26.2
Skill: Application

53) In his 1798 book, *An Essay on the Principle of Population*, Thomas Malthus stated that "...the power of [the Earth's human] population [to increase] is indefinitely greater than the power in the Earth to produce subsistence for man." He explained that our population increases exponentially while we can only increase our food supply linearly. Using our modern terminology, what did Malthus mean by "the power of the Earth to produce subsistence for man?"

A) biotic potential

B) birth rate

C) carrying capacity

D) environmental resistance

E) growth rate

Answer: C
Diff: 2   Page Ref: 26.2
Skill: Conceptual

54) A population of rabbits, introduced to an island, has rapid growth for a few years, and then growth slows. The population becomes stable because

A) carrying capacity has been reached.

B) environmental resistance declines.

C) immigration is reduced.

D) *r* declines.

E) Both answers A and D are correct.

Answer: A
Diff: 2   Page Ref: 26.2
Skill: Application

55) In a population of lemmings which followed a boom and bust cycle, a sudden freeze which caused many of the lemmings to die would be a(n) _____ factor.

A) abiotic and density-independent

B) biotic and density-dependent

C) abiotic and density-dependent

D) biotic and density-independent

E) none of the above

Answer: A
Diff: 1   Page Ref: 26.2
Skill: Conceptual

56) When the lemmings ran out of food because there were so many of them, this would be a _____ factor.

A) abiotic and density-independent

B) biotic and density-dependent

C) abiotic and density-dependent

D) biotic and density-independent

E) none of the above

Answer: B
Diff: 1   Page Ref: 26.2
Skill: Conceptual

57) In this situation wolves which ate lemmings whenever they could find them would be a
_____ factor.

    A) abiotic and density-independent

    B) biotic and density-dependent

    C) abiotic and density-dependent

    D) biotic and density-independent

    E) none of the above

Answer: B
Diff: 1   *Page Ref: 26.2*
Skill: Conceptual

58) Exponential growth occurs

    A) only for a limited time in natural populations.

    B) only in laboratory populations.

    C) frequently in natural populations.

    D) at regular intervals in natural populations.

    E) only in theory, never in actual populations.

Answer: A
Diff: 2   *Page Ref: 26.2*
Skill: Conceptual

59) Populations which have been relatively undisturbed by man normally grow without being
limited by their environments. True or False?

Answer: FALSE
Diff: 2   *Page Ref: 26.2*
Skill: Conceptual

60) Prey, such as lemmings, may have a density-dependent effect on predator populations, such
as those of the snowy owl, by enabling the predator to increase the number of predator
offspring at high prey densities. True or False?

Answer: TRUE
Diff: 2   *Page Ref: 26.2*
Skill: Factual

61) Natural populations cannot exceed their carrying capacities. True or False?

Answer: FALSE
Diff: 2   *Page Ref: 26.2*
Skill: Factual

62) When predators and prey both have population cycles, the predator cycle will tend to
_____ the prey cycle.

Answer: lag behind
Diff: 2   Page Ref: 26.2
Skill: Factual

63) Predation is considered to be a density-_____ factor that controls the population size of
prey.

Answer: dependent
Diff: 1   Page Ref: 26.2
Skill: Factual

64) Competition among individual members of the same species is referred to as _____
competition.

Answer: intraspecific
Diff: 1   Page Ref: 26.2
Skill: Factual

65) A species with high biotic potential that is transferred to a new environment where it has little
environmental resistance is referred to as a(n) _____ species.

Answer: invasive
Diff: 1   Page Ref: 26.2
Skill: Factual

66) When a population stops growing because it has reached the maximum number that the
environment can support, we say that the population has reached what?

Answer: its carrying capacity
Diff: 1   Page Ref: 26.2
Skill: Factual

67) Regular population cycles of rapid growth followed by massive die-off are known as what?

Answer: boom-and-bust cycles
Diff: 1   Page Ref: 26.2
Skill: Factual

68) A graph which shows patterns of death or survivorship over time is known as what?

Answer: a survivorship curve
Diff: 1   Page Ref: 26.2
Skill: Factual

69) Bacteria growing in a Petri dish may grow rapidly and experience exponential growth. However, bacteria in the soil, measured as the number of organisms per gram of soil, usually do not increase in population size from one year to the next. Yet no new food is added to the Petri dish after the initial addition of the bacterial inoculum, but new food sources are always added to the soil by way of plant detritus. How can this be true?

Answer: Bacteria in the Petri dish grow exponentially when first added, but the population stabilizes (and will eventually decline) as space and food become limiting. In the field, bacterial populations have already reached equilibrium with food availability. New food is "added" with plant inputs, but old food has been consumed so there is not a net accumulation of food resources.
Diff: 3   Page Ref: 26.2
Skill: Conceptual

70) Although models of population structure in an ecosystem usually assume that populations reach a carrying capacity after time, in reality population size may fluctuate around a mean from year to year. Using a population of mice in a grassland, give (1) an example of a density-independent factor that could cause population size to increase; (2) an example of a density-independent factor that could cause population size to decrease; (3) an example of a density-dependent factor that could cause population size to increase; (4) an example of a density-dependent factor that could cause population size to decrease.

Answer: Density-independent factors may include a mild winter, which reduces death rates and thus causes a population to increase; the accidental spill of a pesticide might cause the population to decrease in a manner that is density-independent. The increase in a predator population would cause a density-dependent reduction in population; the reduction of a competitor species might cause a density-dependent increase in population size.
Diff: 2   Page Ref: 26.2
Skill: Conceptual

71) Predation is considered to be a density-dependent factor that controls the population size of prey species. Give two examples of ways in which predators act in density-dependent ways in response to fluctuations in prey population sizes.

Answer: Predators may not only adjust the number of prey that they eat in response to prey abundance, but they might switch to alternate food sources when prey abundances are low or specialize in feeding on the prey when population sizes are high. In addition, predators may regulate the number of offspring that they produce in response to prey abundances.
Diff: 3   Page Ref: 26.2
Skill: Conceptual

72) Parasites may often kill their hosts, although they do not directly benefit from host death. And yet, many ecologists believe that parasites may have beneficial effects on their host populations. Why might this be so?

Answer: Parasites and predators tend to destroy weaker and less fit prey, leaving the stronger or better-adapted prey to reproduce and pass genes to the next generation. Thus the prey population is regulated but very fit individuals are not eliminated.
Diff: 2   *Page Ref: 26.2*
Skill: Conceptual

73) In high elevation forested ecosystems of New Hampshire and Vermont, ecologists have noticed a serious decline in certain tree species such as red spruce. When the affected trees are studied, it often seems that parasitic beetles or microbes are involved. Other scientists have stated that acid rain might be the cause of red spruce decline. Yet a third group of scientists have argued that both factors are equally involved. How could this third possibility be true, and which cause is likely to be density-dependent, and which is more likely to be density-independent?

Answer: Population size is a result of complex interactions between density-dependent and density-independent regulation. Many parasites will respond to trees in a density-dependent way, but weaken the trees so that a density-independent factor (acid rain) will kill them; the reverse may also be true.
Diff: 3   *Page Ref: 26.2*
Skill: Application

74) How do interspecific and intraspecific competition differ from each other?

Answer: Interspecific competition occurs between two species, while intraspecific competition occurs between members of the same species.
Diff: 1   *Page Ref: 26.2*
Skill: Factual

75) Which tends to be more intense, intraspecific or interspecific competition? Explain why.

Answer: Intraspecific competition tends to be more intense because the individuals of the same species all need very similar resources.
Diff: 2   *Page Ref: 26.2*
Skill: Factual

76) What are the three shapes of survivorship curves, and what does each one tell about the population?

Answer: A late-loss or convex means that most individuals survive to old age; a constant-loss or constant curve means that there is an equal chance of dying at any age; and an early-loss or concave curve means that there is high infant mortality.
Diff: 2   *Page Ref: 26.2*
Skill: Conceptual

77) If most of the individuals of a species die when they are young, that species will exhibit a
_____ survivorship curve.

   A) convex

   B) constant

   C) concave

   D) sigmoid (S-shaped)

   E) declining

Answer: C
Diff: 1   Page Ref: 26.3
Skill: Conceptual

78) If the individuals of a species are very likely to live until old age, that species will exhibit a
_____ survivorship curve.

   A) convex

   B) constant

   C) concave

   D) sigmoid (S-shaped)

   E) declining

Answer: A
Diff: 1   Page Ref: 26.3
Skill: Conceptual

79) If all the individuals of a species have an equal chance of dying at any age, that species will
exhibit a _____ survivorship curve.

   A) convex

   B) constant

   C) concave

   D) sigmoid (S-shaped)

   E) declining

Answer: B
Diff: 1   Page Ref: 26.3
Skill: Conceptual

80) Which survivorship curve is characteristic of many large animals including humans?

    A) early–loss

    B) concave

    C) constant–loss

    D) late–loss

    E) uniform

Answer: D
Diff: 2   Page Ref: 26.3
Skill: Conceptual

81) What is the advantage of a clumped population distribution?

    A) It is easier to search for food.

    B) Mating and caring for offspring are facilitated by grouping.

    C) Predators in groups can hunt more effectively.

    D) Predators may be confused by a large group.

    E) All of these are advantages of a clumped population distribution.

Answer: E
Diff: 2   Page Ref: 26.3
Skill: Conceptual

82) A uniform population distribution may result from

    A) the need for a group to care for offspring.

    B) allelopathy (the release of chemicals by plants to inhibit growth of other plants nearby).

    C) localization of resources.

    D) the need to find a mate.

    E) scarcity of resources.

Answer: B
Diff: 2   Page Ref: 26.3
Skill: Conceptual

83) A random population distribution

    A) is an advantage in avoiding predators.

    B) occurs when resources are evenly spaced.

    C) allows predators to hunt more effectively.

    D) is rare.

    E) is common among organisms that establish breeding territories.

Answer: D
Diff: 2   Page Ref: 26.3
Skill: Conceptual

84) The human population is currently following roughly a J-shaped curve. This means that the population is growing

    A) arithmetically.

    B) sigmoidally.

    C) at a decreasing rate.

    D) by a boom–and–bust cycle.

    E) exponentially.

Answer: E
Diff: 1   Page Ref: 26.4
Skill: Factual

85) Human populations have continued to grow because humans have increased the _____ of the Earth through agriculture, medicine, and technology.

    A) biotic potential

    B) evolutionary pressure

    C) environmental resistance

    D) fertility

    E) carrying capacity

Answer: E
Diff: 2   Page Ref: 26.4
Skill: Conceptual

86) In the 18th and 19th centuries people increased the capacity of the Earth to support more humans by the discoveries of the _____ revolution.

    A) cultural

    B) agricultural

    C) industrial–medical

    D) social

    E) demographic

Answer: C
Diff: 2   Page Ref: 26.4
Skill: Factual

87) Which BEST describes the reason for the very rapid growth of the human population in the last 8,000 years?

    A) Humans have a late-loss survivorship curve.

    B) Environmental resistance does not apply to humans.

    C) Climatic change has allowed the human species to expand its range.

    D) Technology has allowed the species to overcome some environmental resistance.

    E) The biotic potential for humans has increased.

Answer: D
Diff: 2   Page Ref: 26.4
Skill: Conceptual

88) Population growth rates are high in less-developed countries because

    A) medicines have lowered death rates.

    B) wealth has not yet come with its lowered birth rates.

    C) children are often an important economic advantage.

    D) social traditions support large families.

    E) All of these are important reasons why population growth is high in less-developed countries.

Answer: E
Diff: 2   Page Ref: 26.4
Skill: Factual

89) In areas with a stable population, the number of children born in a period of time is

    A) increasing.

    B) decreasing.

    C) approximately equal to the number of adults.

    D) higher than the number of adults.

    E) lower than the number of adults.

Answer: C
Diff: 1   Page Ref: 26.4
Skill: Conceptual

90) In countries such as Nigeria, which have large numbers of children under age 15, the population is

 A) becoming larger.

 B) becoming smaller.

 C) staying the same.

 D) hard to predict.

 E) able to expand their carrying capacity.

Answer: A
Diff: 2   Page Ref: 26.4
Skill: Conceptual

91) If a population's age structure diagram looks like a pyramid, the

 A) population is expanding.

 B) population is remaining the same.

 C) population will expand for at least a generation.

 D) population is showing continuous exponential growth.

 E) population has reached its carrying capacity.

Answer: A
Diff: 2   Page Ref: 26.4
Skill: Conceptual

92) In countries such as France in which the number of children below 15 is approximately equal to the number between 15 and 45, the population is

 A) expanding slowly.

 B) stable.

 C) shrinking slightly.

 D) growing exponentially.

 E) declining drastically.

Answer: B
Diff: 2   Page Ref: 26.4
Skill: Conceptual

93) Developing countries tend to have a(n) _____ age diagram.

    A) rectangular-shaped

    B) inverted triangle-shaped

    C) pyramid-shaped

    D) square

    E) round

Answer: C
Diff: 2   Page Ref: 26.4
Skill: Conceptual

94) If people in less-developed countries reached replacement-level fertility immediately, their populations would

    A) decline slowly.

    B) decline rapidly.

    C) become stable.

    D) continue to grow for many years.

    E) grow for a short time and then decline rapidly.

Answer: D
Diff: 3   Page Ref: 26.4
Skill: Conceptual

95) The population of the United States continues to grow as a result of

    A) immigration.

    B) babies born to baby boom generation parents.

    C) the birth rate being above replacement level fertility during the 1940s through 1960s.

    D) reducing death rates as a result of better medical care.

    E) All of the above are causes of population growth in the United States.

Answer: E
Diff: 3   Page Ref: 26.4
Skill: Factual

96) Americans use about _____ times as much energy as the world average.

    A) 1.5   B) 2   C) 5   D) 10   E) 20

Answer: C
Diff: 2   Page Ref: 26.4
Skill: Factual

97) The United Nations estimates that by 2050 the world's population may reach about _____ billion and still be growing.

    A) 7.0   B) 9.0   C) 12.4   D) 15.6   E) 20.5

Answer: B
Diff: 2   *Page Ref: 26.4*
Skill: Factual

98) If all people in the world were to live at the level which Americans live in terms of technology, wealth, education, etc., the population of the world would have to _____ in order to support them.

    A) double

    B) reduce by half

    C) reduce to a fifth of current levels

    D) reduce to less than a tenth of the current population

    E) decline by 90%

Answer: C
Diff: 2   *Page Ref: 26.4*
Skill: Conceptual

99) Which developed country has the fastest population growth rate today?

    A) France

    B) Denmark

    C) China

    D) the United States

    E) Russia

Answer: D
Diff: 1   *Page Ref: 26.4*
Skill: Factual

100) At present, the Earth's human population is

    A) stable.

    B) declining.

    C) increasing exponentially.

    D) increasing at a constant rate.

    E) increasing at about 10% per year.

Answer: C
Diff: 2   *Page Ref: 26.4*
Skill: Factual

101) A population grows exponentially when

    A) the birth rate and the death rate are equal.

    B) the birth rate exceeds the death rate and there is no immigration or emigration.

    C) emigration exceeds immigration and the birth rate equals the death rate.

    D) the death rate equals the birth rate and immigration is equal to emigration.

    E) the carrying capacity is exceeded.

Answer: B
Diff: 2   Page Ref: 26.4
Skill: Conceptual

102) The blame for rapidly progressing worldwide environmental degradation lies with

    A) the developing countries due to their large and expanding populations.

    B) the developed countries due to their large per capita use of resources and production of wastes.

    C) both the developing and developed countries as each plays a part.

    D) neither the developing nor developed countries as environmental degradation is inevitable.

    E) no one; there is no environmental degradation occurring.

Answer: C
Diff: 2   Page Ref: 26.4
Skill: Application

103) As a developing country passes through the demographic transition

    A) its age structure changes but growth rate remains unchanged.

    B) its birth and death rates decline simultaneously.

    C) its growth rate first falls but later recovers.

    D) first its birth rate declines, followed by its death rate.

    E) first its death rate declines, followed by its birth rate.

Answer: E
Diff: 2   Page Ref: 26.4
Skill: Factual

104) Malthus' prediction that our human population would eventually reach a point where we cannot sustain ourselves has not yet occurred. This is because

A) dramatic reductions in fertility rates have brought an end to population growth before this crisis point was reached.

B) Malthus was wrong; human populations can grow indefinitely.

C) technological advances unforeseen by Malthus have raised carrying capacity more and faster than predicted.

D) the two world wars and AIDS crisis have caused such massive mortality that the human population has stabilized.

E) the human population continues to find ways to enhance environmental quality, allowing more people to be supported.

Answer: C
Diff: 2   Page Ref: 26.4
Skill: Application

105) If adults of reproductive age are having just enough children to replace themselves, then the population is said to have _____ fertility.

Answer: replacement level
Diff: 1   Page Ref: 26.4
Skill: Factual

106) Just after the Industrial Revolution, many countries in Europe had expanding populations: infant mortality went down and family size increased. However, after World War II, many countries in Eastern Europe are actually declining in population as families choose to have either one child or no children. Draw the two age–structure diagrams for a country such as Hungary, with first the post–Industrial Revolution scenario, and then the current scenario. Hint: number of individuals by age is represented on the x–axis, and age is represented on the y–axis.

Answer: The diagrams should look like the expanding and the shrinking diagrams of Figure 26–19 in the textbook.
Diff: 3   Page Ref: 26.4
Skill: Application

107) The U.S. fertility rate is currently 2.03, meaning that the average family has 2.03 offspring. This is below 2.1, which is considered to be replacement level fertility (RLF) in developed countries. Why is the actual RLF not 2? Also, if the United States has replacement level fertility, why is the population still growing rapidly?

Answer: RLF is 2.1 because parents must replace both themselves and children who die before reaching maturity. Immigration, and lag timing of the baby boom is causing the U.S. population to expand.
Diff: 2   Page Ref: 26.4
Skill: Factual

108) Where do most of the people in the world live today, in developed or developing countries?

   Answer: Most of the people live in developing countries.
   Diff: 1   *Page Ref: 26.4*
   Skill: Factual

109) Why has it been so hard to come up with an accurate measure of the carrying capacity of the Earth for humans?

   Answer: This has been difficult because humans have the ability to increase their own carrying
          capacity by a series of revolutions in agriculture, industry, and medicine.
   Diff: 2   *Page Ref: 26.4*
   Skill: Conceptual

110) What factors determine the Earth's carrying capacity for humans?

   Answer: Human carrying capacity is determined by the amount of water, light, nutrients, and
          space available to sustain the maximum human population size indefinitely.
   Diff: 2   *Page Ref: 26.4*
   Skill: Conceptual

111) Many people in developed countries consider the expanding populations of developing countries to be responsible for Earth's environmental woes. However, many people in developing countries point to the much greater "ecological footprint" of each person in the developed countries as the principle cause. Who *is* responsible for the unprecedented resource depletion, habitat destruction and pollution we are currently experiencing? Include in your answer a list of at least *four* components of an individual's ecological footprint and how these two groups compare for each.

   Answer: Both groups are responsible. While population growth has slowed in most developed
          countries, each individual uses far more resources and produces far more wastes than
          their counterparts in developing countries. And while their *per capita* consumption of
          resources and production of wastes are far less, the rapidly expanding populations of
          developing countries are also having a major impact. Ecological footprint includes
          demand for food (crops, livestock, fishing, etc.), housing (including timber, concrete,
          etc.), fuel (for cooking and heat), transportation (including fuel and road), and other
          goods and services. All of these are much greater per capita in developed countries.
   Diff: 3   *Page Ref: 26.4*
   Skill: Application

112) Over the past 50 years, the amount of cropland per person has

   A) decreased by 90%.

   B) decreased by over half.

   C) decreased slightly.

   D) stayed about the same.

   E) increased slightly.

   Answer: B
   Diff: 2   *Page Ref: Earth Watch*
   Skill: Factual

Chapter 27 Community Interactions

1) Introduced or exotic species like the zebra mussel often explode in numbers, reaching densities in their new homes far greater than they ever did in their original range. This is most likely because

    A) chemical and physical conditions in the new home are more favorable for growth and reproduction.

    B) food and other resources are more plentiful in the new home.

    C) the highly mobile colonists that reach the new home are usually genetically superior to the sedentary individuals that stay behind.

    D) the competitors, predators, and parasites with which they evolved and which normally keep them in check are not present in the new home.

    E) all of these

Answer: D
Diff: 2   Page Ref: Case Study
Skill: Conceptual

2) In the process called _____ species act as agents of natural selection on each other.

    A) succession

    B) commensalism

    C) competition

    D) symbiosis

    E) coevolution

Answer: E
Diff: 1   Page Ref: 27.1
Skill: Conceptual

3) Which of the following is NOT a major category of interspecific or intraspecific interaction among organisms?

    A) symbiosis

    B) predation

    C) competition

    D) speciation

    E) mutualism

Answer: D
Diff: 2   Page Ref: 27.1
Skill: Conceptual

4) The biologist who studies interactions at the "community" level investigates interactions between

    A) organisms of one species.

    B) organisms of more than one species.

    C) animals of one species.

    D) social animals (like insects).

    E) ecosystems.

Answer: B
Diff: 2   Page Ref: 27.1
Skill: Conceptual

5) Over the course of their evolutionary histories, the timing of flowering, spacing of plants, and nectar rewards of flowering plants have influenced the foraging behavior of bees, which has in turn influenced the morphology of flowers. This is an example of

    A) adaptive radiation.

    B) coevolution.

    C) competitive exclusion.

    D) convergent evolution.

    E) niche partitioning.

Answer: B
Diff: 2   Page Ref: 27.1
Skill: Conceptual

6) Predation in similar to _____ in that both types of relationship benefit one of the interacting species while the other is harmed.

    A) commensalism

    B) competition

    C) mutualism

    D) parasitism

    E) symbiosis

Answer: D
Diff: 2   Page Ref: 27.1
Skill: Conceptual

7) What is the relationship between an ecosystem and a community?

Answer: A community consists of all the interacting populations within an ecosystem. The ecosystem includes the abiotic environment as well as all plant and animal communities.
Diff: 2   Page Ref: 27.1
Skill: Conceptual

8) If you were studying the niche of a species of bird, you might study

    A) the food it eats.

    B) its predators.

    C) the temperatures it needs to survive.

    D) the places where it builds its nests.

    E) all of these

Answer: E
Diff: 1   Page Ref: 27.2
Skill: Conceptual

9) Which of the following is the BEST way to define an ecological niche?

    A) the physical environmental factors needed for survival

    B) the organism's home or habitat

    C) an organism's interactions with predators and prey species

    D) all the aspects of an organism's way of life

    E) the intraspecific behavior of the species

Answer: D
Diff: 2   Page Ref: 27.2
Skill: Conceptual

10) An ecological niche

    A) is formed by the physical environment only.

    B) depends on the weather.

    C) is a constantly changing place.

    D) cannot be shared by two species.

    E) is the same thing as its habitat.

Answer: D
Diff: 2   Page Ref: 27.2
Skill: Conceptual

11) Competition between members of two species is

    A) very intense, and referred to as intraspecific.

    B) most intense when the species are most similar, and referred to as interspecific.

    C) very unusual, and referred to as interspecific.

    D) very common, and referred to as intraspecific.

    E) least intense between similar species, and referred to as interspecific.

Answer: B
Diff: 2   Page Ref: 27.2
Skill: Factual

12) Two species that have a high degree of niche overlap will

    A) compete intensely.

    B) speciate.

    C) interbreed.

    D) be a predator–prey pair.

    E) coexist peacefully.

Answer: A
Diff: 2   Page Ref: 27.2
Skill: Conceptual

13) If similar species each occupy a smaller niche when they live together than they would if they lived alone, they are said to be

    A) involved in succession.

    B) involved in intraspecific competition.

    C) partitioning their resources.

    D) coevolving.

    E) increasing niche overlap.

Answer: C
Diff: 2   Page Ref: 27.2
Skill: Conceptual

14) Which of these outcomes is most likely in a natural situation when two closely related species compete for resources in the same habitat?

    A) Population size and distribution of each species may be reduced.

    B) Interbreeding between the two species will occur.

    C) One of the species will become extinct.

    D) Both species will become extinct.

    E) Distribution and size of both populations will increase.

Answer: A
Diff: 2   Page Ref: 27.2
Skill: Conceptual

15) The concept that two species cannot occupy the same ecological niche is called

A) coevolution.

B) mutualism.

C) succession.

D) the competitive exclusion principle.

E) commensalism.

Answer: D
Diff: 1   Page Ref: 27.2
Skill: Factual

16) Ornithologists visiting an island find two species of bird which appear nearly identical except for bill size. Which of the following is the most likely explanation they could offer to explain their discovery?

A) natural random variability

B) Coevolution of the two species has resulted in resource partitioning between the species.

C) Mutations and natural selection has resulted in an inferior species with defective bills.

D) sexual selection

E) the need to camouflage against prey

Answer: B
Diff: 2   Page Ref: 27.2
Skill: Conceptual

17) In interspecific competition,

A) both species benefit from the interaction because each species expands its ecological niche.

B) both species are harmed because access to resources is reduced.

C) one species is harmed because only one species can expand its ecological niche.

D) Either A or B may be true.

E) Either A or C may be true.

Answer: B
Diff: 2   Page Ref: 27.2
Skill: Conceptual

18) Earthworms live in many grass and forest ecosystems, and aerate soil as they burrow. They also may mix soil horizons as they ingest organic matter and travel between horizons. These traits, taken collectively, refer to the _____ of the Earthworm.

   A) niche

   B) habitat

   C) community profile

   D) ecosystem profile

   E) resource partition profile

Answer: A
Diff: 2   Page Ref: 27.2
Skill: Conceptual

19) Two species of buttercup can be found in the same field in South Dakota; but they emerge at different times: one species emerges and flowers in early spring, and the other species does not emerge until the late summer, after the first species has set seed. This is likely to be an example of

   A) habitat fragmentation.

   B) niche fragmentation.

   C) niche realignment.

   D) resource partitioning.

   E) intraspecific competition.

Answer: D
Diff: 2   Page Ref: 27.2
Skill: Conceptual

20) Two species of buttercup can be found in a field in North Dakota, and they tend to flower at the same approximate time in early spring. When some ecology students decide to conduct an experiment in community dynamics, they selectively remove one species from the field by hand picking all emergent plants. When the one species is removed, the other species shows a significant increase in its population size the next season. This study demonstrates

   A) habitat fragmentation.

   B) niche fragmentation.

   C) niche realignment.

   D) intraspecific competition.

   E) interspecific competition.

Answer: E
Diff: 2   Page Ref: 27.2
Skill: Conceptual

21) On the slopes of the Washington Cascades, ecologists have studied some closely related vole species for decades. Many of these vole species, when they occur on separate mountains from each other, tend to have very similar food size choices. However, when these species occur together on a mountain slope, their food choices tend to differ, with some species selecting small seeds and others feeding exclusively on larger seeds. This may be an example of

   A) niche fragmentation.

   B) resource partitioning.

   C) habitat fragmentation.

   D) intraspecific competition.

   E) intraspecific range diversion.

Answer: B
Diff: 2   Page Ref: 27.2
Skill: Factual

22) In his 1961 paper, "The Paradox of the Plankton," ecologist G.E. Hutchinson noted that several species of algae coexist sharing the same few mineral nutrient resources in homogeneous open water systems. As there is little chance of resource partitioning and niche differentiation in such a situation, the paradox of their coexistence is the apparent violation of

   A) Darwin's theory of evolution by means of natural selection.

   B) the climax theory of succession.

   C) the competitive exclusion principle.

   D) the law of mass action.

   E) the second law of thermodynamics.

Answer: C
Diff: 2   Page Ref: 27.2
Skill: Application

23) In his study of the forging behavior of bumblebees, D.W. Inouye noted that both *Bombus appositus* and *Bombus flavifrons* feed from both larkspur and monkshood flowers when they were the only bumblebee species present. However, when both species were present, *B. appositus* feeds only on larkspur and *B. flavifrons* specializes on monkshood. This is an example of

   A) aggressive mimicry.

   B) commensalism.

   C) intraspecific competition.

   D) resource partitioning.

   E) habitat fragmentation.

Answer: D
Diff: 2   Page Ref: 27.2
Skill: Application

24) Over the past century, sagebrush has dramatically expanded its range over the Colorado Plateau's grasslands. This has been attributed to the overgrazing of the area's grasses by cattle and sheep. This example indicates that

    A) grazing has no effect on the distribution of plants.

    B) sagebrush could not exist anywhere in the absence of cattle and sheep.

    C) sagebrush is the dominant competitor over grasses.

    D) the range of sagebrush is normally limited by competition with grasses.

    E) the relationship between sagebrush and grasses is mutualistic.

Answer: D
Diff: 3   Page Ref: 27.2
Skill: Application

25) The physical home of a species is its _____.

Answer: habitat
Diff: 2   Page Ref: 27.2
Skill: Factual

26) The "occupation" of a species in its community is known as its _____.

Answer: niche
Diff: 1   Page Ref: 27.2
Skill: Factual

27) Choose one of the following kinds of organisms and name as many aspects of its niche as you can think of.
    A. Bear
    B. Oak tree
    C. Crabgrass in your yard
    D. Grasshopper
    E. Rattlesnake

Answer: Students should include both abiotic and biotic aspects of the niche.
Diff: 3   Page Ref: 27.2
Skill: Application

28) What factor most determines the intensity of interspecific competition?

Answer: the degree of similarity between the competing species
Diff: 3   Page Ref: 27.2
Skill: Factual

29) What effect is coevolution most likely to have on niche overlap?

Answer: Coevolution will minimize overlap.
Diff: 2   Page Ref: 27.2
Skill: Conceptual

30) Several ecology students were tracking the population ranges of two species of squirrels that live in the Cascade range of Oregon. These students noted that when both species of squirrels were present in a region, species A could be found from sea level to about 900 feet above sea level, and species B could be found from about 900 feet to 1500 feet above sea level. However, when species B was found alone, then it had a range of about 500 feet to 1500 feet. Why might this be true?

Answer: These observations illustrate the competitive exclusion principle: two species cannot occupy exactly the same niche, so when habitats overlap, one species will exclude the other.
Diff: 2   Page Ref: 27.2
Skill: Application

31) What evidence did Gause and MacArthur find for the competitive exclusion principle?

Answer: Summarize the paramecium experiments and the warbler observations.
Diff: 2   Page Ref: 27.2
Skill: Factual

32) If an insect eats the lettuce seedlings in your yard, it is acting most like a(n)

A) parasite.

B) host.

C) mutualist.

D) commensalist.

E) herbivore.

Answer: E
Diff: 1   Page Ref: 27.3
Skill: Conceptual

33) If you find a brightly colored insect resting on a dead leaf, it is likely to

A) be poisonous or distasteful.

B) be prey for birds.

C) be camouflaged.

D) have startle coloration.

E) have aggressive mimicry.

Answer: A
Diff: 1   Page Ref: 27.3
Skill: Conceptual

34) Which of the following statements BEST describes the reason why bright coloration is an effective defense against predators?

   A) The predators are color blind and cannot see the prey.

   B) The predators can see the color and, either through natural selection (if the prey is toxic) or learning (if the prey is merely unpalatable), avoid the prey.

   C) Predatory animals are not intelligent enough to learn anything, so color is unimportant.

   D) Symbiosis allows predators to coexist with prey so that neither goes extinct.

   E) Commensal relationships such as this are the result of coevolution.

Answer: B
Diff: 1   Page Ref: 27.3
Skill: Conceptual

35) An effective, bright, and very distinct color pattern that can be displayed suddenly by a prey species to scare a predator is an example of

   A) modeling.

   B) aggressive mimicry.

   C) mimicry.

   D) startle coloration.

   E) camouflage.

Answer: D
Diff: 2   Page Ref: 27.3
Skill: Factual

36) A species that is a mimic may

   A) form chemicals that deter predators.

   B) have behavior similar to that of another species.

   C) resemble their surroundings.

   D) use bright colors to warn that they are harmful.

   E) produce "smoke screens."

Answer: B
Diff: 3   Page Ref: 27.3
Skill: Conceptual

37) Which of these describes an effective means that prey species may use to evade predators?

A) mimicry

B) warning coloration

C) chemical warfare

D) startle coloration

E) all of these

Answer: E
Diff: 1   Page Ref: 27.3
Skill: Factual

38) Which of these might a predator use to enable it to catch its prey?

A) startle coloration

B) warning coloration

C) camouflage

D) symbiosis

E) coevolution

Answer: C
Diff: 2   Page Ref: 27.3
Skill: Factual

39) Which behavioral response to the threat of predation is most likely to be selected for in a species that uses camouflage for protection from predators?

A) a quick escape response

B) sudden display to startle the predator

C) cooperative behavior

D) behavior that mimics the behavior of the predator

E) motionless behavior

Answer: E
Diff: 2   Page Ref: 27.3
Skill: Conceptual

40) Trees often produce secondary chemicals to deter herbivores from feeding on their leaves; in turn, many herbivores have produced ways of avoiding or detoxifying these chemicals. This is an example of

A) competitive exclusion.

B) predatory avoidance.

C) coevolution.

D) parasitic evolution.

E) parasite predation.

Answer: C
Diff: 2   Page Ref: 27.3
Skill: Conceptual

41) The term mimicry may refer to

A) prey species imitating the predators.

B) nontoxic prey imitating toxic prey.

C) predators imitating something that is attractive to prey.

D) A and B but not C

E) A, B, and C

Answer: E
Diff: 2   Page Ref: 27.3
Skill: Conceptual

42) The tiny wasp *Ooencyrtus kuvanae* lays its eggs inside the egg masses of gypsy moths. When the wasp larvae hatch, they burrow into the gypsy moth caterpillars and eat them from the inside. When they have completed their development, the adult wasps emerge from the bodies of the moth caterpillars, killing them in the process. While this relationship has several of the characteristics of parasitism, it is more properly classified as

A) commensalism.

B) competition.

C) mutualism.

D) predation.

E) resource partitioning.

Answer: D
Diff: 2   Page Ref: 27.3
Skill: Application

43) Harmless king snakes mimic the color patterns of venomous coral snakes, which serve as models. If avoidance were based solely on prior predator experience with the model, what do you predict would happen in areas where coral snakes were never present?

    A) Predators would initially attack and eat king snakes but soon learn to avoid them.

    B) Predators would attack and eat king snakes.

    C) Predators would avoid king snakes.

    D) Predators would initially avoid king snakes but soon learn to attack and eat them.

    E) No predictions can be made based on the information given.

Answer: B
Diff: 2   Page Ref: 27.3
Skill: Application

44) Over their history, cucumber plants have evolved a number of chemicals to deter herbivorous insects. However, cucumber beetles have evolved ways to detoxify each new plant toxin as it arose. Which of the following statements applies to this situation?

    A) Cucumber beetles are generalist herbivores, eating many different plants.

    B) Cucumbers and cucumber beetles have not acted as agents of natural selection driving each other's evolution.

    C) Many different species of herbivorous insects will be able to feed on cucumbers.

    D) To make their efforts of developing detoxification mechanisms worthwhile, cucumber beetles have come to specialize on eating cucumbers.

    E) all of these

Answer: D
Diff: 2   Page Ref: 27.3
Skill: Application

45) Many plants produce chemicals which are used as medicines. For example the heart drug digitalis, which stimulates the heart, is derived from foxglove, a poisonous plant. What advantage does producing such compounds have for the plant?

Answer: In the plant they are poisons, which we use in small doses as medicines. These protect the plant by making the herbivore sick or killing it.
Diff: 2   Page Ref: 27.3
Skill: Application

46) How may a predator use mimicry to its own advantage?

Answer: It may resemble something attractive, such as food, so that prey will actively come to it.
Diff: 1   Page Ref: 27.3
Skill: Conceptual

47) Write a paragraph comparing the color (or lack of color) that you would most likely see on an insect that is poisonous with one that is slow-moving prey for birds. Explain why there are such differences.

Answer: The student should describe a brightly colored insect and a camouflaged one. They may also mention that the harmless one could be a mimic and look harmful.
Diff: 2   Page Ref: 27.3
Skill: Conceptual

48) There are several species of plain-looking, brownish-gray moths which, when they spread their wings, have large bright red or orange eye-shaped circles on their hind wings. What is this called and what advantage does it give to the moth?

Answer: This is startle coloration. It enables the moth to scare away an approaching predator at the same time that it flies away.
Diff: 2   Page Ref: 27.3
Skill: Factual

49) A close interaction between organisms of two different species which is beneficial to one of the organisms but has no effect on the survival of the other is

   A) mutualism.

   B) commensalism.

   C) parasitism.

   D) mimicry.

   E) symbiosis.

Answer: B
Diff: 1   Page Ref: 27.4
Skill: Factual

50) In its broadest sense, symbiosis includes which of the following relationships between organisms of two different species?

   A) mutualism, predation, commensalism

   B) mutualism, predation, parasitism

   C) predation, commensalism, parasitism

   D) mutualism, commensalism, parasitism

   E) mutualism, commensalism, competition

Answer: D
Diff: 2   Page Ref: 27.4
Skill: Conceptual

51) Which of the following is NOT an example of two organisms in a mutualistic relationship?

    A) humans and malaria protozoan

    B) flowering plants and pollinators

    C) ants and acacias

    D) clown fish and sea anemone

    E) nitrogen–fixing bacteria and legumes

Answer: A
Diff: 2   *Page Ref: 27.4*
Skill: Factual

52) Which of the following is NOT an example of two organisms in a parasitic relationship?

    A) carnivorous plant and the insect it captures

    B) Human Immunodeficiency Virus (the AIDS virus) and an infected human

    C) lamprey eel and the fish whose blood it feeds on

    D) tapeworm and the goat whose digestive tract it lives in

    E) flea and the cat it lives on

Answer: A
Diff: 2   *Page Ref: 27.4*
Skill: Conceptual

53) What characteristic best distinguishes predators from parasites?

    A) Predators feed on large animals, parasites attack small organisms.

    B) Predators are long–lived, parasites are short–lived.

    C) Predators kill their hosts immediately, parasites usually do not kill their hosts immediately.

    D) Predators attack both healthy and weak organisms, parasites attack primarily weakened or old organisms.

    E) Predators always harm their prey, parasites have a mutualistic relationship with their hosts.

Answer: C
Diff: 2   *Page Ref: 27.4*
Skill: Factual

54) Tapeworms in the human gut are an example of

    A) predators.

    B) parasites.

    C) hosts.

    D) commensalists.

    E) prey.

Answer: B
Diff: 2   Page Ref: 27.4
Skill: Factual

55) Sap-feeding insects that feed on plants without consuming them completely may be classified as

    A) predators.

    B) parasites.

    C) hosts.

    D) commensalists.

    E) prey.

Answer: B
Diff: 2   Page Ref: 27.4
Skill: Application

56) Many plants are mycorrhizal, where their roots are infected with a specialized fungus. The plant supplies carbon to the fungus, and the fungus supplies nutrients to the plant. The relationship between these plants and the mycorrhizae fungi is an example of a _____ association.

    A) mutualistic

    B) commensalistic

    C) parasitic

    D) successional

    E) predator/prey

Answer: A
Diff: 2   Page Ref: 27.4
Skill: Conceptual

57) Remoras are tiny bony fishes that temporarily attach to the sides of sharks and feed on scraps of food left over when the sharks dine. The remoras get food and transportation out of the relationship while the sharks are unaffected. This is an example of a

A) commensalism.

B) competitive relationship.

C) mutualism.

D) parasitism.

E) predatory relationship.

Answer: A
Diff: 2   Page Ref: 27.4
Skill: Conceptual

58) The Masai tribesmen of Africa regularly consume the blood and milk of their cattle. Based on this information alone we might classify this relationship as a _____. However, if it turns out that the cattle actually derive a net benefit as the herdsman also protect them from predators and help them find water and food, this relationship would instead best be classified as a _____.

A) commensalism; mutualism

B) mutualism; competition

C) parasitism; commensalism

D) parasitism; mutualism

E) predation; parasitism

Answer: D
Diff: 3   Page Ref: 27.4
Skill: Application

59) Aphids pierce the tissues of plants with their tubular mouthparts and suck out their phloem juices. Since this food is mostly sugar water with a low concentration of protein, they have to process large volumes of it to obtain sufficient protein. Most of the excess sugar and water passes right through the aphids' digestive tracts and are defecated as "honeydew," which is actively sought out and eaten by some ants. The ants will even "milk" honeydew by stroking the aphids. In return, ants protect their aphids from predators, even going as far as taking them inside overnight! The relationship between the aphids and plants is a _____, while that between aphids and ants is a _____.

A) commensalism; mutualism

B) mutualism; competition

C) parasitism; commensalism

D) parasitism; mutualism

E) predation; parasitism

Answer: D
Diff: 3   Page Ref: 27.4
Skill: Application

60) Nitrogen fixing bacteria get a place to live and energy while supplying nitrogen to a plant. What ecological relationship is being described?

A) predation

B) parasitism

C) mutualism

D) commensalism

E) competition

Answer: C
Diff: 1   Page Ref: 27.4
Skill: Conceptual

61) A bat pollinates a plant while obtaining nectar from it. What ecological relationship is being described?

A) predation

B) parasitism

C) mutualism

D) commensalism

E) competition

Answer: C
Diff: 1   Page Ref: 27.4
Skill: Conceptual

62) Birds pick parasitic insects from the skin of large animals such as elephants or bison. What ecological relationship is being described?

A) predation

B) parasitism

C) mutualism

D) commensalism

E) competition

Answer: C
Diff: 2   Page Ref: 27.4
Skill: Conceptual

63) Fleas feed on the blood of dogs, cats and people. What ecological relationship is being described?

   A) predation

   B) parasitism

   C) mutualism

   D) commensalism

   E) competition

Answer: B
Diff: 2   Page Ref: 27.4
Skill: Conceptual

64) Insectivorous plants capture and consume insects. What ecological relationship is being described?

   A) predation

   B) parasitism

   C) mutualism

   D) commensalism

   E) competition

Answer: A
Diff: 1   Page Ref: 27.4
Skill: Conceptual

65) Hawks and owls eat field mice. What ecological relationship is being described?

   A) predation

   B) parasitism

   C) mutualism

   D) commensalism

   E) competition

Answer: A
Diff: 1   Page Ref: 27.4
Skill: Conceptual

66) Birds follow animal herds to catch insects that are disturbed as the large animals walk through the grass. What ecological relationship is being described?

   A) predation

   B) parasitism

   C) mutualism

   D) commensalism

   E) competition

Answer: D
Diff: 2   Page Ref: 27.4
Skill: Conceptual

67) Humans contract bacterial infections like tuberculosis or syphilis. What ecological relationship is being described?

   A) predation

   B) parasitism

   C) mutualism

   D) commensalism

   E) competition

Answer: B
Diff: 3   Page Ref: 27.4
Skill: Conceptual

68) Parasites kill their hosts, while predators do not. True or False?

Answer: FALSE
Diff: 1   Page Ref: 27.4
Skill: Factual

69) Commensalism is a relationship in which one species benefits and one species is harmed. True or False?

Answer: FALSE
Diff: 1   Page Ref: 27.4
Skill: Factual

70) Parasites are generally smaller than their prey. True or False?

Answer: TRUE
Diff: 1   Page Ref: 27.4
Skill: Factual

71) In a symbiotic relationship, both species benefit from the association. True or False?

Answer: FALSE
Diff: 2   Page Ref: 27.4
Skill: Factual

72) Most bacteria can reproduce very quickly, allowing their population sizes to rapidly increase. Describe the evolutionary process which prevents most human disease-causing bacterial parasites from causing the human population to become extinct.

Answer: Coevolution between parasites and their hosts favors selection for hosts that can survive infection (until after they have reproduced) and parasites which maintain their infectious capabilities.
Diff: 3   Page Ref: 27.4
Skill: Conceptual

73) In what ways are *Pseudomyrmex* ants and bull's-horn acacias dependent on each other? What type of interspecific interaction is this?

Answer: This is a mutualistic relationship; ants get sugar and protein, and acacias get protection.
Diff: 3   Page Ref: Scientific Inquiry
Skill: Factual

74) A species that plays a major role in determining the structure of its ecological community is

A) a predator.

B) a dominator species.

C) the most abundant species in the community.

D) a keystone species.

E) the species with the largest size.

Answer: D
Diff: 2   Page Ref: 27.5
Skill: Factual

75) The African elephant is considered to be a keystone species because

A) removal of elephants from their community would result in drastic changes in the ecological structure of the community.

B) it is the largest organism in its community.

C) elephants live in large cooperative herds that dominate other smaller groups within the community.

D) elephants eat more food than any other species in their community.

E) elephant populations are larger than any other populations of organisms in their community.

Answer: A
Diff: 2   Page Ref: 27.5
Skill: Conceptual

76) Ecologist Paul Ehrlich likened species in a community to rivets holding together an airplane. He stated that airplanes can lose some of their rivets with no ill effects, but may suffer catastrophic failures if too many are lost. We could extend this analogy to state that some rivets are so crucial that they must be retained for the integrity of the airplane. These latter rivets represent

  A) climax species.

  B) keystone species.

  C) pioneer species.

  D) primary producers.

  E) top carnivores.

Answer: B
Diff: 3   Page Ref: 27.5
Skill: Conceptual

77) A certain species of animal represents just 3% of the biomass in its ecosystem. We might classify this as a keystone species if its elimination

  A) allowed an even rarer species to increase in numbers and take its place.

  B) caused 2% of the other species in the community to disappear.

  C) caused the diversity of the plant community to decline by 40%.

  D) caused plant biomass to increase 5%.

  E) had no effect on the community whatsoever.

Answer: C
Diff: 2   Page Ref: 27.5
Skill: Application

78) You suspect that the American alligator is a keystone species in specific habitats in Florida. How might you experimentally prove or disprove this hypothesis?

  Answer: You could conduct removal experiments. If removal of the species in question dramatically alters the composition of the community, it was likely a keystone species.
  Diff: 2   Page Ref: 27.5
  Skill: Conceptual

79) When all vegetation is removed from a site by human activity or by natural forces such as volcanic activity, _____ species are the first to colonize the site.

A) prokaryotic

B) pioneer

C) climax

D) deciduous

E) eukaryotic

Answer: B
Diff: 2   Page Ref: 27.6
Skill: Factual

80) Which of the following is NOT TRUE of the general trend from recently disturbed to stable self-sustaining community?

A) An increase in depth and organic content of soil occurs.

B) Long-lived species become dominant in the community.

C) Productivity increases.

D) The rate at which populations replace each other increases.

E) All of the choices above are true of a community that is developing towards a climax community.

Answer: D
Diff: 3   Page Ref: 27.6
Skill: Conceptual

81) Succession which begins on bare rock after glaciers have passed, or on newly formed volcanic islands, is

A) primary.

B) secondary.

C) allogenic.

D) pioneer.

E) autogenic.

Answer: A
Diff: 2   Page Ref: 27.6
Skill: Factual

82) A sand dune in Georgia might take several _____ years to reach a climax community, whereas a former corn field that has been left unfarmed is likely to take a couple of _____ years to reach the same climax.

    A) hundred; hundred

    B) thousand; hundred

    C) thousand; thousand

    D) hundred; thousand

    E) million; thousand

Answer: B
Diff: 2   Page Ref: 27.6
Skill: Factual

83) The first community that forms on bare rock often has organisms such as

    A) herbs and conifers.

    B) grasses and weeds.

    C) broad–leaf trees and conifers.

    D) lichens and moss.

    E) woody shrubs and conifers.

Answer: D
Diff: 2   Page Ref: 27.6
Skill: Conceptual

84) When succession occurs after a field is abandoned in the southeastern U.S., the rich soil and intense sunlight allow fast–growing species such as _____ to thrive.

    A) ragweed and crabgrass

    B) mosses

    C) pine trees

    D) oaks and maples

    E) tulip poplars and sweetgum

Answer: A
Diff: 3   Page Ref: 27.6
Skill: Factual

85) Which of the following statements is TRUE of climax communities?

   A) All areas will have the same climax community if enough time is allowed for succession.

   B) The climax community which develops is determined by many factors such as temperature, rainfall, elevation and type of rock.

   C) The climax community at a site changes rapidly.

   D) As the Earth gets older the area covered by climax communities is increasing.

   E) Climax communities are made up of all the species that were found in each successional community.

Answer: B
Diff: 2   Page Ref: 27.6
Skill: Conceptual

86) After a forested area such as a national forest is clear cut, what type of succession occurs?

   A) primary

   B) secondary

   C) subclimax

   D) climax

   E) biome

Answer: B
Diff: 1   Page Ref: 27.6
Skill: Conceptual

87) The next time you need to mow the grass, you can excuse yourself on the basis that by mowing you are helping to maintain a man–made _____.

   A) climax community

   B) subclimax community

   C) biome

   D) ecosystem

   E) population

Answer: B
Diff: 2   Page Ref: 27.6
Skill: Conceptual

88) When a community like the tallgrass prairie is maintained by regular disturbances such as periodic fires set by Native Americans or by lightning, a _____ community exists.

  A) pine forest

  B) subclimax

  C) climax

  D) pioneer

  E) deciduous

Answer: B
Diff: 2   Page Ref: 27.6
Skill: Conceptual

89) What ecological process changes a lake to a marsh over a long period of time?

  A) eutrophication

  B) competitive exclusion

  C) succession

  D) extinction

  E) coevolution

Answer: C
Diff: 2   Page Ref: 27.6
Skill: Conceptual

90) Which of the following is NOT likely to characterize pioneer plant species involved in primary succession?

  A) able to tolerate intense sunlight

  B) able to tolerate low nutrient levels

  C) produces many small seeds that can travel great distances

  D) slow-growing, long-lived perennial

  E) small plant size

Answer: D
Diff: 3   Page Ref: 27.6
Skill: Conceptual

91) Shade tolerant plant species are generally found early in succession, and are replaced by hardier, shade intolerant species. True or False?

Answer: FALSE
Diff: 2   Page Ref: 27.6
Skill: Factual

92) A farmer decides to retire, but he cannot find anyone to take over his farm. When he returns to look at the old place 15 years later, he finds that there are small trees and shrubs that grew in his fields. This is a result of the process known as _____.

Answer: secondary succession
Diff: 2   Page Ref: 27.6
Skill: Conceptual

93) The community that tends to persist in an area after succession is known as the _____ community.

Answer: climax
Diff: 1   Page Ref: 27.6
Skill: Factual

94) The productivity of an ecosystem usually _____ through succession.

Answer: increases
Diff: 1   Page Ref: 27.6
Skill: Factual

95) Succession in small ponds and lakes is usually dependent on the input of _____ from outside the ecosystem.

Answer: nutrients
Diff: 2   Page Ref: 27.6
Skill: Factual

96) Similar climax communities distributed over a very large geographical area are known as _____.

Answer: biomes
Diff: 1   Page Ref: 27.6
Skill: Factual

97) Succession after a catastrophic disturbance such as a volcanic eruption is referred to as a _____ succession.

Answer: primary
Diff: 1   Page Ref: 27.6
Skill: Factual

98) Succession after a disturbance such as forest harvest or a landslide is referred to as a _____ succession.

Answer: secondary
Diff: 1   Page Ref: 27.6
Skill: Factual

99) How do organisms help to cause the changes that result in their own replacement in succession?

Answer: They change the physical environment in ways that favor their competitors.
Diff: 3　　*Page Ref: 27.6*
Skill: Conceptual

100) What happens to the soil in an area as succession proceeds?

Answer: It increases in depth and organic material content.
Diff: 2　　*Page Ref: 27.6*
Skill: Factual

101) Which is the more rapid process, primary or secondary succession? Why?

Answer: Secondary succession is more rapid because soil and seeds are already present.
Diff: 2　　*Page Ref: 27.6*
Skill: Factual

102) What kinds of plant species are likely to be pioneers in secondary succession? Explain why.

Answer: Fast–growing annual weeds are likely to be pioneer species because they grow easily in direct sunlight, their seeds are already present, and they are able to root in the soil that is already present.
Diff: 3　　*Page Ref: 27.6*
Skill: Factual

103) After forest harvest in an old–growth forest of the Oregon Cascades, an ecologist noted that the species that were present after 5 years differed from the species that were present 25 year later, and these differed from the species that were present 75 years later. What are the general characteristics of the species at each stage, and why does the community change over time?

Answer: This is an example of secondary succession. The first species to colonize the cleared site are generally fast–growing, easily dispersed weedy species that are intolerant of shade. Fast–growing tree species eventually replace these weeds, and these in turn are replaced by shade tolerant, slow–growing tree species that can outcompete the other species to form a relatively stable climax community.
Diff: 3　　*Page Ref: 27.6*
Skill: Conceptual

104) Fire is increasingly used as a management tool in both forest and grassland ecosystems to increase species diversity. How might fire influence the occurrence of a climax community and species diversity?

Answer: Fire can encourage the growth of subclimax plants that generally occur earlier in successional development. This vegetational diversity may also encourage a greater animal diversity.
Diff: 3　　*Page Ref: 27.6*
Skill: Application

105) One species of walking stick insects may be dividing into two species because the two varieties

 A) have evolved different camouflage coloration.

 B) prefer to feed on different plants.

 C) prefer to mate with similarly-colored individuals.

 D) A and B only

 E) A, B, and C

Answer: E
Diff: 2   Page Ref: Evolutionary Connections
Skill: Factual

106) To a biologist, the term "exotic" means

 A) an unusual species in a tropical environment.

 B) a particularly beautiful species.

 C) a species that has been introduced into a different ecosystem from the one in which it evolved.

 D) a very desirable species cultivated for the benefit of humans.

 E) an extinct species.

Answer: C
Diff: 2   Page Ref: Case Study Revisited
Skill: Factual

107) Kudzu, a leguminous vine native to Japan, is considered an exotic invader in this country but not in its native habitat. In many parts of the United States, kudzu is rapidly expanding and outcompeting native species. Why might this be so?

 Answer: Because kudzu did not evolve in this country, there are no native predators, parasites or competitors that coevolved with it. Thus kudzu found a niche that was unexplored in this country and other species are not keeping its population in check.
Diff: 2   Page Ref: Earth Watch
Skill: Conceptual

108) Which of the following is NOT a concern with the introduction of an exotic species into a non-native ecosystem?

 A) displacement of native species

 B) rapid spread of the exotic species from the introduction area to other areas

 C) alteration of the ecosystem

 D) alteration of the climate

 E) predation on native species by the exotic species

Answer: D
Diff: 2   Page Ref: Earth Watch
Skill: Conceptual

109) You have a job as an agricultural agent. You learn of a plant that will slow the growth of a weed that is destroying crops in your area. Would you import the plant that controls the weed? Why or why not?

Answer: Answers will differ, but presumably the student will say that they would not import the plant because it is an exotic and might become a problem. However, an advanced student could also correctly answer that many species have successfully been used as biocontrol agents, which have reduced the need for herbicides or pesticides.

Diff: 3   Page Ref: Earth Watch
Skill: Application

Chapter 28 How Do Ecosystems Work?

1) Which of the following statements BEST describes the movements of energy and nutrients in ecosystems?

    A) energy and nutrients flow through

    B) energy cycles and nutrients recycle

    C) energy increases and nutrients cycle

    D) energy flows through and nutrients cycle

    E) energy and nutrients cycle

Answer: D
Diff: 1   Page Ref: 28.1
Skill: Conceptual

2) The energy that powers the flight of an eagle

    A) came originally from the sun and will eventually return to space.

    B) has been recycled for billions of years on Earth.

    C) has not been degraded in form or diminished in quantity as it passed from organism to organism.

    D) was obtained by the eagle directly from its abiotic environment.

    E) all of these

Answer: A
Diff: 2   Page Ref: 28.1
Skill: Conceptual

3) The atoms that make up the molecules in our bodies

    A) cannot be rearranged to make different molecules under any circumstances.

    B) have nearly all been on Earth for its entire history.

    C) traveled to the Earth as electromagnetic waves.

    D) were all formed recently by nuclear fusion on the sun.

    E) will be lost back to space soon after we die.

Answer: B
Diff: 2   Page Ref: 28.1
Skill: Conceptual

4) One of the basic laws of ecosystems that describe the complex interaction of organisms is that _____ flows through the community.

Answer: energy
Diff: 2   Page Ref: 28.1
Skill: Factual

5) One of the basic laws of ecosystems that describe the complex interaction of organisms is that _____ cycle within the community.

Answer: nutrients
Diff: 2   Page Ref: 28.1
Skill: Factual

6) What happens to 99% of the energy that reaches the Earth's atmosphere?

    A) It is captured by plants and used in photosynthesis.

    B) It is destroyed by the atmosphere.

    C) It is used as heat by animals.

    D) It is absorbed by rocks on the Earth's crust.

    E) It is reflected or absorbed by the atmosphere.

Answer: E
Diff: 1   Page Ref: 28.2
Skill: Factual

7) How much of the energy that reaches the Earth's outer atmosphere from the sun is available for photosynthesis in plants at the surface?

    A) 25%   B) 21%   C) 14%   D) 5%   E) 1%

Answer: E
Diff: 2   Page Ref: 28.2
Skill: Factual

8) Only a small percentage of the energy that arrives at the outer atmosphere of Earth reaches the surface and is then captured within ecosystems. What percentage is captured by the photosynthetic organisms?

    A) 5%   B) 3%   C) 1%   D) 0.03%   E) 0.0001%

Answer: D
Diff: 3   Page Ref: 28.2
Skill: Factual

9) How much of the light energy that reaches a plant is captured by photosynthesis to make sugar?

    A) 100%

    B) 25%

    C) 15%

    D) 8%

    E) 3% or less

Answer: E
Diff: 3   Page Ref: 28.2
Skill: Factual

10) If a bird eats an insect that ate a plant, the bird would be considered a(n)

A) autotroph.

B) primary producer.

C) primary consumer.

D) secondary consumer.

E) tertiary consumer.

Answer: D
Diff: 2   Page Ref: 28.2
Skill: Conceptual

11) If a wolf eats a rodent that ate a smaller insect that ate a plant, the wolf would be a(n)

A) autotroph.

B) primary producer.

C) primary consumer.

D) secondary consumer.

E) tertiary consumer.

Answer: E
Diff: 2   Page Ref: 28.2
Skill: Conceptual

12) If the plants in a community produce 500 grams of organic matter per square meter per year that is available for animals in the community to eat, this amount (500 g per m^2 per yr) is known as the

A) availability factor of the community.

B) net primary productivity of the community.

C) consumership of the community.

D) secondary productivity of the community.

E) trophic factor of the community.

Answer: B
Diff: 3   Page Ref: 28.2
Skill: Conceptual

13) The amount of life that can be supported by an ecosystem is determined primarily by the

   A) efficiency of the consumers.

   B) number of producers and their efficiency.

   C) number of heterotrophs.

   D) number of chemoautotrophs.

   E) efficiency of the heterotrophs.

Answer: B
Diff: 2   *Page Ref: 28.2*
Skill: Conceptual

14) Organisms that must rely on the complex high energy molecules produced by other organisms for survival are

   A) heterotrophs.

   B) producers.

   C) autotrophs.

   D) denitrifying bacteria.

   E) cyanobacteria.

Answer: A
Diff: 1   *Page Ref: 28.2*
Skill: Conceptual

15) Which of the following would NOT be likely to limit the primary productivity of an ecosystem?

   A) the species of consumers

   B) the amount of light

   C) the temperature

   D) the availability of nutrients

   E) the amount of water

Answer: A
Diff: 2   *Page Ref: 28.2*
Skill: Conceptual

16) The first trophic level of an ecosystem consists of

    A) primary consumers.

    B) detritus feeders.

    C) secondary consumers.

    D) producers.

    E) heterotrophs.

Answer: D
Diff: 1   Page Ref: 28.2
Skill: Conceptual

17) When researchers measure the increase in the amount of plant biomass in an ecosystem over some period of time, they are measuring the

    A) carnivores.

    B) phytoplankton.

    C) net primary productivity.

    D) autotrophic potential.

    E) trophic levels.

Answer: C
Diff: 2   Page Ref: 28.2
Skill: Conceptual

18) A carnivore is usually a

    A) primary producer.

    B) secondary producer.

    C) primary consumer.

    D) secondary consumer.

    E) tertiary consumer.

Answer: D
Diff: 2   Page Ref: 28.2
Skill: Conceptual

19) Which best illustrates the movement of energy through an ecosystem?

    A) food chain

    B) food web

    C) biological magnification

    D) nutrient cycles

    E) trophic chain

Answer: B
Diff: 2   *Page Ref: 28.2*
Skill: Conceptual

20) An important and often overlooked group of organisms that releases nutrients to soil or water is

    A) producers.

    B) heterotrophs.

    C) decomposers.

    D) tertiary consumers.

    E) autotrophs.

Answer: C
Diff: 2   *Page Ref: 28.2*
Skill: Conceptual

21) Without decomposers and detritus feeders in an ecosystem

    A) plants would eventually die.

    B) plants would soon develop nutrient deficiencies.

    C) dead material would accumulate.

    D) the soil quality would get poorer.

    E) all of these

Answer: E
Diff: 2   *Page Ref: 28.2*
Skill: Conceptual

22) The energy lost as it passes from one trophic level to another is approximately

    A) 99%.   B) 90%.   C) 75%.   D) 63%.   E) 50%.

Answer: B
Diff: 2   *Page Ref: 28.2*
Skill: Factual

23) If a field contains approximately 1000 kilocalories of energy in grass, which is eaten by crickets, which are eaten by birds, approximately how many kilocalories of energy could be in the birds which live in this field?

A) 1000   B) 900   C) 100   D) 90   E) 10

Answer: E
Diff: 3   Page Ref: 28.2
Skill: Application

24) A carnivorous plant, such as a sundew, can be considered a _____ when it eats a predaceous spider.

A) tertiary consumer and a producer

B) secondary consumer and a producer

C) primary consumer and a producer

D) primary consumer and a secondary consumer

E) primary consumer and a tertiary consumer

Answer: A
Diff: 2   Page Ref: 28.2
Skill: Conceptual

25) The amount of energy captured by plants and made available to consumers in an ecosystem is termed

A) net primary productivity.

B) energy pyramid.

C) biological magnification.

D) nutrient cycling.

E) secondary trophic level.

Answer: A
Diff: 2   Page Ref: 28.2
Skill: Factual

26) Certain bacteria and fungi that are important in nutrient recycling because they release nutrients from dead organisms back into the ecosystem are

A) autotrophs.

B) carnivores.

C) detritus feeders.

D) decomposers.

E) recyclers.

Answer: D
Diff: 2   Page Ref: 28.2
Skill: Factual

27) Herbivores may be classified as

 A) autotrophs.

 B) producers.

 C) heterotrophs.

 D) metatrophs.

 E) A and B

Answer: C
Diff: 1   Page Ref: 28.2
Skill: Factual

28) Autotrophs gain energy from

 A) primary producers.

 B) secondary consumers.

 C) secondary producers.

 D) omnivores.

 E) the sun and/or chemical energy.

Answer: E
Diff: 1   Page Ref: 28.2
Skill: Factual

29) Net primary production is

 A) energy that photosynthetic organisms make available to other organisms over a given time.

 B) energy stored by secondary consumers from primary biomass.

 C) energy made by autotrophs minus energy consumed by heterotrophs, and measured as biomass.

 D) heterotrophic production per unit land per unit time.

 E) heterotrophic production minus autotrophic production per unit land per unit time.

Answer: A
Diff: 1   Page Ref: 28.2
Skill: Factual

30) Carnivores are usually

    A) secondary consumers.

    B) primary consumers.

    C) omnivores.

    D) detritus consumers.

    E) consumer producers.

Answer: A
Diff: 1   Page Ref: 28.2
Skill: Factual

31) Detritus feeders consume

    A) herbivores.

    B) plants and plant debris.

    C) secondary consumers and primary debris.

    D) dead organic matter.

    E) fungi and bacteria.

Answer: D
Diff: 1   Page Ref: 28.2
Skill: Factual

32) Detritus feeders serve to

    A) reduce organic matter accumulation.

    B) return nutrients to the soil.

    C) allow autotrophs to continue to produce indefinitely.

    D) A and B

    E) A, B, and C

Answer: E
Diff: 1   Page Ref: 28.2
Skill: Factual

33) A snake that eats a small rabbit that feeds on grass would be classified as a(n)

    A) autotroph.

    B) primary producer.

    C) secondary consumer.

    D) primary consumer.

    E) tertiary consumer.

Answer: C
Diff: 2   Page Ref: 28.2
Skill: Conceptual

34) In a Kansas grassland, 1000 grams of grass are produced per square meter per year by all the different grass species. A theoretical upper limit to the biomass of secondary consumers that can be supported in this ecosystem is

    A) 1000 grams.

    B) 100 grams.

    C) 10 grams.

    D) 1 gram.

    E) 0.1 grams.

Answer: C
Diff: 3   Page Ref: 28.2
Skill: Conceptual

35) In open–water marine ecosystems, the _____ occupy the same trophic level as the giant sequoias (redwoods) in the forests of California.

    A) fast–swimming, fish–eating tuna

    B) giant, squid–eating whales

    C) microscopic bacteria that decompose all the other organisms once they have died

    D) microscopic, single–celled algae (protists) called phytoplankton ("plant–like drifters")

    E) tiny, multicellular zooplankton ("animal drifters") that feed on phytoplankton

Answer: D
Diff: 2   Page Ref: 28.2
Skill: Conceptual

36) Bacteria that live in deep–sea thermal vents use energy from inorganic hydrogen sulfide (H_2S) to make organic molecules from carbon dioxide and are thus

    A) decomposers.

    B) primary consumers.

    C) producers.

    D) secondary consumers.

    E) tertiary consumers.

Answer: C
Diff: 2   Page Ref: 28.2
Skill: Conceptual

37) As many people in "developing countries" become more affluent, they increase the amount of meat, poultry and fish in their diets, eating less grain, vegetables, and fruits. If they raise all their food locally

 A) this will increase their exposure to any fat-soluble and persistent pesticides used.

 B) this will increase the number of people that can be fed from a given area of farmland.

 C) this will reduce the number of people that can be fed from a given area of farmland.

 D) both A and B

 E) both A and C

Answer: E
Diff: 2   Page Ref: 28.2
Skill: Application

38) The community of heterotrophic protists and invertebrate animals like Earthworms, pillbugs, mites, and pseudoscorpions that lives in the leaf litter on the shady floor of a deciduous forest obtains its energy and nutrients primarily from

 A) carbohydrates formed in the roots of the trees that leach out into the surrounding soil.

 B) chemosynthesis by green and purple sulfur bacteria living on the surface of the leaves.

 C) decomposition of the leaves of deciduous trees that fall on the surface of the soil.

 D) photosynthesis or algae living in the soil beneath the leaves.

 E) all of the above

Answer: C
Diff: 2   Page Ref: 28.2
Skill: Conceptual

39) Herbivores occupy the trophic level of _____.

Answer: primary consumer
Diff: 1   Page Ref: 28.2
Skill: Conceptual

40) Organisms that produce their own food in photosynthesis are known as producers or

_____.

Answer: autotrophs
Diff: 1   Page Ref: 28.2
Skill: Conceptual

41) Suppose a gardener puts a chemical on his or her garden that kills off all the detritus feeders and decomposers. What would happen to the garden?

Answer: Nutrients could not be recycled, leaf litter would increase, and the productivity of the garden would drop.
Diff: 3   Page Ref: 28.2
Skill: Conceptual

42) When a rabbit eats the lettuce in your garden, all of the energy in the lettuce is used by the rabbit. Is this statement True or False? Defend your answer.

Answer: False, because the transfer of energy between trophic levels is inefficient. This is true because the lettuce has used some of its energy for its own metabolism and for making indigestible cellulose.
Diff: 3   Page Ref: 28.2
Skill: Conceptual

43) Explain how the world food supply may be affected by whether people primarily eat meat or vegetables.

Answer: If people eat plant materials, approximately 90% more food is available to them than if they eat meat. (10% Law)
Diff: 3   Page Ref: 28.2
Skill: Conceptual

44) What is meant by the term *trophic level*?

Answer: A trophic level is a feeding level of organisms in a food chain.
Diff: 1   Page Ref: 28.2
Skill: Conceptual

45) What one word best describes the transfer of energy from one trophic level to the next?

Answer: inefficient
Diff: 1   Page Ref: 28.2
Skill: Conceptual

46) Approximately what percentage of the energy in one trophic level is available for the next level?

Answer: 10%
Diff: 1   Page Ref: 28.2
Skill: Factual

47) Which ecosystems are more productive, tropical rain forests or northern coniferous forests, and why?

Answer: Tropical rain forests, because the abundance of resources such as light and moisture allows greater primary productivity to occur in tropical forests.
Diff: 2   Page Ref: 28.2
Skill: Conceptual

48) Draw a food web for a vacant city lot that has weeds, seed–eating mice, cats, and grasshoppers. Explain what would happen if an animal came in that ate both mice and cats.

Answer: varied
Diff: 3   Page Ref: 28.2
Skill: Application

49) Explain why a food web gives a better picture of a community than does a food chain.

   Answer: The food web portrays the interactions between animals in which many animals eat from more than one level.
   Diff: 2   Page Ref: 28.2
   Skill: Conceptual

50) Explain why decomposers and detritus feeders are so important to ecosystems.

   Answer: They recycle nutrients to simple molecules which are returned to the abiotic environment for use again by plants, thus maintaining the ecosystem.
   Diff: 2   Page Ref: 28.2
   Skill: Conceptual

51) Describe which trophic level, primary consumers or secondary consumers, has more biomass in most ecosystems and explain why.

   Answer: Primary consumers generally have more biomass because there is a 90% loss of energy available to be converted to biomass with each step to a higher trophic level.
   Diff: 2   Page Ref: 28.2
   Skill: Conceptual

52) Plants produce biomass by taking in energy, CO_2 and nutrients from the environment; consumers eat much of this biomass, but not all. However, ecosystems do not indefinitely accumulate large quantities of organic matter over time. Why not?

   Answer: When consumers eat plant organic matter, much of the carbon is respired, and the nutrients are returned to the soil. Decomposers also recycle much of the remaining organic matter. Many ecosystems do accumulate organic matter, but not indefinitely.
   Diff: 2   Page Ref: 28.2
   Skill: Factual

53) Draw a typical energy pyramid for a grassland ecosystem. Give examples of trophic levels with potential organisms that occupy the different trophic levels. Explain why the energy pyramid is shaped the way that it is.

   Answer: Examples: Tertiary consumers: hawk that eats an insect–eating bird; Secondary consumers: insect–eating bird, wolf, spider; Herbivores (or primary consumers): rabbit, insect, giraffe; Primary producers: tree, grass. The energy contained in each tropic level decreases as you move up the energy pyramid because energy transfer is inefficient.

   Tertiary consumers
   Secondary consumers
   Herbivores
   Primary producers

   Diff: 3   Page Ref: 28.2
   Skill: Factual

54) Three major reservoirs of carbon are

    A) rocks, atmosphere, guano.

    B) acid precipitation, carbon–fixing bacteria, oceans.

    C) soil, water, atmosphere.

    D) fossil fuels, legumes, micronutrients.

    E) oceans, atmosphere, fossil fuels.

Answer: E
Diff: 2   *Page Ref: 28.3*
Skill: Factual

55) Oceans, atmosphere, and fossil fuels are large reservoirs of

    A) nitrogen.

    B) oxygen.

    C) water.

    D) carbon.

    E) phosphorus.

Answer: D
Diff: 2   *Page Ref: 28.3*
Skill: Factual

56) Which of the following is NOT involved with the carbon cycle?

    A) limestone

    B) ammonia

    C) calcium carbonate

    D) decomposers

    E) cellular respiration

Answer: B
Diff: 1   *Page Ref: 28.3*
Skill: Conceptual

57) Which of the following is NOT involved with the nitrogen cycle?

    A) fixation

    B) legumes

    C) decomposers

    D) crystalline rock

    E) ammonia

Answer: D
Diff: 2   *Page Ref: 28.3*
Skill: Conceptual

58) Plants need nitrogen to synthesize all the following EXCEPT

    A) amino acids.

    B) nucleic acids.

    C) complex polysaccharides.

    D) vitamins.

    E) proteins.

Answer: C
Diff: 2   Page Ref: 28.3
Skill: Factual

59) By which of the following ways can nitrogen be made available to plants?

    A) decomposers

    B) nitrogen fixation by bacteria

    C) electrical storms

    D) burning forests and fossil fuels

    E) all the above

Answer: E
Diff: 3   Page Ref: 28.3
Skill: Factual

60) The phosphorus cycle includes *all but which* of the following components?

    A) atmosphere

    B) some rocks and soil

    C) producers

    D) consumers

    E) decomposers

Answer: A
Diff: 2   Page Ref: 28.3
Skill: Conceptual

61) Phosphate fertilizers have increased the amount of phosphate in lakes and other bodies of water. What effect does this have on the producers in the water?

A) It kills them.

B) It stimulates their growth.

C) It increases their likelihood of getting eaten.

D) It causes them to form toxic compounds.

E) It reduces their photosynthetic capacity.

Answer: B
Diff: 2   *Page Ref: 28.3*
Skill: Conceptual

62) A crucial nutrient reservoir of phosphorus that is available to organisms is

A) atmosphere.

B) sedimentary rocks.

C) oceans.

D) autotrophs.

E) consumers.

Answer: B
Diff: 2   *Page Ref: 28.3*
Skill: Factual

63) Phosphorus, which is very commonly a limiting nutrient in ecosystems, is very important because it

A) is needed for molecules such as ATP, cell membranes and nucleic acids.

B) evaporates quickly.

C) is found *only* in sedimentary rocks.

D) is necessary for the production of cellulose so that autotrophs can grow and provide food for heterotrophs.

E) is part of the hydrologic cycle.

Answer: A
Diff: 2   *Page Ref: 28.3*
Skill: Factual

64) The hydrologic cycle is different from other nutrient cycles in that

A) water is chemically unchanged throughout the cycle.

B) the ocean is involved.

C) the atmosphere is involved.

D) the soil is not involved.

E) water is not recycled, but flows one way through ecosystems.

Answer: A
Diff: 2   Page Ref: 28.3
Skill: Conceptual

65) Nitrogen fixation

A) is due to a lack of decomposers, and causes nitrogen to accumulate in dead organic matter.

B) is the conversion of ammonia to nitrate.

C) is the conversion of nitrate to ammonia.

D) is undertaken by denitrifying bacteria.

E) is the synthesis of ammonia from nitrogen gas by certain bacteria and cyanobacteria.

Answer: E
Diff: 2   Page Ref: 28.3
Skill: Factual

66) Limestone is part of the biogeochemical cycle of

A) N, because denitrifying bacteria gain energy from shell organisms.

B) C, because limestone represents a marine sink for carbon.

C) N, because marine producers may use shell organisms for cellular respiration.

D) C, because shell organisms represent the highest trophic level in marine waters.

E) both A and C

Answer: B
Diff: 2   Page Ref: 28.3
Skill: Factual

67) Which of the following statements about the hydrologic cycle is *incorrect*?

A) The hydrologic cycle is driven by solar energy that evaporates water.

B) The ocean is the major water reservoir for the entire planet.

C) Little water is used in the synthesis of other molecules in living organisms.

D) Freshwater ecosystems use a hydrologic cycle which is separate from the marine hydrologic cycle.

E) Gravity acts to pull water from the atmosphere in the form of precipitation.

Answer: D
Diff: 3   Page Ref: 28.3
Skill: Conceptual

68) Each summer a large "dead zone" devoid of fish and other animals develops where the Mississippi River flows into the Gulf of Mexico. This has been attributed to

A) acid rain making the Gulf's water too acidic to support fish.

B) global warming increasing making the river water too hot for the fish to tolerate.

C) high levels of mercury in the river water.

D) high levels of pesticide use in the Mississippi River basin.

E) runoff of large quantities of fertilizer from farm fields into the Mississippi River.

Answer: E
Diff: 2   Page Ref: 28.3
Skill: Factual

69) Micronutrients

A) are needed in smaller quantities than macronutrients but are just as essential.

B) are smaller molecules than macronutrients.

C) benefit organisms if they are present but are not essential.

D) include water, carbon, nitrogen, and phosphorus.

E) are rarely found in the environment.

Answer: A
Diff: 2   Page Ref: 28.3
Skill: Conceptual

70) Farmers often include legumes as part of their normal crop rotation. This increases the overall production of their crops by

    A) adding nitrogen to the soil.

    B) adding phosphorus to the soil.

    C) helping the soil retain water better.

    D) making the soil less acidic.

    E) suppressing the growth of weeds.

Answer: A
Diff: 2   Page Ref: 28.3
Skill: Application

71) In nitrogen–limited ecosystems, legumes often dominate over other plants because they

    A) do not need nitrogen at all.

    B) have long taproots that can extract nitrogen from deeper down in the soil.

    C) have unique access to the large atmospheric pool of nitrogen thanks to their symbiotic bacteria.

    D) inhibit the growth of denitrifying bacteria around their roots, keeping more nitrate in the soil.

    E) obtain supplemental nitrogen by trapping insects and other prey.

Answer: C
Diff: 2   Page Ref: 28.3
Skill: Conceptual

72) Plants absorb small amounts of carbon from the soil in the form of simple sugars or monosaccharides. True or False?

Answer: FALSE
Diff: 2   Page Ref: 28.3
Skill: Conceptual

73) In the _____ cycle, water is cycled between the atmosphere, oceans, and living organisms.

Answer: hydrologic
Diff: 2   Page Ref: 28.3
Skill: Conceptual

74) One of the largest reservoirs for CO_2 on the planet is the _____.

Answer: oceans, or atmosphere
Diff: 2   Page Ref: 28.3
Skill: Factual

75) The global hydrologic cycle begins with precipitation falling to Earth, and the cycle is completed by _____.

Answer: solar energy, or evaporation
Diff: 2   Page Ref: 28.3
Skill: Conceptual

76) For which nutrient cycle is rock the major reservoir?

Answer: phosphorus
Diff: 2   Page Ref: 28.3
Skill: Conceptual

77) Since plants cannot fix nitrogen, why are legumes often called nitrogen fixers?

Answer: They have N-fixing bacteria in nodules in their roots.
Diff: 3   Page Ref: 28.3
Skill: Conceptual

78) What would happen if there were no denitrifying bacteria?

Answer: The atmosphere would have less nitrogen gas available for nitrogen fixation.
Diff: 3   Page Ref: 28.3
Skill: Factual

79) What is the driving force behind the hydrologic cycle?

Answer: solar energy
Diff: 2   Page Ref: 28.3
Skill: Conceptual

80) Why is phosphorus so important to living organisms?

Answer: In the form of phosphate, it is a component of ATP, NADPH, DNA, RNA, and phospholipids as well as bones and teeth.
Diff: 3   Page Ref: 28.3
Skill: Conceptual

81) The global phosphorus cycle is described as a "cycle" yet there is no atmospheric component. P weathers from rocks, and enters the soil. Once P is incorporated into plants or animals, how is it returned to the rock phase?

Answer: Decomposers return P that remains in dead bodies or plants back to soil and water in the form of phosphate; it may then be bound into sediment and eventually reincorporated into rock through geologic activity.
Diff: 3   Page Ref: 28.3
Skill: Conceptual

82) Nitrogen is fixed by soil bacteria and is then incorporated into plant biomass, and eventually into the food chain. What process(es) complete the global N cycle?

Answer: Decomposers return N in dead plant and animal bodies into soluble forms of N in soils or water; denitrifying organisms convert these soluble inorganic forms of N into gaseous forms of N that enter the atmosphere.
Diff: 3   Page Ref: 28.3
Skill: Conceptual

83) The assaults of acids dissolved in precipitation and dry particles of sulfuric acid are together known as

   A) acid rain.

   B) acid precipitation.

   C) acid deposition.

   D) acid fog.

   E) decomposition acid.

Answer: C
Diff: 2   Page Ref: 28.4
Skill: Factual

84) Which of the following BEST describes a lake that has been severely polluted by acid rain?

   A) cloudy water with few organisms

   B) cloudy water with many algae crowding out other organisms

   C) cloudy water with large numbers of insect larvae

   D) crystal clear water with large numbers of algae, but no animals

   E) crystal clear water with few organisms

Answer: E
Diff: 2   Page Ref: 28.4
Skill: Conceptual

85) Which of these is NOT a result of acid rain?

   A) dead lakes

   B) damaged statues

   C) global warming

   D) injured plants

   E) increased exposure to mercury

Answer: C
Diff: 1   Page Ref: 28.4
Skill: Factual

86) Acid precipitation is the result of interference with which biogeochemical cycles?

   A) sulfur and nitrogen

   B) sulfur and hydrologic

   C) hydrologic and nitrogen

   D) hydrologic and phosphorus

   E) sulfur and phosphorus

Answer: A
Diff: 2   Page Ref: 28.4
Skill: Conceptual

87) When you observe a lake that has been affected by acidic deposition, you might expect to find

   A) a clear lake with high levels of metals.

   B) a murky lake with excess algal growth from the deposition of anthropogenic N.

   C) low levels of toxic metals and nutrients essential for growth of biotic organisms.

   D) excess carbon that will contribute to global warming.

   E) high levels of dissolved sulfur dioxide.

Answer: A
Diff: 2   Page Ref: 28.4
Skill: Application

88) Acid rain is a serious problem in the Adirondack Mountains of New York State but not in the prairies of western Kansas because

   A) plant species in the Midwest are naturally more acid tolerant than those in the northeast.

   B) prevailing winds take most of the acids produced in the Ohio Valley over New York, not Kansas.

   C) the soils in the Adirondacks cannot buffer added acids as well as those in Kansas.

   D) all of the above

   E) both B and C

Answer: E
Diff: 2   Page Ref: 28.4
Skill: Conceptual

89) Following implementation of the Clean Air Act of 1990

    A) acid rain is no longer a problem anywhere in the United States.

    B) carbon dioxide levels in the atmosphere have fallen dramatically.

    C) emissions of both sulfur dioxide and nitrogen oxides have fallen dramatically.

    D) emissions of sulfur dioxide and nitrogen oxides continue to rise unabated.

    E) emissions of sulfur dioxide have fallen but emissions of nitrogen oxides continue to rise.

Answer: E
Diff: 2   *Page Ref: 28.4*
Skill: Factual

90) Why is acid rain more of a problem in certain areas, such as New England, than in others?

Answer: 1. Rocks and soils there are unable to neutralize the acid. 2. Prevailing winds carry them to those areas.
Diff: 2   *Page Ref: 28.4*
Skill: Factual

91) List and discuss 3 effects of acid rain on forests.

Answer: Choose from: 1. Leaches essential nutrients such as calcium and potassium; 2. Kills decomposer microorganisms; 3. Plants weaker and more subject to infection; 4. Plants more subject to insect attack; 5. Root shrinkage
Diff: 3   *Page Ref: 28.4*
Skill: Conceptual

92) Sulfur dioxide is a natural product of volcanoes and hot springs, and is by itself not acidic. How then is excess sulfur dioxide linked to acid rain?

Answer: Human industrial activities account for 90% of the sulfur dioxide that is emitted to the atmosphere; combined with water vapor in the atmosphere, sulfur dioxide is converted to sulfuric acid which returns to the Earth in precipitation or as particulates.
Diff: 2   *Page Ref: 28.4*
Skill: Conceptual

93) On a field trip with your class to a series of mountain lakes in Vermont, you come across a beautiful clear lake that is deep, and you can see the pebbles at the bottom of the lake. Why does your classmate hypothesize that this lake has been subjected to acidic deposition?

Answer: The reason that the lake is clear is because plants, algae, and aquatic organisms are dead.
Diff: 2   *Page Ref: 28.4*
Skill: Conceptual

94) A major ecological concern, the Greenhouse Effect, is caused by

    A) the release of heat energy from burning fossil fuels.

    B) the release of carbon dioxide from the burning of wood, coal, and oil.

    C) the destruction of ozone in the upper atmosphere.

    D) overuse of fertilizers in farming.

    E) global warming.

Answer: B
Diff: 2   Page Ref: 28.5
Skill: Conceptual

95) Why is the concentration of carbon dioxide rapidly increasing in the Earth's atmosphere?

    A) The Earth is warming.

    B) More photosynthesis is occurring.

    C) The ozone layer has become much thinner.

    D) Many human activities release carbon dioxide.

    E) The oceans are cooling.

Answer: D
Diff: 2   Page Ref: 28.5
Skill: Factual

96) How do carbon dioxide and other greenhouse gases cause the temperature of the Earth to increase?

    A) by allowing greater transmission of incoming solar radiation

    B) by absorbing heat energy and holding it near the Earth

    C) by increasing plant respiration

    D) by reducing photosynthetic rates

    E) by increasing the amount of radiation from the Earth's surface

Answer: B
Diff: 3   Page Ref: 28.5
Skill: Conceptual

97) Burning coal and oil to release energy also releases _____ which are overloading nutrient cycles of Earth.

    A) sulfur, carbon, nitrogen

    B) sulfur, oxygen, acid

    C) phosphorous, carbon, nitrogen

    D) oxygen, methane, sulfur

    E) nitrogen, phosphorus, potassium

Answer: A
Diff: 2   *Page Ref: 28.5*
Skill: Conceptual

98) What are the sources of sulfur in the atmosphere?

    A) Equal amounts of sulfur are released from natural and human sources.

    B) volcanoes, hot springs, but mostly (about 90%) from human activities such as burning coal

    C) mostly (over 90%) from volcanoes, and photosynthetic bacteria

    D) mostly from transportation sources such as autos, trucks, and planes

    E) decomposition and small amounts from pollution

Answer: B
Diff: 2   *Page Ref: 28.5*
Skill: Factual

99) Which of the following would NOT be an expected result of global warming?

    A) ocean level rise

    B) acidified lakes

    C) change in forest composition

    D) change in rainfall patterns

    E) agricultural disruption

Answer: B
Diff: 1   *Page Ref: 28.5*
Skill: Conceptual

100) Human-caused disturbances of which biogeochemical cycle may be contributing to global warming?

   A) hydrologic

   B) carbon

   C) nitrogen

   D) phosphorus

   E) sulfur

Answer: B
Diff: 1   Page Ref: 28.5
Skill: Conceptual

101) Possible consequences of global warming include

   A) rise in sea level.

   B) shifts in temperature and rainfall patterns.

   C) alteration of range and species composition of forests.

   D) changes in ocean currents.

   E) all of the above

Answer: E
Diff: 2   Page Ref: 28.5
Skill: Conceptual

102) By the end of the 21st century, global warming is expected to increase average global air temperatures by how much?

   A) less than 1°C (less than 1.8°F)

   B) 1.6 to 4.6°C (3.5 to 8.0°F)

   C) 5.8 to 12.6°C (10.4 to 22.7°F)

   D) 12.6 to 25°C (22.7 to 45°F)

   E) more than 25°C (more than 45°F)

Answer: B
Diff: 2   Page Ref: 28.5
Skill: Factual

103) The greenhouse effect is

    A) the ability of sulfur dioxide and nitrogen oxides to retain heat in the lower atmosphere.

    B) the ability of sulfur dioxide and nitrogen oxides to retain heat in the upper atmosphere.

    C) the ability of certain gases to absorb solar heat and reflect the heat as short-wave radiation to the Earth.

    D) the ability of certain gases to retain solar radiation as heat energy.

    E) the ability of structures created by humans to retain solar energy as short-wave radiation.

Answer: D
Diff: 2   Page Ref: 28.5
Skill: Factual

104) Global warming is now causing some of the normally permanently frozen soil (permafrost) in the Arctic to thaw each summer. This allows bacteria to decompose much or the organic matter in these soils, releasing its stored carbon into the atmosphere as carbon dioxide. The likely result of this is to

    A) accelerate global warming in a positive feedback loop.

    B) decrease global warming in a negative feedback loop.

    C) have no effect on the carbon cycle or global warming.

    D) decrease acid rain by slowing the nitrogen and sulfur cycles.

    E) both A and D

Answer: A
Diff: 3   Page Ref: 28.5
Skill: Application

105) The present range of the sugar maple in North America extends from the Atlantic Ocean west to the Mississippi River and from southern Ontario, Quebec, and New Brunswick south to Tennessee and Virginia. If the global climate warms 10ºC in the future, those same climatic conditions will be found where?

    A) further north

    B) further south

    C) further west

    D) In the same place; global warming will not affect the location of climatic regions.

    E) Nowhere; those conditions will not occur anywhere on the continent.

Answer: A
Diff: 3   Page Ref: 28.5
Skill: Application

106) The primary cause of the current rise in atmospheric CO_2 is due to the human use of _____.

Answer: fossil fuels
Diff: 1   Page Ref: 28.5
Skill: Factual

107) Ornithologists have noted that Mexican Jays in Arizona are nesting 10 days earlier in the springtime today than they did in the 1970s. They suggest that this is evidence of _____.

Answer: global warming
Diff: 1   Page Ref: 28.5
Skill: Conceptual

108) Why is it so hard to make definite predictions about the amount and timing of global warming as a result of greenhouse gases?

Answer: There are so many interacting factors that it is difficult to know how all of these will respond to rising levels of greenhouse gases.
Diff: 2   Page Ref: 28.5
Skill: Conceptual

109) Discuss the idea that many Americans have that we should not get too excited about global warming, because we really haven't seen any effects yet.

Answer: The student's answer should address the idea that we are already seeing some possible effects (changes in species' ranges; advancement of springtime events to earlier dates) and the idea that the result of ignoring this problem may be catastrophic. Also, by the time we actually *see* effects, it could be too late to reverse the trend.
Diff: 3   Page Ref: 28.5
Skill: Conceptual

110) It has been said about global warming that "one human in a developed country is not equivalent to one person in a developing country." What is meant by this?

Answer: Each individual in a developed country produces many times more greenhouse gas emissions than an individual in a developing country. With less than 5% of the world's population, Americans are responsible for over 20% of the world's greenhouse emissions.
Diff: 2   Page Ref: 28.5
Skill: Conceptual

111) Forests alongside rivers in the Pacific Northwest that have lost their salmon populations are less productive because

   A) the dams that prevented the fish from migrating also flooded the forests.

   B) the fishers who over-harvested the salmon also compacted the soil in the process.

   C) the global warming that wiped out the fish has also harmed the trees.

   D) the pollution that killed the fish has also directly affected the trees.

   E) the nitrogen the fish brought from the ocean and contained in their tissues has been lost.

Answer: E
Diff: 2   *Page Ref: Case Study Revisited*
Skill: Factual

112) In the Pacific Northwest, salmon provide nearly _____% of the nitrogen to the trees and shrubs near the streams they inhabit.

   A) 1   B) 5   C) 10   D) 25   E) 40

Answer: D
Diff: 2   *Page Ref: Case Study Revisited*
Skill: Factual

113) About 6 tons of greenhouse gases per _____ per year are produced in the U.S.

   A) person

   B) family

   C) household

   D) hundred people

   E) community

Answer: A
Diff: 2   *Page Ref: Links to Life*
Skill: Factual

114) An individual can reduce the amount of greenhouse gases released into the atmosphere by

   A) using ceiling fans rather than air conditioning.

   B) insulating his or her attic.

   C) using public transportation rather than driving.

   D) using fluorescent rather than incandescent bulbs in light fixtures.

   E) All of these will help to reduce greenhouse gas emissions.

Answer: E
Diff: 2   *Page Ref: Links to Life*
Skill: Conceptual

115) Which of these toxic materials is known to cause human health problems because of biological magnification?

A) DDT

B) mercury

C) PCBs and other chlorinated hydrocarbons

D) all of these

E) none of these

Answer: D
Diff: 2   Page Ref: Earth Watch
Skill: Factual

116) What ecological effects are suspected or have been linked to biological magnification of chlorinated hydrocarbons such as DDT, dioxin, and PCBs?

A) declining insect populations

B) water pollution

C) interference with animal reproduction

D) disruption of the carbon cycle

E) interference with the hydrological cycle

Answer: C
Diff: 2   Page Ref: Earth Watch
Skill: Factual

117) Which of the following practices would NOT reduce your exposure to DDT if you had to eat fish from a DDT–contaminated body of water?

A) Bake, broil, or barbecue the fish in a way that allows the fat to drip away.

B) Before cooking, remove the fatty skin and cut away any fatty tissue from the belly or dorsal areas.

C) Consume more fish that are herbivores or omnivores, and fewer fish that are top carnivores.

D) Consume smaller amounts of fish more often, instead of large amounts less frequently.

E) Reduce your overall consumption of fish as much as possible.

Answer: D
Diff: 3   Page Ref: Earth Watch
Skill: Application

118) In 1956, people in Minamata, Japan, began to exhibit severe neurological disorders and birth defects. This was eventually attributed to methylmercury, a water-insoluble and breakdown-resistant chemical formed from mercury dumped into the adjacent bay by a local factory. People who ate which of the following seafoods would you expect were most affected?

   A) kelp, large, multicellular, photosynthetic protists

   B) krill, small crustaceans that eat tiny microscopic algae

   C) mussels that feed on tiny microscopic algae

   D) sea urchins that feed on kelp

   E) tuna that feed on smaller fish that feed on krill that feed on algae

Answer: E
Diff: 2   Page Ref: Earth Watch
Skill: Application

119) The tendency of toxic substances to accumulate in increasingly higher quantities at higher trophic levels is known as _____.

Answer: biological magnification
Diff: 2   Page Ref: Earth Watch
Skill: Conceptual

120) If you were a researcher trying to design a pesticide which was not going to accumulate by biological magnification, what 2 properties should the pesticide have?

Answer: 1. It should break down quickly to harmless compounds. 2. It should not be fat soluble.
Diff: 3   Page Ref: Earth Watch
Skill: Application

121) Why are toxic chemicals which accumulate by biological magnification not removed from the body in the urine?

Answer: They are fat soluble, not water soluble.
Diff: 2   Page Ref: Earth Watch
Skill: Conceptual

122) Why do substances such as DDT undergo biomagnification in the food web?

Answer: DDT and many other pesticides are fat soluble and not water soluble, and thus are retained in fatty tissues of organisms rather than being excreted in urine. Because each trophic level must eat much more biomass while retaining the toxic substances, concentrations of DDT can increase with each rise in trophic level.
Diff: 3   Page Ref: Earth Watch
Skill: Conceptual

123) Why might "eating high on the food chain" subject humans to higher concentrations of certain toxic substances than eating "low" on the food chain?

Answer: because biomagnification causes increased concentrations of certain compounds with increasing trophic status

Diff: 2   Page Ref: Earth Watch
Skill: Conceptual

Chapter 29 Earth's Diverse Ecosystems

1) The Earth is generally hotter at the equator because

   A) the Earth's rotation on a tilted axis creates more atmospheric friction at the equator.

   B) the natural curve of the Earth places the equator nearer the sun.

   C) the sun shines over the equator more hours in the day.

   D) there are large oceans near the equator to absorb large amounts of heat.

   E) the sun's rays strike the Earth at nearly a right angle at the equator.

   Answer: E
   Diff: 2   Page Ref: 29.1
   Skill: Conceptual

2) At about 30° north and south of the equator there are very dry regions on the Earth. Why does this occur?

   A) Cool air falls, is warmed and absorbs moisture.

   B) Warm air falls and absorbs moisture.

   C) Cool air rises and water condenses.

   D) Warm air rises and water is evaporated.

   E) Air flows laterally across the land from the temperate zone.

   Answer: A
   Diff: 2   Page Ref: 29.1
   Skill: Factual

3) The prevailing winds in the Glacier Park area of Montana are from the west. Which side of this mountainous region receives the most rain and snow?

   A) east

   B) west

   C) north

   D) south

   E) There is insufficient information to answer this question.

   Answer: B
   Diff: 2   Page Ref: 29.1
   Skill: Conceptual

4) An area which is very dry because the air in that region has passed over a mountain and lost most of its moisture is called a(n)

A) basin.

B) chaparral.

C) tropical desert.

D) adiabat.

E) rain shadow.

Answer: E
Diff: 1   Page Ref: 29.1
Skill: Conceptual

5) The Earth is warm enough to support life because

A) solar energy is trapped in the atmosphere and the Earth's crust as heat.

B) metabolism by all living organisms generates enough heat.

C) human activities such as industry and auto emissions generate the heat necessary.

D) plants capture solar energy and release it as heat.

E) geothermal heat diffuses outward from the Earth's core of molten rock to heat the Earth's surface.

Answer: A
Diff: 2   Page Ref: 29.1
Skill: Conceptual

6) Why are mountain tops colder than valley bottoms?

A) It snows more on mountains, making it colder.

B) Cold air rises, so mountains accumulate more cold air.

C) Mountain tops are farther from the Earth's core, so they receive less geothermal heat than valleys do.

D) Mountains are all at northern latitudes and valleys are closer to the equator.

E) The atmosphere is thinner and retains less heat at higher elevations.

Answer: E
Diff: 2   Page Ref: 29.1
Skill: Conceptual

7) Nearly all the incoming solar energy to the Earth's surface is returned to space as

A) infrared radiation.

B) visible light.

C) ultraviolet radiation.

D) cosmic rays.

E) A and B

Answer: E
Diff: 3   Page Ref: 29.1
Skill: Factual

8) The tropics occur very near the equator because

A) cool air, which sinks, flows north and south from the equator.

B) water condenses as rain from warm air as air rises from the equator.

C) the Earth's rotation causes warm air to be retained about 10° away from the equator.

D) cool dry air is dense, so it sinks and becomes warmed by the Earth.

E) both A and D

Answer: B
Diff: 1   Page Ref: 29.1
Skill: Factual

9) A rain shadow is caused by

A) ocean currents that heat and cool more quickly than do air or land masses.

B) ocean currents that heat and cool more slowly than do air or land masses.

C) cool, dry air that warms as it moves down over a mountain, picking up moisture.

D) warm, moist air that cools as it moves down over a mountain, releasing moisture.

E) large mountain masses in the center of continents that restrict air flow.

Answer: C
Diff: 1   Page Ref: 29.1
Skill: Factual

10) Incoming sunlight is modified by the Earth's atmosphere; for example, the ozone layer absorbs much of the sun's _____.

    A) high-energy UV radiation

    B) low-energy UV radiation

    C) high-energy IR radiation

    D) low-energy IR radiation

    E) low-energy UV as well as high-energy IR radiation

Answer: A
Diff: 2   Page Ref: 29.1
Skill: Factual

11) Higher latitude ecosystems experience more pronounced seasons than ecosystems at equatorial latitudes because

    A) air currents generated by Earth's rotation have stronger effects at higher latitudes.

    B) heated air rises at the equator, and falls at mid-latitudes, giving rise to distinct seasons.

    C) the Earth is tilted on its axis as it orbits the sun annually.

    D) continental mass is greater at the equator, evening out temperature variations in ocean circulation.

    E) ocean currents moderate near-shore environments.

Answer: C
Diff: 1   Page Ref: 29.1
Skill: Factual

12) Rising air _____; this causes water vapor to _____.

    A) heats; evaporate

    B) heats; condense

    C) cools; evaporate

    D) cools; condense

    E) changes in composition, but not in temperature; condense

Answer: D
Diff: 2   Page Ref: 29.1
Skill: Conceptual

13) The major driving force behind winds, ocean currents, and the global water cycle is

   A) geothermal heating from beneath the surface of the Earth.

   B) heating by the sun.

   C) the Earth's magnetic field.

   D) the gravitational pull of the moon.

   E) the rotation of the Earth.

Answer: B
Diff: 1   Page Ref: 29.1
Skill: Factual

14) In the Northern Hemisphere, north-facing slopes often have vegetation found on level sites further north, while south-facing slopes have vegetation characteristic of level sites further south. This is most likely because

   A) north-facing slopes receive cold prevailing northerly winds while south-facing slopes receive warm prevailing southerly winds.

   B) north-facing slopes receive sunlight more straight-on in the summer than do south-facing slopes, which receive it at a shallower angle, as do sites further north and south.

   C) prevailing winds from the south warm south-facing slopes by friction as they pass over them.

   D) seeds cannot cross over the mountaintop, limiting the species on each side.

   E) south-facing slopes intercept warm, moist air coming from the tropics, so they have higher rainfall and hence more rainforest species than north-facing slopes.

Answer: B
Diff: 3   Page Ref: 29.1
Skill: Application

15) Coastal areas along the Atlantic coast of the United States and Western Europe have climates much warmer than their latitudes alone would predict. This is because

   A) coastal areas heat up more quickly but cool more slowly than sites further inland.

   B) frequent El Niños push warm, moist air up against these coasts.

   C) these areas are at elevations below sea level, resulting in thicker and warmer air there.

   D) the Gulf Stream brings warm waters from the Caribbean.

   E) upwelling of warm waters from the ocean's depths heats these coastlines.

Answer: D
Diff: 2   Page Ref: 29.1
Skill: Factual

16) The periodic decline in Pacific tradewinds causes a phenomenon known as

   A) a rain shadow.

   B) El Niño.

   C) the Coriolis effect.

   D) a gyre.

   E) La Niña.

Answer: B
Diff: 1   Page Ref: 29.1
Skill: Factual

17) An El Niño results in

   A) flooding in Peru.

   B) drought in Indonesia.

   C) flooding in east Africa.

   D) drought in south Africa.

   E) all of the above

Answer: E
Diff: 2   Page Ref: 29.1
Skill: Factual

18) A La Niña event results from

   A) complex interactions between the ocean and atmosphere following an El Niño.

   B) drought in Africa.

   C) a reduction in the Pacific tradewinds.

   D) higher rainfall amounts in Florida.

   E) all of the above

Answer: A
Diff: 2   Page Ref: 29.1
Skill: Factual

19) Between the fall of 1997 and spring of 1998, 1,400 square miles of Indonesian rainforests burned, aided by a severe drought caused by

  A) an unusually severe El Niño that year.

  B) an unusually mild El Niño that year.

  C) an unusually severe La Niña that year.

  D) an unusually mild La Niña that year.

  E) the absence of either an El Niño or a La Niña that year.

  Answer: A
  Diff: 3   Page Ref: 29.1
  Skill: Application

20) Anchovies are small marine fish that feed on plankton. Every 3 to 7 years, the normally huge harvests of anchovies off the coast of Peru shrink considerably. This is most likely due to

  A) collapse of the plankton communities due to periodic sunspot activity during these years.

  B) El Niños during these years reducing the upwelling of nutrient–rich waters, causing the food chain to collapse.

  C) La Niñas during these years causing flooding on the land, washing huge amounts of nutrient–rich water into the ocean.

  D) periodic reversals of the Gulf Stream, pulling cold water down from the Arctic, freezing the fish.

  E) unusually cold water temperatures in these years due to "mini ice ages."

  Answer: B
  Diff: 3   Page Ref: 29.1
  Skill: Application

21) A _____ is a circular ocean current caused by the presence of continents.

  Answer: gyre
  Diff: 1   Page Ref: 29.1
  Skill: Factual

22) What factors determine the patterns of ocean currents?

  Answer: The patterns of ocean currents are determined by Earth's rotation, wind, heating by the sun, and the presence of continents.
  Diff: 2   Page Ref: 29.1
  Skill: Conceptual

23) Explain why there are enormous deserts in the area of the United States known as the Great Basin, which is east of the Sierra Nevada Mountains and west of the Rockies.

  Answer: The air coming off the Pacific was pushed up over the Sierras where it dropped its moisture. As the air drops back to lower elevations, it warms, causing dry, warm air to prevail in the Great Basin.
  Diff: 3   Page Ref: 29.1
  Skill: Conceptual

24) The weather at the equator is both fairly constant seasonally, and quite warm. What physical factors of the Earth's position relative to the sun are responsible for these observations?

Answer: At the equator, sunlight hits the Earth's surface at nearly a right angle, whereas farther north or south the sun's rays strike Earth's surface at a greater slant, spreading the same amount of sunlight over a greater area. Also, the Earth is tilted on its axis, so higher latitudes experience considerable variation in the directness of the sunlight throughout the year.
Diff: 2   Page Ref: 29.1
Skill: Factual

25) Western Oregon generally has cooler summer temperatures and warmer winter temperatures than do same–latitude states that are inland; similarly, Cape Cod (a coastal peninsula southeast of Boston) generally has a more moderate climate than interior Massachusetts does. Why might this be true?

Answer: Coastal areas tend to have less–variable climates than do areas near the center of continents due to the moderating effects of ocean currents. Because water both heats and cools more slowly than does land or air, ocean currents tend to moderate temperature extremes.
Diff: 3   Page Ref: 29.1
Skill: Application

26) If you wanted to do research on desert animals, to what latitude would you travel to find the most information?

Answer: Deserts tend to be located at about 30° north and south latitude.
Diff: 2   Page Ref: 29.1
Skill: Factual

27) List at least one of the two geographical circumstances under which most deserts are found.

Answer: 1. Approximately 30° north and south latitude; 2. Rain shadow of large mountain ranges
Diff: 2   Page Ref: 29.1
Skill: Factual

28) Which fundamental resources are required to support life?

A) nutrients, oxygen, sugar, appropriate temperatures

B) water, nutrients, energy, appropriate temperatures

C) water, energy, oxygen, nutrients

D) oxygen, carbon, nitrogen, water

E) oxygen, water, energy, carbon

Answer: B
Diff: 2   Page Ref: 29.2
Skill: Conceptual

29) The thick, green stems and spike-like leaves of cacti and euphorbias are adaptations to

    A) collect light in light-limited environments.

    B) conserve water in dry environments.

    C) increase gas exchange in oxygen-poor environments.

    D) speed heating and cooling in environments with little fluctuation of temperature.

    E) take up atmospheric nitrogen in nutrient-poor environments.

Answer: B
Diff: 1   Page Ref: 29.2
Skill: Factual

30) Similar groups of plants are found in areas in which the _____ is similar.

Answer: climate
Diff: 1   Page Ref: 29.2
Skill: Factual

31) Explain why climate is the primary factor in determining the type of ecosystem in an area.

Answer: Climate is determined by sunlight, water, and temperature which are three of the four basic requirements for life. Thus plants with similar requirements tend to be found in areas with similar climate.
Diff: 2   Page Ref: 29.2
Skill: Conceptual

32) Which of the following factors is (are) frequently limiting in terrestrial environments?

    A) water

    B) appropriate temperatures

    C) oxygen and nutrients

    D) nitrogen gas

    E) both water and appropriate temperatures

Answer: E
Diff: 2   Page Ref: 29.3
Skill: Factual

33) Large areas with similar environmental conditions and characteristic plant communities are

    A) climatic zones.

    B) biomes.

    C) ecosystems.

    D) climax communities.

    E) biospheres.

Answer: B
Diff: 1   Page Ref: 29.3
Skill: Conceptual

34) Which of the following is NOT a characteristic of tropical rain forests?

    A) very high species diversity

    B) vegetation grows in layers

    C) fertile soil

    D) high temperatures

    E) arboreal animals

Answer: C
Diff: 2   Page Ref: 29.3
Skill: Conceptual

35) The greatest diversity of plants and animals is found in

    A) temperate deciduous forests.

    B) tropical rain forests.

    C) chaparral.

    D) taiga.

    E) savannas.

Answer: B
Diff: 1   Page Ref: 29.3
Skill: Conceptual

36) Which of the following is NOT a serious result of destroying the tropical rain forest?

    A) potential extinction of rhinoceros and elephants

    B) greenhouse effect made more severe

    C) loss of potential drugs

    D) acid rain

    E) loss of biodiversity

Answer: A
Diff: 2   Page Ref: 29.3
Skill: Conceptual

37) A region with grasses as the dominant vegetation form, widely spaced trees and thorny shrubs, and a pronounced dry season is

    A) tropical deciduous forest.

    B) savanna.

    C) desert.

    D) tundra.

    E) chaparral.

Answer: B
Diff: 2   Page Ref: 29.3
Skill: Factual

38) Which of the following North American biomes has been almost completely destroyed and used for agriculture?

    A) desert

    B) temperate deciduous forest

    C) grassland

    D) tundra

    E) taiga

Answer: C
Diff: 2   Page Ref: 29.3
Skill: Factual

39) Why do most of the flowers in a temperate deciduous forest bloom in the spring?

    A) Most of the rain falls at that time.

    B) The deciduous tree leaves do not block the light then.

    C) The largest number of insect pollinators are available at that time.

    D) Nutrients are most available then.

    E) The trees do not block the wind and thus prevent wind pollination.

Answer: B
Diff: 2   Page Ref: 29.3
Skill: Conceptual

40) In the fall, trees in the temperate deciduous forest lose their leaves primarily as an *adaptation* to

    A) changing light.

    B) cooler temperatures.

    C) lack of accessible nutrients.

    D) excess rainfall.

    E) lack of available water.

Answer: E
Diff: 2   *Page Ref: 29.3*
Skill: Conceptual

41) When a tree falls in a dense forest it opens a gap in the canopy which allows seedlings to grow on the fallen tree, receiving light through the gap and nutrients from the dead tree. The fallen tree is called a

    A) bole log.

    B) gapper log.

    C) timber log.

    D) nurse log.

    E) mound tree.

Answer: D
Diff: 1   *Page Ref: 29.3*
Skill: Factual

42) A cold region with evergreen coniferous trees as the dominant vegetation is the

    A) savanna.

    B) tundra.

    C) taiga.

    D) arctic.

    E) chaparral.

Answer: C
Diff: 2   *Page Ref: 29.3*
Skill: Factual

43) The vast treeless region near the Arctic Ocean is the

    A) savanna.

    B) tundra.

    C) taiga.

    D) permafrost.

    E) grassland.

Answer: B
Diff: 1   Page Ref: 29.3
Skill: Factual

44) Permafrost is associated with which of these biomes?

    A) littoral

    B) arctic tundra

    C) taiga

    D) temperate deciduous forest

    E) northern coniferous forest

Answer: B
Diff: 2   Page Ref: 29.3
Skill: Factual

45) The striking dissimilarities in plant communities among different biomes with the same average yearly amount of rainfall can be explained by the fact that

    A) plant communities are not influenced by rainfall.

    B) plant communities evolve more slowly than changes in weather patterns.

    C) temperature interacts with rainfall to influence plant communities.

    D) plant communities occur randomly, depending on where seeds are blown or carried to.

    E) plant communities are influenced more by the acidity of rain than by the amount of rainfall.

Answer: C
Diff: 2   Page Ref: 29.3
Skill: Conceptual

46) The tropical rain forest is characterized by tall, broadleaf trees with a very high biodiversity, in part because

A) soils are very fertile, leading to a great ecological expansion of plants.

B) virtually all of the nutrients in a rain forest are tied up in the vegetation.

C) exposed soil is rich in iron and aluminum.

D) evenly warm and evenly moist conditions prevail.

E) both A and C

Answer: D
Diff: 2   Page Ref: 29.3
Skill: Factual

47) If global warming makes the southeastern U.S. warmer but does not alter rainfall, we might expect to see a shift from the present temperate deciduous forest biome there to

A) alpine tundra.

B) chaparral.

C) tropical deciduous forest.

D) taiga.

E) tropical rainforest.

Answer: C
Diff: 3   Page Ref: 29.3
Skill: Conceptual

48) For centuries before Europeans arrived on the continent, Native Americans prevented the encroachment of forests further west and maintained the tallgrass prairies throughout the area that now includes Missouri, Iowa, and Illinois by

A) clear-cutting forests in the area for timber and fuel.

B) establishing an extensive irrigation system to increase soil moisture, favoring grasses.

C) plowing much of the land for agriculture.

D) restricting the migrations of their bison, causing them to browse heavily on tree seedlings, killing them.

E) setting fires periodically to kill the trees.

Answer: E
Diff: 2   Page Ref: 29.3
Skill: Factual

49) Which biome probably contains the largest number and most diverse group of large mammals?

A) tropical rain forest

B) tropical deciduous forest

C) savanna

D) desert

E) chaparral

Answer: C
Diff: 2   Page Ref: 29.3
Skill: Factual

50) Which biome is also known as the prairie?

A) tropical rain forest

B) tropical deciduous forest

C) savanna

D) desert

E) grassland

Answer: E
Diff: 1   Page Ref: 29.3
Skill: Factual

51) Which biome contains plants with small, waxy leaves which can withstand dry summers and fire?

A) tropical rain forest

B) tropical deciduous forest

C) savanna

D) desert

E) chaparral

Answer: E
Diff: 2   Page Ref: 29.3
Skill: Factual

52) In the northern part of which biome would you expect to find wolverines, snowshoe hares, moose, wood bison, and deer in large numbers?

    A) tropical rain forest

    B) temperate deciduous forest

    C) savanna

    D) taiga

    E) chaparral

Answer: D
Diff: 3   Page Ref: 29.3
Skill: Factual

53) Which biome receives large amounts of rainfall, but during only part of the year?

    A) tropical rain forest

    B) tropical deciduous forest

    C) savanna

    D) desert

    E) chaparral

Answer: B
Diff: 3   Page Ref: 29.3
Skill: Factual

54) Which biome is a "freezing desert"?

    A) tundra

    B) tropical deciduous forest

    C) savanna

    D) desert

    E) chaparral

Answer: A
Diff: 1   Page Ref: 29.3
Skill: Factual

55) In which biome do most animals only come out at night?

    A) tropical rain forest

    B) tropical deciduous forest

    C) savanna

    D) desert

    E) chaparral

Answer: D
Diff: 2   Page Ref: 29.3
Skill: Factual

56) Which biome is rapidly expanding into Sub–Saharan Africa?

    A) tropical rain forest

    B) tropical deciduous forest

    C) savanna

    D) desert

    E) chaparral

Answer: D
Diff: 2   Page Ref: 29.3
Skill: Factual

57) Which biome is near the equator, but with distinct wet and dry seasons?

    A) tropical rain forest

    B) temperate rain forest

    C) savanna

    D) desert

    E) chaparral

Answer: B
Diff: 2   Page Ref: 29.3
Skill: Factual

58) In which biome are soils stabilized and enriched by cyanobacterial crusts?

    A) tropical rain forest

    B) tropical deciduous forest

    C) savanna

    D) desert

    E) chaparral

Answer: D
Diff: 3   Page Ref: 29.3
Skill: Factual

59) Which biome is currently being destroyed at the fastest rate?

   A) tropical rain forest

   B) tropical deciduous forest

   C) savanna

   D) desert

   E) chaparral

Answer: A
Diff: 1   *Page Ref: 29.3*
Skill: Factual

60) Which biome is characterized by widely spaced trees surrounded by grasses?

   A) tropical rain forest

   B) tropical deciduous forest

   C) savanna

   D) desert

   E) chaparral

Answer: C
Diff: 2   *Page Ref: 29.3*
Skill: Factual

61) Which biome is characterized by stratification of tree layers?

   A) tropical rain forest

   B) tropical deciduous forest

   C) savanna

   D) desert

   E) chaparral

Answer: A
Diff: 2   *Page Ref: 29.3*
Skill: Factual

62) Explain why it would probably be a money-losing venture to establish a plantation to grow corn in an area which was previously a tropical rain forest.

Answer: The soil is very infertile because the nutrients were tied up in the vegetation. What few nutrients are available after the forest is cut or burned tend to wash away in the heavy rains. Tropical soils also do not retain nutrients well.
Diff: 2   *Page Ref: 29.3*
Skill: Conceptual

63) Every year certain parts of California have fires which sweep rapidly through the area burning or endangering homes. What type of biome is found here and why does it burn so frequently?

Answer: This biome is chaparral. The plants found there are adapted to dry summers by having waxy leaves which burn easily while leaving the plants unharmed.
Diff: 3   Page Ref: 29.3
Skill: Conceptual

64) One of the most popular hikes in the Rocky Mountain National Park is the tundra trail. What effects would you expect from hundreds of people walking on this trail every day during the season?

Answer: because the plants are so small, such as 50-year-old willows that are a few inches tall, the damage done by a single careless hiker may last for many years
Diff: 3   Page Ref: 29.3
Skill: Conceptual

65) What type of biome predominates in tropical areas of the world such as much of India in which there are extremely wet and dry seasons?

Answer: This biome is tropical deciduous forest.
Diff: 2   Page Ref: 29.3
Skill: Factual

66) Which biome contains the most fertile soil? Why?

Answer: Grassland or prairie has the most fertile soil because the grasses that grew there partially composted over thousands of years.
Diff: 2   Page Ref: 29.3
Skill: Factual

67) What main factors determine the location of terrestrial biomes?

Answer: The particular biome is determined by availability of water and appropriate temperatures.
Diff: 2   Page Ref: 29.3
Skill: Conceptual

68) In one area is a desert ecosystem, in another area a tundra. What two fundamental resources are most likely to make the difference in ecosystems between these two areas? Why are these two more important than other fundamental resources?

Answer: They would differ in appropriate temperature and moisture, because these are more unevenly distributed than nutrients and energy.
Diff: 3   Page Ref: 29.3
Skill: Conceptual

69) Why do plants dominate and define communities on land?

Answer: This is because plants cannot escape from the weather; they tend to be precisely adapted to the climate in an area.

Diff: 2   Page Ref: 29.3
Skill: Conceptual

70) Why are most of the trees in the temperate rain forests evergreens?

Answer: There is an abundance of precipitation in winter months and the ground seldom freezes, so there is little need for the trees that grow there to lose their leaves.

Diff: 2   Page Ref: 29.3
Skill: Conceptual

71) Describe the climate in the taiga and explain how that climate favors the type of forest found there.

Answer: Extremely cold winters with short summers favor small-needled conifers which evaporate little water, but allow the trees to photosynthesize as soon as conditions are favorable.

Diff: 3   Page Ref: 29.3
Skill: Conceptual

72) Explain, in ecological terms, why cattle ranchers and conservationists have waged battle with one another over cattle-grazing practices in the western shortgrass prairie biome of the American West.

Answer: Overgrazing of grasses by cattle has altered the ecosystem to favor growth of desert plants such as sagebrush, thus threatening the organisms native to the shortgrass prairie.

Diff: 3   Page Ref: 29.3
Skill: Conceptual

73) In many parts of the Amazon Basin, farmers have cut the tropical rainforest trees and planted crops. However, these croplands are often abandoned after a few years, and farmers have moved on. What are some of the possible reasons for this?

Answer: Soils are very nutrient-poor in the tropical rainforest, in part because the nutrient capital of the forest is tied up in vegetation. Even if the trees are burned for nutrient release, the abundant rains will wash the "fertilizer" away quite quickly.

Diff: 2   Page Ref: 29.3
Skill: Conceptual

74) As large tracts of rainforest disappear due to human activities, the region tends to become drier. Why?

Answer: This is because trees can take up the water that falls to the ground very quickly, and much of the rainfall in a rainforest comes from water transpired from the forest's leaves, thus produced an internal, regional cycle of water.

Diff: 2   Page Ref: 29.3
Skill: Conceptual

75) In what biome do plants tend to be spaced very evenly with large, shallow root systems, and why?

Answer: This happens in deserts, because water is very scarce, and intense competition among plants leads to a partitioning of resources which produces an even spacing pattern. Because desert storms can be brief and intense, shallow roots can soak up the water very quickly.
Diff: 2   Page Ref: 29.3
Skill: Conceptual

76) Both the taiga and the temperate rain forest are dominated by evergreen vegetation. What are the reasons in each biome?

Answer: In the taiga, the growing season is very short, and the few months of warm weather are too short to allow trees the luxury of regrowing leaves in the spring. The abundance of water in the temperate rain forest during winter months means that trees do not need to shed leaves.
Diff: 2   Page Ref: 29.3
Skill: Conceptual

77) The major limiting factors in aquatic ecosystems, determining the distribution of organisms, are

A) availability of water and appropriate temperatures.

B) excess water and nutrients.

C) appropriate temperatures and excess water.

D) energy and excess water.

E) energy and nutrients.

Answer: E
Diff: 2   Page Ref: 29.4
Skill: Factual

78) The open water zone of a lake can be divided into the _____ and _____ zones.

A) limnetic; littoral

B) limnetic; profundal

C) profundal; stratification

D) temperate; taiga

E) littoral; benthos

Answer: B
Diff: 2   Page Ref: 29.4
Skill: Factual

79) The zone near the edge of a lake where a diverse group of organisms lives, and where light and nutrients are abundant is

    A) phytoplankton.

    B) littoral.

    C) stratification.

    D) limnetic.

    E) profundal.

Answer: B
Diff: 1   Page Ref: 29.4
Skill: Factual

80) Oligotrophic lakes have

    A) clear water with deep penetration of light.

    B) high nutrient levels.

    C) low oxygen concentrations.

    D) dense "blooms" of algae.

    E) the largest numbers and diversity of organisms.

Answer: A
Diff: 1   Page Ref: 29.4
Skill: Factual

81) Eutrophic lakes have

    A) clear water.

    B) high nutrient levels.

    C) high oxygen concentrations in deep water.

    D) very little productivity.

    E) few phytoplankton.

Answer: B
Diff: 2   Page Ref: 29.4
Skill: Factual

82) Water from sewage treatment plants, even after processing, usually has high concentrations of
_____ and _____ which support excessive growth of phytoplankton.

    A) oxygen; nitrogen

    B) oxygen; carbon dioxide

    C) phosphates; nitrates

    D) carbon; phosphates

    E) acid; oxygen

Answer: C
Diff: 2   Page Ref: 29.4
Skill: Factual

83) Which of the following best describes a lake that has been heavily polluted with excess
nutrients?

    A) devoid of life

    B) low carbon dioxide

    C) excess oxygen

    D) full of life

    E) low pH

Answer: D
Diff: 2   Page Ref: 29.4
Skill: Conceptual

84) The profundal zone is home to organisms which are

    A) photosynthetic.

    B) decomposers and detritus feeders.

    C) eutrophic.

    D) intertidal.

    E) adapted to high light.

Answer: B
Diff: 1   Page Ref: 29.4
Skill: Factual

85) Regions of upwelling in the oceans are important because

    A) warm water causes more rapid growth of phytoplankton and fish so they are important fishing regions.

    B) warm water containing nutrients is rising from the depths of the ocean.

    C) cold, nutrient rich water rises because of winds along coastlines, supporting growth of phytoplankton.

    D) cold water carries nutrients down and mixes the oceans; this allows fish to flourish at greater depths.

    E) cold water favors the growth of phytoplankton by decreasing the number of plankton feeders in the area.

Answer: C
Diff: 3   Page Ref: 29.4
Skill: Conceptual

86) A coral reef is the result of

    A) volcanic activity in warm tropical waters.

    B) rising ocean levels.

    C) skeletons from some types of Cnidarians and algae.

    D) sea floor settling.

    E) cool water settling over warmer water.

Answer: C
Diff: 2   Page Ref: 29.4
Skill: Factual

87) Organisms that spend their lives in open water swimming or floating are

    A) pelagic.

    B) benthic.

    C) littoral.

    D) intertidal.

    E) profundal.

Answer: A
Diff: 1   Page Ref: 29.4
Skill: Factual

88) As a result of human activities, a factor which currently threatens the survival of coral reef communities is

    A) lack of nutrients.

    B) fluctuations of ocean salinity.

    C) temperature fluctuations.

    D) increased amounts of silt.

    E) excess oxygen.

Answer: D
Diff: 2   Page Ref: 29.4
Skill: Factual

89) In the unique sea floor vent community, the primary producers are

    A) sulfur bacteria.

    B) phytoplankton.

    C) tube worms.

    D) plants.

    E) giant snails.

Answer: A
Diff: 2   Page Ref: 29.4
Skill: Factual

90) In hydrothermal vent communities the primary productivity is based on

    A) photosynthesis.

    B) herbivory.

    C) detritivores.

    D) chemosynthesis.

    E) bacterial decomposition.

Answer: D
Diff: 2   Page Ref: 29.4
Skill: Factual

91) Large numbers of animals and plants live in the clear, blue waters of the tropics.

    A) true

    B) false, because although many plants are found there, there are few animals

    C) false, because tropical waters are typically greenish and murky

    D) false, because tropical waters lack plants but have large numbers of animals

    E) false, because clear, blue waters are deficient in nutrients which support life

Answer: E
Diff: 3   Page Ref: 29.4
Skill: Factual

92) What is the ecological significance of shallow bays and coastal wetlands such as estuaries and salt marshes?

    A) They are the breeding grounds for a wide variety of sea-dwelling animals.

    B) They are an important source of crude oil.

    C) They serve as the habitat for many endangered species.

    D) Coral reefs occur in these areas.

    E) They are safe from most human impact, since humans do not live in these areas.

Answer: A
Diff: 2   Page Ref: 29.4
Skill: Factual

93) What has been the primary impact of human activities on wetlands in the United States?

    A) Most are seriously polluted.

    B) They have suffered little negative impact.

    C) Almost 50% have been filled in or dredged.

    D) Almost 75% have become choked with exotic plant species.

    E) Global warming has altered their native species composition.

Answer: C
Diff: 2   Page Ref: 29.4
Skill: Factual

94) Why is the human-caused damage to coral reefs of particular concern?

A) The physical structure of reefs has an important influence on the movement of ocean currents.

B) Reefs represent unique ecosystems which obtain energy through chemosynthesis rather than photosynthesis.

C) Reefs function in the detoxification of marine pollutants.

D) Reefs provide food and shelter for the world's most diverse collection of marine invertebrates and fish.

E) Reefs are not particularly sensitive to human-caused disturbance.

Answer: D
Diff: 2   Page Ref: 29.4
Skill: Factual

95) Which of the following is NOT a threat to coral reef communities?

A) silt

B) over fishing

C) eutrophication

D) physical damage

E) acid precipitation

Answer: E
Diff: 2   Page Ref: 29.4
Skill: Factual

96) Plankton are

A) drifting plants which include photosynthetic bacteria and algae.

B) drifting protozoa and crustaceans which are not photosynthetic.

C) decomposers and detrital feeders.

D) herbivorous fish and crustaceans.

E) both A and B

Answer: E
Diff: 1   Page Ref: 29.4
Skill: Factual

97) Primary producers in aquatic systems are

    A) drifting plants which include photosynthetic bacteria and algae.

    B) drifting protozoa and crustaceans which are not photosynthetic.

    C) decomposers and detrital feeders.

    D) herbivorous fish and crustaceans.

    E) both A and B

Answer: A
Diff: 1   Page Ref: 29.4
Skill: Factual

98) The major concentrations of life in the oceans are found in

    A) the aphotic zone due to high light levels.

    B) deep, large oceans due to high nutrient concentrations.

    C) the oligotrophic zone due to clear and clean water.

    D) regions of upwelling and in shallow coastal waters.

    E) the anoxic zone.

Answer: D
Diff: 1   Page Ref: 29.4
Skill: Factual

99) Reef building corals enter into a mutualistic relationship with _____ as a means of obtaining food.

    A) decomposer phytoplankton

    B) decomposer algae

    C) photosynthetic dinoflagellates

    D) multicellular algae

    E) phytotropobores

Answer: C
Diff: 1   Page Ref: 29.4
Skill: Factual

100) The "dead zone" in the Gulf of Mexico may be caused by

   A) toxins from the Mississippi River that kill off photosynthetic organisms, the base of the food chain.

   B) toxins from the Mississippi River that kill of zooplankton, the food for fish and higher organisms in the Gulf.

   C) oxygen-depleted waters entering from the Mississippi River that mix with the oxygen rich water of the ocean.

   D) nutrient-laden sediment from agricultural runoff.

   E) both A and C

Answer: D
Diff: 2   Page Ref: 29.4
Skill: Factual

101) Many small lakes in the Adirondack Mountains of New York State have been rendered nearly lifeless by

   A) acid rain.

   B) eutrophication.

   C) heavy runoff of nutrients and silt from agriculture.

   D) inadvertent oil spills.

   E) overfishing.

Answer: A
Diff: 1   Page Ref: 29.4
Skill: Factual

102) The tropical rainforest is the most diverse and productive of the terrestrial biomes, and a potential source of many new products and drugs. The aquatic ecosystem that shares many of these properties is the

   A) coral reef.

   B) intertidal zone.

   C) oligotrophic lake.

   D) open ocean.

   E) profundal zone.

Answer: A
Diff: 2   Page Ref: 29.4
Skill: Conceptual

103) If global warming raises sea levels rapidly due to melting of glaciers but does not change water temperatures, what would likely be the direct effect on coral reefs the world over?

    A) Corals in deeper waters would die as now insufficient light reaches them for photosynthesis.

    B) Corals in shallower waters would now grow more quickly due to added protection against harmful UV radiation.

    C) Corals would be stimulated to grow faster due to the dilution of the salt content of the seawater.

    D) Productivity would go down as the pure water from the glaciers would dilute nutrients in the sea.

    E) Productivity would go up as nutrients trapped in the glacial ice would be released and spread throughout the oceans by currents.

Answer: A
Diff: 3   *Page Ref: 29.4*
Skill: Application

104) Wetlands are extremely productive ecosystems because they have abundant _____, which are limiting in many terrestrial ecosystems, as well as abundant _____, which are limiting in many aquatic ecosystems.

    A) available water and suitable temperatures; nutrients and solar energy

    B) nutrients and available water; solar energy and suitable temperatures

    C) nutrients and solar energy; available water and suitable temperatures

    D) nutrients and suitable temperatures; solar energy and available water

    E) solar energy and suitable temperatures; nutrients and available water

Answer: A
Diff: 3   *Page Ref: 29.4*
Skill: Conceptual

105) The most heat-tolerant organisms presently known come from which type of ecosystem?

    A) chaparral

    B) deep-sea vents

    C) deserts

    D) tropical deciduous forests

    E) tropical rainforests

Answer: B
Diff: 2   *Page Ref: 29.4*
Skill: Factual

106) The Atlantic cod population off the coast of the northeastern U.S. and eastern Canada collapsed during the 1900s due to over fishing. What conservation measure, presently being applied, is most likely to help this fish population recover?

    A) establishing a bounty on sharks and tuna in the area that would otherwise eat the cod

    B) establishing marine reserves in the area that prohibit fishing until stocks recover

    C) fertilizing the ocean here with raw sewage to cause eutrophication, increasing productivity

    D) selective fishing on haddock, turbot, and other species that compete with cod for food

    E) spreading of silt in the water to reduce UV radiation damage to sensitive cod eggs

Answer: B
Diff: 3   Page Ref: 29.4
Skill: Application

107) On the basis of nutrient content, a mountain lake with little sediment or nutrients would be classified as _____.

Answer: oligotrophic
Diff: 2   Page Ref: 29.4
Skill: Conceptual

108) On the basis of nutrient content, a lake that has received large amounts of runoff from farms, feedlots, or sewage, would be classified as _____.

Answer: eutrophic
Diff: 2   Page Ref: 29.4
Skill: Conceptual

109) What environmental limit forms the bottom of the photic zone?

Answer: It is limited by the amount of light necessary for photosynthesis.
Diff: 2   Page Ref: 29.4
Skill: Factual

110) Compare the types of animals you would expect to find in each of the three zones of a lake.

Answer: The littoral zone has small crustacea, insect larvae, zooplankton, snails, frogs, and minnows; the limnetic zone has protozoa, small crustacea, and fish; and the profundal zone has detritus feeders such as snails, certain insect larvae, and fish.
Diff: 3   Page Ref: 29.4
Skill: Conceptual

111) Describe the spatial patterns of light and nutrients in a lake, and explain why these patterns exist.

Answer: Light decreases rapidly from the surface to lower depths because water and suspended particles absorb light. Nutrients are tied up in organic matter, which sinks to the bottom and releases nutrients there through decomposition.
Diff: 2   Page Ref: 29.4
Skill: Conceptual

112) Scientists observing coral reef communities have noted declines in coral reefs in regions with both agricultural runoff and when water temperatures rise. What are the possible reasons for these observations?

Answer: Agricultural runoff may cause eutrophication, which reduces both light penetration and oxygen due to excess algal production. High water temperature may encourage explosions of algal populations which may release specific toxins. In addition, corals expel the symbiotic algae when waters become too warm, thus cutting off the food source for the corals.
Diff: 2   Page Ref: 29.4
Skill: Conceptual

113) You are called to investigate a lake in your home town, where the residents fear that a broken pipe from the local sewage treatment plant has turned the formerly pristine lake eutrophic. Name 3 things that you would measure, or observe, in the lake to determine if the lake is eutrophic.

Answer: A eutrophic lake is generally murky, with high nutrient levels, high concentrations of plant life in the photic zone, and with reduced oxygen levels at depth.
Diff: 2   Page Ref: 29.4
Skill: Application

114) Cultivation of cacao trees for the chocolate industry has resulted in

A) loss of soil fertility.

B) toxic runoff from herbicides and pesticides.

C) clearing of large areas of rain forest.

D) reduction in local species diversity.

E) all of the above

Answer: E
Diff: 2   Page Ref: Links to Life
Skill: Factual

115) In Brazil, the Atlantic rain forest has been reduced to about _____ of its original size.

A) 1%   B) 8%   C) 16%   D) 27%   E) 63%

Answer: B
Diff: 1   Page Ref: Links to Life
Skill: Factual

116) The Earth's ozone layer is extremely important because it

    A) allows high carbon dioxide concentrations to be maintained so that photosynthesis can occur.

    B) traps heat so that the Earth's temperature does not decrease too much.

    C) blocks incoming visible light protecting the Earth against the greenhouse effect.

    D) blocks incoming UV radiation which is damaging to animals and causes a decrease in photosynthesis in plants and algae.

    E) traps harmful infrared rays.

Answer: D
Diff: 2   *Page Ref: Earth Watch*
Skill: Conceptual

117) What are some current or past sources of chemicals which are destroying the ozone layer in the upper atmosphere of Earth and exposing organisms to increased levels of damaging UV radiation?

    A) production of rigid foam, like Styrofoam

    B) refrigerants

    C) cleaners for electronic parts

    D) aerosol propellants

    E) all of these

Answer: E
Diff: 1   *Page Ref: Earth Watch*
Skill: Factual

118) The "ozone hole" over Antarctica and the general decline of ozone levels elsewhere in the stratosphere have been attributed to the ozone-destroying properties of

    A) carbon dioxide and methane.

    B) chlorofluorocarbons.

    C) endocrine-disrupting chemicals.

    D) sulfur dioxide and nitrogen oxides.

    E) all of these

Answer: B
Diff: 1   *Page Ref: Earth Watch*
Skill: Factual

119) Chlorofluorocarbons used as refrigerants and aerosol propellants can damage organisms because they

A) are extremely toxic even in very small quantities.

B) are oxidized in the atmosphere and fall as acid rain.

C) are biologically magnified to dangerous levels in food chains.

D) combine with nutrients like phosphates and nitrates, making them unavailable for uptake.

E) destroy ozone in the stratosphere, increasing levels of damaging UV reaching the surface.

Answer: E
Diff: 1   Page Ref: Earth Watch
Skill: Factual

Chapter 30 Conserving Earth's Biodiversity

1) The ivory-billed woodpecker

    A) was formerly abundant in the southeastern U.S. but is now extinct.

    B) was formerly abundant in the southeastern U.S., and was thought to be extinct, but there may be a small population remaining.

    C) was never abundant in the southeastern U.S. but is now extinct.

    D) was never formerly abundant in the southeastern U.S. but is now widespread.

    E) was never abundant in the southeastern U.S., and was thought to be extinct, but there may be a small population remaining.

Answer: E
Diff: 2   Page Ref: Case Study
Skill: Factual

2) The decline in the ivory-billed woodpecker population in the southeastern U.S. is primarily due to

    A) habitat fragmentation due to human development.

    B) a viral disease infecting the population.

    C) extensive logging.

    D) extinction of the bird's primary food sources.

    E) hunting of the species for its feathers.

Answer: C
Diff: 2   Page Ref: Case Study
Skill: Factual

3) Conservation biology is a field that spans many other disciplines EXCEPT

    A) ecology.

    B) cell biology.

    C) genetics.

    D) the social sciences.

    E) evolutionary biology.

Answer: B
Diff: 1   Page Ref: 30.1
Skill: Conceptual

4) The major goal of conservation biology is to

A) preserve the diversity of living organisms.

B) restore the biosphere to its previously unspoiled condition.

C) make the biosphere more habitable for humanity.

D) increase the population sizes of all species.

E) repair the damage to ecosystems done by introduced species.

Answer: A
Diff: 2   Page Ref: 30.1
Skill: Conceptual

5) Conservation biology operates at all but which of the following levels?

A) individual

B) population

C) species

D) community

E) Conservation biologists make efforts at all of these levels.

Answer: A
Diff: 2   Page Ref: 30.1
Skill: Conceptual

6) One goal of conservation biology is to prevent extinction caused by

A) asteroid impacts.

B) climate changes.

C) predation.

D) human activity.

E) disease.

Answer: D
Diff: 1   Page Ref: 30.1
Skill: Conceptual

7) Genetic diversity within species is important for all of the following reasons except

A) allowing species to live in diverse environments.

B) allowing the species to expand its range into new areas.

C) allowing species to evolve in response to changing conditions.

D) maintaining community interactions among species.

E) All of these are important reasons for maintaining genetic diversity.

Answer: B
Diff: 2   Page Ref: 30.1
Skill: Conceptual

8) Ecosystem services include all of the following except

    A) purifying water.

    B) decomposing waste material.

    C) recycling fossil fuels.

    D) controlling erosion.

    E) recycling oxygen.

Answer: C
Diff: 2   Page Ref: 30.1
Skill: Conceptual

9) Most people ignore ecosystem services because

    A) they are free.

    B) they have little impact on human society.

    C) it is difficult to measure their value.

    D) All of these are reasons that ecosystem services are ignored.

    E) Both A and C are true.

Answer: E
Diff: 2   Page Ref: 30.1
Skill: Conceptual

10) In 2005, the authors of the millennium Ecosystem Assessment concluded that _____% of Earth's ecosystem services are being degraded.

    A) 5   B) 20   C) 40   D) 60   E) 80

Answer: D
Diff: 1   Page Ref: 30.1
Skill: Factual

11) Tropical rainforests provide all of the following except

    A) large supplies of fossil fuels.

    B) wood for cooking by local residents.

    C) traditional medicines.

    D) hardwoods for consumers worldwide.

    E) new medicines for cancer treatment.

Answer: A
Diff: 2   Page Ref: 30.1
Skill: Factual

12) About _____% of prescription medications contain active compounds derived from plants.

   A) 5   B) 10   C) 25   D) 50   E) 75

Answer: C
Diff: 1   Page Ref: 30.1
Skill: Factual

13) Traditional medicines, which are used by about _____% of people worldwide, are primarily derived from plants.

   A) 30   B) 50   C) 70   D) 80   E) 90

Answer: D
Diff: 1   Page Ref: 30.1
Skill: Factual

14) Farming practices that destroy soil are expected to result in

   A) a greater concentration of CO_2 in the atmosphere.

   B) less clean water in the area.

   C) greater crop yield.

   D) an increase in the population sizes of detritivores.

   E) less nitrogen in local bodies of water.

Answer: B
Diff: 3   Page Ref: 30.1
Skill: Application

15) A single inch of soil may take up to _____ to form.

   A) 6 months

   B) a year

   C) 10 years

   D) hundreds of years

   E) thousands of years

Answer: D
Diff: 2   Page Ref: 30.1
Skill: Factual

16) Soil plays a major role in

    A) nutrient recycling.

    B) water purification.

    C) flood control.

    D) decomposition of waste products.

    E) Soil contributes to all of these processes.

Answer: E
Diff: 2   Page Ref: 30.1
Skill: Conceptual

17) Typical soil decomposers include all of the following except

    A) plants.   B) bacteria.   C) fungi.   D) worms.   E) insects.

Answer: A
Diff: 2   Page Ref: 30.1
Skill: Conceptual

18) In the soil, atmospheric nitrogen is converted to ammonia or nitrate, forms that can be used by organisms, by

    A) plants.   B) bacteria.   C) fungi.   D) worms.   E) insects.

Answer: B
Diff: 2   Page Ref: 30.1
Skill: Factual

19) Plants prevent erosion by

    A) releasing water.

    B) supporting animals that consume excess water.

    C) blocking wind.

    D) promoting flooding.

    E) recycling nutrients.

Answer: C
Diff: 2   Page Ref: 30.1
Skill: Conceptual

20) Coastal wetlands, or marshes, serve to

   A) purify water farther upriver.

   B) store phosphorus.

   C) return nitrogen to the atmosphere.

   D) "absorb" water from major storms.

   E) provide a habitat for major predators.

Answer: D
Diff: 2   Page Ref: 30.1
Skill: Conceptual

21) The New Orleans levees, which failed following Hurricane Katrina in 2005 and caused flooding of 80% of the city, were built at great cost to replace the beneficial effects of

   A) coastal wetlands.

   B) older levees.

   C) coastal forests.

   D) offshore barrier reefs destroyed by pollution.

   E) offshore islands destroyed by erosion.

Answer: A
Diff: 2   Page Ref: 30.1
Skill: Factual

22) Forests influence local climates in all of the following ways except

   A) reducing temperature by shading.

   B) increasing the amount of water runoff.

   C) reducing evaporation by blocking wind.

   D) transpiring water to the atmosphere.

   E) absorbing carbon dioxide.

Answer: B
Diff: 2   Page Ref: 30.1
Skill: Conceptual

23) Clear cutting of rain forests may result in the local climate becoming

    A) cooler and drier.

    B) cooler and wetter.

    C) hotter and drier.

    D) hotter and wetter.

    E) Clearcutting rain forests is not expected to affect local climate.

Answer: C
Diff: 1   Page Ref: 30.1
Skill: Conceptual

24) About _____% of the carbon dioxide produced by human activity is a result of deforestation.

    A) 10   B) 20   C) 40   D) 60   E) 80

Answer: B
Diff: 2   Page Ref: 30.1
Skill: Factual

25) It is important to preserve the genetic diversity of the wild relatives of crop plants because

    A) the wild relatives may someday have to replace the crop plants because they are generally more disease–resistant.

    B) the wild relatives are food sources for many domestic animal species.

    C) the wild relatives may someday have to replace the crop plants because they are generally more resistant to insect pests.

    D) the wild relatives are food sources for a large percentage of the human population.

    E) beneficial genes from the wild relatives may be transferred into crop plants.

Answer: E
Diff: 2   Page Ref: 30.1
Skill: Factual

26) The term _____ describes the variety of life, whether organismal, genetic, or among species.

Answer: biodiversity
Diff: 1   Page Ref: 30.1
Skill: Factual

27) The term _____ refers to the ways in which natural communities influence human life.

Answer: ecosystem services
Diff: 2   Page Ref: 30.1
Skill: Factual

28) The industry of _____ is characterized by people traveling to visit unique biological communities.

Answer: ecotourism
Diff: 2   Page Ref: 30.1
Skill: Factual

29) The discipline of _____ measures the trade-offs between the value of human developments and loss of ecosystem services.

Answer: ecological economics
Diff: 2   Page Ref: 30.1
Skill: Factual

30) How did human activity contribute to the amount of flooding in New Orleans following Hurricane Katrina in 2005?

Answer: In the past, the course of the Mississippi River was diverted, and coastal wetlands were subject to development. These activities contributed to the amount and location of flooding in New Orleans.
Diff: 2   Page Ref: 30.1
Skill: Factual

31) Applying ecological economics, how would you decide whether to develop a wetland for vacation property or preserve it?

Answer: You would weigh the costs and benefits of the development, taking into account the potential cost in property damage in future storms that may be minimized by the presence of the wetland, the purifying effects of the wetland, and the loss of habitat for local species.
Diff: 2   Page Ref: 30.1
Skill: Conceptual

32) The most likely explanation for any mass extinction event is

A) loss of genetic diversity due to inbreeding.

B) a gradual increase in global temperature.

C) coevolution of predator and prey species.

D) rapid environmental changes.

E) human activity.

Answer: D
Diff: 2   Page Ref: 30.2
Skill: Conceptual

33) Some biologists believe that life on Earth is in the midst of a sixth major mass extinction event caused by

    A) loss of genetic diversity due to inbreeding.

    B) a gradual increase in global temperature.

    C) coevolution of predator and prey species.

    D) a rapid climate change.

    E) human activity.

Answer: E
Diff: 2   Page Ref: 30.2
Skill: Factual

34) The taxonomic group(s) of species that are currently most rapidly going extinct is/are

    A) birds.

    B) mammals.

    C) birds and mammals.

    D) insects.

    E) This is unknown, because extinction rates for some groups are difficult to measure.

Answer: E
Diff: 3   Page Ref: 30.2
Skill: Conceptual

35) It is difficult to estimate current rates of extinction because

    A) many "extinct" species may still be represented by isolated populations.

    B) extinction is very rare.

    C) there are new species evolving as fast as species are becoming extinct.

    D) the number of species is unknown; there are many that remain undescribed to science.

    E) most species in danger of extinction are microscopic.

Answer: D
Diff: 2   Page Ref: 30.2
Skill: Conceptual

36) A period in which the extinction rate is far above normal is called a(n) _____.

Answer: mass extinction
Diff: 1   Page Ref: 30.2
Skill: Factual

37) A species that is in danger of extinction is described by the World Conservation Union as
_____.

Answer: threatened
Diff: 2   Page Ref: 30.2
Skill: Factual

38) The ecological footprint of the human species

A) is about 20% of the Earth's biocapacity.

B) is about 80% of the Earth's biocapacity.

C) is about equal to the Earth's biocapacity.

D) is about 20% greater than the Earth's biocapacity.

E) is about 80% greater than the Earth's biocapacity.

Answer: D
Diff: 2   Page Ref: 30.3
Skill: Factual

39) Comparison of the human ecological footprint to the planet's biocapacity suggests that

A) the human population is growing slowly.

B) the human population cannot sustain its current level of resource usage.

C) the human population will soon rapidly decrease in size.

D) the human population can continue as its present level of resource usage indefinitely.

E) global warming is seriously damaging most ecosystems.

Answer: B
Diff: 2   Page Ref: 30.3
Skill: Conceptual

40) Coral reefs are threatened by all of the following factors except

A) fungal infection.

B) pollution.

C) global warming.

D) overharvesting of species.

E) Coral reefs are threatened by all of these factors.

Answer: A
Diff: 2   Page Ref: 30.3
Skill: Factual

41) Human farming activities began about _____ years ago.

    A) 400   B) 5500   C) 11,000   D) 120,000   E) 500,000

Answer: C
Diff: 1   Page Ref: 30.3
Skill: Factual

42) About _____% of the world's tropical rain forests have been lost in the last 50 years.

    A) 20   B) 40   C) 50   D) 60   E) 90

Answer: C
Diff: 1   Page Ref: 30.3
Skill: Factual

43) Much of the tropical rain forest land that has been lost has been used for

    A) pastures for grazing domestic animals.

    B) wildlife preserves.

    C) human dwellings.

    D) recreational areas.

    E) farmland.

Answer: E
Diff: 1   Page Ref: 30.3
Skill: Factual

44) The largest threat to global biodiversity, as identified by the World Conservation Union, is

    A) global warming.

    B) introduced species.

    C) phosphate pollution.

    D) loss of habitat.

    E) lack of farmland.

Answer: D
Diff: 2   Page Ref: 30.3
Skill: Factual

45) Loss of habitat is a problem for over _____% of threatened amphibians, mammals, and birds.

    A) 25   B) 45   C) 65   D) 75   E) 85

Answer: E
Diff: 2   Page Ref: 30.3
Skill: Factual

46) Many large mammals and birds require _____ acres of continuous suitable habitat for food and territory.

    A) several

    B) dozens

    C) hundreds

    D) thousands

    E) millions

Answer: C
Diff: 2   Page Ref: 30.3
Skill: Conceptual

47) The minimum viable population level of a species is determined by many factors, including

    A) the number of offspring produced per female.

    B) the amount of food available to the population.

    C) the average lifespan of each individual.

    D) the amount of habitat available to the population.

    E) All of these factors influence the MVP.

Answer: E
Diff: 2   Page Ref: 30.3
Skill: Conceptual

48) Overexploitation is a problem for over _____ % of threatened mammals and birds.

    A) 30   B) 40   C) 50   D) 60   E) 70

Answer: A
Diff: 2   Page Ref: 30.3
Skill: Factual

49) Many marine mammal species are threatened because

    A) they are overexploited as a human food source.

    B) they are overexploited for the oil and other products in their bodies.

    C) they are caught in nets along with the species being fished.

    D) their habitats, coastal wetlands, are disappearing.

    E) their food sources are disappearing.

Answer: C
Diff: 2   Page Ref: 30.3
Skill: Conceptual

50) In less–developed countries, many species are being harvested unsustainably because

A) they are hunted as a danger to humans.

B) the people must eat or sell the species' products to survive.

C) they are hunted and killed because they carry human diseases.

D) people thoughtlessly destroy what they do not need.

E) pollution has reduced their population sizes dramatically.

Answer: B
Diff: 2   Page Ref: 30.3
Skill: Conceptual

51) An introduced species is termed "invasive" if

A) it is a threat to humans.

B) it cannot successfully maintain a population in the new habitat.

C) it survives in its new habitat and forms mutualistic relationships with native species.

D) it outcompetes native species in its new habitat.

E) it does not cause significant harm to native species.

Answer: D
Diff: 1   Page Ref: 30.3
Skill: Conceptual

52) Species that live _____ are particularly vulnerable to invasive species.

A) on islands

B) in lakes

C) in trees

D) both A and C

E) A, B, and C

Answer: D
Diff: 2   Page Ref: 30.3
Skill: Conceptual

53) Pollutants such as _____ may affect the development or reproduction of organisms.

A) endocrine disruptors

B) carbon monoxide

C) flame retardants

D) plasticizers

E) pesticides

Answer: A
Diff: 1   Page Ref: 30.3
Skill: Factual

54) Which of the following elements is NOT a potential pollutant?

    A) sulfur

    B) mercury

    C) nitrogen

    D) lead

    E) All of these are potential pollutants.

Answer: E
Diff: 1   Page Ref: 30.3
Skill: Factual

55) Atmospheric carbon dioxide has increased as a result of

    A) the destruction of coastal wetlands.

    B) burning of fossil fuels.

    C) deforestation.

    D) both B and C

    E) A, B, and C

Answer: D
Diff: 2   Page Ref: 30.3
Skill: Factual

56) As a result of global warming,

    A) the ozone layer is being degraded.

    B) species' ranges are shifting toward the equator.

    C) there are greater extremes in weather patterns.

    D) species are becoming active later in the spring.

    E) forests are expanding in range.

Answer: C
Diff: 2   Page Ref: 30.3
Skill: Conceptual

57) The _____ of the human species is the area of the Earth's surface used to generate resources and process wastes.

Answer: ecological footprint
Diff: 2   Page Ref: 30.3
Skill: Conceptual

58) The _____ of the planet is the area of the Earth's surface that is actually available to generate resources and process wastes.

Answer: biocapacity
Diff: 2   Page Ref: 30.3
Skill: Conceptual

59) _____ occurs when human developments break natural ecosystems into smaller areas.

Answer: Habitat fragmentation
Diff: 1   Page Ref: 30.3
Skill: Conceptual

60) The _____ is the smallest natural population that can subsist in an isolated habitat.

Answer: minimum viable population (MVP)
Diff: 1   Page Ref: 30.3
Skill: Conceptual

61) _____ happens when people hunt, fish, or harvest a species above its natural capacity to sustain itself.

Answer: Overexploitation
Diff: 1   Page Ref: 30.3
Skill: Conceptual

62) What two factors are most responsible for the decline in worldwide biodiversity?

Answer: First, the amount of resources used to support human lifestyles is increasing; and second, human activities are causing direct damage to habitats.
Diff: 2   Page Ref: 30.3
Skill: Conceptual

63) What is the difficulty with establishing small isolated reserve areas for the preservation of threatened species?

Answer: The species may require large areas of continuous habitat, and may be injured or killed in trying to cross nonreserve areas.
Diff: 2   Page Ref: 30.3
Skill: Conceptual

64) The goals of conservation biologists include all of the following except

A) cataloguing the number of species.

B) studying the natural impacts of human activities.

C) working toward resource sustainability.

D) reversing the loss of biodiversity.

E) maintaining and restoring natural ecosystems.

Answer: A
Diff: 2   Page Ref: 30.4
Skill: Conceptual

65) Core reserves must

A) not be used by humans for recreational purposes.

B) be large enough to support sustainable populations.

C) be as isolated as possible from all human activities.

D) be protected from major environmental events, such as fires, to be successful.

E) All of the above are necessary features of core reserves.

Answer: B
Diff: 2   Page Ref: 30.4
Skill: Conceptual

66) The buffer zones of core reserves are areas where

A) humans are forbidden from entering.

B) wildlife species benefit from extensive conservation programs, including nurseries and clinics.

C) human activities that have low impact on the native wildlife are allowed.

D) humans have irrevocably destroyed the local ecosystem.

E) humans are allowed to use and develop as they see fit.

Answer: C
Diff: 2   Page Ref: 30.4
Skill: Conceptual

67) Natural areas that are protected from human development are called _____.

Answer: core reserves
Diff: 1   Page Ref: 30.4
Skill: Conceptual

68) _____ are areas of protected land that allow animals to travel between core reserves.

Answer: Wildlife corridors
Diff: 1   Page Ref: 30.4
Skill: Conceptual

69) Landowners in areas of Costa Rica with threatened species are offered tax incentives, called
_____, if they do not develop their land.

Answer: conservation easements
Diff: 1   Page Ref: 30.4
Skill: Factual

70) How do non–biologists contribute to the field of conservation biology?

Answer: Governments have the ability to establish laws affecting environmental policy,
environmental lawyers can enforce those laws, social scientists can provide
understanding about the relationship between groups of people and their environment,
and educators can help individuals understand the issues.
Diff: 2   Page Ref: 30.4
Skill: Conceptual

71) All of the following criteria are necessary for sustainability of ecosystems except

A) use of renewable energy sources.

B) a biological community with a large number of interacting species.

C) efficient use and recycling of resources.

D) sufficient distance from human settlements.

E) populations remaining at or below their carrying capacities.

Answer: D
Diff: 2   Page Ref: 30.5
Skill: Conceptual

72) The U.N. has established a network of Biosphere Reserves, each of which consists of

A) a core reserve.

B) a core reserve and buffer zone.

C) a core reserve, buffer zone, and transition area.

D) a core reserve, buffer zone, transition area, and remediation zone.

E) a core reserve, buffer zone, transition area, remediation zone, and education center.

Answer: C
Diff: 1   Page Ref: 30.5
Skill: Conceptual

73) In the U.S., most Biosphere Reserves are found in

   A) national parks and national forests.

   B) national zoos.

   C) the Rocky Mountain region.

   D) the Appalachian Mountain region.

   E) coastal regions.

Answer: A
Diff: 1   Page Ref: 30.5
Skill: Conceptual

74) The transition zone of a Biosphere Reserves is an area where

   A) there are captive breeding programs to allow threatened species to increase their population sizes.

   B) there are many human residents, and the goal is sustainable development.

   C) only research and tourism are allowed.

   D) the government funds educational programs, stressing conservation, in public schools.

   E) low–impact human activities and development are permitted.

Answer: B
Diff: 2   Page Ref: 30.5
Skill: Conceptual

75) Unsustainable farming practices include

   A) planting different crops in the same field in alternating years.

   B) abandoning fields and allowing them to go through natural succession.

   C) abandoning the use of irrigation to water fields.

   D) the use of herbicides and pesticides.

   E) mulching fields after harvest.

Answer: D
Diff: 2   Page Ref: 30.5
Skill: Conceptual

76) Organic farming involves

    A) the use of organic pesticides and herbicides.

    B) cultivation of non–genetically engineered crops only.

    C) germination of crop plants in the laboratory before planting.

    D) the addition of organic fertilizers to soil.

    E) the allowance of natural predators to control pests.

Answer: E
Diff: 2   *Page Ref: 30.5*
Skill: Conceptual

77) Food that is produced using unsustainable farming practices tends to be

    A) less susceptible to pest damage.

    B) have a longer shelf life.

    C) be cheaper.

    D) have a lower fat content.

    E) have more complex carbohydrate content.

Answer: C
Diff: 2   *Page Ref: 30.5*
Skill: Factual

78) Which of the following is not a renewable energy source?

    A) wave energy

    B) fossil fuels

    C) wind energy

    D) solar energy

    E) All of these are renewable energy sources.

Answer: B
Diff: 1   *Page Ref: 30.5*
Skill: Conceptual

79) The principle of _____ means that the human species takes only from nature what it can replenish.

Answer: sustainable development
Diff: 1   *Page Ref: 30.5*
Skill: Conceptual

80) The practice of _____ farming is to leave leftover "cover crops" in fields after harvest to mulch the next year's crops.

Answer: no-till
Diff: 1   Page Ref: 30.5
Skill: Conceptual

81) How can sustainable fishing be accomplished?

Answer: There must be limits placed on catches, technological development to minimize damage to other species, and preservation of the spawning grounds of fished species.
Diff: 3   Page Ref: 30.5
Skill: Conceptual

82) Why is the term "sustainable development" nearly an oxymoron?

Answer: "Development" often means the destruction of natural ecosystems and their replacement with human settlements, which by definition is not sustaining ecosystems.
Diff: 3   Page Ref: 30.5
Skill: Conceptual

83) What is the single most important factor that makes worldwide sustainable development very difficult?

Answer: The size of the human population is probably at a level that makes sustainability very difficult, and continues to grow.
Diff: 2   Page Ref: 30.5
Skill: Conceptual

84) How can you, as an individual consumer, conserve energy?

Answer: Many answers are possible; these include ways to save heating and cooling costs, transportation costs and use of fuels, conserving hot water usage, and reducing appliance usage.
Diff: 2   Page Ref: Links to Life
Skill: Application

85) How can you, as an individual consumer, conserve materials?

Answer: Many answers are possible; these include ways to recycle waste materials, reusing "trash", restricting water usage, and purchasing products containing recycled material.
Diff: 2   Page Ref: Links to Life
Skill: Application

86) The possibility of a breeding pair of ivory-billed woodpeckers in Big Woods has resulted in

A) a policy of access to only researchers to the entire Big Woods area.

B) no change in policy; public access to the entire Big Woods area.

C) closing of the Big Woods area to everyone.

D) a policy of public access to the area surrounding the sighting, but restricted access to the rest of Big Woods.

E) a policy of access to only researchers in the area surrounding the sighting, but public access to the rest of Big Woods.

Answer: E
Diff: 2   Page Ref: Case Study Revisited
Skill: Application

87) What are the advantages and disadvantages of publicizing the discovery of living members of a species feared to be extinct?

Answer: Advantages include public awareness of efforts to conserve biodiversity and fundraising for conservation efforts. The disadvantages include large numbers of well-meaning people who would want to visit the area and see for themselves, which may do more harm than good.
Diff: 2   Page Ref: Case Study Revisited
Skill: Application

88) The project to straighten the Kissimmee River in the mid-20th century and the subsequent loss of wetlands resulted in

A) a decline in populations of invasive species.

B) a pollution problem.

C) an increase in the average temperature locally.

D) enhanced natural water purification.

E) an increase in native plant populations with an accompanying decline in herbivore species.

Answer: B
Diff: 2   Page Ref: Earth Watch: Restoring the Everglades
Skill: Application

89) The Comprehensive Everglades Restoration Plan begun in 2000 has already resulted in

A) a rebound in populations of native plants, birds, and fish.

B) the need to build more water treatment facilities.

C) restoration of the Kissimmee River to its original flow pattern.

D) an improvement in water quality.

E) an increase in populations of invasive species.

Answer: D
Diff: 2   Page Ref: Earth Watch: Restoring the Everglades
Skill: Application

90) The hunting of bushmeat in Africa has recently caused problems because

A) hunters have used modern technology to penetrate deeper into the forest and hunt more efficiently.

B) the focus has switched to smaller animals, causing the collapse of food chains.

C) species have been systematically hunted to extinction.

D) waste products from processing have fouled local water sources.

E) species are being driven into areas settled by humans.

Answer: A
Diff: 2   Page Ref: Earth Watch: Tangled Troubles
Skill: Application

91) The recent increase in the hunting of bushmeat in Africa may be providing a source of protein formerly obtained from

A) beef.

B) soybeans.

C) fishing.

D) terrestrial animals now designated as threatened.

E) legumes grown locally.

Answer: C
Diff: 1   Page Ref: Earth Watch: Tangled Troubles
Skill: Factual

92) The biggest threat to African great apes is currently

    A) poor water quality.

    B) habitat loss.

    C) global warming.

    D) invasive species.

    E) hunting.

Answer: E
Diff: 2   *Page Ref: Earth Watch: Tangled Troubles*
Skill: Factual

93) Adult sea turtles are primarily threatened by

    A) beach development.

    B) hunting.

    C) polluted ocean waters.

    D) beach development and hunting.

    E) beach development, hunting, and polluted ocean waters.

Answer: D
Diff: 2   *Page Ref: Earth Watch: Saving Sea Turtles*
Skill: Factual

94) The greatest threat to newly hatched sea turtles is

    A) beach development.

    B) hunting.

    C) polluted ocean waters.

    D) drowning.

    E) predation by native species.

Answer: E
Diff: 2   *Page Ref: Earth Watch: Saving Sea Turtles*
Skill: Factual

95) The conservation organization TAMAR has had some success in protecting sea turtles by

    A) restricting access to beaches.

    B) engaging the local community in conservation efforts.

    C) lobbying for legislation that supports their cause.

    D) fundraising in wealthier countries.

    E) all of the above

Answer: B
Diff: 2   *Page Ref: Earth Watch: Saving Sea Turtles*
Skill: Application

96) The _____ is a keystone predator in Yellowstone National Park.

   A) wolf

   B) black bear

   C) mountain lion

   D) bison

   E) elk

Answer: A
Diff: 1   Page Ref: Earth Watch: Restoring a Keystone Predator
Skill: Factual

97) The reintroduction of wolves to Yellowstone National Park has indirectly resulted in

   A) an increase in elk populations.

   B) an increase in coyote populations.

   C) an increase in aspen populations.

   D) a decrease in beaver populations.

   E) a decrease in grizzly bear populations.

Answer: C
Diff: 2   Page Ref: Earth Watch: Restoring a Keystone Predator
Skill: Application

98) A(n) _____ is an animal whose predation on other species has major effects on the structure of the biological community.

Answer: keystone predator
Diff: 1   Page Ref: Earth Watch: Restoring a Keystone Predator
Skill: Conceptual

99) The major difference between coffee and most other crops is that

   A) it can be grown in almost any climate.

   B) it can be grown in shade, so forests do not need to be cut.

   C) it has many uses in addition to food.

   D) it does not need much human supervision.

   E) it promotes weed growth.

Answer: B
Diff: 2   Page Ref: Earth Watch: Preserving Biodiversity
Skill: Factual

100) The majority of the world's coffee is grown

    A) in tropical rain forests, while shaded.

    B) in temperate regions.

    C) in full sunlight.

    D) it does not need much human supervision.

    E) in the United States.

Answer: C
Diff: 1   Page Ref: Earth Watch: Preserving Biodiversity
Skill: Factual

101) Coffee grown under shade

    A) preserves tropical rain forests.

    B) does not require herbicides or pesticides.

    C) requires little or no added fertilizer.

    D) helps to support bird populations.

    E) all of the above

Answer: E
Diff: 2   Page Ref: Earth Watch: Preserving Biodiversity
Skill: Application

102) Shade–grown coffee is more expensive in the U.S. market

    A) due to lower yield than coffee grown in full sun.

    B) because of the added cost of herbicides or pesticides.

    C) because of the added cost of fertilizer.

    D) because of a surcharge for bird conservation.

    E) because of the added shipping costs; it is grown in remote areas.

Answer: A
Diff: 2   Page Ref: Earth Watch: Preserving Biodiversity
Skill: Application

Chapter 31 Homeostasis and the Organization of the Animal Body

1) Most body systems maintain homeostasis through

   A) positive feedback systems.

   B) negative feedback systems.

   C) monitoring systems.

   D) alternating systems.

   E) redundant systems.

Answer: B
Diff: 1   *Page Ref: 31.1*
Skill: Factual

2) Hypertension produces damage to the lining of the arterioles of the kidneys, which results in the release of molecules that will further raise blood pressure. This is an example of a(n)

   A) negative feedback loop.

   B) positive feedback loop.

   C) controlling mechanism.

   D) uncontrolled mechanism.

   E) electrochemical mechanism.

Answer: B
Diff: 2   *Page Ref: 31.1*
Skill: Conceptual

3) The principle reason that internal homeostasis must be maintained is

   A) that wild fluctuations in conditions are metabolically costly.

   B) to prevent wasting stockpiles of coenzymes.

   C) to retain the correct three–dimensional structure of enzymes.

   D) that unregulated variations will mutate the cells DNA.

   E) because most organisms have not evolved processes to control positive feedback systems.

Answer: A
Diff: 2   *Page Ref: 31.1*
Skill: Conceptual

4) When describing homeostasis, the term *dynamic constancy* refers to

    A) even though physical & chemical changes do occur, conditions are kept within a range.

    B) a constant movement toward equilibrium.

    C) the direct interaction of each positive feedback system with its corresponding negative feedback system.

    D) the use of ATP to initiate a cascade effect.

    E) a now disregarded theory that suggested there were no external energy requirements to maintain cell homeostasis.

Answer: A
Diff: 1   Page Ref: 31.1
Skill: Factual

5) All of the following statements about endotherms are true EXCEPT

    A) All mammals are endotherms.

    B) Endotherms produce heat by metabolic reactions.

    C) Some large sharks can be considered endotherms.

    D) All birds are endotherms.

    E) Endotherms derive most of their heat from the environment.

Answer: E
Diff: 1   Page Ref: 31.1
Skill: Factual

6) All of the following statements about ectotherms are true EXCEPT

    A) All reptiles are ectotherms.

    B) Ectotherms produce heat by metabolic reactions.

    C) A common behavior for an ectotherm is basking.

    D) Most fish are ectotherms.

    E) Ectotherms derive most of their heat from the environment.

Answer: E
Diff: 1   Page Ref: 31.1
Skill: Factual

7) Temperature maintenance in animals is controlled by

   A) the autonomic nerve system.

   B) the hypothalamus.

   C) positive feedback systems.

   D) reflexive skeletal muscles.

   E) by the cerebral cortex.

Answer: B
Diff: 3   Page Ref: 31.1
Skill: Application

8) A group of cells that perform a similar function are known as

   A) tissues.   B) organs.

   C) organ systems.   D) organisms.

Answer: A
Diff: 1   Page Ref: 31.1
Skill: Factual

9) A biological example of a positive feedback system involves

   A) the cascade of events involving oxytocin during childbirth.

   B) temperature regulation.

   C) pH levels of interstitial fluid.

   D) water balance.

Answer: A
Diff: 1   Page Ref: 31.1
Skill: Factual

10) Walter B. Cannon coined the term homeostasis in the 1920s. True or False?

Answer: TRUE
Diff: 1   Page Ref: 31.1
Skill: Factual

11) Due to the freezing temperatures of the deep ocean, all deep sea fish must be endotherms. True or False?

Answer: FALSE
Diff: 1   Page Ref: 31.1
Skill: Conceptual

12) Positive feedback systems are much more common in living organisms than negative feedback systems. True or False?

Answer: FALSE
Diff: 1   Page Ref: 31.1
Skill: Factual

13) Compare the mechanisms by which endotherms and ectotherms regulate body temperature?

Answer: FALSE
Diff: 2   Page Ref: 31.1
Skill: Factual

14) All animal bodies are made of _____ different types of tissues.

A) 4   B) 8   C) 16   D) 48   E) over 100

Answer: A
Diff: 1   Page Ref: 31.2
Skill: Factual

15) Salivary glands are formed from a type of

A) epithelial tissue.

B) connective tissue.

C) muscle tissue.

D) nerve tissue.

E) undifferentiated tissue.

Answer: A
Diff: 1   Page Ref: 31.2
Skill: Factual

16) Blood is a type of

A) epithelial tissue.

B) connective tissue.

C) muscle tissue.

D) nerve tissue.

E) endothelial tissue.

Answer: B
Diff: 1   Page Ref: 31.2
Skill: Factual

17) The mucus that traps dust particles in the lungs is produced by

A) epithelial tissue.

B) connective tissue.

C) muscle tissue.

D) endocrine glands.

E) epithelial tissue.

Answer: E
Diff: 2   Page Ref: 31.2
Skill: Factual

18) The pads that cushion the vertebrae are formed from

A) bone.

B) cartilage.

C) matrix.

D) fat.

E) smooth muscle tissue.

Answer: B
Diff: 2   Page Ref: 31.2
Skill: Factual

19) Which type of muscle lacks an orderly arrangement of filaments?

A) cardiac

B) smooth

C) skeletal

D) both A and B

E) both A and C

Answer: B
Diff: 2   Page Ref: 31.2
Skill: Factual

20) Nerve tissue is composed of cells called

A) neurons.

B) nerves.

C) glial cells.

D) both A and C

E) both B and C

Answer: D
Diff: 1   Page Ref: 31.2
Skill: Factual

21) Which type of tissue is characterized by continuous loss and replacement?

   A) epithelial tissue

   B) connective tissue

   C) muscle tissue

   D) both A and B

   E) all of the above

Answer: A
Diff: 2   Page Ref: 31.2
Skill: Factual

22) The skin is an example of a(n)

   A) cell.

   B) tissue.

   C) organ.

   D) organ system.

   E) undifferentiated mass.

Answer: C
Diff: 1   Page Ref: 31.2
Skill: Factual

23) Cardiac and smooth muscle are similar in that

   A) both have ordered arrangements of thick and thin protein filaments.

   B) both are under conscious control.

   C) both are involuntary.

   D) both are connected to bones.

   E) both use cAMP as an energy source.

Answer: C
Diff: 2   Page Ref: 31.2
Skill: Factual

24) The vertebrate organ systems that control physiological processes in animals are the nervous system and the

    A) reproductive system.

    B) skeletal system.

    C) muscular system.

    D) endocrine system.

    E) respiratory system.

Answer: D
Diff: 2   *Page Ref: 31.2*
Skill: Factual

25) Cells that store lipids (fats) for long-term energy are found in _____ tissue.

    A) bone

    B) muscle

    C) epithelial

    D) adipose

    E) connective

Answer: D
Diff: 1   *Page Ref: 31.2*
Skill: Factual

26) The type of muscle under voluntary control is

    A) smooth.

    B) cardiac.

    C) epithelial.

    D) skeletal.

    E) oxygen enriched.

Answer: D
Diff: 1   *Page Ref: 31.2*
Skill: Factual

27) Groups of tissues that function together form a(n)

    A) organ.

    B) organ system.

    C) system.

    D) individual.

    E) gland.

Answer: A
Diff: 1   Page Ref: 31.2
Skill: Factual

28) Which of the following tissues contains large amounts of collagen?

    A) nerve   B) adipose   C) blood   D) lymph   E) tendons

Answer: E
Diff: 2   Page Ref: 31.2
Skill: Factual

29) Which of the following tissues is in direct contact with the external environment of an animal?

    A) connective

    B) epithelial

    C) muscle

    D) nerve

    E) endothelial

Answer: B
Diff: 2   Page Ref: 31.2
Skill: Conceptual

30) Connective tissues include lymph, ligament tendons and

    A) cardiac muscle.

    B) exocrine glands.

    C) skin cells.

    D) cartilage.

    E) vessel linings.

Answer: D
Diff: 2   Page Ref: 31.2
Skill: Factual

31) A gland is

  A) a cluster of cells that secretes a product.

  B) a type of tissue that makes cartilage.

  C) a special connection between muscle cells.

  D) a group of cells that replaces the stomach lining every few days.

  E) the functional unit of the skeletal system.

Answer: A
Diff: 1   Page Ref: 31.2
Skill: Factual

32) The circulatory system plays a role in temperature regulation. True or False?

Answer: TRUE
Diff: 2   Page Ref: 31.2
Skill: Factual

33) Why do doctors lower a patient's body temperature during open heart surgery?

Answer: Cold slows metabolic reactions thus decreasing the need for oxygen to the cells. This prevents brain damage from lack of oxygen while the heart is not beating.
Diff: 2   Page Ref: 31.2
Skill: Application

Chapter 32 Circulation

1) Which is NOT a component of all circulatory systems?

      A) blood   B) vessels   C) heart   D) lymph nodes

Answer: D
Diff: 1   *Page Ref: 32.1*
Skill: Factual

2) Which of the following has a closed circulatory system?

      A) spider

      B) insect

      C) snail

      D) Earthworm

      E) clam

Answer: D
Diff: 1   *Page Ref: 32.1*
Skill: Factual

3) What is the advantage of a closed circulatory system over an open one?

      A) It can carry more blood.

      B) It can move blood more efficiently.

      C) There are more blood cells in a closed system.

      D) Blood flows more slowly in a closed system.

      E) The blood comes nearer to each cell.

Answer: B
Diff: 2   *Page Ref: 32.1*
Skill: Conceptual

4) What are advantages of closed systems?

      Answer: Closed systems allow for more rapid and efficient transport of materials. This is
               necessary for survival in large animals with high energy needs.
      Diff: 2   *Page Ref: 32.1*
      Skill: Conceptual

5) Name and discuss at least three important functions of the circulatory system.

      Answer: varied, see text
      Diff: 2   *Page Ref: 32.1*
      Skill: Factual

6) In a grasshopper all the body tissues are bathed in blood that is in the

  A) capillaries.

  B) heart.

  C) tracheae.

  D) spiracles.

  E) hemocoel.

Answer: E
Diff: 1   Page Ref: 32.2
Skill: Conceptual

7) Which heart chamber supplies oxygenated blood to the heart muscle?

  A) right atrium   B) left atrium   C) right ventricle   D) left ventricle

Answer: D
Diff: 1   Page Ref: 32.2
Skill: Factual

8) A three-chambered heart

  A) is found in fish.

  B) has two atria and one ventricle.

  C) has one atrium and two ventricle.

  D) Both B and C are correct.

  E) All of the above are correct.

Answer: B
Diff: 1   Page Ref: 32.2
Skill: Factual

9) The aorta

  A) is the largest artery.   B) is the largest vein.

  C) contains blood with low pressure.   D) connects right and left ventricles.

Answer: A
Diff: 1   Page Ref: 32.2
Skill: Factual

10) In which vertebrate does one see a partial partition in the ventricle?

    A) fishes

    B) amphibians

    C) reptiles

    D) birds

    E) mammals

Answer: C
Diff: 1   Page Ref: 32.2
Skill: Factual

11) Which of the following animals have four-chambered hearts?

    A) all reptiles

    B) all birds

    C) mammals

    D) fish

    E) all of the above

Answer: C
Diff: 1   Page Ref: 32.2
Skill: Factual

12) Which set of chambers supplies blood to the pulmonary circulation?

    A) the atria   B) the ventricles

    C) the right atrium and right ventricle   D) the left atrium and left ventricle

Answer: C
Diff: 1   Page Ref: 32.2
Skill: Factual

13) Which heart chamber is the most muscular?

    A) the right atrium   B) the left atrium

    C) the right ventricle   D) the left ventricle

Answer: D
Diff: 1   Page Ref: 32.2
Skill: Factual

14) The left ventricle is more muscular than the right ventricle because

    A) it must push the blood through the pulmonary circulation.

    B) it must pass the blood through the systemic circulation.

    C) it must push against gas pressure in the lungs.

    D) Both B and C are correct.

Answer: B
Diff: 2   Page Ref: 32.2
Skill: Conceptual

15) The difference between the systolic and diastolic blood pressure is called the pulse pressure. Pulse pressure in a healthy human is about

    A) 10 mm Hg.   B) 40 mm Hg.   C) 80 mm Hg.   D) 120 mm Hg.

Answer: B
Diff: 2   Page Ref: 32.2
Skill: Conceptual

16) In humans, the tricuspid valve is found

    A) between the right atrium and the right ventricle.

    B) between the right ventricle and the pulmonary trunk.

    C) between the left atrium and the left ventricle.

    D) between the left atrium and the aorta.

Answer: A
Diff: 1   Page Ref: 32.2
Skill: Factual

17) Gap junctions

    A) allow rapid passage of electrical signals among heart cells.

    B) prevent backflow of blood from ventricles to atrium.

    C) connect veins and arteries.

    D) are found in white blood cells.

Answer: A
Diff: 1   Page Ref: 32.2
Skill: Factual

18) Why is it important that the atrioventricular (AV) node produce a delay between the contraction of the atria and the contraction of the ventricles?

 A) It allows the heart to rest for a brief period of time.

 B) It allows the ventricles to fill to capacity.

 C) It allows the atria to contract on smooth synchrony.

 D) It allows the ventricles to contract in smooth synchrony.

Answer: B
Diff: 2   Page Ref: 32.2
Skill: Conceptual

19) A person who has an artificial pacemaker has an artificial device that replaces the actions of the

 A) sinoatrial node.   B) atrioventricular node.

 C) atria.   D) ventricles.

Answer: A
Diff: 2   Page Ref: 32.2
Skill: Conceptual

20) The parasympathetic nervous system

 A) increases heart rate.

 B) decreases heart rate.

 C) releases the hormones.

 D) increases epinephrine blood flow to muscles.

Answer: B
Diff: 1   Page Ref: 32.2
Skill: Factual

21) In fish, blood leaving the heart goes directly to the

 A) kidney.   B) gills.

 C) swimming muscles.   D) brain.

Answer: B
Diff: 1   Page Ref: 32.2
Skill: Conceptual

22) The head of a giraffe is 5 meters above its heart. Compared to humans, giraffes have

 A) lower systolic blood pressure.   B) higher systolic blood pressure.

 C) less blood.   D) veins of smaller diameter.

Answer: B
Diff: 2   Page Ref: 32.2
Skill: Conceptual

23) Which of the following has a heart with only two chambers?

    A) hummingbird

    B) human

    C) goldfish

    D) bullfrog

    E) cat

Answer: C
Diff: 1   Page Ref: 32.2
Skill: Conceptual

24) In a mammal, blood with a low oxygen content enters the _____ of the heart.

    A) right atrium

    B) right ventricle

    C) left atrium

    D) left ventricle

    E) aorta

Answer: A
Diff: 1   Page Ref: 32.2
Skill: Conceptual

25) If a person's blood pressure is given as 120/70, the 70 refers to the pressure

    A) during contraction of the left ventricle only.

    B) during contraction of both ventricles.

    C) during relaxation of the ventricles.

    D) during contraction of the vena cava.

    E) between contractions.

Answer: C
Diff: 2   Page Ref: 32.2
Skill: Factual

26) Ventricles force blood directly into

    A) veins.

    B) arteries.

    C) capillaries.

    D) arterioles.

    E) venules.

Answer: B
Diff: 1   Page Ref: 32.2
Skill: Factual

27) The human heart contains muscle cells that

    A) contract.

    C) generate electrical signals.

    B) produce a hormone.

    D) all of the above

Answer: D
Diff: 1   *Page Ref: 32.2*
Skill: Factual

28) The bicuspid valve prevents blood from flowing back into the

    A) right atrium.

    B) right ventricle.

    C) left atrium.

    D) left ventricle.

    E) vena cava.

Answer: C
Diff: 1   *Page Ref: 32.2*
Skill: Factual

29) The _____ valve is between the right ventricle and the pulmonary artery.

    A) atrioventricular

    C) bicuspid

    B) semilunar

    D) tricuspid

Answer: B
Diff: 1   *Page Ref: 32.2*
Skill: Factual

30) The cardiac cycle is

    A) the alternating relaxation and contraction of heart chambers.

    B) the movement of blood from heart to lungs and back to heart.

    C) the passage of electric impulses from AV node to SN node to heart muscle.

    D) the movement of blood from systemic to pulmonary circulation.

Answer: A
Diff: 1   *Page Ref: 32.2*
Skill: Factual

31) Which is NOT TRUE of the SA node?

    A) It directly stimulates the ventricles.

    B) It directly stimulates the atria.

    C) It is the pacemaker.

    D) It is influenced by nerve impulses and hormones.

    E) Its stimulus is stopped by inexcitable tissue at the base of the atria.

Answer: A
Diff: 2   Page Ref: 32.2
Skill: Factual

32) Sympathetic nerve stimulation and epinephrine _____ heart activity.

    A) increase

    B) decrease

    C) have no effect on

    D) The heart responds to hormones, but not to nerve stimulation.

    E) The heart responds to nerve stimulation, but not to hormones.

Answer: A
Diff: 1   Page Ref: 32.2
Skill: Factual

33) Rheumatic fever is a bacterial disease that can result in degeneration of heart valves. That would cause

    A) slower heartbeat.

    B) uncoordinated attraction of ventricles.

    C) faster heart beat.

    D) backfire of blood from ventricle to an atrium.

Answer: D
Diff: 2   Page Ref: 32.2
Skill: Conceptual

34) If you feel like your heart is beating rapidly while you sit here taking this exam, you are probably

   A) right because the somatic nervous system is in control.

   B) right because the parasympathetic system responds to the stress of the test situation.

   C) right because the sympathetic system is responding to the stress of the test situation.

   D) wrong because the pacemaker tends to keep your heart beating at a steady rate even under stress.

   E) wrong because the response of your body to stress is to shift energy to the skeletal muscles from the heart muscle.

Answer: C
Diff: 2   *Page Ref: 32.2*
Skill: Conceptual

35) Which statement is NOT TRUE?

   A) Plasma is primarily water.

   B) Red blood cells carry oxygen.

   C) White blood cells defend the body against disease.

   D) Platelets are large cells that aid in blood clotting.

Answer: D
Diff: 2   *Page Ref: 32.2*
Skill: Factual

36) A person is rushed into the Emergency Room of a local hospital and receives treatment with a drug called Atropine. Atropine is a sympathomimetic, which means it "mimics" the effects of the sympathetic nervous system. What symptom did this patient have that warranted the use of this drug?

   A) a wound that would not clot   B) an accelerated heart rate

   C) very high blood pressure   D) a depressed heart rate

Answer: D
Diff: 3   *Page Ref: 32.2*
Skill: Application

37) When your blood pressure is measured from an artery in your arm, you are measuring pressure produced by the

   A) left ventricle.   B) right ventricle.   C) left atria.   D) right atria.

Answer: A
Diff: 2   *Page Ref: 32.2*
Skill: Conceptual

38) If there is an abnormality in the T wave of the ECG, then the problem is in

A) the electrical tissue of the atria.

B) the electrical tissue of the ventricles.

C) the SA nodal tissue.

D) the AV nodal tissue.

Answer: B
Diff: 2   *Page Ref: 32.2*
Skill: Conceptual

39) In an ECG, you notice that there is an abnormally long delay between the P and the QRS wave. Which of the following might explain this result?

A) Conduction of electrical activity through the AV node is slow.

B) The ventricles are contracting, but they stay contracted for a long period of time before relaxing.

C) The SA node is generating electrical signals at a slower rate.

D) The heart is in ventricular fibrillation.

Answer: A
Diff: 3   *Page Ref: 32.2*
Skill: Conceptual

40) The period of time in which the ventricles contract is known as _____.

Answer: systole
Diff: 1   *Page Ref: 32.2*
Skill: Factual

41) "Tubing out" in front of the TV the average person's heart rate is about 70 beats per minute because the _____ nervous system slows the heart down from the approximately 100 beats per minute that the pacemaker, the _____ node, sets.

Answer: parasympathetic; SA
Diff: 2   *Page Ref: 32.2*
Skill: Factual

42) Why do mammals and birds have 4-chambered hearts, whereas fish and amphibians get by with 2 or 3 chambers?

Answer: Only mammals and birds are warm-blooded and thus have very high metabolic requirements. The 4-chambered heart is the only system that completely separates oxygenated from deoxygenated blood. This allows for each cell to get the maximum amount of oxygen and thus meet its metabolic needs.
Diff: 2   *Page Ref: 32.2*
Skill: Conceptual

43) What three major challenges does the heart face in maintaining proper blood flow and what are the mechanisms which enable the heart to meet them?

Answer: 1. To keep the blood from flowing backwards when the chambers contract—valves 2. To make smooth, coordinated contractions of each chamber—pacemaker (SA node) 3. To coordinate contraction of each chamber—AV nodes and fibers
Diff: 3   Page Ref: 32.2
Skill: Conceptual

44) You are a red blood cell. Describe your "Trek Through the Heart" from when you enter until when you finally exit. You enter the right atrium. What next? What do you pass along the way?

Answer: The red blood cell enters the right atrium and goes into the right ventricle. It is deoxygenated at this point. The red blood cell then gets pumped into the lungs and becomes oxygenated. Blood returns to the heart and enters the left atrium and then goes to the left ventricle. It is then pumped into the aorta and out to the rest of the body.
Diff: 2   Page Ref: 32.2
Skill: Conceptual

45) In Southern Copperhead snake venom, you will find a protein called a disintegrin. Disintegrins bind to a class of membrane receptors called integrins. Platelets use integrin receptors to aggregate at a site of tissue damage. Why do you think the snake venom contains this molecule?

A) After the snake bites its prey, the molecule helps in wound healing.

B) The molecule helps kill the snake's prey by producing large clots that travel in the body and produce heart attacks and strokes.

C) The molecule interferes with clot formation so that the venom can travel more efficiently from the site of the bite to the rest of the body.

D) By binding to the platelets, the molecule inhibits the formation of fibrin.

Answer: C
Diff: 3   Page Ref: 32.3
Skill: Application

46) In a random screening of athletes at a recent event, a runner was disqualified for testing positive for an injected form of erythropoietin. Which of the following represents one of the pieces of evidence that the testers used in this case?

A) low blood pressure

B) The cellular components made up 55% of the blood volume.

C) "thin" blood that does not clot efficiently

D) a low white blood cell count

Answer: B
Diff: 2   Page Ref: 32.3
Skill: Application

47) If a person weighed 100 pounds, what would be the weight of their blood?

    A) 5 to 6 pounds   B) 8 pounds   C) 10 pounds   D) 12 pounds

Answer: B
Diff: 2   Page Ref: 32.3
Skill: Conceptual

48) Red blood cells constitute _____ of the total blood volume in females.

    A) 30%   B) 35%   C) 40%   D) 45%   E) 50%

Answer: C
Diff: 1   Page Ref: 32.3
Skill: Factual

49) If you remove red blood cells, white blood cells and platelets from blood you have

    A) salty water.   B) plasma.   C) lymph.   D) albumin.

Answer: B
Diff: 2   Page Ref: 32.3
Skill: Conceptual

50) The maximum number of molecules of oxygen that can bind with one molecule of human hemoglobin is _____.

    A) 1   B) 2   C) 3   D) 4   E) 5

Answer: D
Diff: 1   Page Ref: 32.3
Skill: Factual

51) How long does the average red blood cell live?

    A) 90 days

    B) 100 days

    C) 120 days

    D) 150 days

    E) It depends upon the amount of oxygen and the amount of hemoglobin the cell carries.

Answer: C
Diff: 1   Page Ref: 32.3
Skill: Factual

52) Erythropoietin

    A) is produced by the kidneys.

    B) is released in response to high carbon dioxide or low oxygen levels in the blood.

    C) is only released in response to hemorrhaging.

    D) stimulates the spleen to release more red blood cells.

Answer: A
Diff: 1   Page Ref: 32.3
Skill: Factual

53) Erythroblastosis fetalis is a pathology that

    A) occurs when an Rh negative mother carries an Rh positive fetus.

    B) occurs when an Rh positive mother carries an Rh negative fetus.

    C) never affects the first fetus that a mother carries.

    D) Both A and C are correct.

    E) Both B and C are correct.

Answer: D
Diff: 2   Page Ref: 32.3
Skill: Factual

54) Which type of white blood cell is NOT found within the vasculature?

    A) lymphocytes

    B) leukocytes

    C) monocytes

    D) macrophages

    E) All are found within the vasculature.

Answer: D
Diff: 2   Page Ref: 32.3
Skill: Factual

55) A person that has an allergy to pollen would expect an elevated level of _____ in their blood during the spring.

    A) leukocytes

    B) eosinophils

    C) basophils

    D) monocytes

    E) neutrophils

Answer: C
Diff: 2   Page Ref: 32.3
Skill: Conceptual

56) Which blood constituent makes up more of the volume of blood?

   A) red blood cells

   B) plasma

   C) white blood cells

   D) blood proteins

   E) They each constitute about 25% of the total volume.

Answer: B
Diff: 2   Page Ref: 32.3
Skill: Conceptual

57) Erythrocytes are produced in the

   A) bone marrow.   B) liver.   C) spleen.   D) heart.

Answer: A
Diff: 1   Page Ref: 32.3
Skill: Factual

58) Plasma that leaks out of the blood in the capillary beds is returned to the venous circulation by

   A) the small intestine.   B) suppressor B cells.

   C) the lymphatic system.   D) the inflammatory response.

Answer: C
Diff: 1   Page Ref: 32.3
Skill: Factual

59) Most of the plasma is

   A) protein.   B) salt.   C) cells.   D) gases.   E) water.

Answer: E
Diff: 1   Page Ref: 32.3
Skill: Factual

60) Approximately 99% of blood cells are involved in

   A) immunity.

   B) transporting oxygen.

   C) eating invaders.

   D) amoeba-like activities.

   E) entering and leaving the blood stream.

Answer: B
Diff: 2   Page Ref: 32.3
Skill: Conceptual

61) Which of the following is NOT TRUE of hemoglobin?

    A) It is found in all blood cells.

    B) It carries oxygen.

    C) It carries carbon dioxide.

    D) It contains iron.

    E) It is red.

Answer: A
Diff: 2   Page Ref: 32.3
Skill: Factual

62) Females need more dietary iron than males because

    A) they have more red blood cells.

    B) they have less bone marrow.

    C) they lose iron during menstruation.

    D) they have a larger volume of blood.

    E) they are less able to absorb iron.

Answer: C
Diff: 2   Page Ref: 32.3
Skill: Conceptual

63) Athletes such as long distance runners like to train at high altitudes because the lack of oxygen there stimulates the

    A) body to produce more lung tissue.

    B) bone marrow to make more erythrocytes.

    C) muscles to contract aerobically.

    D) muscles to contract more strongly.

    E) capillaries to diffuse oxygen more readily.

Answer: B
Diff: 2   Page Ref: 32.3
Skill: Conceptual

64) Some athletes use "blood doping"—adding additional RBC's to the blood for the competition will

    A) make the heart beat faster.   B) increase O_2 delivery to muscles.

    C) decrease blood pressure.   D) change the blood type.

Answer: B
Diff: 1   Page Ref: 32.3
Skill: Conceptual

65) WBC's

A) carry O_2 in blood.

B) protect body from microbes.

C) are formed in the spleen.

D) clot blood.

Answer: B
Diff: 1   Page Ref: 32.3
Skill: Factual

66) Which of the following does NOT play a role in blood clotting?

A) fibrinogen

B) platelets

C) thrombin

D) albumin

E) fibrin

Answer: D
Diff: 2   Page Ref: 32.3
Skill: Factual

67) Which of the following blood cells is phagocytic?

A) red blood cells

B) white blood cells

C) platelets

D) all blood cells

E) none of the above

Answer: B
Diff: 2   Page Ref: 32.3
Skill: Factual

68) Which of the following blood cells have no nucleus in mammals?

A) red blood cells

B) white blood cells

C) platelets

D) All blood cells in mammals lack nuclei.

E) none of the above

Answer: A
Diff: 2   Page Ref: 32.3
Skill: Factual

69) Erythropoietin stimulates the manufacture of which type of blood cell?

    A) red blood cells

    B) white blood cells

    C) platelets

    D) all blood cells

    E) none of the above

Answer: A
Diff: 2   *Page Ref: 32.3*
Skill: Factual

70) Which of the following blood cells include lymphocytes?

    A) red blood cells

    B) white blood cells

    C) platelets

    D) all blood cells

    E) none of the above

Answer: B
Diff: 2   *Page Ref: 32.3*
Skill: Factual

71) Thrombin catalyzes the conversion of the plasma protein fibrinogen into fibrin. True or False?

Answer: TRUE
Diff: 1   *Page Ref: 32.3*
Skill: Factual

72) The fluid portion of the blood is called the _____.

Answer: plasma
Diff: 1   *Page Ref: 32.3*
Skill: Factual

73) Red blood cells are called _____.

Answer: erythrocytes
Diff: 1   *Page Ref: 32.3*
Skill: Factual

74) What is the role of erythropoietin?

Answer: to simulate the bone marrow to produce erythrocytes
Diff: 2   *Page Ref: 32.3*
Skill: Factual

75) Your nose is running and your eyes are watering from an allergy. Which of the white cells is involved?

Answer: basophils
Diff: 2   Page Ref: 32.3
Skill: Conceptual

76) During clotting what happens to the plasma protein fibrinogen?

Answer: It is formed into fibrin, which is a string–like protein that forms a web.
Diff: 2   Page Ref: 32.3
Skill: Conceptual

77) Describe the process of blood clotting.

Answer: response should include platelets, thrombin, fibrin, and clot at the minimum
Diff: 2   Page Ref: 32.3
Skill: Conceptual

78) What is one reason why blood pressure in an artery is higher than in a vein?

   A) Arteries have thick walls that contain layers of muscle and connective tissue.

   B) Arteries have one-way valves to prevent blood from flowing backwards.

   C) Arteries contain only oxygenated blood.

   D) all of the above

Answer: A
Diff: 2   Page Ref: 32.4
Skill: Conceptual

79) When your physician takes your pulse, she is feeling the expansion and contraction of your

   A) arteries or arterioles.   B) capillaries.

   C) veins or venules.   D) Both A and C are correct.

Answer: A
Diff: 2   Page Ref: 32.4
Skill: Conceptual

80) Return of blood to the heart in the systemic venous circulation is driven primarily by

   A) contractions of the left auricle.

   B) muscles squeezing blood through the veins.

   C) ciliated cells lining the inside of the veins.

   D) all of these

Answer: B
Diff: 2   Page Ref: 32.4
Skill: Factual

81) Which is the correct sequence of blood vessels from the heart through the body and back to the heart?

   A) veins venules capillaries arterioles arteries

   B) arterioles arteries capillaries veins venules

   C) arteries arterioles veins venules capillaries

   D) veins venules arteries arterioles capillaries

   E) arteries arterioles capillaries venules veins

Answer: E
Diff: 1   Page Ref: 32.4
Skill: Conceptual

82) Which is smallest?

   A) artery   B) arteriole   C) capillary   D) venule   E) vein

Answer: C
Diff: 1   Page Ref: 32.4
Skill: Factual

83) Which has the lowest blood pressure?

   A) arteries

   B) arterioles

   C) capillaries

   D) venules

   E) veins

Answer: E
Diff: 1   Page Ref: 32.4
Skill: Factual

84) You are about to give blood for the first time. While watching everyone else, you become pale and have to sit down before you faint. The vessels that constricted, producing this pallor are

   A) arteries.

   B) arterioles.

   C) capillaries.

   D) venules.

   E) veins.

Answer: B
Diff: 2   Page Ref: 32.4
Skill: Conceptual

85) Which of the types of blood vessels is directly involved in the exchange of materials between blood and tissues?

A) arteries

B) arterioles

C) capillaries

D) lymphatics

E) veins

Answer: C
Diff: 1   *Page Ref: 32.4*
Skill: Factual

86) What happens to the speed of blood as it passes through the capillaries?

A) increases slightly

B) decreases slightly

C) increases greatly

D) drops almost to zero

E) It depends on the location of the capillaries.

Answer: D
Diff: 1   *Page Ref: 32.4*
Skill: Factual

87) The role of valves in the veins is to

A) keep the blood from flowing backward when the veins are squeezed by the skeletal muscles.

B) push the blood upward toward the heart.

C) slow blood flow in the veins so that the blood can move more slowly in the capillaries.

D) block the flow of blood to the heart until it has time to contract again.

E) push the blood back toward the capillaries so that all the oxygen can be removed.

Answer: A
Diff: 1   *Page Ref: 32.4*
Skill: Factual

88) Accumulation of cell waste would cause nearby precapillary sphincters to

A) relax.

B) contract.

C) lengthen.

D) shorten.

E) It would have no effect on precapillary sphincters.

Answer: A
Diff: 2   *Page Ref: 32.4*
Skill: Conceptual

89) As you sit here taking this test, you would expect the precapillary sphincters in your little toe to be _____ compared with those in the hand you are using to write with.

A) longer

B) shorter

C) more open

D) less open

E) open about the same

Answer: D
Diff: 2   *Page Ref: 32.4*
Skill: Conceptual

90) Which of the following compensations would you expect to see when a person experiences a severe hemorrhage (blood loss)?

A) a decreased heart rate and vasoconstriction

B) an increased heart rate and vasoconstriction

C) a decreased heart rate and vasodilation

D) an increased heart rate and vasodilation

Answer: B
Diff: 2   *Page Ref: 32.4*
Skill: Conceptual

91) The liver is the primary source of albumin production. People with liver failure often show signs of extensive edema (tissue swelling). Which of the following statements explains this relationship?

  A) Albumin is a hormone that causes capillaries to become "leaky" and release fluid into the tissues.

  B) Albumin causes an increase in blood pressure which forces fluid into the tissues from the capillaries.

  C) The failing liver releases excess amounts of albumin into the blood. As the osmotic gradient builds, the protein displaces water into the tissues.

  D) The failing liver releases less albumin. As albumin levels in the blood fall, fluid in the tissues is less likely to return to the blood because of a breakdown in the osmotic gradient.

Answer: D
Diff: 2   Page Ref: 32.4
Skill: Application

92) Explain why the pumping of the heart has relatively little to do with the flow of blood in the capillaries.

Answer: Because the speed of blood flow drops almost to zero in the capillaries, the veins receive very little pressure from the heart. Instead the contractions of skeletal muscles force the blood through the veins.
Diff: 3   Page Ref: 32.4
Skill: Conceptual

93) Explain how the composition of the walls of arteries, capillaries, and veins allows each type of blood vessel to function.

Answer: Arteries—thick-walled, elastic, & muscular allows them to contract and help to push the blood along. Capillaries—one cell thick to allow for gas, nutrient, & waste exchange. Veins—thin-walled and less elastic to hold the slow-moving venous blood.
Diff: 3   Page Ref: 32.4
Skill: Conceptual

94) Children who are severely deficient in protein may develop swollen bodies due to accumulation of fluid in their tissues. In light of the role of albumin proteins explain how this might happen.

Answer: Albumin proteins maintain the osmotic balance of the bloodstream. If the fluid which is forced from the blood vessels in the capillaries cannot be pulled back in, the tissues will swell due to accumulation of fluid.
Diff: 3   Page Ref: 32.4
Skill: Application

95) In what way do lymph capillaries differ from blood capillaries? Lymph capillaries

   A) contain red blood cells.

   B) have a wall of only one cell layer.

   C) begin with blind ends throughout interstitial fluid.

   D) are made by lymphocytes.

   E) contain plasma.

Answer: C
Diff: 2   Page Ref: 32.5
Skill: Conceptual

96) Which statement is NOT TRUE?

   A) Lymphatic vessels resemble veins.

   B) The lymphatic system returns fluids to the blood.

   C) The lymphatic system transports carbohydrates from the small intestine to the blood.

   D) The lymphatic system helps defend the body against disease.

Answer: C
Diff: 2   Page Ref: 32.5
Skill: Factual

97) Which of the following is NOT part of the lymphatic system?

   A) thymus

   B) thyroid

   C) spleen

   D) All of the above are part of the lymphatic system.

   E) None of the above are part of the lymphatic system.

Answer: B
Diff: 1   Page Ref: 32.5
Skill: Factual

98) In an average person, how much fluid leaves the capillaries per day?

   A) 1 liter   B) 2 liters   C) 3 liters   D) 4 liters   E) 5 liters

Answer: C
Diff: 1   Page Ref: 32.5
Skill: Factual

99) Which of the following is delivered from the small intestine to the bloodstream through the lymphatic system?

    A) amino acids   B) proteins   C) carbohydrates   D) lipids

Answer: D
Diff: 1   Page Ref: 32.5
Skill: Factual

100) If you have a sore throat, what lymphatic structures are involved?

    A) tonsils

    B) lymph nodes

    C) thymus

    D) both A and B

    E) All of the above are true.

Answer: D
Diff: 2   Page Ref: 32.5
Skill: Conceptual

101) Which is NOT TRUE of lymph nodes? They

    A) destroy bacteria and viruses.

    B) aid in clotting.

    C) produce certain white blood cells.

    D) are located along lymphatic vessels.

    E) are filled with channels through which the lymph is forced.

Answer: B
Diff: 1   Page Ref: 32.5
Skill: Factual

102) When interstitial fluid enters the lymphatic system, it is known as

    A) plasma.

    B) intrastitial fluid.

    C) globulin.

    D) lymph.

    E) macrophage.

Answer: D
Diff: 1   Page Ref: 32.5
Skill: Factual

103) Which of the following is NOT a function of the lymphatic system?

    A) return of fluid to the circulatory system

    B) return of dissolved materials to the circulation

    C) transport of fats to the circulatory system

    D) defense of the body

    E) transport of oxygen to the lungs

Answer: E
Diff: 1   *Page Ref: 32.5*
Skill: Factual

104) What two organs are considered to be part of the lymphatic system?

    A) the pancreas and the liver

    B) the gall bladder and the kidneys

    C) the spleen and the thymus

    D) the heart and the lungs

    E) the thalamus and the hypothalamus

Answer: C
Diff: 1   *Page Ref: 32.5*
Skill: Factual

105) When surgeries involve the removal of lymph tissue, it is not uncommon to experience chronic edema (swelling) in the area of the body in which the nodes were removed. Which of the following explains this symptom?

    A) The body maintains a constant inflammatory response to the surgery.

    B) The open lymph vessels damaged by the surgery leak fluid into the tissue.

    C) Lymph vessels are responsible for the removal of excess tissue fluid. Their absence leads to fluid accumulation in those tissues.

    D) The body responds by growing a large network of new lymph capillaries to replace those that were lost. These new vessels leak fluid into the tissues.

Answer: C
Diff: 2   *Page Ref: 32.5*
Skill: Conceptual

106) Plasma that leaks from the capillaries into the tissue spaces is known as _____.

Answer: interstitial fluid
Diff: 1   *Page Ref: 32.5*
Skill: Factual

107) Why is the thymus gland considered to be part of the lymphatic system?

Answer: because it produces lymphocytes in infants and young children
Diff: 2   Page Ref: 32.5
Skill: Conceptual

108) What is the role of the spleen?

Answer: to filter the blood
Diff: 1   Page Ref: 32.5
Skill: Factual

109) Which is NOT TRUE of hypertension? It

A) is aggravated by obesity.

B) may be treated with diuretics.

C) may result in a stroke.

D) results in more deaths than there were from this cause twenty years ago.

E) is usually accompanied by a number of warning signals.

Answer: D
Diff: 2   Page Ref: Health Watch
Skill: Conceptual

110) Hypertension may lead to

A) atherosclerosis.

B) stroke.

C) inadequate blood supply to the heart.

D) both A and B

E) All of the above are correct.

Answer: E
Diff: 2   Page Ref: Health Watch
Skill: Conceptual

111) Which is the "good" cholesterol?

A) LDL   B) HDL   C) VLDL   D) VHDL

Answer: B
Diff: 1   Page Ref: Health Watch
Skill: Factual

112) Atherosclerosis

    A) reduces blood flow in arteries.

    B) is another name for high blood pressure.

    C) is a condition of the veins.

    D) is caused by a diet high in salt.

    E) causes a loss of plaque from the walls of the arteries.

Answer: A
Diff: 1   *Page Ref: Health Watch*
Skill: Factual

113) A diagnosis of hypertension is made when blood pressure goes above _____.

    A) 100/80   B) 140/90   C) 120/80   D) 200/100   E) 160/85

Answer: B
Diff: 1   *Page Ref: Health Watch*
Skill: Factual

114) Why is HDL-cholesterol considered to be "good" cholesterol?

Answer: because it is metabolized or excreted and because it helps to remove fatty deposits from the smooth muscles of the arteries and returns these fats to the liver for re-processing
Diff: 2   *Page Ref: Health Watch*
Skill: Conceptual

115) Imagine you are a cardiologist. A patient comes into your office and you perform blood work. You go over the results of your tests. You find that his LDL levels are very high and that is dangerous. He asks what that means. What do you tell him?

Answer: LDL accumulates in artery walls. This accumulation triggers inflammation and attracts macrophages which results in enlargement of the plaque. All of this may block blood from flowing through a blood vessel.
Diff: 2   *Page Ref: Health Watch*
Skill: Application

Chapter 33 Respiration

1) Animals need a respiratory system primarily because each cell of their body does the process of

    A) intracellular digestion.

    B) cellular respiration.

    C) hormone production.

    D) nitrogen fixation.

    E) extracellular digestion.

Answer: B
Diff: 2   *Page Ref: 33.1*
Skill: Conceptual

2) _____ is a waste product of cellular respiration.

    A) ATP

    B) Oxygen

    C) Carbon dioxide

    D) Nitrogen

    E) Glucose

Answer: C
Diff: 1   *Page Ref: 33.1*
Skill: Factual

3) *All* respiratory systems

    A) have a moist gas exchange surface.

    B) have a large surface area.

    C) have thin surfaces.

    D) facilitate gas diffusion.

    E) All are correct.

Answer: E
Diff: 1   *Page Ref: 33.2*
Skill: Factual

4) Which of the following respiratory events utilize bulk flow?

   A) movement of air or water past a respiratory surface

   B) exchange of oxygen and carbon dioxide

   C) transportation of gasses between the respiratory system and the tissues

   D) Both A and B are correct.

   E) Both A and C are correct.

Answer: E
Diff: 2   Page Ref: 33.2
Skill: Factual

5) Why does a fish die when it is not in water?

   A) Gills cannot exchange gasses in air, only in water.

   B) The gills collapse.

   C) The gills are no longer kept moist.

   D) Both A and C are correct.

   E) Both B and C are correct.

Answer: E
Diff: 2   Page Ref: 33.2
Skill: Factual

6) Insect respiratory systems do NOT contain

   A) trachae.   B) parabronchi.   C) tracheoles.   D) spiracles.

Answer: B
Diff: 1   Page Ref: 33.2
Skill: Factual

7) Which of the following can extract the most oxygen from the atmosphere?

   A) amphibians

   B) reptiles

   C) birds

   D) mammals

   E) insects

Answer: C
Diff: 2   Page Ref: 33.2
Skill: Factual

8) In the lungs, oxygen moves from air to blood by

    A) diffusion.

    B) osmosis.

    C) bulk flow.

    D) active transport.

    E) facilitated diffusion.

Answer: A
Diff: 1   *Page Ref: 33.2*
Skill: Factual

9) If a respiratory surface dries out, gas exchange will

    A) increase.

    B) decrease.

    C) stop.

    D) not be affected.

    E) decrease for oxygen, but increase for carbon dioxide.

Answer: C
Diff: 1   *Page Ref: 33.2*
Skill: Conceptual

10) You hear that horsehair worms do not have any respiratory system. Which of the following would you conclude would most likely be TRUE of horsehair worms?

    A) They have thick bodies.

    B) They have a dry skin surface.

    C) They use large amounts of energy.

    D) They have a large surface area compared with their volume.

    E) They would be unable to digest food.

Answer: D
Diff: 2   *Page Ref: 33.2*
Skill: Application

11) Which of the following is NOT a stage in gas exchange in respiratory systems?

A) air moves across system by bulk flow

B) diffusion of O_2 and CO_2 across the respiratory membranes

C) active transport of O_2 into the circulatory system

D) gases transported by the circulatory system by bulk flow

E) gas exchange from the circulation to the tissues by diffusion

Answer: C
Diff: 2   Page Ref: 33.2
Skill: Factual

12) Which of the following has gills for gas exchange?

A) insects

B) Earthworm

C) spider

D) fish

E) jellyfish

Answer: D
Diff: 1   Page Ref: 33.2
Skill: Factual

13) Spiracles are

A) openings between the gills of a frog tadpole.

B) openings into the tracheae of insects.

C) openings into the alveoli of the lungs.

D) openings to the bronchi.

E) the dual voice boxes of birds.

Answer: B
Diff: 1   Page Ref: 33.2
Skill: Factual

14) Which of the following is NOT a respiratory surface?

A) tracheae of a fly

B) bat wings

C) skin of an Earthworm

D) gills of a fish

E) alveoli of a raccoon

Answer: B
Diff: 2   Page Ref: 33.2
Skill: Conceptual

15) The lungs of reptiles are better developed than those of amphibians. This correlates with the fact that reptiles

    A) are larger animals.

    B) have a high metabolic rate.

    C) have a dry, scaly skin.

    D) lay shelled eggs.

    E) live on use oxygen for cellular processes.

Answer: C
Diff: 2   Page Ref: 33.2
Skill: Conceptual

16) An animal that takes up O_2 through its skin is a

    A) desert lizard.

    B) bat.

    C) bird.

    D) frog.

    E) trout.

Answer: D
Diff: 1   Page Ref: 33.2
Skill: Factual

17) Movement of O_2 from the outside air to respiratory surfaces by ventilation of the lungs is an example of

    A) diffusion.

    B) active transport.

    C) facilitated diffusion.

    D) osmosis.

    E) bulk flow.

Answer: E
Diff: 1   Page Ref: 33.2
Skill: Factual

18) Aquatic animals, in general, are more efficient at extracting oxygen during ventilation than are terrestrial animals. This is because

A) there is less oxygen available in water than in air.

B) less energy is required to ventilate gills than lungs.

C) aquatic animals lose ions to the environment.

D) gills have thinner cells than alveoli.

E) parabronchi have double the metabolic rate as spiracles.

Answer: A
Diff: 2   Page Ref: 33.2
Skill: Conceptual

19) Birds are able to sustain long flights at high altitudes because they

A) have thicker blood than other animals with many more red blood cells.

B) can extract oxygen during both inhalation and exhalation.

C) use anaerobic metabolism during flight.

D) decrease the heart rate during flight.

E) are able to lower their body temperatures during flight.

Answer: B
Diff: 2   Page Ref: 33.2
Skill: Conceptual

20) Because gas exchange occurs across a wet surface, ventilation in terrestrial animals is a major route of

A) loss of ions.

B) uptake of glucose.

C) loss of water.

D) uptake of H^+.

E) none of the above

Answer: C
Diff: 1   Page Ref: 33.2
Skill: Conceptual

21) Jellyfish do not have a circulatory system because

    A) they have no immune system.

    B) they breathe air.

    C) their tissues are so thin that diffusion is sufficient for gas exchange.

    D) their rapid metabolic processes insure steep concentration gradients.

    E) all of the above

Answer: C
Diff: 1   Page Ref: 33.2
Skill: Conceptual

22) A surface area to volume ratio (S/V) was calculated for four different animals. Which one of these animals is most likely to use its skin as its primary respiratory surface?

    A) Animal A with an S/V of 11.3   B) Animal B with an S/V of 8.6

    C) Animal C with an S/V of 1.23   D) Animal D with an S/V of 0.12

Answer: A
Diff: 3   Page Ref: 33.2
Skill: Application

23) If I wanted to present a sequence of animals to present examples of how animal respiratory systems evolved, which of the following sequences would I use?

    A) shark—grasshopper—lizard—salamander—bird

    B) shark—grasshopper—salamander—lizard—bird

    C) grasshopper—salamander—lizard—shark—bird

    D) bird—lizard—salamander—shark—grasshopper

    E) lizard—shark—bird—grasshopper—salamander

Answer: B
Diff: 2   Page Ref: 33.2
Skill: Application

24) Which of the following structures is analogous in function to tracheoles in insects?

    A) the skin of an Earthworm   B) the bronchi in a human

    C) the trachea of a bird   D) the skin of a reptile

Answer: A
Diff: 3   Page Ref: 33.2
Skill: Application

25) Which of the following structures is analogous in function to the alveoli in humans?

    A) the spiracles of a grasshopper

    B) the trachea of a frog

    C) the skin of an alligator

    D) the parabronchi of a bird

    E) operculum of a fish

Answer: D
Diff: 3   Page Ref: 33.2
Skill: Application

26) Which of the following features of a respiratory system are shared by fish, frogs, jellyfish and Earthworms?

    A) Respiratory structures are internal.

    B) Gas exchange occurs across the skin.

    C) Gas exchange occurs across a moist respiratory surface.

    D) Respiratory systems all involve a complex network of tubes.

    E) lack of a true circulatory system

Answer: C
Diff: 2   Page Ref: 33.2
Skill: Application

27) When a cell is respiring, carbon dioxide is in _____ concentration inside the cell, causing it to _____; whereas _____ is in high concentration outside the cell, causing it to _____.

Answer: high; diffuse out; oxygen; diffuse in
Diff: 1   Page Ref: 33.2
Skill: Factual

28) Frogs use their skin as a respiratory organ. True or False?

Answer: TRUE
Diff: 1   Page Ref: 33.2
Skill: Factual

29) All respiratory systems must be large compared with the size of the animal involved because diffusion is slow. True or False?

Answer: TRUE
Diff: 1   Page Ref: 33.2
Skill: Factual

30) The large body of a jellyfish requires relatively little oxygen because the internal cells of a jellyfish use relatively _____.

Answer: little energy
Diff: 1   Page Ref: 33.2
Skill: Conceptual

31) When a bumblebee lands on a flower, it pumps its abdomen up and down to move oxygen into its system of _____ through round holes called _____ on its abdomen.

Answer: tracheae; spiracles
Diff: 2   Page Ref: 33.2
Skill: Factual

32) What structures make the surface area for gas exchange large in fish?

Answer: There are many gills. Each gill is made of many filaments. Each filament is covered by thin folds of tissue called lamellae.
Diff: 2   Page Ref: 33.2
Skill: Factual

33) What two constraints control all respiratory systems?

Answer: They must be moist and large.
Diff: 2   Page Ref: 33.2
Skill: Conceptual

34) How can a sponge get oxygen to every cell of their body without a respiratory system?

Answer: by having channels throughout their body which allow water to come near all of the cells
Diff: 2   Page Ref: 33.2
Skill: Conceptual

35) How are cellular respiration and respiratory systems connected?

Answer: Cellular respiration uses oxygen and produces carbon dioxide. Oxygen is supplied over long distances to the cells and carbon dioxide is removed from the cells by respiratory systems.
Diff: 2   Page Ref: 33.2
Skill: Conceptual

36) In what ways do bulk flow and diffusion interact to enable respiratory systems to deliver oxygen quickly to all cells of the body?

Answer: Bulk flow carries oxygen quickly into the system and through the circulation to the cells. Diffusion, a slower process, then only has to move oxygen into the circulation and into the cells.
Diff: 2   Page Ref: 33.2
Skill: Conceptual

37) What is the purpose of an operculum?

Answer: It covers the gills in fish to protect them from predators, streamline the body, and direct the flow of water.
Diff: 1   Page Ref: 33.2
Skill: Conceptual

38) How are birds able to get fresh air even when they are exhaling? Why do they need this?

Answer: They have air sacs which fill with air during inspiration and empty into the lungs during exhalation supplying oxygen to the lungs continuously so that birds can have enough oxygen to supply energy for flight.
Diff: 2   Page Ref: 33.2
Skill: Conceptual

39) Vertebrate lungs probably evolved from the digestive tract of fishes. True or False?

Answer: TRUE
Diff: 2   Page Ref: 33.2
Skill: Factual

40) Which of the following is part of the gas–exchange portion of the human lung?

A) larynx

B) pharynx

C) bronchi

D) bronchioles

E) alveoli

Answer: E
Diff: 1   Page Ref: 33.3
Skill: Factual

41) Which structure prevents foods and liquids from entering the lungs?

A) larynx

B) pharynx

C) epiglottis

D) bronchi

E) bronchioles

Answer: C
Diff: 1   Page Ref: 33.3
Skill: Factual

42) The vocal cords are located in the

    A) larynx.

    B) pharynx.

    C) epiglottis.

    D) trachea.

    E) bronchi.

Answer: A
Diff: 1   Page Ref: 33.3
Skill: Factual

43) Gas exchange in the lungs is due to

    A) active transport of gases between the blood and the alveolus.

    B) active transport of gases between hemoglobin and the alveolus.

    C) passive diffusion of gases between the blood and the alveolus.

    D) facilitated diffusion of gases between the blood and the alveolus.

    E) facilitated diffusion of gases between the hemoglobin and the alveolus.

Answer: C
Diff: 2   Page Ref: 33.3
Skill: Factual

44) Which of the following can bind to hemoglobin?

    A) oxygen

    B) carbon monoxide

    C) carbon dioxide

    D) both A and B

    E) all of the above

Answer: E
Diff: 2   Page Ref: 33.3
Skill: Factual

45) The bulk of the carbon dioxide released from cells is transported as

    A) dissolved carbon monoxide.

    B) bicarbonate ions in the plasma.

    C) carbon dioxide attached to hemoglobin.

    D) sugars, such as glucose.

    E) a solid part of the red blood cells.

Answer: A
Diff: 2   Page Ref: 33.3
Skill: Factual

46) During inhalation the diaphragm

    A) contracts and is dome-shaped.   B) relaxes and is dome-shaped.

    C) contracts and is flattened.   D) relaxes and is flattened.

Answer: C
Diff: 1   Page Ref: 33.3
Skill: Factual

47) How much air enters the lungs in an average breath?

    A) 125 mL   B) 250 mL   C) 500 mL   D) 750 mL   E) 1000 mL

Answer: C
Diff: 1   Page Ref: 33.3
Skill: Factual

48) The respiratory center is located

    A) in the medulla.

    B) in the cortex.

    C) in the spinal cord.

    D) in the midbrain.

    E) in the hypothalamus.

Answer: A
Diff: 1   Page Ref: 33.3
Skill: Factual

49) The respiratory system is regulated to maintain a constant level of _____ in the blood.

    A) oxygen

    B) carbon dioxide

    C) hydrogen

    D) hemoglobin

    E) negatively charged ions

Answer: B
Diff: 2   Page Ref: 33.3
Skill: Factual

50) The epiglottis

    A) covers fish gills.

    B) closes insect trachea.

    C) prevents food from entering the airway.

    D) is part of the vocal cords.

    E) produces the alveolar surfactant.

Answer: C
Diff: 1   Page Ref: 33.3
Skill: Factual

51) After passing through the nasal cavities, incoming air moves next to the

    A) larynx.

    B) bronchi.

    C) pharynx.

    D) trachea.

    E) bronchioles.

Answer: C
Diff: 1   Page Ref: 33.3
Skill: Factual

52) Alveoli

    A) have a moist surface.

    B) are thick-walled.

    C) are not permeable to dissolved O_2.

    D) are found in gills.

    E) are directly attached to the trachea.

Answer: A
Diff: 1   Page Ref: 33.3
Skill: Factual

53) A thin slice of a lung would look like a thin slice

    A) through a blown-up balloon.

    B) of a piece of wood.

    C) of the heart at the level of the ventricles.

    D) of sponge cake.

    E) of carrot.

Answer: D
Diff: 2   Page Ref: 33.3
Skill: Conceptual

54) The cells lining the conducting portion of the human respiratory system secrete

    A) mucus.

    B) blood.

    C) tissue fluid.

    D) hormones.

    E) enzymes.

Answer: A
Diff: 1   Page Ref: 33.3
Skill: Factual

55) Most of the oxygen in the blood is

    A) bound to hemoglobin.

    B) in the white blood cells.

    C) combined with carbon dioxide.

    D) in the plasma.

    E) carried by leukocytes.

Answer: A
Diff: 1   Page Ref: 33.3
Skill: Factual

56) Hemoglobin and hemocyanin are respiratory proteins. Their function is to

    A) increase the oxygen carrying capacity of blood.

    B) assist in blood clotting.

    C) attract lymphocytes to damaged tissues.

    D) remove toxins from plasma.

    E) provide structural integrity to red blood cells.

Answer: A
Diff: 1   Page Ref: 33.3
Skill: Factual

57) Smokers often cough because

    A) nicotine blocks chemoreceptors in the nose.

    B) smoking damages the cilia that normally remove mucus and debris from the respiratory tract.

    C) smoking effects the respiratory center neurons in the medulla.

    D) carbon monoxide in the smoke triggers the cough reflex.

    E) none of the above

Answer: B
Diff: 1   Page Ref: 33.3
Skill: Factual

58) When blood is drawn from a blood vessel in your arm, it is dark red in color. This indicates that it

    A) was taken from an artery.

    B) was going away from the heart.

    C) was taken from a vein.

    D) was on its way to the tissues of the arm.

    E) has just come from the lungs.

Answer: C
Diff: 2   Page Ref: 33.3
Skill: Conceptual

59) Carbon monoxide is poisonous because it

    A) causes breathing to stop.

    B) is toxic to the brain.

    C) prevents the SA node from functioning.

    D) prevents hemoglobin from carrying oxygen.

    E) slows the cilia in the respiratory tract.

Answer: D
Diff: 1   Page Ref: 33.3
Skill: Conceptual

60) A person who has experienced carbon monoxide poisoning tends to look healthy at first glance because

A) their breathing is normal.

B) carbon monoxide works slowly.

C) they are able to use a small amount of carbon monoxide in cellular respiration.

D) carbon monoxide is a brain stimulant.

E) their skin and lips are bright red.

Answer: E
Diff: 1   Page Ref: 33.3
Skill: Conceptual

61) What happens in the lungs?

A) Gases move up a concentration gradient.

B) Blood loses all of its carbon dioxide.

C) Some of the oxygen in the air moves into the blood and some of the carbon dioxide in the blood moves into the air.

D) Air loses all of its oxygen.

E) Gases move by bulk flow into and out of the circulation.

Answer: C
Diff: 1   Page Ref: 33.3
Skill: Conceptual

62) During inspiration

A) the diaphragm is contracted.

B) the rib muscles are relaxed.

C) air is leaving the alveoli.

D) the chest wall moves away from the lungs.

E) the heart pumps blood to the lungs.

Answer: A
Diff: 2   Page Ref: 33.3
Skill: Factual

63) What is the respiratory center?

   A) a small cluster of cells in the lungs which monitor the amount of oxygen present

   B) the alveoli

   C) a part of the pituitary gland

   D) the cells of the capillaries in the lungs

   E) a cluster of nerve cells in the brain stem

Answer: E
Diff: 1   Page Ref: 33.3
Skill: Factual

64) Which of the following is NOT possible?

   A) an involuntary increase in the rate of breathing

   B) inhibition of the respiratory centers in the brain

   C) holding one's breath until death occurs

   D) a voluntary increase in the rate of breathing

   E) a voluntary decrease in the rate of breathing

Answer: C
Diff: 1   Page Ref: 33.3
Skill: Conceptual

65) The respiratory center is very sensitive to changes in _____ levels, but not very sensitive to changes in _____ levels.

   A) blood sugar; hormone

   B) hormone; blood sugar

   C) temperature; blood pressure

   D) carbon dioxide; oxygen

   E) oxygen; carbon dioxide

Answer: D
Diff: 2   Page Ref: 33.3
Skill: Factual

66) A patient is admitted to the hospital after falling from the second story window of her apartment. Tests reveal no other injuries other than some swelling in the brain. Why does her breathing become irregular?

A) Her tissues require more oxygen for healing.

B) The blood returning to the lungs from the brain is too high in oxygen.

C) The respiratory center in the lungs is malfunctioning due to a lack of carbon dioxide.

D) The damage to the brain is affecting the respiratory center in the medulla.

E) a decrease in blood pressure

Answer: D
Diff: 2   Page Ref: 33.3
Skill: Application

67) Which of the following is NOT a mechanism for transporting carbon dioxide in the blood?

A) dissolved in plasma as CO_2 B) carried in plasma as HCO_3^-

C) bound to hemoglobin   D) as CO bound to hemoglobin

Answer: D
Diff: 1   Page Ref: 33.3
Skill: Factual

68) Which of the following structures is NOT part of the conducting portion of the human respiratory system?

A) alveoli   B) trachea   C) bronchi   D) larynx

Answer: A
Diff: 2   Page Ref: 33.3
Skill: Conceptual

69) Which of the following events would cause air to rush out of your lungs?

A) contraction of the diaphragm   B) a sudden rise in atmospheric pressure

C) a sudden drop in atmospheric pressure   D) relaxation of the rib muscles

Answer: C
Diff: 2   Page Ref: 33.3
Skill: Conceptual

70) Which of the following changes would the receptors in the respiratory center be the most sensitive to?

    A) a small drop in blood nitrogen levels

    B) a small drop in blood oxygen levels

    C) a small rise in blood oxygen levels

    D) a small rise in blood carbon dioxide levels

    E) a small drop in blood pH

Answer: D
Diff: 2   Page Ref: 33.3
Skill: Conceptual

71) One of these leads to each human lung.

    A) larynx

    B) bronchi

    C) pharynx

    D) trachea

    E) bronchioles

Answer: B
Diff: 1   Page Ref: 33.3
Skill: Factual

72) Air from the nose and the mouth join here.

    A) larynx

    B) bronchi

    C) pharynx

    D) trachea

    E) bronchioles

Answer: C
Diff: 1   Page Ref: 33.3
Skill: Factual

73) Tiny tubes which carry the air to all parts of mammalian lungs are

    A) larynx.

    B) bronchi.

    C) pharynx.

    D) trachea.

    E) bronchioles.

Answer: E
Diff: 1   *Page Ref: 33.3*
Skill: Factual

74) Closed air sacs in which gas exchange occurs in mammals.

    A) alveoli

    B) bronchi

    C) pharynx

    D) trachea

    E) bronchioles

Answer: A
Diff: 1   *Page Ref: 33.3*
Skill: Factual

75) In the lungs _____ diffuses into the bloodstream where it is in low concentration and _____ diffuses from the bloodstream into the lungs.

Answer: oxygen; carbon dioxide
Diff: 2   *Page Ref: 33.3*
Skill: Factual

76) What effect does smoking have on the movement of mucus in the respiratory tract?

Answer: It slows the cilia so that the mucus cannot be swept upward.
Diff: 1   *Page Ref: 33.3*
Skill: Conceptual

77) What usually causes the respiratory center to stimulate an increase in breathing rate?

Answer: a rise in carbon dioxide
Diff: 2   *Page Ref: 33.3*
Skill: Conceptual

78) Why is blood in the veins bluish, whereas blood in the arteries is red?

Answer: When hemoglobin binds with oxygen it changes shape and color. The presence of oxygen causes it to become bright, cherry red compared with the maroon of deoxygenated blood.
Diff: 1   *Page Ref: 33.3*
Skill: Conceptual

79) Compare the way most oxygen is carried in the blood with the way most carbon dioxide is carried.

Answer: Oxygen—bound to hemoglobin; Carbon dioxide—mostly as bicarbonate ion, small amounts bound to hemoglobin and dissolved in the plasma
Diff: 2   *Page Ref: 33.3*
Skill: Conceptual

80) When you begin running hard, what stimulates you to breathe faster?

Answer: Apparently the forebrain does this because you actually begin to breathe faster before you run low on oxygen or produce excess carbon dioxide.
Diff: 2   *Page Ref: 33.3*
Skill: Conceptual

81) Cigarette smoke can inactivate the cilia of the lungs for

    A) 30 minutes.   B) one hour.   C) 12 hours.   D) 24 hours.

Answer: B
Diff: 1   *Page Ref: Health Watch*
Skill: Factual

82) For smokers who quit smoking, healing begins

    A) immediately.   B) after six months.

    C) after a year.   D) after 5 years.

Answer: A
Diff: 1   *Page Ref: Health Watch*
Skill: Factual

83) "Smoker's cough" is the result of

    A) excess mucus.

    B) irritation in the throat.

    C) emphysema.

    D) nicotine.

    E) dry lungs.

Answer: A
Diff: 1   *Page Ref: Health Watch*
Skill: Factual

84) Which of the following is NOT borne out by research?

A) "Passive" smoking is harmful.

B) Smokers who stop will reverse the harmful effects.

C) Nicotine fights against infection.

D) There is carbon monoxide in cigarette smoke.

E) Cilia are paralyzed for up to one hour by a single cigarette.

Answer: C
Diff: 2   Page Ref: Health Watch
Skill: Factual

85) All of the following are harmful effects of "passive smoking" EXCEPT

A) Children of smokers are more likely to contract bronchitis and ear infections.

B) Children of smokers are more likely to have diminished lung capacity.

C) Spouses of smokers have a 30% higher risk of heart attack.

D) Children of smokers are more likely to develop asthma and allergies.

E) Spouses of smokers are more likely to quit smoking than those with a non-smoking spouse.

Answer: E
Diff: 2   Page Ref: Health Watch
Skill: Factual

86) Make a case to a young smoker about the health risks of smoking.

Answer: Discuss the immediate effects such as paralyzed cilia, impairment of WBC's, irritation due to toxic substances. Tell them about the increase in risk of serious diseases such as emphysema and heart disease. Then reveal the danger to loved ones by passive smoking.
Diff: 2   Page Ref: Health Watch
Skill: Application

87) During countercurrent exchange

A) steep concentration gradients are built.

B) there is a transfer of heat or solute from fluids flowing in opposite directions.

C) there is a transfer of heat or solute from fluids flowing in the same direction.

D) plasma is removed from blood leaving only the solid red blood cells.

E) active transport moves solutes across a membrane via transport proteins.

Answer: B
Diff: 2   Page Ref: A Closer Look
Skill: Factual

88) Fish gills consist of a series of

   A) parabronchi.

   B) opercula.

   C) spiracles.

   D) interconnected bronchioles.

   E) filaments.

Answer: E
Diff: 2   Page Ref: A Closer Look
Skill: Factual

89) Some fish can extract 85% of the O_2 from water flowing through their gills. True or False?

Answer: TRUE
Diff: 1   Page Ref: A Closer Look
Skill: Factual

90) Briefly describe how fish are able to extract O_2 from water.

Answer: Discuss countercurrent exchange and the specific structure of fish gills (filaments, lamellae and capillaries).
Diff: 2   Page Ref: A Closer Look
Skill: Conceptual

Chapter 34   Nutrition and Digestion

1) An essential nutrient

    A) is required in large amounts.

    B) is used for energy storage.

    C) cannot be made by the animal.

    D) can only be found in animal products.

    E) all of the above

Answer: C
Diff: 1   Page Ref: 34.1
Skill: Factual

2) The nutrients that provide energy for animals are

    A) carbohydrates and fats.

    B) carbohydrates and proteins.

    C) fats and proteins.

    D) carbohydrates, fats and nucleic acids.

    E) carbohydrates, fats and proteins.

Answer: E
Diff: 1   Page Ref: 34.1
Skill: Factual

3) The average human body at rest burns _____ Calories per day.

    A) 1050   B) 1250   C) 1450   D) 1550   E) 1850

Answer: D
Diff: 1   Page Ref: 34.1
Skill: Factual

4) Why is linoleic acid an essential fatty acid in humans?

    A) It is required for the synthesis of phospholipids.

    B) It is necessary for the formation of cell membranes.

    C) It must be supplied by the diet.

    D) All fatty acids produced by plants are essential.

    E) Both A and B are correct.

Answer: C
Diff: 2   Page Ref: 34.1
Skill: Factual

5) Minerals required for bone formation include magnesium,

    A) calcium and phosphorus.

    B) iron and sodium.

    C) calcium and sodium.

    D) zinc and potassium.

    E) calcium and zinc.

Answer: A
Diff: 1   *Page Ref: 34.1*
Skill: Factual

6) The molecule used by animals for a source of quick energy is

    A) triglyceride.

    B) protein.

    C) glycogen.

    D) phospholipid.

    E) starch.

Answer: C
Diff: 1   *Page Ref: 34.1*
Skill: Factual

7) Na^+ and K^+ are minerals that are important in the function of nerves and

    A) blood.

    B) hormones.

    C) muscles.

    D) bones.

    E) DNA.

Answer: C
Diff: 1   *Page Ref: 34.1*
Skill: Factual

8) Symptoms of pellagra are due to a lack of which vitamin?

    A) thiamin (B1)

    B) riboflavin (B2)

    C) niacin

    D) pyridoxine (B6)

    E) panothenic acid

Answer: B
Diff: 2   *Page Ref: 34.1*
Skill: Factual

9) Scurvy is due to a lack of

   A) thiamin (B1).

   B) riboflavin (B2).

   C) biotin.

   D) choline.

   E) ascorbic acid (vitamin C).

Answer: E
Diff: 2   Page Ref: 34.1
Skill: Factual

10) Vitamin K is required for

   A) night vision.

   B) blood clotting.

   C) restful sleep.

   D) proper kidney function.

   E) transduction of nerve impulses.

Answer: B
Diff: 2   Page Ref: 34.1
Skill: Factual

11) Vitamin D is added to milk because it increases

   A) calcium uptake from food and promotes bone growth.

   B) digestion of milk protein.

   C) digestion of lipids in milk.

   D) increases the shelf–life.

   E) all of these

Answer: A
Diff: 2   Page Ref: 34.1
Skill: Factual

12) A deficiency of this vitamin has been associated with birth defects.

   A) choline   B) C   C) folic acid   D) biotin   E) K

Answer: C
Diff: 2   Page Ref: 34.1
Skill: Factual

13) Which of the following nutrients do NOT provide energy for animals?

    A) fats

    B) carbohydrates

    C) proteins

    D) vitamins

    E) All of these provide energy.

Answer: D
Diff: 2   *Page Ref: 34.1*
Skill: Factual

14) A mineral important for carrying of O_2 in the blood.

    A) calcium

    B) zinc

    C) sodium

    D) potassium

    E) iron

Answer: E
Diff: 1   *Page Ref: 34.1*
Skill: Factual

15) The amount of energy necessary to raise the temperature of water one degree Celsius is referred to as

    A) a Calorie.

    B) a calorie.

    C) the basal metabolism rate.

    D) the basal energy quotient.

    E) the RDA.

Answer: B
Diff: 1   *Page Ref: 34.1*
Skill: Factual

16) Which of the following would have the highest energy expenditure?

   A) a physically active female

   B) a sedentary female

   C) a physically active male

   D) a sedentary male

   E) All people use approximately the same amount of energy.

Answer: C
Diff: 1   Page Ref: 34.1
Skill: Conceptual

17) A diverse group of molecules that generally contain long chains of carbon atoms and are insoluble in water are referred to as

   A) proteins.

   B) carbohydrates.

   C) minerals.

   D) polysaccharides.

   E) lipids.

Answer: E
Diff: 2   Page Ref: 34.1
Skill: Factual

18) Which category of compound is the most concentrated energy source?

   A) lipids

   B) carbohydrates

   C) proteins

   D) minerals

   E) vitamins

Answer: A
Diff: 2   Page Ref: 34.1
Skill: Factual

19) If you eat 20 grams of potato chips in which 10 grams are potato (carbohydrate) and the other 10 grams are fat, you will get

A) about half your calories from fat and half from carbohydrate.

B) about 40 fat calories and about 90 carbohydrate calories.

C) about 90 fat calories and about 40 carbohydrate calories.

D) all the calories from fat.

E) all the calories from carbohydrate.

Answer: C
Diff: 2   Page Ref: 34.1
Skill: Application

20) These nutrients help reduce the cellular damage that occurs with aging.

A) minerals

B) lipids

C) anti-oxidants

D) monosaccharides

E) cellulose subunits

Answer: C
Diff: 1   Page Ref: 34.1
Skill: Factual

21) Which of the following is NOT true of fat?

A) conducts heat three times faster than other body tissues

B) major storage form for excess energy

C) hydrophobic

D) most concentrated energy source

E) is necessary for the synthesis of cell membranes

Answer: A
Diff: 2   Page Ref: 34.1
Skill: Factual

22) All of the following statements are true of lipids EXCEPT

    A) There are about 3600 Calories in each pound of fat.

    B) Lipids are hydrophilic.

    C) Cholesterol is important in the production of bile.

    D) Triglycerides are used as an energy source.

    E) Phospholipids are a component of cell membranes.

Answer: B
Diff: 1   Page Ref: 34.1
Skill: Factual

23) All of the following statements are true of proteins EXCEPT

    A) The subunits of proteins are amino acids.

    B) Protein breakdown produces urea.

    C) Humans can make all of the amino acids needed to produce proteins.

    D) Enzymes are composed of proteins.

    E) Kwashiorkor is caused by protein deficiency.

Answer: C
Diff: 1   Page Ref: 34.1
Skill: Factual

24) The "fiber" in your diet is

    A) starch.

    B) cellulose.

    C) glycogen.

    D) protein strands.

    E) phospholipid.

Answer: B
Diff: 2   Page Ref: 34.1
Skill: Conceptual

25) After getting up late and leaving without any breakfast, you recognize that you are late to class and begin sprinting to reach the lecture hall two blocks away. Which of the following is the most likely energy source for your activity?

    A) cellulose

    B) fat

    C) protein

    D) phospholipid

    E) glycogen

Answer: E
Diff: 2   Page Ref: 34.1
Skill: Application

26) Which category of organic compound is used the least by humans as an energy source?

    A) lipids

    B) carbohydrates

    C) proteins

    D) water

    E) minerals

Answer: C
Diff: 2   Page Ref: 34.1
Skill: Factual

27) Your roommate tells you that since she has no time to eat properly, she is taking megadoses of vitamins. After having completed this unit of general biology, you warn her that this may be dangerous. Which vitamin would be most dangerous to her?

    A) C

    B) B1 (thiamin)

    C) folic acid (B9)

    D) D

    E) All are equally toxic.

Answer: D
Diff: 2   Page Ref: 34.1
Skill: Conceptual

28) Which vitamin is involved with blood clotting?

    A) A   B) B   C) C   D) D   E) K

Answer: E
Diff: 1   Page Ref: 34.1
Skill: Factual

29) When your mother told you to eat carrots, because they would make you see better, she was

   A) wrong, because they contain large amounts of vitamin C, which will prevent scurvy.

   B) wrong, because they contain large amounts of vitamin A, which helps with the formation of red blood cells.

   C) wrong, because they contain large amounts of vitamin D, which helps to prevent rickets.

   D) right, because they contain vitamin A, which is involved in the production of visual pigment.

   E) right, because they contain vitamin C, which is involved in maintaining the walls of blood vessels in the retina.

Answer: D
Diff: 2   Page Ref: 34.1
Skill: Conceptual

30) Which of the following is a water-soluble vitamin?

   A) A   B) C   C) D   D) E   E) K

Answer: B
Diff: 1   Page Ref: 34.1
Skill: Factual

31) In order to preserve the taste of low-fat food, companies have started to use synthetic fats that cannot be broken down and absorbed by the digestive system. What problem might be associated with a diet that includes large amounts of these synthetic fats?

   A) vitamin C deficiency

   B) malnutrition

   C) vitamin K deficiency

   D) obesity

   E) vitamin B deficiency

Answer: C
Diff: 3   Page Ref: 34.1
Skill: Application

32) In a typical American diet most of the energy comes from carbohydrate sources. True or False?

Answer: TRUE
Diff: 1   Page Ref: 34.1
Skill: Factual

33) Humans are able to synthesize all the specialized lipids they need. True or False?

Answer: FALSE
Diff: 1   Page Ref: 34.1
Skill: Factual

34) Cellulose is the most abundant carbohydrate on the planet.

Answer: TRUE
Diff: 1   Page Ref: 34.1
Skill: Factual

35) You need the mineral, _____ in your diet in order to make thyroid hormone.

Answer: iodine
Diff: 2   Page Ref: 34.1
Skill: Factual

36) List the five major categories of animal nutrients.

Answer: lipids, carbohydrates, proteins, minerals, vitamins
Diff: 2   Page Ref: 34.1
Skill: Factual

37) The current emphasis on spending less time in the sun in order to avoid skin cancer makes it even more important that we include sources of which vitamin in our diets?

Answer: vitamin D
Diff: 2   Page Ref: 34.1
Skill: Application

38) Briefly discuss the major advantage of fats as storage molecules.

Answer: They are the most concentrated energy source, are hydrophobic so the prevent excess accumulation of fluids in the tissues, able to store more calories with less weight, increase the likelihood of survival.
Diff: 2   Page Ref: 34.1
Skill: Conceptual

39) In light of the way the human body uses nutrients, what kind of diet should a person with kidney disease avoid? Explain.

Answer: A diet high in protein because the kidneys must make urea out of all the excess nitrogen from a diet which contains protein used for energy.
Diff: 3   Page Ref: 34.1
Skill: Application

40) List four minerals necessary for humans and briefly discuss the role which each plays.

Answer: varied, see Table 30-2 in the text
Diff: 2   Page Ref: 34.1
Skill: Factual

41) Sea anemones, hydra and jellyfish digest foods in a

    A) lysosome.

    B) food vacuole.

    C) gastrovascular cavity.

    D) gastrointestinal tract.

    E) rumen.

Answer: C
Diff: 1   Page Ref: 34.2
Skill: Factual

42) Wild dogs and cats are

    A) omnivores.

    B) carnivores.

    C) ruminants.

    D) herbivores.

    E) opportunistic parasites.

Answer: B
Diff: 1   Page Ref: 34.2
Skill: Conceptual

43) Which of the following BEST describes the act of bringing food into the digestive tract through an opening?

    A) digestion

    B) indigestion

    C) ingestion

    D) absorption

    E) adsorption

Answer: C
Diff: 1   Page Ref: 34.2
Skill: Factual

44) Which of these uses collar cells to obtain food for intracellular digestion?

A) sponges

B) protists

C) hydra

D) humans

E) Earthworms

Answer: A
Diff: 1   Page Ref: 34.2
Skill: Factual

45) In most of the Animal Kingdom, digestion is

A) extracellular in a gastrovascular cavity.

B) extracellular in a cavity open at both ends.

C) extracellular through the circulatory system.

D) intracellular through collar cells.

E) intracellular through simple absorption.

Answer: B
Diff: 2   Page Ref: 34.2
Skill: Conceptual

46) All of the following are found in the digestive system of birds EXCEPT

A) esophagus.

B) gizzard.

C) crop.

D) a long large intestine.

E) cloaca.

Answer: A
Diff: 1   Page Ref: 34.2
Skill: Factual

47) You are examining the teeth in the skull of an unidentified animal. The incisors are flat, the canines are pointed and both molars and premolars are present. This animal was most likely a (an)

    A) carnivore.

    B) omnivore.

    C) herbivore.

    D) bird.

    E) opportunistic parasite.

Answer: B
Diff: 1   Page Ref: 34.2
Skill: Factual

48) In coelenterate animals, which have a gastrovascular cavity,

    A) digestion is exclusively intracellular.

    B) digestion and elimination occur in this place.

    C) digestion is unnecessary due to the small size of the particles absorbed.

    D) absorption is into collar cells.

    E) digestion is in a tube running through the body.

Answer: B
Diff: 2   Page Ref: 34.2
Skill: Conceptual

49) Ruminant animals

    A) harbor symbionts that digest cellulose.

    B) meditate a lot.

    C) are meat eaters.

    D) are capable of synthesizing vitamins for their own use.

    E) break down their own urea.

Answer: A
Diff: 2   Page Ref: 34.2
Skill: Factual

50) The cellulase in a cow's digestive tract is produced by

    A) the liver.

    B) pancreas.

    C) stomach.

    D) microorganisms.

    E) cells lining the rumen.

Answer: D
Diff: 1   Page Ref: 34.2
Skill: Factual

51) A shipworm is an animal that exists entirely on a diet of wood. What special feature must this animal have to survive on this highly specialized diet?

    A) It produces large amounts of proteases.

    B) It has a gastrovascular cavity.

    C) It has symbiotic microorganisms that produce cellulase.

    D) It relies on intracellular digestion.

    E) It has a four part stomach similar to a cow.

Answer: C
Diff: 3   Page Ref: 34.2
Skill: Application

52) This material contains undigested plant fiber and dead microorganisms that is eliminated from the body.

    A) bile

    B) chyme

    C) feces

    D) secretion

    E) pancreatic juices

Answer: C
Diff: 1   Page Ref: 34.2
Skill: Factual

53) The small, sharp stones in a bird's gizzard grind and crash food much like teeth. True or False?

Answer: TRUE
Diff: 1   Page Ref: 34.2
Skill: Factual

54) Digestion in humans occurs in a gastrovascular cavity. True or False?

Answer: FALSE
Diff: 1   Page Ref: 34.2
Skill: Conceptual

55) List the five tasks that the digestive tract must accomplish.

Answer: 1) Ingestion of food; 2) Mechanical breakdown of food; 3) Chemical breakdown of food; 4) Absorption of food nutrients; 5) Elimination of wastes
Diff: 2   Page Ref: 34.2
Skill: Factual

56) Describe the specialized digestive system that allows ruminants such as cows to live on a diet of grass.

Answer: Multi-chambered stomach housing microorganisms that can break down cellulose. Regurgitating food after it has been partially digested, rumination for further mechanical breakdown, return to rumen.
Diff: 2   Page Ref: 34.2
Skill: Factual

57) Compare how teeth and intestinal length differs between carnivores, omnivores and herbivores.

Answer: Teeth of carnivores have reduced incisors but enlarged canines. Teeth of herbivores have reduced canines, incisors adapted to snipping leaves and wide, flat premolars and molars. Omnivores are similar to herbivores but with pointed canines and flat incisors. Intestines in herbivores are much longer than carnivores because plant material is more difficult to breakdown than proteins of the carnivore diet. Omnivores are intermediate in length.
Diff: 2   Page Ref: 34.2
Skill: Conceptual

58) The part of the digestive tract with the lowest pH is the

A) stomach.

B) small intestine.

C) large intestine.

D) rectum.

E) pancreas.

Answer: A
Diff: 1   Page Ref: 34.3
Skill: Conceptual

59) What type of digestion takes place in the mouth?

    A) ingestion

    B) mechanical digestion

    C) chemical digestion

    D) absorption

    E) both B and C

Answer: E
Diff: 1   Page Ref: 34.3
Skill: Conceptual

60) Amylase is produced by the

    A) salivary glands.

    B) small intestine.

    C) pancreas.

    D) Both A and C are correct.

    E) A, B and C are correct.

Answer: D
Diff: 1   Page Ref: 34.3
Skill: Factual

61) Most digestion occurs in the

    A) mouth.

    B) stomach.

    C) small intestine.

    D) large intestine.

    E) esophagus.

Answer: C
Diff: 2   Page Ref: 34.3
Skill: Factual

62) Bile aids in fat digestion by

A) acting as an emulsifier, thus exposing a large surface area to enzymes.

B) acting as a lipid–digesting enzyme.

C) digesting lipids into smaller components; these can now be digested further by pancreatic enzymes.

D) removing the fatty acid chains from the glycerol.

E) all of the above

Answer: A
Diff: 1   Page Ref: 34.3
Skill: Factual

63) Which of the following are absorbed directly into the bloodstream?

A) amino acids

B) monosaccharides

C) fats

D) both A and B

E) A, B and C are correct.

Answer: D
Diff: 2   Page Ref: 34.3
Skill: Conceptual

64) The bacteria in the large intestine manufacture

A) some B vitamins.

B) vitamin K.

C) vitamin D.

D) vitamin C.

E) Both A and B are correct.

Answer: D
Diff: 2   Page Ref: 34.3
Skill: Factual

65) Which of the following is responsible for stimulating the release of pancreatic enzymes into the small intestine?

A) gastrin

B) secretin

C) cholecystokinin

D) gastric inhibitory peptide

E) pepsin

Answer: C
Diff: 2   Page Ref: 34.3
Skill: Factual

66) Where does digestion begin?

A) mouth

B) pharynx

C) stomach

D) small intestine

E) colon

Answer: A
Diff: 1   Page Ref: 34.3
Skill: Conceptual

67) If you chew on a piece of bread long enough, it will begin to taste sweet because

A) amylase is breaking down starches to disaccharides.

B) lipases are forming fatty acids.

C) disaccharases are forming glucose.

D) proteases are forming amino acids.

E) maltase is breaking down maltose.

Answer: A
Diff: 2   Page Ref: 34.3
Skill: Application

68) What structure prevents the passage of swallowed material into the larynx?

A) tongue   B) pharynx   C) glottis   D) epiglottis   E) pyloris

Answer: D
Diff: 1   Page Ref: 34.3
Skill: Factual

69) The stomach is different from the small intestine in that the stomach

  A) does not secrete mucus.

  B) secretes enzymes.

  C) produces enzymes that work best at a very low pH.

  D) absorbs the products of digestion.

  E) has microvilli.

Answer: C
Diff: 2   Page Ref: 34.3
Skill: Conceptual

70) Where does most digestion occur?

  A) mouth

  B) stomach

  C) small intestine

  D) liver

  E) large intestine

Answer: C
Diff: 1   Page Ref: 34.3
Skill: Factual

71) Which of the following secretions does NOT contain enzymes?

  A) intestinal wall secretions

  B) bile

  C) saliva

  D) pancreatic juice

  E) gastric (stomach) secretions

Answer: B
Diff: 2   Page Ref: 34.3
Skill: Conceptual

72) Which of the following exhibits segmentation movements as well as peristalsis?

  A) esophagus

  B) stomach

  C) small intestine

  D) large intestine

  E) rectum

Answer: C
Diff: 2   Page Ref: 34.3
Skill: Conceptual

73) Which of the following enzymes would catalyze the breakdown of a disaccharide?

    A) sucrase   B) peptidase   C) lipase   D) amylase   E) pepsin

Answer: A
Diff: 2   Page Ref: 34.3
Skill: Conceptual

74) Nutrients move into intestinal wall cells by

    A) diffusion.

    B) facilitated diffusion.

    C) osmosis.

    D) active transport.

    E) both B and D

Answer: E
Diff: 1   Page Ref: 34.3
Skill: Factual

75) The pH of the digestive tract

    A) is neutral throughout.

    B) is high in stomach, low in intestines.

    C) is low in stomach, high in intestines.

    D) is variable, depending on the ingested food.

    E) is variable, depending on the volume present in each structure.

Answer: C
Diff: 2   Page Ref: 34.3
Skill: Conceptual

76) Which of the following play a key role in absorption and distribution of fats?

    A) segmentation movements

    B) lacteals

    C) secretin

    D) villi

    E) cholecystokinin

Answer: B
Diff: 2   Page Ref: 34.3
Skill: Factual

77) Which hormone stimulates the production of sodium bicarbonate into the small intestine?

    A) gastrin

    B) gastric inhibitory peptide

    C) cholecystokinin

    D) secretin

    E) antidiuretic hormone

Answer: D
Diff: 2   Page Ref: 34.3
Skill: Factual

78) Which hormone stimulates the secretion of pancreatic juice and bile?

    A) gastrin

    B) gastric inhibitory peptide

    C) cholecystokinin

    D) secretin

    E) antidiuretic hormone

Answer: C
Diff: 2   Page Ref: 34.3
Skill: Factual

79) The major function of the large intestine is to

    A) digest food.

    B) produce digestive enzymes.

    C) make bile.

    D) reabsorb water.

    E) neutralize chyme.

Answer: D
Diff: 1   Page Ref: 34.3
Skill: Factual

80) Bile is produced by the liver and stored in the gall bladder. The functions of bile are

    A) to dissolve salts and detoxify poisons in food.

    B) raise the pH of food from the small intestine and emulsify fats.

    C) prevent regurgitation of food into the esophagus and activate stomach acids.

    D) emulsify fats.

    E) lower the pH of the stomach.

Answer: D
Diff: 2   Page Ref: 34.3
Skill: Factual

81) The cells lining the small intestine have cytoplasmic projections into the lumen of the intestine and the layer of cells lining the lumen is highly folded to

   A) slow down the diffusion of food.

   B) facilitate counter-current heat exchange.

   C) increase the surface area.

   D) accommodate water retention.

   E) slow the nerve impulses that trigger peristalsis.

Answer: C
Diff: 2   Page Ref: 34.3
Skill: Conceptual

82) Absorbed fats are packaged into _____, which enter the lymph.

   A) chylomicrons

   B) micelles

   C) lipons

   D) bile salts

   E) chyme

Answer: A
Diff: 1   Page Ref: 34.3
Skill: Factual

83) Which of the following digestive enzymes will suffer from the regular consumption of antacids following a meal?

   A) lipase   B) pepsin   C) amylase   D) cellulase   E) sucrase

Answer: B
Diff: 2   Page Ref: 34.3
Skill: Application

84) Which of the following dietary changes will I need to make following surgery to remove my gallbladder?

   A) I need to decrease my consumption of fats.

   B) I need to increase my consumption of fats.

   C) I need to decrease my consumption of protein.

   D) I need to decrease my consumption of starch.

   E) I need to decrease my intake of water.

Answer: A
Diff: 2   Page Ref: 34.3
Skill: Conceptual

85) Which of the following enzymes would catalyze the breakdown of a disaccharide?

A) maltase   B) peptidase   C) lipase   D) amylase   E) protease

Answer: A
Diff: 2   Page Ref: 34.3
Skill: Conceptual

86) In which of the following structures would there be a risk of food entering the lungs as it travels?

A) esophagus

B) stomach

C) pharynx

D) larynx

E) epiglottis

Answer: C
Diff: 2   Page Ref: 34.3
Skill: Conceptual

87) A 50-year-old female visits her doctor with complaints of bruises that will not heal. Her doctor has had her on long-term antibiotic treatment to help control some chronic infections. Which of the following explains how her antibiotic treatment is related to her bruising problem?

A) She is malnourished because the antibiotics have destroyed the "good" bacteria in her digestive system that are responsible for producing the digestive enzymes that she needs to break down her food.

B) The antibiotics have traveled to her liver and are now preventing the liver from producing proteins that circulate in the blood and help with clotting.

C) The antibiotics have destroyed the "good" bacteria in her large intestine that produce vitamin K which is important for proper blood clotting.

D) The antibiotics have destroyed the "good" bacteria in her large intestine that produce vitamin E which is important for proper blood clotting.

Answer: C
Diff: 2   Page Ref: 34.3
Skill: Application

88) If the fluid in the stomach is at a very acidic pH of 1 to 3, how would you explain how this fluid becomes slightly basic almost immediately after it leaves the stomach?

    A) The acids in this fluid become neutralized by sodium bicarbonate as it is secreted from the pancreas.

    B) The acids in this fluid remain in the stomach and only the partially digested food enters the small intestine.

    C) The acids in this fluid become neutralized by amylase as it is secreted from the pancreas.

    D) The acids are absorbed by the small intestine as soon as they leave the stomach.

Answer: A
Diff: 2   *Page Ref: 34.3*
Skill: Conceptual

89) Bile is made in the gall bladder. True or False?

Answer: FALSE
Diff: 1   *Page Ref: 34.3*
Skill: Factual

90) The wall of the small intestine is studded with cells that have digestive enzymes on their external membranes which complete digestion as the nutrient is being absorbed by the cell. True or False?

Answer: TRUE
Diff: 2   *Page Ref: 34.3*
Skill: Factual

91) The small intestine is both the principle site of digestion and the major site of nutrient absorption into the blood. True or False?

Answer: TRUE
Diff: 1   *Page Ref: 34.3*
Skill: Factual

92) The large intestine is the longest part of the digestive tract. True or False?

Answer: FALSE
Diff: 1   *Page Ref: 34.3*
Skill: Conceptual

93) Hydrochloric acid formed in the stomach converts pepsinogen to _____, which enables the stomach to begin the digestion of _____.

Answer: pepsin; protein
Diff: 2   *Page Ref: 34.3*
Skill: Factual

94) The hydrophobic end of bile salts dissolves _____, while the _____ end mixes with water.

Answer: lipids; hydrophilic
Diff: 2   Page Ref: 34.3
Skill: Factual

95) If you take an antibiotic by mouth for a long period of time, it is possible to become deficient in certain vitamins. How can this be true?

Answer: The antibiotic kills off the normal bacteria in the large intestine. Since many of these make vitamins which are absorbed by the body, eventually vitamin deficiencies of a few of these are possible.
Diff: 2   Page Ref: 34.3
Skill: Application

96) List three functions of the stomach.

Answer: 1. storage; 2. mechanical breakdown; 3. secretion of substances active in the chemical breakdown of food; 4. protein digestion
Diff: 2   Page Ref: 34.3
Skill: Factual

97) Describe the relationship between stomach acidity, mucus barrier, and the formation of gastric (stomach) ulcers.

Answer: Pepsinogen is converted to the active protease, pepsin, under the highly acidic conditions of the stomach. The stomach wall is largely protein, but is protected from self–digestion by the mucus layer. An increase in acidity (lower pH) or less mucus barrier will lead to a tendency to ulcers.
Diff: 3   Page Ref: 34.3
Skill: Conceptual

98) When you swallow, you set in motion a series of muscle contractions. Name and describe these.

Answer: Peristalsis. Waves of muscle contractions which as they contract, move the food, and later the digested material through the digestive tract.
Diff: 2   Page Ref: 34.3
Skill: Conceptual

99) Briefly describe the role of the liver in the digestion of fat.

Answer: The liver produces bile salts that are stored and released from the gallbladder. Bile salts act as detergents to emulsify fats into microscopic particles. The greater surface area of these particles.
Diff: 2   Page Ref: 34.3
Skill: Conceptual

100) Explain why pancreatic juice is important in digestion.

Answer: It neutralizes the acidity of chyme, and contains amylases, lipases, and proteases for the digestion of starch, fat, and protein.
Diff: 2   Page Ref: 34.3
Skill: Conceptual

101) Name the two parts of the large intestine and briefly describe the primary functions of each.

Answer: 1) Colon—Transport of left-overs from digestion, bacterial vitamin synthesis, and absorption of vitamins, water, and salts; 2) Rectum—Storage of feces, defecation reflex
Diff: 2   Page Ref: 34.3
Skill: Conceptual

102) An anorexic patient

A) eats a meal and then vomits.

B) eats very little food.

C) is usually overweight.

D) has a bacterial infection in the stomach.

E) is primarily treated with antibiotics.

Answer: B
Diff: 1   Page Ref: Case Study
Skill: Factual

103) A teenaged girl has a lower than normal body weight and teeth that have been eaten away by acid. Your diagnosis is

A) anorexia.

B) ulcer of small intestine.

C) bulimia.

D) pancreatitis.

E) liver failure.

Answer: C
Diff: 2   Page Ref: Case Study
Skill: Conceptual

104) Which of the following is NOT true of an ulcer?

   A) The body's own immune response is a contributing factor.

   B) It involves erosion of the mucosa.

   C) The majority of ulcers are caused by *H. pylori*.

   D) The tendency to develop it may be inherited.

   E) It usually occurs in the esophagus.

Answer: E
Diff: 2   Page Ref: Health Watch
Skill: Factual

105) The bacterium shown to be associated with the majority of gastric ulcers is

   A) *Staphylococcus aureus.*

   B) *Escherichia coli.*

   C) *Streptococcus pyogenes.*

   D) *Helicobacter pylori.*

   E) *Streptococcus lactis.*

Answer: D
Diff: 1   Page Ref: Health Watch
Skill: Factual

106) Briefly describe J.R. Warren and Barry Marshall's Nobel Prize winning research on ulcers.

Answer: correlated the presence of the H. pylori bacterium with ulcers
Diff: 2   Page Ref: Health Watch
Skill: Conceptual

Chapter 35 The Urinary System

1) Which of the following describes a urinary system's role in maintaining cellular homeostasis?

    A) Urinary systems ensure the delivery of the proper amount of nitrogen to the cells.

    B) Urinary systems regulate water balance so that the concentration of dissolved substances is maintained for cells.

    C) Urinary systems are important for the generation of urea, which cells can use as an energy source when carbohydrates become scarce.

    D) Urinary systems filter out diseased and damaged cells that can be excreted from the body.

Answer: B
Diff: 2   Page Ref: 35.1
Skill: Conceptual

2) Osmolarity is defined as

    A) pressure within a closed system.

    B) pH concentration of a solution.

    C) concentration of particles dissolved in water.

    D) the ratio of oxygen to carbon dioxide.

    E) total concentration of sugars in a solution.

Answer: C
Diff: 2   Page Ref: 35.1
Skill: Factual

3) The terms *urinary system* and *excretory system* are interchangeable. True or False?

Answer: TRUE
Diff: 1   Page Ref: 35.1
Skill: Factual

4) What are the two main functions of the excretory system?

Answer: excretion of cellular wastes and regulation of body fluids
Diff: 1   Page Ref: 35.1
Skill: Factual

5) Urinary systems must be in close contact with _____.

Answer: interstitial fluid
Diff: 1   Page Ref: 35.1
Skill: Factual

6) Which of the following most closely resemble a vertebrate kidney?

    A) protonephridia

    B) nephridia

    C) protoglomerulus

    D) flame cells

    E) nephrostomes

Answer: B
Diff: 1   Page Ref: 35.2
Skill: Factual

7) Insect excretory systems consist of

    A) protonephridia.

    B) nephridia.

    C) protoglomerulus.

    D) flame cells.

    E) malpigian tubules.

Answer: B
Diff: 1   Page Ref: 35.2
Skill: Factual

8) The funnel-shaped opening of a nephridium is known as a(n)

    A) convoluted tubule.

    B) Bowman's capsule.

    C) nephrostome.

    D) excretory pore.

    E) flame cell.

Answer: C
Diff: 1   Page Ref: 35.2
Skill: Factual

9) Which organism has an excretory system composed of flame cells?

    A) flatworms

    B) Earthworms

    C) mollusks

    D) birds

    E) sharks

Answer: A
Diff: 1   Page Ref: 35.2
Skill: Factual

10) For a biology experiment it is necessary to collect coelomic fluid from an Earthworm for analysis. You know that the easiest way to do this is from the outside because an Earthworm's coelomic fluid is excreted to the external environment by means of a(n)

A) ureter.

B) urethra.

C) excretory pore.

D) nephrostomy.

E) nephrostome.

Answer: C
Diff: 1   Page Ref: 35.2
Skill: Factual

11) Nephridia are found in

A) flatworms.

B) Earthworms.

C) reptiles.

D) arthropods.

E) birds.

Answer: B
Diff: 1   Page Ref: 35.2
Skill: Factual

12) Which of the following explains why the skin of an invertebrate plays a more important role in excretion than it does for a vertebrate?

A) Invertebrates do not have any specialized structures for excretion, so they rely entirely on their skin.

B) The kidneys in most invertebrates are small and they are not able to handle all of the waste.

C) The blood of an invertebrate passes closer to the skin that it does in vertebrates.

D) Many invertebrates have a very large surface area relative to their volume. This makes the skin an efficient mechanism for the excretion of waste.

Answer: D
Diff: 2   Page Ref: 35.2
Skill: Conceptual

13) The excretory system of an Earthworm consists of two nephridia, a nephrostome, and an excretory pore. True or False?

Answer: FALSE
Diff: 1   Page Ref: 35.2
Skill: Factual

14) Flatworms have simple kidneys called nephridia. True or False?

Answer: FALSE
Diff: 1   Page Ref: 35.2
Skill: Factual

15) Urinary system functions include excretion of waste products and

    A) water balance.

    B) egg maturation.

    C) digestion.

    D) regulation of metabolism.

    E) temperature regulation.

Answer: A
Diff: 1   Page Ref: 35.3
Skill: Factual

16) All of the following are functions of the vertebrate urinary system EXCEPT

    A) water balance.

    B) pH levels.

    C) temperature regulation.

    D) secretion of hormones.

    E) removal of waste products.

Answer: C
Diff: 1   Page Ref: 35.3
Skill: Factual

17) Urea is a product of the breakdown of

    A) lipids.

    B) carbohydrates.

    C) proteins.

    D) vitamin B.

    E) iron.

Answer: C
Diff: 1   Page Ref: 35.3
Skill: Factual

18) Each molecule of urea contains _____ atom(s) of nitrogen.

    A) 1   B) 2   C) 3   D) 4

Answer: B
Diff: 1   Page Ref: 35.3
Skill: Factual

19) Amino acids that are NOT needed by the body are

    A) excreted in the urine.

    B) stored.

    C) used directly for energy in the muscles.

    D) called non-essential.

    E) broken down by the liver.

Answer: E
Diff: 2   Page Ref: 35.3
Skill: Factual

20) Excreting nitrogenous waste as uric acid enables an animal to

    A) excrete hypertonic urine.

    B) conserve water.

    C) excrete sodium more efficiently.

    D) excrete more urine.

    E) survive in an aquatic environment.

Answer: B
Diff: 2   Page Ref: 35.3
Skill: Conceptual

21) Birds excrete nitrogenous waste in the form of

    A) urea.

    B) uric acid.

    C) ammonia.

    D) amino acids.

    E) amine groups.

Answer: B
Diff: 1   Page Ref: 35.3
Skill: Factual

22) One animal that excretes ammonia is a(n)

    A) desert locust.

    B) ostrich.

    C) camel.

    D) catfish.

    E) whale.

Answer: D
Diff: 1   Page Ref: 35.3
Skill: Factual

23) The nitrogenous waste product produced by a desert lizard that has evolved to conserve as much body water as possible. It is

A) ammonia.

B) urea.

C) uric acid.

D) phosphotidyl urea.

Answer: C
Diff: 2   Page Ref: 35.3
Skill: Conceptual

24) Urea is more toxic to the human body than is ammonia. True or False?

Answer: FALSE
Diff: 1   Page Ref: 35.3
Skill: Factual

25) All mammals produce urea. True or False?

Answer: TRUE
Diff: 1   Page Ref: 35.3
Skill: Factual

26) Explain the connection between proteins, amino acids, and the need to produce urine.

Answer: Proteins are made up of amino acids which contain an amino group. When more protein is consumed than can be used for making more protein, the amino group has to be removed in the liver from the amino acids. These amino groups are made into ammonia, which is extremely toxic so the liver immediately changes the ammonia into urea, which is less toxic giving the kidneys time to filter the urea from the blood and excrete it as urine.
Diff: 3   Page Ref: 35.3
Skill: Conceptual

27) Briefly discuss the advantages of uric acid excretion by birds, reptiles, and insects.

Answer: The relative insolubility of uric acid allows it to be secreted as a paste which 1. protects the eggs from being surrounded by wastes 2. allows the animal to carry less water, helping those which fly, 3. conserves water 4. uric acid is less toxic than either urea or ammonia
Diff: 2   Page Ref: 35.3
Skill: Conceptual

28) Urine leaves each mammalian kidney through a muscular tube known as the

A) urethra.

B) ureter.

C) bladder.

D) collecting duct.

E) nephron.

Answer: B
Diff: 1   Page Ref: 35.4
Skill: Factual

29) The basic functional unit of the kidney is called the

A) Bowman's capsule.

B) tubule.

C) nephron.

D) nephrostome.

E) glomerulus.

Answer: C
Diff: 1   Page Ref: 35.4
Skill: Factual

30) Which portion of the nephron receives filtrate from Bowman's capsule?

A) glomerulus

B) proximal tubule

C) distal tubule

D) loop of Henle

E) collecting duct

Answer: B
Diff: 1   Page Ref: 35.4
Skill: Factual

31) Where does most secretion take place?

A) glomerulus

B) proximal tubule

C) distal tubule

D) loop of Henle

E) collecting duct

Answer: C
Diff: 1   Page Ref: 35.4
Skill: Factual

32) Which of the following is not secreted?

A) hydrogen ions

B) potassium ions

C) glucose

D) drug metabolites

E) ammonia

Answer: C
Diff: 2   Page Ref: 35.4
Skill: Factual

33) The force that drives filtration in the kidney is

A) osmosis.

B) smooth muscle contraction.

C) blood pressure.

D) salt gradients.

E) pH gradients.

Answer: C
Diff: 1   Page Ref: 35.4
Skill: Conceptual

34) The most important factor that determines glomerular blood pressure is

A) your heart rate.

B) your blood pressure.

C) the diameter of arterioles entering and exiting the nephrons.

D) your total blood volume.

E) ratio of short to long nephrons.

Answer: C
Diff: 2   Page Ref: 35.4
Skill: Conceptual

35) Glucose and amino acids are reabsorbed from the filtrate by the

A) ureter.

B) proximal tubule.

C) distal tubule.

D) loop of Henle.

E) glomerulus.

Answer: B
Diff: 1   Page Ref: 35.4
Skill: Factual

36) Human kidneys are located

    A) on each side of the esophagus.

    B) in the chest cavity.

    C) around the level of the waist.

    D) at the base of the brain.

    E) below the large intestine.

Answer: C
Diff: 1   Page Ref: 35.4
Skill: Factual

37) The force that moves urine to the bladder is

    A) active transport.

    B) diffusion.

    C) osmosis.

    D) peristalsis.

    E) segmentation movements.

Answer: D
Diff: 1   Page Ref: 35.4
Skill: Conceptual

38) After surgery your grandmother is having difficulty urinating. The doctor orders that she be catheterized (have a tube inserted in her bladder to remove the urine). About how much urine would you expect to come out if she is an average adult?

    A) 63 ml (1/4 cup)

    B) 125 ml (1/2 cup)

    C) 250 ml (1 cup)

    D) 500 ml (1 pint)

    E) 1000 ml (1 quart)

Answer: D
Diff: 2   Page Ref: 35.4
Skill: Conceptual

39) Which is voluntary muscle?

    A) the one where a ureter enters the bladder

    B) the internal urethral sphincter

    C) the external urethral sphincter

    D) kidney

    E) those in the ureter

Answer: C
Diff: 2   Page Ref: 35.4
Skill: Conceptual

40) Which is closest to the external surface of the kidney?

    A) pelvis

    B) cortex

    C) medulla

    D) smooth muscle

    E) glomerulus

Answer: B
Diff: 2   Page Ref: 35.4
Skill: Conceptual

41) The hollow inner chamber of the kidney is called the

    A) pelvis.

    B) cortex.

    C) medulla.

    D) smooth muscle.

    E) glomerulus.

Answer: A
Diff: 1   Page Ref: 35.4
Skill: Factual

42) Which of the following is NOT part of the nephron?

    A) Bowman's capsule

    B) glomerulus

    C) loop of Henle

    D) renal pelvis

    E) proximal tubule

Answer: D
Diff: 1   Page Ref: 35.4
Skill: Factual

43) Which of the following would normally NOT be filtered out of the blood in the kidney?

    A) water

    B) salt

    C) glucose

    D) large proteins

    E) drugs

Answer: D
Diff: 1   Page Ref: 35.4
Skill: Conceptual

44) Your patient is producing red urine due to the presence of hemoglobins. This is probably due to

    A) excess ADH.

    B) too little angiotensin.

    C) damage to the kidney.

    D) too much erythropoietin.

    E) a decrease in ADH.

Answer: C
Diff: 2   Page Ref: 35.4
Skill: Conceptual

45) The blood vessel leaving the glomerulus has a smaller diameter than the blood vessel entering it. This has the effect of

    A) causing blood to move faster when it leaves the glomerulus.

    B) increasing reabsorption.

    C) decreasing reabsorption.

    D) creating pressure that causes filtration.

    E) increasing active transport.

Answer: D
Diff: 2   Page Ref: 35.4
Skill: Application

46) The process of filtration in the kidneys is the result of

A) a high concentration of wastes in the bloodstream and a low concentration in the bowman's capsule.

B) blood wastes diffusing across a membrane.

C) reabsorption of excess water.

D) active transport of wastes into the Bowman's capsule.

E) the arteriole coming out of the glomerulus being smaller than the one going in.

Answer: E
Diff: 1   Page Ref: 35.4
Skill: Conceptual

47) Which of these would normally be found in glomerular filtrate?

A) salts

B) large proteins

C) erythrocytes

D) fat droplets

E) white blood cells

Answer: A
Diff: 1   Page Ref: 35.4
Skill: Conceptual

48) Which of the following constituents of kidney filtrate is reabsorbed by osmosis?

A) water

B) glucose

C) amino acids

D) urea

E) red blood cells

Answer: A
Diff: 1   Page Ref: 35.4
Skill: Conceptual

49) The process by which water and nutrients are passed from the filtrate back into the blood is known as

    A) tubular secretion.

    B) tubular reabsorption.

    C) filtration.

    D) tubular excretion.

    E) tubular elimination.

Answer: B
Diff: 1   Page Ref: 35.4
Skill: Factual

50) Which constituent of kidney filtrate is the most likely to be reabsorbed?

    A) glucose

    B) water

    C) hydrogen ions

    D) urea

    E) ammonia

Answer: A
Diff: 1   Page Ref: 35.4
Skill: Conceptual

51) Wastes are moved from blood to nephron by

    A) filtration.

    B) reabsorption.

    C) secretion.

    D) Choices A, B, and C are all correct.

    E) Choices A and C are correct, but B is not.

Answer: E
Diff: 2   Page Ref: 35.4
Skill: Factual

52) Which correctly traces the path of urine?

A) renal pelvis → urethra → bladder → ureter

B) renal pelvis → ureter → bladder → urethra

C) renal pelvis → uterus → bladder → urethra

D) renal pelvis → bladder → ureter → urethra

E) ureter → urethra → bladder → renal pelvis

Answer: B
Diff: 2   Page Ref: 35.4
Skill: Factual

53) The concentration of the urine is controlled by

A) homeostatic hormone.

B) diuretic hormone.

C) antidiuretic hormone.

D) aldosterone.

E) renal diluting hormone.

Answer: C
Diff: 1   Page Ref: 35.4
Skill: Conceptual

54) This structure collects filtrate from the blood.

A) glomerulus

B) Bowman's capsule

C) proximal tubule

D) loop of Henle

E) distal tubule

Answer: B
Diff: 1   Page Ref: 35.4
Skill: Factual

55) A network of capillaries where fluid is filtered out of the blood.

A) glomerulus

B) Bowman's capsule

C) proximal tubule

D) loop of Henle

E) distal tubule

Answer: A
Diff: 1   Page Ref: 35.4
Skill: Factual

56) Which part(s) of the tubule system in the kidney is sensitive to the effects of ADH?

    A) collecting duct

    B) distal tubule

    C) proximal tubule

    D) loop of Henle

    E) both A and B

Answer: E
Diff: 1   Page Ref: 35.4
Skill: Factual

57) A majority of reabsorption takes place in this part of the tubule system in the kidney?

    A) collecting duct

    B) Bowman's capsule

    C) proximal tubule

    D) loop of Henle

    E) distal tubule

Answer: C
Diff: 1   Page Ref: 35.4
Skill: Factual

58) A person taking antibiotics must take pills several times/day to maintain effective concentrations in the blood. This is because of

    A) erythropoietin.

    B) tubular reabsorption.

    C) tubular secretion.

    D) angiotensin.

    E) the decrease in antidiuretic hormone.

Answer: C
Diff: 2   Page Ref: 35.4
Skill: Conceptual

59) Which is the MOST correct statement?

   A) Most of the water that filters into Bowman's capsule is reabsorbed.

   B) One–half of the water that filters into Bowman's capsule is reabsorbed.

   C) Most of the protein that filters into Bowman's capsule is reabsorbed.

   D) One–half of the glucose that filters into Bowman's capsule is reabsorbed.

   E) None of the salts that are filtered in the Bowman's capsule are reabsorbed.

Answer: A
Diff: 2   Page Ref: 35.4
Skill: Conceptual

60) Which of the following has loops of Henle in the kidney?

   A) crab

   B) Earthworm

   C) robin

   D) frog

   E) rattlesnake

Answer: C
Diff: 1   Page Ref: 35.4
Skill: Factual

61) What percentage of the water that filters into the nephron is reabsorbed?

   A) 25%   B) 75%   C) 85%   D) 99%   E) 100%

Answer: D
Diff: 1   Page Ref: 35.4
Skill: Factual

62) Long loops of Henle correlate with

   A) more concentrated urine.

   B) more dilute urine.

   C) urine hypotonic to the blood.

   D) urine isotonic to the blood.

   E) urine with glucose in it.

Answer: A
Diff: 2   Page Ref: 35.4
Skill: Conceptual

63) The second step in the formation of urine in a mammal, _____ occurs in the _____.

    A) reabsorption; proximal tubule

    B) filtration; glomerulus

    C) excretion; rectum

    D) secretion; distal tubule

    E) concentration; Bowman's capsule

Answer: A
Diff: 2   Page Ref: 35.4
Skill: Factual

64) Which of the following explains why a sample of the filtrate in the proximal tubule would not be ideal for conducting a drug test or toxicology screen?

    A) Many of the toxins and drugs do not enter the filtrate until they are secreted in the distal tubule.

    B) As soon as the toxins and drugs enter the proximal tubule, they are immediately reabsorbed.

    C) Many of the toxins and drugs enter the bladder and become part of the urine as it is stored.

    D) Only a blood test can detect drugs and toxins because they are too big to get into the filtrate at any point along the tubule.

Answer: A
Diff: 2   Page Ref: 35.4
Skill: Conceptual

65) The composition of glomerular filtrate is almost identical to urine. True or False?

Answer: FALSE
Diff: 1   Page Ref: 35.4
Skill: Conceptual

66) Human urine is generally isotonic (having the same osmotic pressure as the blood). True or False?

Answer: FALSE
Diff: 1   Page Ref: 35.4
Skill: Conceptual

67) Your total blood volume has passed through your kidneys 5 minutes after you read this question. True or False?

Answer: TRUE
Diff: 1   Page Ref: 35.4
Skill: Factual

68) Based upon your knowledge of the differences between the male and female excretory systems, why are females at greater risk of urinary tract infections?

Answer: The urethra is about 5 times as long in males as females (8 inches compared with 1.5 inches).
Diff: 2   Page Ref: 35.4
Skill: Conceptual

69) Name the three major parts of the nephron.

Answer: glomerulus, Bowman's capsule, tubule
Diff: 1   Page Ref: 35.4
Skill: Factual

70) Since there is a high concentration of salt in the extracellular fluid around the bottom of the loop of Henle, what happens to water in this area?

Answer: It flows by osmosis out of the tubule into the extracellular fluid.
Diff: 2   Page Ref: 35.4
Skill: Conceptual

71) Where does the highest rate of tubular reabsorption occur?

Answer: the proximal tubule
Diff: 2   Page Ref: 35.4
Skill: Conceptual

72) Explain why the process in the kidneys is called filtration rather than diffusion or active transport.

Answer: The blood is actually forced through a filter in the form of the walls of the blood vessels in the glomerulus. The arteriole coming into the glomerulus is larger than the one going out so that anything small enough to pass through the capillary wall is forced out, filtering the blood.
Diff: 2   Page Ref: 35.4
Skill: Conceptual

73) What is the function of tubular secretion?

Answer: Substances that are harmful to the body, such as drugs, excess hydrogen ions, excess salt ions, etc., may be completely removed from the bloodstream by the tubules actively transporting them into the filtrate.
Diff: 2   Page Ref: 35.4
Skill: Conceptual

74) A man survives for 24 hours in Death Valley with no water to drink. His blood level of ADH is

  A) lower than usual.

  B) higher than usual.

  C) the same as usual.

  D) zero.

  E) impossible to determine.

Answer: B
Diff: 2   Page Ref: 35.5
Skill: Conceptual

75) Which portions of the nephron reabsorb water in response to ADH concentrations?

  A) glomerulus and Bowman's capsule

  B) loop of Henle and distal tubule

  C) proximal tubule and distal tubule

  D) proximal tubule and loop of Henle

  E) distal tubule and collecting duct

Answer: E
Diff: 2   Page Ref: 35.5
Skill: Factual

76) An increase in ADH release will have what effect on blood volume?

  A) It will decrease blood volume.

  B) It will increase blood volume.

  C) Only the plasma (fluid) part of the blood will decrease.

  D) No change will occur due to the feedback system.

  E) It will have no effect upon blood volume, since ADH only affects urine output.

Answer: B
Diff: 2   Page Ref: 35.5
Skill: Conceptual

77) An animal that has a predominance of very long loops of Henle probably lives in a(n) _____ environment.

   A) aquatic

   B) terrestrial

   C) arid

   D) salt water

   E) fresh water

Answer: C
Diff: 1   Page Ref: 35.5
Skill: Conceptual

78) Which hormone(s) produced by the kidney is important in the regulation of blood pressure?

   A) renin

   B) angiotensin

   C) ADH

   D) A and B

   E) A, B and C

Answer: E
Diff: 1   Page Ref: 35.5
Skill: Factual

79) Which directly produces vasoconstriction?

   A) erythropoietin

   B) angiotensin

   C) renin

   D) both A and B

   E) both B and C

Answer: B
Diff: 1   Page Ref: 35.5
Skill: Factual

80) Erythropoietin is released in response to

    A) low blood pressure.

    B) high blood pressure.

    C) dehydration.

    D) low blood oxygen levels.

    E) high blood oxygen levels.

Answer: D
Diff: 1   Page Ref: 35.5
Skill: Factual

81) Antidiuretic hormone is put into the blood by the

    A) hypothalamus.

    B) pituitary gland.

    C) kidney.

    D) liver.

    E) small intestine.

Answer: B
Diff: 1   Page Ref: 35.5
Skill: Factual

82) Antidiuretic hormone

    A) acts to increase the amount of urine formed.

    B) controls the amount of fluid filtered from the blood.

    C) increases the permeability of the collecting tubule to water.

    D) decreases reabsorption.

    E) controls the emptying of the bladder.

Answer: C
Diff: 1   Page Ref: 35.5
Skill: Factual

83) Which of the following symptoms might you find in a person with kidney failure?

    A) changes in blood pressure

    B) anemia

    C) a drop in blood pH

    D) increased urea concentration in the blood

    E) all of the above

Answer: E
Diff: 2   Page Ref: 35.5
Skill: Conceptual

84) Officials associated with International Track and Field competitions have noted an increase in the number of athletes using a synthetic form of erythropoietin. Which of the following explains why these athletes would use this drug?

    A) The drug decreases blood pressure so an athlete can be more focused and relaxed during a competition.

    B) The drug increases urine output so that the athlete can shed weight just prior to an important competition.

    C) The drug increases the number or red blood cells so that the athlete can increase their aerobic capacity for an event.

    D) The drug stimulates the release of ADH which then goes on to cause an increase in the number of red blood cells. This helps athletes increase their aerobic capacity for an event.

Answer: C
Diff: 2   Page Ref: 35.5
Skill: Conceptual

85) Ethanol increases urine output by altering the body's release of anti–diuretic hormone. Therefore, ethanol must decrease ADH release. True or False?

Answer: TRUE
Diff: 2   Page Ref: 35.5
Skill: Conceptual

86) The kidneys regulate blood pressure. True or False?

Answer: TRUE
Diff: 1   Page Ref: 35.5
Skill: Factual

87) Animals produce different types of urine depending on their environment and their need to conserve water. True or False?

Answer: TRUE
Diff: 1   Page Ref: 35.5
Skill: Conceptual

88) What happens to ADH when you drink a lot of water? What effect will that have on your urine output?

Answer: The osmotic concentration of the blood drops as you increase the amount of water in the bloodstream. This causes less ADH to be produced and increases urine output.
Diff: 2   Page Ref: 35.5
Skill: Conceptual

89) Briefly explain why animals living in very dry climates have the longest loops of Henle.

Answer: The longer the loop, the greater the concentrating ability of the kidney, thus facilitating necessary excretion of waste without sacrificing essential water.
Diff: 2   Page Ref: 35.5
Skill: Conceptual

90) When a patient is on a kidney dialysis machine, dissolved substances move from the patient's blood to the fluid in the machine primarily by

A) diffusion.

B) osmosis.

C) active transport.

D) pressure on the blood exerted by the machine.

E) filtration.

Answer: A
Diff: 2   Page Ref: Health Watch
Skill: Conceptual

91) Kidneys can be damaged by

A) excess protein in the diet.

B) low carbohydrate diet.

C) high blood pressure.

D) A and C

E) A, B and C

Answer: D
Diff: 1   Page Ref: Health Watch
Skill: Factual

92) A person in renal failure may eat whatever he likes as long as he goes to dialysis three times a week as scheduled. True or False?

Answer: FALSE
Diff: 1   Page Ref: Health Watch
Skill: Conceptual

93) Describe the process of dialysis.

Answer: Student should include blood flowing through semipermeable membrane suspended in dialyzing fluid which allows wastes to diffuse into the fluid but retains sugar, normal salt levels, and large particles. Also should mention that blood is moved through under pressure to force out excess water.
Diff: 1   Page Ref: Health Watch
Skill: Factual

94) The descending limb of the loop of Henle

    A) is not permeable to water.

    B) is freely permeable to salt and urea.

    C) pulls water from the medulla to make the filtrate more dilute.

    D) loses water to the medulla as the filtrate becomes more concentrated.

    E) reacts to ADH levels.

Answer: D
Diff: 2   Page Ref: A Closer Look
Skill: Conceptual

95) The ascending limb of the loop of Henle

    A) is permeable to water.

    B) is permeable to salt which leaves as the filtrate becomes more dilute.

    C) draws in salt from the medulla to make the filtrate more concentrated.

    D) is the primary site of tubular secretion.

    E) reacts to ADH levels.

Answer: B
Diff: 2   Page Ref: A Closer Look
Skill: Conceptual

Chapter 36 Immunity: Defenses Against Disease

1) When Europeans first came to North America, one of the most disastrous interactions with native populations was the introduction of diseases like smallpox. Given what you know about the immune system, why did these diseases wreak so much more havoc in the Native American populations?

   A) Their immune systems were generally weaker than the Europeans.

   B) Their immune systems had not evolved in the presence of this new microbe.

   C) They were genetically predisposed to be susceptible to smallpox.

   D) The Europeans had all been vaccinated against smallpox.

Answer: B
Diff: 3   Page Ref: 36.1
Skill: Application

2) List the three lines of defense of the human body.

Answer: 1. The skin and mucus membranes 2. The non–specific responses 3. Specific immune responses
Diff: 2   Page Ref: 36.1
Skill: Factual

3) The skin acts as a barrier to microbial invasion because

   A) its moist surface slows bacterial growth.

   B) the dead skin cells contain bacterial nutrients.

   C) secretions from sweat glands and sebaceous glands inhibit bacterial growth.

   D) All of the above are true.

Answer: C
Diff: 1   Page Ref: 36.2
Skill: Factual

4) Which is the first line of defense against microbial attack?

   A) nonspecific responses   B) the immune response

   C) external barriers   D) mucous and ciliary action

Answer: C
Diff: 2   Page Ref: 36.2
Skill: Factual

5) Your four-year-old child comes in crying with a skinned knee. You begin to clean the wound and bandage it. He begins screaming even more loudly "Mommy, why do you have to do that?" You explain that now that the skin is broken, he is more at risk of infection because

    A) his skin normally acts like a bandage to keep germs out.

    B) normally his sweat glands prevent germs from growing, but now that his skin is broken, you must apply antibiotic cream to do this.

    C) germs grow better on wet surfaces like his bloody knee than on his dry skin.

    D) All of the above are true.

    E) None of the above are true.

Answer: D
Diff: 3   Page Ref: 36.2
Skill: Application

6) Chronic smokers are more susceptible to illness than non-smokers. Which of the following effects of chronic exposure to cigarette smoke could accounts for this?

    A) Increased mucus production in the respiratory tract decreases flow of oxygen to the lungs.

    B) Toxins such as nicotine cause paralysis of cilia in the respiratory tract.

    C) Toxins in cigarette smoke impair white blood cell function.

    D) A and B

    E) B and C

Answer: E
Diff: 3   Page Ref: 36.2
Skill: Application

7) Nonspecific internal defenses include

    A) natural killer cells.

    B) phagocytic cells.

    C) inflammatory response.

    D) fever.

    E) all of the above

Answer: E
Diff: 2   Page Ref: 36.2
Skill: Factual

8) How does a natural killer cell prevent infection?

A) by enzymatically degrading viruses

B) by destroying the cells infected with a virus

C) by secreting proteins into the viral membrane, thereby opening a large pore in the membrane

D) Both A and C are correct.

E) All statements are correct.

Answer: B
Diff: 2   Page Ref: 36.2
Skill: Factual

9) Which of the following is NOT a consequence of histamine release?

A) "leaky" capillary walls

B) relaxation of the smooth muscle that surrounds arterioles

C) increased blood flow

D) initiation of blood clotting

Answer: D
Diff: 2   Page Ref: 36.2
Skill: Factual

10) Why do physicians recommend that their patients NOT take aspirin for a low-grade fever?

A) Aspirin depresses the immune response.

B) Fevers increase the amount of interferon produced by the body.

C) Fevers slow down bacterial reproduction rates.

D) Both A and C are correct.

E) Both B and C are correct.

Answer: E
Diff: 2   Page Ref: 36.2
Skill: Conceptual

11) Which of the following is NOT an example of a non-specific response against infection?

A) phagocytic white blood cells

B) antibodies

C) fever

D) inflammation

E) All of the above are specific.

Answer: B
Diff: 2   Page Ref: 36.2
Skill: Factual

12) A patient has suffered an injury while playing softball and has pain in their shoulder. The doctor prescribes a strong anti inflammatory drug but warns that one of the side effects could be contracting pneumonia. What would be an explanation for this?

    A) The drug must interfere with DNA replication.

    B) The drug inhibits a part of the non specific defenses.

    C) The drug gets in the way of the action of the specific defenses.

    D) The drug is causing bacteria to form in the body spontaneously.

Answer: B
Diff: 2   Page Ref: 36.2
Skill: Application

13) Macrophages

    A) can squeeze through capillary walls.

    B) move around in the extracellular fluid.

    C) act by phagocytosis.

    D) "present" microbes to the immune system.

    E) All of these are true of macrophages.

Answer: E
Diff: 2   Page Ref: 36.2
Skill: Factual

14) Natural killer cells

    A) destroy body cells that have been invaded by viruses.

    B) are a type of B cell.

    C) engulf and destroy bacteria.

    D) are located on the skin.

    E) are a type of T cell.

Answer: A
Diff: 2   Page Ref: 36.2
Skill: Factual

15) Which of these is NOT part of the inflammatory response?

    A) presence of histamine

    B) blood clotting

    C) swelling

    D) antibodies

    E) redness

Answer: D
Diff: 1   Page Ref: 36.2
Skill: Factual

16) Why is it a disadvantage to you if your roommate gets a cold and takes aspirin to reduce the fever?

    A) Aspirin will make him more tired and cranky.

    B) Aspirin will reduce his ability to produce interferon, so that he is more likely to give you the cold.

    C) Aspirin will make him get over the cold faster by increasing the amount of toxins which his body releases, but some of these are harmful to you.

    D) Aspirin will reduce his production of toxins so that he feels better, even though he is still sick, so that he is more likely to spend time with you and pass the cold on to you.

    E) Aspirin will make him so tired that he can't study with you.

Answer: B
Diff: 3   Page Ref: 36.2
Skill: Application

17) Which of the following is responsible for starting fevers?

    A) B cells   B) T cells

    C) histamine   D) endogenous pyrogens

Answer: D
Diff: 1   Page Ref: 36.2
Skill: Factual

18) Fever is caused by

    A) the release of histamine by damaged cells.

    B) the effect of pyrogens on the hypothalamus.

    C) increased blood flow to the brain.

    D) all of these

Answer: B
Diff: 2   Page Ref: 36.2
Skill: Factual

19) Interferon

    A) kills bacteria.   B) helps cells resist viral infection.

    C) causes fever.   D) all of these

Answer: B
Diff: 2   Page Ref: 36.2
Skill: Factual

20) Which of the following predictions would be most accurate about a person who had normal external barriers and specific internal defenses, but was missing their nonspecific internal defenses?

 A) They would have many more infections than normal.

 B) They would not be able to build immunity to microbes.

 C) They wouldn't be any different because their external barriers would keep out most pathogens.

 D) They wouldn't be any different because their specific defenses would still kill invading pathogens.

Answer: A
Diff: 3   Page Ref: 36.2
Skill: Application

21) A person with a very low white cell count will not develop pus at the site of an infection. True or False?

Answer: TRUE
Diff: 2   Page Ref: 36.2
Skill: Application

22) As part of the _____ line of defense of the body against invaders the skin produces sweat, which contains _____ acid which inhibits the growth of bacteria and fungi.

Answer: first; lactic
Diff: 2   Page Ref: 36.2
Skill: Factual

23) You know you are getting sick because your nose starts running. What advantages does the extra mucus provide to you?

Answer: It kills bacteria through lysozyme in the mucus, traps microbes in the thick mucus, and enables them to be swept out of your respiratory tract by cilia.
Diff: 3   Page Ref: 36.2
Skill: Conceptual

24) What is pus?

Answer: an accumulation of dead bacteria, damaged tissue, and living and dead white blood cells
Diff: 2   Page Ref: 36.2
Skill: Factual

25) What mechanisms do natural killer cells use to destroy body cells that have been infected by cancer or a virus?

Answer: They open up large holes in the membrane of the infected cells by shooting into them. Water floods in through the holes and destroys the cells. Also they secrete enzymes which break down the cell membranes.
Diff: 3   Page Ref: 36.2
Skill: Factual

26) Briefly explain why inflamed tissues appear red, swollen, and warm.

Answer: In an attempt to "wall-off" infection, affected cells release histamine which makes capillaries leaky and dilates arterioles causing increased blood flow. This causes redness, warmth, and swelling.
Diff: 3   Page Ref: 36.2
Skill: Conceptual

27) Briefly describe how a fever develops in response to infection.

Answer: White blood cells release endogenous pyrogens which trigger the hypothalamus to raise its set point. This causes behaviors such as shivering which makes the person feel the need to keep warm. It also increases fat metabolism to fuel the "fire."
Diff: 3   Page Ref: 36.2
Skill: Factual

28) Your friend cut her hand open on a sharp object in the garden. Later that day, she notices that the area around the cut is bright red, slightly warm and there is an outline of white along the perimeter of the cut. Specifically describe what is occurring inside her body to result in these observations.

Answer: The cut has damaged the first line of defense—the skin. The nonspecific defenses are now activated to defend against invading microbes that have entered through the cut. The redness and warmth are caused by the inflammatory response at work. The white perimeter is the result of white blood cells accumulating in the area to destroy any pathogens.
Diff: 2   Page Ref: 36.2
Skill: Application

29) Which of the following statements is TRUE?

A) There are no genes for entire antibody molecules in the cells of your body.

B) The immune system does not design antibodies to fit invading antigens.

C) Each B cell produces a different antibody, different from those of all other B cells (except for its own daughter cells).

D) Both B and C are correct.

E) All statements are correct.

Answer: E
Diff: 2   Page Ref: 36.3
Skill: Factual

30) Foreign proteins that will bind to an antibody are called

   A) cytotoxins.   B) histamines.   C) interferons.   D) antigens.

Answer: D
Diff: 1   Page Ref: 36.3
Skill: Factual

31) MHC (major histocompatability complex) proteins

   A) control antibody gene expression.

   B) cause cancer.

   C) mark cells as "self".

   D) are released by cytotoxic T cells to kill cells infected with virus.

Answer: C
Diff: 1   Page Ref: 36.3
Skill: Factual

32) Antibodies are

   A) protein molecules.

   B) amino acid molecules.

   C) carbohydrate molecules.

   D) organelles of platelets.

   E) derived from vitamins.

Answer: A
Diff: 1   Page Ref: 36.3
Skill: Factual

33) Antibodies are Y-shaped. The specific part of the Y that binds to an antigen is the

   A) constant region.

   B) tips of the arms.

   C) stem of the Y.

   D) heavy chain.

   E) light chain.

Answer: B
Diff: 2   Page Ref: 36.3
Skill: Factual

34) There is a gene for every antibody.

    A) false, because antibodies are made from proteins

    B) false, because the body makes antigens, not antibodies

    C) false, because genes code for antibody parts, not whole antibodies

    D) false, because antibodies form genes, genes do not form antibodies

    E) true

Answer: C
Diff: 3   Page Ref: 36.3
Skill: Conceptual

35) Which is the BEST statement regarding antibodies?

    A) Each individual, from fetal life on, must make his/her own.

    B) They are not made except in response to antigens.

    C) One antibody will bind to many quite different kinds of antigen.

    D) Antigen encounters its matching antibody by chance.

    E) They cause the body to produce more antigens.

Answer: D
Diff: 2   Page Ref: 36.3
Skill: Factual

36) The genes for antibody parts

    A) do not undergo mutation.

    B) amount to about half of the human genes.

    C) are different for the constant and variable regions of the antibody.

    D) are all on the same chromosome.

    E) are in the shape of a Y.

Answer: C
Diff: 2   Page Ref: 36.3
Skill: Factual

37) Immature immune cells

    A) are unable to produce antibodies.

    B) are destroyed if they have "self" antibodies.

    C) do not have surface proteins.

    D) all undergo maturation and are retained throughout life.

    E) are constantly being formed throughout life.

Answer: B
Diff: 2   Page Ref: 36.3
Skill: Factual

38) The proteins that must be matched as closely as possible between an organ donor and recipient are the _____ proteins.

    A) glyco   B) MHC   C) clotting factor   D) all of these

Answer: B
Diff: 1   Page Ref: 36.3
Skill: Application

39) Antibodies are

    A) bacteria.

    B) viruses.

    C) proteins produced by B cells that bind to foreign proteins.

    D) none of the above

Answer: C
Diff: 1   Page Ref: 36.3
Skill: Factual

40) Malaria organisms evade the immune system by

    A) mutating during each life cycle.   B) killing B cells.

    C) quickly changing surface antigens.   D) all of the above

Answer: C
Diff: 2   Page Ref: 36.3
Skill: Factual

41) If you were building an antibody and you had 10 different genes for the light chain variable region and 10 different genes for the heavy chain variable regions, how many different antibodies could you create?

    A) 2   B) 10   C) 20   D) 100   E) 200

Answer: D
Diff: 3   Page Ref: 36.3
Skill: Application

42) Which of these is NOT associated with antibody function?

    A) promotion of phagocytosis

    B) agglutination

    C) neutralization of toxins

    D) complement reactions

    E) All of these are associated with antibody functions.

Answer: E
Diff: 2   Page Ref: 36.3
Skill: Factual

43) Cell-mediated immunity is provided by

    A) B cells.   B) antibodies.   C) T-cells.   D) NK cells.

Answer: C
Diff: 2   Page Ref: 36.3
Skill: Factual

44) Different B cells produce different antibodies by

    A) activating new ribosomes.   B) activating different enzymes.

    C) genetic recombination.   D) all of these

Answer: C
Diff: 2   Page Ref: 36.3
Skill: Factual

45) Which type of cell secretes antibodies?

    A) plasma cells   B) memory cells

    C) T cells   D) cytotoxic t cells

Answer: A
Diff: 2   Page Ref: 36.3
Skill: Factual

46) Which type of cells are responsible for screening and destroying cancerous cells?

    A) natural killer cells

    B) cytotoxic T cells

    C) helper T cells

    D) both A and B

    E) all of the above

Answer: D
Diff: 2   Page Ref: 36.3
Skill: Factual

47) Immune system cells that mature in the bone marrow are

    A) helper T-cells.   B) B cells.

    C) M-cells.   D) suppressor T cells.

Answer: B
Diff: 1   Page Ref: 36.3
Skill: Factual

48) Each B cell of the immune system produces

    A) only one kind of antibody.

    B) the antibodies specified by its heavy chain gene.

    C) the antibodies specified by its light chain gene.

    D) the antibodies specified by its variable region gene.

    E) the antibodies specified by its constant region gene.

Answer: A
Diff: 2   Page Ref: 36.3
Skill: Factual

49) Which of these is NOT a function of B cells?

    A) responsible for humoral immunity

    B) plasma cells secrete antibodies

    C) some act as memory cells

    D) some act as natural killer cells

    E) All of these are functions of B cells.

Answer: D
Diff: 2   Page Ref: 36.3
Skill: Factual

50) Complement is

    A) an antibiotic.

    B) a phagocytic cell.

    C) a blood protein that assists antibodies.

    D) a non-specific antigen.

    E) what you had better pay your teacher.

Answer: C
Diff: 2   Page Ref: 36.3
Skill: Factual

51) The major function of cell-mediated immunity is to

    A) increase the amount of complement.

    B) increase the number of macrophages.

    C) promote the production of antigen.

    D) destroy cancerous or infected host cells.

    E) agglutinate antigens.

Answer: D
Diff: 2   Page Ref: 36.3
Skill: Factual

52) A cell signals to the immune system that it is infected with a virus by

A) irritating local nerves by secreting histamine.

B) attaching viral proteins to its membrane.

C) releasing steroid hormones.

D) none of the above

Answer: B
Diff: 1   Page Ref: 36.3
Skill: Factual

53) The immune cells of your body have detected that viruses have infected some of your body cells. Which of the following would be called in to best take care of this problem?

A) antibodies   B) phagocyte   C) B cell   D) T cell

Answer: D
Diff: 2   Page Ref: 36.3
Skill: Conceptual

54) Your friend has taken an immunology class and tells you that she is most interested in cell mediated immunity. This means that she finds _____ most interesting.

A) B cells   B) antibodies   C) T cells   D) phagocytes

Answer: C
Diff: 2   Page Ref: 36.3
Skill: Conceptual

55) Which of these is NOT a type of T cell?

A) helper cell

B) plasma cell

C) killer cell

D) suppressor cell

E) memory cell

Answer: B
Diff: 2   Page Ref: 36.3
Skill: Factual

56) What do suppressor T cells suppress?

    A) the formation of antibodies

    B) the immune response

    C) the production of B cells

    D) cell reproduction

    E) the memory of past invasions

Answer: B
Diff: 1   Page Ref: 36.3
Skill: Factual

57) Complement is

    A) a set of proteins in the blood that assemble to kill bacterial cells.

    B) a hormone produced by bone marrow that stimulates T cells.

    C) a protein that helps frogs survive freezing during the winter.

    D) none of these

Answer: A
Diff: 1   Page Ref: 36.3
Skill: Factual

58) If an injury left an adult without a functional thymus, what effect would this have on the immune response?

    A) Loss of T cells would result in a loss of cell–mediated immunity.

    B) Loss of B cells would result in a loss of humoral immunity.

    C) Loss of T helper cells would result in a loss of both the humoral and cell–mediated immune responses leading to death.

    D) None of these is an accurate description of what would happen.

Answer: D
Diff: 3   Page Ref: 36.3
Skill: Application

59) Vaccinations are effective because they stimulate the production of

    A) memory cells.

    B) plasma cells.

    C) cytotoxic T cells.

    D) helper T cells.

    E) all of the above

Answer: A
Diff: 2   Page Ref: 36.3
Skill: Factual

60) Life–long immunity to a disease after a vaccination is due to the presence of

    A) helper T cells.   B) killer T cells.

    C) memory B cells.   D) red blood cells.

Answer: C
Diff: 1   Page Ref: 36.3
Skill: Factual

61) Last month you were stung by a bee for the first time in your life. You developed only a small area of redness and swelling at the site. However, yesterday when you were stung again, you had a very large reaction which occurred more rapidly. You know that this is due to

    A) memory cells.

    B) phagocytosis.

    C) complement.

    D) suppressor T cells.

    E) tissue macrophages.

Answer: A
Diff: 2   Page Ref: 36.3
Skill: Application

62) Which of the following equally healthy individuals will most likely have immunity to the most pathogens?

    A) a 10 year old   B) a 20 year old   C) a 40 year old   D) a 60 year old

Answer: D
Diff: 3   Page Ref: 36.3
Skill: Application

63) Which of the following immune cells have spent some time in the thymus gland?

    A) B cells   B) T cells

    C) both B and T cells   D) none of these

Answer: B
Diff: 1   Page Ref: 36.3
Skill: Factual

64) Which of the following immune cells make plasma cells?

    A) B cells   B) T cells

    C) both B and T cells   D) none of these

Answer: A
Diff: 2   Page Ref: 36.3
Skill: Factual

77) Briefly discuss the functions of helper T cells.

Answer: They are involved in almost all aspects of immunity including stimulating the cellular division and differentiation of both cytotoxic T and B cells and the formation of memory T cells.

Diff: 3   Page Ref: 36.3
Skill: Factual

78) You are telling your friend what you've learned about the immune system and she finds it interesting that antibodies don't actually kill microbes. She asks you, "if they don't kill the bad stuff, why are they do important?" What would you tell her? Remember that she is not a scientist so you have to explain this in terms she can understand.

Answer: Antibodies attach to foreign invaders in the body using their variable arms. Once they are attached they flag that non self invader for destruction. Phagocytes or complement may come in to destroy the invader. Also, the antibodies cause agglutination or neutralization of the invader so that it cannot continue to move throughout or cause damage in the body.

Diff: 2   Page Ref: 36.3
Skill: Conceptual

79) Imagine a microbe is considering invading your body. Write a letter to the threatening microbes to describe to the microbe what it will be up against in your body if it attempts to invade. Be sure to describe each of the different lines of defense.

Answer: Dear Microbe– You do not want to invade my body. I have 3 lines of defense that will attack you. My first line of defense with things like my skin and cilia will try to prevent you from entering. If you do make it past that, the non specific defenses will try to fight you off. Inflammation will heat things up and trap you so that phagocytes can come in, ingest you and then digest you into pieces. Complement may also come in and break you apart. If that doesn't work, the specific defenses will kick in. B cells may produce antibodies that will attach and mark you for destruction. They will call in other immune cells to destroy you. T cells will break you apart. You should think twice about trying to invade my body.

Diff: 3   Page Ref: 36.3
Skill: Application

80) Antibiotics are usually NOT effective against

A) bacteria.

B) viruses.

C) fungi.

D) protista.

E) Antibiotics are effective against all invaders.

Answer: B
Diff: 1   Page Ref: 36.4
Skill: Factual

81) Your roommate was given an antibiotic for strep throat. After three days she is feeling fine and asks you if she should stop taking the antibiotic and save the pills for the next time she has a sore throat. Your best response would be

A) yes, quit taking them, because the role of antibiotics is to give the body's immune system enough time to fight off the infection, so she doesn't need the pills after she feels better.

B) yes, the antibiotics were very potent and able to kill off the infection more quickly than anticipated.

C) yes, if she feels better, she should quit in order to avoid possible side effects from the antibiotics.

D) no, the infection is really not under control yet to the point that her immune system can finish fighting it off.

E) no, because repeated exposure to antibiotics may result in drug resistant strains.

Answer: E
Diff: 3   Page Ref: 36.4
Skill: Application

82) The recent appearance of antibiotic-resistant strains of bacteria is an example of

A) natural immunity.   B) acquired immunity.

C) natural selection and evolution.   D) inflammation.

Answer: C
Diff: 2   Page Ref: 36.4
Skill: Factual

83) Triclosan is an common antibiotic used in anti-perspirants, toothpastes, antibiotic soaps and lotions (if you don't believe this, check your labels). Which of the following is the most likely prediction about this antibiotic?

A) It is as effective now as when it first came out.

B) There are no microbes left that aren't resistant to this antibiotic, given its widespread use.

C) There might be microbes left that aren't resistant to this antibiotic in areas where these products have not been distributed.

D) none of the above

Answer: C
Diff: 3   Page Ref: 36.4
Skill: Application

84) Vaccinations involve injecting _____ into the person.

    A) weakened or killed microbes

    B) antibiotics

    C) the disease itself

    D) antibodies against the disease

    E) antibodies against similar diseases

Answer: A
Diff: 3   *Page Ref: 36.4*
Skill: Factual

85) Vaccinations protect against future exposure to disease organisms by causing

    A) increases in the number of red blood cells.

    B) stimulating of suppressor T cells.

    C) increases in complement proteins.

    D) formation of memory cells.

Answer: D
Diff: 2   *Page Ref: 36.4*
Skill: Factual

86) New flu shots are necessary every year because

    A) flu is caused by bacteria.

    B) flu shots do not result in memory cell production.

    C) flu viruses mutate rapidly.

    D) the anti-viral chemicals in flu shots only last 18 months.

Answer: C
Diff: 2   *Page Ref: 36.4*
Skill: Application

87) Some people who were immunized against polio, are no longer immune to polio. How could this be explained?

    A) Memory cells last for only 20 years, so if the people were vaccinated more than 20 years ago, they would no longer have immunity.

    B) Memory cells can last for months to a lifetime, depending on numbers of memory cells initially formed and random death of memory cells.

    C) Memory cells last for a lifetime, so this could not happen.

    D) None of these explanations is accurate.

Answer: B
Diff: 3   *Page Ref: 36.4*
Skill: Application

88) If you go to a doctor and he says you have a cold, should you request an antibiotic? Why or why not?

Answer: No, because antibiotics are not effective against viruses.
Diff: 2   Page Ref: 36.4
Skill: Application

89) Which is NOT involved in the allergic reaction?

   A) B cells   B) mast cells   C) histamine   D) complement

Answer: D
Diff: 2   Page Ref: 36.5
Skill: Factual

90) Excess secretion of _____ by mast cells occurs in _____.

   A) ACTH; cancer   B) antibodies; malaria

   C) complement; allergies   D) histamine; allergies

Answer: D
Diff: 2   Page Ref: 36.5
Skill: Factual

91) Why do some allergies produce cold–like symptoms and others cause nausea or hives?

   A) Different allergens stimulate the release of different chemicals, other than histamine.

   B) Since mast cells are found in tissues rather than in blood, the symptoms will match where the antigen runs into the mast cell/antibody complex.

   C) Only respiratory allergies involve the release of histamine from mast cells.

   D) none of the above

Answer: B
Diff: 3   Page Ref: 36.5
Skill: Application

92) Which disease may involve "anti–self" antibodies?

   A) juvenile diabetes

   B) SCID

   C) AIDS

   D) cancer

   E) measles

Answer: A
Diff: 1   Page Ref: 36.5
Skill: Factual

93) Which of the following is the most likely way that a viral infection might precipitate the onset of an autoimmune disorder?

  A) by stimulating the inflammatory response

  B) by stimulating T cells with receptors with binding sites that can bind to some self-antigen

  C) by causing a large scale fever

  D) by activating suppressor T cells

Answer: B
Diff: 3   Page Ref: 36.5
Skill: Application

94) HIV selectively destroys which type of immune cell?

  A) suppressor T cells

  B) helper T cells

  C) cytotoxic T cells

  D) plasma cells

  E) memory cells

Answer: B
Diff: 2   Page Ref: 36.5
Skill: Factual

95) Some of the AIDS treatment drugs such as, reverse transcriptase blockers and protease inhibitors

  A) kill cells infected with HIV.   B) prevent HIV from entering cells.

  C) interfere with HIV reproduction.   D) all of these

Answer: C
Diff: 2   Page Ref: 36.5
Skill: Factual

96) HIV is a(n)

  A) cytomegalovirus.

  B) rotavirus.

  C) retrovirus.

  D) arbovirus.

  E) cytokinovirus.

Answer: A
Diff: 2   Page Ref: 36.5
Skill: Factual

97) The AIDS patient dies because

    A) the lack of immune response leads to other serious infections.

    B) he or she lacks HIV antibodies.

    C) there are no drugs to slow the progress of the disease.

    D) the AIDS virus has a high rate of mutation.

    E) HIV destroys the internal organs.

Answer: A
Diff: 1   Page Ref: 36.5
Skill: Factual

98) AIDS spreads primarily by

    A) shaking hands.   B) sharing towels.

    C) sexual contact.   D) sharing cigarettes.

Answer: C
Diff: 1   Page Ref: 36.5
Skill: Factual

99) The AIDS virus is called a retrovirus because

    A) its genetic material is DNA.

    B) its genetic material is RNA.

    C) it contains enzymes.

    D) it undergoes frequent mutation.

    E) it is replicated many times.

Answer: B
Diff: 2   Page Ref: 36.5
Skill: Factual

100) Helping a person who is already infected with HIV may include all of the following EXCEPT

    A) administration of anti–HIV antibodies.

    B) treating opportunistic infections.

    C) administration of reverse protease inhibitors.

    D) prevention of spread.

Answer: A
Diff: 2   Page Ref: 36.5
Skill: Factual

101) Which type of cell is destroyed by the AIDS virus?

    A) suppressor T cells

    B) killer T cells

    C) helper T cells

    D) B cells

    E) plasma cells

Answer: C
Diff: 2   Page Ref: 36.5
Skill: Factual

102) Would you expect someone with AIDS to have a fever in response to an infection?

    A) Yes, because the non-specific defenses should be relatively normal.

    B) Yes, because the specific immune response should be relatively normal.

    C) No, because the non-specific defenses should be compromised.

    D) No, because the specific immune response should be compromised.

Answer: A
Diff: 2   Page Ref: 36.5
Skill: Application

103) Chemotherapy makes patients nauseous because

    A) the drugs stimulate stomach acid production.

    B) the drugs attack rapidly dividing cells including those lining the digestive tract.

    C) the drugs cause fever.

    D) all of these

Answer: B
Diff: 2   Page Ref: 36.5
Skill: Factual

104) The chance of a person in the United States having cancer during his/her lifetime is estimated to be

    A) 10%.   B) 20%.   C) 30%.   D) 40%.   E) 50%.

Answer: D
Diff: 2   Page Ref: 36.5
Skill: Factual

105) Cancer cells that invade other body tissues are

    A) benign.   B) malignant.

    C) tumors.   D) caused by bacteria.

Answer: B
Diff: 1   Page Ref: 36.5
Skill: Factual

106) Treatments for cancer include

    A) chemotherapy.   B) surgery.

    C) radiation.   D) all of these

Answer: D
Diff: 1   Page Ref: 36.5
Skill: Factual

107) People with AIDS have a high incidence of some types of cancer, like Kaposi's sarcoma. Which of the following accurately describes why this happens?

    A) Proteins released by HIV infected cells induce cells to begin dividing uncontrollably.

    B) HIV infects T cells and causes them to become cancerous.

    C) Cancer cells don't typically appear in our bodies.

    D) Cancer cells appear in our bodies on a regular basis, but they are normally recognized and destroyed by our cell-mediated immune system before they can cause cancer.

Answer: D
Diff: 2   Page Ref: 36.5
Skill: Application

108) Juvenile onset, insulin-dependent diabetes is caused by an autoimmune disease. True or False?

Answer: TRUE
Diff: 2   Page Ref: 36.5
Skill: Factual

109) At present there is no effective vaccine for AIDS. True or False?

Answer: TRUE
Diff: 1   Page Ref: 36.5
Skill: Factual

110) No one actually dies directly from infection with HIV, rather HIV weakens their ability to fight off other infections, thus causing these other infections to prove deadly. True or False?

Answer: TRUE
Diff: 1   Page Ref: 36.5
Skill: Conceptual

111) HIV is not associated with heterosexual relationships. True or False?

Answer: FALSE
Diff: 1   Page Ref: 36.5
Skill: Factual

112) Briefly describe the series of events that occurs in an allergic reaction.

Answer: should include B cell recognition, antibodies produced against the allergen binding to mast cells, histamine release, and capillary permeability increase leading to symptoms
Diff: 3   Page Ref: 36.5
Skill: Factual

113) Should an AIDS patient eat raw oysters? Why or why not?

Answer: Uncooked food may contain bacteria that will be able to overcome a weakened immune system.
Diff: 3   Page Ref: 36.5
Skill: Application

114) Briefly explain why children born with SCID often do not experience infection for several months after birth.

Answer: Antibodies from the mother during pregnancy or breast feeding will provide temporary immunity.
Diff: 3   Page Ref: 36.5
Skill: Application

115) What is cancer?

Answer: A group of body cells which have escaped from normal regulatory processes and are growing out of control.
Diff: 2   Page Ref: 36.5
Skill: Factual

Chapter 37 Chemical Control of the Animal Body: The Endocrine System

1) Anabolic steroids are

    A) approved by the US Olympic Committee.

    B) undetectable after 24 hours.

    C) performance enhancing drugs.

    D) all of the above

Answer: C
Diff: 2   Page Ref: Case Study
Skill: Factual

2) Which of the following is the most appropriate analogy for signaling by the endocrine system?

    A) telephone   B) radio

    C) conversation between two people   D) none of the above

Answer: A
Diff: 2   Page Ref: 37.1
Skill: Application

3) Local hormones are

    A) biochemicals released from one cell and transferred via the blood to other (target) cells.

    B) released from a nerve cell and diffuse across a synaptic gap to influence its target cell.

    C) chemicals which are released by a cell into the surrounding interstitial fluids and affect only other nearby cells.

Answer: C
Diff: 1   Page Ref: 37.1
Skill: Factual

4) What are endocrine hormones?

    A) biochemicals released from one cell and transferred via the blood to other (target) cells

    B) released from a nerve cell and diffuse across a synaptic gap to influence its target cell

    C) chemicals which are released by a cell into the surrounding interstitial fluids and affect only other nearby cells

Answer: A
Diff: 1   Page Ref: 37.1
Skill: Factual

5) Neurotransmitters are

   A) biochemicals released from one cell and transferred via the blood to other (target) cells.

   B) released from a nerve cell and diffuse across a synaptic gap to influence its target cell.

   C) chemicals which are released by a cell into the surrounding interstitial fluids and affect only other nearby cells.

Answer: A
Diff: 1   Page Ref: 37.1
Skill: Factual

6) If the receptors for a hormone are blocked, it is the same as if

   A) extra hormone were added.

   B) no hormone had been released.

   C) the receptors were not blocked.

Answer: B
Diff: 2   Page Ref: 37.1
Skill: Application

7) What is a target cell?

Answer: a cell which has receptors for a specific hormone
Diff: 1   Page Ref: 37.1
Skill: Factual

8) How do hormones "know" which cells to target?

Answer: Target cells contain receptors for the specific hormone. Without the receptors to bind to the hormone, the hormone can have no effect on the cell.
Diff: 2   Page Ref: 37.1
Skill: Factual

9) Menstrual cramps are caused by overproduction of

   A) estrogen.   B) progesterone.

   C) oxytocin.   D) prostaglandins.

Answer: D
Diff: 2   Page Ref: 37.2
Skill: Factual

10) Prostaglandins are

   A) modified amino acids.

   B) peptides or proteins.

   C) steroids.

   D) modified fatty acids.

   E) none of these

Answer: D
Diff: 2   Page Ref: 37.2
Skill: Factual

11) You woke up this morning with a headache from staying up cramming last night, so you took an aspirin. This should

   A) help because aspirin inhibits prostaglandin synthesis.

   B) help because aspirin stimulates the production of prostaglandins.

   C) make it worse because aspirin increases the production of endorphins.

   D) help because aspirin blocks the production of endorphins.

Answer: A
Diff: 3   Page Ref: 37.2
Skill: Factual

12) Which of the following is secreted not just by a particular gland but in most types of body cells?

   A) prostaglandins

   B) growth hormone

   C) steroid hormones

   D) ADH

   E) androgens

Answer: A
Diff: 1   Page Ref: 37.2
Skill: Factual

13) Which of the following is a documented effect of a prostaglandin?

   A) pain stimulation

   B) constriction of blood vessels

   C) uterine contractions

   D) arthritis inflammation

   E) all of the above

Answer: E
Diff: 2   Page Ref: 37.2
Skill: Factual

14) Endocrine glands secrete their products

A) directly into the target cells.

B) into the blood stream.

C) into the digestive tract.

D) into glandular ducts.

Answer: B
Diff: 2   Page Ref: 37.2
Skill: Factual

15) A woman with menstrual cramps takes ibuprofen. What will happen to prostaglandin levels in the uterus?

A) Levels of prostaglandins inside the cells stay the same while levels outside of the cells decrease.

B) Levels of prostaglandins inside the cells decrease the same while levels outside of the cells stay the same.

C) Levels of prostaglandins inside and outside of the cells decrease.

D) Levels of prostaglandins inside and outside of the cells stay the same.

Answer: C
Diff: 3   Page Ref: 37.2
Skill: Application

16) All hormones are

A) small proteins.

B) lipid soluble.

C) delivered to their target tissue by the bloodstream.

D) all of these

Answer: C
Diff: 2   Page Ref: 37.2
Skill: Factual

17) You go to the doctor and are given a shot of hormone as treatment for your condition. The doctor tells you that the shot won't start to work for about 18–24 hours. Based on the amount of time that it takes for the hormone to work, which of the following categories is the hormone most likely to belong to?

A) peptide hormones

B) amino acid hormones

C) steroid hormones

D) A and B

Answer: C
Diff: 2   Page Ref: 37.2
Skill: Application

18) Signaling by which of the following hormones would be affected by a disease that compromised circulation?

    A) peptide hormones

    B) prostaglandins

    C) steroid hormones

    D) A and B

    E) A and C

Answer: E
Diff: 2   Page Ref: 37.2
Skill: Application

19) Hormones that react with protein receptors on the surface of the target cell are

    A) peptide–based.

    B) amino acid–based.

    C) steroids.

    D) Both A and B are correct.

    E) All of the above are correct.

Answer: D
Diff: 2   Page Ref: 37.2
Skill: Factual

20) Proteins which identify a cell as a target cell for a hormone are called

    A) c– AMP.

    B) receptors.

    C) neurotransmitters.

    D) response proteins.

    E) neuromodulators.

Answer: B
Diff: 2   Page Ref: 37.2
Skill: Factual

21) Water–soluble hormones bind to molecules in the _____ of the target cell.

    A) nucleus

    B) cytoplasm

    C) plasma membrane

    D) mitochondria

    E) DNA

Answer: C
Diff: 2   Page Ref: 37.2
Skill: Factual

22) Insulin is a water soluble hormone that binds to receptor proteins on the cell surface. What type of response would you expect it to cause?

    A) long–term, slow

    B) altered gene activity

    C) nervous system responses

    D) RNA transcription

    E) rapid, short–term

Answer: E
Diff: 2   Page Ref: 37.2
Skill: Factual

23) A possible "second messenger" in the cytoplasm is

    A) c–AMP.   B) ADP.   C) ATP.   D) DNA.   E) RNA.

Answer: A
Diff: 1   Page Ref: 37.2
Skill: Factual

24) Most of the steroid hormones are synthesized from

    A) insulin.

    B) amino acids.

    C) linoleic acid.

    D) glucose.

    E) cholesterol.

Answer: E
Diff: 2   Page Ref: 37.2
Skill: Factual

25) Could a drug interfere with the action of a hormone in some target cells but not others?

   A) Yes, because a receptor for a peptide hormone could be coupled to different second messenger systems.

   B) Yes, because a receptor for a steroid hormone could be coupled to different second messenger systems.

   C) No, hormones always use the same receptor.

   D) No, hormones always use the same second messenger system.

Answer: A
Diff: 3   Page Ref: 37.2
Skill: Application

26) High metabolic activity by target cells usually has the effect of reducing the production of thyroxine by

   A) positive feedback.

   B) negative feedback.

   C) neurotransmitter activity.

   D) solubility factors.

   E) enzymatic action.

Answer: B
Diff: 2   Page Ref: 37.2
Skill: Factual

27) When you scratch a mosquito bite, you damage some cells. Damaged cells release histamine which causes localized swelling. The swelling can crush cells causing them to release more histamine. This is an example of

   A) positive feedback.

   B) negative feedback.

   C) neurotransmitter activity.

   D) solubility factors.

   E) enzymatic action.

Answer: A
Diff: 2   Page Ref: 37.2
Skill: Application

28) When you eat a bag of cookies, blood sugar levels increase. As blood sugar increases, insulin increases to move the sugar into the cells and lowing the blood sugar level. As the sugar level drops, so does insulin. This is an example of

A) positive feedback.

B) negative feedback.

C) neurotransmitter activity.

D) solubility factors.

E) enzymatic action.

Answer: B
Diff: 2   Page Ref: 37.2
Skill: Application

29) If a person gets a shot of epinephrine, the person almost immediately feels the effects (increased heart and breathing rates, etc.). If the same person gets a shot of a steroid hormone such as cortisone, there is no immediate response. What causes this difference?

Answer: Epinephrine is water soluble and causes an immediate response, whereas steroid hormones cause a slower change by stimulating gene activity.
Diff: 3   Page Ref: 37.2
Skill: Application

30) Anabolic steroids are synthetic steroid hormones. In light of the way steroid hormones act, why is it so very dangerous for athletes to take these drugs?

Answer: Steroids are fat soluble, diffuse through cell membranes, and travel to the nucleus where they change gene activity. Thus anabolic steroids will have many effects in many parts of the body and may change the function of all of the cells they enter.
Diff: 3   Page Ref: 37.2
Skill: Application

31) What does it mean to say that cyclic AMP acts as a second messenger?

Answer: The hormone is the first messenger bringing the message of a needed response to the target cell. Cyclic AMP transfers the message to the chemicals in the cell which enable it to respond. cAMP is an intracellular messenger that is activated by the first messenger. It can then transfer this message within the target cell.
Diff: 3   Page Ref: 37.2
Skill: Conceptual

32) What homeostatic process most often controls the production of hormones?

Answer: negative feedback
Diff: 1   Page Ref: 37.2
Skill: Factual

33) How does aspirin help to stop pain?

Answer: Aspirin blocks prostaglandin production, and prostaglandins are associated with pain
sensations.
Diff: 2   Page Ref: 37.2
Skill: Conceptual

34) Why do ecdysone–based pesticides have no effect on humans?

Answer: Humans lack the cell receptors for ecdysone–based hormones, so they cannot cause
changes in our cells.
Diff: 3   Page Ref: 37.2
Skill: Application

35) Why do fat–free diets affect the production of steroid hormones?

Answer: Steroids are based on the lipid cholesterol. If you have no cholesterol, you cannot make
any of the steroid hormones.
Diff: 3   Page Ref: 37.2
Skill: Application

36) Why is their concern about hormones in cattle feed?

Answer: Vertebrate hormones are very similar and there are concerns that extra hormones from
the feed may transfer to those who eat the meat.
Diff: 3   Page Ref: 37.2
Skill: Application

37) Which of the following is an exocrine gland?

A) mammary

B) adrenal

C) parathyroid

D) thyroid

E) pituitary

Answer: A
Diff: 2   Page Ref: 37.3
Skill: Factual

38) A new substance has been discovered that is produced by a specialized group of cells in the
stomach and affects cells in the vicinity of the cells that produce it. Would you consider this an
endocrine hormone?

A) yes

B) no

C) There is not enough information to decide.

Answer: C
Diff: 2   Page Ref: 37.3
Skill: Application

39) The _____ pituitary releases hormones produced from cells in the hypothalamus.

    A) anterior   B) median   C) posterior   D) ventral   E) dorsal

Answer: C
Diff: 2   Page Ref: 37.3
Skill: Factual

40) Which hormone does the posterior pituitary release?

    A) ADH

    B) growth hormone

    C) cortisol

    D) gonadotropins

    E) ACTH

Answer: A
Diff: 2   Page Ref: 37.3
Skill: Factual

41) The principal function of ACTH is to stimulate the release of

    A) testosterone.   B) glucocorticoids.

    C) epinephrine and norepinephrine.   D) angiotensin.

Answer: B
Diff: 2   Page Ref: 37.3
Skill: Factual

42) The connection between the two control systems of the body, the nervous and endocrine systems, is the

    A) pituitary gland.   B) adrenal gland.

    C) hypothalamus.   D) thyroid.

Answer: C
Diff: 2   Page Ref: 37.3
Skill: Factual

43) All of the releasing hormones of the hypothalamus are

    A) modified amino acids.

    B) peptides or proteins.

    C) steroids.

    D) modified fatty acids.

    E) none of these

Answer: B
Diff: 2   Page Ref: 37.3
Skill: Factual

44) Which of these contains neurosecretory cells?

    A) thyroid

    B) pancreas

    C) anterior pituitary

    D) posterior pituitary

    E) adrenal medulla

Answer: D
Diff: 2   Page Ref: 37.3
Skill: Factual

45) A nursing mother hears a baby crying and "lets down" her milk even though the baby is not hers. The hormone that stimulated this response was

    A) estrogen.

    B) progesterone.

    C) oxytocin.

    D) prolactin.

    E) FSH.

Answer: C
Diff: 1   Page Ref: 37.3
Skill: Factual

46) Nursing a newborn can cause uterine cramping. The hormone responsible is

    A) estrogen.

    B) progesterone.

    C) oxytocin.

    D) prolactin.

    E) FSH.

Answer: C
Diff: 1   Page Ref: 37.3
Skill: Application

47) Which of the following produces hormones that stimulate the secretory activity of the other
endocrine glands?

    A) anterior pituitary

    B) thyroid

    C) pancreas

    D) ovaries and testes

    E) adrenal cortex

Answer: A
Diff: 2   Page Ref: 37.3
Skill: Factual

48) If thymosin is blocked

    A) insulin fails.   B) progesterone production stops.

    C) the immune system fails.   D) bone deteriorates.

Answer: C
Diff: 1   Page Ref: 37.3
Skill: Application

49) If the pituitary is damaged

    A) the skin will not tan,

    B) cell growth stops.

    C) cortisol secretion decreases.

    D) cell metabolism slows dramatically.

    E) all of the above

Answer: E
Diff: 1   Page Ref: 37.3
Skill: Application

50) The cells that control the secretion of all of the hormones produced by the pituitary are in the

    A) adrenal gland.   B) pancreas.

    C) testes.   D) hypothalamus.

Answer: D
Diff: 1   Page Ref: 37.3
Skill: Factual

51) After spending 4 hours in the sun at the beach without sunscreen

    A) your blood concentration of FSH would be higher.

    B) your blood concentration of ACTH would be higher.

    C) your blood concentration of insulin would be higher.

    D) your blood concentration of MSH would be higher.

Answer: D
Diff: 2   Page Ref: 37.3
Skill: Application

52) Dwarfism is due to a lack of the secretion of growth hormone by the

    A) anterior pituitary.

    B) parathyroid.

    C) pancreas.

    D) adrenal medulla.

    E) adrenal cortex.

Answer: A
Diff: 1   Page Ref: 37.3
Skill: Factual

53) If basal metabolism drops, which anterior pituitary hormone would be released to stimulate the thyroid gland to produce its secretion?

    A) thyroxine   B) ACTH   C) FSH   D) prolactin   E) TSH

Answer: E
Diff: 2   Page Ref: 37.3
Skill: Factual

54) Children who are pituitary dwarfs can now grow to normal height due to

    A) the invention of synthetic growth hormone.

    B) genetically engineered production of growth hormone by bacteria.

    C) large supplies of growth hormone from dead animals.

    D) genetic repair before birth.

    E) pituitary transplants.

Answer: B
Diff: 2   Page Ref: 37.3
Skill: Factual

55) After hiking for an hour in the desert, what do you expect your circulating levels of ADH to be?

    A) average   B) above average   C) below average

Answer: B
Diff: 2   Page Ref: 37.3
Skill: Application

56) What is the effect of parathyroid hormone?

    A) It increases blood calcium levels.   B) It decreases blood calcium levels.

    C) It increased metabolism.   D) It decreases metabolism.

Answer: A
Diff: 2   Page Ref: 37.3
Skill: Factual

57) The use of iodized salt eliminates

    A) diabetes.

    B) goiter.

    C) menstrual cramps.

    D) high blood pressure.

    E) gigantism.

Answer: B
Diff: 1   Page Ref: 37.3
Skill: Factual

58) A low secretion of thyroxine during infancy results in retarded mental and physical growth known as

    A) goiter.

    B) beriberi.

    C) diabetes.

    D) cretinism.

    E) acromegaly.

Answer: D
Diff: 1   Page Ref: 37.3
Skill: Factual

59) What is the effect of a high level of thyroxine?

    A) decreased growth

    B) decreased release of TSH

    C) decreased metabolic rate

    D) decreased cell division

    E) decreased insulin production

Answer: B
Diff: 2   Page Ref: 37.3
Skill: Factual

60) Calcitonin _____ blood calcium. Parathyroid hormone _____ blood calcium.

    A) forms; breaks down   B) raises; lowers

    C) breaks down; forms   D) lowers; raises

Answer: D
Diff: 2   Page Ref: 37.3
Skill: Factual

61) Antagonistic hormones have opposite effects. Which pair of hormones are antagonistic?

    A) aldosterone and insulin   B) ADH and growth hormone

    C) calcitonin and parathyroid hormone   D) estrogen and progesterone

Answer: C
Diff: 2   Page Ref: 37.3
Skill: Factual

62) You are an endocrinologist. A patient has been referred to you because he is cold all the time, even when the ambient temperature is 75°F. You immediately suspect that his metabolism is lower than normal due to

    A) too much ADH (anti-diuretic hormone).

    B) too much oxytocin.

    C) not enough thyroid hormone.

    D) not enough aldosterone.

Answer: C
Diff: 2   Page Ref: 37.3
Skill: Application

63) Release of calcium from bones

    A) oxytocin.   B) parathyroid hormone.

    C) insulin.   D) prolactin.

Answer: B
Diff: 2   *Page Ref: 37.3*
Skill: Factual

64) Thyroid hormones have been found to play a role in all but which one of the following?

    A) reproductive rate

    B) metamorphosis of a tadpole

    C) growth of a young vertebrate

    D) metabolic rate of animal cells

    E) development of the nervous system

Answer: A
Diff: 2   *Page Ref: 37.3*
Skill: Application

65) Pregnant or lactating women would most likely have _____ levels of calcitonin circulating in their blood.

    A) average   B) below average   C) above average

Answer: B
Diff: 2   *Page Ref: 37.3*
Skill: Application

66) Which hormone decreases blood glucose concentrations?

    A) glucagon   B) insulin

    C) cortisol   D) growth hormone

Answer: B
Diff: 2   *Page Ref: 37.3*
Skill: Factual

67) If I not eating, which hormone(s) increase blood glucose concentrations?

    A) glucocorticoids

    B) glucagon

    C) insulin

    D) both A and B

    E) All of the above increase blood glucose concentrations.

Answer: D
Diff: 3   *Page Ref: 37.3*
Skill: Factual

68) Diabetes mellitus is due to an inability to respond to, or a lack of

    A) glucagon.

    B) insulin.

    C) thyroxine.

    D) glucocorticoids.

    E) ADH.

Answer: B
Diff: 2   Page Ref: 37.3
Skill: Factual

69) If you eat a meal that is high in sugar, which hormone will stimulate your cells to make fat to store the excess?

    A) glucagon

    B) glycogen

    C) insulin

    D) thyroxine

    E) glucocorticoids

Answer: C
Diff: 1   Page Ref: 37.3
Skill: Factual

70) Glucagon increases blood glucose by activating an enzyme which breaks down glycogen which has been stored primarily in the

    A) heart.

    B) liver.

    C) kidneys.

    D) pancreas.

    E) small intestine.

Answer: B
Diff: 2   Page Ref: 37.3
Skill: Factual

71) Which of the following stimulates the storage of glucose?

    A) oxytocin   B) glucagon   C) insulin   D) prolactin

Answer: C
Diff: 1   Page Ref: 37.3
Skill: Factual

72) When blood glucose levels rise, insulin signals cells to take up glucose and use or store it. Diabetes mellitus is a disorder caused by a dysfunction in the insulin signaling system. There are two types of diabetes. People with Type I diabetes must take insulin regularly, while people with Type II diabetes do not. What does this tell you about where the defect might be in these two disorders?

    A) Type I diabetes is probably caused by a lack of insulin.

    B) Type II diabetes is probably caused by a lack of insulin.

    C) Type I diabetes is probably caused by defective insulin receptors.

    D) A and B

    E) B and C

Answer: A
Diff: 2   *Page Ref: 37.3*
Skill: Application

73) Which hormone stimulates the development of the uterine lining?

    A) estrogen

    B) luteinizing hormone

    C) follicle stimulating hormone

    D) progesterone

    E) oxytocin

Answer: D
Diff: 2   *Page Ref: 37.3*
Skill: Factual

74) Which of the following might BEST explain why anabolic steroid abuse by male athletes can lead to a decrease in testicle size?

    A) Circulating anabolic steroids would increase release of FSH and LH, which inhibit testicle growth and function.

    B) Circulating anabolic steroids would decrease release of FSH and LH, which inhibit testicle growth and function.

    C) High levels of anabolic steroids would decrease production of testosterone, through negative feedback, which would decrease the size of the testes because they produce the majority of testosterone.

    D) High levels of anabolic steroids would increase production of testosterone, through positive feedback, which would decrease the size of the testes because they produce the majority of testosterone.

Answer: C
Diff: 3   *Page Ref: 37.3*
Skill: Conceptual

75) During puberty levels of LH and FSH increase which causes in increase in estrogen in females and testosterone in males. How can males and females use the same hormones to get different effects?

A) They don't—FSH is used by females and LH is used by males.

B) They don't—LH is used by females and FSH is used by males.

C) The structure of FSH and LH are different in males and females.

D) FSH and LH interact with different target tissues in males and females.

Answer: D
Diff: 2   Page Ref: 37.3
Skill: Conceptual

76) The release of aldosterone is stimulated by

A) increased extracellular sodium.

B) decreased extracellular sodium.

C) increased blood glucose concentrations.

D) decreased blood glucose concentrations.

Answer: B
Diff: 2   Page Ref: 37.3
Skill: Factual

77) The production of hormones by the adrenal medulla is controlled directly by the

A) anterior pituitary.

B) posterior pituitary.

C) thyroid.

D) kidneys.

E) nervous system.

Answer: E
Diff: 2   Page Ref: 37.3
Skill: Factual

78) Cancer of the adrenal medulla results in over secretion of its hormones. The result is often death due to

A) heart attack from excess adrenalin.

B) breakage of brittle bones from calcitonin.

C) high blood sugar from cortisol.

D) low blood pressure from aldosterone.

Answer: A
Diff: 2   Page Ref: 37.3
Skill: Application

79) A hormone that is produced by the adrenal gland and is critical to normal function of the immune system is

A) LH (luteinizing hormone).

B) ACTH (adrenocorticotropic hormone).

C) cortisol.

D) MSH (melanocyte stimulating hormone).

Answer: C
Diff: 1   Page Ref: 37.3
Skill: Factual

80) Thymosin stimulates the

A) development of T cells.   B) development of B cells.

C) development of both T and B cells.   D) development of white blood cells.

Answer: A
Diff: 2   Page Ref: 37.3
Skill: Factual

81) Which statement is TRUE regarding atrial natriuretic hormone?

A) It increases blood sodium concentrations.

B) Its actions are similar to angiotensin's.

C) It helps to decrease blood pressure.

D) Both A and B are correct.

E) All statements are correct.

Answer: C
Diff: 2   Page Ref: 37.3
Skill: Factual

82) A hormone that is involved in the regulation of lipid metabolism

A) glucagon.   B) leptin.   C) oxytocin.   D) prolactin.

Answer: B
Diff: 2   Page Ref: 37.3
Skill: Factual

83) The thymus produces a hormone that stimulates the development of T cells. This hormone is

A) thyroxine.   B) ACTH (adrenocorticotropic hormone).

C) testosterone.   D) thymosin.

Answer: D
Diff: 2   Page Ref: 37.3
Skill: Factual

84) Which gland responds to light and is involved in daily rhythms in some animals?

A) thymus   B) adrenal   C) pituitary   D) pineal   E) pancreas

Answer: D
Diff: 1   Page Ref: 37.3
Skill: Factual

85) Decreased levels of ADH will cause

A) hunger.   B) water weight gain.

C) fever.   D) dehydration.

Answer: D
Diff: 2   Page Ref: 37.3
Skill: Conceptual

86) Is saliva an endocrine or an exocrine secretion? Defend your answer.

Answer: exocrine, because it is released to the outside of the body (the digestive tract) through
          ducts
Diff: 2   Page Ref: 37.3
Skill: Conceptual

87) Explain why oxytocin and prolactin are both necessary for nursing.

Answer: Prolactin stimulates the growth of the mammary glands and the production of milk.
          Oxytocin allows the mammary glands to release their secretion. Both are stimulated in
          part by sucking.
Diff: 3   Page Ref: 37.3
Skill: Application

88) The peptide hormones of the hypothalamus are produced by what kind of cells?

Answer: neurosecretory
Diff: 2   Page Ref: 37.3
Skill: Conceptual

89) How does ADH help to prevent dehydration?

Answer: by increasing the permeability of the collecting ducts in the nephrons to water so that
          the urine produced is more concentrated
Diff: 3   Page Ref: 37.3
Skill: Application

90) The anterior pituitary produces hormones that stimulate other endocrine glands to produce
their secretions. What stimulates the anterior pituitary to release its hormones?

Answer: the releasing hormones of the hypothalamus
Diff: 2   Page Ref: 37.3
Skill: Factual

91) What is the main function of thyroxine?

Answer: to increase the metabolic rate of cells
Diff: 1   *Page Ref: 37.3*
Skill: Factual

92) How do insulin and glucagon coordinate to maintain normal blood sugar levels?

Answer: When blood sugar levels are up insulin levels go up and glucagon down. When blood sugar levels drop, glucagon increases and insulin drops.
Diff: 2   *Page Ref: 37.3*
Skill: Application

93) Some doctors will prescribe synthetic thyroxine for weight loss even when circulating levels are normal. Will this work? What side effects are possible?

Answer: Thyroxine will increase metabolism and induce weight loss. However, there are complications with increased heart rate, restlessness, irritability and appetite.
Diff: 3   *Page Ref: 37.3*
Skill: Application

94) How do calcitonin and parathyroid hormone interact to control blood calcium levels?

Answer: As antagonists—calcitonin lowers blood calcium by inhibiting its release from the bones. Parathyroid hormone raises blood calcium by releasing it from the bones.
Diff: 3   *Page Ref: 37.3*
Skill: Application

95) Name or describe the three secretions of the pancreas and indicate briefly the role of each.

Answer: Pancreatic juice (called "digestive secretions" in this chapter)—works in the small intestine
Insulin—lowers blood glucose
Glucagon—raises blood glucose
Diff: 2   *Page Ref: 37.3*
Skill: Factual

96) What changes occur in the body in diabetes mellitus?

Answer: Lack of functional insulin leads to high sugar levels, which increases dependence on fats, leading to high amounts of fat in the bloodstream. This deposits on blood vessel walls potentially leading to high blood pressure, blindness, kidney failure, etc.
Diff: 2   *Page Ref: 37.3*
Skill: Factual

97) Which gland was stimulated to produce hormones as you entered this room to take this test (presumably a somewhat stressful situation) and what two hormones were produced?

Answer: the adrenal medulla—epinephrine and norepinephrine or adrenalin and noradrenalin
Diff: 3   *Page Ref: 37.3*
Skill: Application

98) Explain how both males and females secrete some testosterone.

Answer: The adrenal cortex secretes small amounts in both sexes.
Diff: 2   Page Ref: 37.3
Skill: Application

99) The hormone _____, produced by the pineal gland, may be involved in sleep-wake cycles in humans.

Answer: melatonin
Diff: 2   Page Ref: 37.3
Skill: Factual

100) Rapid loss of blood may lead to shock and death. What series of events do the kidneys initiate to raise the blood pressure of a person who has been severely cut in order to prevent this problem?

Answer: Kidneys produce renin in response to lowered blood pressure. Renin stimulates the production of angiotensin in the bloodstream. Angiotensin constricts arterioles, decreasing bleeding, and reducing blood flow to the kidneys so that less water is lost in urine, increasing blood volume and thus pressure.
Diff: 3   Page Ref: 37.3
Skill: Application

101) Do fat cells function as an endocrine gland?

Answer: Yes, fat cells produce both estrogen and leptin—two hormones.
Diff: 2   Page Ref: 37.3
Skill: Application

102) Stress increases cortisol secretion. Why would diabetics have problems controlling blood sugar levels when they are stressed?

Answer: One of cortisol's functions is to increase blood sugar levels. Adding stress would increase blood sugar levels beyond normal.
Diff: 2   Page Ref: 37.3
Skill: Application

103) Why are pituitary tumors so dangerous?

Answer: The pituitary gland secretes many controlling hormones. Problems with these releasing hormones disrupts the function of the adrenal gland (via ACTH), the reproductive organs (via LH and FSH), cell metabolism (via TSH), and cell growth (via growth hormone).
Diff: 2   Page Ref: 37.3
Skill: Application

Chapter 38 The Nervous System and the Senses

1) Which portion of the neuron typically receives information?

    A) soma

    B) cell body

    C) axon

    D) dendrite

    E) telodendria

Answer: D
Diff: 1   Page Ref: 38.1
Skill: Factual

2) Which portion of the neuron contains receptor proteins?

    A) soma

    B) cell body

    C) axon

    D) dendrite

    E) telodendria

Answer: D
Diff: 1   Page Ref: 38.1
Skill: Factual

3) Which of the following is an important difference between the nervous system and the endocrine system?

    A) The nervous system responds to danger, whereas the endocrine system responds to "normal" activities.

    B) The speed of response is different.

    C) The chemicals that transmit the signal are different.

    D) The nervous system is involved with control, whereas the endocrine is involved with coordination.

    E) The nervous system is entirely electrical in nature, whereas the endocrine system is entirely chemical in nature.

Answer: B
Diff: 3   Page Ref: 38.1
Skill: Conceptual

4) Which of the following is an important similarity between the endocrine system and the nervous system?

A) The transmitters from both cause a change in target cells throughout the body.

B) Both involve both electrical and chemical aspects.

C) The speed of response is the same.

D) Both transmit their compounds into the bloodstream.

E) Both synthesize messenger compounds which are released outside the cell.

Answer: E
Diff: 2   Page Ref: 38.1
Skill: Conceptual

5) The functional unit of the nervous system is the

A) neuron.

B) axon.

C) cell body.

D) neurotransmitter.

E) nerve.

Answer: A
Diff: 1   Page Ref: 38.1
Skill: Factual

6) Which of the following is NOT a function of neurons?

A) receive information

B) conduct a signal

C) form the myelin sheath

D) integrate information

E) coordinate metabolic activities

Answer: C
Diff: 1   Page Ref: 38.1
Skill: Factual

7) Which of the following represents the direction a nerve impulse travels within a single neuron?

    A) synaptic terminal → cell body → axon → dendrite

    B) cell body → dendrite → axon → synaptic terminal

    C) synaptic terminal → axon → cell body → dendrite

    D) dendrite → cell body → axon → synaptic terminal

    E) synaptic terminal → dendrite → axon → cell body

Answer: D
Diff: 2   Page Ref: 38.1
Skill: Factual

8) The part of a neuron that contains a nucleus and other organelles typical of cells is the cell

    A) axon.

    B) dendrite.

    C) Schwann cell.

    D) synapse.

    E) cell body.

Answer: E
Diff: 1   Page Ref: 38.1
Skill: Factual

9) The long process of a neuron is called the

    A) synapse.   B) myelin.   C) axon.   D) ohm.

Answer: C
Diff: 1   Page Ref: 38.1
Skill: Factual

10) Neurons vary enormously in structure. True or False?

Answer: TRUE
Diff: 1   Page Ref: 38.1
Skill: Factual

11) Some nerve cells release hormones known as neurohormones into their synapse. True or False?

Answer: TRUE
Diff: 1   Page Ref: 38.1
Skill: Factual

12) Nerve cells release compounds known as _____ into a synapse with adjacent cells.

Answer: neurotransmitters
Diff: 1   *Page Ref: 38.1*
Skill: Factual

13) People with multiple sclerosis develop areas in which the myelin sheath on their neurons has disintegrated. This disease often results in paralysis and extreme weakness. Using what you know about the myelin sheath, explain why these symptoms might occur.

Answer: The myelin sheath allow nerve conduction to occur at a much more rapid rate than without it; thus impulses travel more slowly to and from the brain, contributing to the symptoms.
Diff: 3   *Page Ref: 38.1*
Skill: Application

14) What are the four main functions of a neuron?

Answer: 1. Receive information; 2. Integrate information; 3. Conduct a signal; 4. Transmit the signal
Diff: 2   *Page Ref: 38.1*
Skill: Factual

15) Describe the main functions of a cell body of a neuron.

Answer: integration of the signal, synthesis, metabolism, normal cell activities
Diff: 2   *Page Ref: 38.1*
Skill: Factual

16) An excitatory postsynaptic potential will stimulate

A) the opening of chloride channels.   B) the opening of sodium channels.

C) the opening of potassium channels.   D) none of the above

Answer: B
Diff: 3   *Page Ref: 38.2*
Skill: Factual

17) Curare is a drug that

A) prevents the opening of sodium channels.

B) prevents the opening of chloride channels.

C) blocks acetylcholine receptors.

D) stimulates acetylcholine receptors.

Answer: C
Diff: 2   *Page Ref: 38.2*
Skill: Factual

18) Antidepressants such as Prozac act to increase the effects of

    A) acetylcholine.

    B) dopamine.

    C) serotonin.

    D) norepinephrine.

    E) endorphins.

Answer: C
Diff: 2   Page Ref: 38.2
Skill: Factual

19) Persons that are "addicted" to stress, or those that must run to feel good are, in fact, addicted to

    A) acetylcholine.

    B) dopamine.

    C) serotonin.

    D) norepinephrine.

    E) endorphins.

Answer: E
Diff: 2   Page Ref: 38.2
Skill: Factual

20) The negative resting potential of a neuron is due to

    A) the action of the sodium–potassium pump.

    B) the trapping of large negative organic molecules inside the cell.

    C) diffusion of potassium ions out of the cell.

    D) all of the above

Answer: D
Diff: 2   Page Ref: 38.2
Skill: Factual

21) The action potential along an axon decreases in strength as the signal moves away from the cell body.

    A) true

    B) false, because action potentials move toward the cell body

    C) false, because action potentials occur only at a synapse

    D) false, because action potentials remain unchanged along an axon

    E) false, because axons transmit only resting potentials

Answer: D
Diff: 3   Page Ref: 38.2
Skill: Factual

22) Neurons (and most other animal cells) have a negative inside potential because

    A) they contain a lot of negatively charged proteins.

    B) they leak potassium through open channels in the plasma membrane.

    C) the phospholipids in the plasma membrane generate electricity.

    D) A and B

    E) A and C

Answer: B
Diff: 2   Page Ref: 38.2
Skill: Factual

23) In neurons, _____ ions are at higher concentration inside the cell and _____ ions are at higher concentration in the extracellular fluid.

    A) Cl; Na

    B) Cl; K

    C) Na; K

    D) K; Na

    E) Cl; organically bound

Answer: D
Diff: 2   Page Ref: 38.2
Skill: Factual

24) In a nerve cell at its resting potential _____ are closed.

    A) potassium channels

    B) sodium channels

    C) sodium potassium pumps

    D) all channels

    E) no channels

Answer: B
Diff: 2   Page Ref: 38.2
Skill: Factual

25) When an action potential reaches a portion of the membrane, _____ suddenly open.

  A) potassium channels

  B) sodium channels

  C) sodium potassium pumps

  D) all channels

  E) no channels

Answer: B
Diff: 2   Page Ref: 38.2
Skill: Factual

26) The resting potential of neurons is between _____ millivolts.

  A) –40 and –90

  B) 40 and 90

  C) –4 and –9

  D) 4 and 9

  E) –400 and –900

Answer: A
Diff: 3   Page Ref: 38.2
Skill: Factual

27) The sodium–potassium pump pumps

  A) both sodium and potassium out of the cell.

  B) both sodium and potassium into the cell.

  C) ATP using sodium and potassium.

  D) sodium in and potassium out of the cell.

  E) potassium in and sodium out of the cell.

Answer: E
Diff: 1   Page Ref: 38.2
Skill: Factual

28) When a neuron reaches threshold for an action potential

  A) sodium channels are closed.

  B) potassium diffuses out of the cell.

  C) sodium channels open.

  D) the plasma membrane is impermeable.

  E) the sodium–potassium pump is turned on.

Answer: C
Diff: 2   Page Ref: 38.2
Skill: Factual

29) A postsynaptic potential is

    A) excitatory only, making the neuron more negative.

    B) inhibitory only, making the neuron less negative.

    C) inhibitory only, making the neuron more negative.

    D) either excitatory or inhibitory.

    E) both excitatory and inhibitory at the same time.

Answer: D
Diff: 2   *Page Ref: 38.2*
Skill: Factual

30) Which is NOT true of a synapse?

    A) Neurotransmitters affect postsynaptic neurons.

    B) Neurotransmitters are released from dendrites.

    C) Many neurons may be involved.

    D) A synaptic cleft separates the neurons of the synapse.

    E) Receptors for neurotransmitters are located in the postsynaptic membrane.

Answer: B
Diff: 2   *Page Ref: 38.2*
Skill: Factual

31) Receptors in the brain for the neurotransmitters endorphin and enkephalin are affected by drugs such as

    A) glutamine and GABA.   B) morphine and opium.

    C) atropine and nicotine.   D) LSD and serotonin.

Answer: B
Diff: 2   *Page Ref: 38.2*
Skill: Factual

32) Axons

    A) form the gray matter of the brain and spinal cord.

    B) carry an action potential in the direction of a synapse.

    C) act independently of the cell body.

    D) have neurotransmitter receptors.

    E) decide whether to transmit an action potential.

Answer: B
Diff: 2   *Page Ref: 38.2*
Skill: Factual

33) Which of the following chemicals is NOT a neurotransmitter?

    A) nitric oxide (NO)   B) acetylcholine

    C) dopamine   D) atropine

Answer: D
Diff: 2   Page Ref: 38.2
Skill: Factual

34) The neurotransmitters released by a presynaptic cell can be either excitatory or inhibitory on the postsynaptic neuron depending on

    A) the specific transmitter released.

    B) the amount of transmitter released.

    C) the size of the postsynaptic cell,

    D) the kind of ion channel integral to the transmitter receptor in the postsynaptic cell membrane.

Answer: D
Diff: 2   Page Ref: 38.2
Skill: Factual

35) Repeated usage of drugs such as cocaine results in a decrease in the response of the neurons to the drug. This is due to

    A) decrease in the size of the cells.

    B) increase in the activity of transmitter inactivation enzymes.

    C) decrease in the number of receptors in the nerve membranes.

    D) none of these

Answer: C
Diff: 2   Page Ref: 38.2
Skill: Factual

36) The repolarization (i.e., the return of the membrane potential from +60 to –70 mV) of the nerve during an action potential is due to mostly movement of which of the following ions?

    A) sodium ions   B) chloride ions

    C) potassium ions   D) calcium ions

Answer: C
Diff: 2   Page Ref: 38.2
Skill: Factual

37) Severe dehydration can lead to delirium. Which of the following BEST explains why this happens?

A) Loss of water in the blood and extracellular fluid would change the concentration of ions outside of cells which would change the resting membrane potential and interfere with electrical signaling.

B) Loss of water in the blood and extracellular fluid would change the concentration of ions outside of the cell which would keep neurotransmitters from binding to their receptors.

C) Loss of water in the blood and extracellular fluid would change the concentration of ions outside of the cell which would synaptic vesicles to dump their neurotransmitters inside the cell instead of into the synapse.

D) none of the above

Answer: A
Diff: 3   Page Ref: 38.2
Skill: Application

38) You are recording from a neuron with an electrode and determine that the resting membrane potential is around −70 mV. What would happen to the membrane potential if you added three times more potassium to the external solution surrounding the cell?

A) The membrane potential would stay the same.

B) The membrane potential would become more positive.

C) The membrane potential would become more negative.

Answer: B
Diff: 3   Page Ref: 38.2
Skill: Application

39) Why do you think neurons are more susceptible to injury or death due to lack of oxygen compared to other cells?

A) Oxygen has a hard time crossing the blood–brain barrier.

B) Neurons use oxygen directly as a neurotransmitter.

C) The sodium–potassium pump uses a lot of ATP constantly pumping these two ions across the membrane against their concentration gradients to help maintain the resting potential.

D) none of the above

Answer: C
Diff: 3   Page Ref: 38.2
Skill: Application

40) You are recording from a neuron with an electrode and determine that the peak of the action potential is around +60 mV. What would happen to the height of the action potential if you added 10 times more sodium to the external solution surrounding the cell?

   A) The peak of the action potential would remain +60 mV.

   B) The peak of the action potential would be larger than +60 mV.

   C) The peak of the action potential would be smaller than +60 mV.

Answer: B
Diff: 3   Page Ref: 38.2
Skill: Application

41) The place where a neuron communicates with a muscle fiber, a gland, or another neuron is known as the _____.

Answer: synapse
Diff: 1   Page Ref: 38.2
Skill: Factual

42) A stimulus which is strong enough to change a resting potential into an action potential is said to be above a _____.

Answer: threshold
Diff: 1   Page Ref: 38.2
Skill: Factual

43) The resting potential is always _____ inside the cell and relatively _____ outside the cell.

Answer: negative; positive
Diff: 1   Page Ref: 38.2
Skill: Factual

44) A patient with Alzheimer's disease has a degeneration of groups of _____ –producing neurons in the brain.

Answer: acetylcholine
Diff: 2   Page Ref: 38.2
Skill: Factual

45) Even TV ads mention endorphins. What makes these compounds so interesting?

Answer: They are natural narcotics which block the transfer of pain sensation.
Diff: 3   Page Ref: 38.2
Skill: Factual

46) Why do negative charges tend to remain inside the cell during both the resting potential and the action potential?

Answer: Most negative charges are attached to large organic molecules which cannot cross the membrane.
Diff: 3   Page Ref: 38.2
Skill: Factual

47) If a neuron receives an IPSP, what happens to it?

Answer: Since this is an inhibitory potential, the neuron will be inhibited from transmitting an action potential.
Diff: 3   Page Ref: 38.2
Skill: Factual

48) What causes the nerve impulse to travel along the membrane?

Answer: The positive charge of an action potential spreads quickly to the next part of the axon causing it to reach an action potential as well.
Diff: 3   Page Ref: 38.2
Skill: Factual

49) Explain how the opioid neuromodulators were discovered.

Answer: The ability of the human brain to respond to opiates such as morphine led researchers to look for natural opiates into whose brain receptors the drugs might be fitting.
Diff: 3   Page Ref: 38.2
Skill: Factual

50) The central nervous system interprets signal frequency as

A) stimulus intensity.

B) stimulus importance.

C) convergence.

D) divergence.

E) a reflex.

Answer: A
Diff: 2   Page Ref: 38.3
Skill: Factual

51) An example of the trend in the evolution of the animal nervous system called centralization is

A) the relatively large, well-developed brain of the octopus.

B) the overlapping nerve nets found in many jellyfish.

C) the presence of chemoreceptors on the feet of a fly.

D) all of the above

Answer: A
Diff: 2   Page Ref: 38.3
Skill: Factual

52) The intensity of the stimulus is indicated by the _____ of action potentials.

 A) frequency

 B) duration

 C) speed

 D) intensity

 E) loss

Answer: A
Diff: 2   Page Ref: 38.3
Skill: Factual

53) Which of the following most accurately describes why your brain can distinguish lights from sounds.

 A) because visual stimuli produce action potentials, while auditory stimuli produce generator potentials

 B) Action potentials generated by visual stimuli are larger than action potentials generated by auditory stimuli.

 C) because the brain monitors which action potentials come from the eye and which action potentials come from the ear

 D) none of the above

Answer: C
Diff: 3   Page Ref: 38.3
Skill: Conceptual

54) John is a synesthete who can see yellow triangles when he hears the key of "C". Which of the following statements is TRUE about John when he hears the key of "C"?

 A) His hair cells and auditory cortex are active.

 B) His cones and visual cortex are active.

 C) His hair cells, auditory cortex, and visual cortex are active.

 D) His cones, auditory cortex, and visual cortex are active.

Answer: C
Diff: 3   Page Ref: 38.3
Skill: Application

55) If you tap the tendon below the kneecap of a person with a complete break or cut in the cervical spinal cord, would this elicit a knee–jerk response?

 A) yes   B) no

Answer: B
Diff: 2   Page Ref: 38.3
Skill: Application

56) The stronger the impulse, the larger the action potential. True or False?

Answer: FALSE
Diff: 1   *Page Ref: 38.3*
Skill: Factual

57) The brain is able to take sensory inputs from many neurons and integrate them into a few association neurons is called convergence. True or False?

Answer: TRUE
Diff: 1   *Page Ref: 38.3*
Skill: Factual

58) Cnidarians are able to have a _____ nervous system because they are _____ symmetric.

Answer: diffuse (neural net); radially
Diff: 1   *Page Ref: 38.3*
Skill: Factual

59) A person responds to touching a pan out of a hot oven by pulling their hand away before they realize that the pan is cold. Why are they able to respond before they can think?

Answer: because this is a reflex that goes to and from the spinal cord before the message has time to get to the brain
Diff: 2   *Page Ref: 38.3*
Skill: Factual

60) Which is not part of the central nervous system?

A) brain

B) spinal cord

C) medulla

D) autonomic nervous system

E) thalamus

Answer: D
Diff: 2   *Page Ref: 38.4*
Skill: Factual

61) Complex motor patterns necessary for flight in birds are stored in the

A) hypothalamus.

B) midbrain.

C) cerebellum.

D) cerebrum.

E) pons.

Answer: C
Diff: 2   *Page Ref: 38.4*
Skill: Factual

62) Which portion of the brain is responsible for primitive emotions?

    A) medulla

    B) pons

    C) reticular formation

    D) limbic system

    E) thalamus

Answer: D
Diff: 2   *Page Ref: 38.4*
Skill: Factual

63) A person you know has been in an automobile accident. After the accident, you notice a dramatic personality change. Before the accident, he was industrious and well-liked; after the accident he is profane, impetuous and incapable of working toward a goal. Which portion of the brain was most likely damaged?

    A) hypothalamus

    B) hippocampus

    C) frontal lobe

    D) parietal lobe

    E) temporal lobe

Answer: C
Diff: 2   *Page Ref: 38.4*
Skill: Application

64) The kinds of peripheral neurons that are responsible for involuntary responses to extreme danger or stress are the

    A) somatic.   B) parasympathetic.

    C) sympathetic.   D) all of these

Answer: C
Diff: 2   *Page Ref: 38.4*
Skill: Factual

65) Which of the following are found in the human central nervous system?

    A) spinal cord   B) forebrain (cerebrum)

    C) hypothalamus   D) all of these

Answer: D
Diff: 1   *Page Ref: 38.4*
Skill: Factual

66) In a goldfish, information from the eyes is processed by the

   A) forebrain.   B) cerebellum.   C) midbrain.   D) hindbrain.

Answer: C
Diff: 2   Page Ref: 38.4
Skill: Factual

67) Which of these neurotransmitters or neuromodulators are found between motor neurons and skeletal muscles?

   A) acetylcholine

   B) dopamine

   C) serotonin

   D) noradrenaline

   E) endorphin

Answer: A
Diff: 1   Page Ref: 38.4
Skill: Factual

68) If a doctor sees a patient with tremors and muscular rigidity, she might suspect that the patient had _____ which is caused by the degeneration of _____ –producing neurons in the brain.

   A) Alzheimer's disease; acetylcholine

   B) schizophrenia; dopamine

   C) myasthenia gravis; acetylcholine

   D) Parkinson's disease; dopamine

   E) depression; serotonin

Answer: D
Diff: 3   Page Ref: 38.4
Skill: Factual

69) Which of these neurotransmitters or neuromodulators are released by neurons of the sympathetic nervous system?

   A) acetylcholine

   B) dopamine

   C) serotonin

   D) noradrenaline

   E) endorphin

Answer: D
Diff: 2   Page Ref: 38.4
Skill: Factual

70) Most brain cells are _____ neurons.

A) sensory

B) association

C) motor

D) saltatory

E) parasympathetic

Answer: B
Diff: 1   Page Ref: 38.4
Skill: Factual

71) What type of neuron will activate the biceps muscle in your arm?

A) sensory   B) association   C) motor

Answer: C
Diff: 2   Page Ref: 38.4
Skill: Factual

72) A nerve net is typical of

A) cnidarians.

B) flatworms.

C) arthropods.

D) molluscs.

E) vertebrates.

Answer: A
Diff: 2   Page Ref: 38.4
Skill: Factual

73) The cell bodies of motor neurons are located

A) in the gray matter of the spinal cord.

B) in the brain.

C) outside the spinal cord.

D) in the muscles.

E) next to the sensory terminals.

Answer: A
Diff: 2   Page Ref: 38.4
Skill: Factual

74) A siesta after meals is probably a good idea because it allows the body to digest the food as a result of the activities of the _____ nervous system.

   A) somatic

   B) central

   C) sensory

   D) parasympathetic

   E) sympathetic

Answer: D
Diff: 2   Page Ref: 38.4
Skill: Factual

75) The autonomic nervous system controls

   A) the skeletal muscles.

   B) the senses.

   C) contraction of involuntary muscles.

   D) reflexes.

   E) integration in the brain.

Answer: C
Diff: 1   Page Ref: 38.4
Skill: Factual

76) If a person gets meningitis, they have an inflammation of the

   A) covering of the heart.

   B) coverings of the brain or spinal cord.

   C) cell bodies of sensory neurons.

   D) myelin sheath.

   E) lining of the muscles.

Answer: B
Diff: 2   Page Ref: 38.4
Skill: Factual

77) If an animal is especially coordinated in its movements, it will probably have a larger than normal

    A) cerebellum.

    B) cerebrum.

    C) amygdala.

    D) limbic system.

    E) hypothalamus.

Answer: A
Diff: 2   Page Ref: 38.4
Skill: Factual

78) Which is NOT true of the reticular formation?

    A) It extends through several brain parts.

    B) It screens sensory information going to conscious brain centers.

    C) It plays a role in sleep.

    D) It is the same thing as the limbic system.

    E) It "decides" what sensory inputs need attention.

Answer: D
Diff: 3   Page Ref: 38.4
Skill: Factual

79) The part of the brain that controls involuntary actions, such as breathing is the

    A) cerebrum.   B) cerebellum.   C) retina.   D) hindbrain.

Answer: D
Diff: 2   Page Ref: 38.4
Skill: Factual

80) Which of the following parts of the brain controls breathing and heart rate?

    A) medulla   B) cerebellum   C) cerebrum

    D) hypothalamus   E) thalamus   F) amygdala

Answer: A
Diff: 2   Page Ref: 38.4
Skill: Factual

81) Which of the following parts of the brain passes information from the senses to the cerebrum with little further processing?

    A) cerebellum

    B) cerebrum

    C) hypothalamus

    D) thalamus

    E) amygdala

Answer: D
Diff: 2   *Page Ref: 38.4*
Skill: Factual

82) Which of the following parts of the brain coordinates movements?

    A) medulla   B) cerebellum   C) cerebrum   D) hypothalamus

Answer: B
Diff: 1   *Page Ref: 38.4*
Skill: Factual

83) Which of the following parts of the brain is involved in interpretation of sensory information?

    A) medulla   B) cerebellum   C) cerebrum   D) hypothalamus

Answer: C
Diff: 1   *Page Ref: 38.4*
Skill: Factual

84) Which of the following parts of the brain controls the autonomic nervous system?

    A) medulla   B) cerebellum   C) cerebrum

    D) hypothalamus   E) thalamus   F) amygdala

Answer: D
Diff: 3   *Page Ref: 38.4*
Skill: Factual

85) Which of the following parts of the brain contains about half the neurons in the human brain?

    A) medulla   B) cerebellum   C) cerebrum   D) hypothalamus

Answer: C
Diff: 1   *Page Ref: 38.4*
Skill: Factual

86) You walk in to take this test and notice that your food is sitting undigested in your stomach, your heart is beating quickly, and you can't sit still. What part of your nervous system is primarily involved?

Answer: sympathetic
Diff: 3   *Page Ref: 38.4*
Skill: Application

87) What is the main purpose of cerebrospinal fluid?

Answer: cushion the brain and spinal cord
Diff: 2   Page Ref: 38.4
Skill: Factual

88) A person who exhibits an inability to speak after a stroke, has had damage to what part of the brain?

Answer: cerebrum (may include most likely the left side)
Diff: 2   Page Ref: 38.4
Skill: Factual

89) How are the sympathetic and parasympathetic nervous systems similar?

Answer: They involve the same organs. The sympathetic prepares for stress, whereas the parasympathetic allows for relaxation. There are also differences in the anatomy of the systems.
Diff: 3   Page Ref: 38.4
Skill: Factual

90) Explain why most adults do not have to think about how to walk even though they did when they were toddlers.

Answer: All the neurons and connections needed for walking are in the spinal cord so that what the brain contributes after the person learns to walk is the initiation of the activity.
Diff: 2   Page Ref: 38.4
Skill: Factual

91) Damage to the right frontal cortex may produce

A) paralysis on the left side of the body.

B) paralysis on the right side of the body.

C) paralysis on the dominant side of the body.

D) paralysis on the non-dominant side of the body.

Answer: A
Diff: 2   Page Ref: 38.5
Skill: Factual

92) The structure responsible for transferring short-term memories into long-term memories is the

A) hypothalamus.   B) hippocampus.

C) amygdala.   D) frontal lobe.

Answer: B
Diff: 2   Page Ref: 38.5
Skill: Factual

93) The corpus callosum links the

  A) thalamus and hypothalamus.

  B) cerebrum and thalamus.

  C) forebrain and midbrain.

  D) right and left cerebral hemispheres.

  E) peripheral and central nervous systems.

Answer: D
Diff: 2   Page Ref: 38.5
Skill: Factual

94) The right cerebral hemisphere

  A) is better than the left at language.

  B) is better than the left at math.

  C) controls the left side of the body.

  D) receives input from the right eye only.

  E) is logical.

Answer: C
Diff: 2   Page Ref: 38.5
Skill: Factual

95) Recent discoveries have shown that women are more able to recover speaking ability after a stroke because they are able to shift more easily from the left brain to the right brain because they have a larger _____ than do men.

  A) hypothalamus

  B) corpus callosum

  C) cerebellum

  D) cerebrum

  E) hippocampus

Answer: B
Diff: 2   Page Ref: 38.5
Skill: Factual

96) People with damage to the hippocampus seem to be unable to remember recent events even though the memory of events before the damage remains intact. This seems to indicate that the hippocampus is involved in

    A) transferring of short–term memory into long–term memory.

    B) the production of neurons in the cerebellum.

    C) the production of hormones which control the memory neurons of the cerebrum.

    D) recognition of similar events.

    E) retrieval of memories.

Answer: A
Diff: 3   Page Ref: 38.5
Skill: Factual

97) Is it possible that brain damage from a stroke or other injury could leave a person, whose hearing is fine, with the ability to comprehend written language but no understanding of spoken language? Why or why not?

    A) yes, because various aspects of language are localized to different parts of the brain

    B) yes, because various aspects of language are localized to individual cells

    C) no, because all aspects of language are processed in the same part of the brain

    D) no, because all aspects of language are processed by the same cell

Answer: A
Diff: 3   Page Ref: 38.5
Skill: Conceptual

98) If a patient presents with a particular memory problem in which they can recall old memories but cannot make new memories, what part of the brain is most likely damaged?

    A) temporal lobes   B) cerebellum

    C) hippocampus   D) cerebrum

Answer: C
Diff: 3   Page Ref: 38.5
Skill: Application

99) Alice's PET (positron emission tomography) scan has a large yellow area in the occipital lobe when taken while Alice is looking a color images. Which of the following is TRUE about Alice's PET scan?

    A) The occipital lobe was the only area of Alice's brain that was active.

    B) The occipital lobe had the highest level of activity, but other brain areas were still active.

    C) The darkest areas of Alice's brain were the most active areas of Alice's brain.

    D) This scan proves the old saying that we only use 10% of our brains.

Answer: B
Diff: 3   Page Ref: 38.5
Skill: Conceptual

100) A receptor that produces a signal in response to stretching of its plasma membrane is most likely a

    A) pain receptor.   B) mechanoreceptor.

    C) chemoreceptor.   D) photoreceptor.

Answer: B
Diff: 2   Page Ref: 38.6
Skill: Factual

101) Receptor potentials are _____ the strength of the stimulus.

    A) unrelated to

    B) the same regardless of

    C) inversely proportional to

    D) directly proportional to

    E) much greater than

Answer: D
Diff: 2   Page Ref: 38.6
Skill: Factual

102) Which of the following is a mechanoreceptor?

    A) olfactory receptor

    B) heat receptor

    C) hair cell

    D) rods

    E) taste bud

Answer: C
Diff: 1   Page Ref: 38.6
Skill: Factual

103) How is a sensory receptor like a hydroelectric plant?

    A) They both transduce one type of energy into another.

    B) They both generate electricity.

    C) They both use the energy of moving water.

    D) A and B

    E) B and C

Answer: D
Diff: 3   Page Ref: 38.6
Skill: Conceptual

104) Why do sensory receptors (or the cells they synapse with) have to turn receptor potentials into action potentials to be effective?

    A) Action potentials are regenerative and can convey information over long distances.

    B) Receptor potentials are regenerative and can convey information over long distances.

    C) Action potentials are passive and diminish in size over long distances.

    D) Receptor potentials are passive and diminish in size over long distances.

    E) A and D

Answer: E
Diff: 3   Page Ref: 38.6
Skill: Conceptual

105) Your friend pokes gently at your shoulder to get your attention. Which receptors would sense this?

    A) chemoreceptors

    B) photoreceptors

    C) thermoreceptors

    D) mechanoreceptors

    E) pain receptors

Answer: D
Diff: 2   Page Ref: 38.7
Skill: Application

106) Hair cells are located on the

    A) tectorial membrane.   B) oval window.

    C) round window.   D) basilar membrane.

Answer: D
Diff: 2   Page Ref: 38.8
Skill: Factual

107) The perception of sound depends on

    A) chemoreceptors.

    B) photoreceptors.

    C) thermoreceptors.

    D) mechanoreceptors

    E) pain receptors.

Answer: D
Diff: 2   Page Ref: 38.8
Skill: Factual

108) If the doctor says that you have a middle ear infection, which of the following would NOT be involved?

    A) the Eustachian tube

    B) the hammer

    C) the tympanic membrane

    D) the anvil

    E) the cochlea

Answer: E
Diff: 2   Page Ref: 38.8
Skill: Factual

109) We are able to perceive the pitch of a sound because

    A) the hammer, anvil, and stirrup vibrate at different speeds.

    B) different parts of the basilar membrane vibrate at different frequencies of sound.

    C) different parts of the tectorial membrane vibrate at different frequencies of sound.

    D) the basilar membrane is stiff and narrow at the end away from the oval window.

    E) the tympanum vibrates more strongly at high pitches.

Answer: B
Diff: 3   Page Ref: 38.8
Skill: Factual

110) The hammer, anvil, and stirrup are located in the

    A) outer ear.

    B) middle ear

    C) inner ear.

    D) Eustachian tube.

    E) cochlea.

Answer: B
Diff: 1   Page Ref: 38.8
Skill: Factual

111) The receptor cells for hearing are located in the

    A) cochlea.

    B) semicircular canals.

    C) saccule.

    D) utricle.

    E) Eustachian tube

Answer: A
Diff: 1   Page Ref: 38.8
Skill: Factual

112) Which of the following accurately represents the sequence of structures through which sound waves travel to stimulate hearing?

    A) outer ear → tympanic membrane → Eustachian tube → cochlea → oval window

    B) outer ear → oval window → middle ear → tympanic membrane → cochlea

    C) outer ear → Eustachian tube → oval window → tympanic membrane → basilar membrane

    D) outer ear → tympanic membrane → middle ear → oval window → cochlea

    E) outer ear → basilar membrane → inner ear → oval window → Eustachian tube

Answer: D
Diff: 3   Page Ref: 38.8
Skill: Factual

113) The oval window is between

    A) the outer ear and the middle ear.

    B) the middle ear and the inner ear.

    C) the cornea and the lens.

    D) the lens and the retina.

    E) the tympanic membrane and the Eustachian tube.

Answer: B
Diff: 1   Page Ref: 38.8
Skill: Factual

114) Which of the following would produce the largest receptor potential?

    A) a high pitched 30 decibel sound

    B) a low pitched 40 decibel sound

    C) a high pitched 40 decibel sound

    D) a low pitched 30 decibel sound

    E) B and C

Answer: E
Diff: 3   Page Ref: 38.8
Skill: Application

115) Humans can detect vibrations ranging from _____ to _____ vibrations per second.

Answer: 30; 20,000
Diff: 2   Page Ref: 38.8
Skill: Factual

116) What symptoms would indicate that the Eustachian tube is blocked? Explain.

Answer: pressure in the middle ear or on the eardrum, because the Eustachian tube connects the middle ear with the pharynx to allow air pressure to equilibrate
Diff: 2   Page Ref: 38.8
Skill: Application

117) How does the ear distinguish between loud sounds and soft sounds?

Answer: The louder the sound, the greater the bending of the hairs. Greater bending leads to higher receptor potentials which leads to more frequent action potentials. Frequent action potentials are interpreted as loudness in the brain.
Diff: 3   Page Ref: 38.8
Skill: Factual

118) Your parents most likely need glasses to read because

    A) vision gradually worsens as one ages.

    B) the lens of the eye stiffens as one ages.

    C) the photoreceptors of the eye are no longer as responsive.

    D) the muscles that change the shape of the lens weaken as one ages.

    E) Both B and D are correct.

Answer: B
Diff: 2   Page Ref: 38.9
Skill: Factual

119) When light energy hits a photopigment, the molecule

A) changes shape, altering membrane permeability.

B) is destroyed.

C) is separated from the plasma membrane.

D) forms an enzyme.

Answer: A
Diff: 2   Page Ref: 38.9
Skill: Factual

120) Ommatidia are found in _____ eyes.

A) flatworm

B) mollusc

C) arthropod

D) amphibian

E) human

Answer: C
Diff: 2   Page Ref: 38.9
Skill: Factual

121) Which invertebrate has a camera–type eye?

A) octopus

B) Earthworm

C) starfish

D) insect

E) flatworm

Answer: A
Diff: 2   Page Ref: 38.9
Skill: Factual

122) The receptor molecules affected by light rays are

A) in the ganglion cells.

B) in the lens.

C) mechanoreceptors

D) photopigments.

E) pacinian corpuscles.

Answer: D
Diff: 2   Page Ref: 38.9
Skill: Factual

123) Which is the correct sequence of structures through which light passes in the eye?

    A) cornea → aqueous humor → pupil → lens → vitreous humor → retina

    B) pupil → vitreous humor → aqueous humor → cornea → retina

    C) lens → pupil → cornea → aqueous → humor → retina

    D) aqueous humor → cornea → lens → pupil → vitreous humor → retina

    E) cornea → lens → vitreous humor → retina → aqueous humor → pupil

Answer: A
Diff: 3   Page Ref: 38.9
Skill: Factual

124) The fovea of the human eye is

    A) mostly rods.

    B) the part of the retina that produces the sharpest image.

    C) in the sclera.

    D) in the cornea.

    E) where the lens reaches maximum focus.

Answer: B
Diff: 1   Page Ref: 38.9
Skill: Factual

125) In humans, how does the shape of the lens change when the eye focuses on a nearby object?

    A) The lens does not change, the shape of the eye changes.

    B) The lens gets longer.

    C) The lens gets shorter.

    D) The lens becomes more rounded.

    E) The lens flattens.

Answer: E
Diff: 2   Page Ref: 38.9
Skill: Factual

126) In a person who is nearsighted

    A) the eyeball is too short front to back.

    B) light is focused in front of the retina.

    C) the lens is not functional.

    D) there is an excess of aqueous humor.

    E) the muscle which controls the thickness of the lens is weak.

Answer: B
Diff: 2   Page Ref: 38.9
Skill: Factual

127) Which is NOT true of the optic nerve?

    A) made up of axons of ganglion cells

    B) connects eye to brain

    C) interprets the action potentials it carries

    D) carries action potentials originating in the retina

    E) forms a blind spot where it passes through the retina

Answer: C
Diff: 2   Page Ref: 38.9
Skill: Factual

128) The blind spot is

    A) the part of the cerebral cortex which interprets action potentials from the eye.

    B) part of the cornea.

    C) an area of the retina which has no receptor cells.

    D) in the vitreous humor.

    E) the place where the lens is not part of the pupil.

Answer: C
Diff: 2   Page Ref: 38.9
Skill: Factual

129) People who wear contact lenses or glasses have a defect in

    A) the length of the eyeball.   B) the rod cells.

    C) the cone cells.   D) the iris.

Answer: A
Diff: 1   Page Ref: 38.9
Skill: Factual

130) In low light everything appears black or white because

    A) no colored light is reflected to the eye.

    B) rods are more sensitive to light than are cones.

    C) few action potentials are stimulated at low light.

    D) only white light is available at night.

    E) the diffused light of night does not fall on the fovea.

Answer: B
Diff: 2   Page Ref: 38.9
Skill: Factual

131) How many types of cones are found in humans?

A) 1   B) 2   C) 3   D) 5   E) hundreds

Answer: C
Diff: 1   *Page Ref: 38.9*
Skill: Factual

132) In humans, depth perception is possible because

A) two eyes are present.

B) each of two eyes "sees" a different image.

C) two eyes have different but overlapping visual fields.

D) two eyes are necessary for any vision to occur.

E) the eyes see identical images.

Answer: C
Diff: 2   *Page Ref: 38.9*
Skill: Factual

133) If you could monitor the activity from the photoreceptors of rods and cones in the retina during a dream, would you expect for these cells to be producing electrical activity? Why or why not?

A) yes, because people's eyes move during REM sleep which is when dreaming occurs

B) yes, because rods and cones reproduce whole images that are then sent to the brain

C) no, because rods and cones can only work when our eyes are open

D) no, because rods and cones transduce light energy into electrical energy and there is no light energy hitting these receptors during a dream

Answer: D
Diff: 3   *Page Ref: 38.9*
Skill: Application

134) Most color vision is in the _____, a depression in the retina where most of the _____ are located.

Answer: fovea; cones
Diff: 1   *Page Ref: 38.9*
Skill: Factual

135) How does an insect see the world?

Answer: as a mosaic of many bright or dim images which probably give a relatively grainy image
Diff: 3   *Page Ref: 38.9*
Skill: Factual

136) What is the "blind spot" and why does it occur?

Answer: The optic disk where the axons of the ganglion cells pass through the retina. There are no receptors in that area.
Diff: 2   Page Ref: 38.9
Skill: Factual

137) What are the two main functions of the choroid layer behind the retina in humans?

Answer: 1. Supply blood to the retina. 2. Absorb light that was not absorbed by the retina to prevent stray light from being reflected around in the eye.
Diff: 2   Page Ref: 38.9
Skill: Factual

138) How is the placement of eyes different on a lion (a predator) from the eyes on a deer (a herbivore)? What advantage does this give to each?

Answer: The eyes of a lion are in front so that it can focus clearly on prey and prepare to pounce. The eyes of prey such as deer tend to be on the side so that predators can be detected from all sides.
Diff: 3   Page Ref: 38.9
Skill: Factual

139) Which is NOT a type of taste receptor?

A) sweet

B) sour

C) salty

D) bitter

E) All are types of taste receptors.

Answer: E
Diff: 2   Page Ref: 38.10
Skill: Factual

140) Smell and taste are detected by

A) chemoreceptors.

B) photoreceptors.

C) thermoreceptors.

D) mechanoreceptors.

E) pain receptors.

Answer: A
Diff: 1   Page Ref: 38.10
Skill: Factual

141) In order for chemicals to be sensed in the nose they must

A) first enter the mouth.

B) bind to taste buds.

C) cause bending of hair cells in the upper nasal cavity.

D) stimulate the cones.

E) diffuse into the mucus and bind to receptors.

Answer: E
Diff: 2   Page Ref: 38.10
Skill: Factual

142) Pain perception is

A) blocked by endorphins.   B) caused by bradykinin.

C) caused by damage to cells.   D) all of these

Answer: D
Diff: 2   Page Ref: 38.10
Skill: Factual

143) Humans are just as good as dogs at detecting many odors but not at discriminating them from one another. What could account for this?

A) Dogs have bigger noses.

B) Dogs rely more on their sense of smell than we do.

C) Dogs have more types of odor receptors.

D) Dogs have more of each kind of odor receptor.

Answer: C
Diff: 3   Page Ref: 38.10
Skill: Application

144) Chemoreceptors produce _____ signals in response to a _____ stimulus.

Answer: electrical/sensory; chemical
Diff: 2   Page Ref: 38.10
Skill: Factual

145) What is the common name for the sense of olfaction?

Answer: smell
Diff: 1   Page Ref: 38.10
Skill: Factual

146) Why does food taste bland when you have a cold?

Answer: because much of "taste" is actually smell, so that when the nose is stopped up, only the 4 basic tastes can be detected
Diff: 1   *Page Ref: 38.10*
Skill: Factual

147) Describe a taste bud.

Answer: A cluster of about 60–80 receptors occur in a pit in the tongue. A pore connects the center of the bud to the surface and allows chemicals to contact microvilli from the receptors.
Diff: 2   *Page Ref: 38.10*
Skill: Factual

148) How do eels find their way through thousands of miles of ocean to their breeding grounds? By sensing

A) sound waves in the sea.

B) electrical fields which they generate.

C) the Earth's magnetic field.

D) chemicals in the water.

E) changes in light levels at different latitudes.

Answer: C
Diff: 2   *Page Ref: 38.10*
Skill: Factual

Chapter 39 Action & Support: The Muscles & Skeleton

1) Describe some of the important functions of muscles and skeletons.

    Answer: The muscles and skeleton allow an organism to move. Muscles play a role in pumping blood for circulation, moving food through the digestive system and breathing. The skeleton is a framework for an organism's body as well.
    Diff: 1   Page Ref: 39.1
    Skill: Factual

2) Skeletal muscle is found in muscles that

    A) line the heart.

    B) squeeze food through the digestive tract.

    C) contract and expand the large blood vessels.

    D) move the body.

    E) all of these

    Answer: D
    Diff: 2   Page Ref: 39.2
    Skill: Factual

3) Which muscle component is smallest?

    A) myofibril   B) myosin filament

    C) sarcomere   D) muscle fiber

    Answer: B
    Diff: 2   Page Ref: 39.2
    Skill: Factual

4) What is the purpose of the sarcoplasmic reticulum?

    A) storage of calcium   B) storage of ATP

    C) transmission of a nerve signal   D) contraction

    Answer: A
    Diff: 2   Page Ref: 39.2
    Skill: Factual

5) Connections between thin filaments and thick filaments are known as

    A) sarcomeres.   B) Z lines.   C) crossbridges.   D) myofilaments.

    Answer: C
    Diff: 2   Page Ref: 39.2
    Skill: Factual

6) The myofibrils of skeletal muscle are organized into units called

    A) A lines.

    B) sarcomeres.

    C) Z lines.

    D) Haversian systems.

    E) T tubules.

Answer: B
Diff: 1   Page Ref: 39.2
Skill: Factual

7) The thick filaments of a myofibril are composed of

    A) lipids.

    B) T tubules.

    C) actin.

    D) myosin.

    E) reticulum.

Answer: D
Diff: 1   Page Ref: 39.2
Skill: Factual

8) The striped appearance of skeletal muscle is due to

    A) the T tubules.

    B) the accessory proteins in thin filaments.

    C) the arrangement of thick and thin filaments.

    D) the wrapping of sarcoplasmic reticulum around the myofibril.

    E) the arrangement of ions on each side of the sarcoplasmic reticulum.

Answer: C
Diff: 1   Page Ref: 39.2
Skill: Conceptual

9) Because muscle fibers have T tubules, all parts of the fiber are

    A) in contact with the blood.

    B) close to the cell membrane.

    C) able to send messages to the brain.

    D) able to form acetylcholine.

    E) oriented at right angles to each other.

Answer: B
Diff: 2   Page Ref: 39.2
Skill: Conceptual

10) The connective tissue that connects muscles to bones is called

    A) tendons.   B) ligaments.

    C) thick filaments.   D) thin filaments.

Answer: A
Diff: 1   Page Ref: 39.2
Skill: Factual

11) Which molecule contains a binding site for crossbridge attachment?

    A) actin   B) sarcoplasmic reticulum

    C) ATP   D) calcium

Answer: A
Diff: 2   Page Ref: 39.2
Skill: Factual

12) An action potential travels into the muscle fiber interior by passing down the

    A) sarcoplasmic reticulum.

    B) T tubules.

    C) myofilaments.

    D) sarcolemma.

    E) sarcomere.

Answer: B
Diff: 2   Page Ref: 39.2
Skill: Factual

13) Muscles used for fine motor control have

    A) motor units consisting of many muscle cells.

    B) motor units consisting of a few muscle cells.

    C) many neuromuscular junctions.

    D) large amounts of ATP.

Answer: B
Diff: 2   Page Ref: 39.2
Skill: Conceptual

14) The point of communication between a neuron and a muscle fiber is called a

    A) receptor.   B) neuromuscular junction.

    C) cross bridge.   D) axon.

Answer: B
Diff: 1   Page Ref: 39.2
Skill: Factual

15) The function of the accessory proteins of the thin filaments is to

   A) facilitate muscle contraction.

   B) prevent the formation of cross–bridges between actin and myosin unless Ca ions are present.

   C) prevent over–contraction of muscle fibers.

   D) prevent the entrance of calcium into the fibers.

   E) remove calcium from the sarcomere.

Answer: B
Diff: 2   Page Ref: 39.2
Skill: Factual

16) The site where calcium binds to a protein and activates skeletal muscle contraction is

   A) myosin.   B) actin.   C) troponin.   D) tropomyosin.

Answer: C
Diff: 2   Page Ref: 39.2
Skill: Factual

17) Which of the following is NOT TRUE according to the sliding filament theory?

   A) When a muscle fiber is not contracting, the thin fibers are not connected to the thick fibers.

   B) When actin pushes the Z lines further apart, the muscle expands.

   C) Sliding occurs when the myosin cross bridges change angle.

   D) The muscle relaxes when calcium ions are pumped back into the sarcoplasmic reticulum.

   E) The energy for contraction comes from ATP.

Answer: B
Diff: 3   Page Ref: 39.2
Skill: Conceptual

18) When a muscle fiber receives an action potential from a motor neuron, how many sarcomeres in the fiber contract?

   A) None of them, it is the motor units which contract.

   B) a number directly proportional to the strength of the stimulus

   C) a number inversely proportional to the strength of the stimulus

   D) a few at first, more later

   E) all of them

Answer: E
Diff: 3   Page Ref: 39.2
Skill: Conceptual

19) How might the body control the strength of leg muscle contractions when lifting a heavy object?

    A) increase the frequency of action potentials sent to the leg muscles

    B) increase the number of thick & thin filaments during contraction

    C) stimulate more motor units to contribute to the muscle contraction

    D) both A and C

Answer: D
Diff: 2   *Page Ref: 39.2*
Skill: Application

20) The term "motor unit" refers to

    A) an entire skeletal muscle.

    B) all of the motor neurons going to a skeletal muscle.

    C) all of the skeletal muscle in one body part.

    D) the group of muscle fibers with which one motor neuron synapses.

    E) a group of sarcomeres in a muscle fiber.

Answer: D
Diff: 2   *Page Ref: 39.2*
Skill: Factual

21) The fluid in the sarcoplasmic reticulum contains a high concentration of _____ ions, which are released when an action potential stimulates it.

    A) calcium

    B) potassium

    C) sodium

    D) iron

    E) phosphorus

Answer: A
Diff: 1   *Page Ref: 39.2*
Skill: Factual

22) A muscle fiber generates maximum contractile force when

    A) it has been stretched excessively.

    B) some of the myofibrils contract and then relax at the same time.

    C) it receives repeated action potentials from a nerve.

    D) it has been exposed to a poison.

    E) it is dying.

Answer: C
Diff: 2   *Page Ref: 39.2*
Skill: Conceptual

23) Skeletal muscle produces force as the _____ "walk" along the _____.

    A) actin heads; myosin

    B) myosin heads; actin

    C) ATPs; microtubules

    D) none of these

Answer: B
Diff: 2   Page Ref: 39.2
Skill: Conceptual

24) The connections between the thick and thin filaments in a muscle fiber are called

    A) actins.   B) kinases.   C) microtubules.   D) cross-bridges.

Answer: D
Diff: 2   Page Ref: 39.2
Skill: Factual

25) In a muscle that is fatigue resistant, such as that of a leg muscle in a marathon runner, you would expect it to have

    A) many mitochondria.

    B) an elevated blood supply.

    C) elevated levels of ATP.

    D) all of the above

Answer: D
Diff: 2   Page Ref: 39.2
Skill: Application

26) In which of the following human muscles would you expect to find large motor units?

    A) facial muscles

    B) leg muscles

    C) abdominal muscles

    D) muscles in the hand

Answer: B
Diff: 2   Page Ref: 39.2
Skill: Application

27) From a skeletal muscle perspective, what might happen if a person had a calcium deficiency?

    A) Cross bridges would not release from actin.

    B) Muscles would not contract as strongly as they should.

    C) Motor neurons would not function properly.

    D) ATP would not fuel muscle contraction.

Answer: B
Diff: 2   Page Ref: 39.2
Skill: Application

28) What would happen to a person if they were poisoned with a chemical that blocked the production of neurotransmitters (such as Acetylcholine) at neuromuscular junctions?

    A) The person's muscles would contract uncontrollably.

    B) The sarcoplasmic reticulum would release its stores of calcium ions.

    C) Their muscles would be unable to contract.

    D) Their muscles would enlarge.

Answer: C
Diff: 2   Page Ref: 39.2
Skill: Application

29) The sinoatrial node

    A) is located in the right ventricle.

    B) is formed from specialized strips of smooth muscle.

    C) serves as the "pacemaker" of the heart.

    D) All are correct.

Answer: C
Diff: 2   Page Ref: 39.2
Skill: Factual

30) In cardiac muscle, increased calcium concentrations are produced when

    A) calcium is released from the sarcoplasmic reticulum.

    B) calcium enters the cell from the extracellular fluid.

    C) an action potential is spread down the T tubules.

    D) Both A and B are correct.

    E) All are correct.

Answer: E
Diff: 2   Page Ref: 39.2
Skill: Factual

31) In skeletal & cardiac muscle, relaxation occurs as _____ are pumped back into the sarcoplasmic reticulum.

    A) sodium ions   B) calcium ions

    C) potassium ions   D) chloride ions

Answer: B
Diff: 2   Page Ref: 39.2
Skill: Factual

32) Which of the following are found in both smooth and cardiac muscle?

A) gap junctions

B) sarcoplasmic reticulum

C) regular arrangement of sarcomeres

D) both A and B

E) All are correct.

Answer: A
Diff: 2   Page Ref: 39.2
Skill: Factual

33) Which type of muscle constricts veins when blood pressure drops suddenly?

A) smooth

B) Haversian

C) striated

D) sarcoplasm

E) cardiac

Answer: A
Diff: 1   Page Ref: 39.2
Skill: Conceptual

34) Smooth muscle

A) contracts when stretched.

B) produces long, slow, sustained contractions.

C) contains actin and myosin.

D) all of the above

Answer: D
Diff: 1   Page Ref: 39.2
Skill: Factual

35) Arrange these muscle tissue groupings in order, from most inclusive to least inclusive: sarcomere, motor unit, thick and thin filaments, myofibril, muscle

Answer: Motor unit – muscle fiber – myofibril – sarcomere – thick and thin filaments
Diff: 3   Page Ref: 39.2
Skill: Factual

36) In light of the role of calcium ions in muscle contraction, what would you expect to happen to a person who was very deficient in dietary calcium? Explain.

Answer: Muscle weakness due to an inability to remove the accessory proteins from their relaxed position which blocks binding and thus sliding.
Diff: 3   Page Ref: 39.2
Skill: Application

37) What ion is found in high concentrations in the sarcoplasmic reticulum?

Answer: calcium
Diff: 2   Page Ref: 39.2
Skill: Factual

38) What two types of motion do smooth muscles perform?

Answer: slow, sustained contractions or slow, wave–like contractions
Diff: 2   Page Ref: 39.2
Skill: Factual

39) Describe the differences between fast twitch and slow twitch muscle fibers.

Answer: Slow twitch muscles fibers twitch slowly and have a lot of mitochondria and a plentiful blood supply. Fast twitch fibers twitch faster and stronger and have a smaller supply and fewer mitochondria.
Diff: 2   Page Ref: 39.2
Skill: Factual

40) Which of these is correctly matched with its type of skeleton?

A) Earthworm – endoskeleton

B) human – exoskeleton

C) lobster – exoskeleton

D) mayfly – hydroskeleton

E) snail – endoskeleton

Answer: C
Diff: 2   Page Ref: 39.2
Skill: Conceptual

41) The chitinous exoskeleton of a crawfish

A) protects the animal's vital organs.

B) provides points of attachment for the muscles.

C) necessitates periodic molts to permit growth.

D) all of these

Answer: D
Diff: 2   Page Ref: 39.2
Skill: Conceptual

42) Earthworms and sea anemones do not have bones. They move by the actions of muscles on a fluid–filled compartment. This system is called

   A) endoskeleton.   B) hydrostatic skeleton.

   C) circular skeleton.   D) longitudinal skeleton.

Answer: B
Diff: 1   Page Ref: 39.2
Skill: Factual

43) How might the movement of a sea anemone be affected if its fluid–filled cavity were ruptured?

   A) It would not be able to shorten its body because its circular muscles could not act on cavity fluids.

   B) It would not be able to lengthen its body because its longitudinal muscles could not act on cavity fluids.

   C) It would not be able to shorten its body because its longitudinal muscles could not act on cavity fluids.

   D) It would not be able to lengthen its body because its circular muscles could not act on cavity fluids.

Answer: D
Diff: 2   Page Ref: 39.2
Skill: Application

44) Which of these is NOT a function of the vertebrate endoskeleton?

   A) provides protection

   B) provides support

   C) makes blood cells

   D) conducts sound

   E) All of the above are true.

Answer: E
Diff: 2   Page Ref: 39.2
Skill: Factual

45) Bones store

   A) magnesium.

   B) amino acids.

   C) glycogen.

   D) calcium.

   E) manganese.

Answer: D
Diff: 2   Page Ref: 39.2
Skill: Factual

46) If a doctor told a patient that their appendicular bones are weak, which of the following bones might the doctor be referring to?

    A) humerus

    B) femur

    C) tibia

    D) radius

    E) All of the above are possibilities.

Answer: E
Diff: 1   Page Ref: 39.2
Skill: Application

47) Scientists have explored the relationship between genes and muscles. They have identified a gene that is the instructions for synthesizing the protein designated IGF. What is the role of IGF–I?

    A) IGF–I is the protein that attaches muscles to bone.

    B) IGF–I increases muscle growth.

    C) IGF–I causes muscles to break down.

    D) IGF–I increases the number of sarcomeres.

Answer: B
Diff: 2   Page Ref: 39.2
Skill: Factual

48) The pectoral girdle is part of the axial skeleton. True or False?

Answer: FALSE
Diff: 2   Page Ref: 39.2
Skill: Factual

49) How can animals with an exoskeleton, such as a crab, move without breaking its body?

Answer: The exoskeleton is arranged in plates that are jointed at the edges.
Diff: 3   Page Ref: 39.2
Skill: Conceptual

50) An exoskeleton would be found in _____ while an endoskeleton would be found in _____.

    A) humans; insects   B) humans; spiders only

    C) insects; humans   D) only some humans; all insects

Answer: C
Diff: 1   Page Ref: 39.3
Skill: Factual

51) If an athlete damages the cartilage in his knee, it will tend to heal only very slowly because

    A) cartilage is dead tissue.

    B) cartilage hardens with age.

    C) chondrocytes cannot divide.

    D) calcium is hard to deposit.

    E) cartilage lacks blood vessels.

Answer: E
Diff: 3   Page Ref: 39.4
Skill: Application

52) Cartilage contains a protein called

    A) actin.   B) myosin.   C) estrogen.   D) collagen.

Answer: D
Diff: 2   Page Ref: 39.4
Skill: Factual

53) Which is more TRUE of cartilage than of bone?

    A) high metabolic rate

    B) high potential for repair

    C) capillaries throughout the matrix

    D) flexibility

    E) type of connective tissue

Answer: D
Diff: 2   Page Ref: 39.4
Skill: Conceptual

54) Which of the following common medical procedures would be much more dangerous if cartilage was not present in the ribcage of humans?

    A) the Heimlich maneuver

    B) setting broken rib bones

    C) CPR

    D) listening to heart sounds with a stethoscope

Answer: C
Diff: 2   Page Ref: 39.4
Skill: Application

55) Bone-forming cells are known as

    A) osteocytes.

    C) osteoblasts.

    B) osteoclasts.

    D) osteoprogenitor cells.

Answer: C
Diff: 2   Page Ref: 39.4
Skill: Factual

56) The basic unit of vertebrate bone is the

    A) compact bone.

    C) spongy bone.

    B) cancellous bone.

    D) osteon.

Answer: D
Diff: 2   Page Ref: 39.4
Skill: Factual

57) Osteoporosis may occur when

    A) the activity of osteoclasts exceeds that of the osteoblasts.

    B) the activity of the osteoblasts exceeds that of the osteoclasts.

    C) the activity of the osteoclasts exceeds that of the osteocytes.

    D) the activity of the osteocytes exceeds that of the osteoclasts.

Answer: A
Diff: 2   Page Ref: 39.4
Skill: Factual

58) Which is NOT a true statement about bones?

    A) Bones are preformed as cartilage in the embryo.

    B) Compact bone tissue forms the surface of bones.

    C) Once they have attained full size, bones do not change their structure.

    D) Bone marrow makes blood cells.

    E) The outer layer of bone is more dense than the inner layer.

Answer: C
Diff: 2   Page Ref: 39.4
Skill: Conceptual

59) Which of the following would increase bone strength?

A) low dietary calcium

B) exercise

C) action potentials directly stimulating bones

D) osteoclast activity

Answer: B
Diff: 2   Page Ref: 39.4
Skill: Application

60) Which of the following people would you expect to have the greatest bone density?

A) a person who has been chronically bedridden

B) a professional bodybuilder

C) an astronaut who has been in space for an extended period

D) a computer programmer

Answer: B
Diff: 1   Page Ref: 39.4
Skill: Application

61) Callus is

A) formed after a bone breaks.

B) involved in bone formation in the embryo.

C) a thickening of the fibrous structure of a muscle.

D) likely to lead to cancer.

Answer: A
Diff: 2   Page Ref: 39.4
Skill: Factual

62) Osteoporosis is

A) loss of calcium salts from hard bone, which most commonly occurs in post-menopausal women.

B) painful swelling of joints.

C) the detachment of a ligament from a bone.

D) none of these

Answer: A
Diff: 1   Page Ref: 39.4
Skill: Factual

63) Why might a minor bone break (such as a small hairline fracture) heal more quickly than a sprain?

   A) Bones have more blood vessels than cartilage, thus can heal more quickly.

   B) The presence of calcium speeds up the healing process in bone.

   C) Cartilage has more blood vessels than bone, thus slows down the healing process.

   D) The presence of chondrocytes slows down the healing process in cartilage.

Answer: A
Diff: 2   Page Ref: 39.4
Skill: Application

64) What advantage does the activity of osteoblasts and osteoclasts impart to vertebrates, even after growth has finished?

   A) It allows additional body size increases in an emergency.

   B) It allows for body size decreases when needed.

   C) It allows for bone lengthening & shortening as needed.

   D) It allows bone to get stronger as physical demands are placed on it, and provides a source of calcium when dietary sources are low.

Answer: D
Diff: 2   Page Ref: 39.4
Skill: Application

65) If you break your leg, the bone will heal by forming a thickened area around the outside of the bone. Over a period of time this thickened area will

   A) be eaten away by osteoclasts.

   B) become a permanent part of the bone.

   C) be digested by enzymes secreted by the muscles.

   D) form osteocytes.

   E) move to the skin surface and be shed as dead skin.

Answer: A
Diff: 2   Page Ref: 39.4
Skill: Factual

66) If you were to remove the calcium salt portion of a bone (such as by immersing it in vinegar for an extended period), what would happen to its structural integrity?

    A) It would become more rigid & inflexible.

    B) It would become extremely flexible.

    C) The bone would disintegrate.

    D) Nothing would happen.

Answer: B
Diff: 2   *Page Ref: 39.4*
Skill: Application

67) What would you expect to happen to an astronaut who went into space for 2 months?

    A) Bone density would increase and muscle mass would decrease.

    B) Bone density would increase and muscle mass would increase.

    C) Bone density would decrease and muscle mass would increase.

    D) Bone density would decrease and muscle mass would decrease.

Answer: D
Diff: 2   *Page Ref: 39.4*
Skill: Application

68) Blood vessels penetrate cartilage. True or False?

Answer: FALSE
Diff: 2   *Page Ref: 39.4*
Skill: Factual

69) During embryonic development the initial skeleton is made of cartilage. True or False?

Answer: TRUE
Diff: 2   *Page Ref: 39.3*
Skill: Factual

70) What type of cell is found in cartilage?

Answer: chondrocytes
Diff: 2   *Page Ref: 39.4*
Skill: Factual

71) The vertebrate skeleton is made up of _____ and _____.

Answer: bone; cartilage
Diff: 1   *Page Ref: 39.4*
Skill: Factual

72) Predict what would happen to the bones of a left-handed professional baseball player.

Answer: The bones associated with the left arm (and left handed activities) would grow thicker.
Diff: 2   Page Ref: 39.4
Skill: Application

73) Describe the way the three types of bone cells work together to remodel bone.

Answer: Osteoclasts tunnel through bone, osteoblasts secrete matrix, osteocytes live in the resulting Haversian systems.
Diff: 3   Page Ref: 39.4
Skill: Conceptual

74) Describe the process by which a bone heals.

Answer: Should include: Clot formation, osteoclasts eat away damaged material, osteoblasts form a callus, remodeling occurs, osteoclasts remove excess bone.
Diff: 3   Page Ref: 39.4
Skill: Factual

75) The muscles of your lower leg are arranged in antagonistic pairs so that you

A) can both flex and extend your leg.

B) can pull with one muscle while pushing with the other.

C) have a backup when one muscle is not strong enough.

D) have a backup if one muscle is damaged.

E) get a stronger contraction.

Answer: A
Diff: 2   Page Ref: 39.5
Skill: Conceptual

76) The end of a skeletal muscle attached to the movable bone on one side of a joint is known as the

A) flexor.   B) extensor.   C) origin.   D) insertion.

Answer: D
Diff: 2   Page Ref: 39.5
Skill: Factual

77) It feels like you broke your ankle, but the doctor says you tore a ligament instead. What did you tear?

   A) the connective tissue that attaches muscle to bone

   B) the connective tissue that joins two bones

   C) the bags of fluid that smooth the movement of a joint

   D) the cartilage which lines the end of a bone

   E) the insertion of a muscle

Answer: B
Diff: 2   Page Ref: 39.5
Skill: Conceptual

78) A joint which is movable in only two dimensions is known as a(n) _____ joint.

   A) ball-and-socket

   B) suture

   C) motor

   D) insertion

   E) hinge

Answer: E
Diff: 1   Page Ref: 39.5
Skill: Factual

79) What attaches bones to one another at a joint?

   A) tendons

   B) ligaments

   C) periosteum

   D) cartilage

   E) bursa

Answer: B
Diff: 1   Page Ref: 39.5
Skill: Factual

80) Which is a ball–and–socket joint?

   A) lower jaw with skull

   B) skull with first vertebra

   C) elbow

   D) shoulder

   E) knee

Answer: D
Diff: 2   Page Ref: 39.5
Skill: Conceptual

81) In a hinge joint

   A) a flexor muscle moves the insertion toward the origin.

   B) an extensor muscle moves the origin toward the insertion.

   C) motion is accomplished when flexor and extensor muscles both contract.

   D) movement in three dimensions is possible.

   E) flexor and the extensor must expand at the same time.

Answer: A
Diff: 3   Page Ref: 39.5
Skill: Factual

82) If a person were "hamstrung" (have the hamstring muscles at the back of their upper leg cut), what would this person be unable to do?

   A) move their leg toward the side of their body

   B) extend their lower leg

   C) move their leg toward the midline of their body

   D) flex their lower leg

Answer: D
Diff: 2   Page Ref: 39.5
Skill: Application

83) What might be a major disadvantage of having a ball–and–socket joint, rather than a hinge joint, in the human knee?

   A) decreased strength   B) decreased joint stability

   C) decreased joint flexibility   D) all of the above

Answer: B
Diff: 3   Page Ref: 39.5
Skill: Application

84) How does a muscle return to its extended condition after contracting?

Answer: It has to be pulled back to the extended position by another muscle that is antagonistic to it.
Diff: 3   Page Ref: 39.5
Skill: Conceptual

85) If you get tendonitis from playing tennis, what part of your body is inflamed?

Answer: the connective tissue that attaches muscles to bone
Diff: 2   Page Ref: 39.5
Skill: Factual

86) Many people are hoping that they will one day be able to travel into space like astronauts. What kind of warnings would you give those interested in these "space vacations" regarding the danger to their bones and muscles?

Answer: Under weightless conditions, these travelers will lose bone and muscle mass because there is no pull of gravity to strengthen the bones and muscles. To maintain bone and muscle mass, they will have to do special exercises each day. If they do not, bones and muscles will atrophy, which could also have other negative side effects on their body physiology.
Diff: 2   Page Ref: Case Study
Skill: Application

Chapter 40 Animal Reproduction

1) Forms of asexual reproduction include

    A) budding.

    B) regeneration.

    C) fission.

    D) parthenogenesis.

    E) all of the above

Answer: E
Diff: 1   Page Ref: 40.1
Skill: Factual

2) How would you define parthenogenesis?

    A) creating new organisms from body parts which have been pinched off the parent

    B) combining genetic material from two parents to produce offspring with a new genotype

    C) eggs from a female developing into offspring without being fertilized

    D) gametes from the male develop into new offspring without combining with an egg

Answer: C
Diff: 2   Page Ref: 40.1
Skill: Conceptual

3) Brittle stars can multiply by regrowing a whole individual from a severed leg. This is an example of

    A) sexual reproduction.   B) regeneration.

    C) parthenogenesis.   D) hermaphrodism.

Answer: B
Diff: 2   Page Ref: 40.1
Skill: Conceptual

4) All male honeybees develop from unfertilized eggs. This is an example of

    A) sexual reproduction.   B) external fertilization.

    C) parthenogenesis.   D) hermaphrodism.

Answer: C
Diff: 1   Page Ref: 40.1
Skill: Factual

5) Some species of reptiles have the ability to produce young without fertilization by a male. This is an example of

    A) sexual reproduction.   B) external fertilization.

    C) parthenogenesis.   D) spawning.

Answer: C
Diff: 1   Page Ref: 40.1
Skill: Factual

6) The asexual process by which some species produce a small offspring by pinching off sections of the adult body is known as

    A) fission.

    B) parthenogenesis.

    C) mitosis.

    D) regeneration.

    E) budding.

Answer: E
Diff: 1   Page Ref: 40.1
Skill: Factual

7) The production of offspring from unfertilized eggs is called

    A) fission.

    B) parthenogenesis.

    C) mitosis.

    D) regeneration.

    E) budding.

Answer: B
Diff: 1   Page Ref: 40.1
Skill: Factual

8) An animal that is hermaphroditic, such as an Earthworm,

    A) reproduces by unfertilized eggs.   B) reproduces by regeneration.

    C) produces both eggs and sperm.   D) spawns.

Answer: C
Diff: 1   Page Ref: 40.1
Skill: Factual

9) Clam fishermen used to cut up sea stars (a predator of clams) and throw the parts back into the ocean, in order to protect the clam beds that they fished. Why, in hindsight, was this not such a good idea?

   A) Sea stars do not eat clams.

   B) This allows the sea stars to reproduce parthenogenically.

   C) Sea stars have the ability to regenerate new individuals from body parts.

   D) This allows sea stars to spawn more easily.

Answer: C
Diff: 2   Page Ref: 40.1
Skill: Application

10) Assume you had a male and female lizard of the same species in captivity. You witnessed them copulating and the female laying eggs, but the young that emerged were all genetically identical to the mother. What method of reproduction occurred here?

   A) fission   B) parthenogenesis

   C) budding   D) sexual reproduction

Answer: B
Diff: 2   Page Ref: 40.1
Skill: Conceptual

11) Production of new phenotypes occurs with

   A) sexual reproduction.   B) regeneration.

   C) parthenogenesis.   D) budding.

Answer: A
Diff: 2   Page Ref: 40.1
Skill: Conceptual

12) The most important function of sexual reproduction is

   A) preserving genetic purity.   B) keeping the genes from changing.

   C) creation of genetic variability.   D) limiting genetic recombination.

Answer: A
Diff: 2   Page Ref: 40.1
Skill: Conceptual

13) How do male gametes differ from female gametes?

  A) Male gametes are small and motile; female gametes are large and nonmotile.

  B) Male gametes are diploid; female gametes are haploid.

  C) Male gametes produce pheromones; female gametes do not.

  D) all of the above

Answer: A
Diff: 2   Page Ref: 40.1
Skill: Factual

14) Salmon reproduce by the females laying eggs in a "nest" scraped into the river bottom, and, shortly after, the males coming by and releasing sperm near the nests. This is an example of

  A) spawning.   B) parthenogenesis.

  C) copulation.   D) hermaphridism.

Answer: A
Diff: 1   Page Ref: 40.1
Skill: Factual

15) One example of external fertilization is

  A) spawning.   B) parthenogenesis.

  C) copulation.   D) fission.

Answer: A
Diff: 1   Page Ref: 40.1
Skill: Factual

16) Courtship rituals in fish are designed to

  A) bring males and females of the species together.

  B) ensure sperm fertilize eggs.

  C) ensure genetic variability in the species.

  D) all of the above

Answer: D
Diff: 2   Page Ref: 40.1
Skill: Application

17) Chemical signals released into the environment are known as

  A) hormones.   B) pheromones.   C) telemones.   D) apomones.

Answer: B
Diff: 1   Page Ref: 40.1
Skill: Factual

18) How would you define a pheromone?

   A) A biochemical signal released from one organism which affect another organism.

   B) Gametes released into the environment for fertilization.

   C) A light or temperature signal that triggers reproduction.

   D) An hermaphroditic organism capable of self-fertilization when a mate is not present.

Answer: A
Diff: 2   Page Ref: 40.1
Skill: Conceptual

19) Animals that have internal fertilization without copulation often package their sperm in
   _____, which are inserted into the female.

   A) spermatozoa

   B) spermatagonia

   C) spermatids

   D) spermatocytes

   E) spermatophores

Answer: E
Diff: 2   Page Ref: 40.1
Skill: Factual

20) Synthetic deer pheromones are sometimes used by hunters to improve their ability to hunt
   male deer. Why might this be effective?

   A) It would mask the scent of the hunter.

   B) It would attract male deer to the position of the hunter.

   C) The odor soothes the nerves of the hunter, making him/her a better shot.

   D) all of the above

Answer: B
Diff: 2   Page Ref: 40.1
Skill: Application

21) What might be some effective ways that animals coordinate the timing of mating activities?

   A) changes in the amount of daylight   B) lunar cycles

   C) environmental temperature shifts   D) all of the above

Answer: D
Diff: 2   Page Ref: 40.1
Skill: Application

22) How can parthenogenetically produced offspring be diploid?

Answer: The chromosomes are replicated either before or after meiosis.
Diff: 3   Page Ref: 40.1
Skill: Conceptual

23) Why must organisms which spawn release huge numbers of eggs and sperm?

Answer: Spawn depends on releasing eggs and sperm into the environment and hoping they
meet. The odds are not in favor of this meeting and so large numbers of eggs and
sperm are produced to increase the likelihood that some will meet.
Diff: 1   Page Ref: 40.1
Skill: Conceptual

24) In order to ensure successful reproduction, males and females of spawning species must
synchronize their gamete release both _____ and _____.

Answer: temporally; spatially (or in time and space)
Diff: 2   Page Ref: 40.1
Skill: Factual

25) Explain the advantage animals that reproduce asexually have over those which reproduce
sexually.

Answer: Animals that reproduce asexually do not require a mate and so can reproduce rapidly.
Diff: 2   Page Ref: 40.1
Skill: Factual

26) Discuss the advantages of sexual vs. asexual reproduction.

Answer: should include increased variability in population for sexual and ease and efficiency for
asexual
Diff: 3   Page Ref: 40.1
Skill: Conceptual

27) What are pheromones and what role do they play in spawning?

Answer: Chemicals released from the body of an animal that affects the behavior of another
animal. Many spawning animals use pheromones to signal sexual readiness.
Diff: 2   Page Ref: 40.1
Skill: Factual

28) It is documented that women who live in close proximity (for example, college roommates)
often have synchronized menstrual cycles. This is called the McClintock effect. What could
explain this?

Answer: It has been theorized that humans also produce small amounts of pheromones which
would synchronize the cycles of women in close proximity.
Diff: 3   Page Ref: 40.1
Skill: Application

29) The hypthalomic hormone that is primarily responsible for the onset of puberty is

   A) gonadotrophin releasing hormone (GnRH).

   B) human chorionic hormone (HCG).

   C) luteinizing hormone (LH).

   D) progesterone.

Answer: A
Diff: 2   Page Ref: 40.2
Skill: Factual

30) If a child developed an anterior pituitary tumor that reduced LH and FSH production, what problems might this cause?

   A) The child would not develop gonads.

   B) Puberty would be delayed or disrupted.

   C) The child would produce excess testosterone or estrogen.

   D) All of the above would occur.

Answer: B
Diff: 3   Page Ref: 40.2
Skill: Application

31) The development of secondary sexual characteristics is due to

   A) decreased levels of GnRH.

   B) increased levels of estrogen or testosterone.

   C) decreased LH levels.

   D) all of the above

Answer: B
Diff: 2   Page Ref: 40.2
Skill: Factual

32) In men, as testosterone increases, LH

   A) decreases.

   B) increases.

   C) remains the same.

   D) moves up or down depending on the point in the cycle.

Answer: A
Diff: 2   Page Ref: 40.2
Skill: Factual

33) Under the influence of FSH, a primary oocyte will next become a _____?

    A) corpus luteum   B) primary spermatocyte

    C) secondary oocyte   D) Sertoli cell

Answer: D
Diff: 2   Page Ref: 40.2
Skill: Factual

34) The only flagellated cells in the human body are

    A) primary spermatocytes.

    B) primary oocytes.

    C) sperm.

    D) mature ova.

    E) all of the above

Answer: C
Diff: 2   Page Ref: 40.2
Skill: Factual

35) Which is a haploid cell?

    A) spermatogonium   B) sertoli cell

    C) primary spermatocytes   D) secondary spermatocytes

Answer: D
Diff: 2   Page Ref: 40.2
Skill: Factual

36) Gonadotropin releasing hormone (GnRH)

    A) is secreted when there is a high level of progesterone in the blood.

    B) is made by the ovary.

    C) stimulates the release of FSH and LH.

    D) is a pituitary hormone.

Answer: C
Diff: 2   Page Ref: 40.2
Skill: Factual

37) What is the function of Sertoli cells?

    A) regulate sperm production

    B) nourish the developing sperm

    C) secreting testosterone

    D) Both A and B are correct.

    E) All of the above are correct.

Answer: D
Diff: 2   Page Ref: 40.2
Skill: Factual

38) What is the function of an acrosome?

    A) It holds large amounts of mitochondria.

    B) It contains enzymes used to dissolve the protective layers around the egg.

    C) It propels the sperm through the female reproductive tract.

    D) It contains a haploid nucleus.

Answer: B
Diff: 2   Page Ref: 40.2
Skill: Factual

39) In the male, the primary target of FSH is the

    A) prostate gland.   B) Sertoli cells.

    C) bulbourethral glands.   D) interstitial cells.

Answer: B
Diff: 3   Page Ref: 40.2
Skill: Factual

40) Which hormone stimulates the production of testosterone?

    A) GnRH   B) LH

    C) FSH   D) chorionic gonadotropin

Answer: B
Diff: 3   Page Ref: 40.2
Skill: Factual

41) For human males, a substance that could block the production of FSH, but not LH, would

   A) stop sperm production.

   B) prevent the acquisition of secondary sex characteristics.

   C) produce impotence.

   D) have no effect upon the male reproductive system.

Answer: A
Diff: 3   Page Ref: 40.2
Skill: Application

42) Sperm are stored in the

   A) epididymis.   B) seminal vesicles.

   C) prostate gland.   D) urethra.

Answer: A
Diff: 1   Page Ref: 40.2
Skill: Factual

43) The acrosome of a sperm cell contains enzymes. The function of the acrosome is to

   A) digest the jelly-like vitelline coat surrounding the unfertilized egg.

   B) dissolve the mucus in the female reproductive tract.

   C) lower the activation energy of fertilization.

   D) all of the above

Answer: A
Diff: 2   Page Ref: 40.2
Skill: Factual

44) In spermatogenesis _____ spermatids are produced from each primary spermatocyte by
_____.

   A) 2; mitosis

   B) 2; meiosis

   C) 4; mitosis

   D) 4; meiosis

   E) 8; meiosis followed by mitosis

Answer: D
Diff: 3   Page Ref: 40.2
Skill: Factual

45) A male could be rendered infertile, but not impotent, by

   A) suppressing FSH but not LH.

   B) suppressing both FSH and LH.

   C) suppressing LH but not FSH.

   D) removal of the prostate gland.

   E) suppressing testosterone.

Answer: A
Diff: 3   Page Ref: 40.2
Skill: Application

46) The epididymis connects

   A) seminiferous tubules and urethra.

   B) vas deferens and urethra.

   C) testis and vas deferens.

   D) vas deferens and seminal vesicles.

   E) prostate and urethra.

Answer: C
Diff: 2   Page Ref: 40.2
Skill: Factual

47) During ejaculation, approximately _____ sperm are released.

   A) 30 – 40 thousand

   B) 300 – 400 thousand

   C) 3 – 4 million

   D) 300 – 400 million

   E) 3 – 4 billion

Answer: D
Diff: 1   Page Ref: 40.2
Skill: Factual

48) Erection of the penis occurs by

   A) striated muscle contracting.   B) smooth muscle contracting.

   C) increased blood flow into it.   D) none of the above

Answer: C
Diff: 1   Page Ref: 40.2
Skill: Factual

49) Which of the following represents the correct path which sperm travel on their way out of the male?

A) epididymis → urethra → vas deferens → seminiferous tubules

B) seminiferous tubules → vas deferens → urethra → epididymis

C) epididymis → seminiferous tubules → vas deferens → urethra

D) urethra → vas deferens → seminiferous tubules → epididymis

E) seminiferous tubules → epididymis → vas deferens → urethra

Answer: E
Diff: 2   Page Ref: 40.2
Skill: Factual

50) What would happen to male hormone levels if his hypothalamus were to continually produce GnRH?

A) LH and FSH levels would be high.

B) Testosterone levels would be high.

C) LH and FSH levels would be low.

D) Testosterone levels would be low.

E) LH, FSH, and testosterone levels would be high.

Answer: E
Diff: 3   Page Ref: 40.2
Skill: Conceptual

51) If the prostate gland failed to add its contribution to semen,

A) lack of fructose would starve the sperm.

B) lack an enzyme prevents the semen from liquefying.

C) lacks lubricating mucus.

D) the sperm will be killed by the acidic vaginal secretions.

Answer: B
Diff: 2   Page Ref: 40.2
Skill: Conceptual

52) If the seminal vesicles failed to add their contribution to semen,

A) lack of fructose would starve the sperm.

B) lack an enzyme prevents the semen from liquefying.

C) lacks lubricating mucus.

D) the vaginal mucus immobilizes the sperm.

Answer: A
Diff: 2   Page Ref: 40.2
Skill: Conceptual

53) Which of the following represents the correct path which sperm travel on their way to fertilize an egg?

    A) cervix → uterine tube → vagina → uterus

    B) uterus→ uterine tube → cervix → vagina

    C) vagina → cervix → uterus → uterine tube

    D) uterine tube → vagina → uterus → cervix

Answer: C
Diff: 2   Page Ref: 40.2
Skill: Factual

54) The corpus luteum produces

    A) estrogen.

    B) progesterone.

    C) luteinizing hormone.

    D) both A and B

    E) all of the above

Answer: D
Diff: 2   Page Ref: 40.2
Skill: Factual

55) The egg that is released from the ovary during ovulation is known as a(n)

    A) zygote.   B) secondary oocyte.

    C) primary oocyte.   D) polar body.

Answer: B
Diff: 2   Page Ref: 40.2
Skill: Factual

56) In the standard menstrual cycle, Day 1 is the day

    A) menstruation begins.   B) ovulation occurs.

    C) the corpus luteum disintegrates.   D) LH levels surge.

Answer: A
Diff: 2   Page Ref: 40.2
Skill: Conceptual

57) In the standard menstrual cycle, Day 14 is the day

    A) menstruation begins.   B) ovulation occurs.

    C) the corpus luteum disintegrates.   D) progesterone levels peak.

Answer: B
Diff: 2   Page Ref: 40.2
Skill: Conceptual

58) In the standard menstrual cycle, Day 26 is the day

    A) menstruation begins.
              B) ovulation occurs.

    C) the corpus luteum disintegrates.
     D) LH levels surge.

Answer: A
Diff: 2   *Page Ref: 40.2*
Skill: Conceptual

59) During menstruation, which layer of the uterus is sloughed off?

    A) the myometrium
              B) the endometrium

    C) the exometrium
              D) the metametrium

Answer: B
Diff: 1   *Page Ref: 40.2*
Skill: Factual

60) Thickening of the endometrium is due to

    A) decreased levels of GnRH.
         B) increased levels of estrogen.

    C) increased levels of FSH.
           D) all of the above

Answer: B
Diff: 2   *Page Ref: 40.2*
Skill: Factual

61) Which hormone(s) result in follicular growth?

    A) estrogen and follicle stimulating hormone

    B) follicle stimulating hormone and luteinizing hormone

    C) estrogen and luteinizing hormone

    D) estrogen, follicle stimulating hormone and luteinizing hormone

    E) only follicle stimulating hormone

Answer: D
Diff: 3   *Page Ref: 40.2*
Skill: Factual

62) Ovulation occurs due to a surge in

    A) LH concentrations.

    B) FSH concentrations.

    C) estrogen concentrations.

    D) estrogen and LH concentrations.

    E) estrogen and FSH concentrations.

Answer: A
Diff: 2   *Page Ref: 40.2*
Skill: Factual

63) Which hormone(s) work together to decrease the levels of LH and FSH in women?

    A) estrogen and progesterone

    B) testosterone

    C) GnRH

    D) estrogen alone

    E) all of the above

Answer: A
Diff: 2   Page Ref: 40.2
Skill: Factual

64) Prior to ovulation, estrogen secretion causes

    A) increased secretion of GnRH.   B) decreased levels of GnRH.

    C) no changes in GnRH levels.   D) none of the above

Answer: A
Diff: 2   Page Ref: 40.2
Skill: Conceptual

65) After to ovulation, estrogen and progesterone secretion causes

    A) increased secretion of GnRH.   B) decreased levels of GnRH.

    C) no changes in GnRH levels.   D) none of the above

Answer: B
Diff: 2   Page Ref: 40.2
Skill: Conceptual

66) Which hormone(s) prevent the breakdown of the corpus luteum?

    A) FSH

    B) LH

    C) chorionic gonadotropin

    D) both A and B

    E) both B and C

Answer: E
Diff: 2   Page Ref: 40.2
Skill: Factual

67) In which respect do spermatogenesis and oogenesis differ?

    A) number of gametes produced   B) number of meiotic divisions

    C) number of chromosomes in gametes   D) occur in the gonads

Answer: A
Diff: 2   Page Ref: 40.2
Skill: Conceptual

68) A polar body

    A) is a discarded set of chromosomes.

    B) can be fertilized by a sperm.

    C) is formed at the same time as a primary oocyte.

    D) is a structure found at one pole of a mature egg.

    E) nourishes the egg until it is fertilized.

Answer: A
Diff: 1   Page Ref: 40.2
Skill: Conceptual

69) In which structure would a corpus luteum be located?

    A) ovary   B) testis   C) penis   D) uterus   E) vagina

Answer: A
Diff: 1   Page Ref: 40.2
Skill: Factual

70) The hormone most directly responsible for ovulation is

    A) LH.

    B) FSH.

    C) GnRH.

    D) progesterone.

    E) chorionic gonadotropin.

Answer: A
Diff: 2   Page Ref: 40.2
Skill: Factual

71) Menstruation occurs due to a decrease in

    A) endometrial thickness.

    B) estrogen and progesterone.

    C) the number of follicles.

    D) FSH and LH.

    E) the number of sperm present.

Answer: B
Diff: 2   Page Ref: 40.2
Skill: Conceptual

72) Ovulation occurs at about the _____ day of the menstrual cycle.

    A) first

    B) seventh

    C) fourteenth

    D) twenty-first

    E) twenty-eighth

Answer: C
Diff: 2   *Page Ref: 40.2*
Skill: Factual

73) A pregnancy test is based on the detection of _____ in the urine of the woman.

    A) chorionic gonadotropin

    B) gonadotropin releasing hormone

    C) progesterone

    D) luteinizing hormone

    E) follicle stimulating hormone

Answer: A
Diff: 2   *Page Ref: 40.2*
Skill: Factual

74) In humans, fertilization normally occurs in the

    A) fimbriae.   B) uterus.   C) oviduct.   D) vagina.   E) ovary.

Answer: C
Diff: 1   *Page Ref: 40.2*
Skill: Factual

75) Theoretically speaking, what would you predict would happen to a woman who did not produce a corpus luteum after ovulation?

    A) She would menstruate earlier.

    B) Sperm could not pass through the oviduct.

    C) The egg could not be fertilized.

    D) A fertilized egg could not implant in the uterus.

Answer: A
Diff: 3   *Page Ref: 40.2*
Skill: Application

76) Some animals, such as rabbits, ovulate immediately upon copulation. Hormonally speaking, how might these animals control such an event?

A) immediate production of a LH surge during copulation

B) immediate production of a FSH surge during copulation

C) immediate production of an estrogen surge during copulation

D) immediate production of a progesterone surge during copulation

Answer: A
Diff: 2   Page Ref: 40.2
Skill: Application

77) As a human, all of the mitochondria in your cells came from your mother. This is because

A) sperm contain no mitochondria.

B) mitochondria cross the placenta.

C) only the nucleus of the sperm enters the egg cell.

D) none of the above

Answer: C
Diff: 2   Page Ref: 40.2
Skill: Conceptual

78) Fertilization of an egg by a sperm initiates the second meiotic division and results in

A) reinforcement of the zona pellucida around the egg to prevent additional sperm from entering.

B) secretion of hormones by the egg that inactivate sperm.

C) release of hormones by the egg that cause uterine contractions.

D) all of these

Answer: A
Diff: 2   Page Ref: 40.2
Skill: Factual

79) Sperm live approximately

A) three hours.

B) one or two days.

C) one week.

D) two weeks.

E) one month.

Answer: B
Diff: 2   Page Ref: 40.2
Skill: Factual

80) Why is it necessary for a number of sperm to be present in order for one to fertilize the egg?

   A) A sperm cannot find the egg by itself.

   B) So that the combined enzymes can digest a path through the corona radiata and zone pellucida.

   C) The combined motion of their flagella enables one sperm to push into the egg.

   D) A mass of sperm is necessary to open the oviduct.

   E) The area is so large that only one sperm can find the egg.

Answer: B
Diff: 2   Page Ref: 40.2
Skill: Conceptual

81) Why do FSH levels drop after ovulation?

Answer: After ovulation the corpus luteum begins producing progesterone which causes a negative feedback mechanism, shutting down FSH secretion.
Diff: 3   Page Ref: 40.2
Skill: Application

82) Ovulation test kits measure the level of LH. Why will this help to predict when ovulation will occur?

Answer: LH surges just prior to ovulation. Knowing then the level peaks will give will give the approximate timing of ovulation.
Diff: 3   Page Ref: 40.2
Skill: Application

83) What role does the corpus luteum play in maintaining the endometrium?

Answer: The corpus luteum secretes estrogen and progesterone. These two hormones are necessary to maintain the endometrium. When levels of estrogen and progesterone drop, menstruation occurs.
Diff: 3   Page Ref: 40.2
Skill: Application

84) What are the three glands that contribute fluid to semen?

Answer: seminal vesicles, prostate, bulbourethral
Diff: 2   Page Ref: 40.2
Skill: Factual

85) Describe or draw a sperm and explain how each part is essential to its function.

Answer: Head—contains haploid nucleus and acrosome which digests an opening into the egg. Midpiece— contains mitochondria to supply energy for swimming. Tail—flagellum enables it to swim.
Diff: 2   Page Ref: 40.2
Skill: Factual

86) Is it possible for a man to be sterile and still produce semen? Explain.

   Answer: Yes, the presence of sperm does not define semen. Semen can continue to be produced from the prostate, the seminal vesicles, and the bulbourethral glands without any sperm being present.
   Diff: 2   *Page Ref: 40.2*
   Skill: Conceptual

87) Why are the secretions of the seminal vesicles, prostate, bulbourethral glands necessary for successful reproduction?

   Answer: They activate swimming by the sperm, provide energy to the sperm, and neutralize the acids of the vagina.
   Diff: 2   *Page Ref: 40.2*
   Skill: Factual

88) Describe oogenesis and indicate how this process forms gametes in humans. Indicate when each event occurs in the life cycle.

   Answer: Oogenesis—fetal oogonia divide mitotically into primary oocytes before birth. Primary oocytes start meiosis I, but stop at prophase I. Meiosis I completes during the menstrual cycle, forming a secondary oocyte (egg) that will only complete meiosis II (producing a haploid gamete) when a sperm penetrates the egg.
   Diff: 3   *Page Ref: 40.2*
   Skill: Conceptual

89) What are the two layers of the wall of the uterus and what is the function of each?

   Answer: Endometrium—Nourish and protect the egg and developing embryo and form the mother's side of the placenta. Myometrium—expel the baby during childbirth.
   Diff: 2   *Page Ref: 40.2*
   Skill: Factual

90) What layers must a sperm penetrate in order to fertilize the egg?

   Answer: the corona radiata and the zona pellucida
   Diff: 2   *Page Ref: 40.2*
   Skill: Factual

91) Vasectomy and tubal ligation result in

   A) a lack of semen or menstrual flow.

   B) atrophy of the gonads.

   C) decreased levels of hormones.

   D) an interruption of the path taken by egg or sperm.

   E) inability to produce eggs or sperm.

   Answer: D
   Diff: 1   *Page Ref: 40.3*
   Skill: Factual

92) If each of the vas deferens of a male human were cut, his semen would not contain

A) acid–neutralizing fluid.   B) sperm.

C) fructose.   D) mucus.

Answer: B
Diff: 2   Page Ref: 40.3
Skill: Application

93) Contraceptive methods that rely on synthetic hormones

A) prevent the implantation of a fertilized egg in the uterus.

B) prevent ovulation.

C) prevent the sperm and egg from meeting.

D) both A and B

E) All of the above are true.

Answer: B
Diff: 2   Page Ref: 40.3
Skill: Factual

94) Other than sterilization, what is the most effective method of contraception?

A) a condom

B) the pill

C) a diaphragm

D) an IUD

E) contraceptive sponge

Answer: B
Diff: 2   Page Ref: 40.3
Skill: Factual

95) Which of these is essentially NOT effective at preventing pregnancy?

A) douching

B) rhythm method

C) spermicide

D) condom

E) diaphragm

Answer: A
Diff: 2   Page Ref: 40.3
Skill: Factual

96) If taken within 72 hours of unprotect intercourse, Plan B or the "morning after" pill should

   A) prevent ovulation.

   B) disrupting formation of the corpus luteum.

   C) preventing implantation.

   D) all of the above

Answer: A
Diff: 2   Page Ref: 40.3
Skill: Factual

97) If a doctor recommends use of a diaphragm to prevent pregnancy, what precautions should she always recommend?

   Answer: Use every time, use with a spermicide, inspect for holes, insert shortly before intercourse, leave in place for at least six hours
   Diff: 2   Page Ref: 40.3
   Skill: Factual

98) How do barrier methods prevent conception?

   Answer: Barriers prevent the egg and sperm from meeting so fertilization cannot occur.
   Diff: 2   Page Ref: 40.3
   Skill: Conceptual

99) How do hormonal methods prevent conception?

   Answer: By disrupting the normal hormonal cycle, ovulation should not occur.
   Diff: 2   Page Ref: 40.3
   Skill: Conceptual

100) Sexually transmitted diseases caused by viruses include herpes, AIDS and

   A) syphilis.   B) gonorrhea.

   C) trichomoniasis.   D) genital warts.

Answer: D
Diff: 2   Page Ref: Health Watch
Skill: Factual

101) Gonorrhea can cause

   A) infertility in females.   B) painful urination in males.

   C) infant blindness.   D) all of these

Answer: D
Diff: 2   Page Ref: Health Watch
Skill: Factual

102) Oozing painful lesions which reoccur are characteristic of

  A) HIV.

  B) genital herpes.

  C) chlamydia.

  D) syphilis.

  E) HPV.

Answer: B
Diff: 2   Page Ref: Health Watch
Skill: Factual

103) A bacterial infection which can produce scarring of the uterine tubes is

  A) HIV.

  B) genital herpes.

  C) chlamydia.

  D) Trichomonas.

  E) HPV.

Answer: C
Diff: 2   Page Ref: Health Watch
Skill: Factual

104) Many STDs cause infertility. How?

  Answer: Many STDs cause infertility by producing scar tissue in the vas deferens and uterine tubes.
Diff: 2   Page Ref: Health Watch
Skill: Application

105) Why are STDs so easily spread?

  Answer: Many STDs are asymptomatic and can be transmitted between unsuspecting partners.
Diff: 2   Page Ref: Health Watch
Skill: Application

Chapter 41   Animal Development

1) The metamorphosis of a caterpillar into a butterfly is an example of

A) direct development.   B) placental development.

C) indirect development.   D) internal development.

Answer: C
Diff: 2   Page Ref: 41.1
Skill: Factual

2) A fertilized oyster egg develops into a free-swimming larval stage called a veliger. The veliger later anchors to a substrate and grows a shell. This is an example of

A) direct development.   B) placental development.

C) indirect development.   D) internal development.

Answer: C
Diff: 2   Page Ref: 41.1
Skill: Conceptual

3) Birds hatch out of their eggs looking like small versions of the adult. Birds display

A) direct development.   B) genetic dwarfism.

C) indirect development.   D) internal development.

Answer: A
Diff: 2   Page Ref: 41.1
Skill: Conceptual

4) The main advantage of indirect development, such as occurs in insects, is

A) that the offspring are born using the same habitat as the parents so they are well adapted.

B) that every individual the animal encounters is a potential mate.

C) that the eggs can survive because they contain a large yolk.

D) that the embryos receive nourishment from their mother's body as they develop.

E) the ability to make large numbers of offspring that can feed themselves very quickly.

Answer: E
Diff: 1   Page Ref: 41.1
Skill: Conceptual

5) Yolk is mostly lipid. Its primary function during development is

    A) to provide phospholipids for membranes.

    B) to control gene expression.

    C) to form a placenta.

    D) to provide energy.

Answer: D
Diff: 1   Page Ref: 41.1
Skill: Factual

6) Which statement is TRUE of direct development?

    A) More eggs are produced than in an organism with indirect development.

    B) The young resembles the adult.

    C) Metamorphosis occurs.

    D) Yolks are always large.

    E) Free–living larvae are formed.

Answer: B
Diff: 2   Page Ref: 41.1
Skill: Factual

7) Which embryo undergoes direct development?

    A) butterfly   B) lobster   C) frog   D) fly   E) bluebird

Answer: E
Diff: 1   Page Ref: 41.1
Skill: Factual

8) Which extra–embryonic membrane lies immediately beneath the shell of a reptile embryo?

    A) allantois   B) amnion   C) chorion   D) yolk sac   E) placenta

Answer: C
Diff: 2   Page Ref: 41.1
Skill: Factual

9) In a reptile egg, which membrane is analogous to a lung?

    A) allantois   B) amnion   C) chorion   D) yolk sac

Answer: C
Diff: 2   Page Ref: 41.1
Skill: Conceptual

10) The allantois in a chicken egg is analogous to the mammalian

A) vessels of the umbilical cord.

B) fetal component of the placenta.

C) bone marrow, forming blood vessels.

D) digestive system.

Answer: A
Diff: 3   Page Ref: 41.1
Skill: Conceptual

11) In placental organisms, the layer which forms the placenta is the

A) allantois.   B) amnion.   C) chorion.   D) yolk sac.

Answer: C
Diff: 2   Page Ref: 41.1
Skill: Conceptual

12) In a bird egg, which membrane provides the watery environment in which the embryo develops?

A) allantois   B) amnion   C) chorion   D) yolk sac

Answer: B
Diff: 2   Page Ref: 41.1
Skill: Factual

13) In a placental organism, which membrane provides the watery environment in which the embryo develops?

A) allantois   B) amnion   C) chorion   D) yolk sac

Answer: B
Diff: 2   Page Ref: 41.1
Skill: Factual

14) Defend the statement: The larval form of a mayfly is the "real" insect.

Answer: The adult only lives for a few hours to a few days, cannot feed, and can only reproduce. The larvae live in streams for a year or more, feeding and carrying out all the functions of life except reproduction.
Diff: 3   Page Ref: 41.1
Skill: Conceptual

15) Why can organisms which employ indirect development produce hundreds of offspring, while those who employ direct development produce relatively few.

Answer: Organisms that use direct development provide greater maternal support in terms of both time and nutrients. Organisms that use indirect development provide little if any parental support and very few nutrients. With the small parental investment, organisms which use indirect development and spread their resources across many, many more offspring.
Diff: 3   Page Ref: 41.1
Skill: Conceptual

16) In what ways are juveniles of direct development species like their parents and in what way are they different?

Answer: They look like and have similar nutritional needs as their parents, but they are sexually immature.
Diff: 3   Page Ref: 41.1
Skill: Conceptual

17) How does direct development of an embryo differ from indirect?

Answer: In direct development, the embryo develops to the point of resembling a small adult. With indirect development, the early forms of the organism look unlike the adult form and must go through a metamorphosis to become an adult.
Diff: 2   Page Ref: 41.1
Skill: Factual

18) Butterflies and caterpillars are the same species, yet occupy totally different environmental niches. How is this possible?

Answer: The larval form has a voracious appetite to fuel its rapid growth and development. The adult forms can live on relatively few nutrients, if any, since there is limited growth. This eliminates competition for food between the adult and the larvae.
Diff: 3   Page Ref: 41.1
Skill: Conceptual

19) A solid ball of small cells that develops through the process of cleavage is known as a

A) morula.   B) blastula.   C) blastocoel.   D) morocyte.

Answer: A
Diff: 1   Page Ref: 41.2
Skill: Factual

20) The embryonic stage which consists of a hollow ball of cells is known as a

A) morula.   B) blastula.   C) gastrula.   D) morocyte.

Answer: B
Diff: 1   Page Ref: 41.2
Skill: Factual

21) The embryonic stage in which cell migration and differentiation occurs is known as a

A) morula.   B) blastula.   C) gastrula.   D) morocyte.

Answer: C
Diff: 1   Page Ref: 41.2
Skill: Factual

22) Which is the BEST definition of embryonic cleavage?

   A) alternating periods of cell division and growth

   B) meiotic division resulting in gametes

   C) yolk accumulation

   D) early rapid division of the zygote

   E) organogenesis

Answer: D
Diff: 1   Page Ref: 41.2
Skill: Factual

23) At the blastula stage, the embryo consists of

   A) a mass of cells each the size of the zygote.

   B) three differentiated layers of cells.

   C) a hollow ball of cells.

   D) cells which have different DNA content.

   E) a cluster of cells which are much larger than normal cells.

Answer: C
Diff: 2   Page Ref: 41.2
Skill: Factual

24) During embryonic cell division

   A) meiosis occurs.

   B) cells eliminate the growth phase of the cell cycle.

   C) metamorphosis occurs.

   D) cells lengthen the chromosomes.

Answer: B
Diff: 2   Page Ref: 41.2
Skill: Factual

25) A difference between a morula and a blastula is that the

   A) morula has larger cells.

   B) blastula has a hollow center, the morula doesn't.

   C) blastula has more cells than the morula.

   D) All of the above are differences between morulas and blastulas.

Answer: D
Diff: 2   Page Ref: 41.2
Skill: Conceptual

26) If an animal is missing its outer layer of skin upon birth, which of the following might cause it?

   A) loss of endoderm   B) loss of mesoderm

   C) loss of ectoderm   D) all of the above

   Answer: C
   Diff: 2   Page Ref: 41.2
   Skill: Application

27) The nervous system forms from the

   A) ectoderm.   B) mesoderm.   C) endoderm.   D) exoderm.

   Answer: A
   Diff: 1   Page Ref: 41.2
   Skill: Factual

28) The brain is derived

   A) from mesoderm.

   B) from endoderm.

   C) from ectoderm.

   D) partly from mesoderm and partly from endoderm.

   E) partly from endoderm and partly from ectoderm.

   Answer: C
   Diff: 2   Page Ref: 41.2
   Skill: Factual

29) The cells which line the inside of the blastopore will become the

   A) skin.

   B) muscles.

   C) nervous system.

   D) skeleton.

   E) digestive tract.

   Answer: E
   Diff: 2   Page Ref: 41.2
   Skill: Factual

30) The result of gastrulation is

A) a morula.

B) a blastopore.

C) the formation of organs.

D) a three–layered embryo.

E) the loss of many cells from the blastopore area.

Answer: D
Diff: 2   Page Ref: 41.2
Skill: Conceptual

31) The developmental event that results in the formation of a primitive gut and the three germ tissue layers is called

A) blastulation.   B) primitive streaking.

C) gastrulation.   D) cleavage.

Answer: C
Diff: 2   Page Ref: 41.2
Skill: Factual

32) The germ layer that forms the skin and nervous system is the

A) endoderm.   B) ectoderm.   C) mesoderm.   D) somite.

Answer: B
Diff: 2   Page Ref: 41.2
Skill: Factual

33) Suppose a mutant fish embryo does not form an endoderm, yet the embryo continues development. What might happen to the embryo?

A) The embryo would have no skin.

B) The embryo would have no heart.

C) The embryo would have no nervous system.

D) The embryo would have no stomach.

Answer: D
Diff: 3   Page Ref: 41.2
Skill: Application

34) What hormone triggers metamorphosis in amphibians?

A) thyroid hormone   B) growth hormone

C) gonadotropins   D) cortisol

Answer: A
Diff: 1   Page Ref: 41.2
Skill: Factual

35) Humans are not born with webs between their fingers due to the process of

A) induction.

B) programmed cell death.

C) organogenesis.

D) both A and B

E) both B and C

Answer: B
Diff: 2   Page Ref: 41.2
Skill: Conceptual

36) Sexual maturity in some song birds is induced by changes in

A) environmental temperature.   B) ability to fly.

C) body weight.   D) day length.

Answer: D
Diff: 2   Page Ref: 41.2
Skill: Factual

37) During the early developmental stages from cleavage through formation of the blastula, the individual cells of the embryo become smaller. Why?

Answer: During the early stages, the embryo does not increase in size, so as the number of cells increase, the individual cell size must decrease.
Diff: 3   Page Ref: 41.2
Skill: Conceptual

38) What happens during development that allows the larger than normal fertilized egg cell to form cells which are smaller in size than adult cells?

Answer: The early cleavage divisions of the embryo occur without any growth before the next division so that the cells get smaller and smaller.
Diff: 2   Page Ref: 41.2
Skill: Conceptual

39) If a mutation causes tadpoles to be unable to produce thyroid hormone, what effect will it have on the organism?

Answer: The frog would retain its tail since thyroid hormone is necessary for the development of enzymes which digest the tail away in the adult frog.
Diff: 2   Page Ref: 41.2
Skill: Factual

40) An embryo was exposed to a chemical during early development. At birth, there is chromosomal damage to the skin linked to the chemical exposure. What other organ system should be examined for the same damage?

Answer: the nervous system, since the ectoderm develops into both the skin and the nervous system
Diff: 3   *Page Ref: 41.2*
Skill: Application

41) An embryo was exposed to a chemical during early development. At birth, there is chromosomal damage to the circulatory system linked to the chemical exposure. What other organ systems should be examined for the same damage?

Answer: the muscles and the bones since the mesodermderm develops into all three of these systems
Diff: 3   *Page Ref: 41.2*
Skill: Application

42) Your biceps muscle is derived from which embryonic cell layer?

Answer: mesoderm
Diff: 2   *Page Ref: 41.2*
Skill: Application

43) What is a gastrula?

Answer: an embryo that has developed three cell layers
Diff: 2   *Page Ref: 41.2*
Skill: Factual

44) What occurs during organogenesis?

Answer: the development of the organs from the three cell layers
Diff: 2   *Page Ref: 41.2*
Skill: Factual

45) What kinds of factors affect the onset of sexual maturity?

Answer: The general pattern is set by genetics, but environmental, internal, and social factors help to determine the precise timing.
Diff: 2   *Page Ref: 41.2*
Skill: Conceptual

46) Differentiation is

    A) the process in which different tissues specialize into specific organs.

    B) the process in which different cells develop into different cell types.

    C) the process in which different organs specialize in function.

    D) the process in which the embryo specializes different sexual organs.

Answer: B
Diff: 1   Page Ref: 41.3
Skill: Factual

47) If a cell divides by mitosis so that one cell eventually becomes part of the brain and the other cell becomes part of a salivary gland, the cells have

    A) lost genes.

    B) increased their genetic variability.

    C) diffused.

    D) taken up genes from surrounding cells.

    E) differentiated.

Answer: E
Diff: 1   Page Ref: 41.3
Skill: Conceptual

48) The process by which embryonic stem cells form many specialized cell types is called

    A) fertilization.   B) growth.

    C) differentiation.   D) gastrulation.

Answer: C
Diff: 2   Page Ref: 41.3
Skill: Factual

49) When Gurdon transplanted the nucleus of an intestinal cell from a tadpole into an egg cell whose nucleus had been destroyed, the egg developed into a normal frog. This indicated that

    A) each cell of an organism has all the genes needed for development.

    B) the homeobox genes in a transplanted nucleus underwent mutation.

    C) a nucleus that is removed from its normal location will be influenced by adjoining cells.

    D) scientists can clone a human being by putting one of his/her nuclei into an egg cell.

    E) genes are lost in differentiation.

Answer: A
Diff: 2   Page Ref: 41.3
Skill: Conceptual

50) What makes the cells of a developing embryo differentiate into various types of cells?

    A) They have different genes.

    B) Different genes are activate.

    C) The DNA of their mitochondria is different.

    D) Once certain genes of a cell have caused it to differentiate, the other genes are lost.

    E) There are special genes in the cytoplasm that cause this.

Answer: B
Diff: 2   *Page Ref: 41.3*
Skill: Conceptual

51) The dorsal lip of the blastopore

    A) becomes the neural tube.

    B) becomes the digestive tract.

    C) induces surrounding cells to differentiate.

    D) forms the chorion.

    E) lacks the genes necessary to develop the embryo.

Answer: C
Diff: 2   *Page Ref: 41.3*
Skill: Factual

52) After induction occurs

    A) cells have different genes.

    B) the "fate" of the cell is permanently fixed.

    C) the DNA of their mitochondria is differentiates into new genes.

    D) transcription of all genes stops.

Answer: B
Diff: 2   *Page Ref: 41.3*
Skill: Conceptual

53) Which of the following is TRUE of stem cells?

    A) They are destined to become stem-like organs.

    B) They determine language learning ability.

    C) They can become other, specialized kinds of cells.

    D) They exist only during the early cleavage stages.

Answer: C
Diff: 1   *Page Ref: 41.3*
Skill: Conceptual

54) Which is TRUE of homeobox genes?

A) They block the transcription of genes.

B) They determine the overall shape of the body and location of its parts.

C) They are found only in frogs.

D) Both A and B are correct.

E) All statements are correct.

Answer: B
Diff: 2   Page Ref: 41.3
Skill: Conceptual

55) A transplant of embryonic eye tissue to the back of a developing tadpole will cause a lens to grow on the back of the tadpole. This is an example of

A) metamorphosis.   B) programmed cell death.

C) induction.   D) cleavage.

Answer: C
Diff: 2   Page Ref: 41.3
Skill: Conceptual

56) Induction refers to

A) the pushing in of cells to form the gastrula.

B) the formation of the nervous system.

C) substances from one embryonic cell influencing the development of other cells.

D) the formation of the mesoderm layer in a gastrula.

Answer: C
Diff: 2   Page Ref: 41.3
Skill: Factual

57) Dr. von Frankenstein has removed regulatory proteins from a yak embryo. What might be the results?

A) a normal yak being born

B) no yak born due to lack of cell development in the embryo

C) no yak born due to excessive organogenesis

D) a yak born with its head in its stomach

Answer: B
Diff: 2   Page Ref: 41.3
Skill: Application

58) If an embryo is divided into three during the morula stage, what happens?

    A) The embryos dies.

    B) The embryos develop severe birth defects due to missing genes.

    C) Normal identical triplets will be born.

    D) Three distinctly different embryos will develop depending on which homeoboxes went with which cell group.

Answer: C
Diff: 3   Page Ref: 41.3
Skill: Application

59) If an embryo is divided into three during the gastrula stage, what happens?

    A) Differentiation has progressed too far and the embryos will die.

    B) The embryos develop severe birth defects due to missing genes.

    C) Normal identical triplets will be born.

    D) Three distinctly different embryos will develop depending on which homeoboxes went with which cell group

Answer: C
Diff: 3   Page Ref: 41.3
Skill: Application

60) The process by which an organism proceeds from fertilized egg through adulthood is

_____.

Answer: development
Diff: 1   Page Ref: 41.3
Skill: Factual

61) How does a liver cell in your body differ from the zygote from which you developed and how are they alike?

Answer: They have the same genetic composition, but different genes are transcribed and translated into proteins, forming cells that no longer resemble the zygote.
Diff: 3   Page Ref: 41.3
Skill: Conceptual

62) What are the two sources of chemicals that control gene transcription and lead to differentiation?

Answer: (1) the cytoplasm, (2) other cells
Diff: 2   Page Ref: 41.3
Skill: Factual

63) Recent studies have shown that cells of the dorsal lip of the blastopore contain active _____ genes that code for proteins that are able to _____ the development of other cells.

Answer: homeobox; induce
Diff: 2   Page Ref: 41.3
Skill: Factual

64) How do undifferentiated cells "know" what to become?

Answer: Interactions between neighboring cells, homeoboxes, and induction all affect transcriptions of specific genes within a cell and determine which genes get transcribed and what the cell will become.
Diff: 2   Page Ref: 41.3
Skill: Factual

65) What are the two sources of chemicals that control gene transcription and lead to differentiation?

Answer: (1) the cytoplasm, (2) other cells
Diff: 2   Page Ref: 41.3
Skill: Factual

66) What are the two sources of chemicals that control gene transcription and lead to differentiation?

Answer: (1) the cytoplasm, (2) other cells
Diff: 2   Page Ref: 41.3
Skill: Factual

67) Adult stem cells derived from fat cells have been used to develop muscle and nerve cells in the lab. How is this possible?

Answer: Since all cells contain all the genes, it is only a matter of deactivating the "fat" genes and activating the "muscle" or "nerve" genes.
Diff: 3   Page Ref: 41.3
Skill: Factual

68) A human embryo is known as a fetus after

    A) 4 weeks.   B) 8 weeks.   C) 12 weeks.   D) 16 weeks.

Answer: B
Diff: 1   Page Ref: 41.4
Skill: Factual

69) In humans, fertilization occurs in the

    A) ovary.   B) testes.   C) oviduct.   D) uterus.

Answer: C
Diff: 1   Page Ref: 41.4
Skill: Factual

70) In humans, implantation occurs

A) just prior to fertilization.

B) immediately after fertilization.

C) when the embryo is blastocyst.

D) when the embryo is a gastrula.

Answer: C
Diff: 1   Page Ref: 41.4
Skill: Factual

71) Three weeks after conception, which of the following has NOT happened in an embryo?

A) gastrulation

B) organogenesis

C) neural tube formation

D) All of the above would not have occurred.

Answer: B
Diff: 3   Page Ref: 41.4
Skill: Conceptual

72) The birth defect spina bifida results in part of the spinal cord lying outside of the body. This defect occurs because of abnormal development of the

A) neural tube.   B) gill grooves.   C) allantois.   D) placenta.

Answer: A
Diff: 2   Page Ref: 41.4
Skill: Factual

73) The structure produced by cleavage of a human zygote is called a(n)

A) chorion.

B) blastocyst.

C) blastopore.

D) embryonic disc.

E) gastrula.

Answer: B
Diff: 2   Page Ref: 41.4
Skill: Factual

74) At what stage does a human embryo implant in the uterus?

A) gastrula

B) embryonic disc

C) morula

D) blastocyst

E) fetal

Answer: D
Diff: 2   Page Ref: 41.4
Skill: Factual

75) The umbilical cord of a mammal connects the

A) fetus and the placenta.

B) amnion and the chorion.

C) yolk sac and the allantois.

D) embryo and the amnion.

E) allantois and the embryo.

Answer: A
Diff: 1   Page Ref: 41.4
Skill: Factual

76) A human embryo is called a fetus at _____ month(s).

A) one   B) two   C) three   D) four   E) six

Answer: B
Diff: 2   Page Ref: 41.4
Skill: Factual

77) At which stage is the human embryo most susceptible to damage?

A) just before birth

B) during cleavage

C) during organogenesis

D) during the 4th and 5th months

E) during the last trimester

Answer: C
Diff: 2   Page Ref: 41.4
Skill: Factual

78) Human embryos differ from bird embryos in that

  A) bird embryos have an extra membrane, the allantois, not found in human embryos.

  B) human embryos have no yolk sac.

  C) human embryos have a yolk sac, but it contains no yolk.

  D) human embryos do not develop into a primitive streak stage.

Answer: C
Diff: 2   Page Ref: 41.4
Skill: Conceptual

79) How is embryonic development of humans similar to that of other vertebrates?

  A) Human embryos have a tail.   B) Human embryos have gill grooves.

  C) Human embryos have notochords.   D) All of the above are similarities.

Answer: D
Diff: 2   Page Ref: 41.4
Skill: Conceptual

80) Suppose a drug taken by a pregnant woman causes incomplete brain formation during fetal development. During which time must have the woman taken the drug for its effect to be realized?

  A) the first two months of development

  B) between the third & fourth month of development

  C) between the fifth & sixth month of development

  D) between the seventh & eighth month of development

Answer: A
Diff: 2   Page Ref: 41.4
Skill: Application

81) Developmentally speaking, what would you predict would happen to a male human fetus whose testes could not produce testosterone?

  A) It would die.

  B) Its testes would produce estrogen instead.

  C) It would develop ovaries instead of testes.

  D) It would not develop male genitalia.

Answer: D
Diff: 2   Page Ref: 41.4
Skill: Application

82) A human embryologist examines a 3–week–old embryo and notices that it has not developed a notochord. Assuming the embryo survives, what organs would it lack?

A) a brain & spinal cord B) a heart & lungs

C) skin & blood vessels D) a stomach & pancreas

Answer: A
Diff: 2   Page Ref: 41.4
Skill: Application

83) Which portion of the blastula becomes the embryonic placenta?

A) chorion B) embryonic disc

C) inner cell mass D) primitive streak

Answer: A
Diff: 2   Page Ref: 41.4
Skill: Factual

84) Which hormone(s) is/are secreted by the placenta?

A) estrogen

B) FSH

C) progesterone

D) LH

E) estrogen and progesterone

Answer: E
Diff: 2   Page Ref: 41.4
Skill: Factual

85) In the placenta

A) chorionic villi are bathed in pools of maternal blood.

B) fetal blood and maternal blood mix.

C) all substances in maternal blood that may be harmful to the fetus are prevented from going through.

D) the amnion and chorion grow into the uterus wall.

E) hormones are absorbed to prevent their influencing the developing fetus.

Answer: A
Diff: 3   Page Ref: 41.4
Skill: Conceptual

86) Which diffuses from fetal blood to maternal blood in the placenta?

    A) oxygen

    B) urea

    C) alcohol

    D) infectious organisms

    E) nutrients

Answer: B
Diff: 2   Page Ref: 41.4
Skill: Factual

87) Which of the following cannot cross the placenta?

    A) alcohol

    B) cocaine

    C) AIDS virus

    D) nicotine

    E) All of these cross the placenta.

Answer: E
Diff: 2   Page Ref: 41.4
Skill: Conceptual

88) A woman is exposed to German measles during the second week of pregnancy. The chances of birth defects in the baby are

    A) low because the mother's immune system protects the fetus.

    B) low because the measles virus cannot cross the placenta.

    C) low because even though the virus crosses the placenta, viruses do not damage cells.

    D) high because the virus can cross the placenta and will damage fetal cells at this very sensitive stage of embryonic development.

Answer: D
Diff: 3   Page Ref: 41.4
Skill: Conceptual

89) The placental blood vessels

A) mix maternal and fetal blood.

B) draw oxygen from the fetal blood and pass it to the mother.

C) allows for the exchange of wastes and nutrients but keeps the maternal and fetal circulation separate.

D) manufacture hormones that slow the growth of the embryo, preventing it from outgrowing the uterus.

Answer: D
Diff: 3   Page Ref: 41.4
Skill: Conceptual

90) The placenta consists of

A) chorionic villi.

B) endometrial vessels.

C) hormone–producing cells.

D) cells which actively transport some materials between mother and fetus.

E) all of the above

Answer: E
Diff: 3   Page Ref: 41.4
Skill: Conceptual

91) The fetus can move and respond to stimuli as early as the

A) second month.   B) third month.   C) fourth month.   D) fifth month.

Answer: B
Diff: 1   Page Ref: 41.4
Skill: Factual

92) Most fetuses can first survive outside the womb after a minimum of

A) five months.   B) six months.   C) seven months.   D) eight months.

Answer: C
Diff: 1   Page Ref: 41.4
Skill: Factual

93) What is the main purpose of the last seven months of pregnancy?

    A) formation of major organs

    B) organization of organs into organ systems

    C) formation of the brain

    D) growth

    E) formation of cell layers

Answer: D
Diff: 2   Page Ref: 41.4
Skill: Conceptual

94) Most babies are likely to survive if they are born after at least _____ months of pregnancy.

    A) 4   B) 5   C) 6   D) 7   E) 8

Answer: D
Diff: 2   Page Ref: 41.4
Skill: Factual

95) Developmentally speaking, which of the following events occurs over the longest time for a human?

    A) cleavage   B) fertilization   C) growth   D) implantation

Answer: C
Diff: 1   Page Ref: 41.4
Skill: Conceptual

96) The secretion of milk is promoted by the hormone

    A) colostrum.   B) oxytocin.   C) progesterone.   D) prolactin.

Answer: D
Diff: 2   Page Ref: 41.4
Skill: Factual

97) Babies that are nursed rather than fed formula

    A) grow faster.   B) grow slower.

    C) gain antibodies from maternal milk.   D) none of these

Answer: C
Diff: 2   Page Ref: 41.4
Skill: Factual

98) The longevity of a cell depends upon

    A) where it is located.   B) its ability to repair damaged DNA.

    C) its ability to manufacture ATP.   D) its lineage.

Answer: B
Diff: 2   Page Ref: 41.4
Skill: Conceptual

99) Chromosomal structures that shorten with each cell division are called

    A) homeoboxes.   B) telomeres.   C) centromeres.   D) histones.

Answer: B
Diff: 1   Page Ref: 41.4
Skill: Factual

100) Longevity in animals appears to be most related to the ability of their cells to repair damage to their own DNA.

    A) True

    B) False, because DNA is protected from damage by its position inside the nucleus.

    C) False, because longevity is most related to the ability of the organism to continue to reproduce.

    D) False, because DNA cannot be repaired once it is damaged.

    E) False, because all animals have an equal ability to repair DNA.

Answer: A
Diff: 2   Page Ref: 41.4
Skill: Conceptual

101) The cells of an aging animal function less efficiently because

    A) their metabolic rate is very low.

    B) they lose their organelles.

    C) they cannot repair their DNA.

    D) protein synthesis has stopped.

    E) they cannot divide by mitosis.

Answer: C
Diff: 2   Page Ref: 41.4
Skill: Conceptual

102) A recent series of television commercial promoted the idea that a woman who wants a healthy baby must begin eating well and avoiding some medication and alcohol BEFORE she knows she is pregnant. Why?

Answer: Gastrulation and differentiation of embryonic cells occurs before most women have missed their first period, so many don't even know they are pregnant yet. At these earliest stages when important organ systems are being laid down, the embryo is very sensitive to drugs and nutrient levels.
Diff: 3   Page Ref: 41.4
Skill: Conceptual

103) The mother's part of the placenta is made from the _____; whereas the baby's part is made from the _____.

Answer: endometrium; chorion
Diff: 2   Page Ref: 41.4
Skill: Factual

104) Why should a woman planning on becoming pregnant notify her health care provider of any medications she is taking?

Answer: Many medications can produce developmental damage to a developing embryo or create high-risk pregnancies.
Diff: 2   Page Ref: 41.4
Skill: Application

105) How is blood flow in the placenta maintained so that there is maximum opportunity for the exchange of materials while still keeping the mother's and baby's bloods separate?

Answer: The mother's capillaries break down so that the chorionic villi are bathed in the mother's blood to allow maximum exposure, but the baby's blood remains in capillaries inside the chorionic villi to maintain separation.
Diff: 3   Page Ref: 41.4
Skill: Conceptual

106) If your roommate smokes and she gets pregnant, what dangers would you warn her about?

Answer: Smoking increases miscarriages, low birth weight, infant mortality, and possibly retardation, both social and mental.
Diff: 3   Page Ref: 41.4
Skill: Conceptual

107) German measles is a very mild infection, so why is vaccination against German measles required by most colleges?

Answer: While German measles is mild in most people, an embryo, especially in the first trimester, is very sensitive to the virus. In the embryo it may cause severe birth defects. By requiring college students to be vaccinated, a population most likely to be having children in the next few years are protected.
Diff: 3   Page Ref: 41.4
Skill: Conceptual

Chapter 42 Plant Anatomy and Nutrient Transport

1) While hiking, you find a plant with unusual fruit around the seed and leaves with parallel veins. In which major group does it belong?

    A) monocots; has parallel veins

    B) uncertain; depends on if it's woody or not

    C) monocot or dicot; depending on flower type

    D) dicots; these are the only angiosperm with fruits

    E) cannot differentiate between monocot or dicot; number of cotyledons is the only difference between these groups

Answer: A
Diff: 2   Page Ref: 42.1
Skill: Application

2) Which of the following characteristics could help differentiate between a monocot & dicot?

    A) presence of vascular tissue

    B) seeds covered by a fruit

    C) number of flower parts

    D) whether the plant gains length from an apical or lateral meristem

    E) presence or absence of pollen grains

Answer: C
Diff: 2   Page Ref: 42.1
Skill: Factual

3) Increases in plant *length* occur from cell division

    A) equally throughout the plant body.

    B) only in apical meristems at shoot/root tips.

    C) only from lateral meristems (cambia).

    D) from cell division of differentiated cells.

    E) none of the above

Answer: B
Diff: 2   Page Ref: 42.1
Skill: Conceptual

4) As a child of 7 you helped your mom nail a bird house 7 feet high on a 10 foot maple tree. The tree grew an average of 12 inches per year, except for a dry year, when it only grew 2 inches. How high in the tree was the bird house when you were 18?

   A) 17 feet

   B) 17 feet 2 inches

   C) 7 feet

   D) 14 feet

   E) 18 feet

Answer: C
Diff: 3   Page Ref: 42.1
Skill: Application

5) All of the following are major functions of roots except

   A) produce hormones.

   B) transport water & minerals.

   C) store excess sugars.

   D) interact with soil fungi.

   E) phytosynthesis.

Answer: E
Diff: 1   Page Ref: 42.1
Skill: Factual

6) You discover an unidentified weed that you cut with a lawn mower almost to the ground. Soon it is as tall as it was before you cut it. This growth is likely due to what growth region?

   A) shoot apical meristem (note: apical meristem was removed, lateral buds take over)

   B) lateral bud

   C) root apical meristem

   D) vascular cambium

   E) cork cambium

Answer: B
Diff: 3   Page Ref: 42.4
Skill: Conceptual

7) All of the following are part of the plant's shoot system except

A) stem.

B) buds.

C) mycorrhizae.

D) leaves.

E) flowers.

Answer: C
Diff: 2   Page Ref: 42.1
Skill: Factual

8) Plant cells which are actively dividing are _____ cells.

A) differentiated

B) conducting

C) vascular

D) ground

E) meristem

Answer: E
Diff: 1   Page Ref: 42.1
Skill: Factual

9) What cell type permits the continued growth of a plant throughout its life?

A) differentiated cells

B) ground tissue cells

C) meristematic cells

D) mesophyll cells

E) secondary cells

Answer: C
Diff: 1   Page Ref: 42.1
Skill: Factual

10) If you were studying a plant which had only primary growth and no secondary growth, it would NOT have any

A) stem elongation.

B) expansion of its root system.

C) vascular tissue.

D) development of thicker woody branches.

E) flowers.

Answer: D
Diff: 2   *Page Ref: 42.1*
Skill: Conceptual

11) What type of cell activity is characteristic in meristematic regions of plants?

A) large proportion of cells undergoing mitosis

B) cells exhibiting secondary growth

C) active photosynthesis

D) increased water uptake of cells

E) storage of sugar within cells

Answer: A
Diff: 1   *Page Ref: 42.1*
Skill: Factual

12) Apical meristems are located

A) scattered throughout the plant.

B) in cylinders along the side of the root.

C) between the xylem and the phloem.

D) in clusters in the parenchyma.

E) at the ends of the roots and stems.

Answer: E
Diff: 1   *Page Ref: 42.1*
Skill: Factual

13) Both primary and secondary growth is accomplished by mitotic cell division. Compare and contrast these two types of growth.

Answer: Primary involves apical meristem cells & occurs in growing tips of roots and shoots. Differentiation following division is responsible for specialized plant structures. Secondary growth occurs by division of lateral meristem cells and causes stems and roots to become thicker and woodier.
Diff: 3   *Page Ref: 42.1*
Skill: Application

14) The flowering plants are commonly called the _____.

Answer: angiosperms
Diff: 1   Page Ref: 42.1
Skill: Factual

15) Plants cells which are no longer involved in mitosis are said to be _____.

Answer: differentiated
Diff: 1   Page Ref: 42.1
Skill: Factual

16) Compare the functions of roots with those of shoots. How would they be similar, how different?

Answer: The student should mention the major functions of these plant parts and show that both are involved in hormone production, support, and transport.
Diff: 2   Page Ref: 42.1
Skill: Conceptual

17) If you found a plant while hiking and wanted to show off your understanding of the differences between monocots and dicots, what characteristics could you see with your naked eye that would help you impress your friends?

Answer: number of flower parts, leaf venation, leaf shape, possible root–type
Diff: 2   Page Ref: 42.1
Skill: Conceptual

18) You move into a new home and discover several woody bushes growing in your garden. Is it safe to assume that these are perennials? Why or why not?

Answer: Yes. Woody, secondary growth only occurs in in perennials.
Diff: 2   Page Ref: 42.1
Skill: Application

19) _____ cells that convert sugar to starch in mature roots are part of the _____ tissue system.

   A) Phloem; vascular

   B) Periderm; dermal

   C) Xylem; vascular

   D) Parenchyma; ground

   E) Companion cells; ground

Answer: D
Diff: 2   Page Ref: 42.2
Skill: Conceptual

20) Which of the following tissue types are found throughout young plant bodies?

  A) epidermis

  B) periderm

  C) vascular

  D) all of the above

  E) A and C

Answer: E
Diff: 2   Page Ref: 42.2
Skill: Conceptual

21) You are not likely to find a nucleus in which of these cell types?

  A) parenchyma

  B) collenchyma

  C) sclerenchyma

  D) companion cell

  E) tracheid

Answer: C
Diff: 2   Page Ref: 42.2
Skill: Conceptual

22) Water conducting cells that are narrow with small central cavities are

  A) vessel elements.

  B) tracheids.

  C) sieve elements.

  D) companion cells.

  E) collenchyma.

Answer: B
Diff: 1   Page Ref: 42.2
Skill: Factual

23) Dermal tissue forms what?

  A) vascular tissue

  B) pith

  C) xylem

  D) epidermis

  E) seeds

Answer: D
Diff: 1   Page Ref: 42.2
Skill: Factual

24) Cells that are alive, have thickened corners, and function in mechanical rigidity are

    A) parenchyma.

    B) sclerenchyma.

    C) trichomes.

    D) collenchyma.

    E) vessel members.

Answer: D
Diff: 1   Page Ref: 42.2
Skill: Factual

25) Some plant tissue you are examining in the laboratory is quite rigid. It does not flex or bend. Tests show that it is not consuming oxygen gas as would be expected of aerobic respiration were occurring. This tissue is probably which cell type?

    A) sclerenchyma

    B) primary

    C) collenchyma

    D) parenchyma

    E) ground

Answer: A
Diff: 3   Page Ref: 42.2
Skill: Application

26) Periderm consists mostly of

    A) epidermis.

    B) cork cells.

    C) lateral meristem.

    D) undifferentiated cells.

    E) endodermis.

Answer: B
Diff: 1   Page Ref: 42.2
Skill: Factual

27) Of the major tissue systems associated with land plants, which system covers the outer surface of the primary plant?

   A) ground tissue

   B) meristematic tissue

   C) dermal tissue

   D) vascular tissue

   E) parenchyma tissue

Answer: C
Diff: 1   Page Ref: 42.2
Skill: Factual

28) The soft, thin-walled, living ground tissue cells that make up most of a leaf such as lettuce are

   A) collenchyma.

   B) xylem.

   C) sclerenchyma.

   D) phloem.

   E) parenchyma.

Answer: E
Diff: 1   Page Ref: 42.2
Skill: Factual

29) Thick-walled metabolically active cells of parenchyma typically form

   A) phloem.

   B) xylem.

   C) cork.

   D) ground tissue.

   E) epidermis.

Answer: D
Diff: 1   Page Ref: 42.2
Skill: Factual

30) Of the types of ground tissues, which is generally most abundant?

    A) parenchyma

    B) sclerenchyma

    C) collenchyma

    D) tracheids

    E) vessel elements

Answer: A
Diff: 1   Page Ref: 42.2
Skill: Factual

31) Which of the following plant structures is composed of meristematic tissue?

    A) cortex

    B) root cap

    C) cambium

    D) parenchyma

    E) xylem

Answer: C
Diff: 1   Page Ref: 42.2
Skill: Factual

32) Where are parenchyma cells located?

    A) cortex

    B) central cylinder

    C) mesophyll

    D) pith

    E) all of these

Answer: E
Diff: 1   Page Ref: 42.2
Skill: Factual

33) The hard outer covering of peach pits is made up of

    A) parenchyma cells.

    B) sclerenchyma.

    C) vascular tissue.

    D) periderm.

    E) collenchyma cells.

Answer: B
Diff: 1   Page Ref: 42.2
Skill: Factual

34) Sclerenchyma has all of the following characteristics EXCEPT

   A) found in both xylem and phloem.

   B) is dead at maturity.

   C) made up of cells with thickened secondary cell walls.

   D) contains lignin.

   E) often storage site for sugars and starches.

Answer: E
Diff: 2   Page Ref: 42.2
Skill: Factual

35) The formation of sieve plates between phloem sieve cells allows

   A) the dead phloem cells to form an empty tube.

   B) each cell to function independently.

   C) mesophyll cells to connect with xylem cells.

   D) water to transpire from each surface.

   E) each adjacent cell to connect via membrane-lined channels.

Answer: E
Diff: 2   Page Ref: 42.2
Skill: Conceptual

36) Which of these plant cells is alive but has no nucleus?

   A) companion cell

   B) parenchyma

   C) sieve-tube element

   D) vessel element

   E) collenchyma

Answer: C
Diff: 2   Page Ref: 42.2
Skill: Factual

37) Vascular plants, the tracheophytes, have _____ which enable them to survive especially well on land.

   A) pollen produced at the top of the plant

   B) specialized conducting cells arranged in vessels

   C) elongated roots

   D) parenchyma tissue

   E) seeds which are produced from spores

Answer: B
Diff: 1   Page Ref: 42.2
Skill: Factual

38) In vascular plants, transport of sugar solutions is through tubes constructed of cells called

   A) vessels elements.

   B) companion cells.

   C) tracheids.

   D) sieve-tube elements.

   E) parenchyma.

Answer: D
Diff: 2   Page Ref: 42.2
Skill: Factual

39) All the following are TRUE of companion cells EXCEPT

   A) companion cells fuse together to form the sieve plates of sieve-tube elements.

   B) companion cells provide direct nourishment for sieve-tube elements.

   C) companion cells regulate the movement of sugar into and out of sieve-tubes.

   D) sieve-tube plasma membrane may be repaired by companion cells.

   E) companion cells are connected to sieve-tube elements via plasmodesmata.

Answer: A
Diff: 2   Page Ref: 42.2
Skill: Factual

40) What type of tissue transports the sugars which are the products of photosynthesis to the rest of the plant?

  A) xylem

  B) mesophyll

  C) phloem

  D) parenchyma

  E) endodermis

Answer: C
Diff: 1   Page Ref: 42.2
Skill: Factual

41) All the following are TRUE of xylem EXCEPT

  A) tracheids and vessel elements are the two types of cells that form xylem.

  B) water and minerals are transported through xylem.

  C) companion cells provide nutrition for tracheids.

  D) tracheids are characterized by pits.

  E) at maturity xylem is dead.

Answer: C
Diff: 1   Page Ref: 42.2
Skill: Factual

42) All the following may be found in xylem EXCEPT

  A) tracheids.

  B) sclerencyma fibers.

  C) companion cells.

  D) vessel elements.

  E) end walls with pits.

Answer: C
Diff: 1   Page Ref: 42.2
Skill: Factual

43) Most conifers possess only tracheids. What is the structural feature that allows water and minerals to pass from one tracheid to the next tracheid?

   A) sieve plates

   B) secondary cell walls

   C) pits

   D) stomata

   E) plasmodesmata

Answer: C
Diff: 1   Page Ref: 42.2
Skill: Factual

44) Since most of the trunk of a tree is made of xylem cells, it is safe to say that most of the tissue of a tree is

   A) rapidly dividing.

   B) used for storage.

   C) manufacturing sugars.

   D) conducting sugars.

   E) dead.

Answer: E
Diff: 1   Page Ref: 42.2
Skill: Conceptual

45) Ground tissue is found in the primary plant only, never in the secondary plant. True or False?

Answer: FALSE
Diff: 1   Page Ref: 42.2
Skill: Factual

46) When you crack a nut, the hard, dead cells which make it strong are a type of ground tissue called _____.

Answer: sclerenchyma
Diff: 1   Page Ref: 42.2
Skill: Factual

47) Phloem sieve tube cells are able to remain alive because adjacent _____ cells nourish them.

Answer: companion
Diff: 1   Page Ref: 42.2
Skill: Factual

48) Using a rose bush or a bean plant as an example, give one example for how each of the following tissues is critical to the survival of the plant.

Answer: The student should mention at least one function for each of these tissues.
Diff: 2   Page Ref: 42.2
Skill: Application

49) What is the source of energy for plant roots?

Answer: Photosynthesis in the shoot (leaves) forms sugars using the sun's energy. The sugar must be transported to the plant roots in the phloem. Cellular respiration then makes this energy available to the root.
Diff: 2   Page Ref: 42.2
Skill: Conceptual

50) Discuss the origin and development of primary tissues including their locations in stems and probable functions.

Answer: Cells from the apical meristem mature into the ground meristem which matures into (from outside in) cortex (water storage, photosynthesis), phloem (conducts food), vascular cambium (makes secondary tissues), xylem (moves water) and pith (stores water).
Diff: 2   Page Ref: 42.2
Skill: Conceptual

51) Which of the following is plant tissue derived from a lateral meristem?

A) flower bud

B) leaf bud

C) stem branch

D) bark

E) primary xylem

Answer: D
Diff: 2   Page Ref: 42.3
Skill: Factual

52) Which leaf cell type is most responsible for regulating diffusion of CO_2 availability for photosynthesis?

A) epidermis

B) cuticle

C) guard cells

D) stomata

E) parenchyma

Answer: C
Diff: 2   Page Ref: 42.3
Skill: Conceptual

53) How does carbon dioxide enter a leaf?

    A) The CO_2 simply passes through openings called stomata on the leaf surface.

    B) The CO_2 diffuses through the epidermal cells into the mesophyll.

    C) CO_2 is moved by active transport into the leaf by special cells called guard cells.

    D) Atmospheric pressure forces CO_2 through pits on the leaf surface.

    E) CO_2 travels dissolved in the water in the xylem.

Answer: A
Diff: 2   Page Ref: 42.3
Skill: Conceptual

54) Leaf primordia are

    A) compound leaves.

    B) developing leaves.

    C) leaves of excellent quality.

    D) the stalk–like base of leaves.

    E) flower buds.

Answer: B
Diff: 1   Page Ref: 42.3
Skill: Factual

55) Where is sugar converted to starch and the starch stored as a food reserve in the stems of plants?

    A) mesophyll layer

    B) central vascular cylinder

    C) sclerenchyma

    D) parenchyma cells in both cortex and pith

    E) collenchyma associated with xylem cells

Answer: D
Diff: 1   Page Ref: 42.3
Skill: Factual

56) In a young dicot stem, which tissue(s) are found between the pith and the cortex?

A) vascular cambium

B) vascular cylinder

C) xylem

D) phloem

E) all of the above

Answer: E
Diff: 1   Page Ref: 42.3
Skill: Factual

57) Which of the following is the correct placement of the tissues in a young dicot stem from the center out?

A) pith–cortex–phloem–xylem–vascular cambium–epidermis

B) pith–phloem–cortex–xylem–vascular cambium–epidermis

C) cortex–vascular cambium–xylem–phloem–epidermis–pith

D) cortex–xylem–vascular cambium–phloem–pith–epidermis

E) pith–xylem–vascular cambium–phloem–cortex–epidermis

Answer: E
Diff: 2   Page Ref: 42.3
Skill: Factual

58) What tissue is located between the epidermis and the vascular bundle in a young dicot stem?

A) pith

B) xylem

C) cortex

D) phloem

E) ground tissue

Answer: C
Diff: 1   Page Ref: 42.3
Skill: Factual

59) Why don't trees have annual rings in the secondary phloem?

    A) It's not as dense as the secondary xylem.

    B) It is crushed and sloughed off as cell division in the vascular cambium occurs over the years.

    C) There is not secondary (woody) phloem, only primary phloem.

    D) Secondary phloem is replaced by cork.

    E) There is a life record of annual rings in phloem that is useful in estimating the age of a tree.

Answer: B
Diff: 3   *Page Ref: 42.3*
Skill: Application

Use the figure below, anatomy of a log, to answer the following question(s).

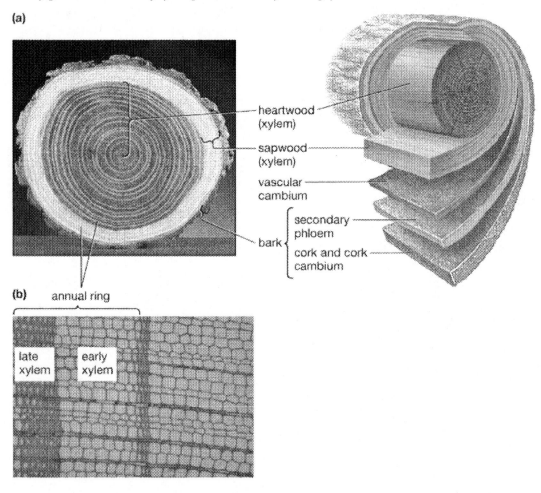

60) Use the photograph in the figure above to estimate the age of this tree in years.

    A) 6   B) 11   C) 16   D) 21   E) 25

Answer: C
Diff: 3   *Page Ref: 42.3*
Skill: Application

61) (Refer to the figure above.) How many (if any) of the years had substantially less rainfall?

    A) 0   B) 2–3   C) 4–5   D) 6–7   E) 8–9

Answer: B
Diff: 3   Page Ref: 42.3
Skill: Application

62) As an oak tree ages, the trunk becomes thicker and more woody due to

    A) primary growth.

    B) secondary growth.

    C) tertiary.

    D) meristematic.

    E) differentiated.

Answer: B
Diff: 1   Page Ref: 42.3
Skill: Factual

63) If a beaver eats the bark all the way around a tree trunk (a process called "girdling"), why does the tree eventually die?

    A) The tree is more susceptible to insect and fungal diseases.

    B) The phloem is damaged and the transport of sugars is interrupted.

    C) Cells of the lateral meristem can no longer continue to divide.

    D) The supply of water and minerals to the leaves is no longer possible.

    E) The tree cannot continue to photosynthesize.

Answer: B
Diff: 3   Page Ref: 42.3
Skill: Application

64) A tree of known age is cut down and its growth rings are examined. The tree is relatively young and the year of its germination is known. There are *more* growth rings than the age of the tree in years. How can you account for the excess growth rings?

    A) Some years had an above average temperature.

    B) Some years had an above average rainfall throughout the season.

    C) Trees normally make several growth rings in each of their 10th through 15th years.

    D) Drought in the middle of some summers resulted in two growth rings in each of those years.

    E) The tree was growing in a tropical area.

Answer: D
Diff: 2   Page Ref: 42.3
Skill: Conceptual

65) A tree has its heartwood rot out. How will this affect the tree?

    A) The tree is more mechanically stable than normal and less likely to be blown down in a storm.

    B) The tree can move water up more easily than before through the large pipe-like cavities left where the heartwood used to be.

    C) The tree is more likely to be blown over in a storm.

    D) The movement of water up the tree will be cut off.

    E) The tree will be unable to move carbohydrates from leaves to roots.

Answer: C
Diff: 2   Page Ref: 42.3
Skill: Conceptual

66) Examination of a woody stem reveals that some tissues are dead at maturity. What are these dead tissues?

    A) cork and heartwood

    B) sapwood and bark

    C) vascular cambium and young phloem

    D) xylem and phloem

    E) epidermis and periderm

Answer: A
Diff: 1   Page Ref: 42.3
Skill: Factual

67) Most of the trunk of a tree is composed of

    A) primary xylem.

    B) secondary xylem.

    C) primary phloem.

    D) secondary phloem.

    E) meristem tissue.

Answer: B
Diff: 1   Page Ref: 42.3
Skill: Factual

68) Casparian strips are similar in composition to the

    A) cuticle.

    B) epidermis.

    C) xylem.

    D) phloem.

    E) pith.

Answer: A
Diff: 3   Page Ref: 42.3
Skill: Conceptual

69) In a carrot, a root adapted for carbohydrate storage, most of the carrot is

    A) phloem.

    B) xylem.

    C) cortex.

    D) endodermis.

    E) pericycle.

Answer: C
Diff: 2   Page Ref: 42.3
Skill: Conceptual

70) From which of the following do root hairs develop?

    A) cortex

    B) endodermis

    C) Casparian strip

    D) epidermis

    E) pericycle

Answer: D
Diff: 2   Page Ref: 42.3
Skill: Conceptual

71) The location of the pericyle is best described as

    A) the outermost layer of the vascular cylinder.

    B) just beneath the epidermis.

    C) adjacent to the apical meristem.

    D) between layers of primary xylem and primary phloem.

    E) lining the cells of the endodermis.

Answer: A
Diff: 1   Page Ref: 42.3
Skill: Factual

72) Under the influence of hormones branch roots develop from what region of a growing root?

A) endodermis

B) pericycle

C) central cylinder

D) epidermis

E) Casparian strip

Answer: B
Diff: 2   Page Ref: 42.3
Skill: Conceptual

73) Many root epidermal cells have projections called _____ which extend from their surface and help in the absorption of water and minerals.

A) root hairs   B) villi   C) cilia   D) rhizoids   E) rhizomes

Answer: A
Diff: 1   Page Ref: 42.3
Skill: Factual

74) On the tip of the root the apical meristem forms the _____ which prevent the meristem from being worn away as it pushes through the soil.

A) cortex

B) epidermis

C) endodermis

D) root cap

E) pericycle

Answer: D
Diff: 1   Page Ref: 42.3
Skill: Factual

75) Which of the following pathways BEST summarizes the route of a mineral that is absorbed by a plant?

A) root hairs → pericycle → endodermis → endodermis → cortex → xylem

B) root hairs → epidermis → endodermis → cortex → xylem

C) root hairs → endodermis → cortex → pericycle → xylem

D) root hairs → epidermis → cortex → endodermis → pericycle → xylem

E) root hairs → cortex → epidermis → phloem → xylem

Answer: D
Diff: 2   Page Ref: 42.3
Skill: Conceptual

76) When water entering the root encounters the endodermis, it is forced to pass through the cytoplasm of these cells by the

    A) pericycle.

    B) attraction of water to cellulose in the cell walls.

    C) cortex.

    D) attraction of water to the proteins in the cytoplasm.

    E) Casparian strip.

Answer: E
Diff: 2   Page Ref: 42.3
Skill: Conceptual

77) Because the secondary meristems are arranged in cylinders around stems, secondary growth results in the formation of stronger, thicker stems. True or False?

Answer: TRUE
Diff: 2   Page Ref: 42.3
Skill: Conceptual

78) Plants need to minimize water loss while maximizing carbon dioxide intake. How have these conflicting needs been met in the structure of a plant leaf?

Answer: mention the cuticle, guard cells, stomata, and possible leaf shape
Diff: 2   Page Ref: 42.3
Skill: Conceptual

79) A deer eats the bark off of a tree *half way around*. How will this affect the tree and why?

Answer: The continuity of the phloem will be destroyed in that area. The tree would survive but growth on the injured side, including leaf and flower development and branch growth, would be reduced. The part of the tree trunk on the side of the wound may die.
Diff: 3   Page Ref: 42.3
Skill: Application

80) Why would you expect to find that lateral buds and leaves are always found at the same places on stems?

Answer: Since both leaf primordia and lateral buds are formed from the clusters of meristem cells which are left behind as the apical meristem moves upward in the stem, each leaf is accompanied by a lateral bud.
Diff: 2   Page Ref: 42.3
Skill: Conceptual

81) In a young dicot stem between the pith and the cortex is the _____.

Answer: vascular cylinder or xylem and phloem
Diff: 1   Page Ref: 42.3
Skill: Factual

82) How do young dicot stems remain upright without the physical support of sclerencyma or collenchyma cells?

Answer: turgor pressure formed by the water entering the cells of the pith and cortex
Diff: 2   Page Ref: 42.3
Skill: Application

83) What is the Casparian strip?

Answer: a waxy layer on endodermis cells of the root which forces water and minerals to enter the endodermal cells
Diff: 1   Page Ref: 42.3
Skill: Factual

84) Branches from a stem develop from the _____, whereas branches from a root develop from the _____.

Answer: lateral buds; pericycle
Diff: 1   Page Ref: 42.3
Skill: Factual

85) Trees are among the largest and oldest living things on Earth. Like all life on Earth the majority of the biomass is carbon based. What is the source of this major nutrient?

A) water

B) crushed rock and water

C) organic layer of the soil

D) air

E) fertilizers

Answer: D
Diff: 3   Page Ref: 42.4
Skill: Application

86) Diffusion doesn't require energy. Why do plants expend energy in active transport to transport minerals into root hairs?

A) Mineral concentrations in the soil are too low for diffusion.

B) Mineral concentrations in the soil are too high for diffusion.

C) Minerals are too large for diffusion.

D) B and C

E) none of the above

Answer: A
Diff: 3   Page Ref: 42.4
Skill: Application

87) Mycorrhizae are associated with which plant organ?

    A) leaf   B) stem   C) root   D) flower   E) seed

Answer: C
Diff: 1   Page Ref: 42.4
Skill: Factual

88) Which of the following accounts for the movement of most minerals from soil into root hairs?

    A) diffusion

    B) osmosis

    C) active transport

    D) hypotonicity

    E) hypertonicity

Answer: C
Diff: 1   Page Ref: 42.4
Skill: Factual

89) Plasmodesmata are

    A) root hairs which are adapted for mineral transport.

    B) organelles which form ATP in roots.

    C) the transport channels for sugars.

    D) nutrients which can only be used by plants.

    E) pores which allow plant cells to connect with nearby cells.

Answer: E
Diff: 1   Page Ref: 42.4
Skill: Factual

90) What cellular feature allows a mineral such as manganese to diffuse from cell to cell after mineral uptake by roots?

    A) plasmodesmata

    B) secondary cell walls

    C) sieve plates

    D) microtubules

    E) microfilaments

Answer: A
Diff: 1   Page Ref: 42.4
Skill: Factual

91) Comparison studies of plant root tissues and the surrounding soil where the plant grows normally reveal a much higher concentration of iron in the root tissues than in the soil. What is indicated by results such as these?

    A) Iron is actively transported into the plant root cells.

    B) Iron is a macronutrient that moves easily by diffusion into the root tissues.

    C) The root hairs are much more permeable to positively charged molecules than to negatively charged molecules.

    D) Iron-containing molecules are produced metabolically by this plant and are transported to the roots for storage.

    E) The water coming into the plant is able to dissolve large amounts of iron.

Answer: A
Diff: 3   Page Ref: 42.4
Skill: Application

92) What would happen if water and minerals could pass **between** endodermal cells rather than through the endodermal cells of a plant root?

    A) An increased concentration gradient of the minerals in the extracellular space of the vascular cylinder would be better maintained.

    B) Too much energy would be needed to move the minerals between endodermal cells.

    C) The minerals would enter the conduction vessels of the vascular cylinder much more rapidly.

    D) Minerals would leak back out of the extracellular space of the vascular cylinder as fast as they were pumped into it.

    E) Root hairs would lose their ability to take up minerals.

Answer: D
Diff: 2   Page Ref: 42.4
Skill: Conceptual

93) What type of relationship is a mycorrhiza?

    A) parasitic

    B) codominant

    C) symbiotic

    D) commensal

    E) predatory

Answer: C
Diff: 1   Page Ref: 42.4
Skill: Factual

94) A mycorrhiza is a

    A) commensal relationship between a fungus and the leaves of a land plant.

    B) parasitic relationship between bacteria and the roots of a land plant.

    C) mutualistic relationship between a fungus and an alga.

    D) symbiotic relationship between a fungus and the roots of a land plant.

    E) symbiotic relationship between bacteria and the roots of a land plant.

Answer: D
Diff: 1   Page Ref: 42.4
Skill: Factual

95) Why are plants not able to use N_2 directly as a nutrient?

    A) Plants lack the enzymes necessary to convert N_2 into NO_3^- of NH_4^+.

    B) Plant hormones are not capable of carrying out nitrogen fixation.

    C) Most soils are depleted of N_2 as a nutrient.

    D) N_2 diffuses out of leaves as quickly as it diffuses in so it has to be "fixed" to remain in leaves.

    E) The N_2 molecule is too large to enter the root hairs.

Answer: A
Diff: 1   Page Ref: 42.4
Skill: Factual

96) Which root tissue primarily contributes to the formation of nodules, particularly in the legume family?

    A) epidermis

    B) xylem

    C) cortex

    D) phloem

    E) endodermis

Answer: C
Diff: 1   Page Ref: 42.4
Skill: Factual

97) If you found a plant that you thought was a legume and you wanted to see if it had N-fixing bacteria, what would you look for?

    A) absence of root hairs

    B) an enlarged taproot

    C) fungal strands called hyphae extending from the plant roots

    D) nodules present on the roots

    E) an extensive fibrous root system

Answer: D
Diff: 2   *Page Ref: 42.4*
Skill: Conceptual

98) Water and minerals are mainly absorbed through which root structure?

    A) root cap

    B) apical meristem

    C) lateral branch buds

    D) the epidermis of large woody roots

    E) root hairs

Answer: E
Diff: 1   *Page Ref: 42.4*
Skill: Factual

99) Bacteria containing nodules in the roots of legume plants aid in the utilization of what by the plant?

    A) carbon dioxide

    B) trace elements

    C) water

    D) phosphates

    E) nitrogen gas

Answer: E
Diff: 1   *Page Ref: 42.4*
Skill: Factual

100) The concentration of nutrients in plants is approximately the same concentration of nutrients in the surrounding soil. True or False?

Answer: FALSE
Diff: 1   *Page Ref: 42.4*
Skill: Factual

101) In the mycorrhizal relationship how do both the fungus and the plant benefit?

Answer: The plant obtains nutrients from the soil and the fungus gets sugars and amino acids from the plant.
Diff: 1   Page Ref: 42.4
Skill: Factual

102) What evidence is there that plants use active transport to move nutrients into the root?

Answer: The concentration of many nutrients in plants is much higher than in the surrounding soil.
Diff: 1   Page Ref: 42.4
Skill: Factual

103) Describe the process of absorption of mineral nutrients into roots.

Answer: 1. Active transport into root hairs 2. Diffusion through cytoplasm to pericycle cells 3. Active transport into the extracellular space 4. Diffusion into the xylem
Diff: 3   Page Ref: 42.4
Skill: Application

104) Suppose a plant was planted in a soil that was polluted by a chemical spill of a compound (such as certain oils) that could dissolve waxes. What might happen to the endodermis of that plant? What effects do you think this might have on the plant? Why?

Answer: The assumption here is that the plant would live long enough in such a soil that the oil could even penetrate to the Casparian strip. Since this is a critical thinking question rather than an essay question, the main purpose is to allow this assumption in order to get the student to reason about the functions of the Casparian strip. The waxy Casparian strip might break down leading to leakage of minerals from the root into the soil and death of the plant.
Diff: 3   Page Ref: 42.4
Skill: Application

105) The guard cells pictured in the figure below

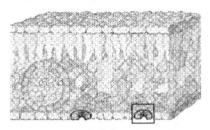

 A) have accumulated potassium.

 B) have lost potassium.

 C) don't contain potassium.

 D) have collapsed.

 E) have lost most of their water.

Answer: A
Diff: 3   Page Ref: 42.5
Skill: Application

106) The movement of water and minerals through xylem is explained by the

 A) pressure–flow theory.

 B) translocation theory.

 C) bulk–flow theory.

 D) cohesion–tension theory.

 E) assisted diffusion theory.

Answer: D
Diff: 1   Page Ref: 42.5
Skill: Factual

107) Water loss through the stomata of leaves is termed

 A) transpiration.

 B) translocation.

 C) guttation.

 D) osmosis.

 E) bulk flow.

Answer: A
Diff: 1   Page Ref: 42.5
Skill: Factual

108) How does water enter roots when transpiration levels are low?

   A) active transport

   B) diffusion: from high to low concentration of minerals

   C) osmosis due to concentration gradient established by actively transported minerals

   D) through stomata

   E) by cohesion

Answer: C
Diff: 2   Page Ref: 42.5
Skill: Conceptual

109) In the cohesion–tension theory the cohesion part refers to

   A) the tendency of water molecules to be attracted to minerals in the water.

   B) the process of osmosis that pulls water into the root.

   C) the evaporation of water from the stomata of the leaf.

   D) the use of water in photosynthesis resulting in a shortage of water in the leaf.

   E) the attraction of water molecules for each other.

Answer: E
Diff: 2   Page Ref: 42.5
Skill: Conceptual

110) In the cohesion–tension theory the tension part refers to

   A) the tendency of water molecules to be attracted to minerals in the water.

   B) the process of osmosis that pulls water into the root.

   C) the evaporation of water from the stomata of the leaf.

   D) the use of water in photosynthesis resulting in a shortage of water in the leaf.

   E) the attraction of water molecules for each other.

Answer: C
Diff: 2   Page Ref: 42.5
Skill: Conceptual

111) What structural feature enables water to move from the extracellular space within the vascular cylinder into the conducting cells of the xylem?

    A) sieve plates in the secondary cell walls

    B) porous pits in the cell walls

    C) plasmodesmata

    D) Casparian strip

    E) microtubules

Answer: B
Diff: 1   Page Ref: 42.5
Skill: Factual

112) The movement of water from outside the Casparian strip into the vascular cylinder is by

    A) osmosis.

    B) hypotonicity.

    C) active transport.

    D) facilitated diffusion.

    E) membrane channels.

Answer: A
Diff: 1   Page Ref: 42.5
Skill: Factual

113) A plant, by opening and closing its stomata, must achieve a balance between

    A) oxygen loss and water uptake.

    B) carbon dioxide loss and sugar uptake.

    C) water loss and carbon dioxide uptake.

    D) sugar loss and oxygen uptake.

    E) carbon dioxide uptake and oxygen loss.

Answer: C
Diff: 2   Page Ref: 42.5
Skill: Conceptual

114) An opening in the epidermis of the leaf through which water evaporates is a

A) guard cell.

B) plasmodesmata.

C) pit.

D) sieve plate.

E) stoma.

Answer: E
Diff: 1   Page Ref: 42.5
Skill: Factual

115) Plant transpiration would occur more rapidly on a day that is

A) cloudy and rainy.

B) humid and hot.

C) cool and cloudy.

D) sunny and windy.

E) very dry.

Answer: D
Diff: 2   Page Ref: 42.5
Skill: Conceptual

116) When potassium ion is transported INTO guard cells, water

A) is actively transported out of the cells.

B) is actively transported into the cells.

C) leaves by osmosis.

D) enters by osmosis.

E) moves to the edge of the cell.

Answer: D
Diff: 2   Page Ref: 42.5
Skill: Conceptual

117) An essential plant nutrient required for the regulation of stomatal opening and closing is

A) potassium.

B) calcium.

C) copper.

D) phosphorus.

E) iron.

Answer: A
Diff: 1   Page Ref: 42.5
Skill: Factual

118) Because abscisic acid is formed in the mesophyll and has its effects in the guard cells, abscisic acid is considered to be a plant _____.

    A) enzyme   B) mineral   C) hormone   D) nutrient   E) ion

Answer: C
Diff: 1   *Page Ref: 42.5*
Skill: Factual

119) Which of the following helps explain the cohesion of water molecules in the cohesion–tension theory?

    A) complete covalent bonds

    B) hydrogen bonds

    C) ionic bonds

    D) peptide bonds

    E) disulfide bonds

Answer: B
Diff: 1   *Page Ref: 42.5*
Skill: Factual

120) Water flows upward in some xylem tubes and downward in others. True or False?

Answer: FALSE
Diff: 1   *Page Ref: 42.5*
Skill: Factual

121) The presence of dissolved substances _____ the free water concentration by binding up the water molecules.

Answer: lowers
Diff: 2   *Page Ref: 42.5*
Skill: Conceptual

122) Plants that live in the desert often have very high concentration of dissolved mineral ions in their xylem. Explain how such dissolved substances change the movement of water molecules and how this might help such plants to get water out of very dry desert soils.

Answer: Such dissolved materials slow the movement of water molecules inside the plant so that water molecules outside the plant will tend to flow into it by osmosis thus contributing to the plant's ability to get water out of very dry soils.
Diff: 2   *Page Ref: 42.5*
Skill: Conceptual

123) After water passes through the endodermal cell of the roots, what happens to it?

Answer: In enters the extracellular space of the vascular cylinder and moves from there into the xylem cells.
Diff: 2   *Page Ref: 42.5*
Skill: Conceptual

124) What two factors contribute to lowering the free water concentration inside the vascular cylinder so that water flows into it?

Answer: 1. The high concentration of minerals in the vascular cylinder 2. The pull of evaporation (transpiration) from the stomata
Diff: 2   Page Ref: 42.5
Skill: Conceptual

125) The type of process by which water moves through the xylem of plants is _____.

Answer: bulk flow
Diff: 1   Page Ref: 42.5
Skill: Factual

126) Explain why the plant does not have to use energy to move minerals in the xylem.

Answer: Once the minerals are dissolved in the water inside the vascular cylinder, they are carried along passively by the bulk flow of the water in the xylem rather like a leaf on a stream.
Diff: 2   Page Ref: 42.5
Skill: Conceptual

127) Why does water move only upward in the plant xylem?

Answer: only the shoot can transpire
Diff: 1   Page Ref: 42.5
Skill: Factual

128) Plants in the tropical rain forest often grow faster than those in temperate forests. Explain how what you know about the factors that affect transpiration would contribute to this.

Answer: Water is abundant in the tropical rain forest, allowing the stomata to open as long as the other factors of light, low CO_2, (temperature, wind speed, etc., not mentioned in text) allow the stomata to remain open.
Diff: 2   Page Ref: 42.5
Skill: Conceptual

129) Plants control the opening of stomata by actively transporting _____ into and out of the guard cells.

Answer: potassium ions
Diff: 1   Page Ref: 42.5
Skill: Factual

130) What is the role of abscisic acid in controlling the closing of stomata?

Answer: It inhibits active transport of potassium ions factual.
Diff: 1   Page Ref: 42.5
Skill: Factual

131) The major factors which affect the opening and closing of stomata are:

Answer: light, carbon dioxide and water.
Diff: 1   *Page Ref: 42.5*
Skill: Factual

132) Tree roots are a _____ of sugars in spring and a _____ in the fall.

    A) source; sink

    B) sink; source

    C) sink; sink

    D) source; source

    E) none of the above—They are not involved in source/sink relationships.

Answer: A
Diff: 3   *Page Ref: 42.6*
Skill: Application

133) Which organism helped biologists determine the contents of phloem?

    A) ants

    B) leafhoppers

    C) aphids

    D) termites

    E) grasshoppers

Answer: C
Diff: 1   *Page Ref: 42.6*
Skill: Factual

134) The most widely accepted explanation for the transport of sugars in phloem is the

    A) pressure–flow theory.

    B) transpiration theory.

    C) bulk flow theory.

    D) root pressure theory.

    E) cohesion–tension theory.

Answer: A
Diff: 1   *Page Ref: 42.6*
Skill: Factual

135) The sugar that is carried in the phloem is in the form of

   A) the simple sugar glucose.

   B) the simple sugar fructose.

   C) table sugar (sucrose).

   D) starch.

   E) glycogen.

Answer: C
Diff: 1   Page Ref: 42.6
Skill: Factual

136) During sugar movement in phloem, water enters sieve tubes from

   A) companion cells.

   B) adjacent xylem.

   C) cortical tissues.

   D) endodermal cells.

   E) the mesophyll.

Answer: B
Diff: 1   Page Ref: 42.6
Skill: Factual

137) In the summer when plants are storing sugar that is being produced in the leaves and roots, the root is the _____ and the leaves are the _____.

   A) xylem source; xylem sink

   B) xylem sink; xylem source

   C) phloem source; phloem sink

   D) phloem sink; phloem source

   E) xylem source; phloem sink

Answer: D
Diff: 3   Page Ref: 42.6
Skill: Application

138) Describe sieve tube fluid.

   Answer: A concentrate (up to 25%) of sugar in water (There are also numerous other components, but these are the most common).
   Diff: 1   Page Ref: 42.6
   Skill: Factual

139) In the spring when sugars are being moved from the root of a plant to the developing buds, the root is phloem _____ and the bud is the phloem _____.

   Answer: source; sink
   Diff: 2   Page Ref: 42.6
   Skill: Application

140) Describe the sequence of events that allows sugars to move from source to sink.

   Answer: At the source end sucrose is loaded by companion cells into the sieve cells. Water follows from the xylem into the sieve tubes by osmosis. This causes hydrostatic pressure to build up on the source end, pushing the sugar solution through the tube. On the sink end the source is actively transported into the surrounding tissue. Water flows back into the xylem by osmosis lowering the hydrostatic pressure on the sink end.
   Diff: 2   Page Ref: 42.6
   Skill: Application

141) A sweet potato has no "eyes" such as those found on a white potato because sweet potato is a _____ adapted for food storage, whereas the white potato is an underground _____ which is adapted for the same purpose.

   A) stem; root

   B) root; stem

   C) leaf; root

   D) leaf; stem

   E) root; leaf

   Answer: B
   Diff: 1   Page Ref: Evolution Connections
   Skill: Factual

142) If you plant irises entirely below the surface of the ground, they will not flower due to a lack of exposure to light. This is because the thing we often call an iris "bulb" is actually a _____ called a _____.

   A) stem; rhizome

   B) root; tendril

   C) leaf; rhizoid

   D) root; mesophyll

   E) stem; node

   Answer: A
   Diff: 1   Page Ref: Evolution Connections
   Skill: Factual

143) An onion bulb is made up of _____ which are specially adapted for food storage.

   A) roots   B) flowers   C) leaves   D) stems   E) branches

   Answer: C
   Diff: 1   Page Ref: Evolution Connections
   Skill: Factual

144) The leaves of round oak seedlings on the forest floor are often much larger than those of their parents. Suggest a reason why this is a good adaptation to survival in a dense forest.

   Answer: Low light levels on the forest floor make large leaves an advantage especially where there is sufficient moisture.
   Diff: 2   Page Ref: Evolution Connections
   Skill: Conceptual

145) Carnivorous plants, such as Venus flytrap, trap insects as a source of _____ which is difficult to obtain from the boggy soils in which they live.

   Answer: nitrogen
   Diff: 1   Page Ref: Evolution Connections
   Skill: Factual

146) When tropical rain forest is cut, what happens to rainfall in the area? Why?

   Answer: It decreases because less water is transpired so that the moisture in the air is lower.
   Diff: 2   Page Ref: Earthwatch
   Skill: Conceptual

Chapter 43   Plant Reproduction and Development

1) Spores and gametes are both haploid, reproductive cells. What is the difference between spores and gametes?

   A) Spores germinate and grow into a multicellular, haploid gametophyte.

   B) Gametes fuse and form a diploid zygote that eventually becomes the sporophyte.

   C) Spores are found in plants that reproduce asexually and gametes are found in plants that reproduce sexually.

   D) A and B

   E) A and C

Answer: D
Diff: 3   Page Ref: 43.1
Skill: Application

2) Why do ferns and mosses need water for sexual reproduction?

   A) They have swimming sperm.

   B) Pollen is transported to nearby plants by rainsplash.

   C) Water is required for sperm production.

   D) Water is required for spore dispersal.

   E) none of the above

Answer: A
Diff: 2   Page Ref: 43.1
Skill: Conceptual

3) If a plant such as an iris reproduces asexually most of the time, it probably

   A) is found in a changing environment.

   B) produces offspring that move into new environments.

   C) lacks the ability to make flowers.

   D) forms spores.

   E) has offspring that live in the same environment as the parents.

Answer: E
Diff: 2   Page Ref: 43.1
Skill: Conceptual

4) You see a moss plant near the base of a tree in your yard. The green leafy plants are

   A) sporophyte.

   B) gametophyte.

   C) gamete.

   D) spore.

   E) zygote.

Answer: B
Diff: 2   Page Ref: 43.1
Skill: Conceptual

5) If you are looking at an oak tree, you are looking at

   A) sporophyte.

   B) gametophyte.

   C) gamete.

   D) spore.

   E) zygote.

Answer: A
Diff: 1   Page Ref: 43.1
Skill: Factual

6) In general, plant evolution has moved from _____ to _____.

   A) dominant gametophyte; dominant sporophyte

   B) dominant sporophyte; dominant gametophyte

   C) dominant spore; dominant gamete

   D) dominant gamete; dominant spore

   E) dominant gamete; dominant gametophyte

Answer: A
Diff: 1   Page Ref: 43.1
Skill: Factual

7) In general, plant evolution has moved from _____ to _____.

   A) nonseed; seed

   B) seed; nonseed

   C) fruit; nonseed

   D) no fruit; no spores

   E) 2N; 1N life cycle

Answer: A
Diff: 1   Page Ref: 43.1
Skill: Factual

8) In an alternation of generations life cycle (ferns, for example), what alternates?

    A) male plants and female plants

    B) reproductive plants and vegetative plants

    C) eggs and sperm

    D) sporophytes and gametophytes

    E) flowers and spores

Answer: D
Diff: 2   *Page Ref: 43.1*
Skill: Conceptual

9) The sporophyte produces

    A) spores by mitosis.

    B) spores by meiosis.

    C) gametes by mitosis.

    D) gametes by meiosis.

    E) gametes by mitosis followed by meiosis.

Answer: B
Diff: 2   *Page Ref: 43.1*
Skill: Factual

10) In alternation of generation when a spore germinates, what is formed?

    A) a plant which produces spores when mature

    B) an increased number of spores

    C) a plant which meiotically produces sex cells

    D) a haploid stage called the gametophyte

    E) a haploid stage called the sporophyte

Answer: D
Diff: 2   *Page Ref: 43.1*
Skill: Factual

11) A diploid fertilized egg is termed a/an

    A) embryo.

    B) zygote.

    C) archegonium.

    D) pollen grain.

    E) ovum.

Answer: B
Diff: 1   *Page Ref: 43.1*
Skill: Factual

12) In the life cycle of a fern the large fern plant that we normally see is the

A) spore.

B) sporophyte.

C) gamete.

D) gametophyte.

E) zygote.

Answer: B
Diff: 1   Page Ref: 43.1
Skill: Factual

13) In the fern life cycle, how do spores and gametes differ from each other?

A) Gametes are easily visible to the unaided eye and spores are not.

B) Spores are produced mitotically and gametes are produced meiotically.

C) Meiotic cell division produces haploid spores and mitotic cell division produces haploid gametes.

D) Gametes are diploid and spores are haploid.

E) Gametes are produced by the sporophyte.

Answer: C
Diff: 2   Page Ref: 43.1
Skill: Conceptual

14) What process results in the production of spores in plants?

A) fertilization

B) germination

C) meiosis

D) spermatogenesis

E) mitosis

Answer: C
Diff: 1   Page Ref: 43.1
Skill: Factual

15) Which of the following has an "alternation of generations" life cycle?

    A) pine tree

    B) moss

    C) grass

    D) rose

    E) all of the above

Answer: E
Diff: 1   Page Ref: 43.1
Skill: Factual

16) Which of the following is "male" in the life cycle of angiosperms?

    A) embryo sac

    B) megaspore mother cell

    C) pollen grain

    D) seed cone

    E) endosperm

Answer: C
Diff: 2   Page Ref: 43.1
Skill: Conceptual

17) Asexual reproduction is rare in plants. True or False?

Answer: FALSE
Diff: 1   Page Ref: 25.1
Skill: Factual

18) In primitive land plants such as mosses and fern how does the sperm get to the egg?

Answer: The sperm must swim through a film or drop of water.
Diff: 2   Page Ref: 43.1
Skill: Conceptual

19) In temperate deciduous forests most of the small flowers that grow on the forest floor must complete their life cycle quickly before tree leaves shade out most of the light. Many of these plants reproduce asexually by runners or rhizomes most of the time. What advantages does this have for such plants?

Answer: The environment that the offspring occupy is the same as that of the parents so are likely to do well if they are identical to the parents. If the flowers do not get pollinated due to their brief life span, the plant is still able to reproduce. The offspring get nutrition from the parent.
Diff: 2   Page Ref: 43.1
Skill: Conceptual

20) Describe the process of alternation of generation in plants.

Answer: should include haploid gametophyte produces gametes by mitosis and diploid
sporophyte produces spores by meiosis
Diff: 2   *Page Ref: 43.1*
Skill: Conceptual

21) In flowering plants the sperm does not have to swim to the egg because the sperm reaches the eggs by

A) wind pollination.

B) a pollen tube.

C) borrowing through the embryo sac wall.

D) cell division within the spore case.

E) digestion of the seed coat.

Answer: B
Diff: 1   *Page Ref: 43.2*
Skill: Factual

22) The earliest seed plants are thought to be the

A) gymnosperms.

B) flowering trees.

C) angiosperms.

D) tree ferns.

E) beetle pollinated flowers.

Answer: A
Diff: 1   *Page Ref: 43.3*
Skill: Factual

23) A pollen grain is actually the

A) male gametophyte.

B) female gametophyte.

C) combination of male & female gametophytes.

D) a megaspore mother cell.

E) primitive egg cell, which will develop into the embryo.

Answer: B
Diff: 1   *Page Ref: 43.2*
Skill: Factual

24) Conifers do not have flowers to attract pollinators. Instead fertilization occurs

    A) via wind pollination.

    B) because both male and female gametophytes are formed within the woody cone.

    C) endosperm can take the place of the male gametes.

    D) when insects coated with pollen are trapped in the sticky resin.

    E) when birds transfer pollen in their droppings after eating the pine seeds.

Answer: B
Diff: 1   Page Ref: 43.2
Skill: Conceptual

25) During a late summer walk through a park you notice a tree with remnants of many flowers but no fruit or seed developing. There are no other trees like this one in the area. What could explain this occurrence?

    A) It is a male tree (contains only male flowers) and so will not form fruit.

    B) It is a female tree and no male trees of the same species are near enough for pollination to occur.

    C) Either of the above are possible explanations.

    D) None of the above is a possible explanation.

Answer: C
Diff: 3   Page Ref: 43.2
Skill: Application

26) In angiosperm but not conifers pollen grains can form pollen tubes. True or False?

Answer: FALSE
Diff: 1   Page Ref: 43.2
Skill: Factual

27) Since they do not have flowers, where do gymnosperms produce pollen and eggs?

Answer: in male and female cones
Diff: 1   Page Ref: 25.2
Skill: Factual

28) Grass flowers lack petals and sepals. Which of the following statements is/are TRUE?

    A) They are wind pollinated.

    B) They are pollinated by flies, which don't require sweet scented petals.

    C) They are imperfect flowers.

    D) They are incomplete flowers.

    E) A and D

Answer: E
Diff: 2   Page Ref: 43.3
Skill: Factual

29) Flowers that make pollen only and no seeds lack which part?

   A) petal   B) sepal   C) stamen   D) carpel   E) filament

Answer: D
Diff: 1   Page Ref: 43.3
Skill: Factual

30) Which of the following flower structures are modified leaves?

   A) petals

   B) carpels

   C) sepals

   D) stamens

   E) all of these

Answer: E
Diff: 1   Page Ref: 43.3
Skill: Factual

31) If a flower is incomplete, it

   A) lacks one or more of the four basic floral parts.

   B) maintains the bud stage and does not bloom.

   C) produces sterile seeds.

   D) manufactures infertile pollen.

   E) is incapable of self-fertilization.

Answer: A
Diff: 1   Page Ref: 43.3
Skill: Factual

32) All of the following are parts of the male parts of a flower EXCEPT

   A) stamens.

   B) ovules.

   C) pollen.

   D) anthers.

   E) All of these are associated with the male parts.

Answer: B
Diff: 1   Page Ref: 43.3
Skill: Factual

33) The American holly tree requires a "male" tree and a "female" tree for the production of red berries in the winter. This indicates that the male flowers lack _____, while the female flowers lack _____.

    A) anthers; stamens

    B) sepals; anthers

    C) carpels; stamens

    D) petals; ovules

    E) petals; carpels

Answer: C
Diff: 2   Page Ref: 43.3
Skill: Conceptual

34) Where is pollen produced by a flowering plant?

    A) stigma   B) ovule   C) fruit   D) anther   E) style

Answer: D
Diff: 1   Page Ref: 43.3
Skill: Factual

35) Theses modified leaves are often green and surround the flower bud.

    A) filaments   B) ovules   C) petals   D) stigma   E) sepals

Answer: E
Diff: 1   Page Ref: 43.3
Skill: Factual

36) Theses modified leaves are often brightly colored and fragrant.

    A) filaments   B) anthers   C) petals   D) stigma   E) sepals

Answer: C
Diff: 1   Page Ref: 43.3
Skill: Factual

37) This structure produces pollen.

    A) filament   B) anther   C) stigma   D) stamen   E) sepal

Answer: B
Diff: 1   Page Ref: 43.3
Skill: Factual

38) The female reproductive structure, the carpel, consists of

    A) filament, anther, pollen.

    B) sepals, petals, ovary.

    C) stigma, style, ovary.

    D) stamen, sepals, filament.

    E) stigma, filament, sepals.

Answer: C
Diff: 1   Page Ref: 43.3
Skill: Factual

39) Which of the following represents the correct relationship for female reproductive structures in angiosperms?

    A) The stamen includes the filament and pollen producing anther.

    B) The sepals are contained within the petals which enclose the carpel.

    C) The carpel includes a stigma, a style and ovules enclosed within an ovary.

    D) The filament and anther enclose the stigma and style.

    E) The style, which is vase–shaped contains ovary, stigma and anther.

Answer: C
Diff: 2   Page Ref: 43.3
Skill: Conceptual

40) The male reproductive structure, the stamen, consists of

    A) the filament and the anther.

    B) a single sepal, 4 or more petals plus the entire carpel.

    C) the stigma, style and ovary.

    D) one or more sepals, the style plus one or more anthers.

    E) a carpel enclosed in first the petals, then the sepals.

Answer: A
Diff: 1   Page Ref: 43.3
Skill: Factual

41) Which of the following statements is correct?

    A) When mature, the carpel will become the seed and the anther will become the fruit.

    B) When mature, the ovules will become seeds and the ovary will develop into a fruit.

    C) When mature, the stamen will become the seed and the stigma will become the fruit.

    D) The filament and anther enclose the stigma and style.

    E) The style, which is vase–shaped contains ovary, stigma and anther.

Answer: C
Diff: 2   Page Ref: 43.3
Skill: Conceptual

42) Pollen is produced by cell divisions inside of the

    A) anther.   B) filament.   C) carpel.   D) stigma.   E) sepal.

Answer: A
Diff: 1   Page Ref: 43.3
Skill: Factual

43) What is the evolutionary significance of a flower with larger, brightly colored petals?

    A) The wind is a significant factor in pollination especially because of the large petals.

    B) Such plants are usually self–pollinators and do not rely on external factors for pollination.

    C) In general, these are aquatic plants and water aids in pollination, irrespective of color and odor.

    D) These flowers are more attractive to animals as pollinators.

    E) Such flowers produce only microspores or megaspores, not both.

Answer: D
Diff: 2   Page Ref: 43.3
Skill: Conceptual

44) Meiosis produces this which will eventually give rise to an egg in an unfertilized seed.

    A) microspore

    B) pollen tube

    C) sporophyte

    D) megaspore

    E) sepal

Answer: D
Diff: 1   Page Ref: 43.3
Skill: Factual

45) Which of the following undergoes meiosis in the development of pollen grains?

    A) microspore mother cell

    B) megaspore mother cell

    C) microspore

    D) megaspore

    E) generative nucleus

Answer: A
Diff: 1   Page Ref: 43.3
Skill: Factual

46) All of the following are processes that occur during angiosperm reproduction EXCEPT

    A) microspore mother cell undergoes meiosis to produce four haploid microspores.

    B) megaspore mother cell undergoes meiosis to produce four haploid megaspores.

    C) the generative cell forms two sperm cells via mitosis.

    D) 1 megaspore degenerates, the other three divide once to produce the 6-celled embryo
       sac.

    E) the tube cell produces the pollen tube.

Answer: C
Diff: 2   Page Ref: 43.3
Skill: Factual

47) In the development of an embryo sac of a plant what results?

    A) an embryo sac made up of eight haploid, uninucleate cells

    B) an embryo sac made up of seven diploid cells and one haploid cell

    C) an embryo sac made up of seven cells: six haploid cells and one cell with two nuclei

    D) an embryo sac with seven binucleate cells and one haploid cell

    E) an embryo sac with an egg and a sperm

Answer: C
Diff: 2   Page Ref: 43.33
Skill: Conceptual

48) In flowering plants, the haploid female gametophyte is the

    A) endosperm.

    B) embryo sac.

    C) pollen grain.

    D) embryo.

    E) polar nucleus.

Answer: B
Diff: 1   *Page Ref: 43.3*
Skill: Factual

49) How many sperm are produced by an angiosperm pollen grain when it grows its pollen tube?

    A) 1   B) 2   C) 3   D) 4   E) many

Answer: B
Diff: 1   *Page Ref: 43.3*
Skill: Factual

50) Endosperm is one of the main reasons the flowering plant group has become the most numerous and diverse. What does the endosperm accomplish?

    A) It's a type of male gamete.

    B) It provides nutrition for the developing embryo, therefore increasing survival rates.

    C) It is the hard outer seed coat and protects the embryo.

    D) It is responsible for dispersal of seeds after they mature.

    E) It is the ripened ovary tissue involved in seed dispersal and protection.

Answer: B
Diff: 2   *Page Ref: 43.3*
Skill: Conceptual

51) What is the function of endosperm?

    A) It provides nutrients for developing flowers.

    B) It supplies nuclei necessary for double fertilization.

    C) It stores food for the developing embryo in angiosperms.

    D) It is a source of nutrition for developing cones in gymnosperms.

    E) It forms the first pair of leaves for the young plant.

Answer: C
Diff: 2   *Page Ref: 43.3*
Skill: Conceptual

52) What are the results of double fertilization?

   A) diploid zygote and diploid endosperm

   B) egg cell and sperm cell

   C) embryo sac and pollen sac

   D) triploid endosperm and diploid zygote

   E) a zygote and an embryo

Answer: D
Diff: 1   Page Ref: 43.3
Skill: Factual

53) Around the world the most common types of plants are the flowering plants. True or False?

Answer: TRUE
Diff: 1   Page Ref: 43.3
Skill: Factual

54) Megaspore mother cells are diploid. True or False?

Answer: TRUE
Diff: 1   Page Ref: 43.3
Skill: Factual

55) The embryo sac of angiosperms consists of 8 diploid cells plus a haploid egg cell. True or False?

Answer: FALSE
Diff: 1   Page Ref: 43.3
Skill: Factual

56) The process in flowering plant reproduction in which the first sperm unites with an egg to form a zygote and the second sperm unites with two haploid polar bodies to form diploid endosperm is called double fertilization. True or False?

Answer: FALSE
Diff: 2   Page Ref: 43.3
Skill: Conceptual

57) Discuss the two key adaptations in plants that were necessary for insect pollination to be successful.

Answer: sufficient amounts of pollen or nectar produced in proximity to the stigma plus 'advertising' in the form of petals to attract the insect to the area
Diff: 2   Page Ref: 43.3
Skill: Conceptual

58) What is the function of the stigma of a flower?

Answer: to serve as a sticky landing site for pollen
Diff: 2   Page Ref: 43.3
Skill: Conceptual

59) What are the advantages to producing gametes within a flower?

Answer: This helps with reproduction on land because the male gamete and the embryo are produced within waterproof coats. This allows the plant to invade dryer environments. In addition the sperm can be released within the female gametophyte.
Diff: 2   Page Ref: 43.3
Skill: Conceptual

60) In some areas of the world where there are large numbers of conifers such as pines, in the spring everything (cars, homes, streets, etc.) is covered with a yellow dust that turns out upon examination to be pollen. Why must conifers produce so much pollen and why do we not see as much pollen produced by, for example, a field of flowers?

Answer: Conifers are wind–pollinated so must produce enormous amounts of pollen in order to ensure that some of the pollen reaches the female cones. Flowering plants are more likely to be pollinated by animals, thus helping to ensure that they actually get pollinated and reducing the need for enormous amounts of pollen.
Diff: 3   Page Ref: 43.3
Skill: Application

61) In the embryo sac, which two cells with a total of three nuclei will be fertilized?

Answer: the two polar nuclei in the primary endosperm cell and the egg cell
Diff: 2   Page Ref: 43.3
Skill: Conceptual

62) Why is fertilization in flowering plants called "double fertilization"?

Answer: One sperm fertilizes the egg cell and the other fertilizes the endosperm cell.
Diff: 2   Page Ref: 43.3
Skill: Conceptual

63) How many sperm nuclei are necessary for successful fertilization of flowering plants?

Answer: two
Diff: 1   Page Ref: 43.3
Skill: Factual

64) The first leaves produced by an embryo while still inside the seed are

A) cotyledons.

B) endosperms.

C) embryosacs.

D) coleoptiles.

E) epicotyls.

Answer: A
Diff: 1   Page Ref: 43.4
Skill: Factual

65) The reserve food in angiosperm seeds is either stored in the cotyledons or in a special tissue called

A) gametophyte.

B) megaspore.

C) endosperm.

D) ovary wall.

E) sporophyte.

Answer: C
Diff: 1   Page Ref: 43.4
Skill: Factual

66) In the processing of wheat to make white all–purpose flour, the wheat is passed through rollers which pop off the embryo and the ovary wall. My grandmother used to add "Wheat Germ" to the white flour of her baked goods to increase the protein content of these products, giving them almost as much protein as if she had used whole wheat flour. What is "Wheat Germ"?

A) the wheat fruit

B) the wheat flour

C) the embryo

D) the endosperm

E) the bran

Answer: C
Diff: 3   Page Ref: 43.4
Skill: Application

67) The seed coat develops from the

    A) ovary wall.

    B) integuments of the ovule.

    C) endosperm.

    D) female gametophyte.

    E) wall of the pollen sac.

Answer: B
Diff: 2   Page Ref: 43.4
Skill: Factual

68) A fruit is a mature

    A) integument.

    B) embryo.

    C) endosperm.

    D) ovary wall.

    E) ovule.

Answer: D
Diff: 1   Page Ref: 43.4
Skill: Factual

69) When we consume rice or barley, we are eating endosperm. True or False?

Answer: TRUE
Diff: 1   Page Ref: 43.4
Skill: Factual

70) Briefly describe how a seed develops from the ovule.

Answer: Two processes: 1) triploid central cells undergoes mitosis, absorbs nutrients and becomes endosperm 2) zygote develops into embryo
Diff: 2   Page Ref: 43.4
Skill: Conceptual

71) When you eat a cherry you know that the fruit was derived from the _____ and the seed was derived from the _____.

Answer: ovary; ovule
Diff: 2   Page Ref: 25.5
Skill: Conceptual

72) You have some freshly produced seeds which refuse to germinate when placed in moist soil. What is one thing you might do to encourage the seeds to germinate?

    A) boil them

    B) freeze and thaw them

    C) put them in the dark

    D) treat them with abscisic acid

    E) put them in the sun

Answer: B
Diff: 2   Page Ref: 43.5
Skill: Conceptual

73) Plants in a/an _____ geographical area most likely do not require drying, exposure to cold, or disruption of seed coat to break dormancy.

    A) northern temperate

    B) arctic

    C) wet tropical

    D) desert

    E) B and D

Answer: C
Diff: 2   Page Ref: 43.5
Skill: Conceptual

74) Cotyledons and endosperm both provide nutrition. What is the difference between these two?

    A) Cotyledon(s) provide nutrition for the developing embryo and endosperm provides nutrition for the young seedling.

    B) Endosperm provides nutrition for the developing embryo and cotyledon(s) provide nutrition for the young seedling.

    C) Endosperm is always photosynthetic and cotyledons are usually not.

    D) Cotyledons are found in flowering plants and endosperm is found in young ferns.

    E) Endosperm is only found in monocots and cotyledons are found in dicots.

Answer: B
Diff: 2   Page Ref: 43.5
Skill: Conceptual

75) Which of these is most likely to preserve seeds alive for the longest period of time prior to their germination?

A) darkness

B) exposure to sunlight

C) slating down as is done with some fish

D) low humidity

E) high humidity

Answer: B
Diff: 2   Page Ref: 43.5
Skill: Conceptual

76) A dicot with mutations that prevent formation of a hypocotyl hook during germination

A) should germinate and grow like a normal plant.

B) will probably have damage to the apical meristem while the seedling emerges from the soil.

C) will probably have damage to the cotyledons while the seedling emerges from the soil.

D) will probably have damage to the emerging root tip.

E) will not be able to germinate.

Answer: B
Diff: 3   Page Ref: 43.5
Skill: Application

77) Desert plants often have _____ in their seed coats which keep them dormant until there is sufficient water to complete their life cycle.

A) drying agents

B) cold–sensitive compounds

C) digestive enzymes

D) wetting agents

E) inhibitory compounds

Answer: E
Diff: 1   Page Ref: 43.5
Skill: Factual

78) In many dicots the first pair of leaves look completely unlike all the rest of the leaves that form on that plant. In such plants the first pair of leaves is

A) derived from the root, not the shoot.

B) cotyledons which have elongated and turned green.

C) made from the opening and greening of the coleoptile.

D) made out of the epicotyl hook.

E) formed from the endosperm.

Answer: B
Diff: 1   Page Ref: 43.5
Skill: Factual

79) In monocots, the shoot tip is protected by

A) a slime layer formed by the shoot cells.

B) cotyledons.

C) the hypocotyl.

D) the coleoptile.

E) the epicotyl.

Answer: D
Diff: 2   Page Ref: 43.5
Skill: Factual

80) In dicots, the shoot tip is protected by

A) a slime layer formed by the shoot cells.

B) the coleptile.

C) forming in the hook of the hypocotyl.

D) forming in the hook of the hypocotyl.

E) either C or D.

Answer: E
Diff: 2   Page Ref: 43.5
Skill: Factual

81) When a bean seed germinates, a hypocotyl hook comes out of the ground first. What part of the young plant is this?

Answer: the area below the cotyledons but above the root
Diff: 1   Page Ref: 43.5
Skill: Factual

82) When a seed germinates, what usually comes out of the seed coat first?

Answer: the root, because it can absorb water and nutrients from the soil
Diff: 1   Page Ref: 43.5
Skill: Factual

83) Plants that live in temperate latitudes often make seeds that exhibit dormancy. What is the advantage of having dormant seeds for plants living in these areas?

Answer: With dormancy a warm fall season would cause the seeds to germinate. The seedlings would then be killed by winter weather.
Diff: 2   Page Ref: 43.5
Skill: Conceptual

84) Both monocots and dicots have ways of protecting their young shoots as they emerge from the soil. Describe the way each group accomplishes this protection.

Answer: The student should explain each of these: Monocots¹coleoptile, Dicots—epicotyl or hypocotyl hook.
Diff: 2   Page Ref: 43.5
Skill: Conceptual

85) Some very showy desert flowers avoid desiccation of delicate tissues by blooming at night. How can they possibly be pollinated?

A) wind   B) bees   C) moths   D) bats   E) C or D

Answer: E
Diff: 2   Page Ref: 43.6
Skill: Conceptual

86) Yucca flowers are pollinated only by yucca moths. This ensures the plant has seed for the next generation and a food source for the larvae. What is a potential disadvantage of this very specific interaction?

A) The plant will be consumed by the larvae.

B) If the moths are killed, for example, by insecticide spray drift, the plant will not be pollinated.

C) Pollination only occurs at night.

D) none of the above

Answer: B
Diff: 2   Page Ref: 43.6
Skill: Conceptual

87) Walking up a riverbank after a swim, you step on a sharp fruit in your bare feet. When you pick it up it rattles, indicating there is an air pocket around the seeds. How is this fruit most likely dispersed?

   A) explosively propelled

   B) wind

   C) water

   D) clinging to animals

   E) being eaten by animals

Answer: C
Diff: 2   Page Ref: 43.6
Skill: Conceptual

88) Which pollinators does one expect to visit a flower that is relatively simple in design and smells like rotting carrion?

   A) beetles

   B) butterflies

   C) hummingbirds

   D) moths and butterflies

   E) bees

Answer: A
Diff: 1   Page Ref: 43.6
Skill: Factual

89) One relative of the milkweed is named for its insect pollinator. This flower is orange; forms a deep, very narrow tube; and produces nectar at the bottom of the tube. The name of this flower is

   A) beeflower.

   B) beetle weed.

   C) hummingbird flower.

   D) butterfly weed.

   E) night–blooming moth flower.

Answer: D
Diff: 2   Page Ref: 43.6
Skill: Application

90) Which of the following is NOT true of the relationship between the yucca and the yucca moth?

   A) The female moth collects yucca pollen.

   B) The developing yucca seeds feed the yucca caterpillars.

   C) The yucca plant is dependent on the yucca moth to reproduce, but the yucca moth can lay its eggs in one of several kinds of flowers.

   D) The moth lays its eggs directly inside the yucca ovary where its eggs hatch into caterpillars.

   E) The yucca moth spreads pollen on the stigma of the yucca flower in which it lays its eggs.

Answer: C
Diff: 2   Page Ref: 43.6
Skill: Conceptual

91) Commercials on TV use food and sex as their most attractive selling points. Explain how flowers use the same two attractants to "sell" their pollen to animals.

Answer: Give examples of sugar-rich nectar and mimicry to illustrate this.
Diff: 2   Page Ref: 43.6
Skill: Conceptual

92) Compare the shape, color, scent, and nectar content of a flower that is pollinated by a bee with one that is pollinated by a hummingbird. Why are they so different?

Answer: The student should mention the deep, narrow shape and lack of a landing lip, the inability of insects to see red clearly, the enormous amount of nectar needed by a hummingbird, and the inability of the bird to smell. The differences in the flowers are the result of the differences in the pollinators.
Diff: 3   Page Ref: 43.6
Skill: Application

93) The aptly named dead horse arum has a heat producing flower. What advantage does this heat provide?

   A) allows blooms to emerge through snow

   B) warms the pollinators, which are usually bats

   C) creates a barrier to invasive plant species

   D) increases the evaporation of the chemical scent, attracting pollinators from greater distances

   E) prevents inappropriate pollinators from wasting the nutrients

Answer: D
Diff: 1   Page Ref: Case Study
Skill: Factual

94) Mexico's fruit-eating bat populations are on the decline. How is this loss connected to the deterioration of Mexico's tropical forests?

   A) Bat guano fertilizes mature trees.

   B) Bats create dens that increase the aeration of the soil.

   C) The bat's predators are dying out causing overgrowth of invasive plant species.

   D) Loss of bat populations has increased the incidence of malaria in the area due to overgrowth of mosquito populations.

   E) The seeds from the fruit the bats eat germinate at much higher rates after passing through the digestive tract of the bats.

Answer: E
Diff: 2   Page Ref: Earthwatch
Skill: Conceptual

95) Using tambalacoque trees and dodo birds as an example, describe how the extinction of one species can affect an ecosystem.

Answer: Tambalacoque trees are in decline due to the extinction of the dodo bird and other island animals. The animals fed on the tambalacoque fruit, cleaning the seed and dispersing it. Now the seed rot and cannot germinate. Thus the aging tambalacoque trees are not being replaced by healthy seedlings.
Diff: 2   Page Ref: Earthwatch
Skill: Application

96) Most 'hay fever' is actually caused by ragweed and not goldenrod. True or False?

Answer: TRUE
Diff: 1   Page Ref: Health Watch
Skill: Factual

Chapter 44   Plant Responses to the Environment

1) The majority of carnivorous plants are found in bogs because

   A) bog soils are naturally low in nitrogen.

   B) insects are a good source of protein.

   C) proteins are a good source of nitrogen.

   D) acidic bog soils inhibit nitrogen–fixing bacteria.

   E) all of the above

   Answer: E
   Diff: 2   Page Ref: Case Study
   Skill: Conceptual

2) A mutant plant has a deficiency in gibberellin production. Which of the following characteristics could be caused by this mutation?

   A) lack of phototropism in the shoots

   B) lack of gravitropism in the roots

   C) fruits that don't ripen

   D) dwarf stem (very short)

   E) stomata that don't close

   Answer: D
   Diff: 2   Page Ref: 44.1
   Skill: Conceptual

3) How a plant cell responds to a hormone vary based on

   A) the cell targeted.

   B) the developmental stage of the plant.

   C) the level of hormone present.

   D) the presence of other hormones.

   E) all of the above

   Answer: E
   Diff: 2   Page Ref: 44.1
   Skill: Conceptual

4) When normal (not mutated) seeds are planted, some of the seedlings do not emerge from the soil. Is it possible that this is due to some of the seeds being planted upside down?

A) Yes, if the seed was oriented so the embryonic shoot pointed down it would grow in that direction since sunlight doesn't reach it.

B) Yes, after seeds are planted, water and settling of the soil may cause them to shift in their orientation.

C) No, auxins in the shoots cause curvature away from gravity.

D) No, sunlight penetrates between soil particles to the depth of seeds and shoots grow towards the sunlight.

E) No, gibberellins and abscisic acid, in balanced concentrations, cause shoots to grow away from gravity.

Answer: C
Diff: 2   Page Ref: 44.1
Skill: Conceptual

5) Why do bananas in a bag ripen so much faster than bananas on a counter top?

A) Ethylene is trapped in the bag and diffuses to the air when bananas are on the counter top.

B) Abscisic acid is trapped in the bag and diffuses to the air when bananas are one the counter top.

C) The bag holds more moisture and the bananas in the bag rot faster than the ones on the counter top.

D) The bag shuts out sunlight so the auxins are not able to accumulate in the skins of the bananas in the bag.

E) Cytokinins are involved in delaying aging and are stimulated by sunlight.

Answer: A
Diff: 2   Page Ref: 44.1
Skill: Application

6) A plant's tendency to bend toward a source of light is called

A) phototropism.

B) lumitropism.

C) gravitropism.

D) amylotropism.

E) thigmotropism.

Answer: A
Diff: 1   Page Ref: 44.1
Skill: Factual

7) Pea tendrils wrapping around a string demonstrate

    A) phototropism.

    B) lumitropism.

    C) gravitropism.

    D) amylotropism.

    E) thigmotropism.

Answer: E
Diff: 1   Page Ref: 44.1
Skill: Factual

8) Planting tomatoes upside down still produces plants which grow upright. The plants are displaying

    A) phototropism.

    B) lumitropism.

    C) gravitropism.

    D) amylotropism.

    E) thigmotropism.

Answer: C
Diff: 1   Page Ref: 44.1
Skill: Factual

9) If a scientist states that he has discovered a new plant hormone, he would have to demonstrate that this compound was

    A) produced in large amounts.

    B) needed by the plant as a major source of energy.

    C) formed in one part of the plant and had an effect in a different part.

    D) capable of stimulating differentiated cells to form meristematic tissue.

    E) made out of cell proteins.

Answer: C
Diff: 2   Page Ref: 44.1
Skill: Conceptual

10) Gravitropism is a plant's

    A) directional response to gravity.

    B) response to stress–inducing situations.

    C) ability to grow upward.

    D) ability to form an abscission layer so that fruits and leaves fall from the plant.

    E) apical dominance.

Answer: A
Diff: 1   Page Ref: 44.1
Skill: Factual

11) A plant placed on a counter leans toward a window. This is an example of

    A) phototropism.

    B) lumitropism.

    C) gravitropism.

    D) amylotropism.

    E) thigmotropism.

Answer: A
Diff: 1   Page Ref: 44.1
Skill: Factual

12) Removing an overripe mushy apple from a container of otherwise good apples helps preserve the good apples. Why?

    A) The bad apple makes ethylene gas which can cause the good apples to become overripe.

    B) Ethanol production in the good apples is inhibited by the lack of ethanol production in the overripe apple.

    C) Chemicals in the overripe apple stimulate the conversion of sugar to starch in the good apples.

    D) The production of cytokinins is inhibited in the remaining good apples.

    E) Gibberellic acid helps preserve the good apples.

Answer: A
Diff: 2   Page Ref: 44.1
Skill: Application

13) Roots turn downward and shoots upward due to the hormone

    A) auxin.

    B) gibberellin.

    C) cytokinin.

    D) ethylene.

    E) abscisic acid.

Answer: A
Diff: 1   Page Ref: 44.1
Skill: Factual

14) The formation of an abscission layer in leaves or fruits can be triggered by

    A) auxin.

    B) gibberellin.

    C) cytokinin.

    D) ethylene.

    E) abscisic acid.

Answer: D
Diff: 1   Page Ref: 44.1
Skill: Factual

15) Seeds germination can be stimulated by

    A) auxin.

    B) gibberellin.

    C) cytokinin.

    D) ethylene.

    E) abscisic acid.

Answer: B
Diff: 1   Page Ref: 44.1
Skill: Factual

16) The hormone which helps plants tolerate drought or cold is

    A) auxin.

    B) gibberellin.

    C) cytokinin.

    D) ethylene.

    E) abscisic acid.

Answer: E
Diff: 1   Page Ref: 44.1
Skill: Factual

17) If I want to encourage cuttings to root, I would treat them with

   A) auxin.

   B) gibberellin.

   C) cytokinin.

   D) ethylene.

   E) abscisic acid.

Answer: C
Diff: 1   Page Ref: 44.1
Skill: Factual

18) Why are plant regulatory compounds considered to be hormones?

Answer: because they are produced in one location and have their effects in another part of the body
Diff: 2   Page Ref: 44.1
Skill: Conceptual

19) Cytokinins cause most of their responses in plants by what mechanism?

Answer: stimulating cell division
Diff: 1   Page Ref: 44.1
Skill: Factual

20) How do auxin and cytokinin interact to affect the shape of a plant?

Answer: Auxin encourages the development of the main stem and inhibits later bud growth. Cytokinin encourages the lateral bud growth. The interactions between the two determine the branching patterns
Diff: 1   Page Ref: 44.1
Skill: Conceptual

21) The only plant hormone that is a gas is _____.

Answer: ethylene
Diff: 1   Page Ref: 44.1
Skill: Factual

22) Defend the statement "Plants are just as capable of responding to their environment as are animals."

Answer: Plants have tropisms like gravitropism and phototropism. Their stomata open and close in response to available moisture to regulate transpiration. Many other examples are possible.
Diff: 3   Page Ref: 44.1
Skill: Application

23) _____ maintains seed dormancy and _____ break dormancy by stimulating enzymes that break down food reserves of the seed to fuel seedling growth.

    A) Gibberellins; abscisic acid

    B) Abscisic acid; gibberellins

    C) Auxins; cytokinins

    D) Cytokinins; auxins

    E) Abscisic acid; ethylene

Answer: B
Diff: 2   Page Ref: 44.2
Skill: Conceptual

24) A species specific ratio of _____ produced in the apical meristem and _____ produced in the root tips, maintains a balance between shoot and root growth.

    A) gibberellins; abscisic acid

    B) abscisic acid; gibberellins

    C) auxins; cytokinins

    D) cytokinins; auxins

    E) abscisic acid; ethylene

Answer: C
Diff: 2   Page Ref: 44.2
Skill: Conceptual

25) What will happen to a long–day plant like spinach if the dark period is interrupted by a flash of light in the night several days in a row, during the spring?

    A) Nothing, development will continue as normal.

    B) The plants will flower early.

    C) The plants will be delayed in flowering.

    D) The plants won't be able to flower that season.

Answer: B
Diff: 3   Page Ref: 44.2
Skill: Application

26) Placing a ripe apple in a bag of green bananas will cause them to ripen quickly. This is because the apple

   A) absorbs cytokinin.

   B) forms digestive enzymes.

   C) makes auxin.

   D) produces ethylene gas.

   E) absorbs heat better than bananas.

Answer: D
Diff: 2   Page Ref: 44.2
Skill: Conceptual

27) Lowering the level of a hedge with a hedge trimmer stimulates the hedge to become bushy because

   A) killing the apical meristems makes more auxin which stimulates lateral branch buds to grow.

   B) killing the apical meristems makes less ethylene which stimulates lateral branches to grow.

   C) killing the apical meristems results in less auxin which then allows lateral branches to grow.

   D) killing the lateral buds results in apical dominance under the influence of cytokinins.

   E) this stimulates the production of ethylene gas.

Answer: C
Diff: 2   Page Ref: 44.2
Skill: Conceptual

28) To encourage the formation of well-developed, heavily-branched roots, you could treat cuttings with

   A) ethylene.   B) gibberellin.   C) auxin.   D) abscisic acid.

Answer: C
Diff: 2   Page Ref: 44.2
Skill: Conceptual

29) You have some freshly produced seeds which refuse to germinate when placed in moist soil. What is one thing you might do to encourage the seeds to germinate?

    A) boil them

    B) treat them with gibberellin

    C) treat them with auxin

    D) treat them with abscisic acid

    E) put them in the sun

Answer: B
Diff: 2   Page Ref: 44.2
Skill: Conceptual

30) Which of the following maintains dormancy in seeds?

    A) auxin

    B) abscisic acid

    C) ethylene

    D) cytokinin

    E) gibberellin

Answer: B
Diff: 1   Page Ref: 44.2
Skill: Factual

31) If you were running a tree nursery and wanted to keep your trees dormant until the customer could get them planted, which hormone might you spray on the trees?

    A) auxin

    B) gibberellin

    C) cytokinin

    D) abscisic acid

    E) ethylene

Answer: D
Diff: 2   Page Ref: 44.2
Skill: Conceptual

32) Oranges and other fruits can be picked before they fully ripen then treated with _____ when needed for market.

A) ethylene

B) gibberellin

C) abscisic acid

D) auxin

E) cytokinin

Answer: A
Diff: 1   Page Ref: 44.2
Skill: Factual

33) Two hormones involved in seed germination and seed dormancy are

A) auxin and ethylene.

B) abscisic acid and gibberellin.

C) ethylene and cytokinin.

D) gibberellin and auxin.

E) cytokinin and auxin.

Answer: B
Diff: 1   Page Ref: 44.2
Skill: Factual

34) Abscisic acid

A) stimulates seed germination.

B) inhibits closing of stomata.

C) maintains bud dormancy.

D) promotes fruit abscission.

E) causes stem growth.

Answer: C
Diff: 1   Page Ref: 44.2
Skill: Factual

35) Ethylene

    A) promotes gravitropism.

    B) inhibits stem elongation.

    C) prevents leaf senescence.

    D) stimulates seed germination.

    E) causes phototropism.

Answer: B
Diff: 1   Page Ref: 44.2
Skill: Factual

36) Auxin

    A) inhibits stem elongation.

    B) promotes phototropism.

    C) stimulates flowering.

    D) promotes cell division.

    E) causes the development of an abscission layer.

Answer: B
Diff: 1   Page Ref: 44.2
Skill: Factual

37) Elongation of cells in stems is promoted by

    A) ethylene and cytokinins.

    B) auxins and gibberellins.

    C) enzymes and phytochromes.

    D) abscisic acid and ethylene.

    E) cytokinins and abscisic acid.

Answer: B
Diff: 1   Page Ref: 44.2
Skill: Factual

38) How does abscisic acid enforce dormancy of seeds?

    A) waterproofing the seed coat

    B) preventing endosperm development

    C) activating gibberellin

    D) preventing growth of the embryo

    E) blocking the micropyle

Answer: D
Diff: 2   Page Ref: 44.2
Skill: Conceptual

39) How does abscisic acid prepare woody plants for winter dormancy?

    A) suppressing ethylene production

    B) preventing endosperm development

    C) inhibiting gibberellin

    D) preventing growth of the embryo

    E) opening stomata

Answer: D
Diff: 2   *Page Ref: 44.2*
Skill: Conceptual

40) The leaf drop as woody plants for winter dormancy is due to

    A) suppressed auxin production.

    B) increased chlorophyll development.

    C) inhibition of gibberellin.

    D) ethylene.

    E) opened stomata.

Answer: D
Diff: 2   *Page Ref: 44.2*
Skill: Conceptual

41) Which of the following induces dormancy in seeds and buds and causes stomata to close?

    A) auxin

    B) ethylene

    C) abscisic acid

    D) cytokinin

    E) gibberellin

Answer: C
Diff: 1   *Page Ref: 44.2*
Skill: Factual

42) When auxin accumulates on the lower side of a shoot of a germinating seed, it

    A) slows cell elongation on the lower side of the shoot.

    B) increases cell elongation on the lower side of the shoot.

    C) decreases the use of energy by the cells in the shoot.

    D) increases the use of energy by the cells in the shoot.

    E) has no effect on the shoot, only on the developing root.

Answer: B
Diff: 1   *Page Ref: 44.2*
Skill: Factual

43) When auxin accumulates on the lower side of a root of a germinating seed, it

A) slows cell elongation on the lower side of the root.

B) increases cell elongation on the lower side of the root.

C) decreases the use of energy by the cells in the root.

D) increases the use of energy by the cells in the root.

E) has no effect on the root, only on the developing shoot.

Answer: A
Diff: 1   Page Ref: 44.2
Skill: Factual

44) The relative sizes of root and shoot systems is regulated by interactions between

A) auxins and cytokinins.

B) abscisic acid and cytokinins

C) cytokinins and ethylene.

D) ethylene and abscisic acid.

E) gibberellins and abscisic acid.

Answer: A
Diff: 1   Page Ref: 44.2
Skill: Factual

45) If I want to stimulate flower formation, I could treat the plants with

A) abscisic acid.

B) auxin.

C) cytokinin.

D) gibberellin.

E) ethylene.

Answer: D
Diff: 1   Page Ref: 44.2
Skill: Factual

46) Which of the following causes cell elongation, promotes apical dominance, promotes root branching and stimulates formation of adventitious roots?

    A) abscisic acid

    B) auxin

    C) cytokinin

    D) gibberellin

    E) ethylene

Answer: B
Diff: 1   Page Ref: 44.2
Skill: Factual

47) Most scientists believe that the lateral buds nearest the top of a tree are most inhibited from sprouting because they

    A) are most exposed to the light.

    B) are shaded by the apical bud and the top of the tree.

    C) produce gibberellins.

    D) receive the most auxin from the apical bud.

    E) are the most pulled down by gravity.

Answer: D
Diff: 1   Page Ref: 44.2
Skill: Factual

48) Most scientists believe that the lateral buds farthest from the top of a tree are the least inhibited from sprouting because they

    A) receive the least light.

    B) receive the most cytokinin from the root.

    C) produce gibberellins.

    D) are shaded by the top of the tree.

    E) are the least pulled down by gravity.

Answer: B
Diff: 1   Page Ref: 44.2
Skill: Factual

49) If a plant is living under conditions that limit root growth, shoot growth will be

    A) limited as well, due to less cytokinin being produced by the root.

    B) limited as well, due to more auxin being produced by the apical meristem.

    C) stimulated, due to less cytokinin being produced by the root.

    D) stimulated, due to more auxin being produced by the apical meristem.

    E) unaffected by the amount of root growth.

Answer: A
Diff: 2   *Page Ref: 44.2*
Skill: Conceptual

50) A plant that blooms only when the duration of light is greater than a critical length is a

    A) long–day plant.

    B) short–day plant.

    C) neutral–day plant.

    D) phytochrome system plant.

    E) gibberellin–regulated plant.

Answer: A
Diff: 1   *Page Ref: 44.2*
Skill: Factual

51) If I want to be sure my flowers look best at the flower show—no leaf drop, flowers still brilliant—I could treat my plants with

    A) abscisic acid.

    B) auxin.

    C) cytokinin.

    D) gibberellin.

    E) ethylene.

Answer: C
Diff: 1   *Page Ref: 44.2*
Skill: Conceptual

52) If I want to be unethical and sabotage the other plants at the flower show, I could sneak in some _____ before I bring in my plants.

    A) abscisic acid

    B) auxin

    C) cytokinin

    D) gibberellin

    E) ethylene

Answer: C
Diff: 1   Page Ref: 44.2
Skill: Factual

53) An environmental factor that is most significant for flowering is

    A) night length.

    B) temperature.

    C) water availability.

    D) nitrogen availability.

    E) light intensity.

Answer: A
Diff: 1   Page Ref: 44.2
Skill: Factual

54) A short-day plant will flower only if

    A) the length of day light is shorter than some species-specific duration.

    B) phytochrome-mediated responses are inhibited.

    C) abscisic acid is available.

    D) the plant is in the shade.

    E) all of the above

Answer: A
Diff: 1   Page Ref: 44.2
Skill: Factual

55) The pigment responsible for the photoperiod responses of plants is

    A) chlorophyll.

    B) phytochrome.

    C) auxin.

    D) far red light.

    E) ethylene.

Answer: B
Diff: 1   *Page Ref: 44.2*
Skill: Factual

56) Which of the following are TRUE of the relationship between the phytochrome system and the biological clock of plant cells?

    A) The phytochrome system is the biological clock for plants.

    B) The phytochrome system manufactures chemicals which are the biological clock.

    C) The phytochrome system detects light and resets the clock.

    D) The biological clock detects light and sends the information to the phytochrome system.

    E) There is no relationship between the phytochrome system and the biological clock.

Answer: C
Diff: 2   *Page Ref: 44.2*
Skill: Conceptual

57) At night when there is little red light available to the plants in an area,

    A) P_r and P_{fr} are both destroyed.

    B) P_r and P_{fr} are both formed from inactive phytochrome.

    C) P_r is converted to P_{fr}.

    D) P_{fr} is converted to P_r.

    E) P_r stimulates flowering.

Answer: D
Diff: 1   *Page Ref: 44.2*
Skill: Factual

58) The process of aging is called

    A) maturation.

    B) elongation.

    C) abscission.

    D) death.

    E) senescence.

Answer: E
Diff: 1   Page Ref: 44.2
Skill: Factual

59) A hormone most associated with the inhibition of plant processes and slowing down of metabolism is

    A) auxin.

    B) abscisic acid.

    C) ethylene.

    D) gibberellin.

    E) cytokinin.

Answer: B
Diff: 1   Page Ref: 44.2
Skill: Factual

60) Senescence in plants usually involves

    A) shade from other plants.

    B) formation of an abscission layer.

    C) presence of cytokinins.

    D) apical dominance.

    E) the development of photosynthetic enzymes.

Answer: B
Diff: 1   Page Ref: 44.2
Skill: Factual

61) If a storm breaks the top off a tree, within a year or two, one of the lower branches will grow upward and become the tree top. This is an example of

    A) ethylene's influence.

    B) formation of an abscission layer.

    C) presence of cytokinins.

    D) apical dominance.

    E) phytochrome inhibition.

Answer: D
Diff: 1   Page Ref: 44.2
Skill: Factual

62) If a storm breaks the top off a tree, within a year or two, one of the lower branches will grow upward and become the tree top. This apical dominance is due to

    A) ethylene's influence.

    B) formation of an abscission layer.

    C) presence of cytokinins.

    D) the interaction of auxin and cytokinin.

    E) phytochrome inhibition.

Answer: D
Diff: 1   Page Ref: 44.2
Skill: Conceptual

63) The lower branches on a tree tend to be more heavily branched due to

    A) ethylene's influence.

    B) formation of an abscission layer.

    C) higher levels of cytokinins compared to auxins.

    D) higher levels of auxins.

    E) phytochrome inhibition.

Answer: C
Diff: 1   Page Ref: 44.2
Skill: Conceptual

64) Several days of dark, rainy weather encourages

   A) P_r and P_{fr} are both destroyed.

   B) P_r and P_{fr} are both formed from inactive phytochrome.

   C) P_r is converted to P_{fr}.

   D) P_{fr} is converted to P_r.

   E) P_r stimulates flowering.

Answer: D
Diff: 1   Page Ref: 44.2
Skill: Conceptual

65) Plants that flower in the United States only in May are

   A) day neutral plant.

   B) long–day plant.

   C) short–day plant.

   D) indeterminate day plant.

   E) night determinate plant.

Answer: C
Diff: 1   Page Ref: 44.2
Skill: Conceptual

66) Plants that flower in the United States between April and early June are

   A) day neutral plant.

   B) long–day plant.

   C) short–day plant.

   D) indeterminate day plant.

   E) night determinate plant.

Answer: C
Diff: 1   Page Ref: 44.2
Skill: Conceptual

67) Plants that flower in Canada in August and in the United States in July are

   A) day neutral plant.

   B) long–day plant.

   C) short–day plant.

   D) indeterminate day plant.

   E) night determinate plant.

Answer: B
Diff: 1   Page Ref: 44.2
Skill: Conceptual

68) I have a new type of strawberry plant that produces fruit all summer and right up to the fall frosts. It would be a

   A) day neutral plant.

   B) long–day plant.

   C) short–day plant.

   D) indeterminate day plant.

   E) night determinate plant.

Answer: A
Diff: 1   Page Ref: 44.2
Skill: Conceptual

69) Stem grows up and roots grow down due to

   Answer: geotropism most likely due to starch–filled plastids.
   Diff: 1   Page Ref: 44.2
   Skill: Factual

70) One of the old gardening folk traditions uses a "tea" made by soaking the stem tips of willows in water over night and then using the tea to water cuttings. This is supposed to encourage root formation. Would it work? Why or why not?

   Answer: Yes, it works. The stem tips contain high levels of auxin which leaches into the tea. When used to water the cuttings, it acts as a hormone treatment, encouraging root formation.
   Diff: 2   Page Ref: 44.2
   Skill: Application

71) Shortly after converting the house to natural gas, the plants in my house begin to drop leaves. What would this signify?

   Answer: There is a high probability that there is a small leak and small amounts of gas are leaking in. One component of natural gas is ethylene which causes leaf drop.
   Diff: 2   Page Ref: 44.2
   Skill: Conceptual

72) If you were selling trees at a local store and noticed that people seemed to like to see leaves on their trees when they bought them, what hormone might you apply to them to cause them to break dormancy? Explain your choice.

Answer: gibberellins, because they are involved in causing buds to sprout
Diff: 2   *Page Ref: 44.2*
Skill: Conceptual

73) Why does "one rotten apple spoil the lot"?

Answer: As the apple ages it produces ethylene which, since it is a gas, spreads to the other apples causing them to age as well so that all the apples in a container tend to rot at the same time.
Diff: 2   *Page Ref: 44.2*
Skill: Conceptual

74) In seeds from northern areas, what plant hormone will often need to be removed to get them to germinate and how can this be accomplished?

Answer: Abscisic acid can be destroyed by chilling.
Diff: 2   *Page Ref: 44.2*
Skill: Conceptual

75) Why would some seeds require cold stratification (chilling for a specific period of time) before they will germinate?

Answer: Abscisic acid can be destroyed by cold. Some plants coat their seeds with high levels of abscisic levels.
Diff: 2   *Page Ref: 44.2*
Skill: Conceptual

76) In the late winter as seeds prepare to germinate, levels of _____ in seeds should be declining as levels of _____ are increasing.

Answer: abscisic acid; gibberellins
Diff: 2   *Page Ref: 44.2*
Skill: Conceptual

77) The same hormone is believed to be responsible for shoots turning upward toward the light and roots turning downward into the soil. What is this hormone and why do scientists believe that it is able to have such different effects in the root and the shoot?

Answer: Auxin seems to be able to cause these opposite responses as a result of the root being more sensitive to auxin than the shoot so that large quantities of auxin inhibit elongation of root cells while stimulating elongation of shoot cells.
Diff: 2   *Page Ref: 44.2*
Skill: Conceptual

78) I build a greenhouse and fill the windows with stained glass in a green forest motif—lots of different leaf patterns in ever shade of green I can get. My plants grow very rapidly, much more so than before I added the stained glass. Why?

Answer: Green light converts P_r to P_{fr}. P_{fr} stimulates leaf growth and chlorophyll formation.
Diff: 2   Page Ref: 44.2
Skill: Application

79) If you have a coleus plant that has gotten tall and spindly, what can you do to cause it to develop lateral branches so that it becomes bushier? Why does this work?

Answer: You can cut or pinch off the topmost (apical) bud so that apical dominance is lowered, allowing the lateral buds to develop. This process is thought to be due to the interaction of auxin and cytokinins.
Diff: 2   Page Ref: 44.2
Skill: Conceptual

80) Explain how the conical shape of a spruce tree, for example, can be explained by the interaction of auxin and cytokinin.

Answer: Auxin is transported down from the apical bud so that the greatest concentration of auxin is near the top. Cytokinin is produced by the root and transported upward. Since auxin depresses the sprouting of the lateral buds and cytokinin induces their sprouting, the buds at the bottom grow the most and those at the top grow the least, forming a conical shape.
Diff: 3   Page Ref: 44.2
Skill: Application

81) Why are auxins used in rooting powders?

Answer: Auxins encourage the formation of well-branched roots.
Diff: 1   Page Ref: 44.2
Skill: Factual

82) Why can flowers be brought into bloom out of season by changing the patterns of light and dark?

Answer: Plants measure season by the length of continuous darkness. Altering the light/dark pattern can trick the plants into thinking it is the appropriate time to bloom.
Diff: 1   Page Ref: 44.2
Skill: Application

83) The use of flashes of light indicate that plants are able to measure the length of the _____ using the _____ system.

Answer: night; phytochrome
Diff: 2   Page Ref: 44.2
Skill: Conceptual

84) When a peach blossom gets pollinated, _____ and/or _____ stimulate the development of fruit from the ovary.

Answer: auxin; gibberellin
Diff: 2   Page Ref: 44.2
Skill: Conceptual

85) As a leaf or fruit ages and prepares to fall from a tree, it forms what type of a layer?

Answer: an abscission layer
Diff: 1   Page Ref: 44.2
Skill: Factual

86) What kinds of hormonal changes occur as trees prepare for winter dormancy?

Answer: Cytokinin and auxin levels decrease. Ethylene levels increase. Abscisic acid cause bud dormancy.
Diff: 2   Page Ref: 44.2
Skill: Conceptual

87) What is the most likely hormone that will stimulate the defenses of a plant near a plant under attack by beetles?

A) abscisic acid

B) gibberellins

C) auxin

D) ethylene

E) cytokinin

Answer: D
Diff: 2   Page Ref: 44.3
Skill: Conceptual

88) Leaves of the Venus fly trap and mimosa recover much more slowly than they snap closed. This is most likely because

A) there is no need for a fast recovery time.

B) they recover their original orientation as quickly as they moved in response to the environmental stimulus.

C) hormones involved move more slowly.

D) there is no electrical stimulus, just diffusion of ions and a return to water balance.

Answer: D
Diff: 2   Page Ref: 44.3
Skill: Conceptual

89) Some plants under attack by viruses or insects can communicate this information to other parts of the same plant and to nearby plants by

    A) ultrasonic vibrations.

    B) releasing chemicals into their roots.

    C) releasing chemicals into the air.

    D) low frequency sound waves.

    E) releasing chemicals into the water around their roots.

Answer: C
Diff: 1   *Page Ref: 44.3*
Skill: Factual

90) Tobacco and many other plants make this chemical from which aspirin is made.

    A) auxin

    B) acetaminophen

    C) acetic acid

    D) salicylic acid

    E) volantin

Answer: D
Diff: 1   *Page Ref: 44.3*
Skill: Factual

91) Maize plants release chemicals that attract a parasitic wasp. The wasp protects the maize plants from destruction by

    A) caterpillars.

    B) root worms.

    C) other wasps.

    D) too dry soils.

    E) stinging bees.

Answer: A
Diff: 1   *Page Ref: 44.3*
Skill: Factual

92) Misting tomato plants with wintergreen tea can help prevent mosaic virus from infecting the plant. How?

Answer: Plants have the ability to convert airborne methyl salicylate into salicylic acid. The acid enhances the plants immune response, making it more resistant to the virus.
Diff: 1   *Page Ref: 44.3*
Skill: Conceptual

93) Venus fly traps trap insects in order to supplement their input of

   A) meat.

   B) magnesium.

   C) nitrogen.

   D) humus.

   E) potassium.

Answer: D
Diff: 1   Page Ref: 44.3
Skill: Factual

94) What mechanisms do plants use to discourage predation?

Answer: Plants produce bitter covering on seeds, produce bitter chemicals within the plant itself, and cause leaves to droop.
Diff: 1   Page Ref: 44.3
Skill: Factual

95) If a poplar forest is attacked by gypsy moths, trees around the infected area tend to become somewhat resistant. How?

Answer: Plants which are attacked by insects tend to release hormones into the air which "warn" neighboring plants.
Diff: 1   Page Ref: 44.3
Skill: Conceptual

96) When an insect twice touches a Venus fly trap hair, this changes the _____ that causes the trap to close.

   A) electrical potential

   B) action potential

   C) osmotic pressure

   D) spring tension on the leaf

   E) pH

Answer: A
Diff: 1   Page Ref: 44.3
Skill: Factual

97) When a Venus fly trap closes, much of the leaf's what is consumed?

A) nitrogen

B) protein

C) magnesium

D) ATP

E) electricity

Answer: D
Diff: 1   *Page Ref: Case Study Revisited*
Skill: Factual

98) Why should you not "torment" your Venus fly trap with toothpicks or other indigestible objects, just to show off its ability to close its trap?

Answer: The trap cells use up almost 1/3 of their ATP every time the trap closes.
Diff: 3   *Page Ref: Case Study Revisited*
Skill: Application